Contemporary Business Reports

SHIRLEY KUIPER

Professor Emerita, Management
Moore School of Business
University of South Carolina

DORINDA CLIPPINGER

Lecturer Emerita, Management
Moore School of Business
University of South Carolina

FIFTH EDITION

SOUTH-WESTERN
CENGAGE Learning·

Australia • Brazil • Japan • Korea • Mexico • Singapore • Spain • United Kingdom • United States

SOUTH-WESTERN
CENGAGE Learning·

**Contemporary Business Reports,
Fifth Edition**

**Shirley Kuiper &
Dorinda Clippinger**

Vice President of Editorial, Business:
Jack W. Calhoun

Acquisition Editor: Jason Fremder

Senior Developmental Editor: Ted Knight

Editorial Assistant: Megan Fischer

Marketing Manager: Michelle Lockard

Senior Marketing Communications Manager:
Sarah Greber

Permissions Acquisitions Manager:
Amber Hosea

Media Editor: John Rich

Manufacturing Planner: Ron Montgomery

Senior Art Director: Stacey Shirley

Internal Designer, Production Management,
and Composition: PreMediaGlobal

Cover Designer: Lou Ann Thesing

Cover Image: © iStock Photo

For product information and technology assistance, contact us at
Cengage Learning Customer & Sales Support, 1-800-354-9706

For permission to use material from this text or product,
submit all requests online at **www.cengage.com/permissions**
Further permissions questions can be emailed to
permissionrequest@cengage.com

Library of Congress Control Number: 2011944789

ISBN-13: 978-1-111-82085-5

ISBN-10: 1-111-82085-6

South-Western
5191 Natorp Boulevard
Mason, OH 45040
USA

Cengage Learning products are represented in Canada by Nelson
Education, Ltd.

For your course and learning solutions, visit **www.cengage.com**

Purchase any of our products at your local college store or at our
preferred online store **www.cengagebrain.com**

Printed in the United States of America
1 2 3 4 5 6 7 16 15 14 13 12

Brief Contents

Contents

Preface

Contemporary Business Reports, Fifth edition, is designed to help students develop business research and reporting skills. The text contains general guides for report writing; specific guides for a variety of common business reports; illustrations and examples of the guides presented; extensive discussion of and step-by-step guides for using Internet tools and Microsoft Office 2010 in the research and reporting processes; and an abundance of application exercises that encourage students to practice their research, writing, and presentation skills.

Purpose, Scope, and Structure

The primary purpose of *Contemporary Business Reports* is to enable students to approach their reporting responsibilities with confidence. Guides for effective reports emphasize the importance of all steps in the report planning, writing, and presentation processes. Guides are also given for completing those processes effectively in collaboration with team members and for increasing efficiency in the research and reporting processes by taking advantage of leading-edge technologies. In addition, ethical concerns are addressed.

The book contains 16 chapters. Those chapters observe the pedagogical practice of moving from the simple to the complex. Through reading, discussion, and application of knowledge, students are led through the essential stages for production of effective simple or complex reports. The book may be characterized as follows:

- The first nine chapters provide the fundamentals of written and oral business reports.

  Chapters 1 through *4* define a business report, discuss business report characteristics, present a process for planning and writing the report, help students understand and implement appropriate writing styles, alert writers to frequently occurring writing lapses, and introduce students to Web-based tools that can increase their efficiency, particularly in collaborative projects.

  Chapters 5 and *6* present ways to illustrate and format a report, including advanced features of Microsoft Excel and Word 2010.

  Chapters 7 and *8* give guides for and illustrations of typical simple reports. Simple reports are defined as those which address a relatively uncomplicated situation that does not require extensive research. Some of those reports are classified as routine (for example, a trip report or a meeting report); others are classified as nonroutine (for example, a feasibility report or an exception report). These chapters also explore how Web conferencing and social media, especially Twitter, are related to report preparation.

Chapter 9 provides strategies for planning and delivering an oral report, including managing the backchannel and avoiding "Death by PowerPoint" when using electronic presentations.

- The remaining chapters apply the fundamentals to more complex business situations.

Chapters 10 and *11* focus on techniques for planning business research, including writing a research proposal and selecting appropriate data sources. The chapters include treatment of engines for searching the visible and invisible Web and website evaluation.

Chapters 12 through *15* provide extensive discussions of using secondary and primary data sources, analyzing data, and documenting data sources, using the latest editions of the three most-used style manuals. Technology treatment here includes on-line surveys and polls and project management tools (PM software, blogs, and wikis).

Chapter 16 gives an example of and guides for communicating research results by way of a formal analytical report. Coverage includes collaboration tools, such as tracking changes and handling the security risks inherent in file sharing.

Special Features

Contemporary Business Reports has several strong features to benefit students and instructors.

- An abundance of contemporary business examples and illustrations.
- Emphasis on the ethical aspects of business research and reporting.
- Techniques for successful collaboration in the research and reporting processes.
- A variety of end-of-chapter activities ("Topics for Discussion" and "Applications") that reinforce the concepts and guides presented in each chapter.
- Up-to-the-minute technologies with hands-on directions in every chapter and included in end-of-chapter exercises.
- A three-piece set of textbook supplements:
  - *An Online Instructor's Resource Manual that supports all instructors in the optimum use of this text.*
  - *An Online Test Bank with True-False, Multiple-Choice, and Fill-In questions for each chapter.*
  - *A visually rich Microsoft PowerPoint slide show for each of the 16 chapters.*

As a package, the book provides instruction in the fundamental requirements for preparing effective business reports as ethical individuals working in a collaborative, high-tech, and global business environment. This flexible book can be used in many ways. The text can be used for seminars or for courses ranging from a few weeks to a full quarter or semester. Some instructors may find that Chapters 1 through 9 adequately address the objectives of their courses. Chapters 10 through 16 are useful in courses that include research strategies, data analysis, and the communication of research results. Instructors may also use parts of the text to complement other teaching materials by requesting custom publication of desired chapters.

Acknowledgments

Several people have influenced the production of this edition of *Contemporary Business Reports*. To name some runs the risk of omitting others; but we shall take that risk.

- The influence of Earl A. Dvorak, who mentored both of us during our graduate studies at Indiana University, is present throughout this book. He gave us a solid foundation in business research and reporting. Fully as important was his insistence that we set high goals and stick to a task until the goals are reached.
- Cheryl M. Luke, a former colleague, hammered out the first edition with Shirley Kuiper. Her influence still lives in this fifth edition.
- Shirley's husband, Tom Fitzpatrick, and Dorinda's husband, William Jewell, were unfailingly supportive. Their wit, patience, and love kept us going.

During our combined 80+ years of teaching, research, publishing, and business ownership, many students and colleagues have influenced our thinking about communication and education for business. We owe a huge debt to them.

CHAPTER 1

Report Characteristics

LEARNING OBJECTIVES

After you have read this chapter, you should be able to:

1. Explain the functions of business reports.

2. Classify typical business reports.

3. Describe the characteristics of effective reports.

4. Identify ethical concerns related to report writing.

5. Identify behavior that contributes to effective collaboration.

6. Describe how to use audioconferencing effectively while working on a collaborative project.

7. Begin to apply writing skills and ethical guides to create effective, ethical reports.

WHAT DO A BANK MANAGER, a retail store manager, a broker for an import-export company, and an executive director of a nonprofit organization have in common? Although their job descriptions may show considerably different duties, one task is common to all: preparing reports.

For many students, the word *report* suggests a term paper, a book review, or a case analysis. But those documents differ from on-the-job reports in many respects. Whereas you may write a term paper to demonstrate your knowledge of a subject, you will write business reports to influence the actions of other people. Although school reports usually flow upward (from student to instructor), business reports move up, down, and across the formal organizational structure and even across organizational boundaries. You may use the Internet or books and journals from your university library as the major data sources for a term paper, but your business reports will frequently contain data drawn from company files or your experience and observations as well as from print and electronic media. The quality of a term paper may affect your course grade, but the quality of a business report can determine the success or failure of your career—and that of your company.

Such differences characterize what is known as a genre: a distinctive type or category of composition. You are familiar with different music genres, such as classical, jazz, and hip-hop. Although some elements of music overlap those genres, each also has style elements and conventions that are unique, differentiating one genre from another. The same is true of writing genres. The writing style used in a critical essay, a lab report, or a poem usually is not effective in a business report. Business writing is a genre that uses certain conventions not common to scientific or literary writing. Those conventions are based on the function that each document serves and require thoughtful analysis of the writer's purpose and the audience's needs.

Functions of Business Reports

Business reports are organized, objective presentations of observations, experiences, or facts used in the decision-making process. To understand the functions of business reports, several words in the definition need further analysis: organized, objective, and decision-making process.

Organized

As an organized presentation, a report must be planned and presented with both the receiver's needs and the sender's objectives in mind. Effective report writers* define the report objective in terms of desired action—what the sender wants the receiver to do. But to achieve that action, the sender must consider the receiver's needs—both information needs and ego needs. Information needs are the data that will enable the receiver to understand and fulfill the sender's desires. Ego needs are a person's desire for recognition and an acknowledgment of that person's worth to the organization. A report may provide all the information a person needs; but unless the report also satisfies ego needs, the receiver may have no motivation to act. Information needs and ego needs influence the structure of a report as well as its content.

Two basic structures for most messages are the indirect and the direct structure. Indirect structure is patterned after inductive reasoning, which moves from specific examples or facts to generalized conclusions. Direct structure simulates deductive reasoning, which moves from generalizations to specific examples or facts to support those generalizations. The following paragraphs illustrate indirect and direct structures.

> *Indirect Structure:* Last year's 15 percent increase in office staff has required us to examine the efficiency of our space usage. Since many employees already telecommute as many as three days a week, approximately 60 percent of our desks are vacant at one time. Instead of renting additional office space to accommodate staff growth, we will be redesigning the current office space. The goal is to reduce the average amount of individual work space and increase the amount of collaborative work space.
>
> Consequently, in the office redesign, the number of individual work spaces will be reduced, and each space will be shared by two employees. The amount of common work space will be increased and will be appropriately configured for both individual and collaborative work as well as client meetings.

*The authors of this text acknowledge that reports may be written or oral. To avoid the awkward repetition of *sender*, the word *writer* is sometimes used when the person originating the report could be either writing or speaking.

> *Direct Structure: In the redesign of our office space, the number of individual work spaces will be reduced, and each space will be shared by two employees. The amount of common work space will be increased and will be appropriately configured for both individual and collaborative work as well as client meetings.*
>
> *Last year's 15 percent increase in office staff has required us to examine the efficiency of our space usage. Since many employees already telecommute as many as three days a week, approximately 60 percent of our desks are vacant at one time. Instead of renting additional office space, we will be redesigning the current office space, with the goal of reducing the average amount of individual work space and increasing the amount of collaborative work space.*

Direct structure is effective when the receiver is likely to agree with the main point of the message. That structure is also effective with receivers who are efficiency conscious—they want to know your main point immediately, whether or not they agree with it. Indirect structure is effective for complex or controversial information. For such a message, the reader may need exposure to the detailed data before being able to understand and accept the conclusions and recommendations of the report.

Objective Presentation of Observations, Experiences, or Facts

Since reports are used in the decision-making process, a user must be able to trust the information contained in a report. Objectivity refers to the selection of report content as well as to the presentation of that content. Deliberately excluding information that may be unpleasant to the writer or the receiver violates the objectivity criterion, which requires that all available relevant data be presented.

Report data may be drawn from a variety of sources. It is not uncommon for a report to contain the observations of the writer. For example, a manager may observe that employees are abusing the privilege of using personal cell phones in their work spaces; a report could follow in which the manager describes the observed practices and reminds the employees of a company policy about conducting personal business on company time. In another example, if an employee writes a trip report after attending a technical conference, much of the report content would be based on the employee's personal experiences during the trip; but the report would likely also include data about new products or techniques as well as facts about the costs incurred for travel, food, and lodging. Although report writers may present personal observations or experiences in addition to impersonal facts, all information must be presented objectively—without distortion by feelings, opinions, or prejudices.

The Decision-Making Process

Some reports supply information necessary for decision making; others convey information about decisions that have been made and must be implemented. Since people at all levels of an organization must make or carry out decisions, reports are used in every kind of job. For example, a report may be as simple as a bank manager's oral reassignment of a teller from an inside workstation to a drive-up window after the manager observes that cars are lining up at the window. Or a report may be as complex as a retail store manager's written analysis of the store's operations, competition, and goals, concluding with a recommendation that the business be relocated.

The function of business reports in the decision-making process is shown in Illustration 1.1. The illustration suggests several reports related to one business situation, entering an international market. The first report is an informal oral report by a sales associate of J Pac, a (fictitious) U.S. manufacturer of gas grills, to the vice president for marketing. The sales associate recently returned from a vacation in Brazil, which is a significant regional producer and consumer of meats. While in Brazil, the sales associate noticed that many restaurants serve meats grilled to order—including lamb, beef, pork, fish, and fowl—and noticed that many families enjoy outdoor grilling as well. However, the grilling is done primarily over charcoal. Although gas is readily available to homes and restaurants, the use of gas grills is minimal at this time. The sales associate thinks there is a potential opportunity to enter the Brazilian market with J Pac's top-of-the-line gas grills.

The initial oral report by the sales associate could lead to a series of reports related to the feasibility of marketing gas grills in Latin America (see Illustration 1.1). Those reports may be simple or complex, oral or written, formal or informal. Moreover, reporting occurs at every level of the organizational structure. Reports perform many functions in the organization, but the primary function is to improve the decision-making process and the quality of actions based on those decisions.

Classifications of Business Reports

Reports are not standardized messages. As the previous examples show, reports are used by many people, in many organizations, and for many purposes; consequently, reports take many forms. Report classifications can help you decide what type of report will best help you achieve your reporting objective. To understand the similarities and differences among reports, consider six ways in which reports may be classified: by function, frequency, subject matter, level of formality, reader-writer relationship, and communication medium.

Function

Reports typically serve one of two major functions: to inform or to analyze. An information report presents facts, observations, or experiences only. These facts or experiences may include requests for specific actions, such as the request for a feasibility study mentioned in Illustration 1.1. The first five reports in that illustration are information reports.

An analytical report, sometimes called an examination report, identifies an issue or problem, presents relevant information, and interprets that information. The interpretation is often carried through to a logical conclusion or conclusions. The report may also offer recommendations for action. The last two reports in Illustration 1.1 are analytical reports.

Frequency

Reports are often classified by frequency of transmission. Periodic reports are transmitted at stated times, such as daily, weekly, monthly, quarterly, or annually. A sales

ILLUSTRATION 1.1   REPORTS AND DECISIONS

Sender	Receiver	Report Content	Report Characteristics	Decision/Action
J Pac sales associate	J Pac sales manager	Consumers in Brazil enjoy grilled meats; most use charcoal; potential market for our gas grills	Oral; informal	Sales manager does preliminary research; relays information to vice president for marketing
Sales manager	Vice president for marketing	Burgeoning consumer market is attracting many U.S. companies to Brazil; few of our competitors are currently selling gas grills in Latin America	Written; semiformal; supplemented by oral summary	Vice president for marketing asks director of market research to conduct further research about feasibility of entering Latin American market
Vice president for marketing	Director of market research	Summary of previous reports; request to study feasibility of entering Latin American market	Written; semiformal	Director of market research assigns task to research staff; requests research proposal
Director of market research	Research staff	Summary of vice president's reports; requests for research proposal	Oral; informal; part of weekly staff meeting	Staff begins work on research proposal
Research staff	Director of market research	Proposed plan for feasibility study	Written; formal	Director approves plan; staff conducts study
Research staff	Director of market research	Findings, conclusions, recommendations of feasibility study	Formal; written; perhaps supplemented by oral presentation	Director asks staff to present report to management committee
Research staff and director of market research	Management committee	Background; summary of preliminary studies; findings, conclusions, recommendations of feasibility study	Oral/visual presentation; written summary of key findings and recommendations	Management authorization of budget for marketing division to begin efforts to establish distributorships in Brazil

© Cengage Learning 2013

representative's weekly summary of calls is an example of a periodic report, as is a company's annual report to its stockholders. In contrast, a special report relates to a one-time or an infrequent event, such as the feasibility study mentioned in Illustration 1.1. Another type of periodic report is a progress or status report, presented at appropriate intervals to inform decision makers about the status of an ongoing, usually large-scale project.

Subject Matter

Some organizations classify reports by broad subject areas, often corresponding to functional divisions of the organization, such as accounting, production, finance, marketing, or engineering. Within the broad subject areas, narrower subject classifications may also exist: audit or tax reports within the accounting department or unit reports within the production division.

Level of Formality

Level of formality includes both tone and structure. In some contexts, formal tone and structure are expected; other contexts justify informality.

A formal report typically uses impersonal language and follows a prescribed format. Although formal reports may be written in memorandum or letter format, they are often presented in manuscript form. The format usually includes headings to guide the reader through the report content. If presented in manuscript format, the report generally includes a title page. As report length and complexity increase, other features, such as a table of contents and appendices, may be included. The final report of the feasibility study could well include a table of contents and appendices.

Informal reports project a more personal tone than do formal reports. First-person and second-person pronouns as well as near-conversational language may be used. Many informal reports are presented orally or in memorandum or letter format. In Illustration 1.1, the sales associate's initial report to the sales manager is an informal report.

Reader-Writer Relationship

Reader-writer classification refers to the relationships that those parties have to one another. An internal report passes between a writer and reader in the same organization. Within an organization, other reader-writer relationships are suggested by such terms as management report, staff report, or committee report. All reports listed in Illustration 1.1 are internal reports.

External reports move across organizational boundaries. A professional report by a consultant to the managers who employed the consultant is an example. Similarly, an audit report presented by an independent accounting firm to a client is an external report.

Communication Medium

When classified by the dominant communication tool or medium, reports are called written or oral, narrative or statistical, illustrated or unillustrated. Most report preparers use combinations of communication tools for multimedia reports. The last report listed in Illustration 1.1 is an example of a multimedia report.

In recent years, social media, such as Facebook and Twitter, have become important media for communicating with an organization's audience. For example, in 2009, Ford Motor Company spent approximately one-quarter of its marketing dollars on digital and social media, successfully launching the American Ford Fiesta (Roman, 2011).

The classifications of reports demonstrate that reports are presented in many forms. Those forms will be amply illustrated in subsequent chapters. Although report forms may vary, effective reports share common characteristics.

Characteristics of Effective Reports

Effective reports are understood by the reader as the writer intended, and they influence the reader to act as the writer desired. The writer's objectives are most likely to be achieved if they correspond with the needs and objectives of the reader. An effective report is empathetic, accurate, complete, concise, and clear. Above all, an effective report presents information ethically.

Empathy

Empathy is being sensitive to and vicariously experiencing the needs or feelings of another. A successful report writer attempts to understand the reader's needs and to fulfill those needs through report content, structure, and tone.

One need that the receivers of most reports have is to use time economically. Many readers want to skim a report, determining quickly what the report is about and its major points. A writer can demonstrate empathy with that need by supplying all necessary information in an easily comprehended structure. Coherent paragraph structure, logical organization of a report, and the use of headings, bullet points, or numbers guide the reader and provide high skim value. Similarly, a courteous and respectful tone demonstrates empathy. Compare the following examples of nonempathetic and empathetic writing. Although the nonempathetic example is a well-structured paragraph, its structure is hidden in the density of the text. In contrast, the empathetic example directs the reader's attention to each clearly stated recommendation.

> *Nonempathetic: After reviewing the plans to redesign our office space, I have several suggestions that may improve our employee's acceptance of the plans. First of all, schedule an e-conference at a time when most employees are able to participate to ensure that all employees get accurate information at the same time, thereby reducing rumors. Secondly, help employees appreciate the need for the office redesign by sharing the statistics about our current space usage and the costs associated with inefficient use of that space. Thirdly, assure employees that the office redesign will in no way impact our current telecommuting policy. This reassurance should relieve any concerns that employees may have about major changes in their current work styles. Finally, ease the discomfort that some employees may experience when confronting change by assuring them that their individual work styles, needs for communal space, and needs for private space with clients will be considered when work stations are assigned.*

Empathetic: After reviewing the plans to redesign our office space, I have several suggestions that may improve our employee's acceptance of the plans:

1. *Schedule an e-conference at a time when most employees are able to participate. Unpleasant rumors can best be avoided by giving all employees accurate information at the same time and allowing discussion of that information.*
2. *Share with the employees the statistics about our current space usage and the costs associated with inefficient use of that space. These statistics should help them appreciate the need for the office redesign.*
3. *Assure employees that the office redesign will in no way impact our current telecommuting policy. Employees must be confident that the office changes will have little effect on their current work styles.*
4. *Assure employees that their individual work styles, needs for communal space, and needs for private space with clients will be considered when work stations are assigned. This assurance should ease the discomfort that some employees may experience when confronting change.*

Accuracy

Effective decisions can be made only if they are based on accurate information. Consequently, a primary criterion for effective reporting is accuracy. The effective reporter attempts to gather accurate, objective data; verifies data when necessary; and presents the data accurately. Correct data are conveyed through accurate number use, word choice, spelling, grammar, and punctuation. Careful use of visual aids also promotes correctness. Compare the following examples of incorrect and correct portions of reports.

Incorrect: The projector cost is $49.50; $30.00 for labor, $9.50 for materials, and $20.00 for indirect costs.

Correct: The projected cost is $59.50 per unit: $30.00 for labor, $9.50 for materials, and $20.00 for indirect costs.

OR

The projected per-unit cost is:

Labor	*$30.00*
Materials	*$9.50*
Indirect costs	*$20.00*
Total	*$59.50*

Completeness

Although completeness is an aspect of accuracy, it deserves special attention. Incomplete messages that omit essential data are likely to be inaccurate. Senders of incomplete messages tend to assume that the reader knows or will "fill in" certain details that the reader, in reality, may not know or cannot supply. Consequently, receivers of incomplete messages often interpret them quite differently from the way the sender intended. Compare the following incomplete and complete presentations of information. Which versions are more effective?

Incomplete: The Lake Lure Artists welcome anyone who is interested in joining us. We meet on the second and fourth Thursdays of each month.

Complete: The Lake Lure Artists welcome anyone who is interested in joining us. We meet at 10 A.M. on the second and fourth Thursdays of each month in the Hickory Room of the Mugan Community Center.

OR

IMPORTANT NOTICE

What: Lake Lure Artists Meetings
When: Second and fourth Thursdays, 10 A.M.
Where: Hickory Room, Mugan Community Center

New members always welcome. Contact Lynn Blaine, 555-1234, for additional information.

Incomplete: Orders from Oxford Tool and Supply Company have declined during recent months. Please let me know soon what you plan to do to revive this account.

Complete: Orders from Oxford Tool and Supply Company for saw blades and router bits went down 10 percent each month during August, September, and October.

Please give me a detailed action plan for that account before November 15. Include in your plan the number of calls you have scheduled, whom you will contact, the questions you intend to ask, and the special offers, if any, you will make to revive that account.

Conciseness

Conciseness is a necessary complement to completeness. In an attempt to provide complete information, some report writers include more information than is necessary. An effective writer, however, uses the least number of words necessary to convey information accurately, completely, clearly, consistently, and empathetically. Concise writing is characterized by lack of trite expressions, redundancies, or unnecessary words. Compare the following examples.

Trite, commonplace expressions:

I look forward to serving you soon.
Let us supply all your hair needs.
Thank you in advance for your business.

> *Concise, relevant language:*
>
> *I'll service your copier each Friday morning.*
> *Hair Trimmers carries a complete selection of Head Turners shampoos and conditioners.*
> *I would be pleased to provide your tax service during this new year.*
>
> *Redundant:* *This report presentation provides the necessary information essential for reaching an informed decision regarding your plans and prospects for success in a profitable venture in that part of the city, that is, a new branch office.*
>
> *Concise:* *This report provides information about the potential profitability of a branch office in the Shady Grove area.*

Conciseness does not mean brevity above all; conciseness means to avoid unnecessary words. Compare the following examples of accurate, clear, empathetic, and concise writing with those that violate one or more of those criteria.

> *Concise but incomplete, nonempathetic:* *Call me tomorrow.*
>
> *Concise, complete, empathetic:* *Please call me (555-5974) between 8 A.M. and 11:30 A.M. tomorrow.*
>
> *Concise but incomplete:* *Amy's fee is less.*
>
> *Concise and complete:* *Amy's fee is $500 less than Matt's.*
>
> *Wordy, unclear, incorrect modification:* *Keeping in mind the objective of facilitating timely processing of rebate requests, it appears that a personnel increase in the neighborhood of 10 percent of our current staff will be essential.*
>
> *Concise, clear, correct modification:* *To fulfill rebate requests promptly, we will need 20 additional employees.*

A writer who supplies unnecessary or redundant information runs the risk of violating another criterion of effective reports: clarity.

Clarity

Since communication is an extremely complex process, the risk of misunderstanding is always present. A general guide for clarity is to use simple rather than complex words, sentences, and paragraphs.

Simple words are those that are familiar to both the sender and receiver. For example, most users of American English understand the words *dog* and *cat*, but fewer understand their synonyms *canine* and *feline*.

The relative simplicity of words is also related to the context in which they are used. Jargon, the technical or special language of a specific group, may simplify communication within that group; but when used with persons outside that group, jargon becomes a communication barrier. The following paragraph contains simple words; but to anyone other than a seasoned woodworker, it is probably meaningless:

> Here's a way to dial in your miter gauge for tricky angles, such as for a seven-sided frame. Cut a piece of ¾″ MDF wider than your miter gauge…. Then center a dado in one face to fit your miter-gauge bar, and add the base, support block, and hold-down. ("Set Precise Angles," 2010)

Study the following examples of sentences using complex and simple words.

> **Complex:** *Subsequent to perusing the vendor's missive, Austin declaimed his opposition regarding the egregious proposition.*
>
> **Simple:** *After reading the seller's letter, Austin loudly rejected the extremely bad offer.*

Another guide for clear writing is to use concrete, vivid words and descriptions rather than abstractions. Concrete words permit a narrow range of interpretation, but abstract words may be interpreted in many ways. For example, the abstract term *writing instrument* may suggest objects as diverse as pencils, pens, typewriters, and computers. But the concrete terms *pen* and *computer* are not likely to bring to mind images of a pencil or a typewriter. The following examples illustrate abstract and concrete language.

> **Abstract:** *Please return the questionnaire as soon as possible. Your responses are valuable to us and other consumers.*
>
> **Concrete:** *Please complete and mail the questionnaire to 123 Blake Street, Citizen, OH 00000-0000, before April 30, 2013. Your responses will help us determine whether to add Saturday banking hours to our array of customer services.*

Sentence structure also contributes to or distracts from clarity. The simplest sentence follows the subject-verb-complement structure. That structure clearly identifies the actor, the action, and the receiver of the action, leaving little possibility of misinterpretation. However, excessive use of simple sentences can result in a choppy, nearly childlike writing style. An appropriate balance of simple sentences and longer, more complex sentences contributes to clear, interesting writing. Compare the following examples.

> **Complex:** *Because there was insufficient evidence of carrier responsibility, the carrier refused the damage claim that was filed by the customer only three days after the shipment arrived.*
>
> **Too simple:** *The shipment arrived. Three days later the customer filed a damage claim. There was no evidence of carrier fault. The carrier refused the claim.*

> ***Appropriate balance:*** *The customer filed a damage claim three days after the shipment arrived. The carrier refused that claim because there was no evidence of carrier fault.*

Clear writing also requires correct use of pronouns. Indefinite pronoun reference—using a pronoun without a clear antecedent—destroys clarity because the reader or listener is not sure which noun is replaced by the pronoun. Compare the following examples.

> ***Indefinite reference:*** *After customers return the questionnaires to the company, they will analyze them.*
>
> ***Clear reference:*** *After customers return the questionnaires to the company, the research staff will analyze the responses.*
>
> ***Indefinite reference:*** *Ignoring customers' comments about unsatisfactory service will soon affect the bottom line. That is something we must correct immediately.*
>
> ***Clear reference:*** *Ignoring customers' comments about unsatisfactory service will soon affect profits. We must respond to customers' comments promptly, and we must correct the service problems immediately.*

A final aspect of clarity is grammatical, structural, and logical consistency. Grammatical consistency (parallelism) exists when a writer uses the same grammatical structure for equivalent sentence or paragraph components. Compare the following examples of nonparallel and parallel grammatical structures.

> ***Nonparallel:*** *One day I would like to coach high school basketball and teacher.*
>
> ***Parallel:*** *One day I would like to coach high school basketball and be a teacher.*
>
> *OR*
>
> *One day I would like to be a high school coach and teacher.*
>
> *OR*
>
> *One day I would like to teach and coach basketball in a high school.*
>
> ***Nonparallel:*** *Harter, Monk, and Ms. Adamson are analyzing the customer survey.*
>
> ***Parallel:*** *Mr. Harter, Mr. Monk, and Ms. Adamson are analyzing the customer survey.*
>
> *OR*
>
> *Harter, Monk, and Adamson are analyzing the customer survey.*

Structural consistency is achieved by maintaining the same structure for parallel units of a report. For example, the wording and placement of headings in a report contribute to or distract from structural consistency. Compare the following examples of inconsistent and consistent headings in a report comparing purchased with free antivirus software.

Inconsistent:
1. *Purchased antivirus software*
   a. *Firewall*
   b. *Parental controls*
   c. *Spam controls*
   d. *Browser toolbars to prevent phishing*
2. *Free*
   a. *No cost at start-up*
   b. *Less protection*
   c. *No technical support*

Consistent:
1. *Purchased antivirus software*
   a. *Start-up costs*
   b. *Protection features*
      ◆ *Firewall?*
      ◆ *Parental controls?*
      ◆ *Spam controls?*
      ◆ *Antiphishing controls?*
   c. *Technical support*
2. *Free antivirus software*
   a. *Start-up costs*
   b. *Protection features*
      ◆ *Firewall?*
      ◆ *Parental controls?*
      ◆ *Spam controls?*
      ◆ *Antiphishing controls?*
   c. *Technical support*

Effective writers also strive to achieve logical consistency. Logic is a form of reasoning that imposes order on information. Logical reasoning contributes to truth, but fallacies (false or invalid arguments) distract from truth. Four common fallacies that report writers should avoid are *post hoc, ergo propter hoc* ("after this, therefore, because of this"); *non sequitur* ("it does not follow"); begging the question; and hasty generalization.

The *post hoc, ergo propter hoc* fallacy confuses passage of time with cause and effect. A writer guilty of this fallacy assumes that if one event occurred before another, the first event caused the second. Compare the following example of a *post hoc, ergo propter hoc* fallacy with the logical statement that follows it. Note that the complete, correct logical statement is longer than the fallacy. Logical consistency should not be sacrificed for conciseness.

> ***Post hoc, ergo propter hoc:*** *District A sales have increased 1 percent each month since Sanchez became district manager. He has turned that territory around.*
>
> ***Logical statement:*** *Although economic conditions have not changed in District A, its sales have increased 1 percent each month since Sanchez became district manager. He has personally helped each sales representative develop a sales plan. That management technique appears to have improved the district's performance.*

A *non sequitur* states a conclusion based on faulty or insufficient evidence. The following sentences contrast a *non sequitur* with a logical statement.

> ***Non sequitur:*** *We received 200 calls in response to Sunday's newspaper advertisement. Our sales are sure to pick up this month.*
>
> ***Logical statement:*** *We received 200 calls in response to Sunday's newspaper advertisement. If only 10 percent of those respondents order by February 28, February's sales will be 2 percent above January's.*

Begging the question is a fallacy in which an assumption or conclusion is restated instead of being supported by logical reasons or evidence. "I should be more assertive because I need to assert myself" merely repeats the need to be assertive but does not supply a reason. "I need to be more assertive because people often take advantage of me" supplies a reason for the conclusion. The following example further contrasts begging the question with a logical statement.

> ***Begging the question:*** *I rejected this proposal because I cannot accept it in its present form.*
>
> ***Logical statement:*** *I rejected this proposal because the cost data were incomplete.*

In a hasty generalization, a person reasons that because something is true in some instances, it is true in the case under discussion. Compare the following examples.

> ***Hasty generalization:*** *Sandy has more education than any other applicant. Sandy is the best person for this position.*
>
> ***Logical statement:*** *Sandy scored higher than any other applicant on all selection criteria. Sandy is the best applicant for this position.*

Grammatical consistency, structural consistency, and logical consistency improve report clarity. Moreover, presenting data and conclusions logically makes a report and its writer believable, whereas fallacies tend to cast doubt on the report content and its writer.

As you compose reports, evaluate your writing by the criteria of empathy, accuracy, completeness, conciseness, and clarity. Those criteria are exemplified in the memo shown in Illustration 1.2.

ILLUSTRATION 1.2 REPORT CHARACTERISTICS

Quik-Host Neighborhood Stores

Memo

To:	Quik-Host Store Managers
From:	Harold Sweetman, VP-Corporate Marketing
CC:	Gerald Montero, CEO
Date:	1/22/2013
Re:	Customer Service Etiquette, Training Update

Problem Encountered

Quik-Host has hired Secret Shoppers to evaluate customer service in Quik-Host stores. Recent reports from Secret Shoppers show that some Quik-Host cashiers keep a customer waiting at the counter while the cashier processes an incoming telephone call.

Requested Action

Please remind all cashiers that a customer standing at a counter always takes precedence over an incoming call. Review with your employees the following procedures that must be followed when a telephone call comes in while a customer is at the cashier's counter.

1. Complete the transaction with the customer at the counter before answering the telephone.
2. If no other employee has answered the telephone after five rings:
   - Say to the customer, "Please excuse me while I take this call."
   - Answer the telephone, saying, "Thank you for calling Quik-Host. Please hold briefly."
   - Immediately put the caller on hold; page another employee to take the call.
   - Return to your customer; apologize for the interruption.
   - Complete the transaction with the customer.
   - If the caller is still on hold, take the call and apologize for the wait.

Expected Results

This procedure will show respect for the person who has visited your store while maintaining goodwill with the caller, who may be a potential customer or supplier. We all benefit when our customers are treated courteously.

© Cengage Learning 2013

Notice that the memo fits the characteristics of a report: It is an organized, objective presentation of a fact, and it is written to influence action. The organizational structure is evidenced by headings as well as numbered and bulleted items. The organization and format help the reader easily focus on the main points (skim value), thereby demonstrating empathy for the reader. The tone of the message, courteous yet firm, also demonstrates empathy. Beginning with the description of the problem adds to the accuracy and completeness of the data, helping the reader understand the importance of the requested action. Notice that the language is clear and concrete, avoiding such trite expressions as "It has come to our attention that...." The requested action is also written in clear, concise language, providing a concrete procedure to be followed. The comment about expected results again demonstrates empathy, showing that the requested action will benefit the reader of the memo, not just the sender.

A final element of reporting must be considered: the ethical dimension. Since the objective of a report is to bring about good decisions, the writer has an ethical responsibility. As will be shown in this book, ethical considerations apply to all aspects of reporting: timing, content, structure, word choice, and illustrations.

Ethical Considerations

Individuals, organizational leaders, and government agencies do not always agree about what constitutes ethical behavior. Most people agree that persons or organizations that are in a position to influence the lives of others ought to behave ethically—they should "do the right thing." But "oughts" or "shoulds" are themselves ethical judgments, indicating the complexity of the ethical arena. To achieve some degree of consistency and consensus about what is good, people and organizations develop ethical systems or frameworks.

Bruce Weinstein, also known as The Ethics Guy®, provides these maxims for ethical behavior (Weinstein, 2007a):

- Do no harm
- Make things better
- Respect others
- Be fair
- Be compassionate

More often than not, ethical questions concern right versus right rather than right versus wrong. Right-versus-right questions vary in complexity and cannot be resolved with easy solutions such as "do the right thing." Weinstein purports that when conflicts between right and right arise, the closer someone is to you, the stronger is your duty to do no harm, make things better, and act with respect, fairness, and compassion. Weinstein (2007b) suggests that an approach to resolving right-versus-right issues may be seen as a series of circles as shown in Illustration 1.3.

For example, suppose you are offered a job promotion that will increase your salary significantly but requires that you relocate to Cairo, Egypt. While trying to do no harm, make things better, respect others, be fair, and be compassionate, you would likely face many conflicts. According to the Weinstein model, your obligations to

ILLUSTRATION 1.3 MORAL OBLIGATION RELATIONSHIPS

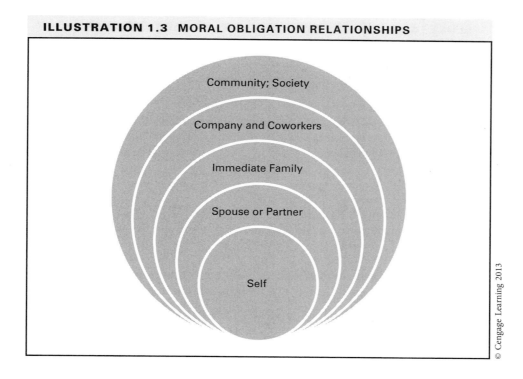

Community; Society

Company and Coworkers

Immediate Family

Spouse or Partner

Self

© Cengage Learning 2013

your spouse or partner should outweigh your obligations to your company (boss, coworkers, assistants, and stockholders) and even to the larger communities of which you are a member.

In a similar vein, another ethicist, J. L. Badaracco (1997), proposes that some ethical issues involve responsibility to self alone; others include responsibility to self and for others; and still others concern an added responsibility—that which is shared with other groups in society. In each category, a person who wants to act ethically and wisely should answer a series of questions to promote a well-reasoned decision, as opposed to a simplistic or impulsive one (see Illustration 1.4).

For example, when applying for a job in an accounting firm, a woman who has passed the CPA exam is offered a position as an office manager rather than as a member of the audit staff. She may face this dilemma: "Should I accept this offer because it provides secure employment near my home? Or should I reject it because it seems to be a case of sexism?" In another instance, when a manager is asked to dismiss a young man whose wife recently lost her job, should the manager consider the needs of the company above the needs of the employee? A further example: When a company president who enjoys attending ballet performances proposes that the company make a generous contribution to a local ballet company, the president's individual values must be balanced against the values of the stockholders and of the community as a whole.

Understanding frameworks for moral judgments, such as those proposed by Weinstein and Badaracco, will help you understand how and why your decisions sometimes differ from those of other well-meaning, moral, rational persons. Ideally, an act is good in itself, the act results in good consequences, the act is prompted by a virtue that is good in itself, and the virtue leads to good consequences (Chewning, 1983).

ILLUSTRATION 1.4 QUESTIONS TO DIRECT MORAL DECISION MAKING

Personal Aspects—Responsibility to Self

1. How do my feelings and intuitions define the dilemma for me?
2. How deep are the moral roots of the conflicting values that are creating the right-versus-right conflict? Which of the responsibilities and values in conflict have the deepest roots in my life and in communities about which I care?
3. Are these the values by which I want to shape my future, as opposed to others who may want to shape my future?
4. What will work in the world as it is? How can expediency and shrewdness, imagination and boldness, move me toward the goals about which I care most strongly?

Organizational Aspects—Responsibility to Self and for Others

1. What is truth? What are the other strong, persuasive, competing interpretations of the situation or problem? What kind of interpretation is most likely to win a contest of interpretation inside the organization and influence the thinking and behavior of others?
2. What is the cash value of this situation and of my ideas for the people whose support I need?
3. Have I orchestrated a process that can make the values I care about become the truth for my organization?
4. Am I playing to win?

Societal Aspects—Responsibility Shared with Others

1. Have I done all I can to secure my position and the strength and stability of my organization?
2. Have I thought creatively and imaginatively about my organization's role in society and its relationship to its stakeholders?
3. Do I have the strength and power to act boldly (like a lion), or should I act more craftily (like a fox)? What allies do I have inside and outside my company? What allies do I need? Which parties will resist or fight my efforts? Have I underestimated their power and tactical skill or overestimated their ethics? Can I respond quickly and flexibly, thereby seizing opportunities?

Source: Summarized from Badaracco (1997).

But when all these ideals cannot be met, moral compromises must be reached. By answering the questions posed in Illustrations 1.4 and 1.5, you should become more skilled in making ethical decisions that result in the greatest good for yourself, for those to whom you have a responsibility, and for the larger society—a responsibility that you may share with others.

Using ethical models to direct judgments made during the communication process can improve the ethical quality of your writing and help you produce more effective

---

ILLUSTRATION 1.5   QUESTIONS FOR ANALYZING THE ETHICS OF COMMUNICATION

1. Is the communication honest and truthful?
2. Am I acting in the company's best interest? In the public's best interest? In my own best interest?
3. What if everybody acted or communicated in this way? If the action or communication is right in this situation, is it right for everyone else in the same situation?
4. Am I willing to take responsibility for the action or communication publicly and privately?
5. Does the action or communication violate the rights of any of the people involved?

Source: Sims (1993).

---

reports. Questions related specifically to the content and tone of a report can direct you toward the production of effective reports, whether you are working on an individual or a team project.

Collaborative Writing

Many reports are produced through collaboration, the process whereby a group of people works together to produce a finished product, such as a report. The first step in producing a collaborative report is to follow these guides for effective collaboration.

- Have empathy for the other collaborators. See their point of view. Do not assume that you know what they are saying or are going to say. Actively listen to what they are saying.
- Be considerate of others. Support the other members of the group with compliments and friendliness. Be supportive by using motivation rather than pressure to inspire people to act.
- Be loyal to the group without agreeing with everything. Tactfully assert yourself when you have a contribution to make or when you disagree.
- Invite criticism of your contributions and be ready to criticize your own ideas. Detach yourself from your ideas and try to see them objectively, as you hope others will. Never attack people personally for their ideas. The criticism should be directed at the idea, not at the person.
- Understand that communication often breaks down. Do not be shocked when you are misunderstood or when you misunderstand others.
- Remember that most ideas that are not obvious seem strange at first, yet they may be the best ideas of all.

Reviewing these guides each time you begin a collaborative project will get you off to a productive start and help bring you to a satisfying end of the project.

In business settings, collaboration is often enhanced through audioconferencing. You may find the discussion in the next section helpful as you embark on collaborative projects.

Audioconferencing

Businesspeople often collaborate during a telephone conference call, involving three to more than a hundred people. This technology, called audio teleconference or simply audioconferencing, is not new; but audioconferencing is more widely used and more advanced than ever. In the simplest conference call, the participants just listen to the caller; but more commonly, calls allow all participants to speak. Early conference calls required the caller to call other participants and add them to the conference. Now, participants are usually able to join a conference themselves by using a telephone number the conference originator provides in advance. In the past, audioconferencing required the use of telephones made specifically for conference calls. Increasingly, companies use ordinary telephones, and special service providers maintain the access numbers and necessary equipment.

Examples of these special service providers include AT Conference, Coms, Intercall, Office Depot, StarConferencing, and others. Both AT Conference and Intercall, like better-known conference call providers such as AT&T, Skype, and Verizon, also offer video (Web) conferencing services, a topic discussed in Chapter 7.

Cutting Business Costs

Conference calls are a means of cutting business costs. Audioconferencing services cost roughly five cents a minute per participant, though service providers offer many, varied rate plans, including plans in which participants share costs of the call. Besides, conference call service providers increasingly use VoIP (Voice over Internet Protocol) phone service, which costs less than conventional telephone service. In any case, collaborating by telephone costs less than online meetings (Web conferencing) and much less than traveling to collaborate in person.

Meeting physically is valuable for building relationships among participants. However, most meetings are held to complete tasks or make decisions or plans rather than to build relationships. These work meetings lend themselves to audioconferencing, eliminating not only the costs of transportation, lodging, restaurant meals, and so on, but also the loss of time and work hours that travel entails. For example, a team of three to seven businesspeople in various locations around the country or world might use conference calls to plan a report, as discussed in Chapter 2. Collaboration often combines an actual meeting with a conference call. Participants in the same office can gather in one room to talk with participants at remote locations, using a speakerphone, a telephone that can be used at short distance without holding it next to the face or without using a headset.

Making Audioconferences Effective

To help ensure successful collaboration, follow these guides for effective conference calls.

- Limit the number of participants. As you would for a physical meeting, invite only the people who need to be included.
- Give clear instructions. Ensure that all participants know the procedures for joining and exiting an audioconference. Provide these directions in writing, along with highlights of conference call etiquette.

- Include all participants in the audioconference. Place a sign with participants' names and/or pictures in front of you as a visual reminder to speak directly to everyone at some point in the conference call.

- Avoid noise. Use a telephone in a quiet area and avoid rustling papers or creating other distracting sounds. If you can, turn off telephone tones, such as call-waiting or paging, that could interrupt the conference call.

- Identify yourself before speaking. Do not assume that other participants will recognize your voice. Even if they know you, a minor distortion in the telephone equipment may make your voice unrecognizable. Identify yourself each time you speak—until other participants tell you they recognize your voice.

- Follow the conference agenda. If you are the conference originator, plan the conference call. Then email or fax the agenda in advance, along with vital handouts. As a participant, look over the agenda and handouts before joining the conference call. Then, as the audioconference unfolds, let the agenda keep you on track.

- Follow the leader. A meeting needs someone to lead it, and one person should manage each conference call. The person in charge should control the order in which participants speak and otherwise keep the conversation organized.

- Wait your turn. Avoid the temptation to speak out of turn, thereby making the audioconference easier for everyone to follow. Besides, some conference call equipment allows only one person to talk. Thus, if you interrupt another participant, you may cut that speaker off midsentence.

- Test audioconferencing equipment periodically. Defective equipment could cause people not to "show up" for an audioconference.

- Ask specific questions, calling on participants by name. In a report planning conference, for example, do not simply ask, "What do you think of this report structure?" Instead, ask, "What do you think of using a cause-effect structure, Nikki?" Likewise, when ending the conference call, do not simply say, "Any comments?" Instead, ask participants to respond in sequence; for example, "Can I hear from Amanda first, then Hendrie and Mikel?"

Summary

Reports are organized, objective presentations of observations, experiences, or facts. Their basic function is to provide information for effective decisions and actions at all levels of an organization. Effective reports contribute to the advancement of the reporter's career as well as to the success of the organization.

To prepare an effective report, evaluate your work for empathy, accuracy, completeness, conciseness, and clarity. Also evaluate the ethical implications of your report: Will it contribute to good or bad decisions and actions? Have you tested your writing decisions against an ethical model?

As you undertake your report-writing activities, you will often be required to work collaboratively. Following basic guides for collaboration—empathy, consideration, loyalty, and openness to criticism and new ideas—should get you off to a good start in any collaborative effort.

Audioconferencing represents a low-cost way of collaborating internally and outside an organization. Common uses of audioconferencing include project planning and updates and regular team meetings. Following basic guidelines—avoid noise, identify yourself, follow the agenda and leader, and wait your turn—will help when you originate or participate in an audioconference.

Topics for Discussion

1. In what ways do business reports differ from a typical college term paper?

2. Business reports are defined as *organized*, *objective* presentations of *observations*, *experiences*, or *facts* used in the *decision-making process*. What is your understanding of each of the italicized terms? Why should you keep each of those ideas in mind as you prepare reports in any organization? What problems could arise if you neglect any one of those factors?

3. Report classifications suggest the pervasiveness of reports as business tools. With which of those classifications are you familiar? Describe to your classmates any experience you have had with various types of reports.

4. Give examples (other than those in the textbook) to demonstrate your understanding of each of the following characteristics of effective reports:
    *   Empathy
    *   Accuracy
    *   Completeness
    *   Conciseness
    *   Clarity

5. Define empathy; give an example of how nonempathetic writing can be changed to demonstrate empathy.

6. Explain this statement: "Conciseness does not mean brevity above all."

7. Explain each of the following forms of consistency. Provide examples of violations of these types of consistency that you have observed in the print media or in business writing:
    *   Grammatical
    *   Structural
    *   Logical

8. Define and give examples (other than those in the textbook) of these fallacies:
    *   *post hoc, ergo propter hoc*
    *   *non sequitur*
    *   begging the question
    *   hasty generalization

9. Discuss ways in which you can contribute to effective collaboration. If you have had experience producing a report collaboratively, describe that experience to your classmates. Was it successful? If so, what contributed to its success? If not, what contributed to its failure?

10. Discuss the relationships between Weinstein's criteria for ethical behavior and collaborative writing behaviors.

11. If you have participated in a conference call with family or friends—using Skype, for example—share the experience with the class. Identify favorable and unfavorable things about the call. What would you and other participants need to do differently in a business audioconference?

12. What do you think the following statement means? A conference call is a meeting that just happens to occur over the telephone, not a telephone call that just happens to be a meeting.

13. An outspoken Russian journalist has attracted many critics, some writing scathing criticisms (and worse) in online blogs and chats. One critic, a novelist, said, "Obscenities and threats are specific features of the Russian blogosphere. Nothing was allowed for 70 years under the Communists, and all of a sudden everything is allowed. You can say anything you want, no matter how vicious or profane, to an unknown person on the Internet. This is a toy, a game. People are not held responsible for their words." Discuss this point of view. Do you agree? Disagree? Is the blogging behavior by one writer (a novelist) regarding another writer (a journalist) ethical? ("Attack on a Journalist," 2010).

14. Steven Katz has been called a "credit terrorist." He wants Americans buried in debt to stop feeling guilty about not honoring their obligations and has founded Debtorboards.com to advise consumers on ways to get out from under their debt loads. Go to Debtorboards.com and review its contents. Discuss the ethics of the website (Thorpe, 2011).

Applications

1. Find an example of a message (report, announcement, business letter, advertisement, and so on) that violates one or more of the characteristics of an effective report presented in Chapter 1. As directed by your instructor, share your findings with your classmates in a brief oral presentation or write a report in a format similar to the memo shown in Illustration 1.2. Explain how the item has failed to meet one or more of the criteria.

2. Select the item that best demonstrates accuracy. Explain your choice by identifying the errors that appear in the remaining items.
   a. Of 300 questionnaire respondents, 35 percent, or 90 people, had seen the Tyler Company TV commercials.
   b. Of 300 questionnaire respondents, 35 percent, or 105 people, had seen the Tyler Company TV commercials.
   c. Thirty-five percent (115) of the 320 questionnaire respondents had seen the Tyler Company TV commercials.

3. Select the item that best demonstrates completeness. Explain your choice.
   a. We should extend our lease.
   b. We should extend our lease on 1212 Parklane.
   c. We should extend our lease on 1212 Parklane Ave. for at least a year.

4. Select the item that least demonstrates clarity. Explain your choice.
   a. Your flight reservation has been confirmed for 9:45 A.M. tomorrow.
   b. Your flight reservation has been confirmed.
   c. Your flight reservation has been confirmed for 9:45 tomorrow.

5. Select the item that best demonstrates correct modification. Explain your choice.
   a. Wanting to improve flexibility and balance, a tai chi class seemed like a good choice.

    b. Wanting to improve flexibility and balance, Dennis thought a tai chi class would be a good choice.

    c. Wanting to improve flexibility and balance, Linda advised Dennis to enroll in a tai chi class.

6. Select the item that best demonstrates grammatical consistency. Explain your choice.

    a. Here's your sandwich and beverage.

    b. Here is your sandwich as well as your beverage.

    c. Here are your sandwich and beverage.

7. Select the item that best demonstrates logical consistency. Explain your choice.

    a. In a recent customer survey, 90 percent of our repeat customers reported that our policy of giving free shipping for online purchases and returns influenced their purchases. We should continue that service.

    b. This report shows that 96 percent of our customers go to our website first when shopping for shoes because we offer free shipping on purchases and returns. That policy gives us an edge on our competition.

    c. This report shows that 96 percent of our customers appreciate our policy of offering free shipping on purchases and returns. That's why we have so many repeat customers.

8. Select the item that least demonstrates empathy. Explain your choice.

    a. Margaret, I need the report of yesterday's sales calls for my meeting with Rachel Mamarchev this afternoon. Will you please find it?

    b. Margaret, I need the report of yesterday's sales calls. Where is it?

    c. Margaret, find the report of yesterday's sales calls.

9. Select the item that best demonstrates conciseness. Explain your choice.

    a. We would ask that you answer each item on the questionnaire.

    b. We request that you answer every single item on the questionnaire.

    c. Please answer each item on the questionnaire.

10. Rewrite each of the following sentences, correcting expressions that are not grammatically parallel. Write concisely while maintaining parallel structure.

    a. Scheduling service calls and to be able to complete them on time are important aspects of this job.

    b. To be able to write concisely and proofreading with precision are skills required of an editor.

    c. An effective secret shopper must be perceptive, objective, and not a time waster.

    d. Betty started a dog-sitting service because she loves dogs and also to satisfy her desire for security and independence.

    e. An effective writer strives for clarity, conciseness, and to show empathy and logical thinking.

    f. Weinstein proposes that ethical people do no harm, make things better, respect others, and acting fairly, and showing compassion.

11. As directed by your instructor, form a team with one or more of your classmates. Select one of the issues from the following list. Discuss the issue getting views of all teammates. Assign one aspect of the issue to each team member and set a time for a meeting at which each person will present a brief summary of her or his findings. Keep the data gathered. This application will be continued in Chapter 2.

- The ethics of outsourcing customer service
- The ethics of downsizing
- The ethics of taking sick-leave days for reasons other than illness
- The values or dangers of buying or selling items on websites such as craigslist.org or eBay.com
- Charter schools: What are they? Advantages? Disadvantages?
- Powering an automobile with waste vegetable oil: How is it done? Advantages? Disadvantages?
- The accuracy or inaccuracy of nutrition and other claims made on food packages (for example, Pepperidge Farm's "Indulge in the perfect combination of chocolate and mocha lusciousness with Pepperidge Farm Petite Cake" ("Food Porn," 2011)

12. Patricia Rogan received the following email message from her supervisor at the investment firm where she works.

> Pat, I just got a call from a man who is 65 years old. Although he retired from real estate sales when he was 62, he has been working part-time since then at Salene's department store and participating in its retirement program. Salene's requires that part-time employees withdraw their retirement funds in a lump sum when they reach 65 or roll the money over into an IRA account. He wants to open an IRA with us and roll the retirement funds into it.
>
> This account isn't going to be worth much. He clearly is not interested in other kinds of investments—doesn't have much money to spare. I don't want to bother with him, so I gave him your name. He'll probably call you. Please handle it.

Using the criteria for effective reports presented in Chapter 1, critique the message. Write an improved version of the message.

13. Go to the website for the International Association of Business Communicators. Find its code of ethics. Choose two articles from that code. In a message to your instructor, explain how those articles do or do not comply with the guides given in Chapter 1. Use the memo format demonstrated in Illustration 1.2.

14. In January 2011, Wal-Mart, the largest retailer in the United States, announced a five-year plan to lower salts, fats, and sugars in packaged foods and drop prices on fresh fruits and vegetables. First Lady Michelle Obama appeared with Wal-Mart executives when the announcement was made and praised the company's efforts to offer healthier food at affordable prices to its customers. Since Wal-Mart sells more groceries than any other company in the United States, this action could have a big impact not only on consumers but also on producers and packagers of foods.

Form a team with two or more of your classmates. Using the guides for ethical decision making given in Chapter 1, discuss potential conflicts the company may face with respect to its owners, its customers, the general public, and its suppliers. Discuss also the ethics of Mrs. Obama's appearance with company executives at the announcement of the program's launch. Summarize your discussion in a message to your instructor. Use the memo format demonstrated in Illustration 1.2.

15. Packaging items for marketing serves many purposes: attracting attention to the product, protecting the product, informing potential purchasers about the product's features, and so on. Environmentalists are increasingly critical of packaging that they consider excessive.

Use the Internet to obtain information about Britain's WRAP project, an effort to encourage household recycling and waste reduction. Some citizens have confronted merchants about excess packaging, considering it a violation of the WRAP ideals. In a memo to your instructor, describe the major features of the WRAP project and citizens' reactions to it.

References

1. Attack on a journalist stirs his allies online. (2010, November 14). *New York Times International*, pp. 5, 16.

2. Baldaracco, J. L. (1997). *Defining moments: When managers must choose between right and right.* Boston: Harvard Business School Press.

3. Chewning, R. C. (1983). *Business ethics in a changing culture.* Richmond, Virginia: Robert F. Dame, Inc.

4. Food Porn. (2011, January/February). *Nutrition Action Health Letter*, 16.

5. Roman, E. (2011, February 1). Lessons from Ford's brilliant use of social medial. Retrieved February 11, 2011, from http://www.huffingtonpost.com/ernan-roman/lessons-from-brilli_b_816605.html?vie.

6. Set precise angles vertically and digitally. (2010, November). *WOOD Magazine*, 10.

7. Sims, B. R. (1993). Linking ethics and language in the technical communication classroom. *Technical Communication Quarterly, 3*(Summer), 285–299.

8. Thorpe, K. (2011). Take this APR and shove it. *Mother Jones, 16–18.*

9. Weinstein, B. (2007a). *Principle no. 3: Respect others (part 1).* Retrieved January 24, 2011, from http://www.businessweek.com/print/careers/content/jan2007/ca20070125_546645.htm.

10. Weinstein, B. (2007b). *Five easy principles?* Retrieved January 24, 2011, from http://www.businessweek.com/print/careers/content/jan2007/ca20070111_219724.htm.

CHAPTER 2
Planning the Report

LEARNING OBJECTIVES

After you have read this chapter, you should be able to:

1. Identify the purpose, audience, and context for a report.

2. Select appropriate report content.

3. Choose an appropriate medium.

4. Choose a report structure that complements its purpose, audience, context, and content.

5. Apply outlining strategies and electronic technology to develop your report structure.

6. Collaborate effectively to plan a report.

7. Use groupware to enhance collaboration.

8. Consider ethical implications that arise during the planning process.

A WELL-PLANNED REPORT CONTRIBUTES TO EFFECTIVE COMMUNICATION, whereas a hastily written report frequently leads to misunderstanding. Some reports require only brief informal plans. Consider, for example, a one-page memo to employees reporting that management has approved an extra holiday, January 2, for all employees. A manager could easily write this report after reviewing notes made in a managers' meeting; but the effective writer would take time to consider the audience, desired effect of the report, exact information to be included, and order of presentation.

In contrast, consider a report from a market researcher to a management committee about a recently completed market survey. Before writing the report, the researcher would develop a formal plan that would likely be presented to a supervisor for evaluation, suggestions, and approval. That plan would include such factors as the intended audience for the report, the purpose of the study, a full description of how the research was conducted, and the results. As a general guide, the formality and length of the report plan are directly related to the complexity of the information to be reported.

Planning the Report

Effective report writers follow a six-step plan before beginning to write, as shown in Illustration 2.1. Although report writers sometimes follow those steps in the order

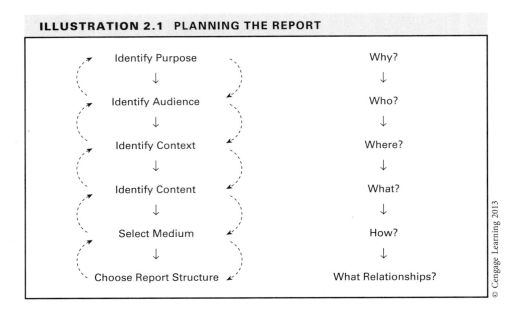

ILLUSTRATION 2.1 PLANNING THE REPORT

Identify Purpose	Why?
↓	↓
Identify Audience	Who?
↓	↓
Identify Context	Where?
↓	↓
Identify Content	What?
↓	↓
Select Medium	How?
↓	↓
Choose Report Structure	What Relationships?

© Cengage Learning 2013

listed, the dotted lines in the illustration indicate that the process is recursive, not linear. The elements are interdependent. For example, identification of the context may help to identify the audience, identification of the purpose may help to define the content, and identification of the content and audience should contribute to selection of the appropriate medium.

Identify Purpose

In some instances, the motivation for the report is that your job description requires you to submit such a report. For example, a sales representative may be required to present a weekly report of calls made, contracts acquired, and plans for the following week. Whether prompted by your job description or by special circumstances, the report will be most effective if you define your purpose in terms of what you want your reader to do or think after reading it. If you do not define the desired outcome, the report may become nothing more than a presentation of data; you will place the burden of interpretation on the reader. The reader may well conclude that action is necessary, but the action may not be what you expected.

Reports can be classified according to their general purposes: production, innovation, or goodwill.* Production messages relate to getting the job done. Assigning an employee a new area of responsibility and reporting a deviation from production standards are examples of production messages. Innovation messages relate to

---

*In a classic study, Farace and MacDonald (1974) identified three purposes of organizational communication: production, innovation, and maintenance. This author has found that students have difficulty associating the term *maintenance* with the idea of maintaining employee morale. Therefore, in this book, the term *goodwill* is used to cover that concept.

initiating change in an organization. A proposal to split an operating division into two units and a memo explaining a company's newly adopted telecommuting policy are examples of innovation messages. Goodwill messages relate to maintaining the loyalty and morale of the people within or outside the organization. Reports about employee accomplishments or plans for the company picnic are examples of goodwill reports. Most short, simple reports are production messages dealing with a single, clearly definable topic and an objective that relates directly to accomplishing the organization's tasks. A sales representative's weekly production report, for example, tells a sales manager about the progress the representative is making toward achieving sales goals; and a policy statement about drug use tells employees what can, must, and will be done to maintain a productive working environment.

By its very nature, innovation often requires review of a problem or presentation of a rationale that requires or justifies an organizational change. For that reason, a well-structured message that will persuade a reader to accept change may require greater length and formality than is typically associated with many short reports. However, context and audience could also justify a relatively short report for an innovation message. For example, a complete analysis of the benefits and disadvantages of telecommuting might be presented in a lengthy, formal report to management. But management's report to employees about the new telecommuting policy could be written in a page or two.

Managers also write short reports for goodwill purposes. A report about employees' volunteer activities with local hospitals or a report identifying and congratulating top sales associates for the month would be written primarily to reinforce the employees' sense of self-worth and worth to the organization—to maintain employee morale.

As you plan your report, it is useful to identify the general purpose as production, innovation, or goodwill. This identification will help you determine the specific purpose (for example, to report last week's sales; to gain approval for a new policy; or to congratulate employees for participation in the United Way campaign), as well as the appropriate content, structure, writing style, and tone for the message.

Assume, for example, that your company, which develops computer software for the insurance industry, has a sick-leave policy. This policy specifically requires employees to inform their supervisors before 8:30 A.M. if they are ill and unable to come to work. The policy allows 1.5 days of leave per month, which may be accumulated to up to 36 days of sick leave. If employees are suspected of misusing the benefit, they may be required to submit medical proof of illness. One of your employees, Janice Widener, has recently taken a part-time job with a start-up software firm that has been somewhat secretive about the type of software it is working on. The job requires her to work from 6 P.M. until 10 P.M. on Tuesday and Thursday. Since taking that job, Widener has frequently called in "sick" on Wednesday or Friday. She has averaged one sick day per week, sometimes two mornings. You have also observed that she often seems sluggish on days following her evening work hours. You have spoken with her about her absences and her lackluster performance, but the pattern persists. When you questioned her about the frequency of "sick" days, she said there should be no problem because she had accumulated 15 days of leave.

You now plan to report the situation to the director of human resources. Before preparing the report, you must define what you want the director to do: Counsel Widener? Make an entry in Widener's personnel records? Advise you about ways to motivate Widener to stop that behavior? Your decision about the report's purpose will influence other reporting steps, such as identification of content and structure, as well as selection of medium.

Identify Audience

Before preparing your report, you must identify your audience, both primary and secondary. In the Widener case, the primary receiver is the human resources director to whom you will send the report. Secondary readers may be current and future human resources staff or higher-level managers—and perhaps Widener herself.

Audience identification requires more than merely identifying who will receive the report. After identifying the primary receiver, try to empathize with that person and identify her or his information and ego needs. If your purpose complements those needs, your writing task is relatively easy. But if your purpose contradicts the receiver's needs, your task becomes more difficult. In such a situation, before you state the main point of your report, you will have to give enough information to overcome possible objections in the receiver's mind.

Consider again the Widener example. One need of the human resources director is to be well informed about all personnel issues. You may also know that the director is altruistic (that is, desires to help others); and as a busy manager, the director likely prefers clear, concise, complete messages that permit immediate action without further clarification. As an effective report writer, you will satisfy all those needs by indicating clearly what you want the director to do, including all necessary information to support that request and excluding unnecessary details. Knowing that the director is altruistic, you might word the request to show that the desired action will help Widener, you, or other employees.

Although your first concern is to address the primary reader, recognize also that others may read the report. Even if you and the human resources director are well acquainted, considering the possible secondary readers should prevent you from using an excessively personal or casual tone in the report. The possibility that Widener herself may have access to the report or that it may become evidence in a disciplinary action should also prompt you to avoid emotional or abstract terms. The report must be objective and unambiguous.

Identify Context

The report context includes the physical and psychological environment of the communication exchange. Many reports are transmitted routinely with little thought about the context in which the message will be received. Many businesspeople, for example, feel burdened by the plethora of emails they face every day. Many of those messages evidence little concern for the physical or emotional context in which the message will be received. But effective communicators send their reports, whether written or electronic, to arrive at a time and place that will encourage the reader to give full attention to the message.

If, for example, you know that the human resources director always has a management meeting on Monday morning, you might be wise to ensure that the director receives the report about Widener on Wednesday or Thursday. That timing would permit the director to dispose of tasks related to the previous Monday's management meeting and give full attention to the report. Appropriate timing would allow the director to consider appropriate action, including what—if anything—about the case should be discussed at the next management meeting. Or assume that you decide to give Widener a final oral warning before reporting her absences and erratic performance. The appropriate place and time for that warning would be privately in your office or at Widener's work station immediately after you observe her breakdown in performance—not at her annual review several months later.

Identify Content

Identifying purpose, audience, and context will help you determine appropriate content for your report. You must include all information the receiver requires to fulfill your purpose, and you must include details that motivate the receiver to act. Fully as important, however, is the caution to exclude unnecessary details that may obstruct understanding. Include all the receiver must know, not necessarily all you know or find interesting. Exclude any information that is not relevant to the purpose of the report.

If, for example, your purpose is to stimulate the human resources director to discipline Widener, you must provide all information justifying such action: a record of Widener's infractions, what you have done to correct the situation, Widener's responses to your actions, and the effects of her behavior. You should not, however, include comments about your personal dislike of Widener or rumors about her plans to leave your company and work full-time for her current part-time employer.

Another critical part of your report-writing plan is to choose a medium to transmit the report.

Select Medium

Media differ in their ability to transmit information. Over 25 years ago, Lengel and Daft developed the medium richness theory, which classifies a medium as "rich" or "lean" on the basis of its ability to meet three criteria: transmit multiple cues, facilitate rapid feedback, and provide a personal focus (see Illustration 2.2). This theory has stood the test of time and has been supported by extensive research (Lengel & Daft, 1988).

The richest medium is face-to-face communication because it meets all three criteria. Impersonal media, such as flyers or bulletin-board announcements, are lean. They can accommodate few cues, allow for delayed feedback only, and have no personal focus. Memos, letters, and reports tailored for a specific receiver are richer than bulletins because they have a more personal focus even though they do not permit immediate feedback. Email is somewhat richer than printed letters or memoranda; while permitting a personal focus, it also enables more rapid feedback than does a printed letter or memorandum. Interactive media, such as the telephone, online conferences, or instant messaging, are richer than memos, letters, or email;

ILLUSTRATION 2.2   EXAMPLES OF MEDIA RICHNESS

Media Richness			
Richest ————————————————————→ **Least Rich**			
Physical Presence (face-to-face discussion; oral presentation with Q/A session)	**Interactive Media** (telephone, e-mail, instant messaging, electronic conferencing)	**Personal Static Media** (memos, letters, reports in personal style)	**Impersonal Static Media** (flyers, bulletins, posters, printout of spreadsheet, generalized reports)

Source: Adapted from Lengel, R. H. & Daft, R. L. (1988). The selection of communication media as an executive skill. *The Academy of Management EXECUTIVE*, 2(3), 226.

they permit both a personal focus and immediate feedback. Although some interactive media (for example, videoconferencing) can accommodate both visual and vocal cues, others (for example, the telephone) cannot. No interactive medium is as rich as face-to-face communication, which can accommodate the full range of vocal and visual cues.

Research has shown that using lean media for communicating about routine management problems and richer media for nonroutine problems contributes to communication effectiveness. In contrast, using a lean medium for a nonroutine problem contributes to communication breakdown. Lean media provide too few cues for the message receiver, resulting in information shortage. Similarly, using a rich medium for a routine problem tends to cause communication breakdown because the message provides excess cues, resulting in information overload or noise (see Illustration 2.3).

Consider again Janice Widener's absences and lackluster performance on days following her night job. The first time you approach Widener to report that this behavior must change, you would probably use face-to-face communication for this nonroutine message. To post a notice on the bulletin board reminding employees of the sick-leave policy would likely have little effect on Widener because the medium is too impersonal. On the other hand, a memo (or email if the director prefers that medium) would be an effective medium to report Widener's behavior to human resources. Neither you nor the director needs immediate feedback, but the memo can be personalized and can become part of Widener's personnel file. A telephone call or a face-to-face conversation could result in miscommunication. The richness of those media could overemphasize the significance of a problem that is routine to most human resources directors, who handle such situations as part of their normal duties. Moreover, although a telephone call or a face-to-face conversation permits immediate feedback, those media provide no immediate record of the communication. In fact, if you were to mention the employee's infraction to the director of human resources over the table during lunch, the director would likely ask you to put it in writing.

ILLUSTRATION 2.3 MEDIA SELECTION

Media Richness	Management Problem	
	Routine	*Non-routine*
Rich ↓ **Lean**	*Communication Failure* Rich medium used for routine situation • Too much data • Excess cues cause confusion and distort meaning	*Communication Success* Rich medium used for non-routine situation • Allows sufficient data • Number, kinds of cues signal significance of messages
	Communication Success Lean medium used for routine situation • Sufficient data • No excess cues to distract receiver	*Communication Failure* Lean medium used for non-routine situation • Insufficient data • Number, kinds of cues downplay significance of messages

Source: Adapted from Lengel & Daft.

Choose Report Structure

The appropriate structure for a report depends on the specific purpose, content, and context of the report. That fact will be demonstrated as you consider nine commonly used structures for entire reports or for parts of reports. These structures may even be applied at the paragraph level.

To help you understand the relationship of report structure to purpose, a specific objective is given in parentheses before each example of structure.

Direct (Deductive)

The direct structure is based on the deductive style of reasoning: from general to specific. A report written in this structure begins with the main point (a generalization), which is followed by supporting data (the facts that justify the generalization). This structure is appropriate when the reader needs little psychological preparation for the main point because it is an expected or easy-to-accept message. The following example demonstrates the direct (deductive) structure. The main point or general statement ("Arriving on time … and we intend to ensure that you do.") precedes the detailed facts about how World Wings has changed flight schedules to and from Atlanta.

(*Objective*: To reinforce customer loyalty)

Arriving on time is important to you, and we intend to ensure that you do.

Our goal at World Wings is to deliver fast and reliable service. One of the ways we hope to achieve this is by adjusting flight schedules to and from Atlanta, the

> *world's busiest passenger airport. Beginning January 31, 2013, our new schedule will offer more than 1,000 daily nonstop flights to nearly 200 domestic and international destinations from Atlanta. The new schedule will give you:*
>
> ◆ *More on-time arrivals and departures*
> ◆ *More flight choices*
> ◆ *Less congestion and smoother check-in and security processes*
>
> *For more information about these changes and other World Wings news, please visit www.worldwings.com.*
>
> *Thank you for flying World Wings.*

Indirect (Inductive)

The indirect structure is based on the inductive style of reasoning, which examines facts and forms generalizations based on those facts. A report written in this structure presents significant data related to the basic purpose of the report, followed by the main point or conclusion supported by those details. This structure is appropriate when the reader requires background details before being able to understand or accept the thrust of the message. The following message demonstrates indirect (inductive) structure. The generalization or conclusion (fewer flights to and from Atlanta) follows the facts that justify the changes.

> *(**Objective:** To maintain customer loyalty and goodwill in spite of schedule reductions)*
>
> *During 2012, several commercial airlines announced reductions in their flight schedules. Knowing that people who spend much of their time flying with us are a key to our success, we at World Wings maintained the number of flights to and from Atlanta, while other carriers were cutting their programs.*
>
> *To demonstrate our appreciation for your loyalty, we will continue to offer all current early morning and early evening flights. This means you will continue to be able to attend business meetings on a timely schedule and easily make connections with most international flights.*
>
> *Security issues, airport congestion, and spiraling fuel costs, however, require that we curtail the less frequently used flights. Therefore, beginning in 2013, we will reduce the number of flights arriving at and departing from Atlanta between the hours of 10:30 A.M. and 5:30 P.M.*
>
> *For more information about these changes and other World Wings news, please visit www.worldwings.com.*
>
> *Thank you for flying World Wings.*

Chronological

Chronological structure uses time as the central organizational component of the message. This structure is appropriate when time is an essential ingredient for understanding the basis of a request or for fulfilling that request. Any time units—minutes, hours, days, weeks, months, years, or eras—relevant to the report may be used. The following example illustrates chronological structure.

> (**Objective**: *To stimulate conference participation and clarify target dates for successful participation*)
>
> *You are invited to participate in the 2013 Association for Human Resource Management Annual Conference. You are especially encouraged to share some of your experience—successful or otherwise—with other human resource managers by presenting a paper or a symposium at the conference in New Orleans, LA, on October 20–22, 2013.*
>
> *Please note these important dates:*
>
> | | |
> |---|---|
> | *April 15, 2013* | *Deadline for submission of proposal for paper or symposium* |
> | *April 25, 2013* | *Acceptance notification* |
> | *August 1, 2013* | *Final copy due at Association Headquarters* |
> | *September 17, 2013* | *Deadline for conference registration* |
> | *October 20–22, 2013* | *Conference in New Orleans, LA* |

The chronological structure may be appropriate for part of a report but not necessarily for the entire report. Chronological structure may also record events by exact time of occurrence; this type of structure is called log structure. The following example illustrates log structure.

> (**Objective**: *To ensure that convention volunteers fulfill their duties completely and accurately*)
>
> *To ensure that all convention participants have an enjoyable experience, we ask all volunteers to adhere to the following schedule on the first day of the convention, October 20, 2013.*
>
> ◆ *6:30 A.M.: Report to Room 398 (Convention Headquarters) in the River View Hotel; receive post assignment and all materials needed at that post.*
> ◆ *7:00 A.M.: Report to post; set up materials.*
> ◆ *7:30 A.M.: Be prepared to greet visitors to your post.*
> ◆ *7:30 A.M.–1:00 P.M.: Answer questions posed by visitors; ask each visitor to complete a visitor's survey.*
> ◆ *1:00 P.M.: Close post; return to Room 398; deposit visitor surveys in box labeled "Surveys"; report any unusual incidents to R. J. Conway, convention chair, who will be on duty in Room 398.*
>
> *Please remember: You are the "face" of AHRM. Please help convention registrants feel welcome when they arrive and be proud of this organization when they leave.*

Problem-Solution

As the name implies, the problem-solution structure presents a problem, followed by a proposed solution. This structure is effective when the problem and proposed solution can be stated concisely and are likely to receive little objection. (Review the first two sections of the memo displayed in Illustration 1.2 in Chapter 1.) When dealing with a complex problem, you may find the inductive style more effective because it gives you greater latitude to describe the details of the problem and the reasons for the proposed solution.

Here is an example of the problem-solution structure. Notice how this structure directs the reader's attention to the major elements of the report.

> (**Objective**: To stimulate the reader to offer a new amenity to hotel guests)
>
> **Problem:** During the past year many of our hotel guests have asked whether we have hypoallergenic rooms. Some potential customers have even declined to make a reservation when they were told we do not have such rooms. Our biggest competitor in this area, The Waterfront, has converted one floor to hypoallergenic rooms and has seen its occupancy rate rise 25 percent over the past year. Meanwhile, our occupancy rate has declined 10 percent during that time. We appear to be losing some customers because we cannot satisfy their requests for rooms that are free of allergens.
>
> **Solution:** We should ask Pure Room and EnviroRooms, two companies that specialize in designing allergy-friendly rooms, to give us a bid on converting the fifth floor of our hotel into a hypoallergenic area. The bid should include the costs of retrofitting that floor and a timeline for completing the job. Ideally, we would be able to offer hypoallergenic rooms before we run our fall holiday promotions.

Cause-Effect

When using the cause-effect structure, the writer identifies and discusses conditions (causes) and a predicted outcome (effect) of those conditions. This structure is similar to the inductive structure because it moves from specific facts to generalizations based on those facts. The cause-effect structure is appropriate when you want to report your perception of a direct relationship between two or more events. Review the last two sections of the memo in Illustration 1.2 in Chapter 1 and the following example of cause-effect structure.

> (**Objective**: To justify an investment in retrofitting hotel rooms to meet hypoallergenic standards)
>
> Three months ago we gave a contract to EnviroRooms to convert the fifth floor of our hotel into a hypoallergenic zone. The work was completed on time and on budget. We are already seeing a return on that investment. The bookings for the Thanksgiving weekend were 10 percent above last year's bookings. Most of that increase can be attributed to the number of reservations for hypoallergenic rooms.

Spatial

The spatial structure is appropriate any time your data can be presented logically in terms of geographic units. Those units may be as large as continents or nations or as small as areas of a parking lot or a room. You may, for example, wish to analyze the layout of an office, parking lot assignments, productivity by sales districts, or market potential by countries. The spatial structure would be appropriate for the presentation of data analysis, conclusions, or recommendations for each of those reports. The following example demonstrates spatial structure in the presentation of recommendations.

> (**Objective**: To meet customer-service needs effectively in all areas of the city)
>
> As you requested, I have analyzed customer assistance calls, complaints about customer assistance, and potential needs for customer assistance in our market area. Based on that analysis, I recommend the following changes in service personnel.
>
> | | |
> |---|---|
> | Central City | Add one service consultant. |
> | Northeast | Add two service consultants and one technician. |
> | Northwest | Add two service technicians. |
> | Southwest | Reassign one technician from this district to the Southeast district. |
> | Southeast | Assign one technician from the Southwest district and add one service consultant. |

Topical

In topical structure, information is organized around major topics of discussion. A report divided into Findings, Conclusions, and Recommendations is organized topically. To be more meaningful, however, topical headings should identify the factors or elements of analysis. For example, a report presenting the results of a survey to determine preferences for employee benefits could be structured effectively in terms of the major categories of benefits, such as medical insurance, retirement plans, child or elder care, and profit sharing. The following example contains headings from a credit union report that was arranged by topic.

> (**Objective**: To present credit union performance on major measures of operating success)
>
> Subject: Credit Union Performance, 2012
>
> Distribution of Consumer Savings
>
> Xxxxxxxxxxxxxxxxxxxxxxxxxxxxxxxxxxxxxxxxxxxxxxxxxxxxxxxxxxxxx
> xxxxxxxxxxxxxxxxxxxxxxxxxxxxxxxxxxxxxxxxxxxxxxxxxxxxxxxx
>
> Composition of Savings
>
> Xxxxxxxxxxxxxxxxxxxxxxxxxxxxxxxxxxxxxxxxxxxxxxxxxxxxxxxxxxxxx
> xxxxxxxxxxxxxxxxxxxxxxxxxxxxxxxxxxxxxxxxxxxxxxxxxxxxxx

Share of Installment Credit Outstanding by Selected Lenders

Xxxxxxxxxxxxxxxxxxxxxxxxxxxxxxxxxxxxxxxxxxxxxxxxxxxxxxxxxxxxxxx
xxxxxxxxxxxxxxxxxxxxxxxxxxxxxxxxxxxxxxxxxxxxxxxxxxxxxxx

Share of Auto Loans Outstanding by Selected Lenders

Xxxxxxxxxxxxxxxxxxxxxxxxxxxxxxxxxxxxxxxxxxxxxxxxxxxxxxxxxxxxxxx
xxxxxxxxxxxxxxxxxxxxxxxxxxxxxxxxxxxxxxxxxxxxxxxxxxxxxx

Average Loan Rates by Credit Union Asset Size

Xxxxxxxxxxxxxxxxxxxxxxxxxxxxxxxxxxxxxxxxxxxxxxxxxxxxxxxxxxxxxxx
xxxxxxxxxxxxxxxxxxxxxxxxxxxxxxxxxxxxxxxxxxxxxxxxxxxxxx

Comparison or Contrast

Comparison or contrast structure examines two or more items in terms of common criteria. Comparison implies examining the qualities of items to discover similarities and differences. Contrasting focuses primarily on differences.

Assume, for example, that you must prepare a report for college seniors who are thinking of pursuing an MBA degree. The purpose of your report is to provide an objective tool for comparing three MBA programs. You would determine the criteria by which the programs should be evaluated, such as admission standards, cost, availability of financial aid, program requirements, quality of faculty, and placement of graduates. Your report could be structured effectively around those criteria, showing how the programs are similar or different on each criterion. One organizational pattern would evaluate each college on all criteria, as shown in the following example.

*(**Objective**: To compare three MBA programs)*

Program A
- *Admission Standards*
- *Cost*
- *Financial Aid*
- *Requirements*
- *Faculty*
- *Placement of Graduates*

Program B
- *Admission Standards*
- *Cost*
- *Financial Aid*
- *Requirements*
- *Faculty*
- *Placement of Graduates*

Program C
- *Admission Standards*
- *Cost*

> ◆ *Financial Aid*
> ◆ *Requirements*
> ◆ *Faculty*
> ◆ *Placement of Graduates*

Another organizational pattern would compare all colleges on each criterion, as shown in the following example.

> *Admission Standards*
> ◆ *Program A*
> ◆ *Program B*
> ◆ *Program C*
>
> *Cost*
> ◆ *Program A*
> ◆ *Program B*
> ◆ *Program C*
>
> *Financial Aid*
> ◆ *Program A*
> ◆ *Program B*
> ◆ *Program C*
>
> *Requirements*
> ◆ *Program A*
> ◆ *Program B*
> ◆ *Program C*
>
> *Faculty*
> ◆ *Program A*
> ◆ *Program B*
> ◆ *Program C*
>
> *Placement of Graduates*
> ◆ *Program A*
> ◆ *Program B*
> ◆ *Program C*

Combination

As you may have inferred, few reports adhere to a single structural pattern. The combination structure employs two or more of the patterns discussed. Look again at the example in Illustration 1.2. That memo uses problem-solution along with cause-effect.

Returning again to the Widener case, assume that you have decided to ask the director to suspend Widener for one day without pay. You could use an inductive structure that begins with a description of the problem and ends with the requested action. Your description of the problem itself could be written in a cause-effect structure, as shown in the following example.

> *(**Objective**: To ask that Widener be given a one-day suspension)*
>
> ***Current problem***: *Widener's frequent absence and poor performance on days following her evening job.*
>
> ***History***
>
> ◆ *Previous observations of absences and lackluster performance*
> ◆ *Previous corrective action*
> ◆ *Most recent incident*
>
> ***Effects***
>
> ◆ *Decline in department morale*
> ◆ *Occasional misuse of sick-leave benefit by other employees*
>
> ***Requested action***: *Suspend Widener without pay for one day*

If you know, however, that the director prefers that reports requesting action begin with the request, your report should be written in the direct structure, and the essential details to support your request could be presented in cause-effect structure.

> ***Requested action***: *Suspend Widener without pay for one day*
>
> ***Widener's misuse of company sick-leave policy***
>
> ◆ *History of absences and lackluster performance*
> ◆ *Previous corrective action*
> ◆ *Most recent incident*
>
> ***Effects of Widener's behavior***
>
> ◆ *Decline in department morale*
> ◆ *Occasional misuse of sick-leave benefit by other employees*

An outline will help you plan the structure of your report. The outline should indicate the relative importance of the facts and their interrelationships.

Outlining the Report

As you develop your outline—whether it is formal or informal—always keep the reader's needs uppermost in your mind. What does the reader already know about the problem? What does the reader look for first? What supporting data does the reader need? What order of presentation best contributes to reader comprehension of the problem and the solution? How will the reader use the information? The final outline of your report reflects your choice of report structure, which in turn reflects your understanding of the reader's needs and the purpose for the report.

Informal Outlines

An informal outline is a list of topics to be included in the report. It often consists of words, short phrases, or combinations of those elements. Such an outline is primarily an idea-generating tool. For many short reports, the informal outline may be the first and final stage of planning before you draft your report.

Assume, for example, that while eating lunch with the director of human resources, you have mentioned Widener's misuse of the company's sick-leave policy. The director has asked you to send her a brief written report about the situation. An effective process for preparing an informal outline includes three steps.

1. List the topics to be included in the report.
   - Widener's part-time job
   - Frequent tardiness or absence after evening work
   - Lackluster performance
   - Other employees' complaints about "picking up the slack"
   - Rumors that Widener plans to leave
2. Edit the list to be sure it contains all essential topics and no unnecessary information. Although the human resources director is the primary reader, the memo may become a part of Widener's personnel file. Include all information relevant to the situation—but *only* that information. Your revised list might look like this:
   - Details about Widener's part-time job: for whom she works, when she works, how long she has worked there
   - Records of tardiness or absences
   - Previous discussions with Widener: when, where, summary of discussion
   - No change in behavior
   - Request suspension
3. Arrange the topics into a sequence that shows relationships of key points and satisfies the communication needs of your readers. Since the human resources director is a busy person who already knows something about Widener's infraction, you may decide to use the direct structure.
   - Request that Widener be suspended one day without pay
   - Details about Widener's part-time job
   - Summary of Widener's tardiness and absences
   - Previous discussions with Widener
   - Results of discussions with Widener

An informal outline will readily communicate necessary information to you, the writer, and will help you compile your report with ease. For a complex situation, however, you may be dealing with a considerable amount of information and an extensive analysis of that data. To help you produce a coherent, well-organized report, you would do well to prepare a formal outline.

Formal Outlines

A formal outline is a useful communication tool both before and as you write the report. If you wish to discuss the content and structure of your report with a supervisor or a colleague before you begin writing, you can use the outline as a guide. If you follow the outline faithfully while writing the report, you will be sure to cover all essential data.

A formal outline employs a structured numbering system to show the various levels into which the report is divided. Phrases or sentences are used to describe the content of each division and subdivision of the report. Depending largely on the preferences of your report readers, you may use either the traditional outline system or a decimal system to number the sections.

The traditional outline system consists of Roman numerals to indicate first-level divisions, uppercase letters for second-level divisions, Arabic numerals for third-level divisions, and lowercase letters for fourth-level divisions. Few outlines progress beyond fourth-level divisions; but when you need such divisions, continue the numbering system by alternating Arabic numerals and lowercase letters. The *Chicago Manual of Style* (2010) recommends that the divisional numerals or letters for the first three levels be set off by periods and that those for the lower levels be set off by single or double parentheses. The manual also gives the sage advice that what is most important in the development of an outline and its numbering system is that the reader be able to see at a glance the level to which each item belongs.

To illustrate the preparation of a formal outline using the traditional system, assume the following facts.

Context: Your company, BestMeters, specializes in the manufacture and service of flowmeters, which are used in many industries that transport a liquid product and must measure the flow of that product during delivery.

The Situation: The company wishes to expand its business by marketing its BESTFLO meter in the South American market. This meter is an electronic unit that is mounted on a truck and measures the flow of liquefied petroleum gas (LPG) at the point of delivery. Preliminary research showed that demand for the product would likely be strongest in Argentina, Brazil, and Venezuela. However, management needs extensive information about the nature of the market before deciding whether to launch a South American venture.

The Report Objective: You were asked to evaluate the potential market for the BESTFLO meter in Argentina, Brazil, and Venezuela. Specifically, you attempted to answer four questions for each of the three countries:

1. What economic conditions influence the development of the LPG industry?
2. What is the general sales potential for BESTFLO?
3. Who are the primary customers and the largest companies distributing LPG?
4. What are the optimal means of distributing and promoting BESTFLO?

Status: You have completed your research and are about to write the report.

Primary Audience: Your report will be presented to the vice president for marketing, Robert Montero. Mr. Montero is familiar with the purpose of the research, and he discussed it at length when he authorized you to conduct the study. You gave him periodic progress reports as you worked on the project. He is eager to learn your findings, conclusions, and recommendations and would be satisfied with an informal outline and an oral report.

Secondary Audience: Mr. Montero will present your report to the executive committee. He wants you to include full background information and details about how you conducted your study so that all members of the committee can understand the situation fully.

A formal outline such as the one shown in Illustration 2.4 would guide your discussion with Mr. Montero and help you prepare an effective written report for the executive committee.

The decimal system, used by many engineering companies, law firms, and government agencies, uses Arabic numerals and decimals to indicate main topics and subtopics. The numbering begins with a single digit (1, 2, 3, and so on) to mark first-level divisions. For each subdivision, a decimal is added and the parts of that subdivision are numbered consecutively (1.1, 1.2; 2.1, 2.2; 2.2.1, 2.2.2; and so on).

Illustration 2.5 shows the decimal system. You can check the accuracy of your decimal numbering system by comparing the numbers with the division level. Notice that every first-level division is marked with a single number; every second-level division has two numbers, separated by a decimal; every third-level division has three numbers, separated by decimals; and so on.

Both systems, traditional and decimal, require that you observe basic outlining guides.

ILLUSTRATION 2.4 A FORMAL OUTLINE

The Feasibility of Marketing BESTFLO in South America

I. Background: BestMeters wants to expand its market for BESTFLO.

II. The Research Question: Is it feasible to promote BESTFLO to the South American LPG industry?
  A. The purpose of the study
  B. The scope of analysis
  C. The method of study
    1. Data sources
    2. Data collection
    3. Data analysis

III. The findings
  A. Economic conditions
    1. Argentina
    2. Brazil
    3. Venezuela
  B. Sales potential for LPG flowmeters
    1. Argentina
    2. Brazil
    3. Venezuela

continued

ILLUSTRATION 2.4 CONTINUED

    C. Primary competitors
      1. Argentina
      2. Brazil
      3. Venezuela
    D. Distribution and promotion strategies

IV. Conclusions
    A. Growing market for flowmeters in the three countries
    B. LPG distribution controlled by few companies
    C. Few competitors in the market
    D. Unique characteristics of each country require country-specific
       adaptations

V. Recommendations
    A. Respond quickly to growing market
    B. Establish BESTFLO as industry standard
      1. Adapt meter for needs of specific countries
      2. Target nine specific LPG suppliers
    C. Educate potential customers
      1. Quality of BESTFLO
      2. Competitive price of BESTFLO

ILLUSTRATION 2.5 PARALLELISM IN OUTLINES

Improving Organizational Effectiveness

1. Define organizational mission
2. Identify organizational goals
   2.1 Unit goals
      2.1.1 Short term
      2.1.2 Long term
   2.2 Department goals
      2.2.1 Short term
      2.2.2 Long term
   2.3 Division goals
      2.3.1 Short term
      2.3.2 Long term
   2.4 Organization goals
      2.4.1 Short term
      2.4.2 Long term
3. Determine performance criteria
   3.1 Unit level
   3.2 Department level

continued

ILLUSTRATION 2.5 CONTINUED

     3.3 Division level
     3.4 Organization level
  4. Assess organizational effectiveness
     4.1 Select indicators
     4.2 Select samples
     4.3 Collect data
     4.4 Apply criteria
     4.5 Interpret findings
  5. Use assessment findings
     5.1 Identify strengths and weaknesses
     5.2 Modify goals
     5.3 Allocate resources

Outline Guides

To communicate report content effectively, your outline must be clear and coherent. Observing the following guides will help you achieve those qualities.

  1. Every division and subdivision must have at least two parts. Logically, nothing can be divided into less than two parts. Therefore, every topic that is divided must have a minimum of two subtopics. The following examples contrast ineffective, illogical outline divisions with effective, logical divisions.

Illogical; Ineffective	*Logical; Effective*
A. *The current system*	**A.** *The current system*
1. *Inefficient*	**1.** *Inefficient*
	2. *Error prone*
	3. *Costly*
B. *The proposed system*	**B.** *The proposed system*
1. *Efficient*	**1.** *Efficient*
	2. *Accurate*
	3. *Cost effective*

  2. Divisions should be balanced. All divisions need not have the same number of topics and subtopics; but if any section of your outline is considerably longer or shorter than other sections, you should reevaluate the outline. Lack of balance may suggest the need to regroup information for a more coherent report structure. The following examples contrast unbalanced, ineffective sections with balanced, effective sections.

Unbalanced; Ineffective	*Balanced; Effective*
A. *The current system*	**A.** *The current system*
1. *Inefficient*	**1.** *Inefficient*
	2. *Error-prone*
	3. *Costly*
B. *The proposed system*	**B.** *The proposed system*
1. *Easily learned*	**1.** *Efficient*
2. *Fast*	**2.** *Accurate*
3. *Accurate*	**3.** *Cost-effective*
4. *Desired by employees*	
5. *Easy to correct errors*	
6. *Inexpensive to install*	
7. *Inexpensive to operate*	
8. *Can use some of old equipment*	

3. Divisions and subdivisions should help the reader focus quickly on significant report content. When any part of an outline contains more than four division levels, you may be focusing the reader's attention on minor rather than major points. The following examples show how the previous outlines can be improved by clarifying major and minor points.

Major/Minor Points Unclear	*Major/Minor Points Clear*
The proposed system:	*The proposed system:*
Easily learned	*Efficient*
Fast	*Fast*
Accurate	*Accurate*
Desired by employees	*Easy corrections*
Easy to correct errors	*Cost-effective*
Inexpensive to install	*Inexpensive to install*
Inexpensive to operate	*Inexpensive to operate*
Can use some of old equipment	*Use some old equipment*
	Acceptable to employees
	Desired
	Easily learned

4. Division headings should be stated concisely. Topic headings, such as those often used in a tentative outline, may be too concise to communicate report content to the reader. If the outline in Illustration 2.5 were a topic outline, the first-level headings might be single words or short phrases, such as *mission, goals, criteria, assessment,* and *use.* Although such an outline may guide the report writer, it conveys little to the reader.

Talking headings, written in parallel phrases or short sentences as in Illustration 2.5, provide more information about the report content. Lengthy talking headings, however, may distract from effective communication. Assume, for example, that Heading 2 in Illustration 2.5 were written in this way: "Identify goals by getting input at all organizational levels." Such a heading burdens the reader with unnecessary words, particularly since the subtopics listed under the heading indicate that goals must be identified at all levels.

5. Division topics must be expressed in parallel grammatical structure. Appropriate parallelism is demonstrated in Illustration 2.5. Notice that first-level divisions (1 through 4) are grammatically parallel; second-level divisions, such as 2.1 through 2.4, are parallel within the division but not necessarily parallel with other second-level divisions, such as 4.1 through 4.5.

Computer-Assisted Outlining

Most word-processing software includes special timesaving tools for creating and re-organizing outlines. Computer-assisted outlining involves a unique display called outline view. This view shows the headings of a document indented to represent their level in the document's makeup, thereby helping a writer lay out and organize ideas. You might be familiar with the outline-numbering feature in your word processing software, which numbers the lines of text (for example, I, II, A, B, 1, 2). However, this type of outline numbering is different from outline view. The two features serve different purposes and are not meant to work together.

As you type the first words in outline view, you will likely see large, bold text. That's because the software labeled it a main or Level 1 heading and assigned it a heading style suited to that level. For example, in Microsoft Word 2010, the Outline view involves nine built-in heading styles, plus body text, used for the paragraphs. As topics are added to the outline, Word continues to apply an appropriate built-in style to each level. Thus, each outline level is tied to a built-in heading style. This linking of outline levels and heading styles is vital to the outlining function, although Word lets users display an outline as plain text if preferred.

Using outline view, you can quickly change the level and order of topics as well as reduce visual clutter by hiding selected parts of an outline. As you work to complete an outline, you may improve your focus if you selectively collapse (hide) subheadings. A small symbol reminds you the collapsed subheadings are there; and, of course, you can easily expand (unhide) them.

While making an outline, you may realize that a subheading is more important or has more subtopics than you thought at first; or you may realize just the opposite: that certain ideas are less important than their current outline level implies. When this occurs, you can rapidly demote (move to the right, a lower level) or promote (move to the left, a higher level) the heading. Additionally, a simple click can move a topic and all its subtopics up or down in the outline.

In a process called capsuling, writers who use outlining software often insert main ideas to be developed under each outline heading and subheading in body text style. Report composition, which may be done in outline view but is usually done in another view, then becomes a relatively easy task of supporting those ideas with data and visual aids. Many writers have found that this technique helps them write clearly and concisely.

Outlining software is also useful for evaluating the organization of a finished report. You can readily see whether report headings are logically and grammatically consistent and whether they summarize the text in each section. Another advantage of computer-assisted outlining: Using the built-in heading styles, the software can generate a table of contents for the report.

A tutorial for using Outline view in Microsoft Word 2010 is available on the Web at http://office.microsoft.com/en-us/word-help/create-a-document-outline-RZ006105145.aspx.

Collaborative Writing

Many of you have worked on collaborative projects; some of you have been disappointed with the experience. As you progress in your career, it will become increasingly important for you to be able to work effectively on a group project.

Understanding the dynamics of group formation may help you function more effectively in groups. A classic study on group formation (Tuckman, 1965) identified four stages of group formation: forming, storming, norming, and performing. A fifth stage, adjourning, was later added.

Forming

During the forming stage, the group is usually at its best behavior. This stage is also called the orientation stage. Group members act courteously toward one another as they become acquainted and test the waters to determine what behaviors will be acceptable and unacceptable to the group. During this stage, the group becomes oriented to the task, sets initial goals, and begins to establish ground rules. A leader may begin to emerge during this stage because members will look to someone for guidance.

Storming

The storming stage is marked by intragroup conflict. The group is typically eager to proceed with the task, but disagreements may arise about goals and procedures. Conflicts can lead to resentments and the development of subgroups. Dysfunctional behaviors (blocking, dominating, competing, withdrawing, and repeating) often characterize this stage.

However, the storming stage can be productive if it teaches team members how to deal with their differences. The storming phase can bring out the creativity of the members if group members are willing to consider all proposals. Effective groups capture the energy generated at this stage and direct it positively. Constructive task-oriented behaviors (initiating discussion, seeking information, giving information, coordinating comments, evaluating suggestions, and summarizing) will help the group keep on task. Process-oriented behaviors (encouraging participation, harmonizing differing viewpoints, opening gates to people who are attempting to join the discussion, and setting standards) will foster greater team unity.

To navigate the storming stage, some groups pause to evaluate what is happening. A form similar to the one shown in Illustration 2.6 can help members identify functional and dysfunctional behaviors that have emerged and decide how to improve the group's work climate.

ILLUSTRATION 2.6 GROUP PARTICIPATION RATING FORM

Enter each group member's name into one of the columns. Rate each group member's behavior, using the following scale: 4 = Frequently; 3 = Occasionally; 2 = Rarely; 1 = Never.

BEHAVIORS	MEMBERS					
Task Oriented						
Initiates Discussion						
Seeks Information						
Gives Information						
Coordinates						
Evaluates						
Summarizes						
Process Oriented						
Encourages						
Harmonizes						
Opens Gates						
Sets Standards						
Dysfunctional						
Blocks						
Dominates						
Competes						
Withdraws						
Repeats						

Norming

If the group successfully navigates the storming phase, it moves into norming. This phase is usually typified by openness to other group members, cooperation, and mutual support. The group becomes more focused on the task, and the members become aware of themselves as a functioning organism with a common goal and group spirit.

Because of the strong focus on task, the threat of "groupthink" exists at this stage. Wanting to move forward, members may hesitate to challenge the prevailing direction of the group. It is especially important that members use their process-oriented skills to encourage all ideas to come forward.

Performing

Having passed through the storming and norming stages, group members should be able to work harmoniously toward achieving their common goal. In the performing stage, the group functions as a relatively cohesive work unit. There is a minimum of emotional interference; emphasis is on task achievement. Typically, group members can function individually or in any combination with other members on parts of the task because goals and norms have been established. Task-oriented behaviors characterize the interactions among group members. Questions still arise, but the group members are able to harmonize differences by practicing their process-oriented skills.

Adjourning

Having completed the task, successful groups pass purposefully through the final stage: adjourning. At this stage, members often feel exhilaration in the successful accomplishment of a task. They may also feel some sadness or anxiety as they recognize that the group will disband and they may never again work together. Successful teams take time to evaluate what has occurred in the group in terms of both task accomplishment and group skill development. The adjournment phase should be seen as an opportunity to appreciate what has been done well, recognize what might have been done more effectively, and acknowledge the behaviors that contributed to successes or failures. Members can then apply that knowledge as they approach a new group assignment.

A Caution

Although the group-formation stages are generally considered to occur in a developmental sequence, it is not uncommon for groups to experience regression to earlier stages. The important thing is to recognize that dysfunctional behaviors may be recurring and determine the reasons. For example, during the performing stage, some members may lag in performing their duties. It is important to deal with the matter promptly: reconfirm or clarify goals, define or reassign tasks, and reinforce norms. A brief period of storming may emerge, but by implementing task-oriented and process-oriented behaviors, the group should be able to minimize conflict and return to productivity.

Collaborative Software: Wiggio

To aid with task-oriented behaviors, teams may use groupware (collaborative software). Groupware is made up of productivity tools that create a collaborative working environment within which people involved in a common task can work together and achieve their goals regardless of their geographical locations.

Groupware includes tools to aid communication, conferencing, and coordination. It may be Web based, with users accessing tools via the Internet, or desktop based, with users installing the collaborative software on their own computers. In addition, groupware ranges from multilayered complex systems down to a combination of simple tools, such as email (communication), chat room (conferencing), and calendars (coordination).

Wiggio—groupware designed for college students involved in team projects—is simple (six tools), Web based (http://wiggio.com), and free of charge. These attributes are helping Wiggio win favor among small businesses and nonprofit organizations even as its popularity among college students continues to grow. Other users include clubs and committees, families, religious organizations, sports teams, and social groups.

Wiggio—the name came from *working in groups*—includes two communication tools (Folder and Messages), a conferencing tool (Meeting), and three coordination tools (Calendar, Poll, and Links).

Folder and Messages

With the Folder tool, all of a team's files are stored in one place, eliminating the need for sending attachments. The users can edit word-processing documents and spreadsheets in Wiggio. When a user uploads, changes, and then downloads a document, Wiggio recognizes it as a new version and saves both the new and the old version.

The Messages function allows three forms of communication: texting, email (nongroup members are blocked), and voice note. In addition, Wiggio integrates with Facebook, allowing users to create a group and then import group members directly from their list of "friends" on Facebook.

Meeting and Coordination

Wiggio also provides for three kinds of meetings: audioconference (using Rondee, a free conference call service), chat room, and Web conference. The Calendar tool allows users to manage group events. Wiggio's calendar interfaces with events on Google Calendar and exports to other popular calendars: Microsoft Outlook, Yahoo!, and iCal.

Poll and Links are two additional functions that aid collaboration. The Poll function is a survey tool that helps users with decision making. It allows group members to ask the whole group questions and receive responses quickly. The Links tool provides a place for pasting hyperlinks so that a team has a shared set of favorite, frequently used websites.

Ethical Considerations

Ethical issues may arise as you plan reports. When deciding on the purpose, audience, context, content, structure, and medium for a report, ethical individuals would ask why each decision is made. Does each decision promote the sender's good only, or does it contribute to the well-being of others also?

Assume, for example, that you have observed safety violations in the manufacturing plant in which you work. You decide to prepare a report in which you will identify each violation and recommend corrections. Is your purpose to improve working conditions or to expose lax management? Will you present both sides of the issue? Should your audience be upper management, or should it include employees and the press? What tone should you use? Should the report be released if your analysis of context reveals that an environmental interest group in the community is attempting to have the plant closed—even though many community members would lose their jobs? Should the report disclose all violations you have observed or only selected ones? Which medium—oral or written—would yield greater "good"?

With the increased use of collaborative writing teams, writers should also consider the ethical issues that may arise under such working conditions. An ethical obligation that would seem obvious is to honor your commitments to others. When you are tempted not to fulfill your share of the assignment, answer these basic questions about your responsibility to yourself and for others.

- Is keeping a promise one of your core values?
- Are you acting as the person you want to be?
- Are you acting in the group's best interest?
- Are you willing to take public responsibility for your action?
- Does the action violate the rights of any other people?

Summary

Following the six steps for a report plan—identify purpose, audience, and context; select content and medium; and choose a structure—will keep you on target as you write your report. Writing a clear, coherent report begins with a logical outline. A well-constructed outline can reveal strengths and weaknesses in the proposed report structure. If weaknesses are evident, you can correct them before you write the report. Outline software permits you to reorganize a report quickly and easily.

At each step of the planning process, an ethical writer evaluates the potential effect of the planning decisions: Do they promote the well-being of others as well as of the writer and the writer's organization?

Effective collaborative writing can occur if writers are aware of the typical stages of group formation. It is perhaps unrealistic to expect success if the group has not taken time to become acquainted, recognizing members' strengths and weaknesses. Successful groups also clearly identify goals and establish behavioral norms. Effective collaboration also requires that all group members act ethically toward one another and fulfill the obligations they have accepted.

Using collaborative software such as Wiggio does not eliminate the forming, storming, and other stages of team development. However, since it removes many frustrations associated with team tasks, it may make those early stages of team formation shorter and smoother.

Topics for Discussion

1. When is an informal report plan justified?
2. Describe the steps to be included in a report plan. Why are the steps called *recursive*?
3. Explain each of these message classifications: production, innovation, and goodwill.
4. What is a primary audience? A secondary audience?

5. What are the characteristics of a lean medium? A rich medium? How does knowledge of these characteristics affect your choice of a medium?

6. One writer has ranked various media in terms of levels of intimacy in the following order, beginning with most intimate: talking, video chat, phone, letter, instant message, text message, email, Facebook message, Facebook status, and Twitter ("Imgur," 2010). In what ways is this classification similar to or different from Lengel and Daft's hierarchy of media richness?

7. Compare or contrast inductive and deductive report structures. Give examples of appropriate uses for each.

8. Give examples of appropriate uses for these structures:
   - Chronological
   - Problem-solution
   - Cause-effect
   - Spatial

9. Compare or contrast topical and comparison structures. Give examples of appropriate uses for each or combinations of the two.

10. Describe the five stages of development that most groups experience. Why is it important that group members understand these stages?

11. Give examples of each of these task-oriented behaviors: initiate discussion, seek information, give information, coordinate, evaluate, and summarize.

12. Give examples of each of these process-oriented behaviors: encourage, harmonize, open gates, and set standards.

13. Give examples of each of these dysfunctional group behaviors: block, dominate, compete, withdraw, and repeat.

14. Identify ethical issues that may arise as you work independently or collaboratively to produce a report.

15. If you have had a collaborative writing experience, share information about that experience with your classmates. Was it successful or unsuccessful? What contributed to its success or failure? How might using collaborative software, such as Wiggio, have increased the team's success?

Applications

1. In a small-group discussion, plan a report for each of the following scenarios. In each situation:
   - Clarify the context of the report. Then identify the audience; the sender's purpose; the receiver's needs; and the appropriate content, structure, and medium for the report.
   - Prepare an outline for the report.
   - Select a member of your group to present to the class an oral summary of the group's decisions, along with reasons for those decisions.
   a. A state board of public education is considering a proposal by an advertising company to post advertisements on school buses. The advertising company will be responsible for posting and maintaining the signs, which will be placed inside each bus above the windows and will be no more than 11 inches tall. The ads could bring in as much as $6 million per year, which

the board proposes to share with the county school districts. Some teachers and parents question the ethics of subjecting children to advertising while they are riding the buses; others think the proposed plan is a way to earn a substantial sum of money for the schools with little effort. Take a position on this matter. As a parent whose children ride the school buses, send a report to the president of the board of public education in which you support your position.

b. Dan Sullivan, a benefits consultant with Gibbs and Associates, helped Mr. and Mrs. McCants apply for long-term-care insurance. After the underwriting company had reviewed the applications and the medical information obtained from the clients' doctors, the company offered Mrs. McCants the coverage she had applied for but rejected Mr. McCants because of certain health conditions. Sullivan thinks he can get another company to underwrite Mr. McCants with slightly less coverage and a 10 percent higher premium. He thinks Mrs. McCants should accept the plan that was approved and that Mr. McCants should apply to the second company. Mr. Sullivan must report this information to Mr. and Mrs. McCants.

c. Assume you are the executive director of Hannah's House, a nonprofit agency that provides emergency shelter for families in trauma. When those families leave the shelter, you provide them with a recycled cell phone that they can use if they must contact you in another emergency situation.

You have learned about a mobile service provider, SoWel (for "social welfare") that contributes 1 percent of its income to approximately 50 nonprofit organizations that are working for peace, human rights, and the environment. Its contributions have averaged nearly $3 million a year. SoWel has a mobile phone plan for businesses that will cost less than what Hannah's House is currently paying to cover phones for its employees and client families. Further, you like the idea of supporting other organizations that are trying to improve society.

Prepare a report that will convince your board of directors to switch your agency's mobile phone service to SoWel.

d. Assume that the Board has given you permission to discontinue your current mobile phone service and sign on with SoWel (Application 1-c). SoWel also has individual and family plans that are competitive with major mobile service providers. You are enthusiastic about the concept of supporting charitable organizations while paying for a necessary service and want to encourage your supporting constituency to switch to SoWel. Prepare a message to inform and persuade.

e. Three employees under Jack Grasman's supervision have each volunteered to spend two weeks of their vacation time working with the local Habitat for Humanity. Simona Jun worked with a prospective home owner to select paint, wallpaper, and window coverings for the new house and scheduled additional volunteers to complete the interior decorating. Rick Kattreh helped frame three houses. Nancy Jones helped the local Habitat director contact businesses to ask for monetary or in-kind (lumber, nails, and so on) contributions. Grasman wants to commend the employees for their volunteer work. He also wants to encourage other employees to participate in the program.

f. The director of the motor pool for a large state agency has been criticized for the vehicle purchase/retention plan in use at the agency. The current plan includes replacing vehicles after three years of use or at 80,000 to 90,000 miles, whichever occurs first. Typically, this has resulted in replacement of about one-third of the fleet each year. Requests for bids are issued in September, with purchases made in November. In the past, the agency has used only gasoline-powered vehicles. The director wonders if the time has come to consider hybrid vehicles for at least part of the fleet. He asks you to determine the cost savings, if any, to be obtained if the agency splits this year's anticipated purchases between hybrid and gasoline-powered vehicles.

g. Assume that you are the executive director of Food for Families, a non-profit agency that provides food to individuals and families in need. Potential food recipients enter a reception area where they participate in an intake interview. After legitimate need is determined, the applicants for food are given a voucher that they redeem at the adjacent warehouse where your food supplies are stored. You have hired a cleaning company, Sani-Clean, to clean your facility twice a week. The task includes cleaning the office and the reception area. Although the cleaning crew has not been asked to clean the warehouse in which you store the food, you have noticed "inventory shrinkage" after some of their visits. The missing inventory has ranged from as little as a case of sodas to as much as several cases of canned fruits and vegetables. You want to report the food loss, along with your suspicions that the cleaning crew may be responsible. Since you know the owner of the cleaning service as a friend and supporter of the agency, you do not want to offend her; yet you cannot afford continued inventory shrinkage. Prepare a report to Christine Miller, owner of Sani-Clean.

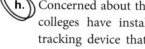

h. Concerned about the safety of their students both on and off campus, some colleges have installed systems that permit students to activate a GPS tracking device that will alert campus security if a student is in potential danger. For example, if a student is returning to campus from an off-campus site, the student can activate the device. If it is not deactivated within 20 minutes, an alarm will sound at the campus police station, and a computer screen will display a dot indicating the student's location, along with a photo and other personal details. The 20-minute interval allows a student to reach her or his intended destination with no interference from the system, at which point the person deactivates the system; but it also ensures that if the student does not reach the destination, help will be on the way. Some colleges require that all students buy a cell phone equipped with a GPS that can be linked to such a system.

Assume that your dean for student services has proposed that your school adopt such technology and require that students link into it. In a report to the dean, express your support for or opposition to such a program. Justify your position.

2. Select one of the scenarios given in Application 1. Write the report, using inductive structure. Write the report a second time, using deductive structure.

3. Using the information you gathered for Chapter 1, Application 11, prepare an outline for a report to your instructor. This application will be continued in Chapter 3.

4. Using the outlining feature in your word processor, develop an outline for a report about one of the following topics:
   - Using Twitter as a marketing tool
   - The major features of Evertune, a guitar that stays in tune.
   - Using Wiggio for collaborative report-writing assignments. (Explore this groupware at http://wiggio.com, including the About Us page.)
   - A comparison of two printer/scanner/copier/fax units to use in your home office or dormitory room
   - Energy drinks: pros and cons
   - Arguments for and against purchasing insurance to protect against identity theft
   - Virus-scanning software: free versus purchased

References

1. *Chicago Manual of Style* (2010). 16th ed. Chicago: University of Chicago Press.
2. Farace, R. V., & MacDonald, D. (1974, Spring). New directions in the study of organizational communication. *Personnel Psychology*, 115.
3. Imgur: The simple image sharer. (2010). Retrieved February 18, 2010, from http://imgur.com/tRnNd.png.
4. Lengel, R. H., & Daft, R. L. (1988). The selection of communication media as an executive skill. *The Academy of Management EXECUTUVE*, 2(3), 225–232.
5. Tuckman, B. (1965). Developmental sequence in small groups. *Psychological Bulletin*, 63(6), 384–389.

CHAPTER **3**

Producing the Report

LEARNING OBJECTIVES

After you have read this chapter, you should be able to:

1. Draft, revise, and edit your report.

2. Collaborate effectively to draft, revise, and edit a report.

3. Use document sharing services to enhance your collaborative writing efforts.

4. Consider ethical issues that arise during the writing process.

AFTER COMPILING AN INFORMAL OR A FORMAL OUTLINE, you are ready to write the first draft of your report. In simple reporting situations, the first draft often is also the final draft. In more complex situations, the draft may be revised and edited several times before it is finally produced and delivered.

Drafting the Report

The steps for drafting a report are diagrammed in Illustration 3.1. As the diagram indicates, these steps in the writing process differ, depending on the complexity of the report and the relationships of the parties involved in the communication. For example, if you were asked to prepare a complex report, such as a study of the feasibility of moving your office to a new location and you did not yet know all that should be included, you would begin at Stage 1, Step 1—Preliminary Draft. A preliminary draft is a working tool for the report writer. It will help you organize (or reorganize) your ideas, make evident any serious gaps in information, and let you experiment with format, including visual aids. After writing and reviewing the preliminary draft, you should be prepared to discuss with a colleague or manager any questions that arose as you wrote it (Stage 1, Steps 2 and 3). Following such a conversation, you would be ready to move to Stage 2, Step 1—Review Draft.

The illustration demonstrates, however, that not all reports need to begin at Stage 1, Step 1. A report presenting your comparative evaluation of three properties considered for the new office location could well begin at Step 1 of Stage 2—Review Draft. If you have already collected and analyzed your data, have prepared a comprehensive outline—and perhaps even had the outline approved—you should be able to begin here. In this stage, you will prepare a draft that you will review thoroughly for

ILLUSTRATION 3.1 DRAFTING THE REPORT

Start with the appropriate stage and repeat the steps through Stage 3

	Preliminary Draft Stage #1	Review Draft Stage #2	Near-final Draft Stage #3
Step 1: **Write a draft.**	**A Preliminary Draft** is a draft that helps you (1) discover what you still need to find out, (2) organize ideas, and (3) experiment with format. **A Preliminary Draft is not** ready for document review or final editing because the writer still needs to do a major revision. **Start here if you** find the writing project to be difficult, **or** have not previously written a similar document, **or** do not yet know what material to include and cannot outline the piece, **or** do not know your manager's preferences and expectations.	**A Review Draft** is a well-organized draft that results from strategic decision-making and is ready to be reviewed for content and organization. **A Review Draft is not** ready for final editing because the writer may still make major changes in content. **Start here if you** understand your manager's expectations and preferences, **and** have made good strategic decisions about content and organization, **and** can create a good, defensible outline of your piece.	**A Near-final Draft** is a draft that is ready for stylistic revision and final editing. **A Near-final Draft** is not a draft that should be reworked in major ways unless it has major omissions. **Start here if you** are writing something simple or familiar, or have planned the document well **and** are under great time pressure.
Step 2: **Review your own draft.**	Use the Writing Review Checklist (1–4). If possible revise before showing to a reader. **Then** develop a list of questions to ask a colleague or project manager. Be sure to control the conversation.	Check the draft using the Writing Review Checklist (1–4). If necessary, revise. **Then** give the piece to a colleague or project manager to review.	Check the draft using the Writing Review Checklist. Review 1–4. Focus on 5–6. **Then** give the piece to a colleague or project manager to review.
Step 3: **Get a helpful reader review.**	**The reader should** tell the writer what is confusing and what questions need to be answered. Return the piece to the writer to revise.	**The reader should** check the draft using the Writing Review Checklist (1–4). Return the piece to the writer to revise.	**The reader should** check the draft using the Writing Review Checklist. Review 1–4. Focus on 5–6. Correct minor problems. Point out major stylistic problems to writer.

Source: Shwom and Hirsch (1994).

accuracy, completeness, clarity, and structure. When you think you have done your best job, you will give the report to someone else—a colleague or a manager—for review. That person may suggest additions, deletions, or other modifications and return the draft to you, leading you to Step 1 of Stage 3—Near-final Draft.

Further, Illustration 3.1 shows that for some reports you may be able to begin at Stage 3, Step 1. This document is a draft that is ready for possible revisions in style and final editing. A simple report announcing that the office will be closed on Monday so that commercial movers can move all furniture and equipment to the new location is an example of such a report. For such a report, you could easily write a near-final draft after consulting your informal outline.

With your outline as a guide, you can draft any report by major sections. Do not, however, feel that you must draft the report in the exact sequence in which it will finally appear. Attempting to write the report from beginning to end as indicated by the outline may create writing barriers that delay the production of the report.

A key to successful writing is to recognize writing barriers and develop strategies for overcoming them. Some writers, for example, begin by writing the easiest sections of the report. This technique provides a sense of accomplishment and stimulates the writer to move on to the more difficult sections. Other writers begin with the sections that they think will be most difficult to write, preferring to complete the hard tasks early in the writing process so that they will not feel pressured toward the end. Many writers move among sections of the document. For example, when you have difficulty with one part of the report, you may find it helpful to work on another section. After some time has passed, you will often find that you have subconsciously removed the writing block and can think more clearly and write more easily about the difficult topic.

One useful technique is to prepare all visual aids—tables, charts, graphs, and so forth—before writing the report narrative. Your primary writing task then is to explain those aids. After writing the explanatory narrative, your next task is to write the transitions between parts of the report. Your final task is to write introductory and summary sections.

Revising and Editing the Report

Before preparing a final copy of your report, read it carefully to evaluate all aspects of the report: content, structure, diction, tone, overall style, and impact. The drafting guide shown in Illustration 3.1 encourages you to review your draft carefully (Step 2 of each stage) and to subject your work to another person's critical review (Step 3 of each stage). The Writing Review Checklist (Illustration 3.2) provides a systematic guide that you and your reviewers can use as you attend to specific parts of your report.

Critical revision and editing often mark the difference between an effective and an ineffective report. Revising a report consists of rewriting sentences, paragraphs, or entire sections of a report or moving them to different locations. Adding or deleting information may also be part of the revision process. As Illustration 3.2 suggests, you should evaluate the power of the introduction and ending, the accuracy and completeness of the report's content, and the report's organization and format. Editing consists

ILLUSTRATION 3.2   WRITING REVIEW CHECKLIST

1. **Do your introductory paragraphs provide sufficient context? Do they**
   - State the purpose of the document (often written as or combined with a "road map" sentence)?
   - State the main point, conclusion, or recommendation?
   - Focus on the reader and reader benefits (especially in persuasive pieces)?
2. **Do your organization and formatting make ideas easy to find? Does your document use**
   - **Cover material:** Would an executive summary or cover letter help a busy reader? If a letter is longer than two pages, can you break it into two documents: a cover letter and a separate report or proposal?
   - **Subject lines:** Are they as short and precise as possible?
   - **Headings and subheadings:** Do they form a logical outline? Does all the material in a section match its heading?
   - **Topic sentences:** Do they state the most important ideas in the paragraph? Do they signal how the paragraph will be organized? Do all the topic sentences, read together, form an outline for the reader?
   - **White space:** Are your pages easy on the eye?
   - **Bullet point lists:** Do you list out key ideas for emphasis? Do bulleted paragraphs begin with the key idea?
3. **Is the information complete and persuasive? Does your document**
   - Stress reader benefits?
   - Answer all questions that a reader may ask?
   - Include sufficient details, explanation, and evidence for each point?
   - Provide rationale and benefits for each recommendation?
   - Present material in an order that will appear logical to the reader?
   - Explain the relevance of attachments?
4. **Is the ending strategic? Do you use the ending to**
   - Emphasize key points?
   - Spell out next steps, if appropriate?
   - Create a positive impression?
5. **Are the sentences easy to read?**
   - Are sentences relatively short?
   - Are subjects and verbs near the beginnings of sentences? Are lists and complicated ideas near the end?
   - Are verbs in the active voice?
   - Are lists parallel?
   - Are words unambiguous?
   - Do sentences and paragraphs include transitions?
   - Is language positive?
6. **Is the document proofread? Is it**
   - Free of typos and misspellings?
   - Free of grammatical errors, such as run-on sentences, pronoun errors, problems in subject-verb agreement?
   - Consistent in typography: headings, subheadings, caps, underlining, indentation?

Source: Shwom and Hirsch (1994).

of locating and correcting errors at the paragraph, sentence, and word levels—such as transitions, sentence structure, spelling, punctuation, word use, subject-verb agreement, pronoun references, and so on. Chapter 4 provides guides to improve the style, tone, and grammatical precision of your reports.

The final draft should be a coherent document that flows smoothly from start to finish, always giving the reader a sense of forward movement. Your summaries and transitions should help the reader understand the relevance of what has been said and anticipate what will be said next. Avoid vague references such as *this*, *that*, and *it* without a clear antecedent. Similarly, avoid comprehensive references like "as stated above" or "the previously mentioned facts." Such statements often require readers to move backward in the document to be sure they understand the reference.

The following examples contrast a style that moves forward with a style that disrupts the message flow. The first example disrupts the flow by requiring readers to return to previous sections of the document if they do not recall the criteria. In the second example, the writer briefly recalls previous information as a transition to a discussion of empathy, thereby moving the reader forward in the document.

> *Disrupted Flow: In addition to the characteristics already discussed, your reports should demonstrate empathy for the reader.*
>
> *Forward Flow: Accuracy, clarity, and conciseness will help the reader understand your message. In addition, your writing should demonstrate empathy for the reader.*

After moving through all steps of Stage 3 (Illustration 3.1), you are ready to prepare the final copy in an appropriate format. Chapter 5 presents guides for document design and commonly used report formats.

Collaborative Writing

As documents and the techniques used to produce them become more complex, the degree of collaboration is likely to increase. The final product should be seamless. That is, the reader should not be able to tell where Joan's work leaves off and Mark's work begins.

In reality, collaborative writing often consists of a combination of collective and independent work, depending on the stage of the project (see Illustration 3.3).

Planning the Report

During the planning stage, the writing team should collectively identify the audience, purpose, and scope of the project. At this stage, the team should review the overall project to be sure everyone understands the expected outcome. After the scope of the project has been identified, the group may assign specific data-collection responsibilities to individual team members.

ILLUSTRATION 3.3 A PROCESS FOR COLLABORATIVE WRITING

Planning the Report—Collective Work

- Clarify task—identify audience, purpose, and scope of project.
- Develop preliminary outline.
- Identify possible data sources.
- Select writing style and format.
- Make data-gathering assignments.

Collecting and Analyzing Data—Independent Work

- Fulfill data-gathering assignment.
- Evaluate adequacy of data.
- Prepare to present your data and its assessment to the group, or continue working until you have met the assignment.

Evaluating Data—Collective Work

- Evaluate data.
- Return to data-gathering stage if data are inadequate.

Drafting and Revising—Independent and Collective Work

- Draft your part of the report.
- Revise and edit until that section is as good as you can make it.
- Review each member's contribution for adequacy and style; provide constructive criticism.
- Revise your section of the report, based on suggestions of team members.
- Deliver a near-final, corrected version of your section to the group.

Producing Final Document—Collective Work

- Assist in merging parts of the document, placing visuals, and so on.
- Review the entire report for accuracy, completeness, and consistency.

© Cengage Learning 2013

The team could also develop a preliminary outline for the final report to ensure that all necessary topics are covered and to guide the team members as they gather data. Team members should always allow for revisions in the outline as new perspectives arise during the data collection and analysis stages.

Another collective task during the planning stage is to agree on a general writing style, formal or informal. (Matters of style will be discussed in Chapter 4.) The team should also make formatting decisions or select a standard template so that all writers use the same software for their drafts; within that software, each should use the agreed-on margins, font, typeface, type size, and type style for the report body and headings. (Guides for formatting reports will be presented in Chapter 5.) These decisions will ease the process of merging individual documents into a single unified document.

Collecting and Analyzing Data

Collectively, the team should identify possible data sources. (Selecting and using data sources will be discussed in Chapters 11–14.) If the research requires the use of primary data, one or two members of the team might be responsible for designing the questionnaires or interview guides, but all members should participate in a critical review of those instruments before they are used. During the data-collection phase, it may be efficient for team members to function independently, each person collecting and interpreting data for the segment of the study for which he or she is responsible.

After the data are collected and analyzed, the group should again work together to plan the draft report. Members should discuss the data, evaluate its adequacy, and agree on its interpretation. (Data analysis will be discussed in Chapter 15.) At this time, the team should also review the report outline and adjust it as necessary.

Drafting and Revising

During the drafting stage, team members may first work independently as each person drafts the parts of the report for which he or she is responsible. Since most collaborative reports are relatively complex, each writer would likely begin at Stage 1, Step 1, of Illustration 3.1. After writing the preliminary drafts of their report sections, the team members should meet to discuss any questions that have arisen (Stage 1, Steps 2 and 3). Each writer would then be ready to move to Stage 2, Step 1, with her or his part of the writing effort.

After individuals have written their review drafts (Stage 2, Step 1), the group would again move into a collective mode. During Stage 2, Steps 2 and 3, every team member should review all parts written by other members; in a group setting, reviewers should provide constructive criticism, and the group should give individual authors directions for the near-final draft. The individual authors should continually evaluate the suggestions of the group and incorporate the best of their advice into the document.

Producing the Final Document

All writers should participate in the production of the final document. Each writer should bring the near-final, corrected version of her or his draft to a group meeting and be prepared to assist with the merging of parts, the preparation and placement of visual aids, and a review of the final document. Individual responsibilities include checking the writer's own section to ensure that it is correct and evaluating the entire report for consistent writing style and format.

Checking the entire document is a particularly important step when the drafting work has been divided among the group members. Even with agreements beforehand about format and style, inconsistencies will no doubt occur. Be aware that differing word-processing skill levels can cause inconsistencies. Fonts, headings, margins, and spacing should be consistent; footnotes or references should all be in the same style; and so on. The final report should be a seamless product in which a reader is unable to distinguish one writer's work from another's.

Google Docs: A Free Document-Sharing Service

During the drafting and revising stage, the use of Google Docs can simplify collaboration. This free service, offered by Google Inc., allows a user to draft and revise or edit files online and then invite others to share those files. Thus, a student team or group of employees can produce files and collaborate on documents from any computer. Files created in Google are saved to the Google servers automatically, and Google automatically saves changes in the file and keeps a revision history, even when multiple users open and revise or edit the same file simultaneously.

Google Docs combines data storage services, online applications (including emailing), word processing, presentations, and spreadsheets. Thus, a user can create a report in Google Docs, import it through the Web interface, or send the report by email.

Besides drafting files in Google Docs, a user can import files in various formats, such as DOC, PPT, and XLS (Microsoft Word, PowerPoint, and Excel, respectively) and HTML (HyperText Markup Language). In addition, files created in Google Docs can be downloaded to a computer in various formats, including Microsoft Word, ODF (OpenDocument for Office Applications), PDF (Portable Document Format), and RTF (Rich Text Format).

Some browsers and operating systems may not support Google Docs, but the most popular systems do, including Chrome, Firefox, Internet Explorer, and Safari running on Microsoft Windows, Apple OS X, and Linux.

Generous limits define document sizes and storage capacity in Google Docs. A word-processing file created as a Google document may contain 512,000 characters, the equivalent of 100 to 250 pages, depending on font size and line spacing. Uploaded files converted to Google documents have a limit of 1 megabyte (MB), or roughly 500 plain-text pages. It is worth noting that a specific format, such as Microsoft Word 2010, would be considerably larger than the same number of plain-text pages. Likewise, photographs inserted into the file would reduce the space available for text, depending on quantity and image quality. Presentations created in Google Docs as well as those uploaded and converted can be up to 200 slides (10 MB). A spreadsheet file created as a Google document may contain 400,000 cells and 256 columns per sheet. Uploaded spreadsheets must have smaller dimensions, but the overall spreadsheet capacity is sizable (20 MB).

Free document storage space—up to a gigabyte—is available for files not converted to Google Doc format, a capacity that exceeds 250,000 plain-text pages. While this total includes Google's email (Gmail), Web albums, and photo storage, most students and many businesses find the free space adequate for long-term needs. In addition, Google will sell storage space ($0.25 per gigabyte per year) to users who run out of free storage space.

Opening a Gmail Account

To make a Google Doc, you need a Gmail account. To open a Gmail account, go to http://www.gmail.com and click "Create an Account." Follow the on-screen prompts to enter your name, desired email address (log-in name), password, and other required

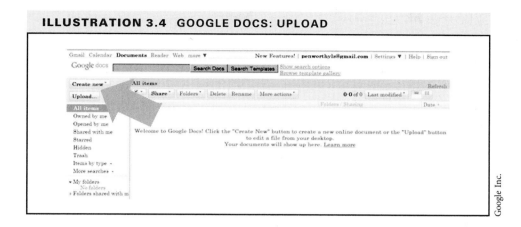

information. (Remember to record your log-in name and password.) Finally, click "I Accept. Create my Account."

To continue creating a report in Google, log in to your Gmail account. Click "Documents" (top left). From here, you may create a new file or upload a document that's already on your computer (see Illustration 3.4). To share an existing file, click the "Upload" button, then click "Select Files to Upload." Follow the on-screen prompts.

Creating a Google Document

To create a file from scratch, click the "Create New" button (top left). Then, from the available options, choose the type of file you want to create: Document (word processing). Other options include Presentation, Spreadsheet, and Forms (see Illustration 3.5). Next, type or paste the report text and images to the blank page.

Google's document menus include File, Edit, View, Insert, Format, Table, Tools, and Help. Here you will find familiar word-processing commands, such as

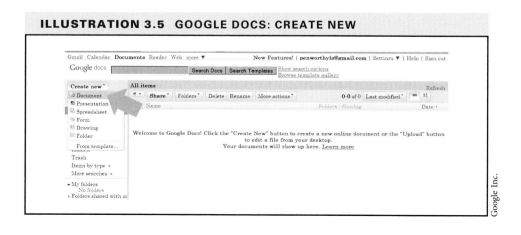

Undo (Edit menu), Header and Footer (Insert menu), and Check Spelling (Tools menu). Be aware, though, that Google may not include every feature found on a particular word-processing program. For example, the hanging-indent feature commonly used to format a bibliography or reference list is unavailable in Google Docs, as is the hyphenation feature normally used to divide long words at line endings.

Sharing a File

When your Google file (report) is ready to share, give your Gmail ID (address) to the people who will collaborate with you and ask them for their Gmail IDs. To share the report file, take these five steps:

1. Click "Share," then "Sharing Settings."
2. In the Sharing Settings dialog box, type the Gmail addresses of people you want to collaborate with. Specify "Can Edit" or "Can View" for each collaborator listed. Keep the recommended setting "Send Email Notifications."
3. Click "Share." This will allow the people you listed to view and/or revise and edit the report (see Illustration 3.6).
4. To open a report you shared or one shared with you, simply click the file name in your mailbox.
5. To access all previous versions of the report, open the File menu and click "See Revision History." The right-hand panel lists the revisions by date and time with the latest revision on top. Use buttons at the bottom to view changes (see Illustration 3.7).

ILLUSTRATION 3.6   GOOGLE DOCS: SHARE

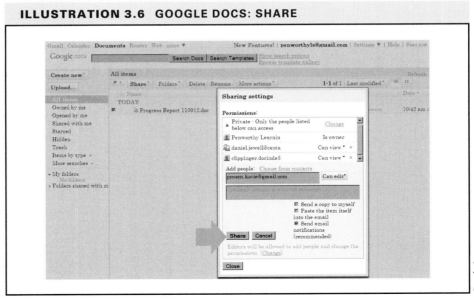

Google Inc.

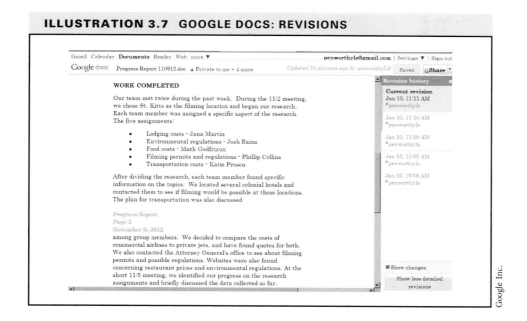

ILLUSTRATION 3.7   GOOGLE DOCS: REVISIONS

Ethical Considerations

A growing ethical issue is the tendency for people to act as though information on the Internet is in the public domain (that is, not subject to copyright laws). In reality, most information contained on websites is protected by copyright. When you obtain copyrighted information from a website, the data must be documented as meticulously as information obtained from other publications. To test your understanding of documentation requirements, you can take a short quiz developed by Ted Frick, an Indiana University professor. The quiz is available at https://www.indiana.edu/~tedfrick/plagiarism/index2.html.

As you draft and revise a report, it is important to check the accuracy of all references to data sources. You should be prepared to provide source information if any reviewer asks for such data. Subsequent chapters will discuss data collection and how to acknowledge data sources. At this point, it is important to remember that ethical writers always properly credit information and ideas obtained from another source, whether primary or secondary. Appropriate documentation establishes your credibility as well as your honesty.

When a report is produced collaboratively, it is the responsibility of each writer to verify and properly acknowledge the sources of the data used in her or his section of the report. In addition, all writers should be alert to the possibility that a writer has, knowingly or unknowingly, inadequately acknowledged a source.

Summary

Effective writers follow a strategy for drafting and revising every report. For complex reports, your strategy will include more write-review-revise cycles than are necessary for a simple report. In all situations, however, you should review your work with a critical eye. Consider especially the accuracy and clarity of all data, your report structure and writing style, and the impact of the opening and closing paragraphs or sections. Verifying the accuracy of source acknowledgments is also a vital part of the review process. Such review should be standard for both individual and team projects.

Google Docs is one of many document-sharing services, but most of them require user fees, whereas Google Docs is free. That fact, in addition to its online accessibility and ease of use, explains the popularity of Google Docs in the business and academic worlds.

Topics for Discussion

1. What is the importance of the write-review-revise strategy that is described in Illustration 3.1?
2. Why will not all report writers begin at Stage 1, Step 1, of the strategy described in Illustration 3.1? Provide examples of situations in which a writer may appropriately begin at Stage 2 or even Stage 3.
3. What would be your duties as a reviewer in Step 3 of any of the stages described in Illustration 3.1?
4. In what ways may an understanding of the drafting strategy described in Illustration 3.1 improve a collaborative writing effort?
5. How may the writing review checklist shown in Illustration 3.2 assist you during the review steps, both as a writer and as a reviewer of another writer's work?
6. What are the advantages and disadvantages of using a document-sharing service such as Google Docs for a collaborative project?
7. What ethical issues may arise during the drafting and reviewing stages of a collaborative project?

Applications

1. Using the outline you prepared for Chapter 2, Application 3, write the report. Draft, revise, and edit your report following the guides given in Illustrations 3.1 and 3.2. Attach the outline to the final version of your report and present both to your instructor.
2. For each of the following situations, form a team with one or two of your classmates. Discuss the issues presented in the scenario. In a report to your instructor, summarize your discussion and provide conclusions or recommendations regarding the issue discussed. Remember to plan, draft, revise, and edit your report before you prepare the final copy to give to your instructor.
   a. Extended warranties are offered on nearly every major purchase: automobile, refrigerator, dishwasher, television, cell phone, and so on. According to the Service Industry Council, U.S. residents bought 250 million warranties in 2010 ("Spending Smart," 2011). Typically, an extended warranty lengthens and often overlaps the manufacturer's warranty. Discuss the advantages and disadvantages of extended warranties.

b. Automobile manufacturers have stepped up their research and development of plug-in electric vehicles. Frequent objections or concerns about electric vehicles include the following (Thorpe, 2011):

- The U.S. electric grid cannot handle the added burden.
- Consumers' electric bills will skyrocket.
- Coal-burning utilities providing electricity for the cars will make emissions worse.
- Electric cars do not handle well.
- The lithium-ion batteries used in the cars are not reliable.
- A driver could run out of power when nowhere near an electrical socket.

Conduct research related to these issues. Discuss the legitimacy of the concerns.

c. Instruction manuals for most electronic devices (for example, cell phones, laptops, iPods, headsets, e-readers, and so on) provide technical information about their use, but they generally omit important information about the etiquette of using such devices. Discuss courtesies and discourtesies that you have seen or practiced. Summarize your discussion and provide recommendations for the courteous use of electronic devices.

d. Obtaining or transmitting information through the use of small electronic devices, such as those mentioned in Application 2-c, has become increasingly fast and easy. Discuss ethical issues that may arise with respect to obtaining and distributing information via such devices.

e. For many years, banks offered credit cards to college students, often including incentives—such as a T-shirt or free food—to sign up for the card. However, the Credit Card Act of 2009, which went into effect in February 2010, tightened the rules for granting credit to individuals under the age of 21. Check the Internet for details of that legislation. Discuss the pros and cons of the restrictions placed on banks and colleges as well as the pros and cons of allowing a bank to promote credit cards on campus.

3. In the 2008 U.S. presidential election, the percentages of voters by age-group were as follows (http://www.historycentral.com):

- 18–24: 10 percent
- 25–29: 8 percent
- 30–39: 18 percent
- 40–49: 21 percent
- 50–64: 27 percent
- 65+: 16 percent

For this task, form a team with one classmate. Assume that you are consultants to the Young Republicans or the Young Democrats (you choose which group) on your campus. Do the following:

- Determine the percentages of voters by age-group in the 2012 U.S. presidential election.

- Write a report to the president of the organization you have chosen. Provide likely reasons for and implications of the changes, if any, that have been observed between 2008 and 2012. Before writing the report, prepare a brief outline that shows you have considered and made decisions about all aspects of the report's content and structure.
- Attach the outline of the final version of this report and present it to your instructor.

4. If you do not have a Gmail account, open one now at http://www.gmail.com; then exchange IDs (Gmail ID) with your teammate for Application 3. In Google Docs, draft a report describing the roles that you and your teammate played while completing Application 3. Did you complete the entire assignment together, or did you alternate between individual and team work? Include all aspects of planning that report; gathering and interpreting the data; drafting, revising, and editing the report; and producing the final report. What did you learn about collaborative writing as you completed Application 2? Collaborate in Google Docs to revise, edit, produce, and print a final draft. Print the two original drafts and attach to the final draft. Present the report to your instructor.

5. To live comfortably during retirement, financial advisors suggest that your retirement income from all sources (personal savings and investments, pensions, Social Security, and so on) should be equivalent to 80 percent of your preretirement income. For this task, do the following:
   - Determine what you may expect to earn when you graduate from your current educational program. Estimate reasonable increases in your employment earnings during your career.
   - Compute how much you must save each year, assuming an average 5 percent return on savings/investments, to reach a retirement goal of 80 percent of your preretirement income. Remember to factor in expected salary increases over time and the age at which you hope to retire.
   - Write a report to your instructor, including this information. Include also an assessment of how realistic it is for you to think you can reach the savings goals you have computed.

6. While she was still an undergraduate student at the Leeds School of Business, University of Colorado, Sarah Schupp founded University Parent, a company that helps parents get information about their children's campuses and the communities surrounding them. Today, more than 180 colleges and universities in more than 38 states are affiliated with University Parent. Thousands of parents follow University Parent on Twitter or are Facebook friends with University Parent ("College Guide for Parents," 2010). If your university is affiliated with University Parent, obtain statistics about the frequency of its use and parents' evaluation of the service. If your university is not affiliated, determine what would have to be done to establish a relationship with University Parent. Present your findings in a brief memo to your instructor, using the format demonstrated in Illustration 1.2.

References

1. College guide for parents. (2010, Fall). *Portfolio*, 14–15.
2. Shwom, B. H., & Hirsch, P. (1994). Managing the drafting process, creating a new model for the workplace. *Bulletin of the Association for Business Communication, 57*, 1–10.
3. Spending smart: The extended warranty debate. (2011, February 1). http://www.thestate.com/2011/02/01/1673282/spending-smart-the-extended-warranty.html.
4. Thorpe, K. (2011, January/February). Take that APR and shove it. *Mother Jones*, 68.

CHAPTER **4**

Writing Style and Lapses

LEARNING OBJECTIVES

After you have read this chapter, you should be able to:

1. Choose a writing style that complements the audience, content, and context of your report.

2. Recognize and revise an inappropriate writing style.

3. Detect these common writing lapses and avoid them or correct them in your or your colleagues' writing:

   • Lapses in noun-pronoun and subject-verb agreement

   • Errors in the use of nouns and pronouns

   • Inaccuracies in sentence structure

   • Problems with punctuation

   • Errors in word choice

4. Use electronic editing tools to improve the quality of your writing.

5. Work effectively with team members to produce a document that is professional in all aspects of writing style and mechanics.

6. Demonstrate responsibility in style choices and language usage while working alone or with others.

STYLE IS A DISTINCTIVE MANNER OF EXPRESSION OR A TECHNIQUE BY WHICH SOMETHING IS DONE OR CREATED. Empathy, accuracy, completeness, conciseness, and clarity are qualities that should be demonstrated in all reports—long or short, simple or complex. To achieve those qualities, you must choose a writing style purposefully instead of just "letting it happen."

Choose a Writing Style

Style involves an element of choice—you can select a style for your report that is appropriate for its content, context, and desired outcome. As you choose a writing style for a particular report, you should empathize with your readers. Consider their needs—both information needs and ego needs. Information needs are the data that will enable the receiver to understand and fulfill the objectives of your report. Ego needs are desires for recognition and acknowledgment of worth. A report may provide all the information a receiver needs, but unless the report also satisfies ego needs, it may not motivate that person to act.

The content, context, and desired outcomes for simple and complex reports may differ considerably. The overall style of simple, relatively short reports (such as a trip report, a production report, or minutes of a meeting) differs from the style of complex, specialized reports (such as a business plan or a business research report). The decisions you make about report tone, level of formality, and objectivity will define your report style.

Choose Report Tone

Tone is evidence of the sender's attitude toward the message and the receiver. Some descriptors of tone are personal, impersonal; formal, informal; positive, negative; courteous, curt; passive, forceful; conciliatory, defensive. In written reports, tone is conveyed by word choice and message structure. In oral reports, tone may be conveyed additionally by vocal pitch or emphasis, posture, and gestures.

The following examples demonstrate how a sender might plan to accommodate a receiver's needs by carefully selecting tone, structure, and presentation mode as well as content. Notice that the sender's objective in both cases is to get the receiver to act. The first example demonstrates a plan for a relatively simple, informal report.

Sender's objective: A bank teller will move to a station that will enable more effective customer service.

Receiver's needs: Information needs—to know when to move, where to move. Ego needs—to be respected as a valued member of the organization

Report structure: Direct—main point followed by brief explanation, if any

Report tone: Courteous, informal

Presentation mode: Oral; no written supplement (Example: "Juan, please close this window and take over the drive-up window. Cars are beginning to line up out there.")

In contrast, a store manager's more complex report to company officers about relocating the business might include these planning considerations:

Sender's objective: Upper management will move the store to a new location so that profits may increase.

Receiver's needs: Information needs—justification for, likely benefits of, and estimated costs of moving the store. Ego needs—recognition of status and decision-making authority; respect for value of reader's time

Report structure: Direct—recommendation to move the store to a new location followed by supporting details: profitability of current location, problems associated with current location, goals for store, cost of move to new location, and benefits of move

> **Report tone:** *Formal and respectful, yet forceful and confident*
>
> **Presentation mode:** *Written, supplemented by oral; both enhanced by visual aids*

Choose Degree of Formality

When you write a report, you must choose the degree of formality you want to convey. Formality is conveyed by language and by inclusion or exclusion of certain parts of a report. You can decide what formal parts to include with your report after you have written the report body. You must, however, decide about the formality of language before you write the body of the report.

Some contexts may justify informality, a style that is most often reserved for situations in which the writer knows the primary reader well or frequently works with that person. Even under those circumstances, however, an informal style may not be appropriate because secondary readers must also be considered. If a report is to pass among many readers, some of whom the writer does not know, a formal style is generally preferable. Similarly, when the primary reader files the report for future use by other people, a formal style is often preferred.

Assume, for example, that two cities are trying to annex a residential area known as Winslow Hills. You are a member of the Winslow Hills Homeowners Association, and its officers have asked you to determine the homeowners' attitudes and preferences with respect to annexation. The officers will circulate the summary of your final report to all homeowners and will present the full report to the competing city councils. In such a situation, an informal style is appropriate for a progress report to the officers of the homeowners' association, whom you know well and with whom you share common concerns. The final report, however, would likely be written in a formal style, which would show respect for the elected officials while impressing them with the seriousness of the annexation issue.

No sharp distinction exists between formality and informality in reports. Consequently, no one can define exactly what constitutes formal or informal language. Nonetheless, the language we tend to use with peers or individuals whom we know well is often characterized as informal language. Informal language includes frequent use of first names, contractions, and first- and second-person pronouns: *I, me, my, mine, we, us, our, ours, you, your, yours*. In addition, colloquial expressions tend to connote informality. Colloquialisms are words and phrases commonly used in conversation (for example, *OK, thumbs up, go-ahead* as equivalents for *agreement, approval*) or those common to certain regions (for example, *crack the window* for *open the window, cut on the light* for *turn on the light*).

In spite of the popularity of text messaging, the conventions of those messages are still considered too informal for business use. The real issue here is the generation gap. Many members of the baby-boomer generation (or earlier generations) have not adapted to text-messaging conventions. Even if they can decipher the message, they may be offended by such informality.

In contrast, the language we tend to use with someone who holds a high-status position or individuals whom we do not know well is characterized as formal language. The major difference between formal and informal language is the presence or absence of words that suggest how well the writer and reader (speaker and listener) are acquainted. Absence of first- and second-person pronouns, use of courtesy or position titles with full names or last names, and avoidance of contractions and colloquial expressions characterize a more formal style. For example, the author of this book met a relatively young college professor from an Asian country at a professional conference. In conversations at the conference and in subsequent email correspondence, the younger woman always addressed the older woman as "doctor" or "professor." She even expressed discomfort with using the older person's first name. Such factors as age, professional experience, and cultural practices prompted her to use a more formal style.

You should not confuse formality with wordiness, unwieldy sentences, and overuse of passive verbs. Even formal writing can be concise, clear, and vigorous. The following examples contrast features of informal and formal writing.

First- and Second-Person Pronouns

Informal: I interviewed your information technology managers and technicians. Your IT crew is eager to have a tai chi class offered on your premises during the lunch hour.

Formal: Interviews with information technology managers and technicians revealed their eagerness to participate in an on-site tai chi class.

Informal: Your IT employees are pumped; you should have a good turnout if you offer a tai chi class during lunch hour.

Formal: Information technology personnel have strong motivation to support an on-site tai chi class.

Names, Titles

Informal: Jean said that IT support increased 12 percent in February.

Formal: Ms. Jean Herriot, IT support coordinator, reported a 12 percent increase in support requests during February.

Informal: If you need additional information, Alex, please let me know.

Formal: If you need additional information, Mr. Padgett, please let me know.

Contractions

Informal: What's your reaction? I'm eager to hear from you. You can reach me at 555-8765.

Formal: Please direct questions or comments about this proposal to Ms. Marlow at Extension 109.

Informal: Your IT guys said they're swamped with support requests.

Formal: Information technology managers and technicians expressed concern about the volume of support requests.

Colloquialisms

Informal: We have to get on the ball and tackle the problem of health insurance for our employees. Let's find out what companies like ours are offering and figure out how we can handle another employee benefit.

Formal: We must consider seriously the issue of health insurance for our employees. We should study what companies similar to ours are offering and whether we can finance another employee benefit.

Informal: Let's look at the numbers. The bottom line is that our employees want a health insurance plan and we can afford to cover half of the employee's premium if we reduce vacation allowances. Some employees said they wouldn't be able to afford a vacation anyway if they had to pay for all of their medical bills.

Formal: The data show two important facts:

1. Washtenaw Electric employees want a health insurance plan.
2. Some Washtenaw Electric employees prefer a modest medical insurance plan over a generous vacation allowance.
3. Washtenaw Electric can afford to cover 50 percent of each employee's premium if it also reduces vacation allowances.

To summarize, informal reports project a more personal tone. They may use first- and second-person pronouns as well as near-conversational language. Many informal reports are presented orally or in memorandum format. Study the scenario diagrammed in Illustration 4.1. The sales associate's report to the sales manager and the research director's report to the research staff are informal reports.

In contrast, a formal report typically uses impersonal language and tone. Although formal reports may be written in memorandum or letter format, they are often presented in manuscript form. The format frequently includes headings to guide the reader through the report content; and, if presented in manuscript format, the report generally includes a title page and perhaps a transmittal message. As report length increases, other preliminary pages may be included to accommodate reader needs, such as a table of contents and an executive summary. Some lengthy formal reports also contain supplements such as a bibliography or source list and an appendix. The feasibility study referenced in Illustration 4.1 would likely be prepared as a formal report because it would go not only to the staff's immediate supervisor but also to upper management. Moreover, the report will contain much technical market information, requiring a table of contents, a source list, and perhaps some appendices. The writer may also provide an executive summary to give readers a concise preview of the report content. These parts, which often differentiate formal from informal reports, are discussed and illustrated in Chapter 16.

ILLUSTRATION 4.1 DEGREES OF FORMALITY

Sender	Receiver	Report Content	Report Characteristics	Decision/Action
J Pac sales associate	J Pac sales manager	Consumers in Brazil enjoy grilled meats; most use charcoal; potential market for our gas grills	Oral; informal	Sales manager does preliminary research; relays information to vice president for marketing
Sales manager	Vice president for marketing	Burgeoning consumer market is attracting many U.S. companies to Brazil; few of our competitors are currently selling gas grills in Latin America	Written; semiformal; supplemented by oral summary	Vice president for marketing asks director of market research to conduct further research about feasibility of entering Latin American market
Vice president for marketing	Director of market research	Summary of previous reports; request to study feasibility of entering Latin American market	Written; semiformal	Director of market research assigns task to research staff; requests research proposal
Director of market research	Research staff	Summary of vice president's reports; request for research proposal	Oral; informal; part of weekly staff meeting	Staff begins work on research proposal
Research staff	Director of market research	Proposed plan for feasibility study	Written; formal	Director approves plan; staff conducts study
Research staff	Director of market research	Findings, conclusions, recommendations of feasibility study	Formal; written; perhaps supplemented by oral presentation	Director asks staff to present report to management committee
Research staff and director of market research	Management committee	Background; summary of preliminary studies; findings, conclusions, recommendations of feasibility study	Oral/visual presentation; written summary of key findings and recommendations	Management authorization of budget for marketing division to begin efforts to establish distributorships in Brazil

Some situations call for a combination of formal and informal style. For example, a lengthy, complex analysis of a business problem may be presented in formal style and format, but it may be accompanied by a transmittal message that is written in an informal tone and supplemented by a semiformal oral summary. The marketing research staff's report to the management committee (Illustration 4.1) is such a situation.

Whether you choose a formal style, an informal style, or a combination of the two, all of your reports must meet the criteria for effective writing: accuracy, clarity, empathy, completeness, and conciseness. Moreover, all data must be presented objectively, not emotionally.

Write Objectively

Objectivity requires that all available, relevant data be presented. Moreover, you should focus on the data, not on what you think or feel about the situation. Each step in data analysis—presenting data, interpreting data, drawing conclusions, and making recommendations—takes you further from the original facts, experiences, or observations. To maintain credibility, you must discipline yourself to keep the analysis free of your biases or emotions and express your conclusions and recommendations in objective language.

For example, a bank loan officer may observe that the number of applications for home equity loans increased substantially after Christmas. But to conclude that borrowers use home equity loans to pay for Christmas debts is an improper conclusion. Such a conclusion may be drawn only if information obtained from customers consistently shows they intend to use the equity loan to pay for holiday purchases. Likewise, to conclude that borrowing on home equity is irresponsible financial management is the expression of an opinion based on a writer's values, not an objective conclusion.

The following examples contrast emotional language with objective language.

Emotional: I was not surprised to find that the vast majority of your clients strongly favored that you move your office to a new location. The current office is in a seedy part of town, and clients are afraid they may be mugged when they leave their cars to come into your office. Therefore, you need to find a new site now or lose your clients.

Objective: Eighty-five percent of the clients surveyed said they are reluctant to come to your office in person. The crime level in this neighborhood is a deterrent. Therefore, I recommend that you immediately begin a search for an office in a safer area.

Although your writing should not contain unjustifiable expressions of opinion or emotion, you should demonstrate confidence in your findings, conclusions, and recommendations.

Express Confidence

Expressing yourself with confidence does not mean being brash or impudent. Instead, it means that when the data are sufficient, you do not hesitate to state your objective findings, conclusions, and recommendations, even if they are contrary to the outcome your reader might have preferred. If, on the other hand, the data are insufficient to support any logical and objective conclusions and recommendations, you also state that fact confidently.

To demonstrate confidence, many writers use imperative sentences when stating recommendations that are clearly supported by the data. The following examples contrast impudent, hesitant, and confident styles.

> *Impudent: This agency has obviously neglected to consider the safety of its clients. That error can be corrected simply by doing two things:*
>
> 1. *Install better exterior lighting at the current location.*
> 2. *Begin an immediate search for an office in a safer area of the city.*
>
> *Hesitant: The agency might want to consider looking for an office in a safer part of town. In the meantime, the agency could probably also install better exterior lighting at the current location.*
>
> *Confident: Our recommendations to Family Counseling are:*
>
> 1. *Install better exterior lighting at the current location.*
> 2. *Begin an immediate search for an office in a safer area of the city.*
>
> *Unjustifiably confident: Approximately 50 percent of the Family Services Board of Directors are eager to relocate the office. With their enthusiasm, you'll probably see them moving to a new facility within a month.*
>
> *Justifiably hesitant: Approximately 50 percent of the Family Services Board of Directors expressed reluctance to relocate the office. Relocation at this time appears to be unwise. Further study to determine how to overcome objections to relocation may be necessary to ensure the eventual success of a plan to move to a new facility.*

Ideally, choices about writing style are made before you begin writing your first draft. It is not unusual, however, for the style to evolve as you experience various stages of drafting and revising your report, as was discussed in Chapter 3. As you draft and revise the report, you should also be alert to frequently occurring writing lapses.

Frequently Occurring Writing Lapses

Whereas choice enters into writing style, the mechanical aspects of writing permit little choice. Following generally accepted standards for grammar and word usage marks the writer as a literate, well-educated individual. Ignoring such standards may tag the writer as either careless or uneducated.

Some writing lapses are minor, others are irritating, but all become distractions when a knowledgeable reader encounters them. To avoid being labeled as a FOWL writer, learn to identify—and avoid—the *frequently occurring writing lapses* (FOWLs) discussed in this chapter.

The items are categorized and numbered for easy reference and to allow your instructor to indicate by number the types of FOWLs that appear in your writing. The following groups of FOWLs are discussed:

- Agreement lapses
- Problems with nouns and pronouns
- Sentence errors
- Punctuation problems
- Language lapses

Agreement Lapses (A1–A2)

Lack of agreement between subject and verb or noun and pronoun may result in reader confusion, misinterpretation, or irritation.

A1: Mixed Singular and Plural Nouns and Pronouns

A pronoun must agree in number with its antecedent. Mixtures of singular and plural pronouns occur most frequently in reference to companies or organizations.

> **FOWLs**
>
> **A.** *Boulware, Inc. has launched an intensive effort to penetrate the Eastern European market for central heating and air conditioning.* They intend to be the first with the best in that region of the world.
>
> **B.** *Management must commit to an extensive advertising campaign.* They have *little time to lose.*

> **Corrections**
>
> **A.** *Boulware, Inc. has launched an intensive effort to penetrate the Eastern European market for central heating and air conditioning.* It [or The company or Boulware] intends *to be the first with the best in that region of the world.*
>
> **B.** *Management has little time to lose.* It *must commit to an extensive advertising campaign.*

> **Exception**
>
> *Although British writers often use a plural pronoun in reference to an apparent singular antecedent (such as* management*), those writers also use a plural verb in such a context. That is, they consistently use the noun in the plural sense, properly followed by a plural verb or pronoun. For example:*
>
> *Manangement* are *firm in* their *decision to expand product offerings.*
>
> NOT
>
> *Management* is *firm in* their *decision to expand product offerings.*

A2: Mixed Singular and Plural Subjects and Verbs

Subjects and verbs must agree in number. Mixtures of singular and plural nouns and verbs occur most frequently when modifying words or phrases are inserted between the subject and verb.

> **FOWLs**
>
> **A.** *The basic writing* ability *of trainees* are *determined by an analysis of scores on a writing examination.*
> **B.** *Communication* skills, *as well as writing ability,* is *expected of all trainees.*
> **C.** This type *of problems* are *seen often.*

> **Corrections**
>
> **A.** *The basic writing* ability *of trainees* is *determined by an analysis of scores on a writing examination.*
>
> OR
>
> *A trainee's writing* ability is *determined by an analysis of scores on a writing examination.*
> **B.** *Communication* skills, *as well as writing ability,* are *expected of all trainees.*
>
> OR
>
> *All* trainees are *expected to have communication skills and writing ability.*
> **C.** These types *of problems* are *seen often.*
>
> OR
>
> *This type* of problem *is* seen often.

Problems with Nouns and Pronouns (PN1–PN7)

Incorrect use of nouns and pronouns also tends to confuse or distract the reader. Avoid the noun and pronoun errors discussed here.

PN1: Possessive Noun Errors

Because many possessive forms of nouns (*company's, employee's*) sound like the plural forms (*companies, employees*), correct punctuation of possessive forms is essential for clarity. Mastery of possessives requires application of the following four guides:

- Recognize the correct spelling of the singular and plural noun forms.
- Form the possessive of the singular noun by adding 's, no matter how the noun ends.
- Form the possessive of a plural noun that ends in s by adding an apostrophe only.
- Form the possessive of a plural noun that does *not* end in s by adding 's.

FOWLs

A. *Many* company's *offer benefits that differ from this* companies *benefits.*

B. *Those* companie's *benefits differ from* other's *in the industry.*

C. *Because our* companies *benefits package allows* employee's *to make choices,* each *employees' package may be designed to fit her or his needs.*

D. Ms. Thomson-Hass' *employer provides on-site child care.*

E. *An* employees *minor* childs' *dental care is covered by our plan.*

F. Employee's *spouses* are *included in the family plan.*

G. *The first* years *coverage for your child includes all well-baby care.*

H. *The first five* years *coverage for your child includes all inoculations.*

I. Childrens' *benefits end when children reach age 21.*

Corrections

A. *Many* companies *offer benefits that differ from this* company's *benefits.*

B. *Those* companies' *benefits differ from* others *in the industry.*

C. *Because our* company's *benefits package allows* employees *to make choices,* each *employee's package may be designed to fit her or his needs.*

D. Ms. Thomson-Hass's *employer provides on-site child care.*

E. *An* employee's *minor* child's *dental care is covered by our plan.*

F. Employees' *spouses* are *included in the family plan.*

G. *The first* year's *coverage for your child includes all well-baby care.*

H. *The first five* years' *coverage for your child includes all inoculations.*

I. Children's *benefits end when children reach age 21.*

PN2: Errors in Pronoun Case

Careless speakers and writers sometimes use an objective pronoun (me, him, her, them) when a nominative pronoun (I, he, she, they) is needed. This error frequently occurs with a plural subject but rarely with a single subject. To avoid the error, ask yourself which pronoun you would use if the sentence had a singular subject. Incidentally, courteous speakers and writers usually place references to self after references to others.

FOWLs

A. Me *and Francis (or Francis and* me) *volunteered to move the office furniture. (Test: would you have said* me *volunteered …?)*

B. Me *and Kate (or Kate and* me) *went to the country music concert. (Test: would you have said* me *went …?)*

Corrections

A. I *and Francis (preferably Francis and* I) *volunteered to move the office furniture.*

B. I *and Kate (preferably Kate and* I) *went to the country music concert.*

PN3: Reflexive Pronoun Errors

Reflexive pronouns serve two purposes: to emphasize (for example, Joe *himself* is responsible for this error) or to reflect the action of the verb toward a noun or pronoun already used in the sentence (for example, Joe asked *himself* how he could have avoided the error). Errors in the use of reflexive pronouns typically occur in the first person when an individual makes a mistakenly modest attempt to avoid using *I* or *me*.

FOWLs

 A. *Lee and* myself *conducted interviews with the clients.*

 B. *The subjects expressed their opinions openly to Lee and* myself.

Corrections

 A. *Lee and* I *conducted interviews with the clients.*

   OR

   I conducted the interviews myself.

 B. *The subjects expressed their opinions openly to Lee and* me.

PN4: Confusion of Contractions and Possessive Pronouns

Possessive pronouns have no apostrophes. A contraction requires an apostrophe to indicate the omission of one or more letters. *It's* is a contraction for *it is*, *they're* is a contraction for *they are*, and *who's* is a contraction for *who is*. *Its*, *their*, and *whose* are possessive pronouns.

FOWLs

 A. *If a company does not communicate quickly during a crisis,* it's *reputation may suffer severe damage.* Its *difficult to recover from the loss of goodwill.*

 B. *Employees should be notified immediately when* their *in potential danger.*

 C. *Investigators try to determine* whose *at fault when an industrial accident occurs.*

Corrections

 A. *If a company does not communicate quickly during a crisis,* its *reputation may suffer severe damage.* It's *difficult to recover from the loss of goodwill.*

   OR

   If a company does not communicate quickly during a crisis, it's *possible that the company's reputation will be damaged.*

> **B.** *Employees should be notified immediately when* they're *in potential danger.*
>
> *OR*
>
> *When* their *work environment is dangerous, employees should be notified of potential hazards.*
>
> **C.** *Investigators try to determine* who's *at fault when an industrial accident occurs.*
>
> *OR*
>
> *Investigators try to determine* whose *error caused the accident.*

PN5: Relative Pronoun Errors

Relative pronouns refer to nouns that immediately precede them. The most common relative pronouns are *who* (for persons), *that* (for persons and things), and *which* (for things). Relative pronouns introduce adjective clauses; in those clauses, the relative pronouns act as subjects or objects and must be in the appropriate case: nominative (who) or objective (whom). Most contemporary writers reserve *which* for nonrestrictive clauses and *that* for restrictive clauses.

> **FOWLs**
>
> **A.** *Is Joan the person* which *shipped this box?*
> **B.** *Joan is the person* who *I saw.*
> **C.** *This is the third box* which *I've delivered today.*
> **D.** *This box* that *Joan sent is heavy. I wonder what's in it.*

> **Corrections**
>
> **A.** *Is Joan the person* who *shipped this box?*
> **B.** *Joan is the person* whom *I saw.*
> **C.** *This is the third box* that *I've delivered today.*
> **D.** *This box,* which *Joan sent, is heavy. I wonder what's in it.*

PN6: Confusion of Conjunctions and Relative Pronouns

The verb *to be* and its forms (*am, are, is, was, were, been*) serve as linking verbs which must be followed by a noun or adjective form to complete the sentence. (Examples: Larry is tall. Larry was kind. Larry has been a police officer for 10 years.) A noun clause introduced by *that* may be used as the complement. (Example: One of Larry's strengths is that he is kind.) The conjunction *because* should be reserved to introduce an adverbial construction and should not follow a linking verb.

> **FOWLs**
>
> **A.** *The* reason *is* because *bond yields are more uncertain as they are projected further into the future.*

> **B.** *A contributor to Larry's kindness is* because *he was reared in a home that valued kindness.*

Corrections

A. *The* reason *is* that *bond yields are more uncertain as they are projected further into the future.*

OR

The reason *is* clear: *Bond yields are more uncertain as they are projected further into the future.*

OR

We may have difficulty finding an underwriter for this issue because *bond yields are more uncertain as they are projected further into the future.*

B. *A* contributor *to Larry's kindness is* that *he was reared in a home that valued kindness.*

OR

Larry is kind because *he was reared in a home that valued kindness.*

PN7: Indefinite References

An antecedent is the noun for which a pronoun substitutes. A pronoun should refer unmistakably to its antecedent; otherwise, the antecedent should be repeated, or the entire sentence should be rewritten for clarity.

FOWLs

A. *Competition in capital markets determines the appropriate trade-off function between risk and return for different classes of securities. This occurs when....*

B. *In the early years of the 21st century, interest rates on adjustable-rate mortgages contributed to loan foreclosures. They rose to an unprecedented level.*

C. *We successfully closed the Conrad contract,* which *pleased us.*

Corrections

A. *Competition in capital markets determines the appropriate trade-off function between risk and return for different classes of securities. This* trade-off *occurs when....*

B. *In the early years of the 21st century, interest rates on adjustable-rate mortgages contributed to loan foreclosures. The rates rose to an unprecedented level.*

Frequently Occurring Writing Lapses   **87**

> **C.** *Successfully closing the Conrad contract pleased us.*
>
> *OR*
>
> *The Conrad contract,* which *pleased us, was successfully closed yesterday.*

Sentence Errors (S1–S7)

A third class of FOWLs includes seven errors in sentence construction.

S1: Dangling and Misplaced Modifiers

A modifier must be structurally and logically related to a word or clause in the sentence. Dangling and misplaced modifiers frequently occur when the writer begins a sentence with a verbal phrase and follows the phrase with a noun that the phrase cannot logically modify. Misplaced modifiers frequently occur when a sentence contains too many modifying words and phrases.

> **FOWLs**
>
> **A.** After completing the audit, a report *was prepared for the client.*
> **B.** Raising EPS to $5.79, *the* annual report *shows diversification has paid off.*
> **C.** *For a family of four with a teenage driver,* which drives 15,000 miles per year, *the CR-V is a more economical vehicle than the Suburban.*

> **Corrections**
>
> **A.** After completing the audit, *the* accountant *prepared a report for the client.*
> **B.** *The annual report shows that diversification has paid off,* raising EPS to $5.79.
> **C.** *For a four-member family* that drives 15,000 miles per year, *the CR-V is a more economical vehicle than the Suburban.*

S2: Excessive Use of Expletives

An expletive is a word or phrase used to fill out a sentence or to provide emphasis. Unless emphasis is desired and can be achieved in no other way, expletives should be avoided. In fact, a more direct style may strengthen the impact of the sentence.

> **FOWLs**
>
> **A.** There are *several conclusions that might be drawn from the study.*
> **B.** It is *apparent that hiring overqualified workers is a costly practice.*

> **Corrections**
>
> **A.** *Several conclusions might be drawn from the study.*
> **B.** *Hiring overqualified workers is a costly practice.*

S3: Excessive Use of Parenthetical Expressions

Parentheses or dashes may be used to show a sudden interruption or shift of thought, to provide a supplementary explanation, or to show emphasis. However, excessive use of parentheses or dashes may obstruct the main idea of the sentence. Using shorter sentences, you can often work the qualifying information into the discussion.

FOWL

Annual fuel costs based on $3.50 per gallon (a fair estimate for this area) would be approximately $2,300 for the CR-V and $3,800 for the Suburban based on 15,000 miles of driving—a reasonable average for a family of four (including a driving teenager).

Correction

A fair estimate for gasoline in this area is $3.50 per gallon. Annual driving mileage for a family of four with a teenage driver is estimated at 15,000 miles. Based on these figures, the family could expect annual fuel costs of approximately $2,300 for the CR-V and $3,800 for the Suburban.

S4: Nonparallel Constructions

Parallelism indicates equality of ideas. To achieve parallelism, balance nouns with nouns, adjectives with adjectives, verbs with verbs, adverbs with adverbs, prepositions with prepositions, conjunctions with conjunctions, and verbals with verbals.

FOWLs

A. *The company's net income differed from its projections because of random events, ignoring relevant assumptions, and when interest rates fluctuated.*

B. *This job requires skills in accounting, management, and the ability to communicate well.*

C. *An employee manual should be revised when:*
   New laws are enacted.
   The company changes benefit plans.
   There are new company policies.
   Changes in company goals and philosophies.

Corrections

A. *The company's net income differed from its projections because of random events, omission of relevant assumptions, and fluctuations of interest rates.*

B. *This job requires skills in accounting, management, and communication.*

C. *An employee manual should be revised when changes occur in:*
   Laws
   Company benefits

> *Company policies*
> *Company goals and philosophies*

S5: Fragmented Sentences, Clauses, and Phrases

Every sentence must contain a subject and a verb and must express a completed thought. Although a subordinate clause contains a subject and a verb, it does not express a completed thought. For example, the first clause of the previous sentence has a subject (*clause*) and a verb (*contains*); but those 10 words (*Although … verb*) are meaningless if they stand alone. The most common fragmentation error is separating a subordinate (dependent) clause from the main (independent) clause to which it is related. Another fragmentation error is separating a phrase (which contains no subject and verb) from the item that it is intended to modify.

FOWLs

A. *Some employees elect not to participate in the company's medical insurance plan.* Although that is a rare occurrence.
B. Even if they think they already have enough life insurance. *Employees should never reject the free life insurance offered by the company.*
C. Foolishly conservative. *Some employees elect not to participate in the company's medical insurance plan.*

Corrections

A. *Some employees elect not to participate in the company's medical insurance plan,* although that is a rare occurrence.
B. Even if they think they already have enough life insurance, *employees should never reject the free life insurance offered by the company.*
C. Foolishly conservative, *some employees elect not to participate in the company's medical insurance plan.*

S6: Run-On or Spliced Sentences

A run-on sentence is one that combines two or more independent clauses without appropriate punctuation or conjunctions. The major punctuation error, in addition to lack of any punctuation, is the use of a comma when a period or semicolon should be used. This is called a comma splice.

FOWLs

A. *When you have made a complete statement, and are ready to move on to the next statement, you must make one of four decisions, end the sentence and begin a new one, link the two clauses with a semicolon, link the two clauses with a comma and a coordinating conjunction, or link the two clauses with a semicolon, a conjunctive adverb, and a comma.*

B. *Some writers have difficulty determining when one sentence should end and another should begin, therefore they just keep going on.*

Corrections

A. *When you have made a complete statement and are ready to move on to the next statement, you must make one of four decisions: end the sentence and begin a new one; link the two clauses with a semicolon; link the two clauses with a comma and a coordinating conjunction; or link the two clauses with a semicolon, a conjunctive adverb, and a comma.*

OR

When you have made a complete statement and are ready to move on to the next statement, you must take one of four actions:
- *End the sentence and begin a new one.*
- *Link the two clauses with a semicolon.*
- *Link the two clauses with a comma and a coordinating conjunction.*
- *Link the two clauses with a semicolon, a conjunctive adverb, and a comma.*

B. *Some writers have difficulty determining when one sentence should end and another should begin. They just keep going on.*

OR

Some writers have difficulty determining when one sentence should end and another should begin; they just keep going on.

OR

Some writers have difficulty determining when one sentence should end and another should begin, and they just keep going on.

OR

Some writers have difficulty determining when one sentence should end and another should begin; therefore, they just keep going on.

S7: Long and Complex Sentences

Some writers mistakenly think that long, complex sentences will impress the reader. Quite the contrary is true. A reader will not be impressed by a sentence if he or she must struggle to extract its meaning.

FOWL

Most investor-owned utilities (IOUs) are vertically integrated, which means that they do not specialize in any of the aspects of the electricity industry (generation, transmission, or distribution); however, three major types of utilities (municipal

> *systems, federal agencies, and state agencies) fall under the broad category known as publicly owned utilities (POUs), which, unlike IOUs, are not vertically integrated but, instead, specialize in either generation or distribution.*

> ### Correction
>
> *Electric utilities fall into one of two categories: investor-owned utilities (IOUs) or publicly owned utilities (POUs). POUs include municipal systems, federal agencies, and state agencies. Most IOUs are vertically integrated; that is, they generate, transmit, and distribute electricity. In contrast, most POUs specialize in either generation or distribution.*

Punctuation Problems (P1–P4)

Punctuation marks are communication signals that improve message coherence. Consider these examples:

- Send this report to Jorge Ray.
- Send this report to Jorge, Ray.
- Raise the gear-release lever.
- Raise the gear; release lever.

The few rules included here should help you avoid the most common punctuation problems.

P1: Comma Omitted or Misused

Use commas for these purposes:

- To punctuate a long introductory phrase, an introductory phrase containing a verbal, or an introductory adverb clause
- To set off a *nonrestrictive* clause or appositive
    Caution: *Do not* use commas to set off a *restrictive* clause or appositive.
    (A *nonrestrictive* clause or appositive *describes* but does not *limit* or *restrict* its antecedent; a *restrictive* clause or appositive *restricts* or *limits* its antecedent to a particular group or category.)
- To set off parenthetical words or phrases, including terms of direct address
- To punctuate independent clauses joined by a coordinating conjunction (*and, but, for, or, nor*)
- To separate whole numbers into groups of three digits (except items such as room numbers, policy numbers, and telephone numbers)

Space once after a comma, except when it is used to divide numbers into three-digit groups ($4,329).

> ### FOWLs
>
> **A.** *After completing the employee survey the human resources division developed a new policy about using personal cell phones on company time.*

> **B.** *Employees, who use personal cell phones on company time, will be disciplined.*
>
> **C.** *Michael who rarely uses his personal cell phone at his desk is not worried about the new policy.*
>
> **D.** *Michael do you approve of the new cell phone policy? Consider if you will the consequences of this policy.*
>
> **E.** *Michael approves of the general policy but he thinks some exceptions should be allowed.*
>
> **F.** *Your bonus is $4329, because you signed up more than 1500 new clients.*

> **Corrections**
>
> **A.** *After completing the employee survey, the human resources division developed a new policy about using personal cell phones on company time.*
>
> **B.** *Employees who use personal cell phones on company time will be disciplined.*
>
> **C.** *Michael, who rarely uses his personal cell phone at his desk, is not worried about the new policy.*
>
> **D.** *Michael, do you approve of the new cell phone policy? Consider, if you will, the consequences of this policy.*
>
> **E.** *Michael approves of the general policy, but he thinks some exceptions should be allowed.*
>
> **F.** *Your bonus is $4,329 because you signed up more than 1,500 new clients.*

P2: Semicolon Omitted or Misused

Although the semicolon is a useful mark of punctuation, many writers avoid it because they are unsure about its use. Others use it often, but incorrectly. The semicolon should be used in the following ways:

- To punctuate independent clauses of a compound sentence when no coordinating conjunction links the clauses
- To separate independent clauses or items of a series when at least one of those items also contains other punctuation, such as a comma or parentheses.
- To punctuate independent clauses of a compound sentence when a conjunctive adverb (for example, *nonetheless, however, therefore, consequently*) is used to link the clauses
- To punctuate transitions (for example, *such as, for example, i.e., e.g.*)

Always use a comma after a conjunctive adverb or transition that is preceded by a semicolon. Space once after the semicolon; do not space before the semicolon.

> **FOWLs**
>
> **A.** *Employees must sign and complete FORM B-290 before October 1 of each year, all changes will become effective on January 1 of the subsequent year.*

> **B.** *To change benefits options employees must sign and complete FORM B-290 before October 1 but changes will not become effective until January 1 of the subsequent year.*
>
> **C.** *Follow these procedures: Pick up FORM B-290, Election of Benefits, at the Human Resources Office, complete and sign the form, give the form to the benefits administrator before October 1.*
>
> **D.** *The Medical Spending Account applies to this year only, therefore any money not spent during the current year will be forfeited.*
>
> **E.** *Olmstead Manufacturing has a flexible benefits plan, that is the company lets employees choose from an array of benefits.*

Corrections

> **A.** *Employees must sign and complete FORM B-290 before October 1 of each year; all changes will become effective on January 1 of the subsequent year.*
>
> **B.** *To change benefits options, employees must sign and complete FORM B-290 before October 1; but changes will not become effective until January 1 of the subsequent year.*
>
> **C.** *Follow these procedures: Pick up FORM B-290, Election of Benefits, at the Human Resources Office; complete and sign the form; give the form to the benefits administrator before October 1.*
>
> **D.** *The Medical Spending Account applies to this year only; therefore, any money not spent during the current year will be forfeited.*
>
> **E.** *Olmstead Manufacturing has a flexible benefits plan; that is, the company lets employees choose from an array of benefits.*

P3: Colon Omitted or Misused

The colon is used for these purposes:

- To present a sentence element emphatically
- To introduce a series or list within a sentence, but not if the list is preceded by a linking verb or a preposition
- To introduce a vertical list
- To introduce a long or formal quotation
- To separate hours, minutes, and seconds when time is stated in figures
- To punctuate the greeting of a business letter in the mixed punctuation style

Space once after a colon in a sentence; do not space after a colon in a time notation; never space before a colon.

FOWLs

> **A.** *I have just one word to say to you, Congratulations!*
>
> **B.** *The traditional management functions are: planning, organizing, activating, and controlling.*

> **C.** *I have proofread everything except: Chapter 13, Chapter 14, and the Appendix.*
> **D.** *The second paragraph of our agreement states you are obligated under this contract to return unused items.*
> **E.** *The conference began at 8:30 A.M.*
> **F.** *Dear Ms. Rossi,*

Corrections

> **A.** *I have just one word to say to you: Congratulations!*
> **B.** *The traditional management functions are planning, organizing, activating, and controlling.*
>
> *OR*
>
> *We will study these traditional management functions:*
> - *Planning*
> - *Organizing*
> - *Activating*
> - *Controlling*
>
> **C.** *I have proofread everything except Chapter 13, Chapter 14, and the Appendix.*
> **D.** *The second paragraph of our agreement states: "You are obligated under this contract to return unused items."*
> **E.** *The conference began at 8:30 A.M.*
> **F.** *Dear Ms. Rossi:*

P4: Hyphen Omitted or Misused

A hyphen should be used:

- To join two or more adjectives (compound adjective) that *precede* a noun and define a single concept (for example: *up-to-the-minute* report; *first-class* work; *five-room* suite)

    Generally, hyphens are not used when a compound adjective *follows* the noun it modifies; for example, *the data appear to be up to date.*
- In compound numbers written as words (for example, *ninety-eight, twenty-nine, seventy-seven,* etc.)
- To clarify intended meanings (for example, junior *high-school* students; *junior-high* school students)

Do not use a hyphen between an adverb and the adjective that it modifies; for example, a *highly effective* presentation.

> ## FOWLs
> **A.** Hard earned *sales growth appeared in the third quarter.*
> **B.** *The customer expected the delivery to be* on-time.

C. Twenty eight *associates got* well deserved *salary increases.*

D. *A* debt reducing *action appears to be essential.*

E. *These* highly-toxic *materials must be labeled clearly.*

Corrections

A. Hard-earned *sales growth appeared in the third quarter.*

B. *The* customer *expected* on-time *delivery.*

OR

The customer expected the delivery to be on time.

C. Twenty-eight *associates got* well-deserved *salary increases.*

D. *A* debt-reducing *action appears to be essential.*

E. *These* highly toxic *materials must be labeled clearly.*

Language Lapses (L1; L2A–Z)

Take care to avoid two common language errors: exclusionary language and the use of wrong words. Both types of errors can jar readers and diminish their respect for and confidence in the writer.

L1: Exclusionary Language

In today's increasingly diverse workplace, sensitive writers avoid language that can be interpreted as exclusionary (that is, excludes one or more members of the audience because of inappropriate word choice). Nonexclusionary language avoids references to gender, age, racial, or physical characteristics unless they are relevant to the context.

FOWLs

A. *In 2011, our Secretary of State, former first lady Hillary Clinton, maintained a grueling travel schedule.*

B. *Leonard Pitts, Jr., a noted black* Miami Herald *columnist, stimulates thinking about controversial issues.*

C. *Amy Tan, a female Chinese-American author, has written several award-winning novels.*

D. *The girls in Printing did a fine job on this brochure.*

E. *Every manager must ensure that his employees accurately report time taken for sick leave.*

Corrections

A. *In 2011, our Secretary of State maintained a grueling travel schedule.*

B. *Leonard Pitts, Jr., a* Miami Herald *columnist, stimulates thinking about controversial issues.*

> **C.**   *Amy Tan has written several award-winning novels.*
> **D.**   *The Printing staff did a fine job on this brochure.*
> **E.**   *Managers must ensure that their employees accurately report time taken for sick leave.*

L2: Wrong Word (L2A–Z)

Wrong-word errors can occur for many reasons. Some words sound alike or nearly alike but have different spellings and meanings. Other words have similar constructions but different meanings. Some words sound somewhat alike and have related but distinct meanings. Other word-use errors involve selection of an incorrect part of speech, such as adverb-adjective or noun-verb confusion. You can avoid wrong-word errors by becoming familiar with this list of frequently misused words.

L2A: Accept/Except/Expect

Use *accept* as a verb, meaning *to receive willingly, to agree to*. Use *except* as a verb, meaning *to take or leave out*; as a preposition, meaning *with the exclusion of*; or as a conjunction, meaning *unless* or *only*. Use *expect* as a verb, meaning *to anticipate, to suppose, to think*, or *to consider reasonable, due, or necessary*.

> *I can* accept *the terms of your offer,* except *paragraph 3.b.*
>
> *The coach* excepted *Carrie from the running drill because she had a sprained ankle.*
>
> *I will* expect *a revision of the offer within a few days.*
>
> *I will be available any day* except *Thursday to discuss the terms, and I* expect *that we can reach an agreement soon.*

L2B: Affect/Effect

Use *affect* as a verb, meaning *to influence or to produce an effect*, or as a noun, meaning *a feeling, emotion, or desire*. Use *effect* as a noun, meaning *a result or impact*, or as a verb, meaning *to bring about or accomplish*.

> *The tornado had a devastating* effect *on the state's economy.*
>
> *In what ways did the tornado* affect *the economy?*
>
> *Have you ever measured a tornado survivor's* affect *about the effectiveness of emergency aid programs?*
>
> *We must* effect *a better way to distribute emergency aid.*

L2C: Among/Between

Both words mean *in company with*. Use *between* when referring to two elements or people; use *among* when referring to more than two.

> *Rewards should be distributed equitably* among *employees.*
>
> *The bonus was distributed equally* between *Ms. Huan and Mr. Arendsen.*

L2D: Amount/Number

Use *amount* with reference to things in bulk or mass; use *number* for things that can be counted as individual items.

> *The* amount *of money needed for this project is more than we anticipated.*
>
> *The* number *of employees who elected to participate in the medical savings account is encouraging.*

L2E: Anxious/Eager

Use *anxious* as an adjective, meaning *worried* or *uneasy of mind*; use *eager* as an adjective, meaning *marked by urgent or enthusiastic desire or interest.*

> *Julie was* eager *to meet her new boss, but she was* anxious *about whether he would value the contributions of a young employee.*

L2F: Chose/Choose

Chose is the past tense of *choose.*

> *I* chose *to attend this university even though my parents wanted me to* choose *another.*

L2G: Complement/Compliment

A *complement* is something that *completes* (notice the *comple-* spelling of both words). A *compliment* is *an expression or act of praise or courtesy.* Each word can be used either as a noun or in an adjective form (*complementary/complimentary*).

> *Hollandaise sauce is a tasty* complement *to steamed asparagus.*
>
> *Jed blushed when he received profuse* compliments *about his musical talent.*
>
> *The* complimentary *close of a letter should* complement *the tone of the letter.*
>
> *Many restaurants offer customers over age 60 a* complimentary *beverage with a food order.*

L2H: Compose/Comprise

Compose means *to create* or *to make up the whole.* Both the active and passive forms are appropriate. *Comprise* means *to contain, to embrace, to include all parts,* or *to be composed of. Comprise* is generally used only in the active voice; *comprised of* is considered nonstandard usage.

> *The advisory committee* composed *the rules for the case-analysis competition.*
>
> *The advisory committee* is composed of *(not* comprised of*) presidents of four local corporations.*
>
> *The advisory committee* comprises *(not* is comprised of*) presidents of four local corporations.*

L2I: Economic/Economical

Economic means *of or relating to economics; economical* means *sparing in the use of resources.* Although *economic* is sometimes accepted in lieu of *economical, economical* should not be substituted for *economic.*

> *Current* economic *(not* economical*) conditions require that we use our resources sparingly.*
>
> Economical *use of our resources is necessary at all times.*
>
> *Your plan appears to be an* economical *(or* economic*) approach to resource management.*

L2J: Fewer Than/Less Than

Use *fewer than* in reference to items that can be counted; use *less than* in reference to bulk or mass.

> *We have* fewer *sales associates in the field this year* than *last year.*
>
> *It is not surprising that this year's sales revenue is* less than *last year's.*

L2K: Incidence/Incident/Incidents/Incidences

Incidence means *rate of occurrence,* an *incident* is *a single occurrence,* and *incidents* is the plural of *incident. Incidences* is a nonstandard word often used incorrectly in place of *incidents.* (If you practice pronouncing the words *incidence, incident,* and *incidents,* you will likely remember their appropriate uses. Do *not* use the nonstandard *incidences.*)

> *The* incidence *of shoplifting has declined dramatically this year.*
>
> *This is the first shoplifting* incident *we have experienced this year.*
>
> *We have had* fewer incidents *of shoplifting this year than last year.*

L2L: Incite/Insight

Incite is a verb, meaning *to arouse to action* or *stir up. Insight* is a noun, meaning *the power, act, or result of seeing into a situation.*

> *Gaining new* insights *into social injustices often* incites *citizens to join activist organizations.*

L2M: *Insure/Ensure/Assure*

Each of these words means *to make secure or certain.* However, they have slightly different connotations and uses. Use *insure* only with reference to guaranteeing the value of life or property. Use *assure* with reference to people, meaning *to set their minds at ease.* Use *ensure* in other situations.

> *You should consider replacement value when you* insure *your property.*
>
> *Let me* assure *you, your property is well protected.*
>
> *I will send the policy by overnight delivery to* ensure *that it arrives tomorrow.*

L2N: *In to/Into*

In colloquial language, *in to* is used with a verb to suggest *the action of submitting or transmitting something from one person to another person or place. Into* is used to express *motion or direction to a point or within, direction of attention or concern,* or *a change of state.*

> *We must turn this report* in to *our professor tomorrow morning.* (Saying you turned your paper *into* your professor suggests an act of magic.)
>
> *Logan's mother finally gave* in to *his persistent plea for a cell phone.*
>
> *Unprepared students walked* into *the room apprehensively.*
>
> *I'll look* into *that matter for you.*
>
> *Please break* into *groups of three.*
>
> *The magician appeared to turn the belt* into *a stick.*

L2O: *Irrespective/Irregardless*

Use *irrespective* as an adjective, meaning *not taking something into account. Irregardless* is nonstandard English. Do not use it!

> Irrespective *of what you may hear, you should never use the word* irregardless.

L2P: *Its/It's/Its'*

Its is a possessive pronoun; *it's* is the contraction for *it is. Its'* is not a standard English form. To avoid the *its/it's* error, always read *it is* when you see *it's.* If that reading doesn't make sense, it's the wrong word.

> *The Hoboken office has surpassed* its *sales goals.*
>
> It's *about time to set new goals for all of our regional offices.*

L2Q: Loose/Lose

Loose is an adjective, meaning *not bound or confined*, or a verb, meaning *to untie, free, relax*, or *slacken*; *lose* is a verb, meaning *to cease to have*.

> *If you carry too much* loose *change in your pocket, you may* lose *some of it.*
>
> Loosing *the constraints on sales territories may provide an incentive for expansion.*
>
> *This division has been* losing *money steadily for the past year.*

L2R: Manufacture/Manufacturer

Manufacture is a verb, meaning *to make a product; manufacturer* is a noun used in reference to *a person or organization that manufactures something.* (If you practice pronouncing the words, you will likely remember their appropriate uses.)

> *A* manufacturer *that does not* manufacture *what the market demands will soon face financial problems.*
>
> *I can* manufacture *that product at less cost than any other* manufacturer *in this area.*

L2S: Perspective/Prospective

Use *perspective* as a noun, meaning *the apparent relation between visible objects* or *the mental view of the relative importance of things*; use *prospective* as an adjective, meaning *expected* or *future*.

> *From this* perspective *the building looks like a pyramid.*
>
> *How many* prospective *clients do we have in Cincinnati?*
>
> *What is your* perspective *on the* prospective *sales for January?*
>
> *An effective business plan provides* prospective *investors with a* perspective *on the company's potential success.*

L2T: Set up/Setup

Use *setup* as a noun, meaning *the manner of arranging*; use *set up* as a verb, meaning *to place in position or assemble.*

> *The hotel will take care of the* setup *for the debate.*
>
> *The debate platform must be* set up *before 5 P.M.*

L2U: Site/Sight/Cite

Use *site* as a noun, meaning *a place or location*; as a verb, meaning *to locate*. Use *sight as a noun, meaning something that is seen*, or as a verb, meaning *to get a view of* or *to take aim*. Use *cite* as a verb, meaning to *quote* or *refer to.*

> *Meg* cited *an Internet* site *on which she caught* sight *of the automobile she wants to buy.*
>
> *While visiting the building* site, *we thought we* sighted *a pine marten.*
>
> *When you prepare a report, always* cite *the sources of your information.*

L2V: Their/There/They're

Their is a possessive pronoun, *there* is an adverb, and *they're* is a contraction for *they are.*

> Their *house is over* there, *but it looks like* they're *not home.*
>
> They're *planning to set up* their *office* there *within the next year.*

L2W: Then/Than

Use *then* to mean at that time; use *than* as the second term in a comparison.

> Then *it became evident that Willie's Filly was faster* than *Harry's Horse and would win the race.*
>
> *I earned less* then than *I do now.*

L2X: To/Too/Two

Use *to* as a preposition introducing a noun or pronoun or with a verb to form an infinitive; use *too* as an intensifier or to replace *also*; use *two* to represent a number or quantity.

> *After you have completed the form, please return it* to *me.*
>
> *I hope I will not have* to *wait* too *much longer for a response.*
>
> *Please check this column* too.
>
> Two *employees volunteered* to *organize a softball team.*

L2Y: Waist/Waste

Waist refers to *the narrowed part of the body between the chest and hips* or *a garment or part of a garment for the upper part of the body.* As a noun, *waste* refers to *an unwanted by-product* or *material left over, rejected, or thrown away.* As a verb, *waste* means *to wear away or diminish gradually*, or *to spend or use carelessly.*

> *Dieters often hope to lose inches from their* waists.
>
> *The* waist *of this dress must be altered.*
>
> *We should* waste *no more time on this project.*
>
> *The lost hikers began to despair as their supplies* wasted *away.*

L2Z: Whose/Who's

Whose is used as a possessive or relative pronoun; *who's* is the contraction for *who is.*

> *I wonder* whose *book this is.*
>
> *Gerry,* whose *book was stolen, will have difficulty studying for the exam.*
>
> Who's *going to help her?*

Electronic Tools Help Identify FOWLs

Electronic tools are readily available to help you reduce common lapses in your writing: proofing options of Microsoft Word 2010, online grammar and spell-checkers, and websites offering free grammar coaching. This information comes with a caveat: Proofing or checker technology is limited, with error detection rates generally in the 20 to 50 percent range, though stand-alone spell-checkers are notably more accurate than grammar checkers. For maximum effect, use three or more checkers on one piece of writing.

Microsoft Word 2010 Proofing Options

Microsoft Word 2010 comes with the ability to check the spelling and grammar of text. You can check both spelling and grammar at once on completing a draft. In Word 2010, select the Review ribbon; in the Proofing group, click "Spelling & Grammar" (see Illustration 4.2). One sentence at a time appears in the top window. Spelling errors appear in red, grammar errors, in green. Buttons on the right allow you to ignore a rule once or throughout the document and move to the next sentence. One or more suggested

ILLUSTRATION 4.2 MICROSOFT WORD 2010 SPELLING AND GRAMMAR DIALOGUE

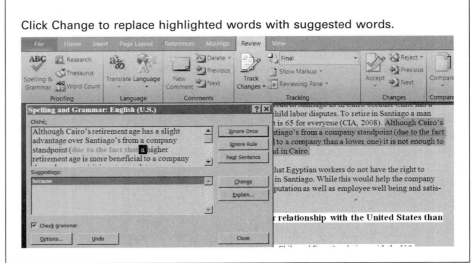

Click Change to replace highlighted words with suggested words.

changes may appear in the bottom window. If so, a "Change" button will be active on the right. Clicking the "Explain" button opens a brief tutorial in Word Help.

Most writers prefer to use the spell-check or grammar check to correct errors while they work. Doing so saves time, especially with long reports. If you use this option, which is active by default, Word shows a wavy red line under words not found in its spelling dictionary and a wavy green line under grammar errors, which may include capitalization, passive voice, punctuation, sentence structure, and nonstandard spacing between words and sentences. In addition, the program can show a wavy blue line under misused words, like "from" instead of "form," "it's" in place of "its," and "to" in place of "too." The Word program refers to these language lapses as "contextual spelling."

To activate contextual spelling, select the File menu; click "Options" (bottom left). Next, at the upper left, click "Proofing." Under "When correcting spelling and grammar," select "Use contextual spelling" (see Illustration 4.3).

In addition to grammar, Microsoft Word will check writing style (21 factors including contractions, hyphenated words, passive voice, sentence length and structure,

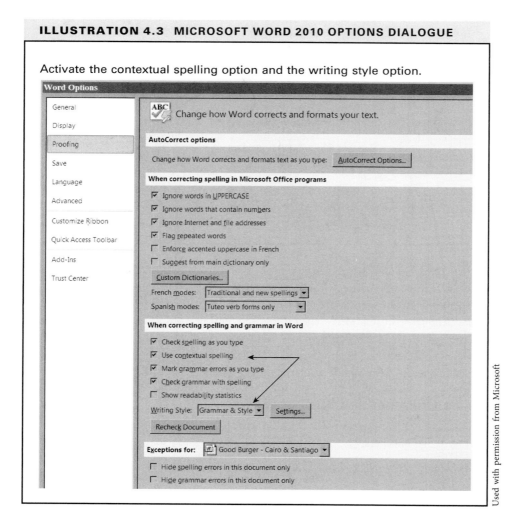

ILLUSTRATION 4.3 MICROSOFT WORD 2010 OPTIONS DIALOGUE

Activate the contextual spelling option and the writing style option.

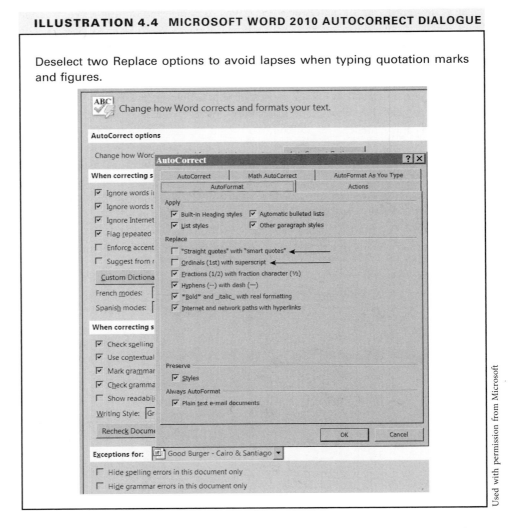

ILLUSTRATION 4.4 MICROSOFT WORD 2010 AUTOCORRECT DIALOGUE

Deselect two Replace options to avoid lapses when typing quotation marks and figures.

unclear phrasing, and wordiness). Activate this feature at the Writing Style text box; click the arrow and choose "Grammar & Writing Style" (see Illustration 4.3).

Become familiar with Word's other proofing options: At the top of the dialog box, click "AutoCorrect Options" and study the options on each tab. The following changes on the AutoFormat tab may help you avoid lapses when using quotation marks or numbers (see Illustration 4.4). Under "Replace," deselect these two options: "Straight quotes" with "smart quotes" and "Ordinals (1st)" with "superscript."

Online Grammar and Spell-Checkers

Ideally, you will supplement Word's built-in error detection with a couple of the following online checkers.

Grammarly (http://ed.grammarly.com/editor/view/Zf=1)

This checker performs 150 grammar checks, including contextual spelling, and returns a summary, a list of the lapses, and a brief analysis of each category. In addition, it rates the writing with a percentage score. For example, the author entered a 100-word sample, including many FOWLs. Grammarly gave it a score of 64 percent and the words "weak, needs revision." In addition, Grammarly offers vocabulary enhancement, suggesting a more appropriate word in some instances, and plagiarism detection. That is, it compares text you enter against many online sources and tells you if any part of the text was taken from an online source. Thus, Grammarly alerts report writers to the need for proper documentation.

PaperRater (http://www.paperrater.com)

Although this checker also detects FOWLs, it is best suited to research reports. Through its vocabulary enhancement feature, it promotes a "sophisticated" vocabulary rather than the short, simple words recommended for business correspondence. Its plagiarism detection is exceptional, asking the writer to enter the reference list along with the report text in order to verify documentation.

Spellchecker.net (http://spellchecker.net)

This checker flags spelling errors on the screen as the writer types or pastes text to the screen, allowing changes to be made swiftly. It does not address grammar errors.

SpellCheckPlus (http://spellcheckplus.com)

This checker accurately identifies misspelled and misused words (contextual spelling) and one-word versus two-word situations. Besides showing correct spelling, it often gives a memory aid. As the name suggests, this program does not check for grammar errors.

WhiteSmoke (http://www.whitesmoke.com)

This checker includes grammar and spelling and has a relatively high error detection rate. It checks only 250 characters at a time (roughly 50 words, or about three sentences) and requires text to be typed (not pasted) on the screen.

Grammar Coaching Websites

Many websites offer writing tips. One in particular, Grammar Monster (http://www.grammar-monster.com), serves as a handbook. Go there to look up your specific problems with grammar and mechanics. The directory on Grammar Monster's home page allows for speedy navigation.

The following sites provide English tutorials, useful for persons studying English as a second language as well as for native English speakers and writers who want to brush up their skills. At each site, coaching involves concise lessons with examples and exercises for applying the rule(s) just taught.

Daily Grammar (http://dailygrammar.com)

A new lesson appears each Monday through Friday on the Daily Grammar blog, with a quiz posted on Saturday. For self-pacing, a user can access any of the 440 lessons from an archive page. Lessons 1 to 90 cover the eight parts of speech, and lessons 91 to 300 cover parts of sentences. Lessons 301 to 440 deal with the mechanics of grammar, including spelling and punctuation. Each short lesson includes five application sentences. The site does not allow users to type answers but does accommodate scrolling to correct answers on the same Web page.

English Page (http://englishpage.com)

This website provides in-depth instruction in just a few areas and includes ample exercises and tests. It gives lively examples and glossaries on various topics, from the aerospace industry to entertaining films. English Page contains over 120 fill-in exercises that require typing a word or two in a text box. The user, if unsure of the answer, can click a "Hint" button to reveal one letter of the answer at a time. Each 10-item exercise can be checked and graded. Incorrect answers remain in place so that the user can change them. A sentence with the correct answer highlighted replaces the writer's correct answers.

Online English Courses (http://www.1-language.com)

This program includes 70 lessons: Starter (1–12), Elementary (13–25), Pre-Intermediate (26–47), and Intermediate (48–70). Each lesson involves two sets of 10-item exercises that receive a percentage grade and a list of correct answers. For some lessons, the second set involves filling in information about one's self (not graded). In every case, the writer can clear her or his answers and redo the exercises.

Using the tools described in this section will not end all FOWLs, as previously noted. As one blogger put it, "The only way to prevent grammar errors is to learn grammar," and the same might be said for spelling. Still, these checkers and tutorials can increase writers' mechanical accuracy, which helps readers view them as literate and well educated.

Collaborative Writing

When a report is written collaboratively, matters of style and avoidance of FOWLs demand attention. The overall style should be agreed on before individuals begin writing their parts of the report. If decisions about tone, degree of formality, objectivity, and confidence are addressed early in the writing stage, the process of merging parts of the document will be simplified.

The issue of writing lapses is somewhat more complex. Few people choose to make the errors enumerated in this chapter, and writers come to the group with different skill levels. Some groups assign the proofreading and editing task to the person most skilled in detecting writing lapses. However, even if one person accepts the task of final editing and proofreading, each writer has a responsibility to present the best copy of which he or she is capable.

If you know you are weak in the mechanical aspects of writing, a first necessary step is to use the electronic tools described in the preceding section. Be aware, however, that those programs are not infallible. You must have enough knowledge about the writing standards presented in this chapter to be able to make a correct choice from the options offered by the tool. Another strategy is to seek help from outside the group so that you do not unfairly burden the group members with your weaknesses. A useful technique is to pair up with someone, exchange copies of your writing, and critique each other's style and mechanics. Even strong writers use this technique because an independent eye often is able to detect errors that you do not notice in your own writing.

Ethical Considerations

Since writing style involves choice, it is not far-fetched to say that choosing a style may have ethical implications. For example, if you use a curt or excessively informal tone in a sensitive situation, you may offend associates or clients and ultimately the health of your company. Is it ethical to say, "Well, that's just my style, and they'll have to get used to it"? Or should you demonstrate enough concern for the company and your associates to try to modify your style? As a manager, what is your responsibility to assist a person who has difficulty choosing and using an appropriate tone?

Another ethical issue that may arise is the legitimacy of asking another person to proofread and edit your work. If you question the honesty of such a practice, you may reach an ethical decision by answering these questions: Is asking someone to review one's work an accepted practice in this organization? Why am I doing this? Am I trying to conceal one of my weaknesses? Have I done all I can to overcome that weakness? Am I exploiting the goodwill of a fellow employee? Will a document with writing lapses negatively affect this organization? Ultimately, the question is, Does this practice yield good results for others or only for me?

Summary

This chapter has juxtaposed two important aspects of writing: style, in which you have a range of choices, and the technical aspects of writing, in which you have few choices.

As you write you must make choices about tone, formality, and objectivity. You must also decide how much confidence you should demonstrate in your writing. Ideally, your choices will reflect an understanding of the possible impact on readers and, ultimately, on your organization.

This chapter has also presented several frequently occurring writing lapses (FOWLs). If you find that you lapse into some of these errors, you should not become discouraged; neither should you become complacent. The lapses presented are some of the most common errors made even by competent, intelligent writers. An occasional lapse is forgiven. However, the writer who does not learn from and correct those lapses runs the risk that all of her or his work will be devalued to some extent. The ready availability of electronic tools to check the style and mechanics of your writing eliminates most excuses for faulty writing.

Although students sometimes underrate the importance of the matters discussed in this chapter, mastering this content may ultimately make or break your career, as is shown in the following anecdote.

An MBA graduate returned to reminisce with his former report writing professor. He related his experience in a highly competitive training program. The program required each trainee to give five presentations; a single lapse, including the kinds presented in this chapter, would result in a failing assessment for that presentation. Three failures would result in expulsion from the program.

How did this man pass the test? He remembered that his professor had urged students to know their weaknesses and to submit all writing to a trusted critic before releasing it to the ultimate audience. In this instance, the audience included readers and listeners who could "make or break" his future with the company. Although some persons might question the ethics of this practice, others would say that it demonstrated appropriate awareness of his strengths and weaknesses and the wisdom to use a strategy to overcome the weaknesses.

Topics for Discussion

1. What is the role of style in planning and writing a report?

2. What is meant by message *tone?* What are some ways to describe tone?

3. Contrast formal and informal writing style, using examples of the following:
   - First- and second-person pronouns
   - Names, titles
   - Contractions
   - Colloquialisms

4. Define and give an example of objective writing style.

5. Give examples to contrast confident and hesitant writing styles.

6. What is the value of learning or reviewing the grammatical rules presented in this chapter?

7. Which of the FOWLs appear most frequently in your writing? Discuss ways to overcome those writing lapses.

8. Which of the rules do you find most confusing? Discuss ways to remember and apply those rules.

9. How do you react when any of the lapses are demonstrated by one of your classmates? A professor? A business or professional person whom you admire?

10. Do you know of a situation in which a person experienced negative reactions when he or she used nonstandard written or spoken English in connection with work responsibilities? If so, share that information with your classmates.

11. Correct all FOWLs appearing in the following sentences. Each sentence contains at least one error; many contain more than one error. More than one revision may be acceptable. Be prepared to defend your revisions. If classmates come up with revisions that differ from yours, discuss the effectiveness of each version.
    a. The rents on this property is excessive. Although the owner of the apartment may disagree.
    b. The rent on that property is within our budget, therefore I recommend that we relocate to that location.
    c. Theirs many ways to do this task: I recommend that you follow my instructions.
    d. Entering the office a half hour late sarcastically his manager asked Howie if he had enjoyed his lunch "hour."
    e. Tired from a long days work, the childrens' pleas to play games did not interest me.
    f. Avoidance of FOWLs are important to writers who want to advance on the job, appear well educated, as well as receiving a positive response from clients.
    g. How many manufactures were sited for not cleaning up there industrial waist?
    h. The highly-professional female cardiologist said anybody that works a job and has a family, you kind of ignore yourself and try to juggle everything else.
    i. Management voted to increase they're employee's vacation allowance accept for employees who had accumulated a years leave time.

j. When was those circuits tested? Was their any problems detected?

k. Unless you plan your report, it may omit some important data.

l. Here's the trip report and my expense voucher.

m. The dieter choose a challenging goal: to loose 5 inches from his waste in 5 weeks.

n. ABC Corp. announced their merger with XYZ which should increase it's market share.

o. Discussing the production schedule, critical specifications was emphasized.

p. Analyzing your companies needs and your customers interest are necessary if you want too maintain market share.

q. Its hard to determine what affect the fall advertising campaign had on the years sales.

r. The IRS treats incidences of tax fraud seriously, however its' tax assistance division generously answers individuals questions about legitimate deductions.

s. Your prospective on the importance of each topic will effect the organization of your report.

t. Cathy, a typical female engineer, was surprised by the affects of her tirade but their was no excuses for her to loose her temper that I can identify.

u. To regain trust she will have to come in early tomorrow review her work schedule with her supervisor and submit an outline a bibliography, and a draft for the exception report—even if its rough—before noon.

v. Each of the presidential candidates has their own economical advisors.

w. Kelsey who's business plan won the entrepreneurship award sites his fathers influence and his own hard-work as the thing that has helped him succeed.

x. Harry said, "Hua and myself have found an economic cite for our new business."

y. Leighton choose to work for Whitney corporation a major manufacture of home appliances who manufacturers products which sell well.

z. The perspective cite which they had located was turned in to a parking lot before they had a chance to make an affective offer.

Applications

For each of the following applications, write the message in the format requested by your instructor. (Examples of letter, memo, and manuscript formats are given in Chapter 6.)

1. Find examples of three writing lapses presented in this chapter. (Hint: Use newspapers, business signage, posters on campus, letters you receive, and so on as sources.) In a message to your instructor, identify the type of lapse and tell where you found it. Use proofing options available in your word-processing software to check your text for grammar and spelling lapses, and then present a corrected version.

2. Review at least two pages of writing you have done for this class, for another class, or at your workplace. Circle any FOWLs that you can now identify.

Exchange papers with a classmate. Review her or his paper and circle any additional FOWLs that you detect. Together write appropriate corrections for all errors detected. Present these corrections, along with the original documents, to your instructor for review.

3. Recent news reports have covered the topics given below. Select one of the topics and research it on the Internet. As directed by your instructor, report your findings in a brief written or oral report.
   - Social entrepreneurship
   - Culinary tourism
   - Consumer access to credit scores
   - Effects of fast food on health

4. Owners of small businesses (under 50 employees) have found it difficult to offer insurance to their employees. Some insurance companies have developed insurance pools that enable such businesses to form a group and obtain group rates that normally are available only to large businesses. Research such pools. Identify factors such as the extent to which they are currently being offered, the states in which they are offered, and major features of the plans offered to employers and employees. Present your findings in a report to your instructor.

5. Owners of small businesses are often advised to carry some or all of the following kinds of insurance coverage:
   - Accounts-receivable insurance
   - Business interruption insurance
   - Boiler and machinery insurance
   - Convention cancellation insurance
   - Key-man insurance
   - Leasehold insurance

   Select one of those types of insurance. Use the Internet to find information about that insurance product. Present your findings in a report to your instructor.

6. If they meet specific criteria, U.S. citizens may take certain credits to their federal income taxes. Some of those credits are:
   - Adoption credit
   - Child and dependent care credit
   - Child tax credit
   - Credit for the elderly or the disabled
   - Earned income tax credit

   Conduct research to identify the major features of two of those credits. In a report to your instructor, give a brief description of your research techniques and report your findings.

7. Sacred Words Bookstore is a small church-sponsored bookstore located on church property. Its sales have declined approximately 15 percent during the past fiscal year. The store manager, Ann Singletary, is convinced that the lack of convenient parking has contributed to the sales decline. The parking lot tends to be filled with church employees' cars, leaving little space for visitors. Although a parishioner has offered free parking in a garage located one block from the church, the church's employees continue to use the limited space in

the church lot. Ms. Singletary has asked the church's administrative manager, Eddie Victor, to require all who work at the church in any capacity to use the garage that is available, leaving the parking lot open for visitors. Church employees include ordained clergy, business office personnel, bookstore personnel and volunteers, building and grounds staff, and the child-care center staff. Mr. Victor has asked Ms. Singletary to compose a message that he can send to the staff requesting that all employees park in the garage.

Acting as Ms. Singletary, write the message. Be prepared to justify the message content, structure, and style to your classmates. Answering these questions should help you as you plan the message:

- What is the purpose of the message? (Hint: What action do you want?)
- Who is the primary audience? the secondary audience?
- What is the context?
- What is the content?
- What is an appropriate structure?
- What is an appropriate tone? level of formality?
- How much emotion should you inject into the message?
- How confident should you be about your request?

8. Pair up with one of your classmates to review the work each person did for Application 7. Use the following procedures:

- Exchange copies of your messages. Read one another's work.
- Provide constructive criticism of the content, structure, tone, formality, objectivity, and level of confidence demonstrated by the writing style. Also examine the messages for possible FOWLs.
- Rewrite the memo, incorporating any worthy suggestions made by your critics. Submit the original and rewritten memos to your instructor for evaluation.

9. The executive director of a small nonprofit agency thinks the director of development is not bringing in enough revenue and wants to discontinue the position entirely. The director of development's major responsibility is to find new revenue sources for the agency. The job includes planning and executing fund-raising events, writing and sending two general fund-raising letters to current small donors each year, soliciting donations from local businesses, and writing grant proposals to eleemosynary organizations. Her current salary is $50,000 per year; during the past year she brought in about $70,000 in new money. The executive director has made an oral request to the board president to bring the matter before the board. There has been no action on that request.

Form a group with one or more of your classmates and do the following:

- Discuss this question: What communication barriers may account for the board president's failure to respond to the executive director's request?
- Plan the message to be sent to the president. Identify the purpose, audience (primary and secondary), context, content, medium, structure, and style for the report. Prepare an outline for the message. Ask your instructor to review the outline and authorize you to write the message.
- After your instructor approves the outline, each member of the group should draft the message, assuming he or she is the executive director.

- Share your draft with the group. Critique all aspects of the messages: awareness of audience, content, structure, style, and mechanics. Submit the best message (or combined elements of the best messages) to your instructor to represent your group's work.

10. Make a copy of the Group Participation Rating form shown in Illustration 2.6. Rate the performance of the group you worked with to complete Application 9. Summarize your evaluation in a brief report to your instructor.

11. Using word-processing software—checking grammar and spelling as you write—compose a message to your instructor identifying and describing at least three computerized reference sources in your school library. Besides correcting all writing lapses identified, be prepared to defend your writing style.

CHAPTER 5

Illustrating the Report

After you have read this chapter, you should be able to:

1.   Explain the purposes of visuals in reports.

2.   Choose appropriate visuals to illustrate your reports.

3.   Choose appropriate graphics software for creating these visuals.

4.   Apply the criteria for constructing and using visuals effectively.

5.   Work cooperatively with team members to generate effective visuals.

6.   Avoid misrepresentation when using visuals.

HAVE YOU EVER TRIED to follow complex written task instructions, such as those for assembling a bicycle, and wished the author had included pictures or diagrams to guide you? Have you noticed that some manufacturers now supply only visuals as directions for use or assembly of their products? Have you ever listened to a detailed explanation of statistical information, such as an insurance salesperson's description of the rate structure, and wished the person would summarize the data in a table? If so, you can appreciate the complementary value of visuals to words, either written or oral.

Purposes of Visuals

Although many writers readily think of using visuals in long reports, such aids can also increase the effectiveness of short reports. You should use visuals to emphasize, clarify, simplify, reinforce, and summarize information in both simple and complex oral or written reports. Further, visuals may be used to add interest, improve credibility, and increase the coherence of written messages.

Emphasize

Newspaper reporters and advertising copywriters are well aware of the value of pictures, diagrams, or charts to emphasize an important fact. For example, a picture of people milling about and waving placards in front of a government building emphasizes the number of people involved in a protest far more effectively than a verbal report that "1,500 people demonstrated in front of the State House." Similarly, a line chart showing steadily increasing sales emphasizes the increase more effectively than does a written narrative alone.

Reports often cover many points, but not all are of equal importance. Visuals can be used effectively within reports to emphasize specific information. In addition, a visual on the report cover can draw the reader's attention to the main point of that report. Assume, for example, that you must prepare a report to employees to show that health insurance claims have increased dramatically while employee contributions to the health insurance plan have increased minimally during the past 10 years. For emphasis, you could prepare line charts showing claims and contributions as percentages of total wages for 10 years. Those charts could be placed strategically within the report. As an alternative, however, you could place a multiple-line chart on the report cover showing the relationships of employee claims and contributions, thereby emphasizing a significant fact to readers as soon as they pick up the report.

Clarify

A second purpose of visuals is to clarify something that may be difficult to express clearly in words alone. Assume you wish to explain to your employees how payments for insurance benefits have been distributed among various benefit categories. Although you could provide that information in narrative form, the same data could be conveyed more clearly in a visual, such as a pie chart.

Simplify

Another purpose for visuals is to simplify data. Simplification involves breaking a complex whole into its component parts while preserving the essential nature of the whole. The previous example of a pie chart used to clarify information is also an example of simplification. The pie chart presents the essential components (amount in each benefit category) while retaining the whole (total benefit payments).

A diagram is another example of a visual often used to simplify a complex process. The diagram you studied in Chapter 2 (Illustration 2.1) simplifies the complex process of planning a report by identifying essential parts and possible sequences in that process.

Reinforce

To reinforce is to make stronger or more pronounced. Repetition is one form of reinforcement that helps people remember something important, but reinforcement is usually most effective when information is presented in more than one way, rather than through mere repetition.

You can increase reader retention and recall of important facts by using visuals to reinforce your report narrative. For example, if you were asked to present a case for your company's participation in a major project, your visuals would probably include information about the company's past performances with projects similar to the one being considered. You would show charts reflecting the creative methods used by the company to keep costs down, performance statistics to indicate your high-quality standards, and your best idea-to-production times to show the audience how adept your company is at meeting target dates.

To be most effective as reinforcers, visuals should be used selectively. If minor as well as major verbal information is supplemented by a visual aid, the visuals become common, and their reinforcing value is reduced.

Summarize

Visuals can effectively summarize detailed information. A summary covers main points succinctly without providing all details. A good summary presents a reader with essential information and minimizes the amount of reading required to obtain that information. If constructed accurately, a single visual, such as a table or chart, can summarize several pages of narrative.

As a summary, the visual cannot fully replace the narrative. The visual provides major points, but the narrative may describe fine points that cannot be included in the summary.

Add Interest

When you pick up a magazine or newspaper, do you immediately begin to read the narrative or do you first look at pictures or charts in that publication? If you are like many people, you are first attracted to the visuals. Similarly, after reading several pages of narrative in a textbook, you probably welcome the sight of a picture or diagram.

Visuals are effective tools to create interest and to relieve the tedium of a lengthy narrative. They make a report more attractive. Even in short reports, visual devices such as bullets (•), squares (□), or pointers (▶) can provide interest.

Improve Credibility

Visuals tend to add a sense of credibility that words alone cannot convey. The statement that profits have "increased dramatically" during the past five years may be interpreted as self-serving puffery. But that same statement may seem credible if it is accompanied by a line chart that shows sharply rising profits.

Graphics and pictures create a sense of precision. Many readers tend to believe that a writer who uses well-designed, accurate visuals is a confident, credible information source.

Increase Coherence

Effective reports are coherent—that is, all parts come together in logical relationships. The report writer may understand the relationships because of extensive exposure to the data, but the report will not be effective unless those relationships are also made clear to the readers. Visuals such as line charts, summary tables, or diagrams can show the relationships among different parts of a report.

As you study the examples of visuals in this chapter, consider which of the purposes—to emphasize, clarify, simplify, reinforce, summarize, add interest, improve credibility, and increase coherence—each visual would serve if it appeared in a report.

Criteria for Effective Visuals

To use visuals effectively in reports, you must be familiar with certain principles that apply to all visuals. In addition, you should follow guides for identification and placement of visuals in reports and adhere to criteria for ethical representation of information.

Principles of Graphics

Well-constructed visuals meet four standards for effective graphics: simplicity, contrast, unity, and balance.

Simplicity

The most effective graphics are simple. Regardless of how complex the subject, the visual itself should include no more information than absolutely necessary to support the author's message. Each visual should focus on one main point. A complex, cluttered visual presents too many stimuli to the viewer, thereby diverting the reader's attention rather than focusing it on the main point to be conveyed. Besides, as the number of stimuli increases, the possible interpretations of the visual also increase, adding to the probability of misunderstanding.

Consider, for example, the simplicity and effectiveness of international traffic symbols. Even when people cannot read or understand the local language, they can interpret those traffic signs. In effect, the simplicity of the signs helps to overcome a language barrier.

© Cengage Learning 2013

Contrast

The second principle that you should demonstrate in your visuals is contrast. To be effective, a visual must be noticed. Therefore, it must first stand out from its field. In written reports, that field is the page of the report. Contrast is achieved by visually separating the graphic from the narrative. This separation can be accomplished by using additional blank space or horizontal lines between the text and visual or by emphasizing borders of the visual.

Second, contrast must be achieved within the visual itself to clarify the comparisons or relationships that are presented. Contrast within the visual is achieved by solid and dotted lines, differing colors, plain and patterned bars, and different shapes to represent contrasted items, as shown in the following examples.

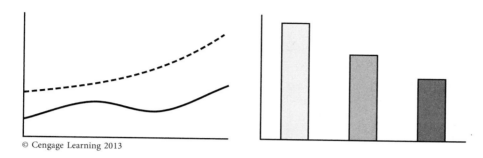

© Cengage Learning 2013

Unity

The third principle to observe is unity. An effective visual gives the impression that all parts belong and fit together. A unified chart or table shows the logical relationship of the parts to one another.

A sense of unity can be achieved by proximity, grouping, connecting lines, common shape, or common base. Some of those techniques are shown in the following examples.

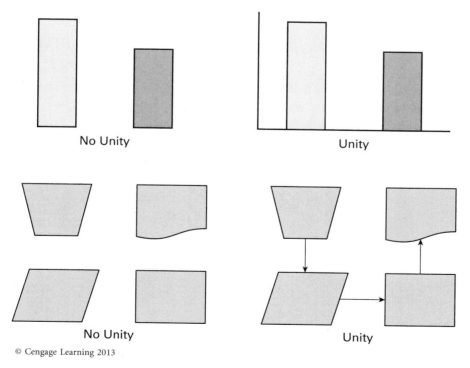

© Cengage Learning 2013

Balance

The fourth principle for graphics construction is balance. Balance refers to a sense of equal weight among the components of the visual. When two or more equal things are being described, balance is relatively easy to achieve. Each item can be presented in exactly the same size, shape, or plane of the visual. That type of balance is called symmetrical balance. In business reports, however, you must often present factors that are not equally weighted. Then you must achieve asymmetrical balance by planning and controlling the location, size, and arrangement of the symbols and labels used in the visual.

In the following examples, symmetrical balance and asymmetrical balance are contrasted with unbalanced presentations. Notice that the balanced presentations are more attractive. An unbalanced arrangement may be justified under some conditions. For example, the unbalanced bar chart shown in the example would be justified if the bars were arranged chronologically. But if the bars represent discrete data, such as sales by region, the balanced presentation is preferable.

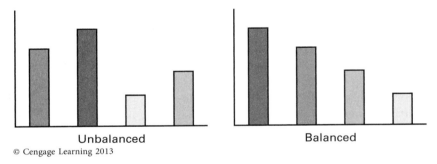

© Cengage Learning 2013

In pie charts, balance can be achieved by beginning the largest segment at the top of the circle. The other segments should follow in a clockwise direction, by size, ending with the smallest. Again, rationale may exist for an unbalanced presentation. If two pies, for example, show contributions of parts to the whole for two different years, logical arrangement would be to place the segments of the first pie according to the principles of balance and the segments of the second pie in the same sequence to facilitate comparison of the related parts.

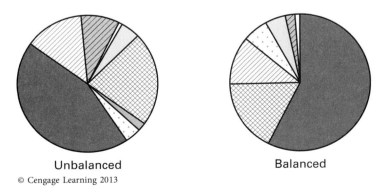

© Cengage Learning 2013

Identification and Placement

When your report contains several visuals, identify each by a label, number, and title. For simplicity, some writers label all visuals as illustrations (for example, Illustration 1, Illustration 2, etc.). An alternative practice is to differentiate tables from other visuals, usually referring to charts, diagrams, maps, and so on as figures or illustrations (for example, Table 1, Table 2, Figure 1, Figure 2, etc.). Some writers use the word

Table for tables and the word *Figure* for all illustrations except tables. Current practice is to use Arabic, not Roman, numerals to number the visuals.

A title must be descriptive but concise. A well-written title answers *what* and *when* questions about the data, and in many cases the title should also answer *who* and *where*. For example, "Microcom Sales by District, 2012 and 2013" is a more meaningful title for a chart than "Microcom Sales" or "Sales by District." Titles of tables are normally placed above the table, while titles of charts or figures may be placed at either the top or the bottom. Because most readers in the Western world read a page from top to bottom, it is reader friendly to place the number and title at the top of all visuals so the reader sees such identifying information before studying the visual. Remember to be consistent with your placement of titles.

Besides identifying the visual by label, number, and title, you should identify the data source. If you used secondary data, the source may be identified in a shortened form, assuming that full identification is provided in the report bibliography or endnotes. An example of noting a secondary source is "Source: *Statistical Abstract of the United States, 2013.*" If the data are from a primary source, the simple notation "Source: Primary" is adequate. As you study this chapter, notice the identification techniques used in the illustrations.

The most effective placement of visuals is within a report, not in a report appendix, unless you know that your primary reader prefers that the visuals be grouped in an appendix. Visuals should be placed where they are needed for emphasis, clarity, simplification, reinforcement, summary, interest, credibility, or coherence. A visual should be placed as near as possible to the accompanying narrative. An effective three-step procedure for incorporating a visual into a report is to introduce the aid, display it, and then discuss it.

Introduce

In the introductory statement, mention a primary fact that the visual illustrates. Focus on the information contained in that visual, not on the visual itself. Following the introduction, identify the aid by number or title to help the reader locate it in the report. If the aid is on another page, also include the page number in the identification. The following examples contrast less effective and more effective introductions.

> *Less Effective: Illustration 1 shows sales for oat bran, rice bran, and wheat bran in 2012.*
>
> *More Effective: Oat bran substantially outsold both rice bran and wheat bran in 2012. (See Illustration 1.)*
>
> *Less Effective: As Figure 1 shows, a research plan contains 12 parts.*
>
> *More Effective: Planning research is a 12-part process, as demonstrated in Figure 1, page 4.*

Display

Following the introduction, display the visual as soon as possible. Separate the visual from the narrative with additional white space or lines to achieve contrast.

If space permits, place the visual on the same page as the introduction. If the visual does not fit on the same page, do not leave a large patch of blank space at the bottom of the page; just continue with your discussion and place the visual at the top of the next page. Visuals must fit within the margins of the report narrative and should not be so large that they distract from the narrative. If necessary, reduce the visual so that it will fit attractively within the report margins while retaining legibility.

When large visuals must be used, they may occupy a full page and may be placed vertically or horizontally. Whenever possible, display full-page visuals on the page immediately following the one on which the visual was introduced.

Discuss

A visual can add interest to a report or summarize essential information, but it is your responsibility as the report writer to interpret the data in that aid. After introducing and displaying the visual, discuss it in an interpretive manner. Interpretation requires more than merely repeating the data presented in the visual. Your discussion must clarify data or add details that cannot be captured visually.

When your discussion requires only one paragraph, you may combine the introduction and discussion. In such a situation, display the visual after the discussion. If the discussion is lengthy, however, the introduce-display-discuss sequence is more effective. Acceptable patterns for introducing, displaying, and discussing visuals are demonstrated in Illustration 5.1.

ILLUSTRATION 5.1   PLACEMENT OF VISUAL

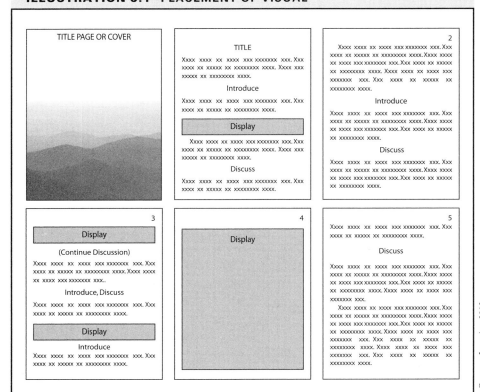

Choosing and Constructing Visuals

Although visuals serve many purposes in reports, those purposes are achieved only if the appropriate aid is chosen. Knowing the characteristics of each type of visual will help you choose visuals to achieve your purposes. Following are specific guides for constructing five types of visuals to increase the effectiveness of your reports: bar charts, pie charts, line charts, flowcharts, factor relationship charts, and tables. Three other visuals—pictures, pictographs, and statistical maps—are discussed briefly.

Bar Charts

A bar chart is a graphic that uses two or more rectangles along with vertical and horizontal axes to represent information. When the rectangles are placed vertically, the chart is sometimes called a column chart; when the rectangles are placed horizontally, the chart is often called a horizontal bar chart.

Uses

Bar charts are used to compare discrete (noncontinuous, distinct, unconnected) quantitative data, such as the numbers of females and males in a training program, the sales volumes of two or more products in a stated time period, or the distribution of time among several activities. A bar chart provides a quick visual impression of the relationships between or among the components that are being compared.

Construction Guides

Following these guides will help you construct effective bar charts:

- Plan size and page location carefully. Allow sufficient space so that the chart, including its title and source notation, will not be crowded. Locate the chart according to the introduce-display-discuss pattern.
- Achieve balance in length and width of bars. All bars must be the same width, and the space between bars should be no less than half the width of the bar itself. For readability, vertical bars should be no longer than seven inches, and horizontal bars should not exceed five inches. Unless it is logical to do otherwise, arrange bars in ascending or descending order by length.
- Draw axes and scale units accurately. Units of measurement must be uniform; that is, all steps of a scale must represent the same unit size and must be placed at equal distances from one another. Place the unit of measurement on the horizontal (x) axis for horizontal bars chart and on the vertical (y) axis for vertical bar charts.
- Label the chart. For each axis, identify scale units and categories of comparison. In multiple bar charts, use sharply contrasting colors to differentiate categories. *Note:* For a monochrome (all-black) printer, use colors that will produce high-contrast shading or use contrasting patterns. Provide a key or legend within the chart to interpret the colors and patterns. Observe how those guides are applied in Illustrations 5.2 through 5.5.

Variations

A simple bar chart compares two or more variables on one dimension, as shown in Illustration 5.2. That chart compares five variables or categories on one dimension—by percent of respondents who participated in each.

A multiple bar chart compares two or more variables on two or more dimensions, as shown in Illustration 5.3. That chart compares two variables (men and women) on five dimensions (leisure-time activities). A segmented bar chart adds another dimension to a comparison, as shown in Illustration 5.4. The parallel, segmented bars clearly show changes in revenue sources and permit ready comparison of those sources in the two years.

Another variation of the bar chart is the bilateral bar chart, which permits display of positive and negative values. (See Illustration 5.5.)

Bar charts are effective aids to compare amounts and percentages. When you wish to emphasize the parts of which a factor is composed, a pie chart is an effective tool.

Pie Charts

A pie chart is a circle divided into segments. The circle represents the whole amount (100 percent), and each segment represents a proportion of the whole. Pie charts are also called circle charts or circle graphs.

Uses

A pie chart is effective when you want to emphasize relative proportions. Pie charts permit comparisons of parts that make up a whole but may be less effective than bar charts in comparing absolute amounts. Two or more pies can also be placed side by side to compare factors at different times, such as expenditures in two different years, or to compare two related factors, such as sources and uses of funds.

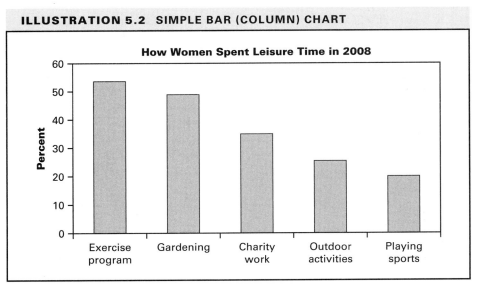

ILLUSTRATION 5.2 SIMPLE BAR (COLUMN) CHART

How Women Spent Leisure Time in 2008

Source: *The 2011 Statistical Abstract: PDF Version*, p. 763.

ILLUSTRATION 5.3   MULTIPLE BAR CHART

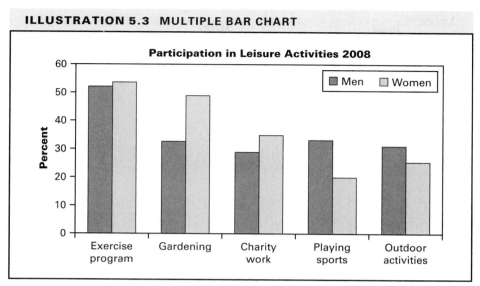

Source: *The 2011 Statistical Abstract: PDF Version,* p. 763.

ILLUSTRATION 5.4   SEGMENTED BAR CHART

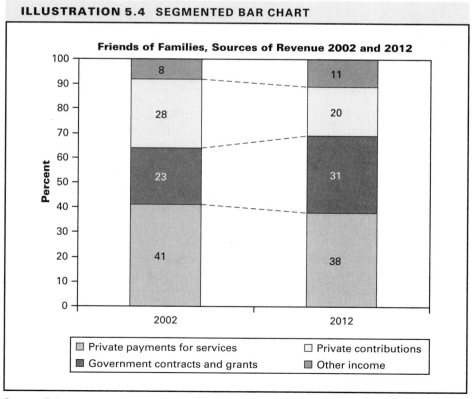

Source: Primary.

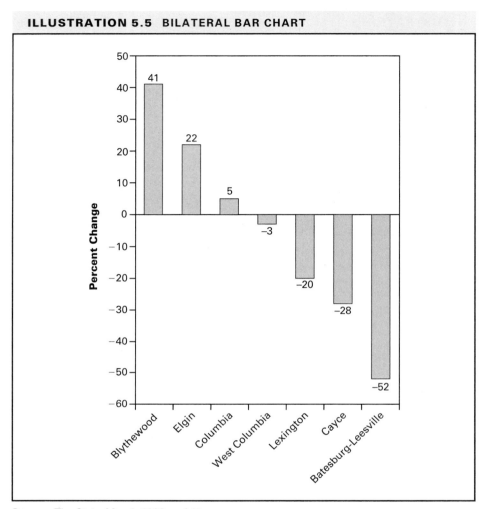

ILLUSTRATION 5.5 BILATERAL BAR CHART

Source: *The State*, May 2, 2008, p. A11.

Construction Guides

To construct effective pie charts, follow these guides:

- Keep the number of segments to a minimum. When a pie chart contains too many segments, the comparisons are difficult to comprehend. Some illustration experts recommend using no more than eight segments.
- Balance the segments. Because people in the Western world tend to read pie charts in a clockwise direction, illustrators recommend placing the largest segment first, beginning at the top. Place other segments around the circle in descending order of size unless logic requires some other arrangement. For example, the data presented in Illustration 5.4 could be presented in two pie charts placed side by side. If that were done, the largest-to-smallest clockwise sequence for 2002 would be Private payment for services, Private contributions, Government contracts and grants, and Other income. It would then be

logical to use that same sequence for 2012, even though the segments would not be in the largest-to-smallest arrangement.

- Label the chart. Appropriate labeling includes a title, a source notation, and identification of the segments. The title must include the factor being analyzed and the time represented by the chart. Give each segment a meaningful name and identify its proportion of the whole. If space permits, place that identifying information on the face of the pie within the appropriate segments. If space is limited, the identifying labels may be placed around the perimeter of the pie, and you may use a short line to connect each label to its segment.

- Show segment values accurately. When segment values are stated in percentages, the segments must always total 100 percent. Although pie chart units are most often in percentages, units may also be in absolute numbers. If you state units in absolute numbers, be sure that each segment size still represents its accurate proportion of the pie.

- Keep the chart simple. Although colors and patterns may be used to add interest to the chart, use patterns sparingly. If it is labeled correctly, a pie chart is quite effective without such additions. Excessive use of interest techniques can impair the readability of the chart.

Variations

Pie charts are either one-dimensional or multidimensional. A one-dimensional pie chart is a simple circle cut into segments, as shown in Illustration 5.6.

Multidimensional pie charts employ various techniques to emphasize certain segments or to increase interest. Common multidimensional techniques are to separate segments or "explode" one segment. Only the segment that is being referred to should be exploded. Another technique is to draw the circle with a shaded or patterned area to suggest the factor being discussed or to add a bar or brackets to explain one of the segments. Those techniques are demonstrated in Illustration 5.7.

Bar and pie charts permit comparison of discrete, independent items. When you wish to show relationships between or among continuous, dependent variables, a line chart is an appropriate tool.

Line Charts

A line chart consists of a vertical axis, a horizontal axis, and one or more plotted lines. Each axis contains a measurement scale that identifies the factors of comparison: income, age groups, time periods, percents, rates, amounts, and so on. Traditionally, the horizontal dimension represents time and the vertical dimension represents values. There are underlying assumptions of continuity and equal intervals in the measurement scales. For example, a time scale is based on the assumption that time is a continuous variable and that all scale points represent equal intervals of time.

Uses

Line charts show the relationship between the variables plotted on the vertical and horizontal axes. In business reports, one of the most commonly used line charts is a

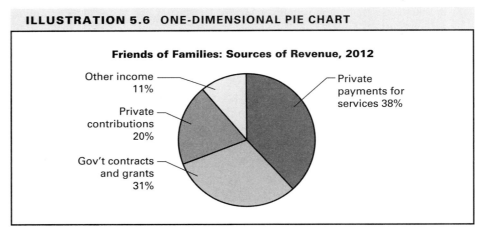

ILLUSTRATION 5.6 ONE-DIMENSIONAL PIE CHART

Friends of Families: Sources of Revenue, 2012

Other income 11%

Private contributions 20%

Gov't contracts and grants 31%

Private payments for services 38%

Source: Primary.

time chart, which shows trends or changes in a variable over time. Another frequently used line chart is a frequency distribution, which shows the relationship between two factors (excluding time), such as anticipated sales at various unit prices or unit costs at various production levels.

Line charts should not be used to compare obviously independent items, such as sales in each of several districts. A bar or pie chart appropriately compares that kind of data.

Construction Guides

The following guides, which are applied in Illustrations 5.8 through 5.12, will help you construct effective line charts:

- Plan the chart size for readability. The maximum size should occupy less than a full page of the report so that there will be enough space for the title and other identifying information. If you are tempted to use a chart that is larger than a full page, reconsider. You are probably trying to present too much data in a single chart. The minimum width and height should be two to three inches so that the title, scales, and labels are legible.
- Follow standard plotting rules. Use the horizontal axis to designate the independent variable or the method of classification (for example, time, scores, age-groups, etc.). Use the vertical axis to show the dependent variable, amounts, or frequency (for example, sales volume, numbers in classification ranges).
- Use accurate, nondistorting scales. To avoid distortion, follow the "three-quarter rule" whenever possible. That rule, observed by many statisticians, states that the height of the vertical axis should be about three-quarters the length of the horizontal axis. On each axis, the distance between markers must be the same. A good guide is to attempt making distances on the x-axis and y-axis approximately the same. Vastly different scale units can distort the data. For example, reducing distances on the vertical scale of a time chart tends to minimize differences across time, whereas expanding the distances tends to maximize those differences. *Note:* Charting software, such as Microsoft Excel, generally complies with this guide. The vertical scale must begin at zero. If the entire plotted line lies

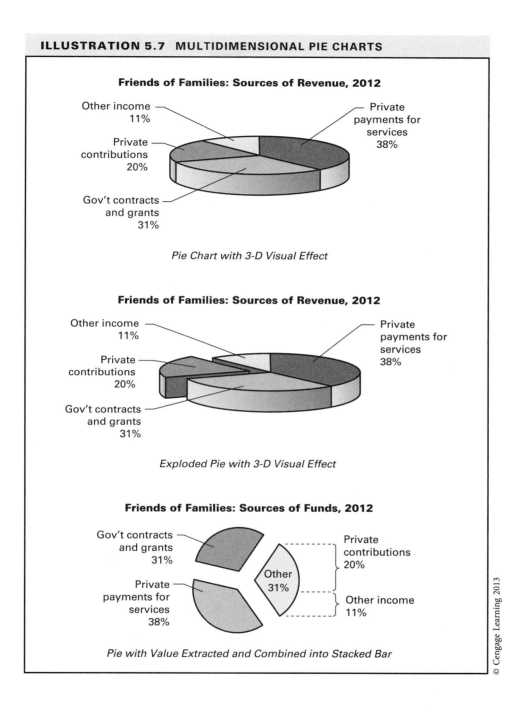

ILLUSTRATION 5.7 MULTIDIMENSIONAL PIE CHARTS

Friends of Families: Sources of Revenue, 2012

Other income — 11%

Private contributions — 20%

Gov't contracts and grants 31%

Private payments for services 38%

Pie Chart with 3-D Visual Effect

Friends of Families: Sources of Revenue, 2012

Other income — 11%

Private contributions — 20%

Gov't contracts and grants 31%

Private payments for services 38%

Exploded Pie with 3-D Visual Effect

Friends of Families: Sources of Funds, 2012

Gov't contracts and grants 31%

Private payments for services 38%

Other 31%

Private contributions 20%

Other income 11%

Pie with Value Extracted and Combined into Stacked Bar

considerably above zero, you may break the vertical scale to show omission of unnecessary data. This technique is appropriate *only* when the entire line can be plotted above the scale break.

• Label the chart. Identify the x-axis and y-axis scale units. In multiple-line charts, use sharply contrasting colors to differentiate the variables and provide a legend

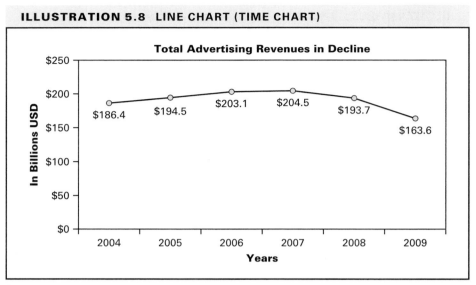

ILLUSTRATION 5.8 LINE CHART (TIME CHART)

Total Advertising Revenues in Decline

Source: *Statistical Abstract of the United States, 2011*, Table 1278.

within the chart to interpret those lines. ***Note:*** In a hand-drawn chart, use one solid line along with dotted or broken lines. As with all charts, full identification includes an appropriate title and source notation.

Variations

A basic line chart contains one plotted line showing the changes of the variable plotted on the vertical axis as the variable on the horizontal axis changes. In a basic time chart, that line represents the changes in a variable over time. (See Illustration 5.8.) A multiple-line chart permits comparison of both trends and relationships. For example, two types of advertising expenditures can be compared with a multiple-line chart, such as the one shown in Illustration 5.9.

An area chart or band chart is a stacked variation of the line chart. In this chart, the factors that contribute to a total are identified. A line is plotted for each factor. The areas between the plotted lines represent the respective contributions of the factors to the total, and the top line represents the sum of all factors. The data plotted in Illustration 5.9 could also be plotted as a band chart, as is done in Illustration 5.10.

Notice that the band chart effectively demonstrates total revenues for television and online advertising and the proportion attributed to each spending category, but the amount of each category is somewhat difficult to determine. The multiple-line chart (Illustration 5.9) more effectively displays the actual amounts contributed by each.

A bilateral line chart permits plotting of both positive and negative values. To accommodate negative values, the vertical scale must continue below the zero point, as is shown in Illustration 5.11.

The high-low chart is an interesting variation of the line chart. This chart permits you to show variations in values for a factor during a time period as well as the average value of the factor. A bar marks the high and low values, and a line is plotted

ILLUSTRATION 5.9   MULTIPLE-LINE CHART

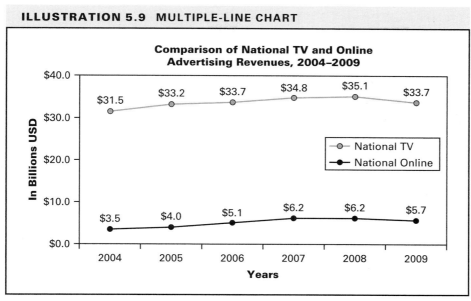

Source: *Statistical Abstract of the United States*, 2011, Table 1278.

ILLUSTRATION 5.10   AREA CHART (STACKED LINE CHART)

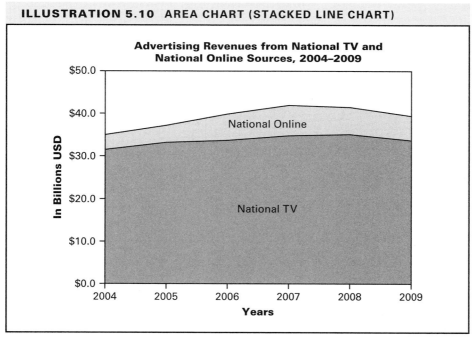

Source: *Statistical Abstract of the United States*, 2011, Table 1278.

through the bars to show the average values. Quarterly stock prices for a hypothetical company are shown in the high-low chart in Illustration 5.12.

Whereas line charts show quantitative relationships, the next section presents two charts used to show nonquantitative information.

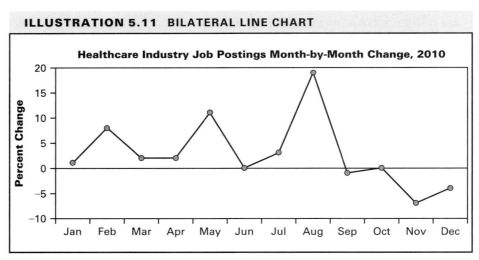

ILLUSTRATION 5.11 BILATERAL LINE CHART

Healthcare Industry Job Postings Month-by-Month Change, 2010

Source: *Indeed.* http://www.indeed.com/jobtrends/healthcare-industry?date-2010-06.

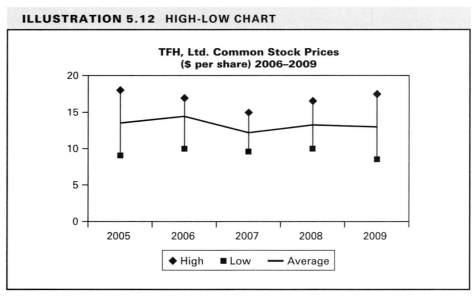

ILLUSTRATION 5.12 HIGH-LOW CHART

TFH, Ltd. Common Stock Prices ($ per share) 2006–2009

Source: Primary.

Relationship Charts

A relationship chart shows how several nonnumeric factors act together. Two relationship charts that you may find useful in reports are the flowchart and the factor relationship chart.

Flowchart

A flowchart shows pictorially how a series of activities, operations, events, and other factors fit together to accomplish a full cycle. Complex flowcharts are often used as engineering or systems analysis tools. But simple flowcharts also can be used effectively in business reports to condense, clarify, or simplify a description of a series of activities.

A flowchart consists of a title, shapes (squares, rectangles, triangles, etc.) to represent various elements in the process, labels to identify each element, and lines or arrows to connect the shapes and show the direction of flow. Although simple flowcharts may use a rectangle or a square for each element, many flowchart designers use these standard flowchart symbols.

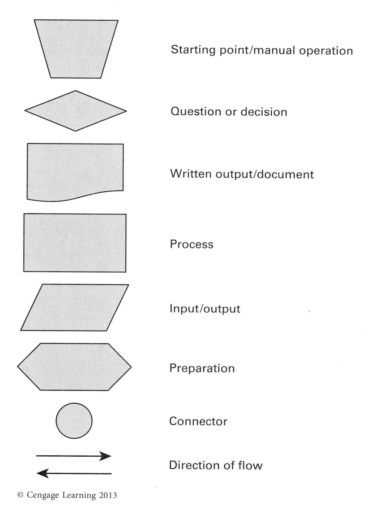

A flowchart describing the procedures for copying copyrighted materials is shown in Illustration 5.13.

Factor Relationship Chart

A factor relationship chart is useful to describe nonlinear relationships. Such a chart shows how a primary factor and secondary factors interact with one another. The chart consists of a title, shapes to represent various factors that interact with one another, labels to identify those factors, and multiple arrows to show how the factors interact. The layout of this chart should draw the eye to the primary factor and clearly indicate how other factors interact with one another and with the primary factor.

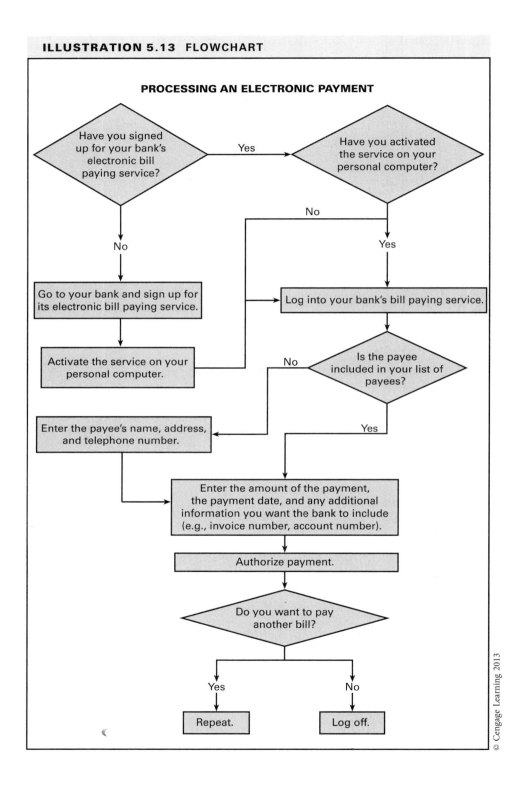

ILLUSTRATION 5.13 FLOWCHART

PROCESSING AN ELECTRONIC PAYMENT

© Cengage Learning 2013

At the end of this chapter, a relationship chart (Illustration 5.21) summarizes the collaborative writing process. That chart shows how various tasks and activities should interact for successful collaboration.

Although bar charts, pie charts, line charts, and relationship charts effectively summarize and simplify information, the amount of information that can be shown in such charts is limited. When numeric detail is desired, a table is the best visual.

Tables

Both formal and informal tables are used in reports. A table consists of columns and rows of quantitative data, along with labels to identify the data. A formal table also has a title and generally has more identifying information than does an informal table.

A table surpasses all charts in ability to present detailed information. Consequently, you should use a table when you want the reader to compare exact figures. As the number of dimensions to be compared increases, the need for identifying labels also increases. Therefore, formal tables are required for presentation of complex data.

Formal Table

As with charts, a formal table is separated from the report narrative and is identified by title. A formal table may also be numbered and show a source notation. In addition to columns and rows of numbers, other features of a formal table include column heads, stubs to identify rows, and stub heads. Some formal tables also contain a spanner head, which unifies the column heads. For clarity, you may use horizontal and vertical lines to separate heads. In long tables, you can improve readability by leaving a blank row about every five rows. Features of a formal table are identified in Illustration 5.14.

Informal Table

An informal table is a brief tabulation inserted directly into the text. This type of table has no title, and column and stub heads may also be omitted if the text clearly

ILLUSTRATION 5.14 FORMAL TABLE

U.S. SCHOOL ENROLLMENT BY ETHNICITY, 2000–2008		WHITE		BLACK		HISPANIC	
YEAR	TOTAL	NO. (000)	%	NO. (000)	%	NO. (000)	%
2000	75,300	54,257	72	11,115	15	9,928	13
2005	79,102	55,715	70	10,885	14	12,502	16
2008	80,420	55,886	69	10,944	14	13,590	17

Source: *Statistical Abstract of the United States*, 2011, p. 146.

identifies the table's contents. The following examples demonstrate techniques for including informal tables in a report.

Between 2006 and 2009, the median earnings of women increased by 11.6 percent, while the median earnings of men increased by 11.5 percent. Nonetheless, the median earnings for women was still nearly 77 percent of earnings for men.

	Median Earnings		
	2006	*2009*	*% change*
Females	*$32,515*	*$36,278*	*+11.6*
Males	*$42,261*	*$47,127*	*+11.5*
Female/Male earnings ratio	*0.769*	*0.770*	*+0.001*

Source: (Income, Poverty, and Health Insurance Coverage in the United States: 2009)

Brazil's unemployment rate of 8.1% is lowest of the countries compared in this study, and the quality of labor in Brazil is relatively high (CIA World Factbook, 2010). Besides, Brazil's unemployment rate has decreased in recent years, as shown in Table 5.1

TABLE 5.1 BRAZIL'S UNEMPLOYMENT RATE, 2004–2010

Year	Unemployment Rate	Percent Change
2004	12.30%	
2005	11.50%	−6.50%
2006	9.80%	−14.78%
2007	9.60%	−2.04%
2008	9.30%	−3.13%
2009	7.90%	−15.05%
2010	8.10%	2.53%

Source: Index Mundi at http://www.indexmundi.com.

Source: (Income, Poverty, and Health Insurance Coverage in the United States: 2009)

Although charts and tables are the most common visuals in reports, other visual aids are also used to add interest.

Other Visuals

Three visuals that are especially effective to add interest to a report are pictures, pictographs, and statistical maps.

Pictures

Because of their universal appeal, photographs effectively capture reader attention, a fact that prompts many corporations to use photos extensively in annual reports. You may also find opportunities to use pictures effectively in other business reports. Many report writers, for example, incorporate photos into an oral presentation that supplements a written report.

Pictures tend to add a sense of reality to a report. With digital cameras, high-quality photographs are easy to take and integrate within reports. Viewers know that pictures can be posed and that good photographers compose a picture; nonetheless, many readers perceive pictures as truth. Because of that fact, an ethical obligation exists to ensure that pictures represent accurately the conditions they are intended to portray. For example, a picture of employees at work should accurately portray the environment in which the majority of employees work. Picturing the most favorable working conditions that perhaps only a few enjoy would present a distorted view of reality.

Pictograph

A pictograph, or pictogram, is a bar chart or line chart that uses pictures or symbols to depict its data. For example, when reporting results of a survey about a population's favorite ice cream flavors, you might create a bar chart of variously colored ice cream cones in place of the bars. The simple images in a pictograph add interest and emphasis and, according to many people, make the data easier to read and remember. Notice how the pictograph in Illustration 5.15 emphasizes the goal of Women for Women International, which is to help women around the world, particularly in war-torn countries, improve their economic well-being.

Statistical Maps

A statistical map presents numerical data superimposed on a map of the geographical units to which the data are related. Although the same data could be presented in a table or a bar chart, the map image helps the reader associate the data more directly with specific geographic areas.

Many variations of statistical maps can be designed, including separating and enlarging or exploding part of the map. One statistical map technique is demonstrated in Illustration 5.16.

ILLUSTRATION 5.15   PICTOGRAPH

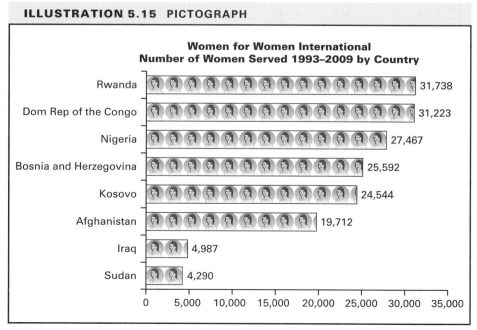

Source: *Women for Women International.* 2009 Annual Report, http://www.womenfor women.org.

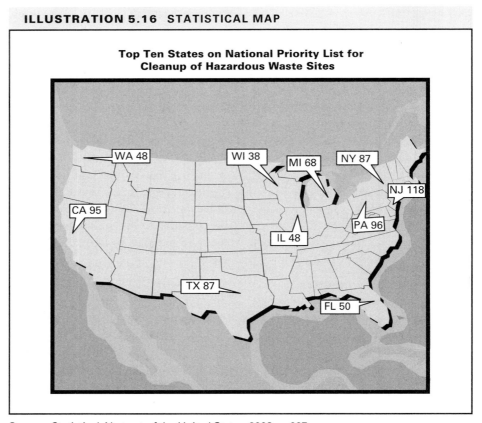

ILLUSTRATION 5.16   STATISTICAL MAP

**Top Ten States on National Priority List for
Cleanup of Hazardous Waste Sites**

Source: *Statistical Abstract of the United States*: 2008, p. 227.

All visuals discussed in this chapter can be constructed with traditional tools: pen and pencil, ruler, stencil, graph paper, camera, and so on. Many corporations have graphics departments to help report writers prepare visuals. However, most report writers now design visuals efficiently and effectively with their own computers, using the graphics tools in their spreadsheet and word-processing applications along with digital cameras and online image and map services.

Graphics Tools for Creating Visuals

As noted, report visuals can be created manually, but today most are created with graphics software or, more specifically, with built-in graphics tools in spreadsheet and word-processing software. The job of these graphics tools is to let you generate readable charts, diagrams, and so on. With minimal practice, all business report writers can produce professional-looking visuals for illustrating their reports.

Although graphics tools actually prepare the visuals, you are obligated to evaluate the effectiveness of each illustration. Some report writers get carried away with the many options available and overload their reports with visuals. To use graphics tools well, you must first decide which data should be illustrated. Then select the most appropriate visual to achieve your purpose and follow the principles for effective visuals discussed earlier in this chapter. Avoid the temptation to demonstrate your skill with graphics software. Instead, demonstrate your total report-writing skill. Here are some guidelines for creating effective visuals:

- Designate the visual as a figure or table and assign it a number.
- Use the introduce-display-discuss procedure to incorporate the visual at the most advantageous location in the text.
- Ensure that the title accurately states the desired message.
- Include blank space around the visual so that it will stand out.
- Remove any unnecessary decorations or clutter.
- Cite the source, if applicable, using proper bibliographical form.

The following paragraphs describe graphics features available in Microsoft Office 2010, specifically, Excel and Word.

Chart Creation Tools

Microsoft Excel 2010 supports a dozen types of charts, including the bar, pie, and line charts discussed earlier. To create a chart in Excel, enter numeric data for the chart on a worksheet. Then you can select and plot that data. On the Insert tab in the Charts group, select the chart type you want to use.

Some chart elements, such as a legend, display by default; you will need to add others, such as axes titles and chart title. Excel allows you to modify a basic chart to meet your (and your readers') needs. For example, you can add tick marks to an axis to make it easier to read, hide a legend from a chart depicting only one variable, and move a legend from beside the chart to above or below it. (Selecting the chart and clicking the Layout tab will provide you such options.) This graphics software also permits you to modify appearance of your charts. (Select the chart, and then select Chart Tools for this purpose. For more design tools, click Excel's Design tab and Format tab.) In addition, while creating charts in Excel, you can open Excel Help for detailed directions on altering a basic chart to suit your purposes. (See Illustration 5.17.)

To incorporate a chart in your report, you can simply copy it in the charting application and copy it as a picture into the word-processing application. (Microsoft Word offers another way to insert a chart in report narrative. On the Insert tab, click Chart. Then on the Insert Chart dialog, select the type of chart you want. An Excel worksheet opens with simulated data and a corresponding chart in it. After you replace the simulated data with your data, the chart will be complete. Naturally, you can resize the chart in Word and use Chart Tools and the Format and Styles tabs to modify chart appearance.)

In addition, the Microsoft Office applications allow you to link a chart pasted into Word to the original worksheet in Excel. Thus, if you change the worksheet data, the chart in your report will change with it. To do this, follow these steps:

1. Select and copy the Excel chart. In Word on the Home tab, Clipboard group, click the Paste down arrow, then Paste Special.
2. Next, in the Paste Special dialog, click Microsoft Excel Chart Object.
3. At the left, select Paste Link, then click OK.

Later, when you open the Word file, a screen prompt will remind you that it's linked to another file and ask if you want to update this Word file to match the

ILLUSTRATION 5.17   EXCEL HELP

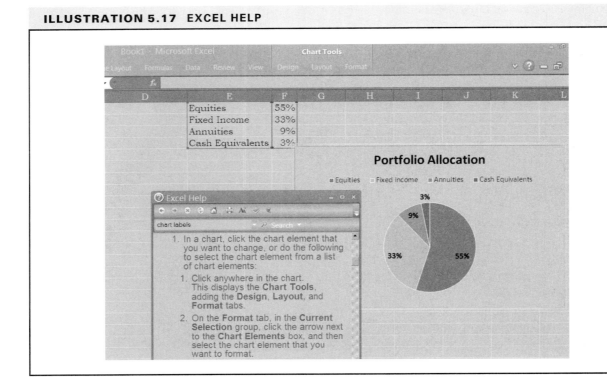

source. Thus, you may choose to incorporate worksheet changes into your report visual or to leave the visual unchanged.

Follow these guidelines for charts in your report:

- Choose colors and patterns that are easily differentiated from one another. For example, in a pie chart, use sharply contrasting colors for side-by-side slices.
- Size the visual according to its complexity. For example, a pie chart with three or four slices may be clear at a width of two inches, but a chart with seven or eight slices needs to be three to four inches wide.
- Include a legend when there are two or more variables in the chart. When only one variable is present, use the title and axes to identify it.
- Label the axes so that they can be read without rotating the visual.
- Choose simple chart layouts, styles, and formats and apply these choices consistently throughout your report to give it a uniform appearance.

Table Creation Tools

As you know, a table is an orderly arrangement of text and numeric data in columns and rows, so the grid arrangement of a spreadsheet is an obvious tool for creating a table. The table can be sized and formatted before or after it is copied into the report text. The ability to link the table to its spreadsheet source is particularly advantageous if the table involves formulae and the data may change before the final draft.

Linking Report Table and Worksheet

To link the report visual and worksheet in Microsoft Office, follow these steps:

1. Create and copy your table in Excel.
2. In Word on the Home tab, Clipboard group, click the Paste down arrow, then Paste Special.
3. Next, in the Paste Special dialog, click Microsoft Excel Worksheet Object.
4. At the left, select Paste Link, then click OK.

When opening the Word file later, you will see a reminder of the link and the option to update the table to match any changes made in the worksheet.

Showing Trends in a Report Table

Data presented in a table are useful, but patterns can be hard to see at a glance. The context of table data can be shown by inserting a tiny chart, called a Sparkline, in a single cell next to the numbers. Ideal placement of a Sparkline is on the same row as the data it depicts, in the right-hand column.

Like a full-sized chart, a Sparkline gives a *picture* of data. For instance, a sales manager might use a Sparkline to show sales trends throughout a year, to show whether the year had a gain or a loss, or to highlight high and low sales amounts. Unlike full-sized charts, a Sparkline is not an object. It is embedded in the cell, which means that you can type text—like an extremely abbreviated chart title—in the same cell. The Sparkline appears behind the text. You can make color, format, and style choices for these miniature charts.

Take these steps to insert a Sparkline in Excel 2010:

1. Select the empty cell(s) where you want to insert a Sparkline.
2. Then, on the Insert tab, Sparklines group, click the type of chart you want to create. The options include column (vertical bar) chart, line chart, and win/loss (gain/loss) chart.
3. In the Create Sparklines dialog, type the range of the cells containing data you want represented. (See Illustration 5.18.)
4. Finally, use the Design tab to modify the tiny chart(s). To customize your Sparkline further, use Excel Help.

Using Word Processing to Insert Tables

Other ways of adding a table involve the word-processing application used to draft the report. Word processors generally provide more than one way to insert a table. For example, in Microsoft Word 2010, you can insert a table by (1) choosing from a gallery of preformatted tables, (2) drawing a table, or (3) indicating in a dialog box the number of columns and rows you want. Option 1 is an ideal choice if all tables in the report fit a built-in option. Option 2 is the best choice for a complex table, such as one containing cells of unequal heights or a varying number of columns in a row. For general use, Option 3 is the most efficient way to include a table.

In Word 2010, there are two ways to use the Insert Table dialog. One way allows partial formatting of the table before it's inserted. Take the following steps to insert a plain table:

1. Click where you want the table to appear. On the Insert tab, Tables group, click Table.

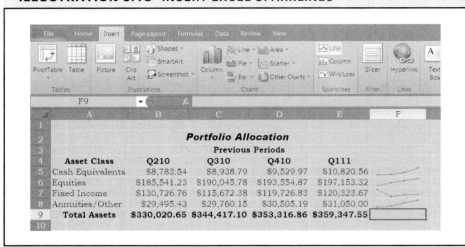

Note: Mark the quarters in your Sparklines: Select the Sparkline cell; at top of screen, click Sparkline Tools. Then in the Show group, click Markers. For the illustration, in the Sparklines group, select the Line option to highlight it.

2. On the Insert Table dialog, drag the pointer to select the number of rows and columns you want. Notice that the Insert Table heading changes to show table capacity—from 1x1 (one column, one row) to 10x8 (10 columns, 8 rows).

3. Click the pointer to insert the table grid. The unformatted grid extends from the left to right margin regardless of the number of columns.

To move from cell to cell when typing text, press Tab, but when entering numbers on the keypad, tap the down arrow. You can add or delete columns and rows as needed.

- To enlarge the table, right-click; select Insert and choose the desired action.
- To reduce the table, select the unused column(s) or row(s), right-click, and choose Delete cells. From the Delete Cells dialog, select Delete entire column or Delete entire row.

Take steps to enhance a table's appearance and readability. The following suggestions are in keeping with guidelines presented earlier:

- Place the table's number and title above the table or in the top row. First, join the cells. Select that row and right-click; from the pop-up menu, choose Merge Cells.
- Shrink column width to fit the contents. Right-click anywhere in the table. Select AutoFit and then AutoFit to Contents.
- Choose a font that contrasts with report paragraphs. For example, use a plain font, such as Calibri. Use Size 10 for the table, even if the paragraphs are Size 11 or 12.
- Change how text aligns in the columns. Select the column, right-click, and choose Cell Alignment; then select the desired option. Generally, left-align the stub, which usually contains text, and right-align columns containing numbers. In decimal numbers, add zeros on the right to align the decimal points.

ILLUSTRATION 5.19 FORMAT TABLE WITH BORDERS AND SHADING

						Estimated	
HOLDINGS IN MUTUAL FUNDS **January 1, 2012–January 31, 2012**							
Symbol	**Description**	**Beginning Value**	**Quantity**	**Ending Price**	**Ending Value**	**Annual Income**	**Yield**
CLVFX	Croft Value	$18,755.72	823.0510	$24.100	$19,835.53	$473.00	2.39%
HINX	Harbor Intl.	$21,343.56	355.7260	$60.820	$21,635.26	$237.00	1.10%
MNFAM	MFS Family	$14,559.85	610.4760	$24.150	$14,743.00	$0.00	0.00%
TAGRX	J Hancock	$24,812.89	954.3420	$26.370	$25,166.00	$283.00	1.13%
TEBIX	Beacon Grp.	$18,464.02	1,508.4990	$12.410	$18,720.47	$570.00	3.05%
Total Mutual Fund Holdings					**$100,100.26**	**$1,563.00**	

Source: Exam Personal Financial Services Report, February 10, 2012.

- Vary row height and change the table's placement on the page. Right-click in a row you want to change and select Table Properties. On the Table Properties dialog, click the Row tab. Specify an exact row height in inches. A common practice is to make the header row(s) noticeably higher than data rows, which are all the same height.
- Place the table attractively in relation to the report text. Right-click in the table and choose Table Properties. On the Table Properties dialog, click the Table tab; select left, center, or right alignment; and choose the desired text wrapping. *Suggestion:* Place the table at the left and wrap text around it on the right or center the table between the margins with no text wrapping.
- Use the Shading and Border tools on the Design tab. (Click in the table to display this tab.) The 8x9 table in Illustration 5.19 shows shading, borders, and other enhancements mentioned in this list.

Diagram Creation Tool

Sometimes the most appropriate visual is a diagram. In those situations, you may use SmartArt, a tool in Microsoft Office 2010. SmartArt is a diagramming tool that lets you illustrate dynamics, such as an organizations hierarchy, a process in action, or relationships among work teams. If you want to incorporate photos into your diagram, SmartArt makes it easy to do so.

With some software tools, you can experiment until you get the result you planned. With SmartArt, though, you need to choose a diagram according to your specific plan. Think about what you want to show, the order of the information, and what relationships are involved; then take a moment to sketch it on paper. Next, click through the diagram options to become acquainted with them (cycle, hierarchy, list, matrix, picture, process, pyramid, relationship). You will notice that each of these types involves several different layouts. Choose the SmartArt diagram that appears best for the message you want to convey. Before proceeding, draft text for the diagram. Make it so concise that *a few clear words* contain what you want the diagram to say.

Follow these steps in Word 2010 to create a SmartArt visual:

1. On the Insert tab, Illustrations group, click SmartArt.
2. In the Choose a SmartArt Graphic dialog, click the diagram type (at the left) and then the layout you want. (See Illustration 5.20.)

ILLUSTRATION 5.20   INSERT A SMARTART DIAGRAM

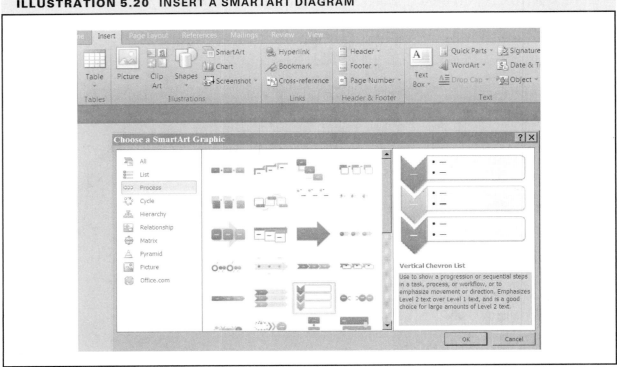

Used with permission from Microsoft

3. Insert any additional text boxes you will need. Click the text box closest to where you want to add one. On the Design tab, Create Graphic group, click the arrow under Add Shape. Now click Add Shape After or Add Shape Before.
4. Enter text: Click the Text pane and type it or paste it from another location.

You can change the layout, but remember that choosing a different type of diagram may alter the *meaning* of your information. (For example, a process diagram with arrows pointing to the right does not send the same message as a cycle diagram with arrows going in a circle.)

You can control the size, color, and style of your text. In addition, you can add various heading styles and graphic elements, or themes, as well as apply a range of designer effects, formats, and layouts. If you choose SmartArt's picture diagram, you can easily add photos and then use the picture-formatting tools provided to perfect them. Consult Word Help as needed for the steps involved. ***Note:*** For the most effective diagrams, keep your SmartArt simple.

Google Maps

Google Maps (http://maps.google.com/maps) is a mapping service provided on the Web by Google, Inc. Google Maps (for noncommercial use) powers many map-based services of which the Google Maps website is most relevant to report writers.

Google Maps offers detailed, high-resolution street maps for most urban areas in the United States, Canada, and the United Kingdom as well as parts of Australia and many other countries. Direction buttons let you pan a map in all four directions, and

ILLUSTRATION 5.21   INSERT A GOOGLE MAP

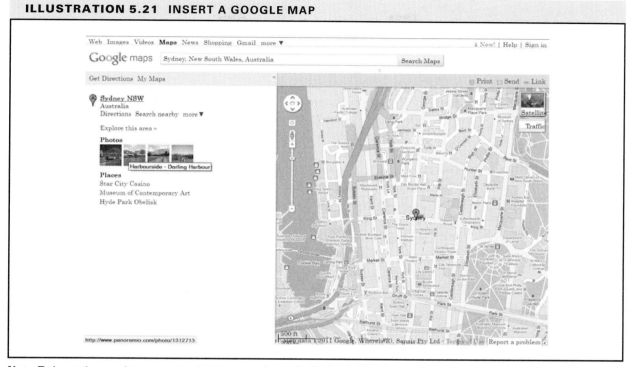

Note: To insert the map into a report, print the screen (press PrtScn key); then paste the picture into Microsoft Word. Use Picture Tools (Crop) to trim the excess, but do NOT trim off the copyright line. Finally, copy the revised map and paste it into your report.

Zoom In/Out buttons enable you to focus on one small area of a city or to see the city in relation to its entire country. (See Illustration 5.21.)

In many instances, you can also see a street view if you search for a specific address. For example, enter the exact address in Rio de Janeiro, Brazil, of the Golden Tulip Hotel, and a picture of the hotel and surrounding buildings appears over the Rio street map. **Note:** A separate Google website called Street View (http://maps. google.com/help/maps/streetview) lets you zoom, rotate, and pan photographs of streets and buildings (inside and outside) in the world's major cities.

In addition, Google has blurred some map areas for security (mostly in the United States). Not all map areas are covered in the same resolution; less populated areas usually have less detail. Google Maps is intended to cover the world, but initial service tends to be heavier in English-speaking areas. Although Google uses the word *satellite*, most of the images are aerial photography taken from aircraft flying 800 to 1,500 feet. Therefore, Google's maps are not in real time but may be several months or years old.

Comparable mapping services include Bing Maps (http://www.bing.com/maps) and Yahoo! Maps (http://maps.yahoo.com).

Ethical Considerations

A final criterion for effective visuals is that all visuals must be ethical representations of data. Although you may use visuals effectively to emphasize, summarize, and so on, you should avoid distortion of data. Visuals can sometimes have more impact than their accompanying text for three reasons:[1]

- Visuals have an emotional impact that words lack.
- Skimmers of items will see visuals even when they do not read the text.
- Readers remember visuals longer.

A report narrative may present comprehensive and accurate data, but readers tend to gain first impressions of information from visuals. Those first impressions and images often influence the reader more strongly than does the verbal narrative.

You can avoid distortion by attending carefully to scale dimensions and sizes of symbols (bars, circles, boxes, etc.) used in your visuals. Line charts are especially vulnerable to distortion; when improperly drawn or when a scale is collapsed, they can exaggerate growth or minimize problems. The distance between all units of measurement on each axis must be equal. (An exception is proportional-line charts, which are too complex for inclusion in this discussion.) On a line or bar chart, you can avoid distortion by making units on the horizontal and vertical axes approximately the same size. Further, if you use symbols to compare items, draw those symbols to an accurate scale so that relative size represents appropriate comparisons. Charts can also mislead if they are incomplete. Remember that a key element for preparing effective reports is completeness.

The following examples demonstrate the distortion that may result from changing the size of scale units or of objects used in comparisons. Notice that changing the horizontal scale units makes the rise in expenses appear more gradual and that showing expenses with a smaller circle makes expenses appear to be considerably smaller than revenue, even though no data about amounts are given.

Collaborative Writing

Previous chapters have introduced you to collaborative writing and ways to improve the collaborative process. You have probably come to realize that effective collaboration includes many kinds of activities that occur before, during, and after the actual writing activity. In a work setting (and in many classrooms), some of the prewriting tasks are undertaken by someone in a supervisory position. For example, a supervisor or instructor defines the goal of a project and sets up the conditions that will foster collaborative work. (See Illustration 5.22, pre–collaborative writing task.)

After the group members have been notified of the task, they must first form a team as opposed to a mere collection of people. Only after team formation can the group members effectively move on to planning the task and producing the document. After the document has been produced, perhaps in its near-final version, the effective team engages in purposeful windup work. (See Illustration 5.22, collaborative writing task.)

If the collaborative writing task is to be a learning experience with benefits for both the team members and the organization, the task-related activities extend beyond the point at which the document is approved. In addition to delivering the document to the appropriate recipients, the team and its supervisor can benefit from reviewing the process and analyzing the lessons learned from working together. (See Illustration 5.22, post–collaborative writing task.)

Whenever you are assigned to a collaborative writing group, the model shown in Illustration 5.22 can serve as a guide to ensure that essential tasks are not omitted.

ILLUSTRATION 5.22 COLLABORATIVE WRITING TASKS AND ACTIVITIES[2]

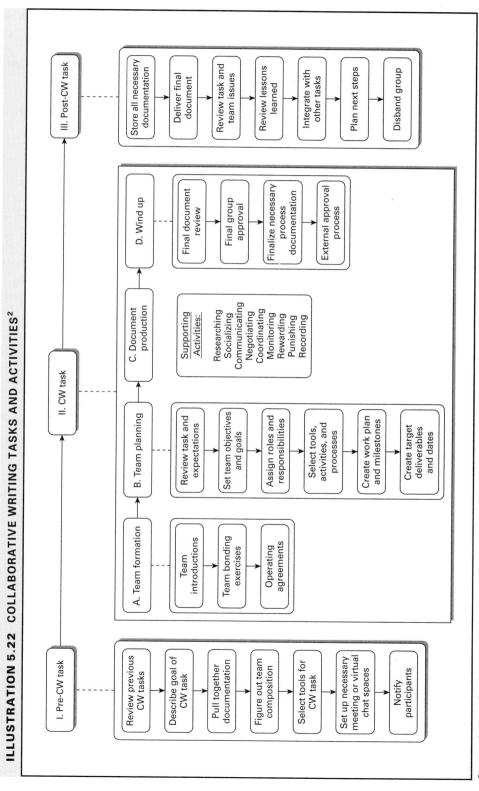

Source: Lowry, Curtis, and Lowry, p. 73

Awareness of all aspects of collaborative writing should improve your collaborative writing experiences.

Summary

Visuals may be used to emphasize, clarify, simplify, reinforce, or summarize report data. In addition, effective visuals add interest to a report, improve the credibility of the report and its writer, and increase report coherence.

Effective visuals demonstrate simplicity, contrast, unity, and balance. All parts of the aids must be identified fully, and each visual must be identified by title and referred to in the report. The most effective placement of visuals is in the report narrative, preferably immediately after a brief introductory statement. Effective visuals are also ethical representations of data; that is, they are accurate "pictures," not distortions of reality.

Useful visuals include bar, pie, line, and relationship charts; flowcharts; formal and informal tables; and pictures, pictographs, and statistical maps. Graphics tools in spreadsheet and word-processing software, including Microsoft Excel and Word, enable you to construct visuals. In your dual role of graphics designer and report writer, apply the principles for effective visuals given in the chapter. Become familiar with the chart, diagram, and table creation tools in the software you use. Whenever a geographical map is the most appropriate visual, use a mapping website, such as Google Maps, to obtain the precise area and level of detail needed in the report.

During your career, you will likely be part of a collaborative writing team or a supervisor who requests that a team produce a document. Whether you are a supervisor or a team writer, attention to the wide array of prewriting, writing, and postwriting tasks will contribute to successful collaboration.

Topics for Discussion

1. Identify and explain the eight purposes of visuals in reports.
2. Explain the significance of each of the following principles of graphics:
   a. Simplicity
   b. Contrast
   c. Unity
   d. Balance
3. Explain what is needed in a well-written title for a visual.
4. Improve the following introductory statements for visuals:
   a. Table 1 shows advertising expenses for Alpha Company, Beta Corp., and the Gamma Group in 2013.
   b. As Figure 1 indicates, collaborative writing tasks can be grouped into three stages.
   c. The following bar chart shows coffee production by country in 2012.
5. Describe the three-step technique for incorporating visuals into a report.
6. Compare and contrast the following visuals:
   - Multiple bar chart and bilateral bar chart
   - Simple bar chart and basic line chart
   - Multiple-line chart and band chart

- Flowchart and factor relationship chart
- Formal table and informal table
- Photograph and pictograph

7. Give guides for constructing and preventing distortion in each of the following visuals:
   - Bar chart
   - Pie chart
   - Line chart

8. Discuss your experience using the graphics tools in Microsoft Excel and Word with two or more classmates. Which tools were easiest to master? Which ones were most difficult? Choose one unfamiliar tool in each category, then search Help for using each tool.

9. Collaborate with two or more other students to identify ways in which data may be misrepresented in visuals. Try to recall/show specific examples from print media, product packages, and/or the Web.

10. Explain the three major stages of collaborative writing. What special challenges may arise if a writing team must incorporate several visuals into its report?

Applications

1. Which visual would be the most appropriate to illustrate the following types of information? Be prepared to support your decision while recognizing that, for some items, several alternatives may be possible.
   a. A comparison of in-state tuition, housing, and student fees at three universities in your state or region
   b. The number of U.S. nationals and foreign nationals enrolled in your school by year, 2003–2012
   c. The mean, maximum, and minimum temperatures for your city for each month of the year
   d. Women's Summer Olympic participation by nation in the years 1996, 2000, 2004, 2008, and 2012
   e. The relative market share for the top three cell phone service providers in the United States
   f. An explanation of how to assemble a gas barbecue grill
   g. Sales, profits, and assets of the five largest U.S. industrial corporations
   h. A breakdown of auto production by country (four countries) and model types (three types)
   i. A breakdown of your monthly budget
   j. The number of male and female inmates in state and federal prisons during the years 2008–2012
   k. U.S. Treasury bond yields in the years 2007–2011, with three maturity terms
   l. The percent of households owning four kinds of pets by annual household income (five categories)
   m. Expenditures per consumer unit for four forms of entertainment by four regions of the country

     n. Dollars given in one year by an endowment fund distributed among six categories of recipients

2. Locate a visual that needs improvement. You may want to look online or in newspapers, magazines, textbooks, brochures, newsletters, or computer manuals. Revise and enhance or re-create the visual. Submit it to your instructor, along with a copy of the original and a memo explaining your improvements.

3. Compare and contrast the visuals used in two corporation's annual reports. Critique those visuals, applying criteria you have learned while studying this chapter. Present the criteria and your critique in a three-page manuscript report to your instructor. See a sample manuscript report in Chapter 6, page 168.

4. Conduct research and develop a visual to illustrate one or more of the following sets of data. Incorporate the visual into a short memorandum report, applying the introduce-display-discuss technique presented in this chapter. (**Hints:** Use websites such as U.S. Government Directory [http://www.govengine.com], State and County Quick Facts [http://quickfacts.census.gov], or Census Bureau Home Page [http://www.census.gov]. See a sample memorandum report in Chapter 6, page 159.)

     a. How managers spend time during a typical day

     b. The number of auto registrations in your state (or county) for these vehicle types: SUVs, vans, pickups, hybrids, and sedans

     c. The number of violent crimes in your city during each of the past six months

     d. The number of female lawyers in the United States by type of practice in the years 2007 and 2011.

     e. The U.S. labor force participation rates of males and females in 2010 by level of education

     f. The costs of treating substance use disorders in the U.S. by type of treatment (inpatient, outpatient) and length of treatment, average cost per admission, and estimated annual costs

     g. International tourism arrivals (selected major countries) in 2008, 2009, and 2010

     h. Quarterly changes in U.S. e-commerce, from the first quarter of 2009 through the first quarter of 2010

     i. Foreign-born and native-born populations in the U.S. civilian labor force by gender, 2009

     j. U.S. noninstitutional population enrolled in nursery school and above in the years 1990, 2000, and 2010

5. Prepare a visual for each of the following sets of data. Using the introduce-display-discuss technique, write a brief report interpreting the data.

     a. Prestige of occupations in the United States (by percent of 1,010 respondents who said the profession had very great prestige): firefighter, 62%; scientist, 57%; doctor, 56%; nurse, 54%; teacher, 51%; military officer, 51%; police officer, 49%; priest/minister/clergy, 41%; engineer, 39%; farmer, 36%; architect, 29%; member of Congress, 28%; lawyer, 26%; business executive, 23%; athlete, 21%; entertainer, 17%; journalist, 17%; union leader, 17%; banker, 16%; actor, 15%; stockbroker, 13%; accountant, 11%; real estate agent/broker, 5% (Source: *Harris Poll*, July 7–14, 2009)

b. Made in America. U.S. adults' reaction to a Made in USA label or advertisement in percent of respondents who said they would be more likely to buy: total, 61%; age 18 to 34, 44%; age 35 to 44, 61%; age 45 to 54, 66%; age 55 and over, 75% (Source: *Harris Poll*, July 27–29, 2010)

c. The percent of adult population considered to be obese, in selected countries in 2007: United States, 34.3; Canada, 15.4; Greece, 16.4; Mexico, 30.0; New Zealand, 26.5; United Kingdom, 24.0 (Source: *Statistical Abstract of the United States: 2008*, p. 832)

d. Carbon dioxide emissions from consumption of fossil fuels by selected countries in 2004 and 2008 in millions of metric tons (Source: *Statistical Abstract of the United States: 2011*, p. 868)

	2004	2008
World	27,620	30,317
United States	5,965	5,833
China	5,132	6,534
Russia	1,644	1,729
India	1,132	1,495
Germany	871	829

e. Projected percent changes in population for selected states in the years 2000–2030: United States, 29.2; Arizona, 108.8; District of Columbia, −24.2; Florida, 79.5; Idaho, 52.2; Iowa, 1.0; Nevada, 114.3; New York, 2.6; North Dakota, −5.5; Texas, 59.8; West Virginia, −4.9 (Source: *Statistical Abstract of the United States: 2008*, Table 14; http://www.census.gov)

f. Military expenditures by percent of gross domestic product in 2009: United States, 4.1; Turkey, 5.3; Syria, 5.9; Saudi Arabia, 10; Libya, 3.9; Israel, 7.3; Iraq, 8.6; Greece, 4.3; Cuba, 3.8; China, 4.3 (Source: *Statistical Abstract of the United States: 2011*, p. 878)

g. Cell phone subscribers (rates per 100 persons), 2008: Saudi Arabia, 142.85; United Kingdom, 126.34; South Korea, 94.71; United States, 86.79; Japan, 86.73; Brazil, 78.47; China (People's Republic and Taiwan), 47.95; India, 29.36 (Source: *Statistical Abstract of the United States: 2011*, p. 869)

6. Devise a pictograph that shows the composition of LifeStyle decorative paint products. ***Note:*** You will need to create this visual manually. Each gallon of paint contains the following percentages of ingredients:

Titanium Dioxide	18.4%
Silicates	10.4%
Calcium Carbonate	5.0%
Tinting Colors	1.0%
Water and Synthetic Rubber Emulsion Base	65.2%

7. Devise a visual that shows the percent of minimum daily requirements (based on a 2,000-calorie diet) provided by a one-third-cup serving of Aunt Minnie's Southern Style Rice: fat, 1; sodium, 28; potassium, 5; carbohydrate, 14; vitamin A, 6; vitamin C, 8; calcium, 2; thiamin, 20; folate, 20; iron, 15; niacin, 15.

8. In 2013, Nobuko Company (hypothetical) had sales of $2.9 million. Broken down, the revenue came from the following product lines: jewelry, 39%; personal care products, 34%; food products, 21%; novelties, 4%; other products, 2%. The company's pretax profit totaled $870,000 and came from the same lines as above but in the following percentages: jewelry, 47%; personal care products, 29%; food products, 14%; novelties, 6%; other products, 4%.

   Incorporate the data into an illustration to show the relationship between the sales of each product line and the pretax profits from the same lines.

9. You are a sales manager for Santiago and Sons, Inc., a large local furniture store in your area. You must report to your supervisor, the owner, about the annual efforts of your sales area and of the individual efforts of your sales force. In one section of your report, you decide to show the percentage of change from last year's sales for each of your sales associates. These are your data (name of associate, percentage of change): James Cummings, −6.2; Sophie Davis, +6.5; Teresa Davis, −13.1; Victor Heldago, −8.0; Arlis Jamison, +7.1; Jean March, −7.3; Seung Hwang, −1.5; Jose Ruiz, +4.8; Harrison Toomey, −11.2; Amy Wilson, +10.3.

   Prepare a visual to depict this information, write the sentence that will precede the illustration, insert the visual into the narrative, and write the discussion that will follow it. Remember to interpret the data; don't merely repeat it.

10. You work as an aide to Inez Torringa, who is considering a run for a congressional seat for your district. She intends to use health and nutrition as one of her campaign issues. Using the following data, write a brief report to Ms. Torringa, suggesting a position that she could take. Include at least one visual in your report to substantiate that position.
    - Health expenditures as a percent of gross domestic product, 1990 and 2007, respectively, for selected countries: United States, 12.2, 16.0; France, 8.4, 11.0; Greece, 6.6, 9.6; Ireland, 6.1, 7.6; Spain, 6.5, 8.5; Switzerland, 8.2, 10.8; United Kingdom, 5.9, 8.4 (Source: *Statistical Abstract of the United States: 2010*, p. 845)
    - Uninsured individuals in the United States: 1997, 42,359,000; 2007, 45,657,000 (Source: *Income, Poverty, and Health Insurance Coverage in the United States: 2007*, p. 58)
    - Persons in the United States having problems with access to food (2008): adults with low food security, 20,320,000; adults with very low food security, 12,115,000; children with low food security, 57,433,000; children with very low food security, 16,673,000 (Source: *Household Food Security in the United States, 2008*, Economic Research Report No. 83, 2009)
    - Individuals below poverty level in your home state (go to http://www.quickfacts.census.gov/qfd to get data about your state)

11. A major state university released the grade-point averages of its athletes, overall and by team. Here are the data: overall, 2.886; baseball, 3.005; men's basketball, 2.910; women's basketball, 2.992; equestrian, 2.980; football, 2.217; men's golf, 3.502; women's golf, 3.671; men's soccer, 2.703; women's soccer, 3.356; softball, 3.266; men's swimming and diving, 2.850; women's swimming and diving, 3.303; men's tennis, 3.538; women's tennis, 3.369; men's track and field, 2.831; women's track and field, 3.265; volleyball, 2.769. Construct an appropriate visual aid to represent some or all of the data (depending on the main point you want

to convey). Incorporate that visual into a memorandum report sent from the director of athletics to all academic department heads. Remember to use the introduce-display-discuss technique.

12. You have been asked to improve a brochure intended to attract entering students into your department or college of business. The text of the brochure looks intimidating, sounds confusing, and could actually drive students away from majoring in business. After reading the following statement, develop a visual that could follow the narrative and clarify it.

> Entering students must have a minimum of a 2.5 grade-point average (A = 4.0); then they, in their chosen majors, work through several modules of courses. First, there are the introductory courses, like Introduction to Business (BUS 240), Personal Finance (FIN 220), and Careers in Business and Industry (BUS 230). Then there are the skills courses, like Business Writing (BUS 260), Statistics (MAT 150), and Business Law (BUS 270). Next come the core courses, like Management Concepts (BUS 340), Principles of Marketing (MKT 310), Principles of Accounting (ACT 350), and Foundations of Economics (ECO 325). Finally, the capstone course, Business Policy (BUS 480), should be completed. Students must also select four courses in their selected majors. Please see your department for an updated list of major courses.

13. You work as a research associate for a major publisher. Your company wants to capture more of consumers' discretionary spending by stimulating people to read more books. You have been asked to find out how much U.S. citizens currently spend on various categories of discretionary spending. This is what you have found (Source: *The 2011 Statistical Abstract PDF version* at http://www.census.gov/prod/2011pubs/11statab/income.pdf).

Discretionary spending per consumer unit (annual averages, in dollars)

Year	Entertainment	Tobacco Products	Reading
2004	2,218	288	130
2006	2,376	327	117
2008	2,835	317	116

Construct an appropriate visual to represent some or all of the data (depending on the main point you want to convey). Incorporate that visual into a memorandum report (example on page 159) sent from you to the director of marketing. Use the introduce-display-discuss technique.

References

1. Kienzler, D. D. (1997, April). Visual ethics. *Journal of Business Communication,* 34, 171–187.

2. Lowry, P. B., Curtis, A., & Lowry, M. R. (2004). Building a taxonomy and nomenclature of collaborative writing to improve interdisciplinary research and practice. *Journal of Business Communication,* 41(1), 66–99.

CHAPTER **6**

Formatting the Report

LEARNING OBJECTIVES

After you have read this chapter, you should be able to:

1. Apply current business protocols for formatting memoranda, letters, and manuscripts.

2. Plan an effective, readable design for a simple or complex document.

3. Use word processing tools to improve the appearance and readability of your reports.

4. Work effectively with team members to plan and produce an appropriate, effective format for a report or other document.

5. Demonstrate ethical responsibility with respect to accessing and disseminating data electronically.

AFTER PLANNING, WRITING, REVISING, AND EDITING YOUR REPORT, you may feel confident that you have prepared an effective message. However, you must also consider how to "package" that fine product. An effective format will entice the receiver to read the report, lead the reader effortlessly through the information presented, maintain the reader's interest, and, ideally, stimulate the reader to respond to the report as you had hoped.

You can produce professionally formatted reports by mastering three commonly used report formats (letter, memo, and manuscript) and following a few basic guides for document design.

Formatting Reports

Most business reports are written in memorandum, letter, or manuscript format. Whichever of those formats you choose, you should apply the following general guides.

General Guides

To maintain a consistent image, companies often adopt document standards and require that all employees adhere to those specifications. Applying these guides will help your reader scan the document, quickly determine its content, and focus attention on specific information.

Spacing

Most printed business documents omit blank lines between text lines. Therefore, this kind of spacing, called single spacing, is used for memorandum and letter reports. The trend is also to use single spacing for manuscript reports, although some organizations use double spacing (blank line between text lines).

A small amount of blank space roughly equivalent to a line of text separates paragraphs of single-spaced documents. Generally, single-spaced paragraphs have no paragraph indentations. Double-spaced documents have no extra blank space between paragraphs but have a paragraph indentation of one-half inch.

Some word-processing programs use different spacing protocols than those just described. For example, Microsoft Word 2010 uses 1.15 (Multiple) instead of 1 (Single) as the default line spacing. In fact, many examples in this textbook use this spacing, which looks much like single spacing. However, you should not automatically use default settings. Instead, determine the preferences of your readers (your employer, instructor, or other readers) and change the settings to meet their expectations. (In Word, on the Home tab, click the Paragraph down arrow. In the Paragraph dialog, set line spacing (Single, Double, Multiple, etc.) at the lower right. The Multiple setting requires a number in the **At** text box. As already noted, the default setting is Multiple At 1.15.)

Regulate the amount of space between paragraphs at the lower left under Spacing. The default setting is **Before** 0 and **After** 10. When using Single line spacing, change the After setting to 12. For Double line spacing, set **Before** and **After** to 0.)

Typography

Typography—your selection of typeface (font), font style, and font size—affects the appearance and readability of your report. The primary goal of typography is to create a document that is consistent, harmonious, and balanced. Too much variety can be distracting to a reader.

Typeface, or *font*, refers to the shape or design of letters and characters. As the fonts shown in Illustration 6.1 demonstrate, some typefaces are considerably more intricate—and often less readable—than others. Fonts are also identified as serif or sans serif. *Serif* refers to the fine lines that cross the bottom of a letter. (Notice the lines at the bottom of *f*, *k*, *l*, *m*, *n*, and *r* in the previous sentence.) *Sans serif* fonts do not have lines at the ends of letters. A third way to classify fonts is by spacing characteristics. Monospaced fonts allocate equal space to each letter; examples include Consolas and Lucida Console (sans serif) and Courier, Courier New, and Letter Gothic (serif). (These monospaced fonts look like old-fashioned typewriter characters.) Most computer typefaces are proportionally spaced, meaning the fonts allocate more space to wide letters, such as *W*, and less space to narrow letters, such as *l*. Along with choosing a font, you must consider font style and size. Most of your report text should be produced in regular or plain style. Bold, italic, and bold-italic may be used sparingly for emphasis or to clarify the text. For example, bold is often used for headings and subheadings and italics for names of publications or for emphasis. Limit underlining to subheadings and a few words in paragraphs. Readers recognize words by their shapes; underlining tends to obscure the descending portions of letters like *g*, *j*, *p*, and *y*. (Note the slight distortion when *these letters* are underlined: g, j, p, y.)

Font size is measured in points (1 inch = 72 points) from the top of the characters' ascenders (letters like *d* and *k*) to the bottom of its descenders (letters such as *p* and *q*). Font size for report text should be 10 to 14 points. Size 10 may be too small

ILLUSTRATION 6.1   COMPARATIVE FONTS, FONT SIZES, AND FONT STYLES

Serif Fonts	Sans Serif Fonts
Cambria, 12 point, regular	Calibri, 12 point, regular
Cambria, 14 point, bold	**Calibri, 14 point, bold**
Cambria, 16 point, italics	*Calibri, 16 point, italics*
Times New Roman, 12 point, regular	Tahoma, 12 point, Regular
Times New Roman, 14 point, bold	**Tahoma, 14 point, bold**
Times New Roman, 16 point, italics	*Tahoma, 16 point, italics*
Palatino Linotype, 12 point, regular	Univers, 12 point, regular
Palatino Linotype, 14 point, bold	**Univers, 14 point, bold**
Palatino Linotype, 16 point, italics	**Univers, 16 point, italics**
Harrington, 12 point, regular	Eras Light, 12 point regular
Harrington, 14 point, bold	**Eras Light, 14 point, bold**
Harrington, 16 point, italics	*Eras Light, 16 point, italics*

for some readers, but it is sometimes used when the writer wants to limit the pages in a document or shrink a document to one page. Any size larger than 14 points is considered a display font and should be reserved for headings. Using anything larger than 12 points for the main text may give the impression that you are trying to pad the report. You may use a hierarchy of sizes, with headings larger than the text.

Again, you are cautioned to check the default font in your word-processing program. For example, Microsoft Word 2010 uses Calibri, a *sans serif* font, as the default setting. Traditionally, *serif* fonts, such as Word's Cambria, have been used for the main text of a document because the serifs create a line to lead a reader's eye from left to right. Thus, serif text is easier to read. If the default setting in your program does not correspond with the standards set by your instructor or your employer, change the settings to meet expectations.

Emphasis Techniques

When you want to emphasize certain information in a report, you may use one of several emphasis techniques, such as full capitalization (ALL CAPS), bold style, italics style, bulleted lists, numbered lists, and shading.

Use ALL-CAPS in short spans, such as a main heading or a few key words in a long paragraph. LONG STRINGS OF CAPITALIZED TEXT ARE HARD TO READ. Moreover, using all uppercase letters has come to be equated with shouting. E-mail protocols, for example, discourage use of all capital letters except for headings or occasional emphasis within a message.

Use **bold** in moderation. Apply it to a few words or phrases up to a short sentence or two that are altogether worthy of emphasis. (In Word, select the text; on the Home tab, Font group, click B.)

Likewise, use *italics* sparingly. When too many things are emphasized, nothing receives appropriate attention. Besides italicizing made-up words and the titles of complete published and artistic works that contain subdivisions, use italics *when you want readers to slow down and read more carefully.* (In Word, select the text; on the Home tab, Font group, click I.)

Grouping and bulleting or numbering closely related items focuses attention on that information. To group items effectively, follow these guides:

- Use an introductory sentence or phrase to unify the group. The sentence immediately preceding this list is an example of such a sentence. Include at least two or three items in your list. Logically, you cannot have a group of one.
- Write all items in parallel grammatical structure. For example, each item in this list begins with an imperative verb and is followed by additional information.
- Use bullets if order of the items is irrelevant. Use numbers if the list represents a sequence, such as the steps in a procedure.
- In a report, choose one bullet style for all lists in that document. For a formal report, use a traditional bullet style (large, solid circle, or square), reserving more exotic characters for less formal documents, such as a newsletter. (In Word, on the Home tab, in Paragraph group, click Bullets or Numbering or click the down arrow to launch the Bullets or Numbering dialog and choose a bullet style or number format. To add bullets or numbers after typing the list, select the text; then click Bullets or Numbering.)
- Put the same space between bulleted or numbered items that appears between regular paragraphs. (To adjust vertical spacing in Word, open the Paragraph dialog. Change the spacing after paragraphs to match the spacing elsewhere. Then deselect this checkbox: Don't add space between paragraphs of the same style. Align bulleted or numbered items at the paragraph point. (In Word, select the bulleted or numbered items. On the Home tab, Paragraph group, click Decrease Indent to move items toward the left margin; then click Increase Indent to move the items to the right.)
- Use the hanging indentation style for bulleted and numbered items. This style aligns the text 0.25 inch or 0.5 inch to the right of the bullet or number. (To add or change this indentation, select the bulleted or numbered items and open the Paragraph dialog. Under **Indentation/Special**, select Hanging; at **By**, click the up or down arrow to increase or decrease the indentation.
- Shading may be used selectively to separate report sections and highlight examples, set off long quotations, or draw attention to other text. Use light shading behind text (as illustrated throughout Chapter 4) and strips of medium to dark shading as dividers. (In Word, select text to be shaded. On the Home tab, Paragraph group, click the Shading down arrow. Choose a shading color. To use shading as a divider, click where you want the separator; then click the Shading down arrow and choose a color.)

Headings

Headings should represent the outline of your report and guide the reader through its content. When you use headings, their appearance must convey the relationship of report sections. All first-level headings, which indicate major divisions of the report, must be printed in uniform style, and all second-level headings, which identify subdivisions of the major divisions, must be printed in a uniform style that clearly distinguishes them from first-level or third-level divisions. One acceptable style for headings is shown in Illustration 6.2. In that illustration, first-level headings are centered, second-level headings are placed at the left margin, and third-level headings are placed at the beginnings of paragraphs. (Illustration 6.2 shows all headings in the same font and font size as they should be in a memo or letter report. To enhance the appearance and readability of a report in manuscript format, you might use a sans serif font for the title and Level 1 and 2 headings and use different sizes, such as 18, 16, and 14, respectively. For Level 3 headings, use the same serif font and font size as the paragraphs.)

Each heading should be close to the text it covers. For example, if a heading appears on the last line of a page, force it to the top of the next page. (In Word 2010, click in front of the heading; press/hold Control and tap Enter.) Also, insert text below each heading. For example, if the report contains Level 1 and 2 headings, a Level 2 heading should not appear immediately below a Level 1; instead, text below the Level 1 heading should introduce the Level 2 topics.

As you study the illustrations of reports throughout this book, notice how the general guides for spacing, typography, headings, and emphasis are applied. In addition, observe the following specific guides for memorandum, letter, and manuscript reports. When you apply those guides, you not only enhance readability; you also demonstrate your knowledge of contemporary business writing protocols that accommodate differences in the content and context of messages.

Memorandum Format

Most relatively brief internal reports are written in memorandum (memo) format. A commonly used memorandum format is shown in Illustration 6.3. The memo heading includes the guidewords *To*, *From*, *Date*, and *Subject*. The date may appear above the name of the recipient. Some organizations include other guidewords, such as *cc* (courtesy copy).

Courtesy and professional titles (Mr., Mrs., Ms., Dr., etc.) are usually omitted in intracompany memos, but position titles (Vice President, Supervisor, etc.) are sometimes included. When you begin a new job in a large organization, it's a good idea to show your department affiliation until others in the organization become acquainted with you. In any case, it is wise to check the organization's office manual or files to determine the preferences within that company. A memo template is a preformatted file containing placeholders and guides for completing a memorandum. Templates are designed to save users' time, and Microsoft Word 2010 offers hundreds of templates in various categories, with over a dozen memo templates.

The memo category contains over a dozen templates. Before using a template, it is important to find a design, such as the Contemporary, Elegant, Personal, Professional, or Simple memo, that conforms to the guidelines of your instructor or organization. It may be necessary to adapt a template to your specifications and save it for future use. Follow these steps to modify a Microsoft Word template:

ILLUSTRATION 6.2 LEVELS OF HEADINGS IN REPORTS

Title	**Organizational Effectiveness**
First Level	Determining Criteria for Effectiveness
	Xxxxxxxxxxxxx xxx xxxxxxxxxxxx xxxxx xxxxx xxxxxx. xxxxxx xxxx. Xxxxxxxxxxxxxx. x…
First Level	Assessing Effectiveness
	Xxxxxxxxxxxxx xxxxxxxxxx xxxxxxx xxxxxxxx…
Second Level	Setting Standards
	Xxxx xxxxxxx xxxxxxxxxx xxxxxxxx xxxxxxxx xxxxxxxx. Xxxxx xxx…
Second Level	Selecting Indicators
	Xxxxxxxxxxxxxx xxxxxx xx xxxxxxx xxx xxxx xxx xxxxx. Xxxxxxxxxxxx xxxxxx x xxxx xxxxx xxx…
Third Level	Outcomes. Xxxxxxxxxx xxxx xxxx xxxxx xx. Xxxxxxx…
Third Level	Processes. Xxxxx xxxxxxxxx xx xxxxx xxx xxxx. Xxxxxxx
Third Level	Structures. Xxxxxxx xxx xxxxxxxxx xxx xxxx xxx. Xxxxxx xxxxxx…
Second Level	Selecting Samples
	Xxxxxxxxxxxxx xxxxx xxxx xxx. Xxxx xxx xxxxxx…
Second Level	Applying Measurements
	Xxxxxxxxx xxxxxx xx xxxxx xxxx. Xxxx xxx xx xxxxxxx…
First Level	Explaining Effectiveness
	Xxxxxxxxx xxxxxxxxxxxx xxxxx xxxxxxxxxxxxxxxxxx xxxxxxxx xxxxxxxx xxxxxxxx xxxx xxx xxxxx…

© Cengage Learning 2013

1. Click the File tab; then click New.
2. From the alphabetic list of template categories on the Office.com dialog, scroll to and click the desired category (Memos).
3. When you see an appropriate template, click it; study the on-screen image at the right, as shown in Illustration 6.4. (**Hint:** The Professional memo template uses a clear, simple format.)
4. At the right, click Download. When the template opens, study it further and make changes that seem necessary. For example, you will note that all text appears in the Arial font, size 10.
   a. To change to a serif font (preferred) and larger size, select all the text, starting at *To*. Then on the Home tab, Font group, click the Font down arrow and choose a serif font, such as Cambria.
   b. Next, click the Font Size down arrow; select the desired size.

ILLUSTRATION 6.3 MEMORANDUM FORMAT

To: Report Writing Students

From: Willis Knight, Instructor   *WK*

Date: September 17, <year>

Subject: Standard Memorandum Format

This illustration demonstrates memorandum format. Notice these features of memo format:

1. The standard heading consists of the captions *To*, *From*, *Date*, and *Subject*. Those captions may be arranged in different ways, but either *Date* or *To* should be the first item, and *Subject* should immediately precede the memo body (message).

2. On a memo, the date may appear as shown or in *mm/dd/yy* format.

3. The subject line must be a brief, meaningful summary of the memo's content.

4. This memo body has one blank line below the heading and below each paragraph.

5. Left and right margins should be at least one inch wide.

6. Numbering focuses the reader's attention on specific information, emphasizing items in top-to-bottom order. Numbered items also permit a reader to identify specific items for response. If a memo contains only one major point, do not number it.

The memo sender frequently writes her or his initials after the typed name to indicate approval of the message. Some writers sign or initial the memo at the end of the message. However, do not use a closing (such as Sincerely or Yours truly) at the end of a memo. Other illustrations of memo reports appear throughout this book. Follow these guides as you prepare memo reports.

ILLUSTRATION 6.4 MICROSOFT WORD'S PROFESSIONAL MEMO TEMPLATE

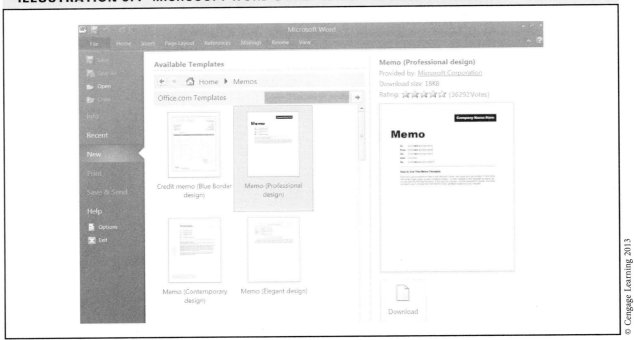

    c. At the top of the template (Company Information Here), click and type appropriate information or select and delete the text box.

    d. Decide whether the courtesy copy notation (cc:) should remain. If you typically indicate courtesy copy recipients below the body of the memo, delete the notation here.

    e. The word Re, which means "in regard to," may be replaced with the word Subject.

5. Save your memo template with a clear file name, in a convenient place. When using this template to prepare a memo, note three critical points:

    a. As soon as you open the template, save it with a new file name that represents the specific document.

    b. Select all placeholder (original) text and replace it with your message or remove it.

    c. Ensure that all text is the same font and size.

Letter Formats

External reports of one to three pages may be written in letter format. If the report is longer than three pages, it should be written in manuscript format, accompanied by a letter to the receiver.

    Three standard letter formats—block, modified block, and simplified block—are shown in Illustrations 6.5, 6.6, and 6.7, respectively. Notice that the body of each letter

ILLUSTRATION 6.5 BLOCK LETTER FORMAT, OPEN PUNCTUATION

Communications Design Associates

801 JACKSON STREET, WEST	TEL: 312-555-9753
CHICAGO, IL 60607-5511	FAX: 312-555-9750

<Date>

Tap Enter twice

Ms. Taylor Pettas
Communications Director
Pettas Fine Foods
1849 N. Halifax Ave.
Daytona Beach, FL 32018-4421

Dear Ms. Pettas

This letter demonstrates block letter format. In block format, all lines begin at the left margin. No letter parts or paragraphs are indented.

The block format is used extensively in business today. Its efficiency and crisp appearance are pleasing to contemporary business writers.

This letter also demonstrates open punctuation, with no punctuation mark after the greeting or the complimentary closing. Mixed punctuation, with a colon after the greeting and a comma after the closing, may be used. However, use of that punctuation style is declining.

I think this block letter format will be useful for your business reports and correspondence, Ms. Pettas. If you have other questions about report formats, I will discuss them with you and provide illustrations.

Sincerely

Jerri Martino   Tap Enter twice

Jerri Martino
Staff Consultant

ILLUSTRATION 6.6   MODIFIED BLOCK LETTER FORMAT, MIXED PUNCTUATION

Communications Design Associates

801 JACKSON STREET, WEST   TEL: 312-555-9753
CHICAGO, IL 60607-5511   FAX: 312-555-9750

<Date>

Tap Enter twice

Ms. Taylor Pettas
Communications Director
Pettas Fine Foods
1849 N. Halifax Ave.
Daytona Beach, FL 32018-4421

Dear Ms. Pettas:

This letter demonstrates modified block letter format. In this format, the date and the complimentary close begin at the approximate center of the page. The letter address and greeting are placed at the left margin. Paragraphs are usually blocked at the left margin. Paragraphs may be indented a half inch, but contemporary business writers rarely use that style.

The modified block letter format is a more traditional style than is the block format. Companies that wish to project a somewhat conservative image to their clients might consider this style.

This letter also demonstrates mixed punctuation, which uses a colon after the greeting and a comma after the complimentary close. Alternatively, open punctuation, with no punctuation marks after the greeting and close, may be used.

If you have questions about the modified block format, Ms. Pettas, please call me at 1-800-555-7777. I will discuss it with you by phone or in your office.

Sincerely,

Jerri Martino   Tap Enter twice

Jerri Martino
Staff Consultant

ILLUSTRATION 6.7 SIMPLIFIED BLOCK LETTER FORMAT

Communications Design Associates

801 JACKSON STREET, WEST   TEL: 312-555-9753
CHICAGO, IL 60607-5511   FAX: 312-555-9750

May 13, <year>

        Tap Enter twice

Taylor Pettas
Communications Director
Pettas Fine Foods
1849 N. Halifax Ave.
Daytona Beach, FL 32018-4421

SIMPLIFIED BLOCK LETTER FORMAT

This letter demonstrates the simplified block letter format. The format has these features:

- All lines begin at the left margin.

- A subject line replaces the traditional salutation. The subject line may appear in all capital letters or in upper- and lowercase letters. Leave a blank line above and below the subject line.

- The complimentary close is omitted. Only two blank lines separate the writer's name from the letter body. The writer's title or department may be included beside the name, separated from it by a comma or hyphen (note the spaces surrounding it) . This signature block may be keyed in all capital letters or in upper- and lowercase.

Although the simplified block style may be used for any correspondence, it is especially useful when you do not know the receiver's courtesy title. On such occasions, omit a title in the letter address and envelope.

Please let me know what you think of this format. Many of our clients have adopted it as a standard letter format.

Jerri Martino   Tap Enter twice

JERRI MARTINO – STAFF CONSULTANT

explains specific features of its format. As you study the illustrations of letters, notice also the following features that apply to all letters:

1. **Identity of sender.** Every letter must include a letterhead or return address to identify the sender. A well-designed letterhead presents the organization favorably and provides all information needed to communicate with that organization, such as address, telephone number, and fax number. Many companies also include an e-mail address and Web address. *Note:* Letterhead is used only for the first page of a letter. Any additional pages are printed on plain paper of the same color and quality.

   If no letterhead is used, the sender's return address appears first. Depending on letter length, the return address should be placed one to two inches from the top of the page. The return address includes *everything but the writer's name,* which always appears in the signature lines at the end of the letter.

2. **Date of letter.** A letter should always contain the date on which it was written and/or mailed. In addition, the date should always appear in the style shown here—the month spelled in full, followed by the date (cardinal, not ordinal, number), a comma, and four-digit year. When letterhead is used, insert one or two blank lines below the letterhead before typing the date. However, when a return address is used, place the date immediately below that address. (In Word 2010, remove excess space between these text lines, as explained in Item 3.)

   Here are examples of return addresses and dates.

1610 Castle Drive	Rt. 1, Box 50
Byron Center, MI 49315	Edgerton, MN 56128
January 11, <year>	May 18, <year>

3. **Address of receiver.** The letter address (receiver's address) is placed about four lines below the date (tap Enter twice). Since messages going outside an organization tend to be more formal than those moving within, etiquette calls for using a person's courtesy or professional title (if it is known) in a formal letter. Do not, however, include a courtesy title if you do not know the person's gender or a woman's title preference. A position title, placed after the name or on the next line, may also be included. The letter address governs the envelope address—the two must be identical. (If your word processing program places blank lines between these text lines, delete the blanks. In Word 2010, select all lines except the last; then on the Paragraph dialog [Home tab, Paragraph group, down arrow] under Paragraph spacing, change the **After** setting to *0.*)

4. **Greeting.** The letter address also governs the greeting. When a courtesy or professional title appears in the address, it is used in the greeting, *without the individual's first name.* For example, the standard greeting for a letter addressed to Ms. Kimberly Hagood is "Dear Ms. Hagood," not "Dear Kimberly Hagood." An exception to that rule is appropriate when the letter writer knows the reader very well. Then a first-name greeting, such as "Dear Kimberly" or even "Dear Kim," is appropriate. When the address has no courtesy title (for example, K. Hagood) or has only a position title (for example, Marketing Director), you

must choose an alternative to the standard greeting. Popular choices include the following:

- The person's name as given in the address (Dear K. Hagood)
- The position title used in the address, when no name is given (Dear Marketing Director)
- The simplified block format, which omits the greeting (see Illustration 6.7)

Sometimes the first line of the letter address is a company name rather than an individual's name, or a letter may be addressed to a company, followed by an attention line that names a person. These are ideal situations in which to use the simplified block format. Although some writers use an impersonal greeting such as "Ladies and Gentlemen" or "Gentlemen and Ladies," that language seems excessively formal for modern business writing. Considerate writers avoid "Dear Sir" or "Dear Sirs" because those words convey an exclusionary, sexist tone. Avoid, also, the excessively impersonal "To whom it may concern"; that greeting may connote that you do not care who reads the message. Moreover, it shifts the responsibility of determining an appropriate reader from you, the sender, to the receiver.

5. Complimentary close. The complimentary close begins the closing lines. Use a traditional complimentary close, such as *Sincerely yours*. (This particular close is appropriate for any formality level.) Leave a blank line between the letter body and the complimentary close.

6. Signature block. The signature block includes the writer's name and, usually, her or his position title or department affiliation. Vertically align the signature block with the complimentary close. The name and title may appear on the same line (separated by a comma) or on separate lines. Leave two blank lines between the complimentary close and your typed name. Sign the letter (black or blue ink) in this blank area.

7. Envelope. If you are not using a window envelope, you must also prepare an envelope for your letter. The envelope address should be identical to the letter address. The address is blocked beginning at the approximate center of the envelope. The first line should be about halfway down from the top of the envelope. Most word-processing programs have an envelope addressing function that will print the letter address onto an envelope. This function also allows you to print a return address on the envelope if your envelope is not already printed with such an address.

Follow these steps to address an envelope in Microsoft Word 2010:

First, in the Word file, select the letter address. Then click the Mailings tab, Create group, Envelopes.

Next, on the Envelopes and Labels dialog, click the Envelopes tab. (The selected address appears in the Delivery address window.) If necessary, type the sender's address in the Return address box.

Then, click Options and check envelope size and fonts. The standard (long, thin) envelope for business correspondence is Size 10. The delivery address font should be the same font used for the letter; you may apply bold and/or increase the size slightly. The default font and font size is acceptable for the return address (if none, select Omit).

Finally, to insert the envelope into the Word file, click Add to Document. (The envelope becomes page 1 of the Word document; the letter begins on page 2.)

Templates available in Microsoft Word 2010 include letterheads and letters. Most report-writing assignments call for a conservative letterhead, such as Business Level, Essential, Realty Classic, or Traditional Elegance.

Word 2010's letter templates include the formats introduced in this chapter; however, template names refer to message content (Apology letters, Collection letters, Sales letters) rather than letter format. Therefore, you might create your own letter template, using the preferred format. Whether you use a letterhead template or a blank document, you can save your creation as a Word template: Click Save. In the Save As dialog at **File name**, type a file name that identifies the letter format and includes the word *Template*. At **Save as type**, click the down arrow; select Word Template.

Manuscript Formats

Internal or external reports that exceed three pages are generally written in manuscript format. A cover letter or memorandum almost always accompanies such a report, and the report usually has a title page. Illustration 6.8 shows the title page and the first page of a report in manuscript format. Notice that the report discusses and demonstrates the general guides for spacing, typography, emphasis, and headings.

In specialized reporting situations, several additional preliminary or supplementary parts are included in the manuscript. Those components will be discussed in Chapter 16. Other publications, such as brochures, newsletters, and annual reports, also require careful attention to document design.

Direct Formatting in Word 2010

To format a manuscript report, start with a blank Word file. To direct format the manuscript, take these steps to set margins, choose the font, design the paragraphs, and emphasize the headings:

- Set report margins on the Page Layout tab, Page Setup group. First, click Margins and choose an option; or at the bottom edge of the Margins dialog, click Custom Margins. Next, set the desired top, left, bottom, and right margins, then click OK.
- Choose the font for report paragraphs. First, in the Home tab, Font group, click the Font down arrow. Then, in the Font dialog, select the font and size you want as default settings for the report. Next, at the bottom left, click Set As Default and click OK.
- Set paragraph spacing and indentations. First, on the Home tab, Paragraph group, launch the Paragraph dialog (click down arrow). Now, set line spacing at the lower right to fit specifications/preferences. (As you know, common choices include Single, Double, and Multiple At 1.15, but the person who assigned the report may specify a different setting.) Next, on the Paragraph dialog, set the blank space between paragraphs under **Spacing**. (*Suggestions:* Use 0 in a double-spaced report, 10 in a report with line spacing at 1.15, and 12 in a single-spaced report.) If using paragraph indentations, set them at the top right under **Indentation**: Under **Special**, select First line. Under **By**, set the size of the

ILLUSTRATION 6.8 MANUSCRIPT REPORT

Format for Manuscript Reports

Prepared for

Mountain View Industries
13666 E. Bates Avenue
Aurora, CO 80014

Green Mountain Ski Resort

Woodland, VT 05409 (802) 555-3265

Prepared by

KC&S Communication Consultants
Suite 116, Castle Complex
1218 Fairview Road
Denver, CO 80202

(303) 555-9154

January 19, <year>

continued

ILLUSTRATION 6.8 CONTINUED

Format for Manuscript Report

This illustration explains one commonly used format for business reports. Notice these features of the report format: title page, margins, fonts and font styles and sizes, report headings, and spacing.

Title Page

A title page may be used to orient the reader to the report and its writer. The title page should include the report title, for whom the report is written, by whom it is written, and the transmittal date. Optional items are the company logo(s), page borders, and other design elements that suggest the report content or nature of the organization. Notice that this information, arranged in four clusters, is <u>centered horizontally and vertically</u> on the page. Although a title page may be optional in some situations, an inventive design can create a positive first impression. Therefore, choose a format that conveys your professionalism.

Margins

Place the title 1½ to 2 inches from the top of the first page of the report. Use a 1-inch top margin for all remaining pages. If the manuscript is unbound or stapled in the upper left corner, use a 1-inch left margin. For a left-bound manuscript, use a 1.5-inch left margin. (Staple the finished report a half inch from the left edge near the top, middle, and bottom.) Right and bottom margins should be approximately one inch on all pages.

Fonts

Use no more than two fonts in your report. This illustration, for example, uses a sans serif font (Calibri) for the title and headings and a serif font (Cambria) for the report text. It would also be appropriate to use the same serif font for headings and report text. You may use bold and italic sparingly for emphasis. *Note:* As noted previously, you may need to change defaults in your word processing program to meet your reader's expectations.

Spacing

This single-spaced, blocked format is used extensively by contemporary business writers. All paragraphs in this example are single-spaced. (Microsoft Word's 1.15 setting would have a more "open" appearance and may be preferred by some readers.) Use two or three blank lines below the title, with one blank line above and below headings and between paragraphs.

Since some readers prefer a double-spaced format, always try to determine reader preference before completing the final copy of your report. If you use double spacing, tradition calls for indented paragraphs (0.5 inch) and no additional space between paragraphs.

continued

ILLUSTRATION 6.8 CONTINUED

Report Headings

Use headings in any report containing more than one major section. Headings should orient the reader to the report content.

Font style and placement must indicate the relationship of headings and subheadings. Notice that the headings in this report are centered and keyed in identical style. If subheadings were used in any section, they would be keyed and placed to distinguish them from the main headings. For example, subheadings might be placed at the left margin.

Summary

Following these format guides will have two results: (1) a report that invites the receiver to read it and (2) a report that leads the reader effortlessly through its pages.

© Cengage Learning 2013

paragraph indentation. (As noted earlier, indented paragraphs are recommended only for double-spaced paragraphs, and 0.5 inch is the recommended indent.)

- Format report headings in a near-final draft. Begin with Level 1 headings and work on one level at a time. Select the first heading and choose the desired font, font size, and font style (Home tab, Font group) and center the Level 1 heading (Home tab, Paragraph group, click Center). Now, with the first heading still selected, double-click the Format Painter (Home tab, Clipboard group). Then select the next heading at the same level to emphasize it. Repeat these steps until all Level 1 headings look the same. Click Format Painter again. Then format headings at each of the other levels.

You can also change the text format for a portion of a document; for example, a double-spaced report may have a single-spaced section or vice versa. In Word 2010, you would need to insert section breaks in order to make such a change. Follow these steps to insert a section break:

1. Click the Page Layout tab; then click Breaks.
2. Select Continuous if you want the different format to take effect on the current page or choose Next Page.
3. Make the desired text format changes on the Home tab in the Paragraph dialog. At the upper left, under **Indentation**, click the arrows to increase (up arrow) or decrease (down arrow) margin width.
4. After typing the differentiated text, insert another section break to revert to your original text format. (If you decide the differentiated text should match the text above it, delete the section break in Draft view: Click View, Document Views group, Draft. Select the section break that you want to delete; press Delete on the keyboard.)

Microsoft Word Styles

Direct formatting works for a short report with one or two heading levels. For longer, more complex reports, though, Microsoft Word's built-in Styles may save you time and effort and minimize formatting flaws. Styles allow you to format major elements quickly in your document, such as headings, titles, and subtitles.

To apply Quick Styles to the text in your report, select the text you want to format. On the Home tab, Styles group, point to any style to see a preview in your document. Click an appropriate style to apply it to your text. *Note:* If you decide you want headings to look different, you can change Heading 1 and Heading 2 styles, and Word will automatically update all instances of them in your report.

You can also apply a different Style Set or a different Theme to change the look of the headings without changing the basic styles. Style sets and themes include graphic elements, such as horizontal lines and shading colors to highlight headings.

To apply a style set, on the Home tab, Styles group, click the Change Styles down arrow. Then point to Style Set and choose an option, such as Formal, Modern, or Simple, from the menu.

To apply a theme, on the Page Layout tab, Themes group, click Themes. Now, from the Built-In dialog, choose one of the 40 themes available in Word or one of the 13 provided at Office.com. Notice that you can change theme colors, fonts, or effects while keeping the selected theme.

Principles of Document Design

You can enhance your report-writing efficiency by resolving some aspects of report format before you begin writing. These guidelines can help you successfully format your report:

- Choose a simple, functional format. You will impress readers most by providing just the information they need in a way that makes it easy for them to find and understand it. An overly elaborate design may give readers the impression that you did not pay enough attention to the content.
- Weigh the value of additions such as a glossary of terms carefully. Add something only if you can justify it on the basis of functionality. For example, if your report contains only a few words that need to be defined, put the definitions in the text. On the other hand, if you use many terms that may be unfamiliar to some of your readers, a glossary is a helpful addition.
- Plan for visuals. While planning your report, look for places where visuals can help explain the points. Instead of giving an array of statistics in your text, turn them into tables and charts. Chapter 5 describes several Microsoft Office tools that make it easy to integrate visuals into your text.
- Know what decisions you can or may make. Your company, for example, may already have a standard format for memos, letters, and manuscripts. You may be expected to use certain templates in Microsoft Word 2010 so that documents in a series look alike; or if someone has adapted or created a template for reports like the one you are writing, you may be expected to use it.

You have already studied general guides for spacing, fonts, emphasis techniques, and the use of headings in reports. As you design any document, you must attend also to page layout and graphics.

Guides for Page Layout

The design of a document should reflect its purpose, content, and intended audience. The annual report of a small nonprofit agency will differ considerably from the annual report of a major for-profit corporation. Since the design of a document will be influenced by funds budgeted for the project and the perceived reading level of the recipients, many experts suggest that you plan a document's layout before you compose the contents. You must decide how many pages will be included, the size of paper you will use, and how the document will be bound or folded.

You should begin with a sketch of how you want the finished document to appear. A useful technique is to sketch the contents on paper by blocking areas for headings, text, and visuals. This sketch will help you plan page layout for effective visual impact. Illustration 6.9 contains a sketch for a four-page newsletter to be printed front and back on 17-inch × 11-inch paper that will be folded in the center, creating an 8.5-inch × 11-inch finished document.

Criteria for effective page design include balance, consistency, contrast, focus, and proportion.

- Balance—visual harmony of top, bottom, and side margins as well as placement of text and graphics on a page. To achieve visual balance and compensate for optical illusion, the bottom margin should be slightly larger than the top margin.

ILLUSTRATION 6.9 NEWSLETTER PAGE LAYOUT

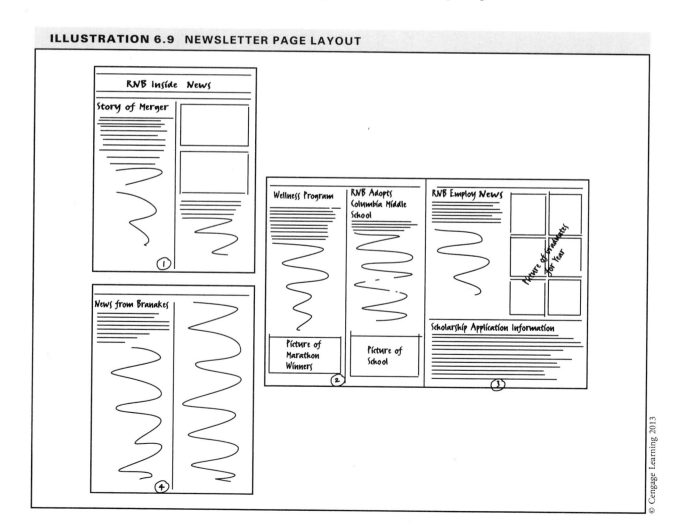

- Consistency—harmony of fonts, font styles, font sizes, heading structure, and visuals. You can mix these elements sparingly and still achieve consistency in appearance.
- Contrast—use of blank space, shaded areas, and visuals in documents. Use contrast techniques to relieve visual tedium.
- Focus—methods used to attract reader attention. Focusing techniques include placement of visuals; emphasis techniques, such as bold, italics, underline, ALL CAPS, and bullets or numbering; and use of color.
- Proportion—relationship of font size in headings and text, the relationship of the size of a visual to the surrounding text, and the relationship of text and blank space. The most important information should have more space assigned to it than the least important information.

As you plan your page layout, follow these guides:

- Allow sufficient blank space. Some experts suggest that 20 percent to 25 percent of a page should be reserved for blank space (margins, above and below headings, between paragraphs, etc.).
- Use text lines that are comfortable for the eye to follow. In a newsletter, for example, aim for 40 to 50 characters per line. Lines that are too short or too long are difficult to read. For a newsletter, this guide suggests that on a page 8.5 inches wide, two or three columns will be more readable than one or four columns.
- Use slightly uneven right margins, which are easier to read than justified (perfectly even) right margins and create a "friendly" appearance. However, the Hyphenation feature should be on so that long words divide automatically at line endings. With justified (perfectly even) right margins, extra spaces are placed between some words; those spaces tend to distract readers and may disrupt the sentence flow.
- Rank the importance of each article. This ranking will help you place material effectively. The most important article or lead story should be placed at the dominant center of visual interest, usually the top left corner of a page. The next most important article should be placed at a secondary center of visual interest, such as at the top right corner, bottom left corner, or bottom center of a page.

Note: In Microsoft Word 2010, more than 60 newsletter templates include some for families and schools in addition to business templates. Cost of producing newsletters from the templates would vary since some examples involve only small shaded areas, while others involve large areas shaded in multiple colors.

Guides for Text

In addition to the guides for fonts given earlier in this chapter, here are some guides to help you plan attractive, readable text:

- Use one *serif* font for content. Serif fonts are more legible because the serifs visually link letters into words.
- Use one *sans serif* font for headings. Those fonts tend to attract the reader's attention.
- Use font styles purposefully to achieve desired emphasis.

- In brochures and pamphlets, use a font size from 9 to 12 points for text. Smaller type sizes are acceptable for footnotes and explanatory comments; larger type is recommended for titles and headings.
- Limit the different type sizes on a single page to six or fewer.
- Use uppercase and lowercase characters (not all uppercase) for text and most headings. When a document has more than one level of heading, some writers use all uppercase characters for the first-level heading.

Guides for Visuals

Word-processing software enables you to integrate visuals with text. In formal written reports, writers often use the introduce-display-discuss technique of incorporating visual aids into reports (described in Chapter 5). With that technique, you first write a statement that highlights a major point the reader should see in the visual, then display the visual and follow it with an interpretive discussion. That strategy is effective for many documents. However, some kinds of writing, such as brochures, newsletters, and annual reports, may benefit from other placement techniques. In those documents, a graphic should be placed where it is most likely to attract reader attention. Visuals can be displayed above, surrounded by, or below related text. Here are some guides for using visuals effectively in promotional materials.

- Keep the number of graphic elements small enough to stand out. A good guide is to use no more than two visuals on an 8.5-inch × 11-inch page.
- Use sufficient blank space around a visual to optimize impact.
- Keep the hierarchy of importance clear. Place the most important visual where it will gain the most attention.
- Consider eye movement when placing visuals on a page. For instance, a profile picture of a person should be placed so that the person is looking into the page rather than off the side of the page.
- When a picture is too large for the space, cut (crop) unnecessary parts from the visual. For example, a picture of a person standing may be cropped to show only the person's head and shoulders.
- When a visual such as clip art or a chart is too large or too small for the space allotted, scale the visual in both height and width. Scaling the visual in one direction only will distort the appearance and sometimes the meaning conveyed by the item.

Illustration 6.10 contrasts a cluttered, inappropriate use of visuals with a balanced, purposeful, focused use of visuals.

Collaborative Writing

Early planning efforts for a group project typically focus on group processes and task requirements. Group members must become acquainted with one another and identify individuals' strengths, weaknesses, work styles, and so on. The group must also clarify the objective of the group project, the kinds of tasks that must be completed to reach a successful conclusion, and individual responsibilities for those tasks. Decisions about the

ILLUSTRATION 6.10 CLUTTERED AND UNCLUTTERED PAGE LAYOUT

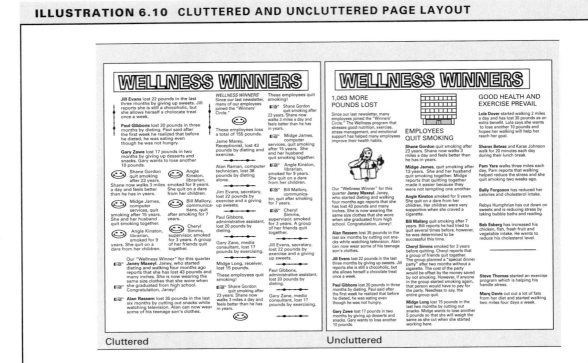

Cluttered

Uncluttered

© Cengage Learning 2013

"deliverable"—the document that must be delivered—are often postponed until late in the collaborative process.

However, postponing decisions about matters related to writing style and format—spacing, fonts, emphasis techniques, headings, page layout, and use of visuals—tends to lead to extra work or inferior quality when individual contributions must be merged. In several places, the chapter notes the importance of consistent format to show readers how each section fits into a report. Since default settings can vary even between different versions of the same word-processing product (e.g., MS Word 2007 and MS Word 2010) and predefined styles can help collaborators with format consistency, it's vital that everyone begins "on the same page" with respect to these matters. It is especially helpful for all group members to share their knowledge of formatting and computer tools that will help the group design and produce a professional-looking document.

Ethical Considerations

Computer technology assists you with more than document design and format. As you progress in your report-writing responsibilities, you will use the computer increasingly to acquire and disseminate data. The capability of technology to provide access to vast amounts of information and to transmit it to a large number of people creates ethical responsibilities in four areas: privacy, ownership, accuracy, and accessibility.[1]

Privacy

Knowledgeable technicians can freely access large amounts of confidential data. Some people are tempted to invade another person's privacy to get information, share it, or tamper with it.

Of particular concern today are the vast amounts of employee and customer information maintained in corporate data banks. In fact, identity theft has become a major privacy and security concern. Most U.S. colleges have discontinued use of Social Security numbers for student identification because of the risks associated with unauthorized use of such numbers. Communicating private or confidential information by e-mail or on websites—including social networking sites—could be extremely damaging to individuals and organizations.

Ownership

Laws are relatively clear about taking someone else's copyrighted material, but the issue of how much electronic modification may legally occur is still being decided. Entering a database or electronic file to obtain, manipulate, or change information that does not belong to you or for which you do not have authorization is equivalent to theft or burglary. The unauthorized copying or pirating of commercial software is illegal as well. In addition, intentionally damaging an electronic file by introducing a virus is a federal offense.

The issue of who owns software, text, images, sound, and video has caused many organizations to take an aggressive stance when protecting themselves and their products. Surprise visits by "software police" representing the industry's trade association have increased as the battle over piracy has intensified. In recent years, colleges and copy services have been charged with copyright infringement because they included copyrighted materials on course websites and in course packages. College students have also been penalized for using college computer connections to download or share music by their favorite artists.

Accuracy

Legal rulings have upheld that the publisher of material, whether hard copy or electronic, is responsible for the accuracy of the content. However, an inexpensive scanner can duplicate images from a variety of sources at minimal cost. Photographs, drawings, and designs can be scanned easily and quickly into a computer, modified slightly, and claimed as one's own work. The effect of appropriating and modifying the work of other people has the potential for profound personal and corporate damage. If the data are altered, the potential for damage increases because responsibility for accuracy may be hard to pinpoint.

Accessibility

Because computers allow storage of vast amounts of information, it becomes increasingly important to consider the types of information to which organizations are entitled, the conditions under which they might obtain information, and the safeguards in place to protect all individuals' rights. Access to databases, whether internal or external to the organization, must be protected to prevent access by information hijackers or software viruses.

Other accessibility issues arise. For example, should employees be able to use their company computers for personal benefit or to access other employees' computer files that are not password protected? The city manager of Columbia, South Carolina, lost her job several years ago after one of her computer files was accessed, which contained potentially offensive comments about certain employees whom she supervised. She asserted that the file was merely her form of brainstorming about a personnel matter. Should she have been protected from the employee who accessed her file? Should she have used the office computer for recording her unique, personal way of thinking through a personnel issue? Did she violate the privacy of the individuals mentioned in her file?

A final issue involves cost. Since organizations pay a fee to access databases or the Internet, should everyone have access to the information or only those whose work is deemed to require it? Should employees be permitted to use those resources for personal benefit during "off" hours?

Clearly, the arguments involving privacy, ownership, accuracy, and accessibility have yet to fully unfold. Competent communicators use their technical knowledge and ability to access information to achieve their goals while acting in an ethical manner.

Summary

An effectively formatted report enhances the report's contents. Whether presented as a letter, memo, or manuscript, the format must entice the recipient to read the report, lead the reader effortlessly through the report, and maintain the reader's interest.

When you are unsure of the reader's preferences regarding report format, you should attempt to determine what will please that reader. If you cannot determine a specific reader's preferences, the guides given in this chapter can help you produce an attractive, reader-friendly report.

Topics for Discussion

1. What spacing guides should you apply to your reports? Compare spacing guides in this chapter with any reports you prepared for school or work and analyze the differences.
2. What guides concerning fonts should you apply to your reports? Compare font guides in this chapter with those you applied in the past and cite three differences.
3. What cautions about emphasis techniques should you observe in your reports?
4. What should guide your use of headings in reports?
5. Identify three commonly used formats for written reports and indicate circumstances in which each would be used.
6. Compare and/or contrast the block, modified block, and simplified block letter formats with respect to these letter parts:
   - Date of letter
   - Letter address
   - Greeting
   - Letter body
   - Complimentary close

7. In business letters in block or modified block format, why is it important to use a traditional rather than a modern greeting and complimentary close and the traditional open or mixed punctuation of these parts?

8. Give an appropriate formal and informal greeting (or other option) for each of these letter addresses:
   - R. S. French, III, 187 Ocean Drive, Jacksonville, FL 32217-1234
   - Director, Office of Consumer Affairs, State of Arizona, P.O. Box 16650, Tucson, AZ 85732-5678
   - Mrs. Jennie Wilson, 755 Camille Lane, Chicago, IL 60643-0910
   - Kites for Tikes, Attn. Customer Services, 808 Dayton Street, Indianapolis, IN 46204-1112
   - Mr. and Mrs. Jeremy Dreise, 1112 Prairie View, Sioux Center, IA 51250-1314
   - Dori Carter and Will Jordan, 227 Esplanade Drive, Dallas, TX 75220-1516

9. Format and print an appropriate envelope address for each of the items in discussion topic 8, using the envelope template or mailing function in your word-processing program.

10. Identify guides to follow as you lay out pages for a newsletter or brochure.

11. Identify guides to follow as you plan placement of visuals in a document.

12. Describe word-processing features that will help you achieve an effective report format. Specifically, describe features that are available in the word processing program you work with most frequently. *Note:* If that program is Microsoft Word 2010, identify features not included in this chapter.

13. Discuss ways in which you can contribute to a group's decisions about document design and format.

14. Discuss the ethical responsibilities you should exercise as you use word-processing software and the Internet in the reporting process. Add issues you perceive in addition to those presented in this chapter.

Applications

1. Study the format and typography of Illustration for Application 1 on page 178. Identify inconsistencies and necessary changes to bring it up to contemporary standards.
   a. Reproduce the letter in block format, using open punctuation. Save the file.
   b. Save the file in Application 1a with a new file name. Then change the letter format to modified block, using mixed punctuation.
   c. Using a letter template in your word-processing program, reproduce this letter.

2. Visually compare the letters produced in Application 1. Applying the guides for document design and report formats given in this chapter, decide which letter format you prefer. In a letter to your instructor, report your decision and give your reasons.

3. Return to Chapter 2, Application 1, in which you were asked to plan eight reports. As directed by your instructor, write one or more of those reports, using an appropriate structure, style, and format.

ILLUSTRATION FOR APPLICATION 6.1

July 3, <year>

Teranne Babcock
Vice President
Integrated Management Systems, Inc.
P.O. Box 10
Charlotte, NC 28223-0010

Dear Mrs. Babcock,

As you requested in our initial meeting, we have researched the feasibility of introducing IMSI products into the Canadian life insurance market. Our macro and micro analyses were based on your initial specified parameters: environment, market potential, and competition.

Based on our analysis, we offer these conclusions:

- Canada's strong economy and current market trends justify IMSI's entry into the Canadian market.

- IMSI should target medium and large life insurance companies with a single product, IMSI-Life.

- Initial market strategy should focus on developing partnerships with two Canadian life insurance companies to minimize cost of market entry.

The research team will present a full oral report to you on July 13 at 10 a.m. in your Charlotte office. At that time, we will also give you a comprehensive written report of our research.

Igor Jakovich, Team Leader

4. Assume that the laptop (notebook) computer you use in your work-related travel no longer meets your needs. The computer performs well for word-processing, spreadsheet, and presentation applications. However, it has a battery life of only 2.5 hours, only one USB port, and an Ethernet port and 56k modem instead of wireless Internet connection. Determine the features you would prefer in a laptop computer. Consult computer sellers' websites, a current newspaper, or a computer catalog to discover the specifications and price of a laptop that meets your requirements. Write a memo to your supervisor, H. J. Cooper, requesting a new laptop (notebook) computer. Be prepared to justify your message content and structure, writing style, and format.

5. In a *New York Times* article (January 21, 2011), Christine Negroni focused on unsafe practices involving laser pointers, such as those used during slide

presentations. Noting the availability of laser pointers powerful enough to cause eye damage in a microsecond, she reported over 2,800 instances in 2010 of laser pointers aimed at airborne planes. Ms. Negroni's article also cited a Federal Aviation Administration official saying that "a ban on lasers or other regulations might be needed...." Read at least one newspaper or magazine article about this issue. (Online publications are acceptable but avoid blogs and other social media in this situation). In a memo to your instructor, give your stance on banning or regulating laser pointers and explain your reasons.

6. Rising food costs have forced college dining halls to implement cost-cutting measures. Some colleges have removed trays from their cafeterias, thinking that if students cannot load a tray, they will take only the food they are prepared to eat, thereby reducing waste. Other colleges have begun to substitute cheaper products, such as refined-grain pasta for whole-grain pasta and chicken thighs for chicken breasts in some recipes. Read at least one article on the rising cost of food products and how dining services are dealing with the issue of cutting costs while maintaining quality. *Note:* Besides newspapers, magazines, and a key word search of the Web, consider these article databases: Articlesbase (http://www.articlesbase.com), HighBeam Research (http://www.highbeam.com), and GoArticles (http://goarticles.com). Select two practices that your college could implement to reduce the cost of operating its cafeterias. Report your findings in a memo to your instructor.

7. Bonnie Gregory drives a company car, which is replaced every two years. At replacement time, the employee has the option of buying the car at 50 percent of its current book value. The limitation is that the car must be purchased for use by the employee or someone in the employee's immediate family. Bonnie wants to buy a car for her 16-year-old son. Although her car has been maintained well, it has nearly 95,000 miles on it, and Bonnie is unsure that she wants to buy that one. Her colleague, Gerry Barber, is also due to get a new company vehicle, but he is not interested in buying his old one. Bonnie wants to buy Barber's car instead of hers. As Bonnie Gregory, determine the book value of her current company vehicle (make reasonable assumptions about make, model, year, and condition) and of her coworker's (again make appropriate assumptions but make it a better vehicle). Write a report to her supervisor, A. L. Cain, providing the details about each car and requesting that Bonnie be permitted to buy Gerry Barber's car. Be prepared to defend your choice of content, structure, style, and format.

8. As the owner of Tranquility Day Spa, you want to sponsor a benefit for a local nonprofit agency. (Choose a local nonprofit agency that interests you.) Your plan is to give the agency 50 percent of all revenues you take in on September 29. That percentage represents your entire profit; the balance goes to cover supplies, overhead, and salaries. You want to suggest that your staff (massage therapists, aestheticians, nail technicians, hair stylists, etc.) make a contribution also. Write a memo to the staff suggesting that they donate all tips received that day. Include enough information about the agency to motivate the staff to comply with your suggestion. Be prepared to defend your choice of content, structure, style, and format.

9. In recent years, lending institutions have been promoting reverse mortgages to elderly people. Read at least one newspaper or magazine article about the pros and cons of reverse mortgages. In a letter report to an elderly person whom you know, present the advantages and disadvantages of such a financial product, along with your recommendation to that person.

10. Your local Chamber of Commerce, which is revising its tourism brochure, has asked your instructor for help. Your instructor convinced the Chamber CEO, Ike Voehringer, to sponsor a contest in which students will write and prepare the brochure. The writer(s) of the winning entry will receive $500 and be honored at the Chamber's annual awards banquet.

   The first phase of the contest is to write descriptions of three major attractions in your city. Limit the description of each attraction to a maximum of 350 words. You are allowed a total of 1,000 words. The Chamber will provide pictures to supplement the winning copy.

   Collect appropriate information, then outline, draft, and revise your description. Remember, at this time you do not have to prepare the brochure, only the text that will be used in a brochure. Prepare the report in manuscript format. Include a title page and a cover letter, addressed to Mr. Voehringer (assume an appropriate address).

   With your instructor's permission, you may collaborate with one or two classmates to complete this application and Application 11.

11. Assume that the content for the brochure in Application 10 has been approved. Now plan and compose the brochure. Remember: You are trying to win a $500 prize.

12. Obtain a copy of a corporate annual report. Critically analyze the style and format of the report, using the guides presented in this chapter. Present your analysis to your instructor in a report prepared in manuscript format.

13. Obtain a copy of a newsletter or annual report of a local nonprofit agency. Considering the likely audience, critically analyze the style and format of the document, using the guides presented in this chapter. Identify both the strengths and the weaknesses of the document and present your analysis, along with suggestions for improvements, in a manuscript report. Write a letter addressed to the agency's executive director to accompany the report.

Reference

1. Hershel, R. R., & Hayes, P. H. (1997, April). Ethical implications of technological advances on business communication. *Journal of Business Communication*, 34(2), 160–170.

CHAPTER 7

Writing Routine Reports

LEARNING OBJECTIVES

After you have read this chapter, you should be able to:

1.   Describe the nature and purpose of routine reports.

2.   Identify frequently used routine reports.

3.   Produce routine reports in appropriate structures and formats.

4.   Describe videoconferencing and Web conferencing and related business meeting technologies.

YOU WILL WRITE AND RECEIVE many kinds of simple reports during your career. A simple report (sometimes called a short report) does not require an extensive search for the necessary information. In many instances you will recall from memory the principal data for the report. In other situations you may refer to minutes of meetings, data from files, notes written during an experience or observation, or messages given to you by other employees or clients.

Although the data-gathering method may be relatively simple, the resulting report is still a significant element in your organization's decision-making process. Your job performance and career advancement will certainly be influenced by simple reports—those written by others and those that you write.

Simple reports can be further classified as routine and nonroutine reports. A *routine* report is one that you will be expected to prepare as a part of your normal work assignment. Its purpose is to keep people informed of how you are accomplishing your regular duties. A weekly production report is an example of a routine report. That report and others are demonstrated in this chapter.

In contrast, a *nonroutine* report deals with an occurrence that is an exception to your daily activities and responsibilities. For example, you may be permitted to grant a potentially lucrative customer a larger-than-normal discount on an initial order. However, since that is not the normal sales procedure, you would likely write an exception report to notify your supervisor of your actions. Chapter 8 presents that type of report and other nonroutine reports.

Typical Routine Reports

To illustrate every kind of report you will encounter is impossible; but the examples that follow illustrate the most common routine reports used in contemporary businesses: form reports, trip reports, production reports, progress reports, and meeting reports.

Form Reports

When an organization requires frequent reporting of the same categories of information, efficiency may be gained by developing a standard form for that report. For example, most health insurance companies send reports to the insured parties indicating how a claim for payment of medical services has been processed. Since an insurance company processes many such claims each day and reports standard categories of information to its customers, using a standard form expedites the reporting process. Illustration 7.1 demonstrates such a form report. Other kinds of reports that may be simplified by the use of a well-designed form are reports related to sales and production, repairs or use of equipment and vehicles, and activity on delivery routes.

Trip Reports

Your career responsibilities will often require that you travel away from your home base for a number of reasons: to attend a convention or trade show, to observe activities at another work site, to interview a potential employee, to sell your company's products or services, and so on. When your supervisor authorizes your travel, that person will be accountable for your time and expenses. Therefore, the supervisor needs information to evaluate whether the company benefits from your travel. The purpose of a trip report is to provide that information.

A trip report should be brief and factual. Although you may comment about the value of the trip, do not clutter the message with personal reflections about the good— or bad—time you had. Provide complete, clear, well-organized information that will permit the supervisor to draw conclusions or take action. Appropriate style and structure for a trip report are demonstrated in Illustration 7.2. Notice that the report uses a concise but complete subject line, topical structure, headings that clearly identify the topics, and a concrete request for response. Other structures, such as a chronological or log structure, could also be appropriate in some circumstances. Many companies use a standard form for reporting trip activities and requesting reimbursement for travel expenses.

Production Reports

Most jobs require periodic reports about individual or group performance—production reports. Sales representatives, supervisors of manufacturing units, service technicians, and some office employees may be required to submit daily or weekly production reports. Other employees, such as insurance claims examiners, college professors, librarians, or loan officers may prepare production reports less frequently—monthly, quarterly, or annually. The closest that some employees come to preparing a production report is the completion of a self-evaluation before a formal performance appraisal; nonetheless, that is also a production report.

ILLUSTRATION 7.1   FORM REPORT TO INSURANCE CLIENT

*L*inden

HEALTH INSURANCE, INC.
4361 STATE STREET
MARION, IN 46952
(317) 555-6580

I.D. Number: 371-14-2209
Patient Name: Thomas Svenson
Relationship: Spouse
Group Number: 002036590
Claim Number: 718941593
Date of Notice: 07/14/2013
Date of Service: 07/08/2013

Policyholder:

Lorraine Svenson
116 Varsity Drive
South Bend, IN 46322

Explanation of Benefits THIS IS NOT A BILL

Service Provider	Date of Service	Amount Charged	Noncovered Amount/Reason		Covered Amount	Copayment	Amount Paid
Bailey Phys. Partners Medical Services	10/11/2013	846.00	471.00	01	375.00	75.00	300.00

Total health benefits paid for this person this benefit period:	797.80	The payment for this claim has been sent to the provider	300.00
Lifetime Health Benefits Paid for this person to date:	9,338.10	Balance due to provider	546.00

Remarks:

01 This amount exceeds the maximum allowable benefit for this service.

ILLUSTRATION 7.2 TRIP REPORT IN MEMO FORMAT

DATE: April 13, 2013

TO: Michael Dreyer

FROM: Noah Isaacs

SUBJECT: Inspection Trip, McNabb Project, April 12, 2013

As you requested, I went to Chesapeake yesterday to inspect the McNabb project and investigate why it has fallen behind schedule. Here is what I learned.

Construction Quality

All completed phases of the project meet our quality standards. Invoices and samples of materials indicate that building materials meet the specifications set forth in our RFPs. Files in the construction office contain reports from local building inspectors showing that requirements of local codes have been met.

Construction Delays

Several factors contributed to construction delays during the past two months:

1. The supplier who was awarded the contract for plumbing supplies initially delivered substandard materials. The construction chief, David Bowen, insisted on the quality specified in the contract. Those materials were delivered two weeks later.

2. Since our policy is to pay skilled-labor crews only when they are actually on the job, Bowen could not pay the plumbing crew while waiting for the materials. Consequently, that crew moved to another construction project.

3. Because of the high demand for and low supply of skilled-labor crews in the Chesapeake area, we lost another week while Bowen tried to hire a new plumbing crew. Naturally, some phases of construction could not be completed until the basic plumbing system was installed.

Requests

Bowen asks that he be authorized to pay skilled-labor crews for up to one week of waiting time when delays are caused by shortages of materials. He acknowledges that weather-related delays are normally considered an occupational hazard for which construction crews are not compensated. But in a tight labor market, we risk losing good crews if we refuse to pay them for other delays.

continued

ILLUSTRATION 7.2 CONTINUED

Michael Dreyer   -2-   April 13, 2013

Additional Information

I have reminded Bowen that he must immediately report the failure of suppliers to meet bid specifications. If he had reported the supplier's actions earlier, perhaps we could have transferred plumbing materials from other projects or put pressure on the supplier to fulfill the contract terms promptly.

I also asked Bowen to submit a monthly progress report detailing what has been completed, problems encountered, and any other information that will help us work with him to meet project goals.

Request for Response

I promised Bowen that I'd give him an answer before April 30 about paying crews for waiting time. Please let me know your decision.

A production report is important employee-to-manager feedback. The purpose of such a report is to let a manager or supervisor know whether individual employees or work units are meeting performance goals. The report usually identifies quantities and units of production (for example, customers contacted, items manufactured, loans closed, claims processed, etc.) during an identified time period. Comments about the production experience, such as difficulties encountered or successes enjoyed, are also appropriate. Many production reports also include a work plan or objectives for the next period. Those kinds of information help managers evaluate an individual employee's contributions to the organization's success. The report may tell the manager that all is well and no intervention is needed, or the report may provide evidence that potential or immediate problems require the manager's intervention or assistance.

A typical production report is demonstrated in Illustration 7.3. Notice that the report form clearly identifies the kind of information the manager needs. The report could have been prepared in memo format if the company had not designed a form. A production report in memo format is shown in Illustration 7.4.

Although most production reports flow from subordinates to superiors, supervisors or managers may also send production reports to their subordinates. These reports are often summaries of the unit's production and may be sent to bolster the morale of a unit with evidence of its accomplishments. An example of a supervisor-to-employees production report is shown in Illustration 7.5. Since the primary purpose of the report is to enhance morale, an informal style and medium—email—are appropriate.

ILLUSTRATION 7.3   FORM PRODUCTION REPORT

FAST TRACK DELIVERIES

Sales Representative: _____Powell Henderson_____

Rep. Number: ____103_____   District: _____7_____

Month: ____April_____   Date Submitted: _____5/1/2013_____

New Clients

    Prospects contacted   ___63___

    New clients from those contacts   ___19___

    Total pickups   ___123___

    Total deliveries   ___51___

    Total revenues related to new clients $2,740.50

Current Clients

    Total pickups   ___326___

    Total deliveries   ___215___

    Total revenues from current clients $8,520.75

    Total revenues for month $11,261.25

Plans for Next Month (Use additional pages if needed.)

The increasing volume of pickups and deliveries restricts the amount of time I can spend calling on prospective clients. I plan to hire a driver to handle most of the pickup and delivery work. I hope to have someone on the job by May 15.

    My goal for May is to add a minimum of 30 new clients and retain those currently using our services. With an assistant to handle the pickups and deliveries, I will have more time to contact potential clients and make follow-up calls on current users.

ILLUSTRATION 7.4 PRODUCTION REPORT IN MEMO FORMAT

Date: May 1, 2013

To: Kira McKimson

From: Powell Henderson, Agent No. 103

Subject: Sales and Delivery Activity, April 2013

By targeting new clients and providing prompt service to established clients, I have been able to increase revenues in my territory by approximately 33 percent in April. Here is a summary of my activity:

New Clients

Prospects contacted	63	
New clients from those contacts	19	
Total pickups	123	
Total deliveries	51	
Total revenues related to new clients		$2,740.50

Established Clients

Total pickups	326	
Total deliveries	215	
Total revenues from established clients		$8,520.75
Total Revenues		$11,261.25

Plans for May 2013

The increasing volume of pickups and deliveries restricts the amount of time I can spend calling on prospective clients. I plan to hire a driver to handle most of the pickup and delivery work. I hope to have someone on the job by May 15.

My goal for May is to add a minimum of 30 new clients and retain those currently using our services. With an assistant to handle the pickups and deliveries, I will have more time to contact potential clients and make follow-up calls on current users.

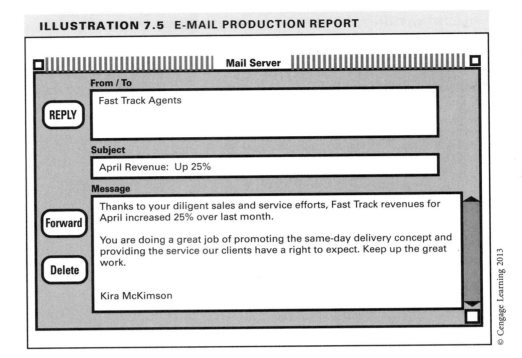

ILLUSTRATION 7.5 E-MAIL PRODUCTION REPORT

Mail Server

From / To

Fast Track Agents

REPLY

Subject

April Revenue: Up 25%

Message

Thanks to your diligent sales and service efforts, Fast Track revenues for April increased 25% over last month.

Forward

You are doing a great job of promoting the same-day delivery concept and providing the service our clients have a right to expect. Keep up the great work.

Delete

Kira McKimson

© Cengage Learning 2013

Progress Reports

A progress report is similar to a production report. However, a progress report is related to a major—usually one-time—project. In some organizations, this report is called a status report.

Progress reports must include all information needed by the manager to evaluate whether the project will be completed as planned. Such information could include the current status and projected completion dates of the entire project or parts of it. Accomplishments since the last report, difficulties encountered (if any), difficulties anticipated (if any), and budget data are also appropriate content for a progress report. Some contracts for major projects provide that a penalty will be assessed if the project is not completed as scheduled. In such instances a progress report is an important tool to ensure that penalties are not incurred for failure to meet scheduled completion dates.

Progress reports are production messages that must be written in a style, structure, and format that permit the manager to learn quickly what is happening on a project for which the manager is accountable. Study the content, style, structure, format, and tone of the progress report in Illustration 7.6. That report demonstrates a combination structure: direct (deductive), topical, and chronological.

Meeting Reports

Much of an organization's business is conducted in face-to-face or electronically mediated meetings. These sessions may range from the meeting of a project team, a

ILLUSTRATION 7.6 PROGRESS REPORT IN MEMO FORMAT

DATE: May 31, 2013

TO: Frederick Cox, VP, Medical Affairs

FROM: Chao-chen Yang, Operations Manager

SUBJECT: Progress on Improving Efficiency of Emergency Room Procedures

We are well on the road to improving the efficiency of emergency room procedures here at City Central Hospital.

Tasks Completed

During the past three months we have established the foundation for improving procedures in the emergency room. Specifically, we have:

- Held meetings with key members of the emergency room staff to inform them of our plans to study our current operations with a goal of reducing patients' wait time.

- Contracted with LeQuire and Associates to study our emergency room procedures and apply current operations and supply chain theory to an analysis of our ER operations.

- Enabled researchers from LeQuire and Associates to observe emergency room procedures and access hospital records related to patient processing time.

- Received a written report from LeQuire and Associates, along with an oral briefing of the findings and recommendations. A major finding was that 85 percent of the problems encountered in moving patients through the ER were related to administrative bottlenecks, not to competencies of doctors and nurses.

- Obtained budget approval for five Patient Flow Coordinators (PFCs) and started recruiting for those positions.

Recommendations for Improving ER Efficiency

LeQuire made two major recommendations:

- Assign each incoming patient to a PFC immediately upon the patient's entering the ER facility. The PFCs will track patients from start to finish through admission, diagnosis, and treatment. This tracking system should ensure that patients are moved through the system more rapidly and also reassure patients that they have not been forgotten.

continued

ILLUSTRATION 7.6 CONTINUED

Frederick Cox   -2-   May 31, 2013

- Require medical personnel to use checklists for procedures (much like those used by airline pilots before they start a jetliner's engines) to ensure that all protocols are followed. The discipline and efficiency of using such a checklist should improve the speed and quality of ER services.

Problems Encountered

Although ER personnel generally favored employing Patient Flow Coordinators, some objected to completing the checklist. However, LeQuire consultants were able to demonstrate the advantages of using a checklist to speed up the diagnosis and treatment process. ER personnel are now on board with that recommended change in operations.

Target Dates for Remainder of Project

We plan to have our patient flow coordination plan fully operational on July 1, the beginning of the next fiscal year. That timing will enable us to do an effective cost-benefit analysis after one year of operation. Specific targets are:

June 15	Complete hiring of Patient Flow Coordinators
June 20	Complete training of PFCs
June 21–25	Conduct trial run of new flow system, including use of checklists by medical personnel
June 25–29	Identify and implement any changes resulting from trial run
June 30	Have all procedures in place and personnel confident about their use

Additional Information

Beginning with five PFCs will enable us to maintain a flexible schedule that will get us through the various ebbs and flows of ER traffic. The ER will be staffed at all times by a minimum of two PFCs; during the busiest days and seasons, it will by staffed by five. That number will be evaluated after three months to determine whether five PFCs are sufficient to handle the heaviest loads. If necessary, we will request budget approval to increase the number.

With the system operating smoothly, we should be able to process more patients through the ER than we have been handling in the past, with a considerable reduction in patient wait time. All indications are that the added cost of the PFCs will be recouped as the ER sees more patients.

City Central has already garnered some favorable publicity about our attempts to improve patient flow in the ER. LeQuire projects that the new procedures will enable us to cut the average time from admission to treatment by half. We intend to keep precise records and evaluate the system's effectiveness every three months.

standing committee, or an ad hoc committee within a company to a major assemblage of members of a professional or trade association. In all cases, the meeting organizer or chairperson is responsible for informing participants—and often company managers—of upcoming activities and results of the meetings. The most common tools for communicating such information are the agenda and minutes.

Meeting Agenda

An agenda provides potential participants with the information needed to prepare effectively for a meeting. A complete agenda includes the name of the person or agency calling the meeting; the date, time, and location of the meeting; and a schedule of business to be conducted. The schedule of business is often structured as follows:

1. Call to order
2. Correction and approval of minutes of [date] meeting
3. Reports of standing committees or subcommittees (identify each that will report)
4. Reports of special committees or subcommittees (identify each that will report)
5. Unfinished business (include appropriate details)
6. New business (include appropriate details)
7. Announcements (may include "good of the order," an opportunity for members to bring information or concerns to the group)
8. Adjournment

Although some meetings may not require all elements listed, an effective agenda includes everything that will enable participants to come to the meeting prepared to conduct business efficiently.

Many organizations today find that the speed and efficiency of email makes it an ideal medium for transmission of a meeting agenda. An example of such an agenda appears in Illustration 7.7.

Minutes of Meetings

To ensure accurate records of its accomplishments, every group that conducts meetings should appoint or elect a recorder or secretary. That person's task is to take notes during the group's deliberations and provide minutes, a written record of the group's decisions. The minutes are sent to meeting participants and other persons who have an interest in that work.

Minutes are summaries of actions taken, not verbatim transcripts of the deliberations. Minutes should include only objective data and actions, not subjective generalities. For example, although members of a committee may comment about the superior quality of a subcommittee's work, the minutes should report only the facts presented by the subcommittee and the action taken by the full group. Unless the group passes an official resolution that includes descriptive words (such as *brilliant, outstanding, superb* or *faulty, inefficient, ineffective*), the recorder should avoid descriptive adjectives. Those terms could be problematic if they are considered to reflect the group's opinion when in fact they represent only the recorder's interpretation of something that occurred in the meeting.

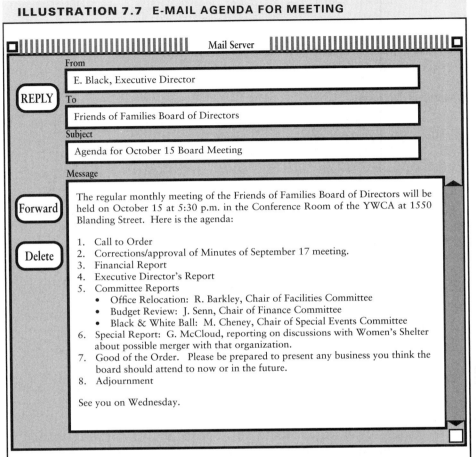

ILLUSTRATION 7.7   E-MAIL AGENDA FOR MEETING

Mail Server

REPLY

From
E. Black, Executive Director

To
Friends of Families Board of Directors

Subject
Agenda for October 15 Board Meeting

Message

Forward

Delete

The regular monthly meeting of the Friends of Families Board of Directors will be held on October 15 at 5:30 p.m. in the Conference Room of the YWCA at 1550 Blanding Street. Here is the agenda:

1. Call to Order
2. Corrections/approval of Minutes of September 17 meeting.
3. Financial Report
4. Executive Director's Report
5. Committee Reports
    • Office Relocation: R. Barkley, Chair of Facilities Committee
    • Budget Review: J. Senn, Chair of Finance Committee
    • Black & White Ball: M. Cheney, Chair of Special Events Committee
6. Special Report: G. McCloud, reporting on discussions with Women's Shelter about possible merger with that organization.
7. Good of the Order. Please be prepared to present any business you think the board should attend to now or in the future.
8. Adjournment

See you on Wednesday.

© Cengage Learning 2013

Minutes usually include the following data:

1. Identification of group
2. Type of meeting (for example, regular, monthly, quarterly, special, emergency)
3. Location, date, and time of meeting
4. Identification of people in attendance and the person presiding
5. Identification of absentees along with reasons for the absences and whether the absence was excused or unexcused
6. Reference to minutes of previous meeting: accepted as presented or amended and then accepted
7. Reports of action on matters previously presented to the group (old business)
8. Reports of action on matters currently presented to the group (new business)
9. Reports of "good of the order" information
10. Place and time of next meeting

11. Time of adjournment

12. Identification of person who prepared the minutes

Formats for minutes vary among organizations, but the format should enable each reader to focus easily on any item that may be of special interest to that person. An example of such a format appears in Illustration 7.8.

ILLUSTRATION 7.8 MINUTES OF MEETING

FRIENDS of FAMILIES

Minutes of Regular Meeting, Board of Directors

Time/Date/Place	5:30 p.m., October 15, 2013, YWCA Conference Room
Presiding Officer	S. A. Cochran-Smith, President of Board
Members Present	D. C. Blackburn, G. E. Bradley, R. Barkley, M. Cheney, S. A. Cochran-Smith, G. McCloud, W. W. Rutstrom, J. Senn, D. Wilson, P. Zahgbie
Member Absent	J. L. Paliz (Representing the Board at the City Council Meeting)
Minutes Approved	Minutes of the September 15, 2013, meeting were approved as distributed.
Financial Report	J. Senn reported that the Finance Committee has conducted its 3rd quarter review. The Committee is satisfied that the Executive Director and staff are handling finances in a responsible manner.
Executive Director's Report	E. Black reported that the agency helped 32 individuals or families during October with vouchers for emergency transportation, housing, medical care, and clothing. Fifteen households were referred to Food Pantry for emergency food supplies.
	The staff has been working closely with the relocation committee to find a facility that will serve our clients more efficiently and with a greater sense of dignity.

continued

ILLUSTRATION 7.8 CONTINUED

Committee Reports

Office Relocation: R. Barkley reported that the Facilities Committee has signed a three-year lease on an office located at 310 Beltline Blvd. The lease begins on November 1, and Barkley has negotiated a successful termination of the lease on our current facilities. The new office is on a main bus line, thereby making it more accessible to clients. It also affords greater privacy for intake interviews. In addition, the facility has a conference room that will permit the Board of Directors to meet there rather than in rented or borrowed facilities around town. Volunteer movers have been recruited, and the entire office will be moved on November 1. The office will be closed that day to accommodate the move, but emergency lines will still be staffed and emergency services will be available throughout the day.

Black & White Ball: M. Cheney reported that all plans for the December 10 ball have been completed. The ball will be held at the Top of the City Club, 8–11 p.m. The Press will publish weekly advertisements—without charge—in the Friday entertainment section throughout November. Tickets are available for the event at $75 per person or $125 per couple. The committee has set a $15,000 (net) goal for this event.

Special Report

B. McCloud reported that after lengthy discussions with members of the Women's Shelter staff and board, the consensus was that neither organization would benefit from a merger because the unique mission of each would be diluted. Consequently, merger talks have ended.

Good of the Order

M. Cheney praised the work of the people who are working on the Black and White Ball and emphasized that all Board members should get behind the event by promoting it to friends and selling tickets.

Next Meeting

President Cochran-Smith announced that the next regular meeting will be held on November 14 at 5:30 p.m. in the conference room of our new office facility.

Adjournment

The meeting was adjourned at 6:45 p.m.

Respectfully submitted,

W. W. Rutstrom

W. W. Rutstrom

Videoconferencing and Web Conferencing

Businesspeople must join in collaborative conversation for various reasons, including assessing needs, generating ideas and strategies, building morale, dividing tasks, making decisions, meeting new clients, negotiating terms, planning projects and reports, presenting new products and services, reviewing outcomes and procedures, setting goals, training personnel, and troubleshooting.

As noted in the section on audioconferencing in Chapter 1, businesspeople have sought alternatives to actual gatherings because of the expansion of businesses nationally and internationally, along with mounting travel costs and the negative impact of travel and large gatherings on the planet. Threats of contagious disease and terrorism provided additional reasons for companies to restrict business travel and look for alternative to face-to-face meetings. In addition, a high percentage of organizations today have employees who telecommute, adding to the need for virtual rather than actual meetings. Over the past 30 years, businesses have developed audiovisual technologies to replace some business get-togethers with virtual meetings. Naturally, the Internet contributed greatly to the growth of these virtual meetings.

Both videoconferencing and Web conferencing are appropriate for meetings in which each person participates actively and contributes to the progress and outcomes of the meeting. Meetings that require no audience participation, except perhaps a brief question-and-answer time at the end (for example, briefings, one-way presentations, and training sessions) use variations of the same technologies. In addition, contemporary businesspeople use collaboration tools known as blogs (Chapter 15) and wikis (Chapter 16).

Managers must, however, be aware that virtual meetings are inappropriate in at least three situations:

- Meeting content is confidential or highly sensitive.
- Participants are unfamiliar with the technology involved or unsupportive of it.
- No bond exists among participants going into a persuasive or problem-solving meeting.

Videoconferencing

A videoconference is interactive audiovisual communication over a distance that is difficult or time consuming to navigate. It uses electronic input devices (video camera, microphones), output devices (television screen, loudspeakers), and an integrated services digital network (ISDN). Videoconferencing equipment may be dedicated (all components in one piece of equipment) or desktop (hardware boards added to a personal computer).

With dedicated systems, participants in a given location generally meet in special conference rooms equipped with cameras and screens for transmitting images and documents to remote participants. These videoconferencing systems vary in size, cost, portability and the number of participants served. Some large, expensive, stationary devices are designed for use in auditorium-sized rooms, while smaller, less expensive, portable or stationary devices are designed for use in small meeting rooms. Both involve a PTZ video camera, that is, a camera that pans to the left and right, tilts up and down, and zooms in and out. A dedicated videoconferencing system designed for a single user has a fixed camera, microphone, and loudspeaker in one portable unit. Desktop systems use dispersed computers rather than a specially equipped meeting room.

The latest videoconferencing equipment has what the industry refers to as telepresence. That is, it's made to create a virtual meeting so realistic that participants look and feel like they are in the same room even when thousands of miles apart. To create this illusion, equipment designers might use a row of 60-inch high-definition screens showing people sitting behind a conference table identical in color and shape to the one used by the viewers. This seamlessness is reinforced by advanced audio that lets everyone talk at once without canceling any voices. Earlier equipment used voice-activated switch technology, meaning other participants could see only the site with the loudest talker. Telepresence equipment permits continuous presence; that is, it displays multiple participants at the same time, and if a participant rises and walks across the room, that person's voice travels with her or him.

Basic systems range from $10,000 to $80,000 per room, but more elaborate displays can easily run $400,000, with network management fees from $6,000 to $18,000 a month. Telepresence systems with broadcast-quality cameras and a row of plasma screens can top $1 million. Naturally, high-end systems are found mostly in large corporations where the need for such equipment is constant and ongoing. Besides business executives and managers, other users include researchers and scientists. Providers of videoconferencing equipment include Hewlett-Packard, LifeSize Communications, Panasonic, Polycom, Siemens, Toshiba, and Visual Systems Group (VSGi).

Web Conferencing

Web conferencing also involves interactive audiovisual communication over long distances. In a Web conference, participants use their own computers, equipped with conferencing software to go online and access a virtual meeting room.

Generally, the leader launches a meeting by sending an email or instant message (IM) to all participants. The attendees then click a link in the IM to join the group at the designated time. When the Web conference begins, attendees see live videos of each other's faces on their computer screens. While the meeting leader controls the displays, participants all see the same website, slide show, or report file on their screens.

Just as they might do in an actual meeting, attendees at an e-meeting can discuss, make presentations, demonstrate products, and collaborate on drafting and revising drawings and text. They interact with each other by typing text in a chat window or by an audioconference call, depending on the amount and speed of interaction required. Naturally, developers of meeting software seek ways to make their products more versatile and the meetings more realistic. Many of today's meeting applications include the following utilities:

- Application/desktop/screen sharing in which participants can view anything the meeting leader has on screen

- Calendar and email interfaces for planning meetings and sharing relevant information in advance
- Markup tools and a remote mouse pointer to engage participants during a PowerPoint slide show
- Meeting recording for later viewing and/or distribution
- Polls and surveys, allowing a presenter to direct questions with multiple-choice answers to participants
- Split screen so that participants can view a presenter and her or his visuals simultaneously
- Streaming or live video capability
- Text chat for question-and-answer sessions, public (transmitted to all participants) or private (between two participants)
- VoIP (Voice over Internet Protocol) through computer headphones and speakers
- Web tours, the ability to push URLs, cookies, scripts, and so on to participants for instant logon and use during a website demonstration
- Whiteboard with annotation, allowing participants to highlight and mark presentation slides and take notes on a blank whiteboard

Providers of Web conferencing software include Fuze Meeting (Fuze Box, Inc.), GoToMeeting (Citrix Online), iMeet (American Teleconferencing Technologies, Inc.), MegaMeeting (Internet MegaMeeting, LLC), Microsoft Office Live Meeting (Microsoft), TurboMeeting (RHUB Communications Inc.), WebEx (Cisco Systems, Inc.), and Yugma (YSL Holdings).

Guidelines for Virtual Meetings

The processes required to schedule and conduct an effective videoconference can be greatly simplified by using MeetingMix (http://meetingmix.com/vhome), an online scheduling and agenda application. You can use this service to schedule meetings, invite attendees, and create meeting minutes all in one place.

To set up a meeting, you first enter the meeting title, date, and time as well as the frequency of a recurring meeting. Then you enter the agenda topics and subtopics, along with the name of the presenter in each instance. After saving the information, you enter email addresses of meeting participants. MeetingMix will automatically email participants with the meeting date, time, and agenda. If you change the date, time, or topics, MeetingMix will send updated emails automatically.

To record minutes, you can select the meeting at the website and enter meeting minutes in the displayed editor. MeetingMix will archive this record of your meeting, and an All Meetings link on the home page will show you a list of all your meetings.

Studies show that although many businesses have virtual meeting technology, few of them use it to the best advantage. A high percentage of business leaders still travel at least once a month, and many telecommuters have no way to collaborate with employees in their offices. The likely reason for these gaps is the lack of a long-term plan for adopting videoconferencing and/or Web conferencing.

After writing a long-term implementation plan, business leaders would do well to follow the virtual meeting guidelines given in Illustration 7.9.

ILLUSTRATION 7.9   GUIDES FOR VIRTUAL MEETINGS

Before the Meeting

- Become familiar with the equipment and surroundings. In the case of videoconferencing, know what technical support is available in your organization and from the service provider. Build a good working relationship with these people.

- Ensure that all participants, especially the most reluctant and least tech-savvy, know how to use the equipment and how to contact customer service and technical support when questions or problems arise. In addition to detailed information about how to use the technology, explain why they should use it, describing the savings potential in personal as well as organizational terms.

- Schedule a virtual meeting only when it fits the meeting's participants and purpose. Ask yourself if key people are willing and able to participate virtually.

- Distribute a meeting agenda. For Web conferences, use the scheduling and email interface available in your meeting software. For videoconferences, use a program such as MeetingMix to schedule the meeting and distribute an agenda.

- Establish rapport with participants before the virtual meeting. Call participants beforehand or e-mail a short questionnaire if necessary to get to know them and their attitudes about main agenda items. Then use any prior dialogue to develop positive interaction during the meeting.

During the Meeting

- Begin a videoconference with a wide-angle shot of the leader making rapport-building comments. Zoom in to signal the first agenda item and to emphasize key points during the meeting.

- Maintain eye contact when speaking to convey an intent, such as conversational turn taking. Video conferencing systems, especially older ones, sometimes give an incorrect impression that a remote participant is avoiding eye contact.

- Don't stare into the camera; do look at the entire audience as you would in a live meeting.

- Speak clearly and energetically. In a videoconference, note any lag between the video and audio transmission and adjust your timing

continued

ILLUSTRATION 7.9 CONTINUED

to avoid distracting listeners or interrupting other speakers. This time lapse (latency) between a gesture or utterance and when it is seen or heard by remote participants becomes quite noticeable at around 150 milliseconds and at 300 milliseconds is observed as unnatural and distracting.

- Project a positive nonverbal message. Relax, smile, and use large, sweeping gestures to reinforce your points, avoiding rapid, diffuse motions.

- Avoid anything that could trigger a voice-activated microphone, such as coughing, throat clearing, and verbal asides.

- When others speak, listen carefully, not just for words but for subtle vocal but nonverbal cues also. You may not always see the speaker's face, such as when someone asks a question.

- Make visuals, such as a PowerPoint slideshow, especially appropriate to the medium. Since text becomes fuzzy when transmitted through compressed video, be especially careful in a videoconference to use large, solid fonts and sharp contrast between text and background. For Web conferences, keep download time to a minimum and avoid elements that may be incompatible with some users' computers.

- Ask a few Web conference participants to collaborate with you in rehearsing your presentation and slides.

- Record minutes. To make your virtual meeting ultimately effective, ask an observer to summarize actions and decisions during the meeting; then, email these minutes to the participants. MeetingMix simplifies the process of recording and distributing minutes. In instances where the proceedings are important—not just the actions, assignments, and decisions—it may be appropriate to create and distribute a copy of the videoconference or Web conference.

Inexperienced participants may feel concern about making an acceptable on-screen appearance, much like the speech anxiety some people experience as presenters. This form of stage fright usually goes away with practice, but a bit of coaching initially may boost everyone's comfort level. With full knowledge of the importance of virtual meetings and appropriate preparation, most participants come to appreciate the economies of time and money that can be realized by using videoconferencing and Web conferencing.

Ethical Considerations

A major ethical challenge that arises during the preparation of routine reports is the need to maintain objectivity. Because the primary data sources for many routine reports are the writer's memory and notes made during or after an observation or experience, the writer must constantly separate her or his feelings and opinions from the objective facts.

For example, as you write a report about your trip to a trade show, you may recall the pleasant experiences you had—building your professional network, eating in fine restaurants, and seeing some of the sights of a city you had not visited before. Although you would enjoy attending another show of this type, you must objectively evaluate the benefit your company receives from sending you to such an event. If, in fact, you learned little or made few contacts that you can use to benefit your organization, your report should include those facts. The report then might end with a recommendation that the company should reevaluate or discontinue its practice of sending a representative to that event.

Similarly, as you write a report about the status of a major project, you must include objective statements about what has been accomplished and any difficulties encountered. If the project is behind schedule, you should include factual statements about what can or cannot be done to bring it back on schedule, not your "feelings" that you can inspire everyone to work hard and get the job done.

Summary

The most common routine reports are form, trip, production, and progress reports, and reports of both face-to-face and virtual meetings. Although these reports are routine in the sense that they are prepared regularly, they are nonetheless significant to the success of the organization. To ensure effectiveness, consider the purpose, audience, context, content, medium, and structure as you plan your reports. In addition, use an appropriate writing style and format for each report, as illustrated in this chapter. Remember that your goal is to help the reader comprehend the message easily, quickly, and accurately.

Topics for Discussion

1. In what ways are routine and nonroutine reports similar? How do they differ from one another?
2. Identify the purpose and characteristics of each of the following routine reports:
   a. Form report
   b. Trip report
   c. Production report
   d. Progress report
   e. Meeting agenda
   f. Minutes of meeting
3. What is the relationship of a progress report to a project's budget?
4. Why are meeting agendas often sent by email?

5. In your judgment, what conditions would justify the use of email for any of the other reports described in this chapter?

6. With two classmates, identify four types of groups you participate in (for example, political, social, work) that meet regularly. Then identify pros and cons of replacing most of these meetings with Web conferences.

7. Identify a major ethical challenge that may arise as you prepare routine reports. If you have had experience preparing such reports, share with your classmates other ethical issues, if any, you have had to resolve.

Applications

1. Assume that you are a consultant to two young men who want to start a "same-day" delivery service. These enterprising young men have seen the success of overnight delivery companies, and they hope to apply some of the principles those companies have followed. Their plan is to guarantee same-day delivery to anyone located within a 300-mile radius of their hub location. The men plan to begin with one hub, located in Greenville, South Carolina. They want to gather accurate information about each delivery so that they can use that information for billing purposes and to determine when and how to expand the business. They ask you to prepare a form that will help route drivers report what they do each day. The form should enable drivers to report the time they left the terminal, each stop during the day, the number of parcels delivered and/or picked up at each stop, and the time they returned to the terminal. In addition, the form should contain space to record identifying information, such as route number, driver's name, vehicle number, and total miles driven. Remember that the form must be easy to handle and complete so that drivers will provide all information each day.

2. Review the content of the progress report given in Illustration 7.6. Assume that Chao-Chen has asked you to draft a form that the PFCs will use to track patient progress through the emergency room. Essential information includes the patient's name, address, and ID number; whether the patient has medical insurance and, if so, directions to attach a copy of the patient's insurance ID card; how the patient arrived at the ER; the time admitted to the ER; the time that the patient was first seen by a doctor or nurse; the first action by the medical staff; the diagnosis; the treatment recommended; the time that the diagnosis and treatment were completed; follow-up instructions to the patient; and the patient's evaluation of the service he or she received. Considering that the PFC may be working with several patients simultaneously, structure the form in such a way that the PFC will be able to keep close track of what is happening to the patient and what the next action should be.

3. Cutco markets high-quality cutlery through Vector Marketing, which is known for employing college students as part-time sales representatives (see http://www.cutco.com). Assume that you have completed the training provided by Vector and are attempting to sell Cutco products in your home community and in the vicinity of your campus. You are now preparing a production report for your first two weeks on the job. This is what you have accomplished: called

four potential customers by telephone, scheduled a demonstration appointment with one of those prospects, and demonstrated the products in the home of your communication instructor who had agreed to critique your presentation. Your instructor was so impressed by your presentation and the products that she placed an order for the Galley Plus 6 set with storage block. She also gave you names of three friends whom you may call using her name as a reference. Your plans for the next two weeks are to follow through on the demonstration appointment that you have made, contact the referrals given by your instructor and attempt to get demonstration appointments with them, and do a demonstration at a party that your mother has set up at her home to help you make contacts. The major problem that you have encountered is managing your time in such a way that you can build up a client base while keeping up with your school obligations. Another problem is the need to get more reliable transportation so that you can keep scheduled appointments.

Prepare a production report in memorandum format. Direct it to your regional manager, Sean Kennedy.

4. Assume that you are Jane Allison, the director of human resources at a company that employs approximately 500 people at your home office in the center of a major city (e.g., Chicago, Illinois; Denver, Colorado; St. Louis, Missouri; Jacksonville, Florida). You recently heard a news report about employees at major companies in New York City, such as Google and the *New York Times*, who commute to work by bicycle. You think some of your employees would like to cycle to work, but your company has done nothing to promote bike commuting. You wanted to learn more about actions companies have taken to encourage bike commuting and how employees have responded to the option. Therefore, you authorized Martha Thomas, one of your personnel counselors, to go to New York and speak with commuting employees and human resources personnel at Google and the *New York Times*. When Ms. Thomas returned, she gave you the trip report shown in Illustration for Application 7.4. Although the information about bicycle commuting interested you, you are not pleased with the quality of the report. You decide to revise it and instruct Ms. Thomas about how to improve her trip reports.

Revise the trip report; in a memo to your instructor, explain your decisions about content, structure, style, and format; attach the revised trip report to that memo.

5. Acting as Martha Thomas (Application 4), write an email proposal to Jane Allison, who authorized that trip. For similar situations in the future, propose the use of virtual meetings instead of business travel. Provide an overview of proposed equipment and/or software and the costs involved. (Search the Web using Bing or Google and combinations of these terms: videoconferencing, virtual collaboration, Web conferencing, benefits, and challenges.) Compare the expense of the actual trip with estimates for meeting electronically. Mention hidden costs (two full days away from your office, downtime while waiting for your return flight, returning at 4 A.M. on a workday). In Application 4, Ms. Allison's interest in bicycle commuting shows her awareness of auto emissions and other "green" issues, so include environmental impact in your proposal, too.

ILLUSTRATION FOR APPLICATION 7.4 TRIP REPORT TO BE REVISED

To: Jane Allison, Director of Human Resources
From: Martha Thomas, Personnel Counselor
Subj.:   Bicycle Commuting

Well, I'm finally back from New York. My return flight was canceled and I had to rebook for a later flight; I did not get home until 4 a.m. this morning. ☹

I had a great time in New York and picked up a lot of good information about bicycle commuting. My first meeting was on May 22 at Google. Although I was supposed to meet with Mr. Hennessey at 10 a.m., he did not show up until 10:30 because he had been called to an emergency meeting. When he finally showed up, he took me to a conference room where I spoke with five employees who regularly cycle to work. They were generally enthusiastic about cycling and gave me some great ideas about personnel policies that might promote bike commuting.

Since I had no appointments scheduled for the afternoon, I was able to do some sightseeing in New York. Great fun! That evening I met my cousin, who lives in New York, for dinner and a Broadway show. Although the tab came to over $300 for the two of us, it was well worth it. (BTW, I have not included those costs in my expense account.)

The next morning I went to the *New York Times*. I had better luck on that visit; the person assigned to escort me (Gerry Flier) was on time and very congenial. She took me to a conference room where I met with eight employees who cycle to work. We had an open discussion on the pros and cons of bike commuting. Again, I picked up some good pointers.

With about two hours to spare before I had to leave for the airport, I was able to do a little shopping on Fifth Avenue. Great fun! However, the fun ended when I got to Kennedy Airport and learned that my flight had been canceled. The airline agents were very helpful in booking me on a later flight; nonetheless, I did not get home until 4 a.m.

I learned that the major factors that encourage employees to cycle to work are feeling confident about cycling in heavy traffic, a cycling safety program sponsored by the company, access to a safe place to park a bike, access to a locker and shower facilities, assurance that company insurance plans cover

continued

ILLUSTRATION FOR APPLICATION 7.4 CONTINUED

injuries sustained while cycling to work, and a financial incentive to participate in the bike commuting movement. The absence of such factors are the major deterrents to bike commuting, along with the need to take children to school or day care, the habit of running errands while driving to and from work, and the need to use an automobile for the job.

Employees also mentioned that a safe bicycle built for the rigors of city commuting can cost as much as $4,000. The major advantages of bicycle commuting cited by the employees were time and money saved compared with auto commuting, improved physical and emotional health, elimination of gym memberships, and feeling good about doing something positive for the environment. Some incentives suggested by the employees were providing all-weather riding gear, perhaps bearing the company logo and cyclist's ID number; loans or reimbursements for bicycle purchases; and convenient, free parking for bikes.

All told, I think the trip was a success. I was able to get a lot of ideas about implementing a successful bike commuting program for our employees.

My out-of-pocket costs, for which I request reimbursement: Round-trip air fare, $729.85; food and lodging (not including the dinner with my cousin), $475.28; taxi fares and tips, $70.

If you need further information, I'll be glad to meet with you at your convenience.

6. Assume that Ms. Allison (Application 4) has authorized you to begin work to set up a bicycle commuting program for your employees. You have worked on the project for about two weeks and now must write a status report directed to Ms. Allison.

    You have accomplished the following:
    - Conducted a survey of employees to determine interest in such a program. Ten employees are strongly interested; five are moderately interested.
    - Identified a place in the parking lot where a bicycle shelter can be built. Obtained an estimate for cost of building such a structure, $1,500.
    - Obtained assurance from your wellness director that shower and locker facilities can be made available before normal working hours so that cyclists can change from cycling clothes to business dress.
    - Arranged a special purchase deal with Out Spokin'; it will give a 10 percent discount on any bicycle and cycling wear purchased by an employee who presents a company ID card.

    Things that you still must do include the following:
    - Develop an incentive plan with the benefits coordinator. You are thinking of asking that employees who commute be paid one cent per mile commuted to

and from work. This incentive would be paid as a monthly bonus. To promote the program, appropriate publicity should accompany those bonus payments.

- Present a proposal for the program to the management committee to get approval for the provisions currently developed.
- If the program is approved by the management committee, prepare and distribute promotional materials to get the program under way.

7. Assume that you are a member of the board of directors for School Aid, a non-profit organization that provides needs-based college scholarships. In the past, your organization has given scholarships to students who attend for-profit colleges as well as private and state nonprofit institutions. A recent study has shown that average tuition and fees at two-year for-profit colleges are nearly five times as high as at state schools. Moreover, graduation rates at four-year public colleges are more than double the rates at four-year for-profit colleges. (*The State*, Money and Opinion, February 20, 2011, p. D1). This report has caused some members of your board to question whether School Aid should continue to grant scholarships to students who plan to attend a for-profit college. One member of your board, Daniel Morales, is a successful entrepreneur, is a graduate of a for-profit college, and strongly supports that type of school as a viable choice for some students. The president of the board of directors has asked you to chair a committee that will study this issue. You have asked Mr. Morales to serve on the committee. You have also asked Ana Greenberg, a graduate of a state college, to serve on the committee. For this application, do the following:

- Do some preliminary research on the issue.
- Prepare an agenda for the first meeting of your committee. At that meeting you will summarize your preliminary research and assign specific areas of study to Mr. Morales and Ms. Greenberg. You may assume that the agenda will be sent to the committee members by email.

8. Form a group with two of your classmates. Let each one assume a role on the committee mentioned in Application 7. Meet with those classmates. In that meeting, plan how you will approach the study of the issue of whether your organization should continue to grant scholarships to students who attend for-profit colleges. Your goal is to eventually present a recommendation to your board of directors. Prepare the minutes of that meeting and present them to your instructor.

9. After meeting with your group (Application 8) at least one more time, write a progress report of your committee's work. This report is to be given to the president of the board of directors, who will likely ask you to present it at the next board meeting.

10. You have been asked to chair a committee to plan your department's annual December holiday party. Two of your coworkers, Jo-Ann Brinkley and Jerry Gluzman, are also on the committee. Your job is to plan a party that will accommodate the cultural differences that exist in your unit. Religious faiths that you are aware of in your unit include Buddhism, Christianity (Eastern Orthodox, Protestant, and Roman Catholic), Islam, and Judaism. Some employees also celebrate Kwanzaa, and several employees do not identify with any religious group. Racial/ethnic heritages include first- to fourth-generation linkages to the

African continent, Brazil, England, France, Germany, Korea, Poland, and Vietnam. The department has 28 employees (13 females and 15 males), and their ages range from 19 to 55 years. Your department supervisor has authorized up to $1,000 in company funds for the party, but you may charge each participant a fee if you think it is necessary.

Your first task is to prepare an agenda for a meeting of the committee. In a memorandum to your instructor, answer the following questions:

- What content must be included? What content is optional?
- What structure do you recommend? Why?
- What tone do you recommend? Why?
- What medium do you recommend? Why?
- What is the best time to transmit the message? Why?

Prepare the agenda and attach a copy to your memo.

11. Complete this application with two of your classmates. Each is to assume the role of one of the committee members referred to in Application 10.

    Hold a meeting to reach decisions concerning the holiday event. Write the minutes of the meeting. You may assume any actions that would be appropriate to your task of planning the event.

12. Assume that two weeks have passed since you held the meeting described in Application 11 and that the party will occur two weeks from now. Write a progress report to your instructor, describing everything the committee has accomplished and what must still be done to ensure that you have a successful party. (Make reasonable assumptions based on the minutes that you prepared for Application 10.)

CHAPTER **8**

Writing Nonroutine Reports

LEARNING OBJECTIVES

After you have read this chapter, you should be able to:

1. Describe the nature and purpose of nonroutine reports.

2. Identify typical nonroutine reports.

3. Produce nonroutine reports in appropriate structures and formats.

4. Describe how social media can be used effectively in business.

THE NEED TO WRITE OR READ REPORTS DIFFERS FOR EACH INDIVIDUAL ALMOST DAILY. As you carry out your work, you will sometimes confront circumstances, make decisions, or take actions that deviate from your normal routine yet fall within your range of responsibility. These situations often require that you report your actions or decisions to management, to your supervisees, or even to the public or stockholders. Those reports may be classified as *nonroutine* reports.

Examples of Nonroutine Reports

It is impossible to illustrate all nonroutine reports that you will encounter. However, among the nonroutine reports that you might send and receive are interview reports, exception reports, justification reports, feasibility reports, staff reports, press releases, executive summaries, and business proposals.

Interview Reports

An *interview report* can be thought of as a special form of a production report. Although you may not interview people regularly in your job, you may on occasion be assigned to a special project that requires you to interview people to obtain critical information. Rather than provide verbatim transcripts of your interviews, you will likely be expected to summarize the information you obtained in a report to your project leader or the members of your project team.

Appropriate content for an interview report would include a statement about when, where, and how the interviews were conducted; a summary of the information obtained; and relevant comments about the experience, such as problems encountered or recommendations related to the interview experience. Illustration 8.1 demonstrates

ILLUSTRATION 8.1 INTERVIEW REPORT

To: R. J. Lin

From: C. G. Gardner

Date: July 22, 2013

Subject: Prospective Mothers' Attitudes About Bucky Bear

Here are the results of the marketing interviews you requested during our staff meeting on June 15. The objective of the interviews was to sample prospective mothers' attitudes toward the new cartoon-like character, Bucky Bear, that we are testing as an imprint on children's bedding and clothing.

Interview Procedures: The market survey team conducted the interviews from 10:30 a.m. until 4:00 p.m., Monday through Friday, during the week of June 14, 2013. With the manager's permission, we set up a display table inside Baby's World, about 30 feet from the entrance. The table contained a banner inviting prospective mothers to ask about a free gift. When a woman stopped to inquire, we offered her a free Bucky Bear crib sheet if she would answer a few questions about the Bucky Bear figure.

Respondents: During the week, we interviewed 83 women. Twenty-four were expecting a first child; 43, a second child; and 16, a child beyond the second.

Reactions to Bucky Bear: The first question asked the shopper to describe the character in one word, using the first word that came to mind. Seventy-five percent of all interviewees described Bucky Bear with words such as "sleepy," "inactive," "sad," or "uninteresting." Only 10 percent of the women described Bucky as "cute," "lovable," or "cuddly."

When asked to suggest how to make the bear more appealing, 73 percent of the respondents suggested showing the bear in more active poses; 41 percent suggested using more brilliant colors; and 62 percent suggested showing the bear in scenes with other characters. (Totals equal more than 100 percent because several interviewees made more than one suggestion.)

Conclusion: These interviews suggest that our current depiction of Bucky Bear does not appeal to the majority of expectant mothers.

Recommendation: Bucky Bear should be sent back to Textile Design for modifications that make it look like a livelier, more sociable creature.

one form of an interview report. It provides the information necessary for others to evaluate the interviews and take action based on those interviews.

Exception Reports

An *exception report* conveys information about deviations from the normal operations of the organization. Exception reports are production-related messages. In fact, some businesses operate under the philosophy of "management by exception"; that is, managers are expected to spend their time and attention on matters that require their particular expertise. In such organizations, individuals are not required to file periodic production reports, but they must prepare an exception report if something occurs that is contrary to expectations, policies, or standards.

An exception report may present facts about the deviation only, or the report may include additional information, such as how the exception was handled, suggestions for handling or avoiding future occurrences, or a request for advice or assistance. Suggested style, structure, content, and format for an exception report are shown in Illustration 8.2. Notice the informative subject line, direct style, and numbered items—all appreciated by busy managers because those techniques simplify and clarify a message.

Justification Reports

A *justification report* describes or proposes an action and the reasons for that action. For example, a notification from an automobile manufacturer to auto owners that they should take their cars to a dealership to check for a possible defect in the steering mechanism is a justification report: The manufacturer requests a specific action and provides reasons for it. Justification reports are similar to exception reports when they describe an exception to a policy or practice and justify that exception. They may also be similar to proposals (discussed later in this chapter) when they propose adoption or rejection of a policy, procedure, or plan.

A typical justification report appears in Illustration 8.3. Notice the courteous, personal, confident tone that is appropriate when a district manager writes to a regional manager. Notice also the subject line, direct structure, and headings, all of which help the reader process the message quickly and respond to the writer's request.

Feasibility Reports

Feasibility report is the term often used to identify a special type of justification report, which analyzes the potential success of a major undertaking. Feasibility studies are often conducted before a company commits itself to a large capital investment, a new product or service, or a new plant location.

Although most feasibility studies result in lengthy, analytical reports, some feasibility reports are presented as short reports. For example, analyzing the feasibility of opening a textile manufacturing plant in South Korea would surely require considerable research and analysis and would result in a lengthy report. In contrast, analyzing the feasibility of changing the hours of operation of a local restaurant would require considerably less data collection and analysis, and the result could be presented in a short-report format.

TO: Ron Ahrendts, General Manager

FROM: Richard Bast, Sales Representative

DATE: March 20, 2013

SUBJECT: Exception to Standard Price, Replacement Windows

Yesterday I approved a special price reduction on an order for seven replacement windows. Here are the details:

1. On March 3, I met with the customer in her home and gave an estimate for replacing all windows in the house. Approximate cost of replacing all windows was $15,000.

2. On March 17, the customer ordered five No. 755 windows, one No. 775, and one No. 739 in white frames, for a total price of $5,770 installed. The customer indicated plans to replace the remaining windows in 12 to 18 months.

3. On March 19, the customer called to say she preferred brown frames. I told her the order could be changed but that brown frames cost 10 percent more than white. She insisted I had not previously mentioned the additional charge, became emotional, and threatened to cancel the entire order.

4. To assure her that we do not use "bait-and-switch" tactics and to improve the chances of getting the order for the rest of the house, I told her I would order the brown frames this time at the price quoted for white frames. However, I indicated she would have to pay the additional charge when she ordered the remaining windows.

I understand your policy is that sales reps must absorb price reductions from commissions if we do not get your prior approval. However, this customer was on the verge of canceling the contract within the 48-hour period allowed by law. I had no time to locate you before making a decision. Since I gave the customer an allowance of $577 to secure a potential $15,000 order, I trust you will not charge that allowance against my commission income.

Please call me (555-1010) if you need further information about this transaction.

ILLUSTRATION 8.3   JUSTIFICATION REPORT IN BLOCK LETTER FORMAT

WORLD-VIEW WINDOWS

201 Leventis Drive
Columbia, SC 29209-1989

March 22, 2013

Mr. Rivers E. Williams
Regional Manager
World-View Windows
P.O. Box 1039
Atlanta, GA 30340-1039

Dear Rivers

Subject: Override of commission policy

I recommend that Richard Bast, one of our Macon, GA, sales representatives, be paid full commission on contract No. 31789, even though he gave the customer a special price on the windows. He should not be required to cover the price differential from his commission in this case.

Justification

This exception is justified for four reasons:

1. Bast made the contract adjustment in good faith, attempting to salvage a sizable account.

2. The evidence is unclear. Bast insists he told the customer that brown window frames cost 10 percent more than white; the customer insists he did not.

3. I have reviewed the sales closing procedure with Bast, and he has demonstrated it to a group of trainees. I am convinced he will not repeat the error nor compromise prices unnecessarily in the future.

4. Bast has experienced excessive medical expense related to his child's illness. The commission is significant to him, but relatively insignificant to the company. This is an opportunity to demonstrate our faith in him and build the morale of a potentially excellent sales representative.

continued

ILLUSTRATION 8.3 CONTINUED

Mr. Rivers E. Williams   – 2 –   March 22, 2013

Request for Action

Please call me before April 15 if you have any questions. If I do not hear from you by that date, I will notify Bast that he will receive the full commission in his April 30 check.

Sincerely

Ron Ahrendts, General Manager
Southeast District

A feasibility report must identify the project that is being analyzed, provide an unequivocal recommendation about the potential success or failure of that project, and supply data to support that recommendation. Feasibility reports usually present the recommendation at or near the beginning of the report because the person requesting the report is interested primarily in the recommendation—whether positive or negative. A short feasibility report appears in Illustration 8.4. Notice its structure, content, style, and format.

Staff Reports

The term *staff report* may be used to identify any report produced by a manager's staff for the manager. A staff report frequently analyzes a problem about which the manager must take action, make a recommendation, or formulate a position. Assume, for example, that a home owners' association objects to rezoning an area bordering its neighborhood from a residential to a commercial designation. The head of the zoning board would likely ask the board's staff to investigate the positions of proponents and opponents and to recommend an action the zoning board should take.

A staff report may be prepared in any format suitable for the nature of the problem and content presented. Managers assign such reports to their staff because managers are often too busy to do the investigation themselves. Therefore, the report should be designed to help the manager extract the essential information quickly.

Notice the structure and format of the staff report shown in Illustration 8.5. The report is presented in a direct structure because the president surely remembers requesting the analysis and is awaiting the results.

Press Releases

A *press release* is a report that is released by an organization for distribution by the mass media: newspapers, magazines, radio, and television. Although large companies typically have a corporate communication division that is responsible for press

ILLUSTRATION 8.4   FEASIBILITY REPORT

MARKET SCOPE, INC.

P.O. Box 1584
Madison, WI 53713-1584

April 24, 2013

Ms. Heather Bonnifield
107 Marlene Drive
Marshall, MN 56258

FEASIBILITY OF MAIL-ORDER BUSINESS: WOMEN'S FASHIONS

In January, you asked that I conduct a study of the feasibility of your beginning a mail-order business to market fashionable easy-care clothing to career women in the 30–45 age range. You planned to operate that business from Marshall, MN, with an initial investment of not more than $1 million.

Recommendation

I recommend that you **not** launch the mail-order business you proposed. Current projections suggest that you will suffer a substantial loss during three years of operation even with relatively optimistic projections. Furthermore, the competition in catalog and Web sales is growing, with the number of small companies up 50 percent in the last five years. Establishing a website to complement the catalog is an imperative in today's market. Therefore, the very real risk exists that at the end of three years you will be looking at the loss of your $1 million investment in addition to an operating loss of more than $400,000.

You can currently invest your money in moderate-risk Exchange Traded Funds (ETFs), some of which have earned 4–5 percent annually in recent years. Assuming an average annual return of 4.5 percent on such an investment, at the end of three years, your money will have grown by more than $100,000.

Findings

Here are the findings that justify my recommendation.

Projected first-year costs and revenues

The first year of operation will require that you conduct marketing tests to establish your customer base; locate and buy appropriate merchandise; develop, print, and mail catalogs; build a website; pay salaries; and cover bad debts and returns. If you send out 500,000 catalogs, you can anticipate that 1 percent of the recipients will respond with an average order of $100, generating $500,000 in sales.

continued

ILLUSTRATION 8.4   CONTINUED

Ms. Heather Bonnifield   – 2 –   April 24, 2013

Your costs to generate those sales are projected as follows:

Catalog development/mkt. tests	$ 60,000
Printing and mailing	275,000
Website development	7,000
Salaries (marketing, merchandising, customer service, telemarketing)	250,000
Cost of merchandise (45–55% of sales)	250,000
Bad debts/returns (1% of sales)	5,000
Total	$847,000

As you can see, your loss from operations would be over $300,000 during the first year.

Projected second-year costs and revenues

If you do not increase your catalog distribution but rely on Web sales for growth, catalog development costs will decline slightly; but your printing and mailing costs will likely increase. Personnel costs will increase also; but we are assuming that with efficiencies derived from experience, they will not increase in proportion to sales. Even if sales double in the second year, you will still not generate a profit. To earn $1,000,000 in revenue you will incur the following expenses:

Catalog development	$ 50,000
Printing and mailing	300,000
Website maintenance	2,000
Salaries	275,000
Cost of merchandise	500,000
Bad debts/returns	10,000
Total	$1,137,000

Projected third-year costs and revenue

Again relying on the Web for increased sales, you should maintain your catalog development costs in the third year of operation. Again, printing and mailing costs, along with salaries, will likely increase, although not in direct proportion to the increase in sales. As the customer base develops, you may expect increased sales, but likely not as large a percentage as in the second year of operation. Another 50 percent increase in sales will be necessary to generate a modest profit in the third year. That will bring in revenue of $1,500,000. Related cost projections follow:

Catalog development	$ 50,000
Printing and mailing	325,000
Website maintenance	2,000
Salaries	300,000
Cost of merchandise	750,000
Bad debts/returns	15,000
Total	$1,442,000

continued

ILLUSTRATION 8.4 CONTINUED

Ms. Heather Bonnifield   – 3 –   April 24, 2013

Summary

To summarize, here is what you can expect during the first three years if you are margin-ally successful.

Year	Revenue	Expenses	Net
1	$ 500,000	$ 847,000	$(347,000)
2	1,000,000	1,137,000	(137,000)
3	1,500,000	1,442,000	58,000
Total	$3,000,000	$3,426,000	$(426,000)

Those projections result in a net loss of over $400,000 during the first three years of oper-ation. In contrast, if you were to invest your $1 million in an EFT averaging 4.5 percent per annum, you would see a gain of approximately $140,000.

Additional Comments

I have enjoyed doing this study for you. If you are interested in an analysis of another entrepreneurial opportunity, please call me.

Heidi Fitzpatrick

HEIDI FITZPATRICK
ENTREPRENEURIAL CONSULTANT

releases, if you work for a small business or nonprofit organization, you may be asked to write a press release. An effective press release contains the following information:

- Name of organization releasing the news
- Target date for publication of the news
- A headline that states the core of the story
- The information source, when applicable
- Answers to the basic communication questions: Who? What? When? Where? Why? How?
- Name of person to contact for further information, along with telephone or fax numbers or email addresses

The body of the press release should be organized in an inverted pyramid form: Answers to basic questions appear first, followed by supporting details. This structure permits the editor to cut the story without deleting vital facts. The news should be written in a style that will appeal to a broad audience. To accommodate the editors of the agencies to whom the release is sent, the news release should have enough

ILLUSTRATION 8.5   STAFF REPORT IN MEMO FORMAT

Welcome Home Hotels

To: Sam Hope, Director of Human Resources

From: Taylor Greene and Logan Dierks

Date: May 2, 2013

Subject: Hiring Parolees

Recommendation

We recommend that Welcome Home Hotels develop policies and procedures for hiring parolees to fill entry-level positions in housekeeping, building maintenance, and food services. This recommendation is based on an extensive review of current literature about hiring parolees and interviews with human resources personnel in three companies that have hired parolees.

Summary of Findings

Welcome Home Hotels can receive both short-term and long-term benefits by developing a program to hire parolees. Companies that have hired parolees cite both altruistic and economic reasons for doing so. Studies have shown that employment is likely to reduce recidivism. A high percent of offenders who violate parole are unemployed, but a small percent of ex-prisoners who are employed end up back in jail. In addition to making a contribution to society, companies reap several practical benefits from hiring parolees.

- Parolees who are seeking employment typically are eager to work and become reliable and loyal workers when offered steady employment.

- Many parolees have gone through training programs while incarcerated and are prepared for jobs at the skilled labor level.

- Incarceration has instilled in the parolees a respect for authority and enabled them to cope with stressful situations.

- The turnover rate for ex-prisoners is lower than for many companies' general employee population.

continued

ILLUSTRATION 8.5 CONTINUED

Sam Hope   -2-   May 3, 2013

In addition to obtaining employees with a good work ethic, a company that hires parolees can receive financial assistance from federal and state government programs that have been established as incentives to hire ex-offenders.

- The U.S. Department of Labor provides a Work Opportunity Tax Credit of up to $2,400 for each qualifying employee. This credit is paid during the parolee's first year of employment. Some states also offer tax credits.

- The Federal Bonding Program, an initiative of the U.S. Department of Labor, provides short term fidelity bonds ranging from $5,000 to $25,000 to protect employers against employee dishonesty.

Next Steps

To get the program under way, we suggest that Personnel take the following actions:

1. Contact correctional systems of the states in which our hotels are located. Many states have established community re-entry projects to help ex-offenders find employment and adjust to their new environments. These re-entry projects will help to identify potential employees.

2. Identify available jobs for parolees and develop standards for hiring and promoting ex-offenders.

3. Schedule an orientation session for all hotel managers at Welcome Home headquarters so that managers will be fully aware of the program's objectives and procedures.

white space to permit a person to write notes or edit the release. Illustration 8.6 demonstrates an effective structure and format for a written press release

Today many companies also use the *video news release* (VNR) as part of their media outreach. A VNR is a professionally produced video presentation that is sent free of charge by satellite link or videocassette to television newsrooms. VNRs can be used to cover product innovations, company milestones, and current consumer issues. Professional associations, such as the National Association of Life Underwriters, have used VNRs to educate the public about the various segments of the industry and to combat misunderstandings.

Networks and local television stations are free to air the tapes or not. Some stations air them as they are presented; others use parts of the presentation or take its ideas and build their own stories. To increase the probability of having the tape aired, companies should produce the tapes in an objective, newsworthy fashion. To attract the interest of the news media, the story must capture the interest of the average consumer in the viewing audience.

Executive Summaries

Another nonroutine report that you may be required to prepare is an *executive summary*. An executive summary often accompanies a lengthy analytical report, but

ILLUSTRATION 8.6   PRESS RELEASE

the
education
foundation

An initiative of the Charleston Metro Chamber of Commerce

FOR IMMEDIATE RELEASE   CONTACT: Emily Watts 843.805.3053
                                                PR & Publications Director
April 19, 2011   Charleston Metro Chamber of Commerce

Boeing Gives $129,000 Grant to The Education Foundation for STEM Education

Charleston, SC – The Education Foundation received $129,000 grant from The Boeing Company today to develop and implement a plan for aligning Science, Technology, Engineering and Mathematics (STEM) education in Berkeley, Charleston, and Dorchester Counties with workforce needs. The ultimate goal of the "STEM in the Workplace" initiative is to ensure a pipeline of graduates who are equipped with knowledge and skills that match our region's economic needs.

The Boeing funds will allow The Education Foundation to provide professional development for teachers of STEM disciplines in three ways: teachers will gain on-site experience in STEM-related businesses; participate in teaching institutes that focus on project-based learning; and implement new methods for teaching STEM to their students.

The growing need for STEM education is largely due to the rapid growth of STEM-related industries globally in recent years. Because STEM industries like Boeing are expanding worldwide, it is crucial to educate students in these fields to provide companies with a competitive workforce.

By doing "externships" in the region's businesses, teachers will see STEM in action, learn first-hand about workplace requirements and simultaneously gain a wealth of ideas for student projects. The practical business experience will be followed by training in project-based learning. The core idea behind project-based learning is that real-world problems capture students' interest and stimulate critical thinking and teamwork as the students apply new knowledge in a problem-solving context. The STEM in the Workplace initiative will give the 60 participating teachers a new arsenal of project-based teaching strategies aimed at preparing students for entry-level jobs that are becoming more and more sophisticated.

"Most teachers go directly from their own education into teaching. This program gives teachers a chance to see and work within the business world and then translate those experiences into 'real world' learning experiences for students," says David Ramey, chairman of The Education Foundation.

continued

ILLUSTRATION 8.6 CONTINUED

There are multiple exit points for students in STEM-related fields, so whether students want to continue their studies through higher education at a 4-year or 2-year college or enter the workforce directly after graduating high school, there are opportunities for them to pursue their goals and interests in STEM. In addition, STEM education increases employability for students and reduces training time and cost for employers. STEM in the Workplace will address a critical regional need by preparing students for success in a work world that increasingly demands high-level skills in science, technology, engineering, and math.

STEM in the Workplace is guided by a steering committee made up of business and education leaders. The committee is currently engaging the support of STEM-related businesses who will offer two-day externships to teachers in the summer of 2011. Businesses interested in participating should contact Angie Rylands, The Education Foundation's Regional STEM Coordinator, at arylands@edfound.net.

About the Education Foundation: The Education Foundation, an initiative of the Charleston Metro Chamber of Commerce, was founded in 1995 to build partnerships between the business community and the schools, mobilize resources, and advocate the changes necessary in our community to prepare all students for the careers of the future.

executive summaries are also used in other circumstances. For example, your state legislature may be proposing more stringent pollution control requirements. Upper management in your company needs an analysis of the proposed legislation and its potential impact on your company. You may be asked to study the issue and prepare an executive summary. Another use for executive summaries is to help the executive keep up with current trends or issues in the industry. You may also be asked to skim several professional or trade journals and write an abstract of pertinent articles or a summary of what you have learned about a particular trend.

Whether you are writing an executive summary of a report you wrote, an abstract of a business article, or a summary of several documents pertaining to a single issue, you should write clearly, concisely, and in your own words. An executive summary should include only the most essential information that its readers need to make informed decisions and act wisely. Such a summary typically includes identification of the issue or problem that is addressed, major findings about the matter, and concise conclusions and recommendations. The guides shown in Illustration 8.7 will help you develop a complete, concise executive summary, whether it is an abstract of a trade journal article or a summary of a major report.

As Illustration 8.8 shows, executive summaries are often presented in direct structure. Because the readers already have some knowledge about the general problem, they are eager to know what you recommend.

Business Proposals

A *proposal* offers a plan of action. The objective of a proposal is to influence others—to persuade someone to act in a way that the proposer considers good or desirable.

ILLUSTRATION 8.7   WRITING AN EXECUTIVE SUMMARY[1]

An Effective Executive Summary

- Emphasizes key points of the report or journal article
- Represents the author's view accurately
- Is written in your own words
- Is concise, specific, and clear
- Is presented in a format that enhances readability
- Is free of spelling, grammar, and sentence errors

How to Prepare an Executive Summary

1. Read the report or each journal article to determine the main idea(s).
2. Write each main idea in a single sentence, using your own words.
3. List key facts or assertions that support the main point(s).
4. Write brief sentences containing the supporting facts or assertions.
5. Reread the report or article for background information needed to understand the main idea(s).
6. Write sentences to present the background information.
7. Combine your sentences describing the background, main idea(s), and supporting information.
8. Revise and edit your summary. Eliminate unnecessary words and sentences; evaluate structure (should it be direct? indirect?); check accuracy of spelling, grammar, and sentence and paragraph structures.
9. Produce the final report in an appropriate format.

© Cengage Learning 2013

Business proposals share that general purpose, even though they have many different specific purposes.

Purposes of Proposals

A proposal may be solicited or unsolicited. A solicited proposal is presented in response to a request for proposal (often abbreviated RFP). In the RFP, the requesting person or agency indicates its needs, and the proposal writer attempts to show that the proposed action can satisfy those needs.

An unsolicited proposal is initiated by the proposer. That individual perceives a need or problem and offers a research plan, a product or service, or an action to satisfy the need. The proposal may be submitted to someone who is unaware of the situation. The writer's purpose is twofold: to convince the reader that a need or problem exists and to show how the proposed action will result in benefits to the reader.

Kinds of Proposals

Business proposals fall into three categories: proposals to investigate or conduct research; proposals to provide a product or service; and proposals to change a policy, procedure, or organizational structure. Each may be independent of the others, but the three may also be related to one another. For example, assume that as a human

ILLUSTRATION 8.8 EXECUTIVE SUMMARY

Promoting FARMCO via Video News Releases

Executive Summary

This report summarizes the current status of Video News Releases (VNRs) as reported in several trade journals.

Recommendation. The literature review supports the following recommendation:

Farmco should contract with a professional video producer, such as TOP-10, to prepare a VNR package about the minimal environmental impact of our pesticides.

Conclusions. Within the past ten years, the VNR has become an increasingly effective tool in a company's media mix. This increased effectiveness can be attributed to the following developments:

- The increasing cost-effectiveness of satellite delivery
- The trend toward content that serves to educate the public
- The push by the Public Relations Society of America to develop a code of good practice for VNR production and use
- The reduced resistance of television news executives to VNR packages that provide flexibility in how the station will use the information

Summary of Findings. Journalists are still debating the ethics of using VNRs. If the station does not control the content of the video, it is considered a breach of ethics to air it. However, today's technology permits stations to exercise substantial control over what is used: video only with a station's reporter doing voice-over, video clips, story line supplemented by the station's own reporting, and so on. Members of the Public Relations profession have worked to establish a quality control program that will guarantee formats and content that will be acceptable to broadcasters.

A VNR can get considerable airing—which is essentially free air time—if it addresses a consumer interest. For example, a VNR prepared for the Irish Tourist Board successfully promoted tourism by tying into St. Patrick's Day. The video was distributed by cassette to 240 stations nationwide, was aired 160 times by 125 different stations, and was viewed by an estimated audience of nearly 8 million.

resources director you recognize that rising worker compensation costs require the company to find alternatives to losing trained employees who have been injured on the job. You first write a proposal to investigate the feasibility of implementing a rehabilitation program for injured employees. On receiving approval for the proposed research, you ask one of your associates to conduct the research. Perhaps the research plan calls for a survey of employees to determine their attitudes about rehabilitating injured employees and integrating them into the workforce. You decide that you want an external agency to conduct that employee survey, and you request that a professional testing agency submit a proposal to provide that service. If the completed research shows that an employee rehabilitation program is a cost-effective way of returning injured employees to the workplace, you will write an operational proposal to management recommending immediate adoption of such a program.

The investigative or research proposal is a formal version of a research plan. (That kind of proposal will be discussed in Chapter 10.) This chapter illustrates a product/service proposal and an operational proposal.

Product or service proposals (sometimes called bids) offer to provide something for the recipient. Such proposals are often solicited. The RFP frequently specifies the exact content and format desired by the receiver. To increase the probability that your proposal will be considered, you must adhere to those specifications.

Some organizations use relatively informal procedures to solicit product or service proposals. For example, a training director may telephone a consultant, describe a training need, and ask for a proposal. In such a situation, the consultant chooses the proposal's content and structure. Both must convince the training director that the consultant understands the need and can satisfy it. Illustration 8.9 demonstrates a service proposal. Notice that it includes everything the reader requires for an informed decision: a general description of the reader's problem or needs, a description of the service that the writer can provide, the cost of the proposed service, the proposed completion date, and the qualifications of the provider. Notice also that the proposal requests a specific action: the approval to proceed.

Organizational or operational proposals set forth suggestions or plans for changes in organizational structure or operations. In some organizations, such proposals are called justification reports. The proposal presents a plan or suggestion and provides objective information to justify it. This kind of proposal is often accompanied by an oral presentation that contains more of the detailed data that constitute the justification.

An example of an operational proposal appears in Illustration 8.10. Notice that the report structure and content complement the readers' needs. The busy members of the executive committee will appreciate the direct, clear statement of the proposed action and the brief, easy-to-read justification for that action. Again, the proposal ends with a clear, concrete statement of the desired action.

Social Media for Business Research

The term "social media" refers to a variety of Internet applications that encourage the exchange of information created by users themselves. You are likely familiar with at least one social networking site, such as MySpace, LinkedIn, and Facebook, and one or more media sharing sites, such as YouTube, Slideshare, and Flickr. In addition, you are probably conversant with Wikipedia and may be aware of other so-called crowdsourcing websites, such as iStockPhoto and Threadless. Perhaps you visit a few Web logs (blogs), like Huffington-Post, Mashable, and lifehacker, regularly and leave comments in response to the content.

Maybe you have used the message and discussion board of an online forum, such as DigitalPoint, to ask and answer questions on specific topics. Social bookmarking sites such as Digg and Delicious are increasing in popularity, as are sites like Yelp, TripAdvisor, and Amazon, where users discuss and rate products and services. In all likelihood, you are aware of Twitter, a microblog that allows users to send 140-character text messages (tweets) to other Twitter subscribers.

ILLUSTRATION 8.9 SERVICE PROPOSAL

K-F COMMUNICATION ASSOCIATES

859 RIVER DRIVE   TELEPHONE: 319-555-4961
IOWA CITY, IA 54441
February 15, 2013

Ms. J. B. McCarthy, President
Board of Directors
Iowa Optometric Association
158 Hawkeye Boulevard
Iowa City, IA 52240

Dear Ms. McCarthy

In response to your February 12 telephone request, I submit this proposal for a study of communication between and among members of the Board of Directors of the Iowa Optometric Association.

Background

My understanding is that the Board of Directors of the Iowa Optometric Association wishes to improve communication among members during and between your monthly board meetings. You have been authorized by your board to solicit proposals for a study of the communication policies and procedures currently in use among board members. Your goal is to improve communication practices and thereby improve the board's productivity.

Procedure

I propose to follow these steps to fulfill your request:

1. Attend your board meeting in March to observe communication practices and interactions among board members during the meeting.
2. Review the Association's constitution, bylaws, and board manual to identify current communication expectations and guides that exist and to suggest improvements needed, if any.
3. Design a questionnaire to assess attitudes of board members about current communication practices between and among board members. You will be given the opportunity to review the questionnaire, and I will test it in an independent focus group before it is distributed to your board members.
4. Administer the questionnaire to your employees electronically. Board members will be sent an email containing a link to the questionnaire, which they will complete online. I am the only person who will have access to the completed questionnaires.
5. Analyze and interpret all data obtained.
6. Present to you a written report containing the findings and recommendations resulting from the study.
7. Give an oral briefing to your Board on a date to be determined.

continued

ILLUSTRATION 8.9 CONTINUED

Ms. J. B. McCarthy   -2-   February 15, 2013

Cost

The cost for this service will be $3,000. I request an initial payment of $1,500 upon acceptance of this proposal; the final payment of $1,500 will be due upon completion of the report.

Completion Date

The final report will be presented to you no later than April 30. Completion by this date will allow you to institute any changes that may seem necessary as soon as the new board members take office in July.

Interim goals:

March 15	Attend meeting of Board of Directors to observe interactions
March 15–April 1	Analyze current constitution, bylaws, and board manual
April 1–5	Prepare, test, review, and upload questionnaires
April 8–12	Board members complete on-line questionnaire
April 13–18	Analyze all data
April 19–20	Complete and deliver report
May ?	Give oral briefing at monthly meeting of the Board of Directors

Qualifications

You indicated that you were referred to me by a client who had used my services in a similar situation. References of other satisfied clients will be provided upon your request.

Request for Approval

Please call me if you have any questions about this proposal. Your approval before February 28 will ensure completion of the study in accordance with your plans for board development.

Sincerely

Carlota Flores

Carlota Flores, Communication Facilitator

At first, most employers viewed social media in the workplace as a distraction with the potential for lowering employees' productivity. As a result, many businesses opposed social media at work, and some still do. On the other hand, many businesses now realize that employees can advocate for the company on social media, especially if the company adopts social media policies for them to follow. Today, about one in

---

ILLUSTRATION 8.10 OPERATIONAL PROPOSAL

To: Executive Committee, Iowa Optometric Association

From: J. B. McCarthy, President of Board   *J.B.M.*

Date: May 25, 2013

Subject: Board Retreat

I recommend that we hold a Board Retreat on July 10–11, 2013.

Justification

Carlota Flores recently completed a study of our board's communication policies and practices. A major recommendation flowing from that study was that we hold a Board Retreat. The ultimate goal of the retreat is to improve our functioning as a board.

You have all received a copy of Ms. Flores's full report and you attended her oral briefing at our regular May meeting. At that time she also presented a proposal to facilitate a Board Retreat to help board members clarify their respective roles and responsibilities and develop more effective communication techniques. The ensuing discussion indicated that current board members strongly support such a retreat. Holding it early in July will permit the newly elected board members to participate. All board members should then be "on the same page" with respect to understanding their roles and responsibilities, and board meetings should run more smoothly.

Additional Information

Baker's B & B in Muscatine, Iowa, has offered us a two-day, one-night package that includes meals, lodging, and use of a meeting room. The cost will be $250 per person. That amount is well within the amount already budgeted for board development.

Request for Approval

I request your approval to accept Ms. Flores's proposal to conduct the retreat, to be held at Baker's B & B, on July 10 and 11. Please email your vote to me (jbm@yahoo.com) no later than May 30 so that I can complete the arrangements for the retreat.

---

four companies, including Zappos, SAP, Monster, Kodak, Intel, IBM, and Coca-Cola, have such a Web participation policy.

Twitter (http://www.twitter.com) is one of many social media that have changed the way businesses and consumers communicate with each other. Businesses pay millions of dollars for case studies, focus groups, think tanks, and reports containing information about the industry and target markets. Twitter represents an inexpensive way to collect such data. Small businesses that cannot afford to spend their marketing budget on more costly data sources can especially benefit from using social media for research; however, small businesses generally have been slow to do so. Any business can supplement existing research efforts with Twitter. Besides, Twitter is a real-time source (no delay between data collection and analysis) for monitoring competitors and a brand's existing users, and it involves no size, location, or time limits.

Some companies use Twitter for direct marketing, posting corporate accomplishments and distributing links to the company's Web pages, press releases, and other promotions. While the easiest way to use Twitter, direct marketing is probably the least effective. Consumers are no longer willing to listen passively to one-way messages sent from businesses. Customers now expect to participate in real conversations not only with companies but also with each other.

Other organizations market indirectly on Twitter by letting employees post tweets. The idea behind indirect marketing is that as individual employees enhance their reputations, the company's reputation is enhanced, too. Employees sending tweets about their work, new products, and industry developments—even if unrelated to the company itself—indirectly generate positive feelings for the organizations they represent. Some companies simply "listen" to Twitter without participating in it. Using Twitter search tools enables business managers to collect product ideas, obtain feedback on existing products, and react immediately to customer complaints. The list of organizations using Twitter for direct or indirect marketing or research includes Best Buy, Comcast, Dell Computer, Etsy!, Ford, International Olympics Committee, Blackbaud, Southwest Airlines, Starbucks, and Whole Foods Market.

Searching Twitter (http://search.twitter.com) is a good way to get news in the making, hours or even days before the information is available anywhere else on the Internet or other news sources. In addition, searching can turn up articles or blog posts that you might not see any other way. At least 60 tools exist for searching Twitter and then gathering and organizing the found information. Some applications also scan blogs, news, and MySpace or Facebook in addition to Twitter. The following list contains a tiny sampling of Twitter search engines:

Twellow (http://twellow.com)—Twellow organizes information gathered from twitter into a Yellow Pages format. Then you can search this "directory" for, say, a specific service or people in a specific profession.

TweetScan (http://tweetscan.com)—The TweetScan search engine tracks key words or phrases that you enter. Then it delivers its findings to you in its search results by email or by an RSS Web feed.

Tweetmeme (http://tweetmeme.com)—This search application shows the most popular tweets across the Web at any given time and then lets you search for topics.

Tweetbeep (http://tweetbeep.com)—This tool lets you monitor a brand, company, industry, and name. (The industry calls this reputation management.) After you set up as many as 10 key word alerts, Tweetbeep automatically gathers the specified information in your emailbox, updating it hourly or daily as you request. Then you can organize and analyze it whenever you see fit.

Topsy (http://topsy.com)—Topsy is a search engine that follows the conversations of 30 million Twitter users and shows what they are talking about *now*.

Searchtastic (http://searchtastic.com)—Like other Twitter search sites, Searchtastic lets you search tweets for a particular key word. Unlike the others, Searchtastic has the ability to pull up tweets from weeks or months ago. In addition, this search tool has the ability to search tweets from particular users, such as the strongest advocates of your brand and the brand's loudest naysayers.

Nearby Tweets (http://nearbytweets.com)—This tool lets you discover tweets from local users. It uses Google Maps to find your location and then shows the tweets by Twitter users near you. This tool is handy for businesses that want to expand their presence in the local area. An application called Areaface (**http://www.areaface.com**) lets you pinpoint a location on Google Maps and then shows you recent tweets and Twitter users in that area.

Monitter (http://www.monitter.com)—Monitter enables you to examine a set of key words on Twitter and narrow the search to a certain geographic location, enabling you to check trends in a particular part of the world. Findings are sorted by category and arranged in columns on your screen. Data collected through social media are unsuitable for the kind of business research you will study in Chapters 10 to 16 for the following reasons:

- You do not select the research subjects (Twitter users) randomly. Therefore, the research participants may differ in their needs and wants and their likes and dislikes from consumers who perhaps do not have Internet access or those who do not use any social media.
- The data collected from tweets are largely unstructured, leaving you no way to measure an element or characteristic of the data (though some Twitter search tools claim to measure intensity of reactions and trends).
- If you send tweets as well as read them, you may cause participants to react a certain way (researcher influence); and doing so in real time means that your study changes constantly.

An executive summary, however, would be a perfect way to report Twitter information to an organization's decision makers. As the researcher, you would select the Twitter search engines; then you would collect, organize, and summarize the results. The executive summary might also include your interpretation, separate from the information contained in the summary. A business leader might also issue a press release if tweets showed widespread misunderstanding of company policies or products. Besides sending a news release to traditional broadcast media, an organization could post the release to its website. Then tweet updates could direct the company's Twitter followers to the press release.

Ethical Considerations

As demonstrated by the illustrations in this chapter, a person preparing a nonroutine report often faces ethical dilemmas. In many instances, the problem is not a choice between a good or bad action; instead, it is a choice between two good actions or outcomes. Should a sales representative seek approval for an action that deviates from a standard operating procedure when the outcome will have a short-term cost to the company, or should the sales representative accept the related cost of her or his action? What is the potential good—or bad—result of a manager's attempt to justify a subordinate's actions? How should a consultant report data to a client when he or she knows the client will be disappointed by the information?

Should a staff member recommend an action that will have a negative impact on some members of a community and a positive impact on others? In early 2011, a major debate among members of the South Carolina General Assembly was whether the state should honor a promise made to Amazon.com during a previous governor's administration to exempt it from collecting sales taxes on sales made to South Carolina residents. That promise, along with other concessions, was given to induce Amazon to establish a distribution center in Lexington County. Opponents insisted that the exemption would discriminate against other retailers in the state who were required to collect the sales tax. Proponents insisted that the employment opportunities and personal income generated by the distribution center would result in a substantial increase in collections of state income taxes and sales tax revenues associated with the increased local spending by Amazon's employees. Reports prepared by legislative staffers could support either position.

Consider also these issues: What kind of "spin" should you put into a press release? How do you draw the line between blatant organizational promotion and news in a VNR? To what extent should you use information obtained by using social media? Should you differentiate information gathered through social media from information acquired by more traditional research techniques? If so, how?

When you respond to a request for a proposal, can you demonstrate that you have the ability to meet the expectations of the potential client—that you have the necessary expertise to provide the requested product or service? Another ethical dilemma may arise as you price your services. How should you value your services? Should you charge "what the market will bear" in all situations? Should you reduce your price for a nonprofit organization and consider part of the work a pro bono contribution, or would that discriminate against for-profit companies that contract your services?

A review of the ethical guides presented in Chapter 1 will help you make some of these difficult decisions about message content and style. Clearly, weighing right versus right is not easy.

Summary

Nonroutine reports address significant problems that are job-related yet not confronted daily. The ability to prepare effective nonroutine reports—such as interview reports, exception reports, justification reports, feasibility reports, staff reports, press releases, executive summaries, and business proposals—will have a significant effect on your career.

The content and structure of those reports must always complement the needs of the receiver and clearly identify the desired action. Because these reports deal with exceptions to normal operations, the writer often faces an ethical dilemma. The content and the style of nonroutine reports should always be scrutinized to ensure that they meet the ethical standards of the organization and its constituencies.

Topics for Discussion

1. Describe the potential role of nonroutine reports in your business career.
2. Identify the purpose and characteristics of each of these nonroutine reports:
   a. Interview report
   b. Exception report
   c. Justification report
   d. Feasibility report
   e. Staff report
   f. Press release
   g. Executive summary
   h. Business proposal
3. What is the general objective of all proposals?
4. Give an example of a solicited proposal and an unsolicited proposal.
5. What is the specific objective of each of the following proposals?
   a. Investigative/research proposal
   b. Product/service proposal
   c. Organizational/operational proposal
6. Identify ethical dilemmas that may arise as you prepare nonroutine reports. In your judgment, are you more or less likely to face ethical dilemmas as you write nonroutine reports than when you prepare routine reports?
7. If you have had experience preparing any of the nonroutine reports described in this chapter, share your experiences with your classmates. Who determined that the report should be written? How did you plan the report? How did you obtain the necessary information? What ethical issues did you have to consider?
8. If you have used any of the social media discussed in this chapter for business purposes, describe how you have used such media and the positive or negative experiences you have had with them.
9. In your judgment, which of the nonroutine reports described in this chapter would be most amenable to Twitter or Facebook distribution?

Applications

1. Form a team comprising you and two or three classmates. You are to make an initial assessment of the need for child care services on your campus by interviewing at least 15 students who have children under the age of five. Use the following procedures for the interviews and report preparation:
   - Meet with your team members to determine the questions you should ask and the interview procedures (where, when, etc.).
   - Write a proposal for the study. Submit it to your instructor, along with a copy of your interview guide.
   - Conduct the interviews. Or, with your instructor's permission, survey those students by using one of the social media described in this chapter.
   - Summarize your findings in a report to be submitted to the director of student services (or another appropriate administrator) at your school. Write the report in memo format.

2. Several cities have enacted no-smoking ordinances for public accommodations, including restaurants and bars. Assume that you are an aide to the mayor of your city. Interview at least 10 students on your campus to determine their opinions about a proposed ordinance to ban smoking in all food establishments, including bars. Summarize your findings in an interview report directed to the mayor.

3. Assume you work for a lawn-care company. Last week while providing service to one of your regular customers, you inadvertently left the backyard gate open, and the customer's dog escaped. You were not aware of the problem until the customer came out of the house, quite irate because someone who lived about a mile away had rescued the dog. Using the identification information on the dog's tags, the rescuer was able to call the owner and inform her that her dog was in good hands. Knowing you had made a serious blunder and wanting to appease the customer, you marked her service ticket "Paid," even though you did not collect the normal $85 fee for the services.

   Prepare an exception report that you will send by email to your supervisor, Cate Peerbolte. Acknowledge your fault and explain why you granted an exception to the normal practice of collecting for services immediately upon their completion. Also request that you not be penalized for the action because $85 would put a serious dent into your family budget. For example, that amount would buy formula for your infant son for nearly a month,

4. Ms. Peerbolte assured the employee (Application 3) that the action taken was appropriate to maintain the customer's goodwill. However, she must convince the company's accountant that the failure to collect the fees was justifiable. Now, acting as Ms. Peerbolte, write a justification report to the company's accountant, Cyril Karsten. Explain why you did not require the employee to absorb the cost of the negligent action. Since this report will become part of the documentation on file in the accounting department, write it in memo format,

5. Bob Guzior, a customer service representative at Big State Credit Union, was visited today by Aline Shelley, a customer who reported that she had requested an electronic payment to one of her creditors the previous month, approximately five days before the payment was due. Yesterday Ms. Shelley got a statement from her creditor with a $35 late payment fee. The payment Ms. Shelley had requested had arrived two days after its due date. Mr. Guzior explained that to ensure timely arrival, requests for electronic payments should be placed at least 10 days before the due date. Ms. Shelley gathered her papers and stood to leave, saying, "I'm disappointed in this service. If you cannot refund that late fee, I'll just have to move my accounts to another institution." Mr. Guzior apologized and said he would credit Ms. Shelley's account for $35 to cover the fee. He promptly took care of the transaction and gave Ms. Shelley a receipt for the deposit. Acting as Mr. Guzior, write an exception report to the branch manager, Dennis Halkyard, explaining what transpired. Supply reasons to justify the action.

6. Bernie's is a small, family-style restaurant located at 335 State Street, Fletcher, North Carolina. The restaurant features steaks, fried-to-order hamburgers, and roasted chicken. As complements to these menu items, the restaurant also offers

baked and french-fried potatoes, salads, a fresh vegetable (the chef's daily choice), and a variety of nonalcoholic beverages, including milkshakes. The restaurant is currently open from 11 A.M. until 8 P.M., Monday through Saturday. The owner, Bernie Dalton, is considering expanding the business in one of two ways: opening at 6:30 A.M. and adding a breakfast menu to be served from 6:30 until 11:00 A.M. or extending the hours until 11:00 P.M. on Friday and Saturday evenings. He has asked you to conduct a study to determine whether either of those options would be feasible.

To obtain data for your study, you prepared a short questionnaire, which the wait staff distributed to diners (one per table) after the customers had placed their orders. The diners were asked to complete the questionnaire while the orders were being prepared, and the wait staff collected the forms when they delivered the food to the tables. Here are the results of your survey:

- One hundred forty-nine questionnaires were completed; these represented 78 families with children, 32 couples, and 39 individuals dining alone.
- Breakfast: 65 percent of the individual diners indicated an interest in eating breakfast at Bernie's at least once a week, with Tuesday and Wednesday mornings being the preferred days; 25 percent of the families indicated an interest in breakfast, with Saturday as the preferred day; 50 percent of the couples indicated an interest, with Friday and Saturday as the preferred days.
- Evenings: No families were interested in extended evening hours on Friday and Saturday; 98 percent of the couples and 96 percent of the individual diners were interested in extended evening hours on Friday and Saturday.
- Food Purchases: The average cost of food purchased during your survey was $42 total for families, $35 total for couples, and $15 total for individuals.
- Anticipated Sales: 89 percent of respondents indicated they would likely eat dinner one additional evening per week if the Friday and Saturday hours were extended; 65 percent of respondents said they would likely eat breakfast at least once a week if a breakfast menu were offered.
- Additional Comments: Eight individuals and 10 couples suggested a Sunday morning brunch; three individuals and one couple suggested offering live music by local talent on Friday and Saturday evenings; seven families and three couples suggested expanding the menu to offer more "heart healthy" items; five individuals and four couples suggested adding beer and wine to the beverage menu.

Based on your interpretation of the data (you may make other reasonable assumptions), write a report for Bernie Dalton. Prepare the report in manuscript format and include a cover letter to Mr. Dalton. Draw a definite conclusion about the feasibility of expanding his business by one or both of the options that he is considering. Provide data to support your conclusion. You may make additional recommendations if you think the data support them.

7. Progressive Corp., an auto insurance company, now offers collision coverage for customers' dogs or cats at no additional premium cost. Assume that you work in the claims department of another major insurance company. Form a team

with one of your classmates. Brainstorm other unique coverages that could make an auto insurance policy more attractive. Knowing that you are looking for promotion opportunities within your company, your supervisor has asked the two of you to prepare a report about the pros and cons of offering collision coverage for pets and at least one additional type of coverage you have generated while brainstorming. Conduct research and prepare the staff report.

8. Assume that you work for Fish Food, a major chain of family-style seafood restaurants. The director of marketing, Raj Patel, wants to evaluate the quality of the company's food and service. He has asked the market research staff to find out how effective "mystery shopping" is as a market research technique. He has asked the staff to do a study of companies that offer mystery shopping services and make a recommendation about whether Fish Food should contract with such a company to evaluate the quality of its food and service. As a member of the research staff, conduct research on this matter and prepare the staff report. Include both benefits and drawbacks of using mystery shoppers. For example, what are typical costs, what input would you have into developing the "shopping" criteria, how reliable are the reports, and how prompt is the feedback obtained from the shoppers? (Hint: Begin your research by entering "mystery shopping" in an Internet search engine.)

9. Assume you are the chair of a committee planning a benefit for PetSave, an agency that rescues and finds homes for abandoned and abused animals. The benefit, Just Fur Fun, will be held on March 15, 2013, at the restored opera house in your city. Features of the evening include a dinner before the performance; wine-and-cheese reception from 6:30 to 7:30 P.M. in the lobby of the opera house; a performance by a famous musician (select one whom you would like to hear); and a reception with the performer after the concert. All proceeds go to PetSave, and donations are tax deductible to the extent allowed by the Internal Revenue Service. Tickets may be purchased online (supply a fictitious Web address) or by telephone (supply a fictitious number). Credit card payments are accepted.

   Pricing options available to donors:
   - $1,000 for four tickets: dinner for four, wine-and-cheese reception, special seating for the concert, and private reception with performer after the concert
   - $600 for two tickets: dinner for two, wine-and-cheese reception, special seating for the concert, and private reception with performer after the concert
   - $150 for two tickets: wine-and-cheese reception, special seating for the concert, and private reception with performer after the concert
   - $50 for one ticket: wine-and-cheese reception and general seating

   a. Write a news release about the event.
   b. Write a progress report in memo format to be sent to the executive director of PetSave, Bettye Leogones. Report these accomplishments:
      - A personal invitation was sent to all previous participants in PetSave fund-raisers during the week of January 15.

- A quarter-page ad was placed in the *Newberry News*, *The State*, and the *Lexington Leader* on January 15.
- Fifty percent of tickets in each category were sold within two weeks of the press release and mailing of personal invitations.

You plan to send a follow-up email to previous participants who have not yet bought tickets for the event.

10. A new trend in street food is gourmet food trucks. In several cities, owners of fine restaurants or chefs wanting to open a new business are going to the streets in trucks from which they sell gourmet sandwiches and light meals. Assume that Ramone Simmons, who has worked as a chef in an upscale restaurant in Atlanta, Georgia, has asked you to study the feasibility of setting up such a business in your community. Use the Internet to get information about mobile gourmet food outlets. Simmons needs information about typical start-up and operating costs, potentially successful menu items or food categories, work hours (food preparation and sales), and so forth. Assume that Simmons projects that he would be able to fill about 20 food orders per hour at an average price of $7.50. Cost of preparing the food (excluding labor) will be approximately 15 percent of selling price. Prepare a feasibility study that will show Simmons how much capital he will need to begin the operation and the sales volume he will need to cover the capital costs, operating costs, and a reasonable return on investment.

11. Read three newspaper, magazine, or journal articles or reliable Web postings on one of the following topics (or another topic assigned by your instructor). Present what you have learned from the articles in an executive summary directed to your instructor.

- Should state development boards give tax incentives to induce businesses to establish a new plant (or other business entity) in your state?
- Have state-operated lotteries resulted in significant increases in funding for elementary and secondary education?
- How do state universities handle security at special events, such as concerts and football games?
- Should age limits be placed on the provision of critical, costly medical services, such as kidney transplants?
- What are the potential positive and negative environmental impacts of mass transition to CF (compact fluorescent) or LED (light-emitting diode) lightbulbs?
- What is the current distinction between "organic" and "natural" as food labels? How helpful are these designations for consumers?
- How effective are "groupons" (group coupons) as marketing tools?
- How can frequent business travelers get the most economical deals on airfares and hotel accommodations?
- What changes should be or are being made in the design of military uniforms for female troops?
- Expansion of the Panama Canal is projected to be completed by the end of 2014. What are the implications of that expansion for major U.S. ports?

- Should a tattoo artist who designs a tattoo specifically for a celebrity (for example, the tattoo around Mike Tyson's eye) be permitted to copyright that "art"?

12. Using Twitter search engines, gather information for the same topic that you selected for Application 11. Summarize the results of your search and write a memo to your instructor, evaluating the effectiveness of search engines for the preparation of an executive summary. Attach your summary to the memo.

13. Assume you are a communication trainer at Samsung USA. You have had extensive experience working with Korean expatriates who have worked for Samsung USA. Professor Suh Kyun-ja at Seoul National University is developing a training program for U.S. expatriates who will be sent to Korea to work as supervisors in various assembly plants for Samsung and other Korean manufacturers. Professor Suh has invited you to deliver a one-day workshop as part of that training program. The program is designed to prepare the U.S. managers for working in Korea.

Professor Suh requested that you prepare a proposal for a presentation to the trainees. He would like the content to be easy to understand, interesting, and inspiring enough to motivate the trainees to feel enthusiastic about working in Korea. Eighty percent of the trainees possess only a threshold level of proficiency in Korean, but you are proficient in Korean and English. The training will be conducted in English.

Write a proposal, addressed to Professor Suh, that he will be able to submit to his dean to request financial support for your trip. The following information will help you develop the proposal:

- Duration of presentation: six hours
    - Morning sessions: 9:00–10:30; 10:45–12:00
    - Refreshment break: 10:30–10:45
    - Afternoon sessions: 13:00–15:00; 15:15–16:30
    - Refreshment break: 15:00–15:15
- Content of presentation
    - Doing business in Korea: general principles and practices
    - Getting to know Korean culture: customs and courtesies
    - Getting to know Korean people: personal attributes and attitudes toward U.S. citizens
    - Keys to success in working and communicating with Korean local employees
    - Major failures of expatriate managers in working and communicating with Korean local employees
    - Korean local employees' work-related expectations from foreign managers
    - Cases of successful and unsuccessful business communication and interpersonal interactions in Korea
- Methods of presentation
    - Lecture with PowerPoint presentation
    - Case study and discussion

- Fees
  - Round-trip airfare: Memphis, Tennessee, to Seoul, Korea (determine current fare)
  - Lodging in Seoul University guest house or nearby hotel
  - Honorarium: U.S.$2,000
14. Review the feasibility study shown in Illustration 8.4. Rewrite the report, assuming that cost of merchandise is 30 percent of sales. You may change any other assumptions about catalog and website development, salaries, and so forth, but be sure to alter the narrative accordingly.

Reference

1. Adapted from Cox, P., Bobrowski, P. E., & Maher, L. (2003). Teaching first-year business students to summarize: Abstract writing assignment. *Business Communication Quarterly*, 66(4), 36–54.

CHAPTER **9**

Planning and Delivering an Oral Report

LEARNING OBJECTIVES

After you have read this chapter, you should be able to:

1. Plan an effective presentation by:

    -   Analyzing the context

    -   Selecting an appropriate delivery style and level of formality

    -   Outlining the presentation

    -   Preparing visual aids, including PowerPoint slide decks

    -   Preparing suitable audience handouts

2. Rehearse purposefully by learning to manage:

    -   Your notes

    -   Symptoms of stage fright

    -   Vocal and verbal aspects of the presentation

    -   Nonverbal aspects of the presentation

    -   Backchannel

3. Manage a question-and-answer session.

4. Apply your presenting skills in a team presentation.

5. Conduct an online presentation (webinar).

AFTER COMPLETING A WRITTEN REPORT, you may utter a sigh of relief. "At last!" you say to yourself. "I've finished that assignment." But in many situations, writing the report is not the final task. You will also be expected to present your information orally to a select audience. That audience may be people at your level, at a lower level, or at a higher level in the organization. In many situations, however, the audience consists of individuals representing various levels in the organization or of persons at the managerial or executive levels.

For that reason, your oral reporting skills will have a significant impact on your career success. In this chapter, you will learn how to construct and deliver effective oral presentations.

Planning the Presentation

Effective oral presentations require extensive preparation. In many ways, preparing an oral report is much like composing a written report. The diagram in Illustration 9.1 will guide you through the preparation steps.

Analyze the Context

The communication context encompasses the internal (psychological) environment and the external (physical) environment. Major aspects of context analysis for an oral report, therefore, are determining the characteristics of the intended audience and the characteristics of the place in which you will deliver the presentation. Those two factors tend also to define the appropriate degree of formality.

Audience

Audience analysis is an attempt to assess the psychological environment for the presentation. In this analysis, you should try to determine who will attend and their

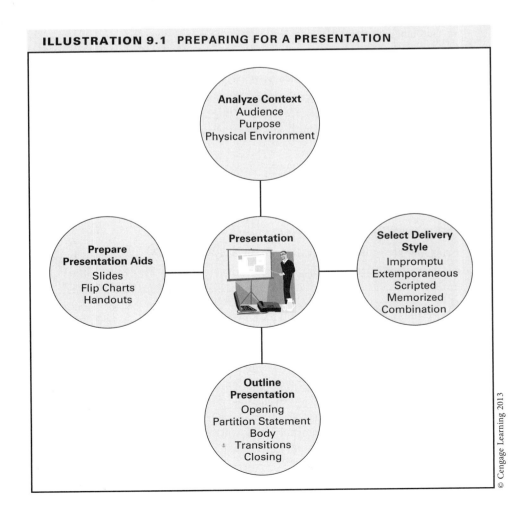

ILLUSTRATION 9.1 PREPARING FOR A PRESENTATION

Analyze Context
Audience
Purpose
Physical Environment

Prepare
Presentation Aids
Slides
Flip Charts
Handouts

Presentation

Select Delivery
Style
Impromptu
Extemporaneous
Scripted
Memorized
Combination

Outline
Presentation
Opening
Partition Statement
Body
Transitions
Closing

© Cengage Learning 2013

motives for attending your presentation. You can expect to give oral reports to four different types of audiences:

- *Clients and customers.* An oral presentation can be a valuable sales technique. Whether you are trying to interest clients in a silicon chip or a bulldozer, you will present its features and its advantages over the competition. Then, after the sale, you will likely narrate detailed operating instructions and maintenance procedures to the users.
- *Colleagues in your organization.* If you are the resident expert on a device, procedure, or technical subject, you will instruct your fellow workers, both technical and nontechnical. After you return from an important conference or an out-of-town project, your supervisors will want a briefing—an oral report. If you have an idea for improving operations at your organization, you probably will write a brief informal proposal and then present the idea orally to a small group of managers. Your presentation will help them determine whether it is prudent to devote resources to studying the idea in greater depth.
- *Fellow professionals at technical conferences.* As you develop in your profession, you might speak about your own research project or a team project carried out at your organization, or you may be invited to speak to professionals in other fields. If you are an economist, for example, you might be invited to speak to real estate agents about interest rates.
- *The general public.* As you assume greater prominence in your field, you will receive invitations to speak to civic organizations and governmental bodies. Since most organizations encourage employees to participate in community service, you will likely be encouraged to give these presentations.

As you analyze your audience, answer questions such as those listed in Illustration 9.2. Answers to such questions will help you define the psychological environment—how receptive your audience is to your message. These questions are equally relevant for online and face-to-face presentations. Assume, for example, that you must present the results of your survey of customer preferences for new services at a local bank. An audience of branch managers who know that the survey was conducted and are eager to increase business in their respective branches will likely be eager to hear your report. Assume further that the managers will meet immediately after your presentation to make a decision based on your recommendations, one of which is to provide online bill payment services. Under those circumstances, the participants will likely listen critically, evaluating every bit of information you present, possibly interrupting with questions and asking for immediate clarification of anything they don't understand. Such an audience would likely be attentive even late on Friday afternoon! Add to your assumption one manager's opposition to your recommendation for online bill payment. In such a situation, you should anticipate the need for an especially convincing presentation. You should also expect challenging, perhaps even argumentative, questions from that manager and be prepared with appropriate responses.

Purpose

Consider the purpose of your presentation, just as you would in writing a report. Are you attempting to inform your audience or to both inform and persuade them? If you

---

ILLUSTRATION 9.2   AUDIENCE ANALYSIS FOR PRESENTATION

As you analyze your audience, ask yourself these questions and write your answers.

- What is the expected size of the audience?
  - Who will attend the presentation?
  - What's the name of the group?
  - What part of the organization does the audience represent?
  - What type of positions do they hold in the company?
  - Are the participants predominantly male or mostly female?
  - What cultures/ethnicities do they represent?
  - How long have they been with the company?
- Does the audience know much about the topic, or do they know little?
- What are their reasons for attending the presentation?
  - Is the audience part of a problem you will discuss?
  - Are participants expected to be part of the solution?
  - Are audience members attending voluntarily?
  - Are they required to attend?
- What are their attitudes toward the topic?
  - Indifference?
  - Opposition?
  - Support?
- What effect will time of the presentation have on participants? Will the audience likely be:
  - Alert or drowsy?
  - Rested or tired?
- What are participants expected to do?
  - Receive information only?
  - Discuss the report?
  - Convey information to other employees?
  - Participate in a group decision?
  - Make a decision at the end of the presentation?
  - Make a decision later?
  - Make individual decisions?

© Cengage Learning 2013

---

are explaining how solar power can be used to generate energy, you have one type of argument. If you are explaining why solar power is an economical means of generating power, you have another type.

Physical Environment

The physical environment also influences the outcome of your presentation. An initially receptive audience can become indifferent or irritable if the physical environment is unsuitable. To define that environment, answer questions such as those listed in Illustration 9.3. These questions relate to face-to-face presentations. You will often lead and participate in Web presentations, which are discussed later in this chapter.

Knowledge about the physical environment, along with an assessment of the psychological environment, can help you plan your presentation strategies. Consider again your presentation to the bank branch managers. If you want to encourage discussion of your findings, conclusions, and recommendations, you should ask for a conference room arrangement with everyone seated at a table. That arrangement tends to foster discussion more readily than does a formal arrangement with the participants seated in rows facing the speaker. If you anticipate serious discussion of the information, use a handout or slide show, such as Microsoft PowerPoint 2010, Corel Presentations, Keynote 5 for Macintosh, or SoftMaker Presentations. (LibreOffice

---

ILLUSTRATION 9.3 EVALUATING THE PHYSICAL ENVIRONMENT

As you evaluate the physical environment, consider the following.

- Where will the face-to-face presentation be made?
  - Auditorium?
  - Part of a divided hotel ballroom?
  - Conference room?
  - Classroom?
  - Office? Whose office?
- What furniture arrangement will be used?
  - Audience in formal rows facing the speaker?
  - Participants and speaker seated at conference table?
  - Audience and speaker seated in office with no table?
- What presentation aids will be available, and where will they be located in the room?
- What arrangements must be made for their use? Who will make those arrangements?
  - Lectern?
  - Stationary or mobile microphone?
  - Flip chart, marker board, or digital whiteboard?
  - Computer hardware?
  - Presentation software—specific brand and version?
  - Projection equipment and screen?
  - Remote control/laser pointer for slide show?
  - Electrical outlets?
- What aspects of the physical environment, if any, may distract from your presentation? Can these potential distractions be removed, controlled, or compensated for?
  - Noise?
  - Lighting?
  - Size of room?
  - Kind of seating?
- What aspects of the environment may you be unable to control? Can you adapt your presentation to accommodate such things?
  - Equipment malfunction?
  - Power outage?
  - Heating, ventilating, and air-conditioning malfunction?
  - Insufficient seating?

© Cengage Learning 2013

[http://www.libreoffice.org] is a free, downloadable application, and Web-based choices include Google Presentations [http://www.google.com; click Documents, Presentations] and Prezi [http://prezi.com]). Prepare to use available markup options (pen, highlighter, and eraser) on the presentation software. If you want to list or summarize ideas generated during the discussion, be sure the room contains a flip chart, marker board, overhead projector, or digital whiteboard and appropriate writing implements.

Recognizing the available options in your physical environment can help you achieve success as a speaker. Selecting the appropriate type of delivery can also enhance your oral report.

Select Delivery Style

Five options are available as you select a delivery mode: impromptu, extemporaneous, scripted, memorized, and combination.

Impromptu delivery consists of speaking spontaneously, without previous rehearsal, with little or no advanced preparation and without text or notes to assist you. You will seldom use this type of delivery for the presentation of a major report. You may use it, however, for spontaneous interim progress reports on a project. After you have completed your data collection and analysis for the bank customer survey, for example, your supervisor could ask you in a staff meeting for a quick update on the project. Your presentation in response to that request would be an impromptu speech.

Although impromptu speeches are spontaneous, following these guides will help you make effective impromptu presentations:

- Anticipate the major topics that may be discussed at a meeting. Play a "What if …" game with yourself. Ask, "What if I am asked to give an update on the bank customer survey?" Answering that question will enable you to consider which information, if any, you will present in the meeting.
- Avoid being surprised. Listen attentively; recognize that the discussion is moving into your area of expertise. You can then anticipate that you may be asked for an impromptu statement.
- Speak for only a minute or two; avoid rambling. Generally, follow this four-step pattern: (1) Restate your topic (one sentence); then (2) state one or two key points. Next, (3) expand on each point; finally (4) tell listeners what you want them to remember.

Extemporaneous delivery appears to be spontaneous but involves extensive planning, purposeful rehearsal, and the use of notes during the presentation. With the notes to aid you and the confidence gained during rehearsal, you can establish and maintain eye contact with your audience and move freely about the presentation area. If you have planned and rehearsed your presentation sufficiently, the information will be accurate, complete, organized, and easy to follow. And if you can think well on your feet, the presentation will have a naturalness that will help participants concentrate on what you are saying.

The following suggestions will help you master extemporaneous delivery:

- Plan every aspect of your presentation, including the use of visual aids and how you will handle questions.

- Write your talk, including notations for visual aids, gestures, audience feedback, and pauses. Read it slowly once or twice to estimate its delivery time. Prepare notes to use during your presentation. Do not memorize your talk.
- Rehearse the presentation until it flows smoothly without giving the impression of being memorized. Include your slides and other visuals in the rehearsal and practice the gestures and moves and pauses you planned. Use your notes only as prompts to keep the presentation flowing smoothly. Time your talk to be sure it fits your allotted presentation time. (In general, the actual talk will take about 25 percent longer.) If possible, rehearse before a small audience and ask them to give you feedback.
- Become thoroughly familiar with the details that you want to present. Understand them; anticipate points that the audience may question.
- Prepare alternative explanations. Adapt to audience nonverbal feedback or questions that indicate the participants do not understand some part of the presentation.

You may use extemporaneous delivery in both formal and informal settings. This delivery style is justified when you are very familiar with the information and exact adherence to a prepared script is less important than maintaining eye contact with the audience.

Scripted delivery involves reading a manuscript verbatim. This delivery style is appropriate when you are presenting technical or controversial information and you want to ensure that no errors are made in transmission of that information.

Scripted delivery tends to be used in formal more often than informal contexts. Advantages of such delivery are that you can feel confident about the accuracy of your speech and can give an exact copy of your message to members of the audience—preferably after your presentation—to ensure that they receive an accurate message. A disadvantage, however, is that you will have difficulty maintaining eye contact and may miss significant nonverbal reactions from your audience.

To prepare for scripted delivery, follow these guides:

- Prepare the manuscript and verify its accuracy.
- Mark the manuscript with delivery cues (arrows, bold type, and underlining) to indicate variations in speed or emphasis.
- Practice reading your manuscript until you can read it fluently. Avoid reading too quickly.
- Concentrate on precise enunciation. Rapid reading frequently leads to slurring or mispronunciation of words.
- Vary your tone or pitch to appropriately emphasize the content of your report as you would in conversation.

When the context justifies scripted delivery, be cautious about impromptu discussion following the speech. Although discussion may be appropriate, listen attentively and answer cautiously to avoid contradicting what you said during the delivery.

Memorized delivery is presentation of a verbatim message learned by rote. An advantage of memorized delivery is that it allows full freedom of movement and permits you to maintain eye contact with your audience. That delivery style can also promote the audience's confidence in your expertise. A disadvantage, however, is that anxiety may cause you to forget or omit part of the presentation, thereby destroying the coherence of the message and possibly destroying your credibility.

Memorized delivery is appropriate when the volume of information is "memorizable" and you want to foster participants' confidence in you. Be cautious, however, about appearing pompous or excessively oratorical. Such an impression tends to alienate an audience. *Combination delivery* employs a variety of delivery styles in a single presentation. You will find this style suitable for many report presentations. In the bank example, for instance, you could deliver a memorized opening statement that will attract attention and stimulate interest in your presentation; that statement could be followed by an extemporaneous presentation of the major findings, conclusions, and recommendations. Perhaps during the presentation of findings, you may choose to read some statements made by survey participants. And, in answer to a question, you may make an impromptu presentation about further research that you think the bank should conduct.

Your analyses of the psychological and the physical environments will also contribute to decisions about how formal or informal your presentation should be.

In a *formal* presentation, such as a scripted speech, you will deliver a carefully structured, controlled message with no immediate verbal feedback from the audience. For formal presentations, you will usually stand at a lectern, facing an audience seated in rows. You may use notes or a manuscript to ensure that you proceed through the presentation as planned. You may also use presentation aids—slides, videos, podcast/audio recordings, flip charts, pass-around objects, and handouts—that you have prepared in advance.

A formal presentation leaves little or no room for spontaneous response from the audience; consequently, you must be aware of nonverbal responses to evaluate whether the listeners understand your message. If nonverbal feedback signifies that the audience does not understand or is becoming restless, you should modify your presentation. When appropriate, you may conduct a question-and-answer session after a formal presentation. (Suggestions for managing question-and-answer sessions are given later in this chapter.)

An *informal* presentation is also a carefully planned, controlled message, but audience verbal feedback is usually encouraged during the presentation. In an informal presentation, your audience will likely be seated at a conference table or in a semicircle to promote interaction among members of the audience. You may also be seated or standing near the group. You will likely speak extemporaneously, relying on brief notes or presentation aids to direct your talk.

Since members of the audience may ask questions or make comments, an informal presentation can veer from its intended course. To achieve the objective of your report, you must maintain control of the discussion and refocus audience attention on your topic after each question or comment has been given an adequate response.

In a *semiformal* presentation, you will strike a middle ground between the formal and informal styles, using a combination style of delivery. In the bank example, for instance, you could give a carefully structured report of your findings as you stand before individuals seated at a conference table, and you might request that they hold their questions until you have presented all findings. Then you could entertain questions about the findings before going on to your conclusions and recommendations. During that part of the presentation, you could sit at the table and permit free discussion of each of the conclusions and recommendations as you present them.

As you plan a presentation, select a degree of formality that complements the topic, the audience, and the physical environment. When the audience is large, a formal presentation may be the most efficient way to present your report. If the findings, conclusions, or recommendations are controversial, you may also choose a formal presentation style so that you can present all information before confronting questions. Deferring questions until the end of the presentation may defuse some issues. When the audience is small, a semiformal or informal style may be effective, especially if you want to promote discussion. When the audience is a mixed group, with various levels of interest in or knowledge about your topic, a formal presentation may be superior to an informal one. The formal style will permit you to control the presentation more closely and be sure that relevant information is presented at a level that is understandable to all members of the audience. For a relatively small, highly motivated, decision-oriented group, an informal style that permits all decision makers to ask questions and evaluate the information is effective.

After choosing a delivery style appropriate for your audience and the context, you are ready to outline your presentation.

Outline the Presentation

A simple yet effective outline structure for an oral report consists of four parts: the opening, a preview or partition statement, the body, and the conclusion. Each must be worded to formulate a coherent speech that accomplishes your reporting purpose, and the parts must be connected by meaningful transitions.

Outlines are extremely useful tools for helping you organize and deliver a presentation. As you prepare, maintain a thorough outline of every element you want to include in the presentation. Organize your outline along the lines presented in Illustration 9.4.

Strong Opening

The opening of the speech must reach out and grab the listeners' attention. An effective opening draws the audience into the message by showing its relevance to them. Such an opening focuses on the audience, not on the speaker. Some effective attention-getting openings are quotations, surprising statements, questions, stories, or relevant statistics.

Some speakers have the mistaken idea that all speeches should begin with a joke. A humorous opening is effective only if the humor relates to the speech topic, offends no one in the audience, and is delivered skillfully.

ILLUSTRATION 9.4   SAMPLE ORAL REPORT OUTLINE

Title of Presentation:

Purpose of Speech:

I. Introduction
  A. Strong opening statement to grab audience attention
  B. Topic of speech
  C. Relevance of topic
    1. Subpoint 1: reason
    2. Subpoint 2: reason
  D. Partition statement

II. Body
  A. Main Point 1
    1. Subpoint 1
      a. Supporting information
      b. Supporting information
    2. Subpoint 2
      a. Supporting information
      b. Supporting information
  B. Main Point 2
    1. Subpoint 1
      a. Supporting information
      b. Supporting information
    2. Subpoint 2
      a. Supporting information
      b. Supporting information
  C. Main Point 3
    1. Subpoint 1
      a. Supporting information
      b. Supporting information
      c. Supporting information
    2. Subpoint 2
      a. Supporting information
      b. Supporting information
      c. Supporting information

III. Conclusion
  A. Summary of main points
  B. Relationship of most important point(s) to purpose of presentation
  C. Strong last sentence to close the presentation

© Cengage Learning 2013

Compare the following examples of ineffective and effective opening statements.

Ineffective: Today I'm going to give you the results of the survey of Midland National Bank customers that Mr. Hector asked me to conduct last month. I think you might be interested in some of the results. (Focuses on speaker; tentatively suggests topic may be relevant to listeners)

Effective: Your customers want innovative bank services that will give them easier access to their accounts. You can give them those services at very little extra cost to your branch. (Focuses on listeners; establishes relevance of message to them)

Ineffective: What's the slowest-moving line in the world? The line at the teller's window I just chose. I always manage to choose the slowest-moving line. Seriously, folks, I'm here to tell you about your recent customer survey and what it suggests about service at your bank. (Trite joke that may offend audience members; focuses on speaker; doesn't recognize participants' needs)

> **Effective:** *Eighty percent of your banking customers are satisfied with Midland services. That's good news. Today I'd like to suggest how you can turn good news into even better news—how satisfied customers can become extremely satisfied customers. (Pleasing statistic involving the audience; shows immediate relevance of speech to participants)*

Meaningful Preview Statement

The preview (partition) statement tells the audience what the speech will cover. This statement should create a mental readiness or "map" that will help the listeners follow your presentation. A partition statement should clearly and interestingly identify the topics to be covered so that participants can anticipate the message that unfolds. Compare the following examples of effective and ineffective partition statements.

> **Ineffective:** *As I said, Mr. Hector asked me to find out what Midland National Bank customers think about some services that we are considering for our customers. So I basically asked them about five different services. In this presentation I'm going to tell you what those services are, how customers responded to the survey, and some recommendations based on their responses. (Continues to focus on speaker; gives no clue about specific content of message or relevance to audience; provides only a structural overview: questions asked, responses, recommendations)*
>
> **Effective:** *My recommendation will be based on two major findings from our study of Midland National Bank (MNB) customer attitudes toward proposed new banking services. MNB customers showed the strongest interest in new services that give them easy access to their accounts. They showed little interest in incentives for some of our standard consumer banking services. Today I'd like to share with you what we found out about consumer preferences, specifically the services they expressed interest in and the services they were indifferent to. I'll also make some recommendations about how we can satisfy MNB customer preferences. (Heightens interest; tells what will be covered; creates a receptive frame of mind because it suggests relevance to audience)*

Well-Developed Main Points

The body of the presentation must adequately develop the points identified in the preview statement. An appropriate sequence of information following the previous effective preview statement would be (1) services preferred by customers, (2) services about which customers were indifferent, and (3) recommendations for providing the preferred services. Development can be achieved by presenting statistics, examples of customer comments, costs of implementing certain services, and any additional data that will support your recommendations and enable listeners to reach an effective decision.

Engaging Language

If people doze off while reading a report you have written, you probably will not know it, at least not until they complain to you later or you realize that the report failed to accomplish its purpose. But if they doze off while you are speaking to them, you'll know it right away. Effective presentations require memorable language.

To help make your language memorable, follow these three techniques:

- **Involve the audience.** People are more interested in their own concerns than in yours. Talk to the audience about *their* problems and *their* solutions. In the introduction, establish a link between your topic and the participants' interests. For instance, in a presentation to the Gafney City Council about waste management, you might begin like this: *Picture yourself on the Gafney City Council two years from now. After exhaustive hearings, proposals, and feasibility studies, you still don't have a waste-management plan that meets federal regulations. What you do have is a mounting debt, as the city is assessed $1,000 a day until you implement an acceptable plan.*

- **Refer to people, not to abstractions.** People remember specifics; they forget abstractions. When you want to make a point memorable, describe it in human terms. *What could you do with that $365,000 every year? You could buy almost 400 personal computers; that's a computer for almost every classroom in every elementary school in Arcadia Township. You could expand your school-lunch program to feed every needy child in the township. You could extend your after-school programs to cover an additional 3,000 students.*

- **Use interesting facts, figures, and quotations.** Do your research and find interesting information about your subject. For instance, you might find a brief quotation from an authoritative figure in the field (Al Gore on global warming?) or a famous person not generally associated with the field (Bill Gates on health and nutrition?).

Purposeful Transitions

Ideas within your presentation must be linked logically and clearly. Transitional words or phrases help the audience understand a discussion by pointing out the direction of the presentation. All parts of the presentation should be linked together by simple transitions that demonstrate the organizational pattern you are using. The introductory preview acts as a transition to the body of the presentation. When you move from one main point to another, use a statement announcing the move: *Now that we have looked at point 1, let's look at point 2.* Likewise, you should announce demonstrations, examples, digressions, or comparisons and contrasts when they occur: *An example of point 2 occurs when ...* Finally, make a clear transition when you begin the conclusion of the presentation: *Now that we have discussed each of the three main points, let's summarize the key elements.*

Weak speakers often overlook these simple transitional sentences, but transitions can be one of your most effective tactics to help the audience follow your points. Because participants do not have the outline of the presentation in front of them, you must verbalize the structure of the outline to keep them on track. Here are several other transition clauses you may find helpful for unifying your presentation.

Enumeration:	"My first point is ..."
Importance:	"A more important fact is ..."
Emphasis:	"The main point to remember is ..."
Addition:	"Another thing to consider is ..."
Tangents:	"This is off the subject, but ..."

Return:	"Let me get back to where I was."
Leading:	"The next thing to look at is …"
Question:	"What is the next thing to consider?"
Preview:	"I will deal with three main ideas."
Internal summary:	"Let me conclude this section."
Summary:	"Let me repeat my main ideas."

Consider the following examples of ineffective and effective transitions.

> *Ineffective:* So that's pretty much what customers thought about services that give them easier access to their accounts. Now let's look at their evaluations of some other kinds of services. (Does not summarize the completed part; provides no clue about content of the next part; gives no indication of how the two parts are related)
>
> *Effective:* As you have seen, our customers gave "important" or "very important" ratings to the two services related to accessing accounts: online funds transfer and bill payment and the Deposit@Mobile application that allows customers to make deposits using their smartphones. In contrast, MNB customers showed little interest in additional ATM locations or Saturday morning teller service. (Summarizes one part of presentation; links it to the next part of presentation)

Memorable Conclusion

The conclusion should clinch the message; that is, it should be what you want the listeners to leave the room with. For an informative talk, the conclusion must help the listeners remember the main points of the message. For a persuasive presentation, the conclusion should stimulate action based on the message. Be sure to link the conclusion to the body of the speech by a meaningful transition.

Effective ways to end a speech include summaries of the report content, requests or proposals for specific actions, examples or anecdotes that reinforce the message, questions that prompt a response or action, or combinations of those strategies. The closing should be a memorable finish for the audience, not a letdown or abrupt stop. Compare the following examples of effective and ineffective conclusions.

> *Ineffective:* That's about all I found out. Based on the findings, it looks like it might be a good idea to provide more online banking options. (Does not summarize or recap the report; tentatively hints at action)
>
> *Effective:* Evidence indicates that MNB customers want more online banking services than we currently provide. The simplest, least costly way to give them those services is to add funds transfer and bill payment to the account statements already available at MNB's website. Only one of our local competitors currently offers funds transfer and bill payment. I recommend that we initiate it by December 1. Doing so will demonstrate to our current customers—and also to some potential ones—that MNB believes in service. (Summarizes major findings; confidently proposes a specific action and the likely outcome of that action)

Outlines vary tremendously because you must adapt them to the situation and the purpose of the presentation. Whatever the case, take care to organize clearly and use a framework that allows you to see at a glance how the presentation is structured. A good outline will help you stay organized as you speak, adjust the presentation to time constraints, add or subtract material, and find your place if you become lost during the presentation. Prepare your outline using complete sentences, partial sentences, key phrases, or key words. Experiment with various forms of outlines until you find one that is particularly useful to you.

Your analysis of your audience and your purpose will affect the content and form of your presentation. Topics, for example, can be arranged to accommodate the audience's needs. You might have to emphasize certain aspects of your subject or ignore others altogether. Meaningful and memorable language will add to the effectiveness of your presentation.

Now that you have structured your presentation, developed your outline, evaluated your language, and incorporated transitional words and phrases, you must find ways to enhance it further. Visual aids are the tools to accentuate the information you want to share.

Preparing and Using Presentation Aids

Presentation aids are any audio or visual tools you use to supplement your spoken message. A microphone, for example, is an audio tool that can improve your presentation in a large room, enabling everyone to hear you well. A large poster displaying a chart is a visual aid that helps you explain or dramatize data. A slide show is an aid that illustrates key points and links you to additional aids on the Web.

Because we live in a visually oriented society, we expect to see as well as hear information. Therefore, effective presenters show as well as tell their points. Two broad categories of visual aids are available to enhance presentations. One category, direct viewing visuals, includes such things as real objects, models, flip charts, diagrams and drawings, photographs, and handouts. The second category, projected visuals, includes slide shows, transparencies, videos/DVDs, and websites.

Selecting Appropriate Presentation Aids

Always remember that presentation aids are just that—*aids.* Adding visuals to a poorly researched, poorly organized presentation will not salvage it. Audio and visual aids should be used to attract and hold attention, clarify meanings, emphasize or elaborate main ideas, or prove a point. Several factors must be considered in selecting the appropriate presentation aid:

- **Constraints of the topic.** Some topics will limit your choice of visual aids. For example, if you were explaining how a large robot operates, you would probably use a video of the robot in operation. That type of aid could also give the audience cues about the sounds such a robot would make while in operation. A scaled-down model of the robot may not be as effective since the scope and movement of the machinery may be a persuasive point. Similarly, a drawing or photograph of the robot would be the least effective visual aid.
- **Availability of equipment.** If the presentation site does not have a microphone, you will have to bring your own or be prepared to project your voice to match the needs of the audience. Likewise, if you plan to project a slide show, you must find

out whether you need to bring a laptop computer and provide a digital projector—and speakers for any audio clips in your slide show. And does the presentation site have a projection screen or a white wall you can use for that purpose?

- **Ownership of the presentation aids.** You may find a visual on the Internet that seems ideally suited to support your presentation. Before including it, however, you must determine whether it is in the public domain or subject to copyright laws. (**Note:** Even some visuals on sites such as Google Images are copyright protected. In that case, legal and ethical use requires permission of the copyright holder [owner of the image]. Plan ahead when requesting permission from the copyright holder, as getting a reply to your request may take several weeks—or even longer. An email or letter to the owner may be enough to obtain the permission you need. In some instances, permission may be denied, or you may need to pay a fee for use of the image. Permission fees vary widely; you may be able to obtain permission for a few dollars, but in some instances, the permission cost could prohibit use of the presentation aid.

- **Cost of the visual.** Easy access to computers, presentation software, and digital cameras allows for low-cost production of professional visual aids. Still, in some instances you may be limited to something like a transparency, flip chart, or handout. Remember, however, that even inexpensive visuals can be effective if used purposefully.

- **Difficulty of producing the visual.** If you have only two days to prepare for your presentation, it may be impossible to assemble the ideal visual. In a talk about preventing motorcycle theft, you would like to use a prototype of an antitheft device you invented. If time is short, however, you may need to show drawings instead.

- **Appropriateness of the presentation aid to the audience.** The type of audience and the nature of the presentation affect the choice of audio and visual aids. If you want to use part of a CD, you must be able to select and play the correct tracks without distracting the audience. Some charts, graphs, and diagrams may be too technical for anyone but specialists to grasp. Detailed and complicated tables and charts that require considerable time to digest should be avoided. Generally, the best visuals are simple to use and comprehend.

- **Appropriateness of the presentation aid to the presenter.** Visual aids require skill for their effective presentation. To use a flip chart, a person must be able to speak clearly, write legibly, and draw well-proportioned diagrams. Projected visuals require skill in handling slides and links to videos and/or websites. If you do not feel comfortable with a particular visual medium, do not use it. (Even when you do prepare to use a particular medium, have a backup plan in case something goes awry—such as a PowerPoint file that will not open or a desired website that is temporarily unavailable.)

- **Appropriateness of the presentation aid to the time limit.** The speaker should carefully check the time required to display and explain a visual aid to make sure the main ideas of the presentation will not be neglected. Any visual that needs too much explanation is a poor one.

To be effective, presentation aids must be incorporated smoothly into your talk. The guides shown in Illustration 9.5 will help you use most audio and visual aids effectively.

ILLUSTRATION 9.5 GUIDES FOR USING PRESENTATION AIDS

To use presentation aids effectively ...

- Prepare the aids in advance; use them in your rehearsal to help you become more confident when using them.
- Check the room in which you will give your presentation to be sure it can accommodate your aids.
- Check all equipment before the presentation to be sure it is operating properly. Be sure that sound equipment, such as a microphone or computer speakers, operates effectively, projecting sound neither too softly nor too loudly. Even so, have a backup plan.
- Use your natural speaking voice when using a microphone. Avoid standing so near to a stationary microphone or holding a handheld one so close that it picks up sibilant speech sounds or noises from the movement of your papers. An appropriate distance for most microphones is six inches from the speaker's mouth. Attach a lapel microphone to the inside of your lapel so your voice can be heard clearly whenever you turn your head to the left or right.
- Designate a specific person to signal you if the microphone volume is too loud or too soft or a visual aid is not visible. Make necessary adjustments before your audience becomes distracted.
- Keep the visuals simple. If necessary, prepare and display several aids instead of crowding too much information into one exhibit.
- Number all visuals; mark your notes or manuscript to indicate when each visual will be used.
- Do not use too many visuals; each one should add something to the presentation, not detract from it.
- Be sure that each visual aid is large enough for your audience to see and detect the detail you want noticed.
- Avoid displaying a visual aid, or any part of it, until you need it in your presentation.
- Do not block your audience's view of the visual aid; use a pointer if necessary. In a slide show, use the mouse pointer or a laser pointer or walk to the screen and point with your index finger.
- Address the audience, not the aid. As you explain portions of the exhibit, face your audience as much as possible.
- Do not remove the visual before the audience has had an opportunity to examine the information.
- Remove the aid from view when it is no longer relevant to your presentation. (When using a slide show, if necessary, blank the screen briefly before advancing to the next slide. To blank the screen in Microsoft PowerPoint, tap "b" on the computer keyboard. Tap "b" again to return to the slide show.)
- Avoid talking about something on a visual aid after you have put it aside.
- After using slides to illustrate your talk, do not end the show. Following the last content slide, include a plain slide or photograph that will not distract the audience as you end your message and answer questions. For other types of audiovisual equipment, turn it off when the projection is finished so that the light and noise will not distract your audience.
- Avoid distributing handouts until you need them in the presentation. Restrict their use to complex information that cannot be presented in other kinds of visual aids or to summarize your message. If you prepare a summary handout, inform the audience at the beginning of the presentation that you will distribute that summary at the end.

Creating a Slide Deck in Microsoft PowerPoint 2010

As you likely know, you can easily produce professional slide shows that include graphics, audio and video clips, and links to websites—as well as print audience handouts and notes pages/speaker notes—with presentation software, such as PowerPoint. You may have heard the expression "Death by PowerPoint." This phrase captures many viewers' attitudes about the number of poorly developed presentations they are subjected to in academic and business settings. The following steps will help you avoid killing *your* audience.

Use the Outline View

You should begin crafting your slide show by using the outline view in the program. This feature helps you divide your topic into main points, subpoints, and supporting information. The outline's main points become slide titles, and the subpoints and supporting information become bullet points. The bulleted text highlights the information you want the audience to remember—never your spoken words. See Illustration 9.6, which shows a portion of the oral report outline (Illustration 9.4) in PowerPoint 2010.

To use the Outline view in PowerPoint 2010, on the View tab, in the Presentation View group, click Normal. Then, in the left pane, click the Outline tab. To indent the first subpoint, on the Home tab, Paragraph group, click Increase List Level. To indent the first supporting information, click Increase List Level again. To type the next main point, click Decrease List Level twice.

ILLUSTRATION 9.6 MICROSOFT POWERPOINT 2010 OUTLINE VIEW

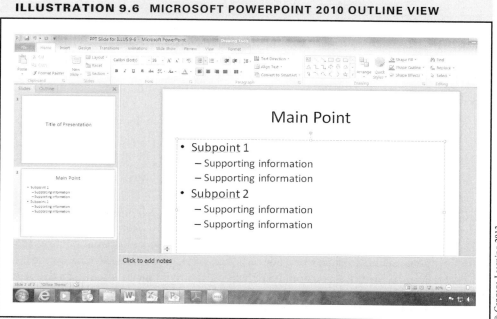

© Cengage Learning 2013

Choose a (Theme) Design Template

Next, choose a design template or theme provided in the software package or develop your own. Select an appropriate design for the context and appropriate colors for good contrast. Generally, light text on a dark background is preferred.

PowerPoint 2010 includes 40 built-in themes (slide design and color scheme), which ensures uniformity of background and font color. A few of the names suggest varying levels of formality: Clarity, Push Pin, Office, Opulent, and Black Tie. Roughly half of the themes, by default, involve light text on a dark background. However, each slide design can be paired with any of the 40 color schemes—1,600 theme possibilities.

To select a theme, on the Design tab, Themes group, click the bottom (More) arrow. Then select and preview an option from the All Themes dialog. To change the color scheme, reopen the All Themes dialog; on the Design tab, Themes group, click Colors. Select one of the 40 color combinations.

Avoid using just a few themes repeatedly. You can do this by downloading free PowerPoint-compatible templates/themes from the Internet. Such websites include fppt.com (http://www.free-powerpoint-templates.com), Microsoft Office (http://office. microsoft.com/en-us/powerpoint-us/free-professionally-designed-templates-for-powerpoint-2010-HA010359-443.aspx), and PowerPoint Styles (http://powerpointstyles.com).

Make Slides Easy to Understand

Also use a readable font size. Projected text is most readable in size 36 (subpoints) and 32 (supporting information), and no text should be smaller than size 24. Make a point of using fonts common to Windows-based computers to avoid possible compatibility problems. Examples include Arial for slide titles and Times New Roman for subtitles and supporting information.

When you display a slide containing text, your audience must choose between reading it and listening to you. Most people automatically block out the presenter momentarily in favor of reading the slide. Therefore, to prevent audience overload, slides should have no more than five to seven lines per slide and no more than five to seven words per line. About one-fourth of any slide should remain blank.

You can avoid overloading your audience using a combination of three methods.

1. Use a text build on each slide that contains bullet points. Thus, you will display only one bullet point at a time as you talk. You may choose to have each line disappear or fade when the next line appears. To use a text build in PowerPoint 2010, select the first bulleted item. On the Animations tab, Advanced Animation group, click Add Animation. Choose an Entrance option (how you want the subpoint to come onto the screen during your slide show), as shown in Illustration 9.7. Generally, the less dramatic entrance options, such as Appear or Fade, are more effective. More extreme options, like Bounce, Swivel, and Zoom, may help recapture audience attention and emphasize a point if used only once in a long presentation. Emphasis can be added to the text (example: Underline)—or to any object placed on your slide (example: Darken). Apply an exit option if you want text to disappear or fade when you display the text below it.

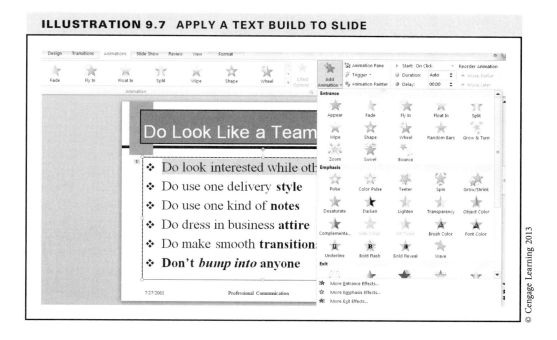

ILLUSTRATION 9.7 APPLY A TEXT BUILD TO SLIDE

Check your work. On the Animations tab, Animation group, click Animation Panel; and on it, click Play. You will see a brief demonstration of the animation(s) you chose. To remove an animation, right click it in the Animation Panel and select Remove. To use the same animation on subsequent lines of text, select this line and click Animation Painter; then select the subsequent lines. If you need to change the animation order, on the Animation Panel, select an out-of-place item. Then click the Re-order arrow (bottom of panel) to move the item up, into place.

2. Another technique to prevent audience overload is the Takahaski Method, named for the Japanese businessman who developed the method several years ago. The technique could be called the Keyword Method because each slide in a deck contains only one short, simple word—in huge letters. Colors and unusual, arty fonts give the text a strong visual quality, making points easy to remember.

   Instead of including up to seven points on a slide, this method involves a separate slide for each key word. A list of four related points might be introduced in the slide show with a gigantic "4."

   This method is easy even for inexperienced presenters. It helps a speaker plan and organize a message and stay on track during delivery. More important, the slides are easy for the audience to comprehend and then recall.

3. Some presenters use slides involving text only in the speaker's notes (introducing and explaining an idea) and slide title (summary of the idea). A directly relevant visual—instead of text—appears in the main slide area. This technique aligns with the notion that most people learn better from words and pictures than from words alone.[1]

Experienced presenters usually create slide decks using a mix of slides with photographs and charts and slides with one word, short phrases, abbreviated sentences, and even short quotations. Their slide shows include whatever they believe will aid them in holding audience attention, clarifying meaning, emphasizing ideas, and proving their point.

Insert Visuals in Slides

Graphics, including charts, photographs, and clip art (line drawings) can add interest and aid comprehension within your presentation. To be effective, each visual must be closely related to the slide's topic and in proper scale. Since business oral reports are expected to convey a professional image, they usually omit clip art in favor of charts and photos. Use such additions to help convey your information, not merely to demonstrate your familiarity with presentation software.

In PowerPoint 2010, the clip art collection includes many current photographs and brief audio and video clips along with line art illustrations. In addition, the program allows you to insert photos from other sources into your slide show. The following paragraphs include how-to information for inserting visuals into your PowerPoint slide deck.

Insert a Photo Album   PowerPoint 2010 makes it easy for you to create a pictures-only slide deck based on any set of photos. Each picture you insert will appear on a separate slide; then you can add appropriate slide titles and separate text slides if you wish. Follow these steps.

1. At the title slide, on the Insert tab, Images group, click Photo Album and New Photo Album.
2. In the Photo Album dialog, at *Insert pictures from*, click File/Disk. Then locate the photos you want included in your slide show. (For efficiency, save all pictures for this deck in a separate folder in advance.)
3. Click one picture; then click Insert at bottom of the dialog. The number and file name appear under *Pictures in album*, and a view of the photo appears under *Preview*. Repeat this step for each photo you want in your slide deck. (The Photo Album dialog in Illustration 9.8 contains eight photos so far.)
4. At the bottom of the Photo Album dialog, click Create. Evaluate your slides in Slideshow view and prepare to edit the deck.
    a. On the Insert tab, Images group, click Photo Album, Edit Photo Album.
    b. On the Edit Photo Album dialog, below the *Pictures in album box*, use the arrow buttons to move a selected photo up or down in the list. Click Remove to delete a selected photo.
    c. To insert text slides between picture slides, under *Insert text*, click New Text Box. You will type in the text boxes after closing the dialog.
    d. To make room for a title on each slide, under Album Layout, click the Picture layout arrow. Then choose this menu option: 1 picture with title. (Other layouts involve two or four pictures per slide with or without a title.)
    e. To modify the shape of each photo or to add a black or white frame, click Frame Shape and select from the seven options.
    f. Now, click Update. Re-evaluate your slides in Slideshow view.

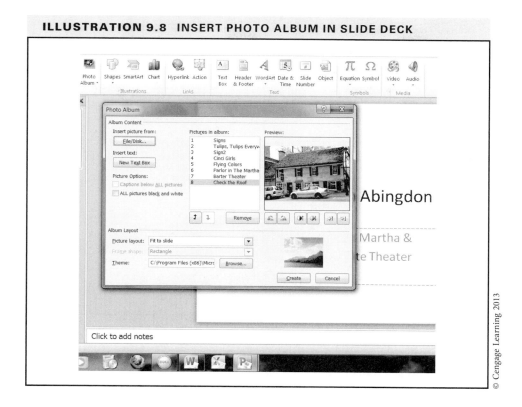

ILLUSTRATION 9.8 INSERT PHOTO ALBUM IN SLIDE DECK

Insert Photo from Clip Art Collection   You can access PowerPoint 2010's Clip Art Collection two ways—from the Insert tab or from the subtopics area of any content slide. Let us assume you are preparing a presentation about business attire (formal and casual) for men and women. You wish to include small photos of a well-attired businessman and businesswoman on your title slide. Follow these steps.

1. At the title slide, on the Insert tab, in Images group, click Clip Art.
2. In the Clip Art dialog at *Search for*, type a category (businessman); at *Results should be*, select the desired media type—photographs, in this case. To include photos online available at Microsoft Office.com, check that box. Then click Go.
3. Scroll the gallery and choose an appropriate image. Click its down arrow; then Insert.
4. Next, resize and place the photo. Click and right-click the image; select Size and Position.
5. On the Format Picture dialog, reduce the height to 2 inches and be sure to select Lock aspect ratio, as shown in Illustration 9.9. Doing so will prevent distortion by reducing the picture width in proportion to the change in height.
6. On the left panel, click Position. Place the figure at least a quarter inch from the top and side, not blocking any text and facing the content. (If necessary, rotate the image to face the content: Launch the Format Picture dialog again. In the left panel, click 3-D Rotation. Under *Rotation* at <u>x</u> [horizontal], type a number up to 180 [degrees] and click Left or Right to "flip" the image.)

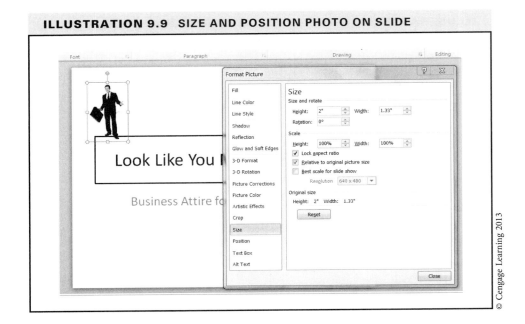

ILLUSTRATION 9.9   SIZE AND POSITION PHOTO ON SLIDE

To complete your plan for this slide, you will need to repeat steps 1 to 4, searching for a photo of a businesswoman. Look for a picture of the same style. Resize it to match the businessman photo; then place and/or rotate it to complement the slide.

Insert a Picture File   Now, let us assume that on the next slide you planned to insert a photo you acquired earlier from Office.com (http://office.microsoft.com/en-us/images/?CTT=6&ver=14&app=powerpnt.exe) and saved on your computer. (**Note:** The procedure would be the same for a photo downloaded from your digital camera or from an online source such as Google Images [http://www.google.com/imghp?hl=en&tab=wi] or one of these sites: Dzineblog [http://dzineblog.com], Dreamstime [http://www.dreamstime.com], FreePixels [http://www.freepixels.com], FreeStock [http://www.freestockfor.us], Kozzi [http://www.kozzi.com], or Stockvault [http://www.stockvault.net]. Avoid files with a bmp extension, opting for one of these formats: .gif, .jpg or .jpeg, .PNG, or .tiff.)

1. In Normal view, click Slide 2 (left panel). Then double-click the Insert Picture from File icon.
2. Use the Insert Picture dialog to locate the desired photograph on your computer.
3. To increase focus on the subject, crop the photo close to the figures.
   a. Select the photo; then on the Format tab, Size group, click Crop.
   b. Align the mouse pointer with the heavy border at the upper right; click and drag to the left, stopping at edge of the image, as shown in Illustration 9.10. Click again.
   c. Align pointer with the heavy border at the lower right; click and drag up. Continue cropping from the lower left and upper left in turn until no margin surrounds the images.

ILLUSTRATION 9.10 CROPPING A PHOTO IN POWERPOINT 2010

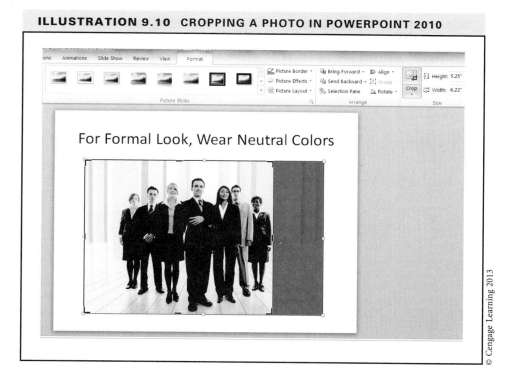

For Formal Look, Wear Neutral Colors

© Cengage Learning 2013

4. Resize the photo to fill the main slide area—roughly 8 inches wide and 5 inches high—and click and drag to center it.
5. Add a picture frame (border) to enhance the image.
   a. Select the photo; on the Format tab, Drawing group, click Shape Outline.
   b. Click Dashes to choose a border style (dashes or solid line).
   c. Click Weight to choose border thickness.
   d. Click a Theme Color or Standard Color or click More Outline Colors and choose from the Standard or Custom tabs.

Insert a Web Link   When using a website or online video in your talk, prepare to go to it smoothly from your slide show. You can use a separate slide displaying the website title and/or the Web address, but to move seamlessly from slides to the Web, simply embed a hyperlink on a content slide (in text or a visual). As an example, the following steps tell how to link a picture to a video titled Dress for Business Success (see Illustration 9.11).

1. Select the text or visual to hold the link—in this case, the picture on the right.
2. Right-click and select Hyperlink. On the Insert Hyperlink dialog, under *Link to*, highlight Existing File or Web Page.
3. Near the bottom, at Address, type or paste the site's URL.
4. At the upper right, click Screen Tip. Type a one- or two-word name for the destination. During your slide show, when you point the mouse at this picture, the description will display, reminding you of what's next. Then click OK.

Of course, these directions presume that your computer is Internet connected during your talk. When running a slide show, you must use the computer mouse to

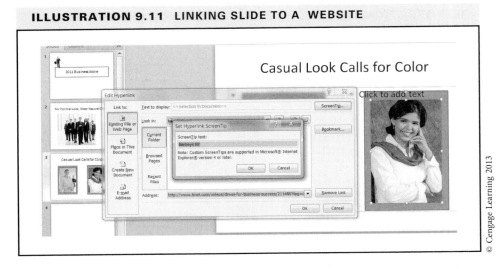

ILLUSTRATION 9.11   LINKING SLIDE TO A WEBSITE

© Cengage Learning 2013

activate a link—not the remote control used to advance slides. If necessary, enlarge the Web page so that the audience can view the details you want them to see. (On your browser, click View, Zoom, and then Zoom In repeatedly or simply press Ctrl and tap the plus key repeatedly.) To resume your slide show after viewing the link, click the slide show on the computer taskbar; then advance to the next slide.

Insert a Chart, SmartArt, or Table   As you may recall, Chapter 5 included directions for creating charts in Microsoft Excel and diagrams called SmartArt and tables in Microsoft Word. These functions for visuals are available—and work the same way—in Microsoft PowerPoint 2010. Starting with a content slide, you can simply click an icon (chart, SmartArt, table) and then create the visual and save it as part of the slide deck.

But beware the size of a PowerPoint *page*. A readable PowerPoint table, for example, can contain a maximum of five columns and five or six rows. Anything more usually results in a slide crowded with excessively abbreviated words and tiny, illegible numbers. Likewise, to be clear to an audience, a chart or diagram has to be downright minimal. If you decide that a table, diagram, or chart is the most appropriate way to illustrate a point, consider creating the visual in Word or Excel and then putting a link to it in your slide show. The steps are similar to linking to a Web page.

1.   Select the text or visual to hold the link.
2.   Right-click and select Hyperlink. On the Insert Hyperlink dialog, under *Link to*, highlight Existing File or Web Page.
3.   At *Look in*, locate the Excel or Word file on your computer.
4.   At the upper right, click Screen Tip and type a short name for the visual. Then click OK.

Save the Excel or Word file on the same medium as the PowerPoint file. When you click this link during your presentation, the file will open in Excel or Word. To enlarge that page, click + (Zoom In) at the bottom right of your computer screen. The Zoom level increases 10 percent with each click; use a level of 150 percent to 200 percent.

Insert a Media Clip   Music and voice recordings as well as movies, if used sparingly, can enrich your slide show. For example, you might want music playing as your audience enters and leaves the presentation room. You could set a mood by softly playing a movie theme song for a slide or two or add flair by playing a voice recording of advertising slogans. A video quote from a company's product manager may be the most effective way to make a point about a new product or a short documentary movie may be ideal for a fund-raising event.

Insert an Audio File   As noted, you can find 10- to 60-second music and sound effect files in PowerPoint's Clip Art dialog. For a wider selection of such sound files, you might use Office.com (linked to the Clip Art dialog) or WavCentral (http://wavcentral.com). WavCentral offers an extensive collection of audio clips from movies, television commercials, and special effects that you can search by name. File formats compatible with PowerPoint 2010 include .aiff, .au, .mid or .midi, .wav, and .wma. PowerPoint 2010 will support the .AAC format provided that an appropriate codec, such as Apple QuickTime Player or ffDShow, is installed. Before downloading an audio clip, find out if it involves a one-time fee and/or a royalty. Select a clip to reveal this information.

In PowerPoint 2010, take these steps to insert a Clip Art sound or a sound file downloaded from another source.

1. On the Insert tab, Media group, point to Audio; then click the appropriate option: Audio from File or Clip Art Audio.
2. In the Insert Sound dialog or Clip Art dialog, find the desired sound.
3. In the Insert Sound dialog, click Insert. In the Clip Art dialog, right-click the selected sound; then click Insert.

After adding a sound, a megaphone icon appears on the slide for use during your slide show. You can move the icon and change its color and size (right-click the icon to display options).

Taking the following steps, you can record your own sound clip and insert it into a PowerPoint 2010 slide (if you have a microphone attached to your computer).

1. On the Insert tab, Media group, point to Audio; then click Record Audio. PowerPoint will display the Record Sound dialog.
2. Use controls in the dialog to record your sound; click OK. You can choose when the sound clip will play in your slide show. Select the sound icon; then on the Playback tab, Audio Options group, click the Start down-arrow and choose Automatically (sound plays when slide is displayed), On Click (sound plays when you click the megaphone icon), or Across Slides (sound plays automatically until you click to stop it). Notice in the Editing group (Playback tab) that you can trim the audio clip, that is, change its duration.

Insert a Video Clip   The so-called video clips in the Clip Art dialog are simply animated line drawings; at Office.com, these items are called Animations. Avoid them. You may find appropriate video clips among shared documents on your company's network, or you could use a video camera to create your own clip. Another possibility is to download video clips from an online source, such as Clipcanvas (http://www.clip-canvas.com), VideoBlocks, (https://www.videoblocks.com), or Video Scavenger (http://www.videoscavenger.com/index.jhtml). Video file formats compatible with PowerPoint

2010 include .asf, .avi, .mpg or .mpeg, and .swf or .wmf. Videos in the .mp4, .mov, and .qt formats can be played in PowerPoint 2010 if the Apple QuickTime Player is installed. Before downloading and saving a video clip on your computer, find out if the clip involves a one-time fee and/or a royalty charge (for material under copyright). To save disk space and improve playback performance, compress your media files. To use your video during a slide show, ensure that the computer used for your presentation is equipped with a sound card, speakers, and enhanced video card.

To embed a video from a file into PowerPoint 2010, follow these steps.

1. On the Insert tab, Media group, click the arrow under Video; then click Video from File.
2. In the Insert Video dialog, find and click the video you want to embed; now, click Insert.
3. Set how you want the video to play: automatically or when clicked. Click the video frame on the slide; next, on the Playback tab, under Video Tools, Video Options group, in the Start list, choose Automatically (video will play when the embedded slide appears) or On Click (video will play when you click the video frame during your presentation). See PowerPoint Help for additional options for video clips.

Remember the following rules for creating successful slide shows. These principles will remain relevant regardless of the presentation software brand or features it provides you.

- Visuals should *enrich* the message, not *become* the message. The presenter's discussion of relevant content should be the focus of audience attention.
- An effective slide show reflects more than just technical features of the software. The overriding goal is effective communication of easy-to-grasp content that facilitates extemporaneous delivery by a well-rehearsed, confident speaker.
- The value of slides should be weighed against the need for audience interaction. Slide presentations tend to flatten discussion, sacrifice the richness of dialogue, and reduce audience involvement.
- Presentation software outlines and templates should never direct or control your presentation. An effective presentation must begin with a worthy *message* that you are able to formulate and support, can organize and effectively deliver, and can inspire listeners to attend to.[2]

Printing Handouts and Notes Pages (Microsoft PowerPoint 2010)

Handouts and notes pages provide benefits for presenters and audiences alike, as one blogger noted: Handouts allow you to simplify your presentation and avoid information overload, and they eliminate concern that you may forget to say some of the details. Handouts help your audience remember your message, and they can follow up with you using your contact information on the handouts. Handouts allow audience members to relax about taking notes, but if they like taking notes, they can write on the handout. Anyone inspired by your topic can get extra information from the handout; anyone who needs a refresher later can get that from the handout, too.[3]

Printing Audience Handouts

You may be familiar with PowerPoint handouts because instructors often distribute them before or after their in-class presentations. If so, you know the value of handouts in tracking a complex talk or in recalling a presenter's message days or weeks later.

PowerPoint 2010 prints handouts with one, two, three, four, six, or nine slides on a page. A handout with three slides per page includes lines that an audience can use to take notes—especially helpful when slides omit text and the topic is somewhat complex. PowerPoint Help suggests posting your slides in a shared location instead of printing handouts for your whole audience. Then, before your presentation, tell your audience where the handout is located. (If notified in advance, audience members who want it can print the handout and bring it with them. Or you can notify the audience as you begin your talk, and they can print it afterward from the shared location.) This practice conserves not only effort and time but also paper and printer ink.

Set the Slide Size, Page Orientation, and Starting Slide Number   Follow these steps before adding content to the slides. If you change the slide size or orientation after adding content, the content may be rescaled.

1. On the Design tab, Page Setup group, click Page Setup.
2. On the Page Setup dialog, under *Slides sized for*, select the size paper on which you will print. (**Note:** Generally, under Orientation, keep the Landscape setting; the Width and Height will set automatically.)
3. Under *Number slides from*, enter the number that you want to print on the first handout page.

Set Printing Options and Print Your Handout   Printing options include number of copies, printer, which slides to print, number of slides per page, and color options. To set these options and then print your slides, follow these steps.

1. On the File tab, click Print. In the Print dialog at the top, enter the number of copies that you want to print; and under Printer, select the printer you want to use.
2. Under Settings, at Print All Slides, specify the slides to include in your handout: all slides, selected slides (press Ctrl and make selection in Slides panel of Normal view), current slide (displayed at right), or custom range (at *Slides*, type slide numbers in this manner: 1-4,6,8-10). (**Note:** In this 10-slide example, PowerPoint will omit slides 5 and 7 from the handout.)
3. At Full Page slides, under Handout, select the layout you want. Choose either horizontal or vertical arrangement when selecting four, six, or nine slides per page (see Illustration 9.12).
4. At Collated, choose whether you want your slides to print collated (all pages assembled in sets) or not.
5. At Color, select from three color options: Of course, the Color option prints in color to a color printer. The Grayscale option prints images that contain various gray tones between black and white. Backgrounds are printed as white so that the text will be legible. (Sometimes grayscale appears the same as Pure Black

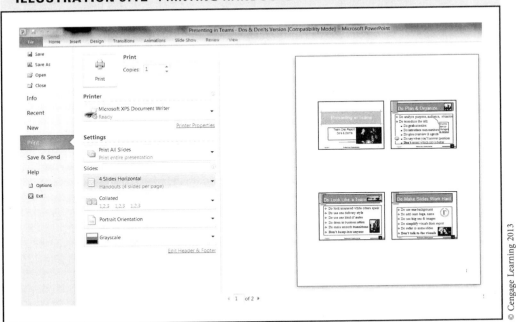

ILLUSTRATION 9.12   PRINTING HANDOUTS FROM POWERPOINT 2010

and White.) As the name implies, the Pure Black and White option prints the handout without gray shades. Since this option is the least costly, use it for all tryout copies.

6.   To include a header and/or footer, click the Edit Header & Footer link. In the Header and Footer dialog, Notes & Handouts tab, select/enter your information. (**Note:** Always include your name and company affiliation on the handout along with the date. If presenting at a convention, include the name or sponsor of it and consider including contact information, such as your email address.)

7.   Finally, click Print.

Creating and Printing Speaker's Notes (Notes Pages)

Presentation experts generally agree that simply printing the slide deck does not make a good handout—because of the absence of explanatory text. A presentation should inspire listeners to want more about the topic, and the handout should provide it. To include additional information in your PowerPoint handout, use PowerPoint's Notes Pages.

You can create notes pages as you build your slide deck. Besides including notes pages in your handout, you can refer to these speaker's notes while delivering your talk.

Create Notes Pages   Use the Notes pane in Normal view to write notes about your slides. Here, you can type and format your notes as you work, but to see how your notes pages will print, switch to Notes Page view. (On the View tab, Presentation Views group, click Notes Page. Also use this view to enlarge, reposition, or format the slide image area or notes area.) Each notes page shows a miniature slide, together with the notes that accompany that slide. In Notes Page view, you can add charts, photographs, and other visuals to your notes. These additions will appear on your printed notes, but not on your screen in Normal view.

Print Notes Pages A notes page consists of a slide on the top half of the page and an equal space for notes below it. If you need more space for your notes, change one page or all pages.

- To change one slide: In Normal view, on the Slides tab, click the slide to which you want to add more space for notes. Then, on the View menu, Presentation Views group, click Notes Page. Next, delete the slide (click it and press the Delete key) or reduce it by dragging a sizing handle on the slide. Finally, enlarge the notes space by dragging the sizing handle on the top border of the notes section.
- To change all pages: Use the Notes Master (in the View Tab, Master Views group, select Notes Master). Then proceed to delete or reduce the slide and expand the notes section. See PowerPoint Help if you need more than one notes page for a slide.

Using PowerPoint for the Written Report

A minor trend in business involves the use of Microsoft PowerPoint to create written reports. Some of these reports consist of little more than a printout of a presenter's slide deck, while others consist of notes pages, showing the slides used in an oral report and the complete oral report narrative.

While written reports in PowerPoint may have merit for some report types (for example, a monthly progress report) it is not recommended for research-based reports or reports on which critical decisions are based. Among the reasons: too little informative detail, lack of text to explain and interpret data and visuals, content that's incomprehensible to anyone not somehow involved in developing it, and lack of organizing and formatting models and standards.

If required to use Microsoft PowerPoint for written reports in your career, make optimal use of notes pages to adequately explain each slide. Include a traditional title page and add a table of contents to reports of more than three pages. Write the slide titles so that they reveal the gist of the report. And, to the extent possible, follow the guidelines in previous chapters of this book.

Follow these guides for preparing a slide deck and audience handouts.

- As you plan and prepare the slides, start with an outline for your presentation, which may be based on a written report. Plan to use visuals only or mark the outline at points where visuals will emphasize or simplify your message. Choose a theme that sets the tone for your presentation and ensures a uniform *look*. On the opening slide, include your name and organization and the title of your talk.
- The slides must not contain your full message—just simple, precise text that introduces or supports the points that you illustrate and then explain when speaking. Write grammatically and logically, making bullet items parallel. Minimize slide density, using a large font and no more than seven words per line and seven lines per slide.
- Use special effects frugally. Any animation and sounds must fit your topic and tone. Provide visual as well as oral transitions by using a preview slide and

divider slides as you move from point to point and into the question-and-answer session.

- Incorporate flexibility and audience interaction into your presentation. Take breaks to discuss your topic with the audience; link to documents or websites for up-to-the-minute information; use stories, metaphors, anecdotes, and demonstrations to enliven your talk.
- Put explanatory information for each slide on a notes page. Then print the notes pages—rather than simply printing your slides—as a handout.

After you have planned and organized the content of your presentation, developed your notes or outline, and prepared your presentation aids, you are ready to rehearse your presentation.

Rehearsing the Presentation

Some of history's greatest speakers—such as Abraham Lincoln and Winston Churchill—were known to practice extensively before delivering a speech.[4] In our day, Steve Jobs developed legendary presentation skills by rehearsing for hours. "To be more precise: many, many hours over many, many days."[5] You should practice your presentation until you are confident that you can handle all aspects with finesse. Rehearse not only the verbal content of the message but also your posture, gestures, and use of presentation aids. As you practice, time your presentation to be sure it fits into your time allotted. In addition, anticipate possible questions and rehearse appropriate answers.

Manage Your Notes

During rehearsal, experiment with different ways of managing your notes or manuscript. Some presenters use cards for extemporaneous talks; others write their notes on sheets of paper. Whatever method you prefer, you should practice so that your notes or manuscript are unobtrusive. The following hints can help you develop those skills.

- **For notes or manuscripts:** Use large, legible letters that you can easily read from your delivery position. Highlighting the key points with color will help you focus on those statements. Include symbols or verbal signals in your notes or manuscript to indicate when you must use a presentation aid.
- **For note cards:** Record only key points on 3-by-5 or 4-by-6 cards. Do not use too many cards; try to limit yourself to one card for the opening, one for each main point in the body, and one for the closing. Number these cards. Arrange them in numerical sequence with a rubber band around them. Remove the band just before your presentation. Hold the cards in the palm of your hand or place them on the lectern. If you hold them in your hand, slip each card to the back of the deck as you complete its use. If you place the cards on the lectern, put the used cards in a stack next to the deck. Some presenters staple their cards in sequence inside a file folder and place the opened folder on the lectern. Others record all notes on a single 5-by-8 card.
- **For note sheets:** Use note sheets only if you will have a lectern on which to rest the sheets. If you do use this technique, use a font size that is easy to read from

an erect standing position; double-space the text and use only the upper two-thirds of the page. This technique promotes better eye contact. It keeps you from dropping your head and eyes to read to the bottom of the page. Number the sheets and arrange them numerically. Slide each sheet unobtrusively to the side as you complete its use. You may find that placing your finger on each point as you discuss it will keep you from losing your place in your talk. If using a slide show, you may print your slides to use as notes. Another option: Add speaker's notes to each slide—as shown in Illustration 9.13—and print. (Directions for typing and printing notes pages from PowerPoint 2010 appear on page 264.) Speaker's notes contain your explanation of the slide's topic and are not projected for the audience to see. (***Note:*** In Microsoft PowerPoint 2010, you can use Presenter View to view your presentation with speaker notes on one computer [for example, your laptop] while your audience views the notes-free presentation on a different monitor [projected on a larger screen].)

ILLUSTRATION 9.13   SPEAKER'S NOTES IN POWERPOINT 2010

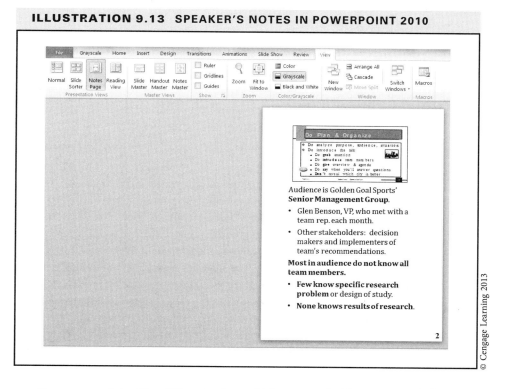

© Cengage Learning 2013

- **For manuscripts:** Use different colors of ink, arrows, bold type, or underlining to highlight key points or to provide signals for emphasis, such as raising or lowering your voice, pausing, or speeding up. Use the partial-page technique described in the previous paragraph to avoid dropping your head and losing eye contact.

If possible, rehearse before an audience—even if it's only one person, such as a helpful family member or roommate—who will provide honest feedback about the message content and your delivery style. When possible, rehearse in the room in which you will give the presentation.

If you cannot rehearse before an audience, make an audio or video recording of your rehearsal so that you can do a critical self-analysis. As you evaluate your rehearsal, consider all aspects of structure given in the previous section and the guides given later in this chapter. As you rehearse you should practice techniques to control three factors: stage fright, the vocal and verbal aspects of a presentation, and the nonverbal aspects of a presentation.

Manage Symptoms of Stage Fright

It is estimated that nearly 75 percent of people suffer from fear of public speaking. For some individuals, the fear is only discomfort at the thought of making a speech, which they overcome by thorough preparation. For others, the fear may be so strong that they become physically incapable of speaking when they appear before an audience. *The Wall Street Journal* reported that stage fright afflicts 20 million people at some point during their lifetimes, and *The Daily Mail* reported that fear of public speaking is the most common phobia worldwide. So if you experience some stage fright, you have lots of company.

A small amount of tension before a presentation can be beneficial. The tension that accompanies anticipation of an important event can make you alert and prompt you to prepare thoroughly for your speech. But excessive nervousness is often an indication that you are focusing on the wrong things: Instead of attending to your audience and your message, you may be placing attention on yourself and others' reactions to you. To avoid stage fright, follow these guides.

- **Justify your presentation.** The fact that you have been asked to give a presentation justifies your talk. Remind yourself that you have been asked to present the information because you possess information that others need or want.
- **Bolster your self-confidence.** Remind yourself of previous successful communication experiences. Make a list of all you know about the topic that your audience likely does not know. List reasons why your audience needs the information you must convey. Remember that the audience is not there to look at you; it is present to hear what you have to say.
- **Trust your audience.** Most audiences are empathetic, receptive, and friendly. They become bored or antagonistic only after a speaker has demonstrated incompetence or lack of respect for the audience. If you attract favorable attention with your opening words and show that you respect your audience's intelligence and needs, you will likely be respected in return.
- **Prepare for the presentation.** Prepare so thoroughly that you know your information, can vary your presentation to meet audience needs, and can enjoy the opportunity to *communicate* important data to others. Think of the presentation as an opportunity to have an informed, animated conversation about a topic that is important to you *and* your audience.
- **Arrive early.** Allow enough time to become comfortable with the room and to check such things as seating arrangements and equipment that will influence your presentation. In addition, chat with audience members who arrive early. Doing so will make you seem friendly, relaxed, confident—and credible. As you begin your presentation, not everyone in the audience will be a stranger.

- **Use stress reduction techniques just before your presentation.** Some stress reduction techniques that speakers use successfully are listed in Illustration 9.14. Those techniques tend to focus the audience's attention on you, give you a few seconds to collect your thoughts before delivering your opening statement, and promote speaker-audience rapport.

ILLUSTRATION 9.14   STRESS REDUCTION TECHNIQUES

Before assuming your speaking position ...

- Take a few deep breaths. This technique tends to relax the body and supplies necessary oxygen for clear thinking.
- With arms hanging loosely at your side, clench your fists and then relax the fingers. Imagine and feel the tension flowing out of your body through the tips of your fingers.
- Swallow a few times and wiggle your jaw to relax the muscles that control your throat and jaw.
- Pause before beginning your presentation. Sweep your eyes over the audience. Select one person at whom you will look directly and imagine beginning a conversation with that individual. Smile, unless the topic is so serious that a smile is inappropriate.
- Begin your speech with a confident tone. Conveying confidence helps establish rapport with your audience. Once you "connect" with the audience, you will likely be confident throughout the presentation.

© Cengage Learning 2013

In addition to controlling stage fright, effective speakers demonstrate control of the vocal and verbal aspects of speech.

Manage Vocal and Verbal Aspects

The vocal aspect of speech communication relates to the quality of sounds that come from your mouth; the verbal aspect relates to the clarity of words that come from your lips.

Vocal quality is controlled by the inhalation, phonation, and resonation phases of speech. *Inhalation* is the process of taking air in through your mouth and nostrils for temporary storage in your lungs. That air is the "fuel" that powers speech and supplies oxygen to your brain. When you breathe deeply, using your diaphragm (area between lower ribs and waistline), you take in a larger supply of fuel than you do when you breathe shallowly.

Practice breathing exercises frequently to improve control of inhalation and exhalation. The following exercises will help you control your breathing:

1. Place your hand lightly on your diaphragm. Inhale gently but firmly so that the air seems to flow to the area where your hand is resting. As you inhale, that area should move outward; as you exhale, it should move inward. In contrast, when you breathe shallowly, you will feel little or no movement in the abdominal region. Instead, you will feel short, panting movements in the upper chest.

2.   Inhale deeply. See how far you can count on one breath. Talk rapidly but *enunciate* each word. Work toward a goal of counting as far as 45 to 60. Men should be able to reach higher counts than women because men generally have larger chest cavities.

Sound is produced in the *phonation* phase. As you exhale, pushing the air out of your lungs, the air passes through your larynx, commonly called the voice box. The voice box has membranous surfaces called vocal folds. Those folds vibrate as air passes over them, producing sound or vocal pitch. If the folds vibrate quickly, which occurs when the throat muscles are tense, the sound is high pitched. When the folds vibrate slowly, which occurs when the throat muscles are relaxed, the sound has a lower pitch. In general, a lower pitch is more pleasing to audiences than is a high pitch. Therefore, relaxing the vocal folds during speech is an important speaking skill to master.

The following exercises will help to relax your throat and shoulders. Practice them often and do one or more in private—not in front of the audience—shortly before giving your presentation.

- Drop your head gently forward; slowly rotate it toward your left shoulder, then backward, then toward the right shoulder, then forward again. Do this exercise slowly and smoothly, not jerkily, until you feel the muscles of your shoulders and throat relax.
- Yawn. Feel your throat muscles relax.
- Think "forward" so that you try to project the sound beyond the region of your throat. Do not force the sound from your throat. Instead, imagine the sound flowing outside your body to a spot on the wall. Read the following paragraph, directing your tone to that one spot.
  I am seeing my grandmother at the back of the room. I am talking to Granny and only to Granny. But Granny does not hear very well, and I must project my voice or she will miss my message. Listen, Granny—hear what I say. My voice is clear; the room is quiet—hear me, if you will.
- Say *one* in the lowest tone you can produce with a clear, controlled, unstrained voice. Move up the musical scale, saying "*two, three, four, …*" until your voice feels slight strain. Move down the scale as far as you can without strain in your voice. Repeat. Through frequent practice, you should be able to extend your vocal range and reduce vocal strain.

After passing through your voice box, the air enters the resonating cavities of your head. In this *resonation* phase, vocal timbre (quality) is determined. The cavities act as echoing chambers. If sound is permitted to resonate freely in the cavities, a rich, warm sound is produced. But if the cavities are constricted or closed, a strident or nasal sound is produced.

To produce rich, pleasing sounds, use these techniques:

- Swallow to relax your throat muscles; flare your nostrils to open the nasal passages and protrude your lips slightly as though preparing to utter the letter "o."
- Create a mental image of roundness instead of flatness. This practice tends to open the cavities and permit full resonation of sound.

- Relax your lips and cheeks, and keep your teeth covered. Do not expose your teeth in a tight smile; this practice tends to produce a nasal sound.
- Try to keep the throat and resonating cavities open as you practice sentences given in Illustration 9.15.

ILLUSTRATION 9.15 RESONATION AND ARTICULATION PRACTICE

To develop a rich, resonant sound and crisp, clear enunciation, practice saying these sentences aloud.

- Fight fiercely and boldly for firm beliefs but not biases.
- Wet your whistle with water at the well.
- Teresa thought that she and Patty had parted ways too abruptly.
- Many men and women experience stress in modern America, and they must spend some time in mental institutions.
- Must we meet Millie at the milliner?
- Cal can scheme to shoot skeet, but his twin is a twit whose tales are always tame.
- Evaluate the effect of Edward's efforts to study serious spending habits of students.
- After you had discussed those details with your doctor, was your affect toward such affectations altered abundantly?
- What was the incidence of unjustifiable, incidental charges entered on your invoice? Was this the first such incident?

© Cengage Learning 2013

Although you can create sound by inhalation, phonation, and resonation, you do not form words until the *modification* or *articulation* stage of speech. In this stage, you use your lips, teeth, tongue, and palate to form vowels, diphthongs, and consonants—the components of words. A vowel is any sound that continues indefinitely as long as there is breath to support it (for example, *a-a-a-a, e-e-e-e,* etc.) A diphthong is a combination of two vowels that blend rapidly seeming to produce one sound (for example, *ei* sounding like long *i; ie* sounding like long *e*). A consonant is a sound other than a vowel or diphthong, many of which stop or interrupt themselves no matter how much breath is available (for example, *k, p, l*).

Understandable speech results from precise articulation of all word components. One way to improve articulation is to practice the pronunciation and enunciation of difficult letter and word combinations. The sentences given in Illustration 9.15 can also be used to improve articulation.

Understanding the four phases of speech will help you realize that, through practice, you can control and improve the vocal and verbal qualities of speech. Through that control, you can improve the understandability of your oral reports. You can also improve communication by gaining greater control of the nonverbal aspects of your presentations.

Manage Nonverbal Aspects

The major nonverbal communication factors that require control during an oral presentation are your appearance, posture, gestures, and facial expressions.

Appearance   The first impression that your audience forms of you is derived from your appearance. If you want to be judged as a competent, professional person, you must present yourself as one. In a formal context a suit, dress shirt, and tie are recommended for a man, and a conservative suit or dress is recommended for a woman. In less formal settings, a man may safely wear a sports jacket and slacks, and a woman may wear a skirt and blouse. Be sure your clothes are comfortable and that the colors complement you. In addition, wear a neat hairstyle that complements your features but draws no excessive attention to itself. Jewelry, if worn, should not be distracting. In all situations, avoid gaudiness and extremes.

Dress in such a way that people do not notice specific items that you are wearing but get an overall impression that you are well groomed. A safe guide especially for women: If you would wear a particular garment for leisure, sport, or an after-five party, do not wear it for a presentation.

Posture   Your posture should suggest that you are in control of the presentation. Avoid slouching or rigidity as you stand or sit before your audience. Slouching connotes indifference or carelessness; rigidity indicates nervousness. In contrast, sitting or standing erectly tends to signify self-confidence, interest, alertness, readiness, and enthusiasm.

As you stand, place your feet 10 to 12 inches apart, with one slightly in front of the other (to reduce any tendency to sway from side to side). Balance your weight evenly on both feet; let your hands hang loosely at your sides; keep your spine erect, shoulders back, and stomach in. That position permits you to inhale and exhale properly for effective speech. From that stance, you can also use your hands easily and naturally for gestures and move gracefully to a new position.

If you sit at a conference table with your audience, move comfortably to the back of the chair, permitting it to support your back and feeling the edge of the seat behind your knees. Place both feet flat on the floor, one slightly in front of the other, to keep yourself balanced and to prevent yourself from slouching or twisting in the chair.

Gestures   Effective speakers do not remain stiffly in one position throughout a presentation. Use gestures—body movements—to complement your words. You probably use gestures spontaneously during interpersonal communication; try to achieve that same spontaneity in your more formal presentations. (But carefully avoid touching your face/head or fixing your hair.) One way to improve gestures is to use them deliberately while practicing, but do not think about gestures during the actual delivery. If you practice your presentation several times, concentrating on large, sweeping gestures, they will tend to become spontaneous and provide appropriate emphasis during your talk. (Bigger audiences need larger gestures.) Although some gesturing can improve your presentation, excessive body movement can become distracting. Use gestures *purposefully* to emphasize or clarify, not merely to release excess energy.

A clenched fist brought down on the lectern may be used to emphasize or to express anger; arms raised quickly, to express surprise; fingers raised sequentially, to enumerate; finger pointing, to single out a person or object; arms and hands moved, to suggest size, shape, or motion. If, however, your audience is an international one, be aware that gestures have different connotations in different cultures. Illustration 9.16 lists some gestures that are common in the United States but may be offensive in another culture.[6]

ILLUSTRATION 9.16   PRESENTATION GESTURES: POSSIBLE CROSS-CULTURAL MEANINGS

Action	U.S. Use/Meaning	Meaning in Another Culture
Pointing with index finger	Emphasis; identification of person in a group, such as pointing to someone in the audience who raises a hand to ask a question	Considered rude in many cultures, especially in Asian countries
Thumbs-up	"Good job"; "That's great"; agreement	Obscene in many countries, including Nigeria, Australia, and some Middle Eastern countries; no meaning for many Southeast Asian cultures
Crooked finger	"Come here"; sometimes used to signal that a member of the audience should come to the front of the room	Obscene in Asian cultures
Speaker's eye contact with listener/ audience	Connecting with listener; considered essential in U.S. presentations; among urban youths, may be considered an invitation to fight	Impudence, disrespect in many African, Asian, and Latin American cultures
Lack of eye contact	Speaker's lack of confidence during presentation; disrespect or disinterest in interpersonal conversation	Respect for authority figure in many African, Asian, and Latin American cultures
Smiling	Friendliness	Japan: sadness, happiness, apology, anger, confusion Korea: shallowness, thoughtlessness Puerto Rico: "Thank you"; "you're welcome"; "excuse me, please"

© Cengage Learning 2013

Mobility   Purposeful walking during your oral report helps you hold audience attention and support your spoken message. Before your presentation, choose a spot on-stage to stand when starting and ending your talk. Then plant your feet on that spot and stay there for at least 30 seconds before walking to a new place. Then take at least two steps and plant your feet again for another 30 seconds or more. (Staying put for a minimum of 30 seconds guards against the appearance of pacing.)

Time your mobility to coincide with point-to-point transitions in your report, whether you talk or stop talking as you walk. Doing so emphasizes what you just said and signals a shift in topic. Walk to the center of the available space when you introduce or review your main message or theme. Thus, you equate your central idea and the center of the space. To create closeness with the audience during your presentation, walk slowly toward them while talking softly. Doing this indicates a need to share personal information.[7]

Facial Expressions Facial expressions convey emotions with remarkable accuracy. When you give an oral report, your facial expressions should suggest your enthusiasm for the topic. Moreover, your expressions should show your interest in your listeners and your desire to communicate with them. Those feelings will be conveyed if you develop a positive mental attitude toward your topic and your audience. In contrast, if you are nervous and unsure about your presentation, those feelings will likely be registered in your facial expressions. Therefore, an excellent way to control facial nonverbal communication is to be thoroughly prepared for and confident about your presentation.

Eye Contact In most Western cultures, eye contact is considered essential for effective communication. Lack of such contact suggests discomfort, uncertainty, or embarrassment. Through eye contact, you convey your interest in and concern about the audience. In addition, by maintaining that communication link with your audience, you can detect the reactions of individuals to your message. You will see enthusiasm, understanding, interest—or their opposites. When you get negative feedback through eye contact, you have an opportunity to adjust your presentation to meet the needs of your audience. Eye contact will then tell you whether your adjustments are effective.

To make proper eye contact, you must look at individuals' eyes—not over their heads. Stick to a "Z" pattern for systematic but varied eye contact. (The top of the "Z" represents people in the back row; the bottom of the letter, people in the front row.) Start with a friendly or familiar face or the first person on your left in the back row; look in the eyes for a few seconds (finish a thought). Instead of eying the person seated next, skip a few people. (When you look directly at one person, the people around him or her feel included in your glance.) Continue to look and skip in a "Z" around the room. On finishing the "Z," return to an individual you skipped near the beginning.

In a very large audience, where individual eye contact may become impossible, divide the room into quadrants and look to each quadrant in turn, making sure to include people in the far corners. Everyone in that section will likely feel included in your eye contact.

You can improve the effectiveness of your oral reports through careful preparation and rehearsal of your presentation. That kind of preparation tends to reduce stage fright and help you manage the verbal and nonverbal aspects of your talk.

In addition to planning the content of your presentation, preparing your presentation aids, and rehearsing your talk, you must prepare to deal with the backchannel.

Managing the Backchannel

The backchannel is a secondary conversation about a presentation/presenter that takes place electronically during the presentation. More and more, these background conversations are becoming just another part of presenting and attending presentations. Many presenters today encourage audiences to transmit questions and feedback to them and to share comments with one another and other interested people outside the presentation room.

Today, many college instructors encourage the use of Twitter (social media) or collaboration tools and laptops or cell phones for backchannel participation in class, and some institutions have built-in backchannel tools. But the backchannel is not limited to academic settings, where student interaction can enhance instruction even in huge classes. Increasingly, the concept—especially the Twitter backchannel—is a fact of life for business presenters.

Not all presenters and audience members agree on the value of the backchannel. Some people on both sides find it distracting, while others find it enriching. It's easy to imagine that multiple conversations occurring at the same time could dilute focus on the presenter and his or her message. Furthermore, people post comments/questions anonymously in the backchannel, which naturally leaves room for a variety of unhelpful comments. On the other hand, the backchannel allows audiences to discuss presentation topics with others in their field—a primary reason for attending presentations. Often, a presenter's ideas are discussed in the backchannel with interested people not in attendance, thus expanding audience size.

Since you will almost certainly have to deal with the backchannel in the business world, begin by realizing that audience members may not always return your eye contact as they look down to type on their laptops or smartphones. The following list includes additional things you can do to manage the backchannel.[8]

- Use the backchannel medium to collect input from people who will attend your presentation. Ask them about the challenges they face that you can help resolve and ask for suggestions for what you should cover in your talk.
- As you begin, publicly welcome audience members who will be using the backchannel and let them know you will read what they write and may read it aloud to the whole audience. Tell them also that you will give a better presentation if they look up and make eye contact with you when not communicating in the backchannel.
- Do not monitor the backchannel while presenting. Focus instead on delivering the talk you planned, prepared, and rehearsed. If there is a live display of the comments, ask to be in control of it. Then turn it off while you talk.
- Take backchannel breaks. During the break in your presentation, respond to questions from the backchannel and live audience. The next section provides guides for managing question-answer sessions. (Display backchannel questions for attendees who are not following it.)
- Afterward, use the stream of backchannel comments—where you can see how the audience reacted moment by moment—to evaluate your presentation.

In addition to planning the content of your presentation, preparing your presentation aids, rehearsing your talk, and preparing for the backchannel, you must decide how to handle questions and answers.

Managing Question-and-Answer Sessions

Some speaking situations require that the speaker give the audience an opportunity to ask questions during the talk. At other times, the speaker may simply involve the audience by following a presentation with a question-and-answer session. As you plan your presentation, you should decide the ground rules for questions. Before you begin the presentation, you or the person who introduces you should tell the audience how questions will be handled. Generally, the time allowed and the formality of the situation influences your management of a question-and-answer session. However, you must always be prepared to answer a question that cannot be forestalled. If the chief executive officer asks a question, you may be wise to answer it when he or she asks, no matter what ground rules you have set.

Informal Presentations

During informal presentations with lax time limits, you may permit or encourage participants to interrupt your presentation as questions arise. If you permit that questioning strategy, you must be able to redirect the discussion to your topic as soon as the question has been answered.

The following techniques will help you resume the discussion:

- Graciously remind the audience of the topic that was being discussed before the diversion: *Thank you for your comments. They were stimulated by the statement that customers want online bill payment. Let's return to that point briefly before we look at other services our customers requested.*
- Solicit other questions on the topic to assure the audience that relevant questions or comments are welcome: *Before we examine other options to expand customer services, does anyone have another question or comment about online bill payment?*
- Summarize the discussion and show its relevance to the last point or the next one to be discussed: *You seem to agree that online bill payment service is not your first choice. Let's look at other options suggested by our customers.*
- Politely stop a person who is monopolizing the question session: *You've asked some good questions. The last one is more closely related to the next topic that I want to cover. Let's hold that one for a while.*

Formal Presentations

For a formal presentation, you will usually ask people to hold their questions until the end of the presentation. If you have allowed time for questions, you can be embarrassed if no one asks a question; conversely, your listeners may be dissatisfied if they are not given enough time for questions. The first rule in managing a formal question-and-answer session is to allow a realistic amount of time as is dictated by the content of your message and the context in which it is given.

The following techniques will help you manage specific problems that arise in formal question-and-answer sessions:

- Anticipate specific questions. You can usually expect questions related to the most complex or controversial parts of your presentation. Be prepared with answers to expected questions.

- "Plant" a question with one member of the audience. Sometimes people are reluctant to ask questions. Ask one person in the audience to ask a specific question if the session begins slowly. That question and its answer may stimulate questions from other people.

- Ask a question yourself. If the questioning begins slowly or lags, suggest a question by saying, "Some of you may be wondering why …" As you answer that question, someone may be stimulated to ask another.

- Acknowledge *each* question with a comment along the lines of "That's a good question" or "I often get that question." Recognizing the questioner increases your rapport with the audience and gives you an additional split second to formulate an answer.

- Restate the question while looking at the person who asked it. Thus, you help ensure that everyone in the audience heard the question, a basis for understanding your answer. By repeating the question, you ensure your grasp of it, and you give the questioner an opportunity to edit the question before you begin answering. Instead of repeating a short, simple question, just paraphrase it as part of your answer.

- Do not let one person monopolize the session. Politely suggest that you will continue the discussion later (*Let's discuss that over a cup of coffee*) and turn to receive a question from someone else.

- While answering, keep eye contact with the entire audience, not just the questioner. Otherwise, you may quickly lose the attention of all but that person.

- Give a direct answer and brief explanation—even if your presentation obviously contained the answer.

- When you finish an answer, look at the questioner and say something like, "Did I answer your question?" In this way, you clear up any confusion before taking the next question or closing the session.

- When the allotted time has elapsed, politely thank the audience for its participation and interest. Offer to be available later (give time and place) for further discussion. Do not hold an audience beyond the stated time. Some members may have other commitments.

- What if you cannot answer a question during or after your presentation? You might give a partial answer and suggest a source—magazine or website—where the questioner could seek a complete answer. Or you might ask if anyone present can give a more complete answer. Alternatively, you might promise to provide an answer within a few days. (Make the promise only if you intend to follow through, and be sure to get the questioner's name and email address.) Above all, be aware that much credibility is lost when a presenter attempts to "bluff" through an answer.

- If questions lag before the allotted time has elapsed, thank the audience for its participation and interest and dismiss the group. Most people appreciate the consideration of being given some free time rather than being held for a redundant discussion.

The previous guides for presentations have suggested that you will give a solo performance. Although you will often present reports alone, you will also be required to participate in group presentations during your business career.

Presenting in Teams

Oral reports are often developed and delivered by teams of presenters. This is especially true if the presentation requires the input of people with different expertise. For example, individuals from accounting, marketing, and human resources all may be involved in a team presentation regarding the creation of a team to manage a new business account. The best team presentations are "seamless." That is, each segment supports the presentation's overall purpose and is linked to but does not repeat the material in the other segments. In addition, performances are coordinated as each person acts according to a carefully developed plan intended to maintain the focus of the full presentation.

A team presentation should be a carefully orchestrated performance that gives the impression of a single, unified report rather than a series of individual presentations. The following guides will help you achieve coherent team presentations:

- As the report is prepared, individuals should be given responsibility for specific parts of the presentation. Ideally, each person will assume primary responsibility for a part about which he or she is most knowledgeable.
- All members of the team should be familiar with the total report, not only with the parts for which they have primary responsibility.
- Inexperienced teams should use a *distributed* presentation format. In it, team members divide topics in their report outline, one to each person. More experienced teams may accept the challenge of a *merged* presentation format. In it, team members collaborate on a very detailed outline of points and examples; then they take turns presenting *within each point*. Merged format helps keep the listeners' interest, but it works only when (1) all team members know the subject well and (2) the group is willing and able to rehearse extensively.
- One team member should act as coordinator to introduce the presentation, introduce the team members and their respective topics, and moderate the discussion. The coordinator may also be responsible for summarizing the report and moderating the question-and-answer session.
- As an individual completes a section of the report, that person should name the next presenter and topic. If the team is using a slide show, a divider slide can accomplish that task and take attention away from the physical movements of the speakers as they change positions.
- While the current presenter stands before the audience, team members should be seated quietly, giving the presenter their full attention. That procedure permits the audience to focus on the current speaker and topic. The seating arrangement should permit a person to sit down gracefully when finished and allow the next presenter to take the speaking position smoothly.
- Team members should share the responsibility for answering questions. The team may choose to conduct the question-and-answer time in open forum style or panel moderator style. As you might suppose, *open forum* means that audience members "call on" a particular team member before posing a question or "throw out" a question for anyone on the team to answer. Panel moderator style involves designating a team member to take and repeat each question, then answer it or refer the question to the team member most qualified to answer it.

- If you sense that a team member is hesitant or may be about to convey inaccurate information, tactfully step in to answer the question. You can do so by interjecting a statement such as, "I've worked closely with this part of the project ..." Likewise, speak up if you can add important information to a teammate's answer.
- All aspects of the presentation—spoken parts, use of presentation aids, and seating arrangements—should be rehearsed until the group achieves a smooth, comfortable performance. Time the total presentation, including introductions, speaker movements, and the question-and-answer session, to be sure that it conforms to the allotted time.

Many oral reports are made with the audience and speaker occupying the same room. Today, too, more and more presentations are given online.

Presenting a Webinar

As you read in Chapter 7, the term *Web conference* refers to an interactive online meeting for discussion and problem solving. Online meetings that include oral reports/presentations are more commonly called a *webcast* (one-way flow of information to a large audience) or a Web seminar, or *webinar* (interaction consists of polling the audience for feedback and answering audience questions).

A typical webinar involves 3 to 15 participants seated at their own computers, equipped with Web conferencing software that permits them to chat by typing comments and questions and responding to the presenter's surveys. Naturally, a webinar has much in common with presentations in any other setting. For example, one webinar expert was asked to identify the best practices of webinar presenters. He noted the importance of putting the audience's viewpoint ahead of your own, engaging the audience with your voice (since they can't see you), and taking the time to practice every aspect of your talk.[9] But there are also differences between a face-to-face presentation and an engaging webinar, and Illustration 9.17 includes tips for dealing with these differences.

When the technology is available for a webinar, businesses are finding that such presentations can be as effective as face-to-face presentations. Effectiveness is greatly influenced, however, by the presenter's preparation—as it would be for any talk.

Ethical Considerations

In creating a presentation, your goal should be to ensure a common frame of reference between you and your audience; you want them to see and hear how important you consider each idea to be. Your goal is not to mislead the audience; rather, it is to understand their needs, values, and attitudes so you can help them identify with your point. This analysis must be based on a respect for and sensitivity to the participants' position.

Speakers may be tempted to make their points more forceful by exaggerating a point, omitting something crucial, or providing deceptive emphasis. Consider the case of a speaker who attempted to convince employees to accept a change in insurance benefits. The speaker emphasized a small benefit but deemphasized a major

ILLUSTRATION 9.17   GUIDES FOR PRESENTING WEBINARS[10]

Preparation

1. Insert your photograph near the beginning of your slide deck. This picture will help participants visualize you talking to them during the webinar.
2. Use more visuals than you would in a face-to-face presentation. In the absence of visuals, audience attention will be more likely to wander since participants cannot focus on you.
3. On your slides, highlight what you want participants to look at. Use shading, arrows, and drawing tools available in the software to emphasize detail (since you can't actually point to it).
4. Omit slides that you would show for only a few seconds. Some participants may see the slide for only a split second because of a slight lag between advancing the slide and its appearing on the screen. For the same reason, avoid a sequence of slides or text builds that rely on being synchronized with your spoken words.
5. Create a special "questions" slide to display during question-and-answer time. The slide shown before you pause for questions may be irrelevant.
6. Do the extra rehearsal required. First, rehearse your presentation until you know it well; then rehearse using the webinar software.
7. Before starting the webinar, turn off your cell phone and landline and shut your door. Do all that you can to prevent distracting noises during your online presentation.

Delivery

1. Use a remote control (instead of the mouse or space bar) to advance slides, even though you're at your computer. The remote reminds you of presenting face-to-face.
2. Use a clock or watch to monitor the time. Knowing that the presentation is on track helps you relax and attend to the audience.
3. Tell participants when you are going to be silent. Let them know, for example, if you will take a sip of water. If you display a slide you want them to read—a quotation, perhaps—introduce the slide with, *I'll let you read ...* Otherwise, participants may think they have lost the sound.
4. Use shorter pauses than you would face-to-face. Instead of long, dramatic pauses, insert tiny pauses between phrases and sentences.
5. Break for questions at the end of each section in your talk. This way, participants, who will type their questions when they occur, will not have to wait too long to get answers.

reduction in total coverage. Some members of the audience missed the main point. Others recognized the deception, however, and before long the speaker's credibility was lost. A speaker is effective only when he or she is believable. If audience members suspect that they are being manipulated or misled or if they find any part of the presentation untruthful, the total presentation fails.

The best approach to making an ethical presentation is to present your information honestly, fairly, and without deception. Be aware of your own biases and prejudices so that you do not unconsciously distort data.

Summary

Effective oral presentations begin with comprehensive preparation. That preparation includes analysis of the context, selection of delivery style, outlining the presentation, devising effective transitions between parts, preparing visual aids, and rehearsing the presentation until you have perfected all aspects of delivery.

Effective delivery of an oral presentation requires control of stage fright, the vocal and verbal aspects of speech, and nonverbal communication cues. In addition, you should develop skill in managing the backchannel, using presentation aids to give additional impact to your oral reports, and preparing suitable handouts.

The ready availability of presentation software requires a concentrated effort to make every slide or panel meaningful. Begin with a worthy message. Avoid the temptation to overload slides and to use unrelated sounds, unnecessary animations, or trite clip art.

Team oral reports require careful coordination of all aspects of the presentation. Team members must be knowledgeable about all parts of the report, not only the parts for which they have specific responsibility. Both individual and team reports may be presented in a webinar as well as face-to-face.

The goals of an ethical communicator include telling the truth, labeling opinions so that they can be distinguished from facts, being objective, writing and speaking clearly, and giving credit when using others' ideas or words.

Topics for Discussion

1. Explain the purpose and methods for doing an analysis of the speech context, including the audience and physical environment.
2. Explain how the style of a presentation is related to the audience and the physical environment. Give examples to demonstrate your understanding of the audience-environment relationship.
3. Describe the main characteristics of each of these types of delivery:
   - Impromptu
   - Extemporaneous
   - Textual/scripted
   - Memorized
   - Combination
4. Describe the desired characteristics of these aspects of a presentation:
   - Opening
   - Partition statement
   - Body
   - Language style
   - Transitions
   - Conclusion

5. Discuss factors that must be considered when selecting a visual aid.

6. Compare the advantages and disadvantages of the following media for oral reports:
   - Presentation software
   - Transparencies
   - Flip chart
   - Objects
   - Handouts

7. Discuss recommendations for preparing a slide show. With two or three classmates, share examples of effective and ineffective slide use. Consider slide appearance/composition and speaker's use of the slides.

8. Describe effective ways to rehearse individual and team presentations. Try to add tips from your experience not included in this chapter.

9. Describe ways to reduce stage fright. If you use any techniques not described in this chapter, share them with your classmates.

10. Explain what occurs in each of these speech phases and their relevance to a pleasing delivery style:
    - Inhalation
    - Phonation
    - Resonation
    - Modification

11. For each of the following categories, give examples of specific nonverbal behaviors and how they can enhance or detract from an oral report:
    - Appearance
    - Posture
    - Gestures
    - Mobility
    - Facial expressions

12. With two or three classmates, identify pros and cons of participating in a backchannel. Base the response on your combined experiences. If you have no personal experience to share, ask businesspeople you know about their backchannel experience or do a brief online search of the topic.

13. Explain how to manage question-and-answer sessions to reinforce a presenter's credibility.

14. Identify characteristics of team oral reports that are not concerns of individual presenters.

15. Explain why a printout of a presenter's slides may not be a suitable handout.

Applications

1. Plan an informative presentation (about five minutes long) for delivery to your classmates. Select a topic with which you are comfortable and knowledgeable. Try to select a topic that is not familiar to your classmates. Examples of appropriate topics include an unusual hobby, a unique travel experience, a creative idea for a new product or service, your position on a

controversial issue, a person whom you admire, or an outstanding graduate of your school. As you prepare a preliminary outline, consider the following:

- Audience for the presentation
- Reasons the audience may need or enjoy the information
- Relevant audience interests and needs
- Purpose of the presentation
- What the audience already knows about your topic
- Additional information to be researched
- Resources for gathering needed information

Build your presentation to include an attention-getting beginning that draws the audience into your talk; a preview statement that clearly and interestingly defines your main points; interesting, adequate development of the points; meaningful transitions; and a memorable conclusion. Follow any additional guides for preparation or delivery that your instructor may give.

2. Team up with a classmate. Act as one another's audience as you both rehearse your presentations (Application 1). Provide constructive criticism. Modify your message and delivery style in response to that criticism. Give the presentation to a larger audience, such as your entire class.

3. Write a memo to your instructor in which you evaluate a presentation presented by one of your classmates. In your evaluation, include specific strengths or weaknesses related to the following:

- Opening of presentation
- Preview statement
- Body of the talk
- Transitions
- Conclusion
- Verbal and vocal aspects of delivery
- Nonverbal aspects of delivery
- Effectiveness of presentation aids (if applicable)
- Handling questions (if applicable)

4. Interview a person who gives presentations frequently. For example, you may want to talk to a salesperson, a teacher, a member of the clergy, or someone else who regularly talks to large audiences. Ask that person how he or she organizes, constructs, practices, and actually delivers his or her presentations. In a memo, share your findings with your instructor.

5. Prepare and deliver a short presentation (five to seven minutes) in which you demonstrate effective use of presentation software. Use a topic of your choice or one assigned by your instructor. Include at least one of each of the following types of slides in your presentation:

- A title slide
- A slide containing bulleted subtopics and a text build
- A slide containing a photograph
- A slide containing a bar chart, line graph, pie chart, or table
- A slide containing a hyperlink

6. This application will give you experience thinking on your feet. You will need a container to gather topics. Each member of the class writes two impromptu

topics on pieces of paper and puts the papers into the container. Each speaker then draws a topic from the container. After three minutes of preparation, each speaker gives a two-minute presentation to the class on that topic, followed by a minute of question-and-answer.

7. After giving the impromptu presentation (Application 6), do additional research to get information needed for a 7- to 10-minute presentation on the same topic. Develop an outline and at least three visual aids to accompany the presentation. As directed by your instructor, deliver the presentation.

8. Select one of the topics below. Gather enough information for a 7- to 10-minute presentation. Outline your talk. Prepare three interesting and relevant opening statements, previews, and concluding statements for it. Select the best opening statement, preview, and conclusion and incorporate them into your outline, along with appropriate transitions between main points. Plan the kinds of visual aids that would assist you in creating interest in and understanding of your topic. Select the two or three visual aids you would most likely use in your presentation and roughly sketch each of these aids. Also indicate how you would present each aid.

- Advantages and pitfalls of payday loans
- What you can learn from doubletongued.org or howjsay.com
- Importance of beginning your retirement fund now
- Business adoption of "green" (environmental friendly) construction
- Costs and benefits of owning a companion animal (pet)
- Podcasting in business
- Paying off debt the smart way
- Turning gift cards into dollars
- Women in military combat
- Exercising without leaving your office cubicle
- Cycling to work or school
- Extra challenges facing female leaders
- A U.S. company that has grown in recent years because of production for the military

9. Using the topic you selected in Application 8, pair up with a classmate. Exchange your presentation outlines and sketches of visual aids. Offer constructive criticism to one another.

10. Incorporate any valuable suggestions received from your classmate in Application 9. Complete your preparation and rehearsal for the presentation. Deliver the presentation at a time and place chosen by your instructor.

11. Select an article from a recent issue of a business periodical such as *The Economist*, *Fortune*, *Money*, or *Smart Money*. In a memo report to your instructor, identify each of the following:

- Attention-getting device(s)
- Intended audience and audience adaptation(s)
- Preview/partition statement
- Main points
- Conclusion

12. In a memo to your instructor, identify the changes you would make in the structure or content of the article used in Application 11 if you were to present the same information to members of your class, to a group of businesspeople, or to the news media.

13. In a memo to your instructor, provide guidelines for effective backchannel participation. Recall your own experience and the experience of others (Discussion Topic 12).

14. Attend a presentation by a guest lecturer on your campus, a meeting of a business or professional organization (such as Rotary, Kiwanis, or Business and Professional Women), or a student chapter meeting of a professional association. In a memo to your instructor, critique the speaker in terms of the following categories:
    - Introduction:
        - How clear were the topic and the purpose of the talk?
        - What attention-getting devices did the speaker use?
        - How effective were the devices in building rapport and interest?
    - Body:
        - Were the main points clearly organized?
        - What kind of information did the presenter use to support the main points?
        - What visual aids did the speaker use? Were they incorporated into the presentation effectively?
    - Conclusion:
        - What concluding techniques did the speaker use?
        - How effective were the techniques in ending the presentation?
    - Language:
        - Did the speaker use memorable language? Give examples.
        - Was the level of formality appropriate for the audience and context?

15. Form a group with three or four of your classmates. Examine *That Used to Be Us* by Thomas L. Friedman and Michael Mandelbaum. Using information from that book, supplemented by your research, give a presentation on three major challenges, besides globalization, that America faces. Offer at least three significant steps the audience can take toward reversing the country's seeming loss of can-do spirit. Answer a question people asked before the book was released: Does it have a happy ending?

References

1. Atkinson, C. (2008). *Beyond bullet points*. Redmond, WA: Microsoft Press, 208, 209.
2. Jones, G. H. (2004). Message first: Using films to power the point. *Business Communication Quarterly, 67*, 88–91.
3. Mitchell, O. (2010, July 23). 13 best practice tips for effective presentation handouts [Web log post]. Retrieved from http://www.speakingaboutpresenting.com/delivery/presentation-handouts
4. Ramki. (2011, January 30). Methods for speaking preparation [Web log post]. Retrieved from http://www.speakfreaks.com/methods.html

5. Gallo, Carmine. (2010). *The presentation secrets of Steve Jobs: How to be insanely great in front of any audience.* New York: McGraw Hill, 179.

6. Adapted from Dresser, N., *Multicultural manners: Essential rules of etiquette for the 21st century* (Rev. ed.). New York: Wiley, 2006), 12–35.

7. Templeton, M., & FitzGerald, S. S. (1999). Nonverbal techniques of communication. In *Schaum's quick guide to great presentations* (pp. 139–153). New York: McGraw-Hill. On the importance of motion to effective presentations, see also Booth, D., Shames, D., & Desberg, P. (2010). Physical grammar. In *Own the room: Business presentations that persuade engage & get results* (pp. 167–182). New York: McGraw-Hill.

8. These items are a synthesis of two sources: Atkinson, C. (2010, March 7). 5 ways to use Twitter to avoid a backchannel disaster [Web log post]. Retrieved from http://mashable.com/2010/-3/-7/twitter-backchannel; Mitchell, O. (2009, December 2). 8 tips for managing the Twitter backchannel during your presentation [Web log post]. Retrieved from http://socialtimes.com/8-tips-for-managing-the-twitter-backchannel-during-your-presentation_b1502

9. WebinarHero (2010, April 2). Ask the experts: Ken Molay, president, Webinar Success [Web log post]. Retrieved from http://webinarhero.wordpress.com/2010/04/02/ask-the-experts-ken-molay-president-webinar-success

10. These guides adapted from Mitchell, O. (2010, September 30). 18 tips on how to conduct an engaging webinar [Web log post]. Retrieved from http://www.speakingaboutpresenting.com/presentation-skills/how-to-conduct-engaging-webinar

CHAPTER **10**
Planning the Research

LEARNING OBJECTIVES

After you have read this chapter, you should be able to:

1. Explain the value of a comprehensive research plan.

2. Recognize the steps in planning business research.

3. Identify the information that should be included in a research plan.

4. Write a research proposal that clearly articulates your research plan.

MANAGERS MUST OFTEN MAKE DECISIONS that will have a major impact on the success of their organizations. Should a would-be entrepreneur begin the business that he or she has long contemplated? Should an automobile manufacturer discontinue a product line? Should an advertising agency give a substantial amount of money to a state university to establish a business communication center? Should an insurance company change its policy about medical insurance coverage for domestic partners?

These and other questions require extensive research before they can be answered with confidence. The first step in the research process is to create a plan that clearly identifies the problem to be studied and its scope as well as the purpose of the study and the audience to whom the information will be reported. All factors related to the study, including costs and time required, may be presented formally in a research proposal.

Planning the Research

A report about a complex problem begins with a *research plan*, which becomes a guide for collecting data, analyzing data, and reporting the results of the analysis.

A research plan, as indicated in Illustration 10.1, includes twelve parts: obtain or review authorization, identify the audience, define the problem, clarify the purpose, narrow the scope, state delimitations and limitations, plan data collection, plan data analysis, estimate time schedule, estimate resources needed, plan the presentation of results, and seek approval to proceed.

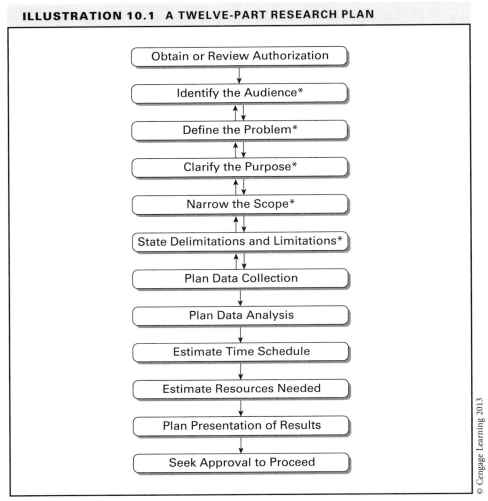

ILLUSTRATION 10.1   A TWELVE-PART RESEARCH PLAN

- Obtain or Review Authorization
- Identify the Audience*
- Define the Problem*
- Clarify the Purpose*
- Narrow the Scope*
- State Delimitations and Limitations*
- Plan Data Collection
- Plan Data Analysis
- Estimate Time Schedule
- Estimate Resources Needed
- Plan Presentation of Results
- Seek Approval to Proceed

© Cengage Learning 2013

*Two-way arrows suggest that a reiterative approach to these parts of the research plan may improve its overall quality.

Obtain or Review Authorization

When a project requires extensive research, you must be sure that you are authorized to spend time or money on the project. In some situations, your job description will require that you prepare specific reports; then you need no additional authorization to initiate a research plan for that report. But you may also discover the need to analyze a unique problem related to your work; then part of your plan is to be sure you are authorized to do the research. In addition, your supervisor may ask you to work on a special project; then your research plan must include a review of the request to demonstrate that you understand what the supervisor wants you to do.

Identify the Audience

As when preparing a simple report, you must have a clear understanding of your audience, both primary and secondary. The authorization facts may tell you who the receivers are, or you may need to determine who they will be. When you initiate a research plan, decide whom you want to influence with the report. When asked to work on a project, clarify who is—and is not—to have access to the information.

Assume, for example, that you must prepare a report investigating the feasibility of relocating a grocery store currently located in an economically distressed neighborhood. The intended primary audience would likely be upper-level corporate managers, and releasing information prematurely to anyone not authorized to receive it could result in negative attitudes and behaviors among employees and customers. After deciding to relocate the store, management may ask you to write a report to the employees, who become your primary audience. But (unless employees can be prevented from sharing this information with acquaintances) the potential secondary audience—such as neighborhood leaders, customers, and news media—must also be considered and may influence report content, structure, and tone.

Sometimes you cannot determine the full audience until you have clearly defined the problem. The definition of the problem may provide a clearer view of potential audiences for the report.

Define the Problem

The *problem* is the central focus of the research. A clear, concise statement of the problem keeps the researcher on target. To conduct business research, you must distinguish between the managerial problem (or symptoms of a problem) and the research problem.

The observable phenomena about which a decision must be made make up the managerial problem. Such phenomena are also called the symptoms of the problem. For example, a manager may observe that the office support personnel often are tardy for work, turn in poor-quality work, and complain about eyestrain, wrist strain, and backache. These are all symptoms that something is amiss in the office support system. A manager who considers only one symptom at a time may decide that the resolution to the "problem" is to reprimand tardy employees, give negative work evaluations to employees who do inferior work, or buy new office chairs and wrist rests. But a manager who looks at several symptoms may decide that a deeper problem exists. Perhaps the question that must be addressed is, How can we improve the productivity of our office support staff? That question would become the *research problem* or *research question*.

Clarifying the purpose of the report frequently helps the researcher define the problem.

Clarify the Purpose

Whereas the problem defines *what* is to be investigated, the purpose identifies *why* the research should be conducted. When the research is completed, the *purpose* guides the formulation of recommendations.

In some situations, the problem and purpose are nearly identical. For example, the purpose of investigating ways to improve office productivity would be to improve productivity. When the problem and purpose are similar, they may be stated as the objective of the study. The objective is the overall outcome or goal of a report.

In other cases, the problem and purpose must be differentiated from one another. Consider the following situation. The new administrator of Peaceful Village, a retirement center that has been in operation for three years, observes several phenomena.

1. The facility has averaged 90 percent occupancy during the past year, whereas the goal is 99 percent.
2. Three new facilities have opened during the past year in the Peaceful Village service area.
3. Three months ago, Peaceful Village's dietician/cook took a job with a competing facility. Since then the residents have complained frequently that the meals served differ considerably from the posted menus. Although the menus sound appetizing, the food is not.
4. Although five potential residents toured the facility during the past month, only one became a resident. That person complained about the intake interview and procedures and almost refused to sign the contract.
5. The head nurse conducts the intake interviews in the medical office. Personnel who need supplies from the office or must ask the nurse a question frequently interrupt the interviews.

The phenomena suggest a major managerial problem. If the facility continues to operate at less than optimal capacity, it will lose money. If it cannot satisfy its residents, it will likely not operate at full capacity. Several approaches could be taken to solve the managerial problem. After some preliminary investigation, the administrator authorizes a study to investigate ways to attract and retain residents. That investigation is the research problem. The purpose of such a study is to enable the facility to reach its goal of 99 percent occupancy.

Having defined the problem and purpose, your next step is to identify the scope of the investigation.

Narrow the Scope

By narrowing the scope of the analysis, you identify the specific factors or elements to be analyzed. A perfect study would investigate all possible aspects of the research question. But time and money constraints require that you focus your study on the factors most likely to yield relevant data. Preliminary research often leads to the identification of those elements. After identifying the factors, you will concentrate the remainder of your research on those items.

In the Peaceful Village example, the scope could include these factors regarding attracting and retaining residents:

A. Advertising
   1. Cost/benefit analysis of current program
   2. Analysis of competitors' advertising

   B. Intake Procedures
       1. Work-flow analysis of current procedures
       2. Analysis of procedures used in other facilities
       3. Residents' evaluation of current procedures
   C. Services to Residents
       1. Food
       2. Recreation
       3. Entertainment
       4. Personal and medical services
       5. Maintenance of private rooms
       6. Maintenance of common areas

Notice that the scope remains focused on the problem of attracting and retaining residents. It does not, for example, include looking at alternative uses for the building and grounds. That factor is outside the scope of this research problem.

State Delimitations and Limitations

Two concepts—delimitations and limitations—relate to narrowing the project's scope. *Delimitations* are additional boundaries or restrictions that you place on the study. For example, in the Peaceful Village study, a decision to interview only current residents is a delimitation. *Limitations* are potential shortcomings or inadequacies of the study. Some limitations arise from circumstances beyond your control; others derive from the way you define the scope and delimitations. Interviewing only current residents prevents you from knowing why former residents left and why people who toured your facility did not become residents. Failure to acquire that information may seriously limit the validity of your conclusions. If, however, you do not delimit your study in this way, you may find it extremely difficult and costly to locate those nonresidents. Practical constraints may make the delimitation necessary.

Delimitations and limitations are not required in all research plans. But effective planners include those items when they are relevant. Stating delimitations tends to clarify and refine the scope; stating limitations demonstrates that the researcher understands and is willing to acknowledge the weaknesses of the proposed study.

Having carefully defined the problem, purpose, and scope of the study, you are now ready to plan how you will collect relevant data.

Plan Data Collection

The first step in *data collection* is to identify potential sources. Researchers use two kinds of data: primary and secondary. Information that has been collected and published by others is secondary data. Books, magazines, journals, and corporate annual reports found in public or private libraries are examples of secondary data sources. Many traditional secondary sources are now available as online or CD-ROM services. Primary data consist of information that is collected at its origin. People and company files are major sources of primary data used in business research.

You will learn methods for collecting primary and secondary data when you study Chapters 11 through 13. Recognize now, however, that the scope of the research problem directs the selection of data sources. To ensure the validity of the data, sources must be chosen for their relevance, not their convenience.

Plan Data Analysis

Data analysis is the process by which researchers find meaning in the many facts and figures they have accumulated. Both quantitative and qualitative analysis procedures are used in business research. *Quantitative analysis* involves the use of statistics to derive meaning from numerical data. *Qualitative analysis* is the use of logical thought processes to discover relationships and meaning in data. You will learn more about data analysis when you study Chapter 15. At this time, observe that even before you collect data, you must decide how you will analyze them. (Please note that *data* is the plural form of *datum*. Always refer to *data* with a plural pronoun and accompany the word with a plural verb.)

Although some people consider quantitative analysis to be the more objective form of analysis, that method also has a subjective component. Selection of a statistical procedure and interpretation of the computations rest on subjective judgments. In both quantitative and qualitative analysis, the researcher must avoid faulty reasoning. For example, a researcher could make a hasty generalization about the interrupted intake interview referred to in the previous example of the retirement center. In a hasty generalization, the researcher concludes that something that was true in one instance is true in all cases. If the observed instance was an unusual situation resulting from unexpected events on that day, the researcher would be in error to design a study to determine how to improve intake interviews. The interview situation could also be a symptom of a larger management problem, such as the lack of standard procedures for several aspects of the operation.

The manager must also know when the project will be completed. Therefore, the proposal should include a realistic estimate of time required for the work.

Estimate Time Schedule

The purpose of a time schedule is twofold. It ensures the manager that you have considered carefully the time required and are making a commitment to keep to that schedule. It also serves as a checklist for people working on the project to remind them of obligations at various stages. The terms of a proposal often become part of a formal contract; some contracts include penalties if the project is not completed on time or bonuses if completed ahead of schedule.

An effective time schedule includes target dates for completion of various segments of the project as well as a projected date for presentation of the results. It may also include dates on which interim or progress reports will be made. When a researcher has been given a deadline for a project, an effective method for developing a time schedule is to work backward from that date and allocate the maximum length of time that can be devoted to each phase of the project. If no deadline has been given, the proposal writer may work forward from the date of the proposal and project the amount of time required for each phase.

Estimate Resources Needed

Research always requires time; in addition, some research requires special equipment or supplies. Before approving a project, a manager must know how much of the company's resources the project will consume. A research plan should include realistic estimates of the costs of necessary labor (researchers and assistants), supplies, equipment, travel, and so on. The manager can then evaluate the potential benefits against the projected costs of the research.

In many companies, the accounting department has developed standard costs to apply when employees prepare proposals. For example, when you prepare a proposal, you will often follow standard cost procedures for determining the value of the time that you and your associates will spend on a project. However, it is your responsibility to make a realistic estimate of the kinds of personnel and the number of hours a project will require. You can usually obtain costs for equipment and supplies from vendors, but it is your responsibility to assess realistically the quantities of such materials that will be required. You can get reasonably accurate estimates of costs for airfare and lodging from a travel agent or online services provided by airlines and hotels. Company policy may require that you use a company vehicle for land travel. If you are permitted to use your own vehicle, apply your employer's standard mileage allowance or the Internal Revenue Service's allowance.

Plan Presentation of Results

Research has no value until the results have been communicated. A complete research plan indicates how the findings, conclusions, and recommendations will be presented.

Since research deals with a nonroutine problem, a relatively rich medium must be chosen. That medium is usually a carefully designed, comprehensive written report, perhaps supplemented by an oral presentation. A tentative outline for the written report may be included in the research plan as evidence that the researcher has thought the project through to its completion.

Seek Approval to Proceed

By now you can probably appreciate that one more item must be included in a research plan: a request for approval. Since research addresses a nonroutine problem and may consume substantial resources, the researchers and managers must agree on all items in the plan. Even when authorized to prepare the plan, effective researchers do not assume that it is automatically approved. They specifically request feedback and approval. That request opens the door for clarification, possible modification, and approval of the plan. On approval, the researcher can work confidently, knowing that carrying out the plan will contribute to both individual and organizational goals.

To obtain approval, most researchers write the research plan and present it in a formal document called a research or project proposal. The proposal may also be presented orally so that managers can ask questions immediately and clarify any ambiguities or request changes before giving their approval.

Searching the Visible and Invisible Webs

As an Internet user, you are likely so familiar with the Google search engine that you use its name as a synonym for the verb *search*. You probably also use other search engines, such as Yahoo!, Ask, Bing, Blekko, Duck Duck Go, and Entire Web.

To plan for data collection for business reports, you can benefit from other search utilities, including meta-search engines and deep-search engines. A meta-search engine is one that sends your requests to several other search engines and delivers a combined list of the search results. A deep-search engine is designed to search the invisible or hidden Web that regular engines cannot reach.

Search Engines

You have likely heard a search engine referred to as a "spider" that crawls around the Web seeking websites. The spider reads the found websites, so to speak, and arranges the text on them (or part of it) into a large index, or database, that you, the user, can access. No search engine covers more than about 30 percent of the Internet, though some of them—especially Ask, Bing, Google, and Yahoo!—are huge.

Some smaller search engines are powered by larger ones. For example, Blackle (http://www.blackle.com) receives search service from Google, while Yahoo! powers the ecologically motivated Ecosia (http://ecosia.org). In addition, hundreds of small engines operate independently.

Still other search engines are called *Web portals* because they provide not only search capabilities but also a point of entry to a range of Web services, such as email, news, social media, stock market quotations, popular videos, and weather. Portal examples include AOL (http://www.aol.com), Excite (http://www.excite.com), iGoogle (http://www.google.com/ig?aig=0&reason=1), MSN powered by Bing (http://www.msn.com), Netvibes for Business (http://www.netvibes.com/en), and Yahoo! (http://www.yahoo.com).

Meta-Search Engines

Meta-search is based on the premises that the Web is too vast for any one search engine to index all of it and that more complete search results can be found by merging results from multiple engines.

Unlike Google, Yahoo!, and other conventional engines, a meta-search engine lacks a database. Instead, it creates a virtual database by taking your search request, sending it to several diverse engines, and then compiling hits in a particular way based on the engine's unique set of rules.

Each meta-search engine is different. Some search only popular search engines; others combine lesser-known engines and other sources. These engines also differ in the number of search engines they use and how they present search results.

Two notable meta-search examples include Dogpile (http://www.dogpile.com) and Yippy (http://www.yippy.com). Dogpile searches Ask, Bing, Google, and Yahoo!, while Yippy searches Open Directory in addition to Ask, Bing, and Yahoo!. (**Note:** *Open Directory* refers to results of the Open Directory Project, an attempt to create and edit a comprehensive directory of the Internet by an enormous group of volunteers.)

Some meta-engines, like Srchr (http://www.srchr.com/default.aspx), group hits by the engines and databases involved in the search. Others simply list results in order of relevance, concealing which search engine returned those results, thus eliminating duplicate hits.

The meta-searcher SurfWax (http://www.surfwax.com) includes a feature called LookAhead that works like the auto-complete feature in a word processor. As a user types the first few letters of a query, the engine picks up the suggestion and lists articles and blogs of possible interest. For example, when you type s-u-s-t, SurfWax promptly will list any current articles on the subject of sustainability. In addition, a feature called SearchPal offers semantics- and lexicon-based search options. The lexicon goes beyond an index to the words on a website. Instead, SurfWax logically associates concepts, products, and terms in a way that delivers results based on their related meaning, not just the words. For instance, if you type sust+sea, the engine will list current articles involving sustainability and sea life, anything from seafood recipes to shipping. In this respect, SurfWax is related to the deep-search engines discussed later in this section. Copernic Agent Personal, software that you can download free of charge (http://www.copernic.com), also searches lexically and semantically, comparable to SurfWax.

A relatively new meta-searcher, Wolfram/Alpha (http://www.wolframalpha.com), processes natural language (in place of Boolean search terms) and computes answers to your queries from a structured database in place of listing Web pages that *may* contain the answer. Specializing in mathematics or computation, Wolfram/Alpha deals with a range of question types, including facts, lists, and definitions; how and why questions; and hypothetical and other complex questions.

In addition to the meta-search engines already named, the following list contains names of a select few.

Meta-Search Engine and Location	Searches These Engines	Comment
Fazzle (http://www.fazzle.com)	Bing, Google, Project Gutenberg, Wikipedia, Wolfram/Alpha, Yahoo!	Project Gutenberg searches well-known and classic books.
Info.com (http://www.info.com)	About, Bing, Google, Yahoo!	Includes access to major online encyclopedias, dictionaries, and so on. Includes search for flights, images, jobs, products, and videos.
Ixquick (http://www.ixquick.com)	Undisclosed	Includes five-star rating of sites: one star for each engine that chooses it. Many stars mean that the site was chosen for many reasons.
MetaCrawler (http://www.metacrawler.com)	Undisclosed	Includes image, news, and video search as well as business and people finders.

continued

Meta-Search Engine and Location	Searches These Engines	Comment
MonsterCrawler (http://www.monstercrawler.com)	Bing, GigaBlast, Google, Yahoo!	
Pandia Metasearch (http://www.pandia.com/metasearch/index.html)	Undisclosed	
WebCrawler (http://www.webcrawler.com)	Bing, Google, Yahoo!, and others	Includes image, news, and video search as well as business and people finders.
ZapMeta (http://www.zapmeta.com)	Altavista, Bing, Entireweb, Gigablast, Yahoo!	Includes image, MP3, and video search.

Meta-Browser

The search engine called Quickbrowse (http://quickbrowse.com/qbhomepage.cgi) is technically known as a meta-browser. To use it, you specify websites you want to see by typing or pasting the Web addresses into a text box. Quickbrowse then combines pages of search results into a vertical, continuously scrollable list. In addition to viewing the results, you can save the Quickbrowse page or email it to yourself. Of the half dozen meta-browsers introduced in the late 1990s, only Quickbrowse remains.

Search Aggregators

A search aggregator is a meta-search engine that finds, filters, and sorts results into user-friendly categories. For example, at Leapfish (http://www.leapfish.com), a search for "laser pointer" listed finds in five categories: blog results, image results, news results, shopping results, and Twitter results. The search aggregator Gajeebo (http://www.gajeebo.com) is set up to sort results into a dozen categories: Web pages, news, public views (digg and Twitter), videos, pictures, queries (frequently asked questions), blogs, shopping, people, music, movies, and travel. Gajeebo displays these categories tidily as separate tabs, so you can view just one category at a time, skipping any tab that you deem irrelevant for your report. Within each category, the hits are grouped by source. The Web page category, for example, includes three tabs—Google, Yahoo!, and Wikipedia—and the picture category also includes three tabs—PhotoBucket, Flickr, and Picasa.

Another advantage of search aggregators is greater flexibility in deciding which engines will fill your research needs. Most aggregators allow you to select the engines for a specific search. The aggregator MrSapo provides an example. You can use MrSapo to search over 150 search tools. Once you type a query at the website (http://www.mrsapo.com), you can choose among 250 search tools from which you would like to get results, including eight website search engines: Ask, Bing, Duck Duck Go, Google, Leapfish, Wolframs/Alpha, Yahoo!, and Yauba. Then, as you navigate to your search results, MrSapo's toolbar remains accessible at the top of your screen.

Deep-Search Engines

The visible Web, then, is that part of Web content that standard search and meta-search engines can find and index. Other names for it are Indexable Web and Surface Web. Most of the Web's content, however, is buried far down on pages that do not exist until a specific query generates them. Conventional search engines cannot find this so-called *dynamic content*. Other information below the surface includes Web pages that no other page links to; text written in a format other than HTML; text content using protocols other than HTTP; sites that require users to register and log in, including many searchable databases; sites that block search engines; and ever-changing content, such as news and stock market reports. Common names for these unreachable sites—vastly more numerous than the surface Web—include Deep Web, Deep Net, Hidden Web, Invisible Web, and Undernet.

Unlike a regular search engine's hits, deep-search results cannot be a list of Web addresses. To be meaningful, the results have to show characteristics of each source found. Therein lies the main deep-search challenge: how to find and map similar data from many, dissimilar sources and then present an understandable list of results. As you might expect, more than one modern-day pioneer has taken this challenge, and the following list identifies deep-search resources for your consideration. In addition, various printed and online tools exist for finding information in specific business-related disciplines. Chapter 12 explores many of those tools.

- Biznar (http://biznar.com/biznar) is a deep-Web meta-search engine returning the most relevant results from over 60 authoritative business collections to one Web page. It removes duplicate results and weighs each result for relevance. Advanced features give flexibility in narrowing a search. For example, you can search for specific phrases or complex Boolean terms, and you can specify a particular title or author or year of publication. Biznar allows clustering by topics and includes sort options. In addition, the site issues alerts. You can specify search terms; and when new, relevant content appears, Biznar will notify you by email or RSS feed—a good way to keep up with business developments. Then you can receive the results as email or download your selections to a citation reader for offline use.
- Complete Planet (http://aip.completeplanet.com) accesses about 70,000 dynamic searchable databases on widely varying subjects, including specialized topics like food and drink, media and entertainment, and products and technology. One of the advanced search options allows you to set a date range for your search results.
- DeepDyve (http://www.deepdyve.com) makes millions of articles accessible to businesspeople and publishers from thousands of journals in business and finance, computer science, humanities, information technology and engineering, life sciences, medicine, patents and law, physics and physical sciences, and social sciences. DeepDyve goes beyond key word–based search. It indexes every word in a document, but it also looks at the meaning of a document and uses that sense to compute a relevance statistic, that is, an index of the document's relevance to the search terms. You can browse or preview article abstracts for free. Downloading or printing a resource is not an option, and to read a full article at the DeepDyve site, you would need to rent it at about $1 for 24 hours.

- DeepPeep (http://www.deeppeep.org) is a search engine that aims to index every database on the public Web, including the deep Web. It specializes in Web forms, tracking 45,000 forms across seven domains: airfare, auto, biology, book, hotel, job, and rental. The DeepPeep search engine caters to both casual Web users (for example, forms related to used cars) and serious researches (for example, forms containing salary information).

- IncyWincy (http://www.incywincy.com) acts like a meta-search engine. It taps into other search engines and filters the results. Besides searching the Web, IncyWincy searches directories, forms, and images. The site tells you the number of hits in each of 13 categories (arts, business, computers, games, health, news, recreation, reference, regional, science, shopping, society, and sports); then you can refine your search by clicking one of the categories.

- Infomime (http://infomine.ucr.edu) was built by a consortium of university libraries. The Infomime engine gathers information from online articles, books, databases, directories, journals, and library card catalogs. You can search by subject and then use various options to tweak your search. Two of its links—General Reference and Other Search Tools—turn Infomime into a research portal.

- Infoplease (http://www.infoplease.com) is a feature-rich portal that gives you access to almanacs, atlases, biographies, and encyclopedias in addition to a range of other services. Infoplease contains information in nine broad categories: biography, business, entertainment, health and science, history and government, society and culture, sports, United States, and world. An offshoot called Biosearch is a search engine for biographies.

- ScienceResearch (http://scienceresearch.com/scienceresearch) is a comprehensive science research portal created by Deep Web Technologies, the maker of Bisnar for business research. Bisnar and ScienceResearch have similar features. Related deep-Web portals include Science.gov Alliance (http://www.science.gov/scigov), which searches over 50 million pages of authoritative selected science information provided by U.S. government agencies, including research and development results, and Scitopia (http://www.scitopia.org/scitopia), a search portal of leading worldwide science and technology societies.

- Scirus (http:// http://www.scirus.com) has a scientific emphasis. This far-reaching engine scours courseware, scientists' home pages, and journals. Scirus's coverage of patents and institutional intranets adds relevance for researchers in business. The site includes a knowledge-sharing service for the scientific community and a list of headlines from the journal *New Scientist*.

- TechXtra (http://www.techxtra.ac.uk) focuses on computing, engineering, and mathematics. Besides articles and website information, TechXtra gives you industry news, job announcements, technical data and reports, and teaching and learning resources. A tagline on TechXtra's home page indicates 5 million items from 33 sources, which are listed.

- WorldWide Science (http://worldwidescience.org) is a global science gateway comprised of national and international scientific databases and portals. This search engine provides one-stop searching of databases from around the world and translation of multilingual scientific literature. WorldWide Science was developed and is maintained by an office in the U.S. Department of Energy.

- WWW Virtual Library (http://vlib.org) is known for both the breadth and the depth of subjects and resources. Besides a search bar, the virtual library involves an alphabetized category list, and you can "drill" each subject vertically: agriculture, arts, business and economics, communications and media, computing and computer science, education, engineering, humanities and humanistic studies, information and libraries, international affairs, law, natural sciences and mathematics, recreation, regional studies, social and behavioral sciences, and society.

Deep-Web technologies are in their infancy, nowhere near the ultimate goal of a Web where all data are interconnected and accessible regardless of where held. Scientists and Web visionaries continue working toward systems that connect and integrate unlike data sources. Although we may never reach the ultimate goal, the dozen deep-Web search engines in this list represent an impressive start.

The Research Proposal

The objective of a business proposal is to persuade another person or persons to do something that the proposer thinks will be beneficial for the organization and its stakeholders. In the case of a research proposal, the objective is to persuade the recipient to authorize the time and money required to carry out a significant research project.

The persuasiveness of the proposal will depend on your ability to show that you understand the problem and are capable of conducting the study. Additional persuasive elements are honest, realistic estimates of time and resources needed for the project and evidence that you have considered how you will present your results. Therefore, an investigative or research proposal is a formal version of your research plan.

As you prepare a research proposal, use the 12 parts of the research plan shown in Illustration 10.1 as a guide. Include all parts that are relevant to the proposed investigation. The situation may justify omission of certain parts. For example, stating delimitations or limitations is not necessary if the scope of the project is already stated very narrowly and no obvious limitations are foreseen. The order in which the parts are presented must contribute to the reader's understanding of what you plan to investigate. The presentation sequence should also lead the reader to appreciate the significance of the research.

Since a research proposal is a complex document, structural devices such as headings, enumerations, and columns can be used advantageously. Illustration 10.2 demonstrates effective format and structure for a research proposal.

Although Illustration 10.2 shows the proposal in memorandum format, that proposal could also be presented in letter or manuscript format. Manuscript format usually includes a title page and a transmittal message, which includes the request for approval. Illustrations 10.3 through 10.5 show a proposal presented in manuscript format. The introductory material that might be used in a proposal written in memo format would logically be included in a transmittal message that accompanies a proposal in manuscript format. Similarly, the request for approval is generally excluded from the manuscript when that request is included in the transmittal message. Since the illustrated proposal is going from K-F Urban Design to a potential client, the manuscript format with a transmittal letter would be preferable to the memo format.

ILLUSTRATION 10.2 RESEARCH PROPOSAL*

S. C. Ports Authority

Memo

TO	Bryant T. Joseph, VP, Terminal Development
FROM	Melvin L. Barbara, VP, Government Relations
DATE	1/12/2011
SUBJECT	Citizens' Attitudes toward Cruise Traffic

Background and Authorization

Recent letters to the editor in the *Charleston News and Courier* have indicated mixed attitudes about the docking of cruise ships at Union Pier in the Port of Charleston. For approximately 25 years, the Port of Charleston has been the site of one to three ship departures and arrivals per week. Currently this port serves as a home port and port of call for Carnival Cruise Lines as well as a port of call for other cruise lines. Home porting and port-of-call stops generally do not occur on the same days, except when emergencies, weather conditions, or other nautical events necessitate such multiple dockings. Although some merchants appreciate the increased business associated with the cruise dockings, other merchants and many local residents complain that the increased pedestrian and auto traffic distract from the traditional charm of Charleston. Discussions have been underway to move the cruise terminal to a different location along the Charleston Harbor waterfront in an attempt to alleviate some of the negative aspects of the departure and arrival of cruise ships.

At our management meeting on January 7 we discussed the need to determine objectively how the citizens of Charleston feel about the effects of cruise dockings in the Port of Charleston. We decided it was necessary to know more about those attitudes before launching a major study of the feasibility to relocate the cruise terminal. You asked me to design a study to explore those feelings.

Statement of the Problem

The objective of the study is to determine Charlestonians' perceptions of the economic and social impact of cruise dockings in the Port of Charleston and the possible relocation of the cruise terminal.

Purpose of the Study

The purpose of this study is to assess the business and social climate in which the Ports Authority will operate if it continues with plans to relocate the cruise terminal. Knowledge of that climate will help the Authority develop operational and communication strategies relative to the potential relocation.

continued

*All illustrations that discuss research related to the cruise terminal in Charleston, South Carolina, are based on events taking place at the time of writing. However, all names and data used in the illustrations are fictitious.

ILLUSTRATION 10.2 CONTINUED

Bryant T. Joseph   –2–   1/12/2011

Scope of Analysis

Three factors will be studied:

1. What business impacts do Charleston's downtown residents and merchants perceive to be related to the arrival and departure of cruise ships?
2. What personal and community impacts do Charleston's downtown residents and merchants perceive to be related to the arrival and departure of cruise ships?
3. What knowledge of and attitudes toward relocation of the cruise terminal are evidenced by Charleston's downtown residents and merchants?

Definitions

For purposes of this study, *residents* is used to designate persons living in the Ansonborough section of Charleston. The term *merchants* includes all commercial and professional units within the designated geographical area.

Delimitations

Because cruise passengers primarily frequent the area between the Charleston Harbor and King Street, the sample for this study will be drawn from merchants and residents in an area bounded by East Bay St. on the east, Broad St. on the south, King St. on the west, and Calhoun St. on the north. The sample of residents will be drawn from the Ansonborough district, which is located within those street boundaries.

The study period will be the months of June and August, confined to two days following the departure of a homeport ship and two days following the arrival and departure of a port-of-call ship. Ships will be selected from published cruise schedules, with ships departing at least three days from one another.

Limitations

The data collected will not represent attitudes of the business community or residents outside the downtown area, some of whom may also be affected by the cruise business. However, since the downtown community absorbs the major impact of the presence of cruise ships, the attitudes of that community can best direct decisions related to relocating the cruise terminal.

Since the data will be collected during the summer cruise season, the attitudes expressed may differ from attitudes expressed during an earlier or later cruise season. Nonetheless, the responses should be representative of attitudes developed during a peak tourist season in Charleston.

Methodology

This study will be based solely on primary data gathered by questionnaires completed by members of the target populations.

The sample. All merchants and residents within the defined geographical area will be invited to participate in the study.

continued

ILLUSTRATION 10.2 CONTINUED

Bryant T. Joseph   –3–   1/12/2011

Data collection. The data will be collected in two ways:

1. A letter will be mailed to all merchants inviting them to log onto a specified website on specified dates and complete an electronic questionnaire. The dates will be based on the docking of selected ships.
2. An invitation to attend a town-hall meeting will be mailed to all residential addresses in the Ansonborough district. The meetings will be scheduled to correspond to dockings of selected ships. At each meeting, the purpose of the study will be explained, attendees will be permitted to ask questions, and they will be asked to complete the questionnaire before leaving the meeting.

Data analysis. My staff will code the data obtained from the questionnaires and enter then into a statistical program. Summary statistics will be computed and interpreted.

Time Required

I propose the following schedule:

March	Design, test, and revise questionnaires; test data analysis program
April	Prepare letters to be sent to merchants and residents
May 1–May 15	Prepare and distribute a series of three news releases (newspaper, radio and television) to inform the community about the upcoming survey and encourage participation
May 15–May 30	Mail letters to merchants and half of Ansonborough residential addresses
June 1–5	Send reminder to attend town hall meeting
June 12 & 13	Conduct town-hall meetings following June 1 departure of Carnival cruise ship
June 15 & 16	Conduct town-hall meetings following June 15 port-of-call docking of Carnival cruise ship
June 17–July 30	Begin data entry and analysis regarding June dockings
August 1–5	Mail letters to remaining half of Ansonborough residents; mail reminders to merchants
August 14 & 15	Conduct town-hall meetings following August 13 departure of Carnival cruise ship
August 23 & 24	Conduct town-hall meetings following August 22 port-of-call docking of Carnival cruise ship
September 1–15	Complete data entry and analysis
September 20	Distribute completed written report to management committee
September 22	Discuss report with management during regular meeting

continued

ILLUSTRATION 10.2 CONTINUED

Bryant T. Joseph   –4–   1/12/2011

Resources Needed

All research will be conducted by staff of the Government Affairs Division as part of
our normal duties. We will use approximately 100 employee hours to prepare the data collection
instruments, enter and analyze the data, and prepare the final report. We anticipate spending
approximately 24 employee hours conducting the town-hall meetings. Standard cost allocations for
respective grades will be applied. In addition, the project will incur direct costs for printing, supplies,
postage, and town-hall meetings. The total project budget is $5,750:

Staff Labor	$3,750
Printing and supplies	750
Postage	750
Meeting expenses	500
Total	$5,750

Presentation of Results

I will present our findings, conclusions, and recommendations to the management committee in a
formal written report prior to our September 20 management meeting and will be prepared to discuss the report at that meeting.

Request for Approval

Approval of this proposal by January 20 will permit the Government Affairs division to work this
project into our schedule and adhere to the proposed schedule given in this proposal. Please call me
at extension 597 if you have any questions.

Ethical Considerations

Ethical issues may arise as you plan research and prepare proposals. At each step in
the planning process, ethical individuals would weigh the possible impact of their decisions. Does each decision promote the researcher's good only, or does it contribute
to the well-being of others also?

For example, what are the implications of narrowing the scope of analysis? Researchers are often confronted by the very practical constraint of not being able to
analyze all possible elements of a problem. But the decision to include some elements
and exclude others implies a judgment that one route of analysis will lead to "better"
results than another—in essence, a moral judgment. Discussing a research problem
with a group of colleagues who can judge the work impartially may help you identify
the "best" set of factors to include in the scope of analysis.

For practical purposes, researchers must sometimes accept data sources that are
less than ideal, such as interviewing shoppers in Mall Y because the management of
Mall X would not give permission to conduct the interviews. Because of such practical
constraints, an honest statement of delimitations and limitations is a practice honored
by ethical researchers.

ILLUSTRATION 10.3 TITLE PAGE OF RESEARCH PROPOSAL

THE FEASIBILITY OF RELOCATING
THE CRUISE TERMINAL AT UNION PIER
CHARLESTON, SC

A Proposal

Submitted to

Bryant T. Joseph, VP, Terminal Operations
South Carolina State Ports Authority

Submitted by

D. W. Kirkpatrick, Vice President
K-F Urban Design
456 Capitol Way
Charleston, WV 25301

October 15, 2011

ILLUSTRATION 10.4   TRANSMITTAL MESSAGE FOR RESEARCH PROPOSAL

K-F Urban Design

Designing Tomorrow's Communities Today

456 Capitol Way, Charleston WV 25301
Tel: 888.888.8888 Fax: 888.123.4567

October 15, 2011

Mr. Bryant T. Joseph, VP, Terminal Operations
South Carolina State Ports Authority
P O Box 22288
Charleston, SC 29413

Dear Mr. Bryant

In a telephone conversation with you on September 28, you mentioned your desire to determine the feasibility of relocating the cruise terminal along the Charleston Harbor waterfront. You indicated that you had already conducted a community survey of attitudes about cruise dockings at Union Pier. We discussed your firmly held belief that the cruise business can have a positive impact on Charleston's economy. You also expressed concerns that any plan to relocate the cruise terminal must take community attitudes into consideration and result in better commercial and social use of the Charleston Harbor waterfront.

You requested that I propose a study to determine the feasibility of relocating the cruise pier with the objective of ameliorating the perceived negative impacts of using Charleston as a home port or port of call for major cruise line. The enclosed proposal is a response to that request. I expect to be able to present a written report to you by May 15, 2012.

Approval of this proposal by November 15 will permit K-F Urban Design to begin and end on schedule. If you have any questions about the proposal, please call me at extension 12.

Sincerely

D. W. Kirkpatrick

D. W. Kirkpatrick, Vice President

ILLUSTRATION 10.5 RESEARCH PROPOSAL IN MANUSCRIPT FORMAT

A PROPOSAL:

THE FEASIBILITY OF RELOCATING THE CRUISE TERMINAL

AT UNION PIER, CHARLESTON, SOUTH CAROLINA

A study conducted by the South Carolina Ports Authority in Summer 2011 revealed mixed attitudes about the economic and social benefits of cruise dockings in the Port of Charleston. A sizable majority of merchants approved of the dockings and reported that their businesses had benefited from the cruise traffic. In contrast, a majority of downtown residents expressed considerable dissatisfaction with the increased pedestrian and motor traffic in the area as well as the abrasive announcements made from the ships and pier directed to cruise passengers during embarkation and debarkation.

The Ports Authority is tentatively considering a relocation of the cruise terminal to an area slightly north of its current Union Pier location. Tentative plans call for redirecting motor traffic along the waterfront and increasing public space to provide greater waterfront access to Charlestonians and tourists. The Authority hopes that relocating the cruise port may reduce some of the dissatisfaction expressed by downtown residents and ultimately make a large portion of the waterfront a major community asset. In general, downtown merchants were knowledgeable about the potential economic and social impact of relocating the cruise port; however, residents had incorrect or inadequate information about that impact.

Statement of the Problem

The focus of this study will be to determine the feasibility of relocating the cruise terminal to an area slightly north of its current Union Pier location, including related changes in traffic flows and waterfront usage.

Three factors will be analyzed:

1. Optimal location for a new cruise terminal
2. Infrastructure and traffic needs
3. Public use of Charleston's historic waterfront

Purpose of the Study

The purpose of the study is to generate a concept plan for the Union Pier waterfront that will enable the Ports Authority to serve the contemporary needs of the cruise industry while retaining the traditional ambiance of historic Charleston.

Methodology

Both primary and secondary data will be used in the study. Secondary data will be obtained by a review of current security standards related to cruise embarkations and disembarkations, records of current use of port facilities both as a cruise terminal and a shipping terminal, Charleston County tax assessor's data, and current zoning regulations.

continued

ILLUSTRATION 10.5 CONTINUED

Primary data will be obtained by way of a photographic survey of the entire area under study, followed by engineering and economic studies of pedestrian and vehicular traffic, infrastructure needed to service the port area satisfactorily, and alternative uses for the Port of Charleston waterfront.

To conduct this study K-F Urban Design will assign a team of licensed engineers and economic analysts who will employ standard engineering and economic analysis techniques.

Time Required

This study will be completed within six months of contract signing. An interim report will be provided at the end of three months.

Final Report

A comprehensive written and fully illustrated concept plan will be presented to the Ports Authority. This plan will be accompanied by all engineering and financial studies conducted to formulate the plan.

Qualifications to Conduct Study

K-F Urban Design has a track record of compiling successful concept plans for major urban waterfront renewal projects in North America and Europe. Examples of those projects are available at the website www.KFUrbanDesign.com.

Cost

K-F Urban Design will conduct this study for a turnkey figure of $200,000, with a penalty of $2,000 per day for failure to deliver the final product within six months of contract signing.

Similarly, the request for approval is more than a request for authorization of funds. Do you have (or can you acquire) the skills needed to carry out the research as proposed? The person who gives approval has an ethical responsibility to evaluate the quality of the proposed research, its value to the organization, and the competence of those who will conduct the research. For that reason, some proposal writers include the qualifications of the person or persons who will conduct the study to demonstrate competence to fulfill the proposal.

The public is becoming increasingly concerned about the invasion of privacy and identity theft. If primary data are to be used in the research, both the researcher and managers who authorize the research have a moral obligation to protect the confidentiality of the data and the safety of human and nonhuman subjects. Specific techniques for protecting confidentiality may be included in the proposed plan for data collection.

Individual rights and the good of others are always involved in proposal preparation. Whenever a person attempts to influence others, ethics are involved. When a proposal is solicited, ethical standards require that a person submit a proposal only if he or she is able to satisfy the requester's needs. When presenting unsolicited proposals, ethical individuals address only genuine, verifiable problems that they can competently analyze.

Summary

A research plan guides the investigator toward completion of effective research. Content and context determine the formality of the plan. A complex project requires a research plan that includes these steps: obtain or review authorization, identify the audience, define the problem, clarify the purpose, narrow the scope, state delimitations and limitations, plan data collection, plan data analysis, estimate time schedule, estimate resources needed, plan presentation of results, and seek approval to proceed. As part of planning data collection, consider data that may be available on the visible and invisible Webs. Select meta-search and deep-search engines that seem promising; then use them to conduct preliminary searches and capture search results. A research or project proposal is a formal written version of such a plan.

Ethical issues may arise at each stage of project planning. The ethical researcher considers motives for and likely outcomes of decisions made in each planning step.

Topics for Discussion

1. What is the function of a research plan?
2. What are the parts of a research plan?
3. What is the relationship of a research plan to a research proposal?
4. Differentiate these elements of a research plan: managerial problem, research problem, research purpose.
5. Why must you limit a project's scope?
6. What are delimitations and limitations? Why should these factors be considered when the research is being planned?
7. How do primary and secondary data differ from one another?
8. With two or three classmates, discuss and list your favorite Web search engines, including standard, meta-search, and deep-search engines. For each website in your list, name its main purpose and one or more distinguishing features. If you cannot identify favorites from experience, try out a few engines mentioned in this chapter.
9. Why should data analysis be addressed in a research proposal?
10. Why should a research proposal include estimates of time and resources needed?
11. Why are both authorization of a research project and approval of the project proposal necessary?
12. Under what circumstances is it advisable to include the researcher's qualifications in a research proposal? In your judgment, what would demonstrate a person's ability to conduct the proposed research?

13. If you have conducted business research, share with your classmates some of the ethical issues that you had to consider as you planned the research.

14. If you were asked to provide personal data for business research purposes, what concerns would you have about the use of the data? What evidence would you require to ensure that the researcher would use the data ethically?

Applications

1. For each of the following situations, assume that you are a researcher for Abrams, Beltzer, Cox, and Duoma, LLP, a business consulting firm to small businesses. Each scenario requires that you write a proposal to conduct research that will help the client resolve a problem. You do not have to conduct the research at this time. Just write the proposal, providing the kinds of information the client will need before authorizing you to proceed with the research. In each situation, identify the managerial problem, the research problem and purpose, the scope of your analysis, and possible data sources. Add other factors that will convince the client to hire you to do the research.

   a. Zack Pupchek has observed the growing popularity of resale, consignment, and thrift shops. Many astute consumers have learned to stretch their dollars by buying "nearly new" clothing, toys, tools, and home furnishings in such shops, and they are becoming a growing force in retail markets. Pupchek is considering opening a resale, consignment, or thrift shop that specializes in the resale of tools used in the building trades, woodworking, auto repair, and so forth, as well as electronic games that would appeal to men and boys. He plans to call the shop "Tools and Toys for Men and Boys." Pupchek wants to know the potential for such an enterprise in your city or a nearby town. (**Note:** Check the National Association of Resale & Thrift Shops at http://www.narts.org for distinctions among the three classifications and other information about this industry.)

   b. Natural Fare is a supermarket that specializes in organically grown fruits, vegetables, and other grocery items classified as "natural" or "organic." Its shopping carts have become quite dilapidated and must be replaced. The owner, Hans Grossman, has read about new supermarket carts that are equipped with touch screens that can guide the shopper through the store. Some devices permit a shopper to swipe a frequent-shopper card that will call up the person's shopping list. That list can be sent over the Web or compiled from a shopping history. As the customer strolls the aisles of the store, the cart can point out relevant items and "specials," along with cents-off coupons. Most setups also permit a shopper to order items from the deli or bakery without having to stand in line. Whereas retailers claim the carts help them to manage their supply chain more effectively, some consumer groups have criticized the movement toward "smart carts" as another attempt to surreptitiously gather marketing information.

   Since many of Grossman's customers are busy professional people who don't want to spend a lot of time shopping for food, he thinks the smart carts may be the way to go when he replaces his old equipment. Grossman has asked you to study the advantages and disadvantages of smart carts.

c. Lisa Carswell has completed a dog grooming course and has worked for three years with one of the busiest pet grooming businesses in your city. She thinks she wants to begin a mobile dog grooming business (no cats, please) in which she would take her fully equipped van to homes and groom dogs on their owners' premises. She thinks the service would appeal to retirees who may have difficulty taking their pets to the grooming parlor and also to busy professionals who often cannot find time to take their dogs out to be groomed. Carswell asked you to study the potential for such a business in your town. She also wants information about the advantages and disadvantages of using Facebook to promote her services.

d. Strokes are rising among young and middle-aged Americans while dropping among older ones. Some public health officials consider this a sign that obesity is changing the age at which this disease becomes a burden. Although stroke still takes it highest toll on older people, comparison of hospitalizations in 1994–1995 with those in 2006–2007 showed a 51 percent increase among men ages 15 to 34 and a 17 percent increase among women in that age-group. During that same period, strokes dropped 25 percent among men age 65 and older and 28 percent among women in that age-group ("Strokes Rise Fast Among Young," 2011).

   The State Department of Public Health wants updated research related to this issue so that it can decide what kinds of changes should be made in its educational programs related to stroke.

e. While visiting Japan, Brian Paschal and his wife Victoria were captivated by the rickshaw, a light, two-wheeled vehicle drawn by one or two persons. They currently own a gift shop in a beach resort community. Auto traffic is prohibited in the main shopping area of the town, an area covering four square blocks. Parking lots are located on the perimeter of the shopping square, and customers must walk from their cars into the commercial area. Some shop owners think that the restricted access prevents potential customers from browsing in the shops. Brian and Victoria think that a rickshaw service, transporting people from their cars into the shopping area, could be profitable both for the operator of that service and for merchants who might gain more business by increased customer traffic. They ask you to research the requirements for such a business and its potential success.

f. Several employees who are approaching retirement have asked Regina Papadopolis, Director of Human Resources for West Trust Bank, whether the company will allow them to continue to work part time when they reach retirement age. They have suggested that they should be allowed to work half-time and draw part of their pensions at the same time. Papadopolis would like to keep some of the better employees in part-time positions but would be happy to see the less effective employees retire. Ms. Papadopolis has asked you to research the issue, including potential legal issues.

g. Clinic.com is an online service that will allow individuals who have medical issues to consult with a physician for 10 minutes for $45. Although the service is not intended to replace face-to-face, in-office interaction with a physician, it is offered in recognition that there are circumstances under which a medical issue can be addressed without such personal contact. Columbia Medical Associates are wondering whether they should add this type of service to their practice. This medical group has asked for research to help them address the issue.

h. Jorge Morales, a personal trainer who works out of City Athletic Center, has several clients who have asked his advice about various diet programs. Since he is not a registered dietician, he will not make specific diet recommendations to these clients. However, he would like to be able to discuss the pros and cons of various programs that are currently popular. He has asked you to compare four popular programs: Adkins, Jenny Craig, Nutri-System, and Weight Watchers. He wants to be able to talk knowledgeably about such factors as the costs of the programs, the types of food emphasized, the emotional and social support provided, the satisfaction of clients, and so on.

i. Babar Kahn, owner of City Athletic Center, asks that you research the feasibility of including child care services at his gym. Many gyms are attracting customers by providing play areas or child-care centers on the premises. However, since drop-in care facilities are usually exempt from licensing, parents may be concerned about the quality of care provided. Kahn wants to know how to set up a drop-in facility at his gym that will appeal to parents, thereby attracting more gym clients. Examine such factors as space, ratio of caregivers to children, sanitation practices, how children of various ages are handled, security, and so on.

j. Harrell Lovelace owns two shops that specialize in flooring materials: carpeting, hardwoods, vinyl, and so on. Many customers who come into his shops appear to be pressed for time as they try to fit visits to his shop into busy work and family schedules. Customers often ask to carry samples home to help them make decisions about flooring. Lovelace is thinking about adding a new service to his business: Door-to-Door Floors. His idea is to create a mobile showroom. He wants to equip a van with a wide selection of flooring materials, take those materials to a potential customer's home, and make the whole selection process less stressful. He wants to know the feasibility of adding such a service to his current business. He includes the possibility of closing one of his shops and using current staff to handle the mobile service.

2. Prepare a proposal (in memorandum format) to conduct a study related to a topic of your choice to be approved by your instructor. Select a personal, organizational, or societal problem in which you have a special interest. Here are some suggested topics:

- A significant personal decision (for example, options for a major consumer purchase, such as an automobile, a boat, or a house; feasibility of establishing a particular kind of business; the wisdom of buying health insurance for your pets; buying distressed real estate with the intent of repairing or improving the property and reselling it)

- A communication topic (for example, communication problems and needs of the elderly when dealing with health-care professionals, insurance companies, or social service agencies; effective ways for a nonprofit agency to inform the public of its services; communication problems between expatriate managers and foreign nationals whom they supervise; converting health records in private practices to electronic records that can be easily shared with other health practitioners)

- An organizational or business problem (for example, environmentally responsible or irresponsible actions of X Company; use of hybrid vehicles versus traditional gasoline-fueled vehicles for pizza deliveries; using secret shoppers to evaluate customer service; providing design and construction services to convert an already existing house into a "smart house" that will significantly reduce the residents' carbon footprint)

- A societal or governmental issue (for example, requiring real estate developers to pay impact fees or set aside acreage for public use; offering incentives to lure filmmakers to shoot films in your state; the constitutionality of the 2006 Stolen Valor Act, which is designed to prevent people from misrepresenting themselves as members of the military for a political or business advantage; a request presented to the National Collegiate Athletic Association to recognize collegiate cheerleading as an "emerging sport," which is a precursor to full status as a championship sport; what municipalities can do now to adapt to climate change, especially with respect to new construction and public spaces)

Topics suggested in Application 1 may also be appropriate. Your instructor may discuss other options with you.

Include the following in your proposal:
- Background information that will identify the managerial (general) problem
- The research problem and its scope
- The purpose of the research
- Delimitations and limitations, if relevant
- A preliminary plan for data collection and analysis, including but not limited to names and addresses of five to seven meta- and deep-search engines that will generate current, relevant data
- An estimate of the resources needed to complete the research
- A projected time schedule for completion of the project
- A statement of how you will report your research results
- A request for approval to proceed with your proposed project
  After receiving feedback from your instructor and approval to conduct the research, use the proposal as your guide for data collection, data analysis, and preparation of a report. Chapters 11 to 16 will provide more details to guide your completion of this project.

3. Form a team with two or more of your classmates. Prepare a research proposal as directed in Application 2. Prepare the proposal in manuscript format with a cover letter to your instructor. In the letter, indicate clearly that this is a team project and specify the tasks that each team member will fulfill.

CHAPTER 11
Selecting Data Sources

LEARNING OBJECTIVES

After you have read this chapter, you should be able to:

1. Explain how to determine appropriate data sources for your quantitative research.

2. Discuss criteria for evaluating data sources and websites.

3. Define the characteristics of a valid sample.

4. Identify general guides for determining sample size.

5. Identify kinds of samples used in quantitative research for business.

THE VALUE OF ALL RESEARCH depends on the validity and reliability of the data acquired for the project. GIGO (garbage in, garbage out) is an acronym used often by systems analysts to remind themselves and system users to protect the quality of information that enters the system. That acronym is also an appropriate warning to report writers. The quality of a report can be no better than the quality of the data on which it is based. Therefore, report writers must master the skills of selecting appropriate data sources and using those sources accurately.

Determining Data Sources

Defining potential data sources is part of the development of a research plan, as discussed in Chapter 10. Two questions should guide you as you determine possible sources for research data:

- What kinds of information do I need to answer the research question?
- Should I use primary or secondary data sources—or both—to obtain that information?

Data Need

The research question, divided into appropriate elements or factors of analysis, must direct your search for data. After you have defined the research question clearly and have narrowed the scope, you must focus your attention on finding data directly related to those factors.

Keeping the scope of analysis in mind will make you an efficient, effective researcher. You will be efficient because you will target your data search toward the sources most likely to yield meaningful information rather than wasting time looking at unrelated data. You will be effective because you will be able to judge all data in terms of its relevance to the research problem and will not be tempted to include interesting but irrelevant data.

The chart in Illustration 11.1 shows how the research question guides the selection of information sources. After the research problem and purpose have been defined, the scope of analysis must be narrowed. Then specific kinds of data and specific

---

ILLUSTRATION 11.1 DETERMINING DATA SOURCES

Research Problem: To project market conditions for skilled construction labor in the Northwest United States during the next three years.

Research Purpose: To ensure that Air Waves has an adequate supply of labor to fulfill installation contracts.

ELEMENTS (SCOPE)	DATA NEEDED	POTENTIAL SOURCES
Projected demand for skilled HVAC technicians	a. Sizes of projects under contract by major regional contractors b. Projects to be bid and contracted for during next three years	a. Regional contractors b. State economic development boards
Projected supply of skilled technicians	a. Demographics of crews currently hired by major HVAC contractors in the Northwest b. Projected graduates from technical schools in the Northwest for next three years	a. Regional HVAC contractors; state employment services b. Registrars and placement officers of technical schools
Air Waves recruitment and employment practices	a. Methods currently used to locate skilled HVAC technicians b. Air Waves employment practices that attract technicians to Air Waves c. Air Waves employment practices that deter technicians from working for Air Waves	a. Air Waves director of human resources b. Members of current Air Waves crews c. Former Air Waves technicians

© Cengage Learning 2013

data sources must be identified for each element in the scope. Note that more than one kind of data and more than one data source may be required to analyze a specific element adequately.[1]

Primary versus Secondary Data

Effective business researchers use both primary and secondary data to solve business problems. *Primary data* are data acquired at their sources through observation, experimentation, interviews, questionnaire surveys, and searches through company records. *Secondary data* consist of information that others have accumulated and made available through books, magazines, journals, and other published documents. Other important sources of secondary data include information made available on microform and CD-ROM and, of course, the World Wide Web. Specific techniques for collecting secondary and primary data are discussed in Chapters 12 and 13.

Some researchers mistakenly consider primary data to be better than secondary data. They assume that information "straight from the source" is better information than secondhand data. Others prefer to use primary data because they are stimulated by that data collection process and feel restricted when they must sit in a library searching through documents or in front of a computer monitor using search engines to find secondary information.

In contrast, some researchers—equally mistakenly—suspect the accuracy of primary data. They recognize that people can deliberately distort self-reported information, and researchers can make incorrect observations or lead people to report what the researcher wants to record. In addition, some researchers may feel uncomfortable with the primary data collection process but enjoy the sense of discovery that comes from searching out well-documented information in secondary sources.

Neither attitude can produce consistently effective research reports. When you recognize a problem and the need for research, you should *first* consult secondary sources. Secondary sources often provide information to help define the problem more clearly and to identify elements that should be investigated. After narrowing the scope of the analysis, you must determine whether primary or secondary sources will best answer each element of the problem, as was demonstrated in Illustration 11.1. When the problem you are investigating is unique to your organization, primary data may be the only usable information. But if adequate secondary data are available, you should use those data instead of spending the time and effort required to use primary sources effectively.

Evaluating Primary Data Sources

Before using any data source, you should be sure the source meets three criteria: validity, reliability, and practicality.

Validity

Validity is a measurement concept that refers to the extent to which differences revealed with a measuring tool represent true differences among the people or objects being measured. For example, a test to determine prospective employees' knowledge of and skill in using spreadsheet software is valid to the extent that the test can differentiate among applicants who have various levels of spreadsheet knowledge and skill. The test has *content* validity if it tests or measures what it purports to measure. To have content validity, a test to determine employees' knowledge of spreadsheet software must test enough aspects of software use to be able to assess different levels of competence. A test has *criterion-related* validity if test scores can predict a relevant behavior. The spreadsheet test has criterion-related validity if it can successfully predict which applicants will use spreadsheet software efficiently and effectively as required in their job assignments.

In a broader sense, validity can apply to data sources and the data obtained from those sources as well as to the instruments used to collect data. A data source is valid if it is able to provide objective, accurate information about the research topic. Some sources have greater degrees of validity than others. For example, assume your research requires information about the number of single-parent households in your county. The 2010 U.S. census (secondary source) has greater validity than would a heads-of-household sample in the county conducted by your staff (primary source) because the data come from a more extensive survey than you could conduct yourself. In contrast, assume your research requires data about average cost-of-living pay increases granted in your county last year. In that case, a survey of local businesses could be more valid than the census data because it is more current.

Reliability

Reliability is a measurement concept that refers to the consistency of results obtained with a measuring device. A reliable instrument is relatively free of random or unstable error; such an instrument helps the researcher get as close to the truth as possible. For example, a steel measuring rod is more reliable than a cloth measuring tape to measure distance or height. The steel rod itself changes little with variations in temperature, moisture, or pressure, but a cloth measuring tape may stretch or shrink in response to those conditions.

Two aspects of consistency—stability and equivalence—contribute to reliability. An instrument has *stability* if it gives consistent measurements of the same person or thing at different times; for example, your car odometer records nearly the same mileage each time you measure the distance of the route from your home to your campus or workplace. The instrument has *equivalence* if different people using the instrument at approximately the same time and for the same purpose get consistent results; both you and your spouse or a friend get the same results when measuring distance by the odometer. To illustrate further, assume that two professors will rate your oral report. Such an evaluation can be somewhat subjective, but a reliable instrument can remove much of the subjectivity from the situation. A rating guide would direct both observers to focus on the same evaluation factors. If the two professors give you nearly equivalent scores, the rating instrument may be presumed to have equivalent reliability.

The concept of reliability extends to data sources and data obtained from them as well as to data collection instruments. Assume you operate an upscale women's clothing store and you want to identify services that will attract more customers to your store. A sample of women in a specific income range within the geographic area you plan to serve would be a more reliable data source than would your current customers. Your current customers' perceptions are not representative of people who do not shop at your store.

Ideally, data sources and data collection techniques are both reliable and valid. Valid instruments and sources are also reliable, but reliable sources or instruments are not necessarily valid. Assume, for example, that survey participants mistakenly believe they have used a toothpaste (Product X) that is similar to but different from the toothpaste they have actually used (Product Y). The participants may consistently report satisfaction with Product X (reliability), but the information is not valid because they have never used that product. They are clearly reporting satisfaction with something but not with the test toothpaste.

Another example will illustrate the relationship between validity and reliability. Automobile odometers, which measure travel distance and speed, are calibrated to be used with certain tire sizes. If an auto owner installs a tire larger in diameter than that for which the odometer was calibrated, the odometer will consistently (reliably) register a speed that is slower than the auto is actually traveling. By using a reliable instrument that records incorrect (invalid) data, the driver may have an unpleasant experience with the highway patrol.

As you select data sources, always consider both the validity and the reliability of each source, especially when you search for data on the Internet. Since few restrictions exist with respect to who may post information on the Internet and what may be posted, invalid information from unreliable sources exists there. Guides for evaluating Internet sources are provided later in this chapter.

Practicality

A final criterion by which you must judge potential data sources is practicality. Although business researchers desire validity and reliability, some trade-offs are usually needed between the ideal project and what can be achieved within time and budget constraints.

Practicality refers to both the cost and the convenience of using a data source. Assume, for example, that you are assisting the manager of a Subway franchise restaurant who wants to investigate customer satisfaction with its food and customer service. Your restaurant's customers are certainly a more valid data source than are your employees. Observation of customers interacting with order takers and cashiers and face-to-face interviews with customers may be your preferred data-gathering techniques. The time and cost required to use those techniques, however, may force you to substitute a less expensive survey technique, such as a preaddressed questionnaire given to customers with their orders. As you prepare your questionnaire, you may recall that increasing the number of items is one way to improve questionnaire reliability. However, since survey participants often resist completing a long questionnaire, you may shorten the questionnaire, thereby trading a degree of reliability for practicality.

Another practical decision that you would likely make is that you cannot question all customers about their satisfaction with your franchise's food and service. Most business researchers are confronted with the need to sample data sources rather than attempt to use the entire population.

Sampling Data Sources

To understand sampling concepts, you must understand five terms: population, element, sample, subject, and population frame.

Population refers to the entire group of people, events, or other items of interest that are the focus of a study. If the manager of Coastal City Club, a private club, wants to know members' opinions about the club's services, the population is all members of the club. An *element* is a single unit of the population, that is, one member of the club. The population, therefore, consists of the total collection of elements about which a researcher wishes to make inferences. A *sample* is a subgroup of the population composed of some of the elements, and a *subject* is a single member of the sample.

Before a sample can be drawn from a population, all members of the population must be identified. A *population frame* (sometimes called a sampling frame) is a list of all elements in a population from which a sample could be drawn. In some cases, devising that list is relatively easy; for example, an accurate list of Coastal City Club members should be relatively easy to obtain. In other cases, identifying all members of the population may be nearly impossible, and a list that reasonably approximates the population must be chosen. For example, if the Clermont school board wants to learn how the community rates its performance on major educational issues, identifying all members of the community would be prohibitive. Some researchers use a telephone directory as the population frame when they wish to sample a city population. However, with the current popularity of cell phones, many city residents have no land-based telephones, and others have unlisted numbers. Therefore, the telephone directory is not a true representation of the population. To obtain valid data, a researcher working for the Clermont school board would do well to avoid using that source as its population frame. A list of registered voters in the areas served by that board might be a better population frame for the school board research. That list would presumably include all people who show enough concern for civic matters to be involved, at least to some extent, in the electoral process.

In business research, an investigation may involve hundreds or thousands of potential subjects. Time and budget constraints often prohibit data collection from or about every element that could be studied; therefore, a sample is used. The basic idea of sampling is that elements in a population provide useful data about the characteristics of that population. When you judge the quality of a box of chocolate truffles, for example, you take a sample (one truffle), analyze the characteristics of that sample, and generalize that the entire population (all truffles in the box) has the same characteristics. Similarly, in Coastal City Club's member satisfaction survey, the researcher infers that the characteristics of a sample of those members represent the characteristics of the entire member population. Such inferences, however, are valid only if the sample is valid.

Characteristics of a Valid Sample

A valid sample is one that accurately represents its population characteristics. Sample validity depends on three factors: accuracy, precision, and size.[2]

Accuracy

An accurate sample is free of bias; that is, it neither overrepresents nor underrepresents certain population characteristics. An accurate sample has no systematic variance, which is variation in measurement due to some known or unknown influence that causes the scores to lean in a particular direction. For example, assume that a group of young professionals meets for breakfast at Coastal City Club every Tuesday from 7 to 8 A.M. If the club draws a sample from members who visit the club during those hours, the sample may be systematically biased toward the attitudes of young professionals. The attitudes of retired members who use club services primarily during lunch hours or to entertain dinner guests would be systematically underrepresented.

Inaccuracy sometimes results from use of an inaccurate population frame. Coastal City Club could use a list of all members as a population frame. However, if the member list is not updated daily to indicate new and discontinued accounts, the population frame would be inaccurate and could contribute to inaccuracy in any sample drawn from it.

Precision

No sample can be identical to its population in all respects. A sample statistic (such as the arithmetic mean of the sample) may be expected to vary from its corresponding population value (the arithmetic mean of the population) because of random fluctuations in the sampling process. Such fluctuations or variations are referred to as sampling error. A precise sample has little sampling error.

Assume, for example, that Coastal City Club wants information about its members who are retired. For practical reasons, the researcher may decide to take a sample of customers who come to the club between 11:30 A.M. and 1 P.M. because that is when many retirees visit the club. But a sample taken at that time would contain sampling error if it randomly included guests who accompanied members to the club for lunch that day or young professionals who were lunching at that time.

Sample Size

Precision and accuracy are important sampling issues because a researcher wants to be sure that inferences about the population are justifiable. Sample size can affect the accuracy and precision of your inferences.

Generally, if the characteristics that are being studied are widely dispersed in the population, the accuracy and precision of inferences based on the sample can be improved by increasing the sample size. For example, if the monthly expenditures of Coastal City Club's retired members range from $50 to $3,000, to gain the desired levels of precision and accuracy, the researcher will have to draw a larger sample than would be necessary if the monthly expenditures were $50 to $300. In contrast, if the characteristics are narrowly dispersed in the population, drawing a large sample size may be wasteful and costly. It may be possible to achieve the desired precision and accuracy with a relatively small sample. By following the guides given in the next section, you should be able to select an appropriate sample size for your research.

Guides for Determining Sample Size

Four rules of thumb guide researchers in determining sample size.

1. Sample sizes larger than 30 and smaller than 500 are appropriate for most research. Where samples are to be broken into subsamples (males/females, juniors/seniors, etc.), a minimum sample size of 30 for each category is necessary.

2. If several variables are used in the research, the sample size should be several times (preferably 10 times or more) as large as the number of variables measured in the study. For example, if you are measuring four variables, your sample size should be at least 40.

3. For simple experimental research with tight experimental controls, successful research is possible with samples as small as 10 or 20.

A final consideration in sampling is the kind of sample to use. Several options are available. The nature of your research problem and the desired degree of accuracy determine which sampling technique is appropriate.

Kinds of Samples

Sampling designs fall into two major categories: probability and nonprobability. In *probability sampling*, the population elements have a known chance or probability of being selected. In *nonprobability sampling*, the elements do not have a predetermined chance of being selected.

Probability Sampling

When representativeness of the sample is important, probability sampling is used. This type of sampling can be unrestricted or restricted. *Unrestricted probability sampling* is commonly called simple random sampling. *Restricted* or *complex* sampling designs have been developed to compensate for the inefficiencies of unrestricted sampling. Four of those designs—systematic, stratified random, cluster, and area sampling—are used frequently in business research.

Simple Random Sampling

In *simple random sampling*, every element in the population has an equal chance of being selected as a subject. Assume that Coastal City Club has 1,000 members and wishes to draw a sample of 100. If all names are thrown into a basket and a blindfolded individual draws 100, each member has an equal chance (100 in 1,000) of being drawn. Actually, to retain that 100-in-1,000 chance, each name must be returned to the basket after having been drawn, and the drawing must continue until 100 different names have been selected.

Simple random sampling has the least bias, but the technique can be cumbersome and expensive. In addition, bias can enter the sample if the population frame is not accurate and up to date.

Systematic Sampling

The *systematic sampling* design involves drawing every *n*th element in the population, starting with a randomly chosen element. To draw a systematic sample of 100, the

Coastal City Club researcher would randomly select a member number, such as 128, and then draw every tenth (if that is the chosen n) account thereafter (138, 148, 158, etc.) until 100 have been drawn.

Accuracy of this method depends on an accurate population frame. In addition, researchers using this technique must be cautious to avoid systematic bias. For example, a researcher may decide to draw a systematic sample of 25 companies from the most recent list of the Fortune 500 largest industries, drawing every tenth firm after randomly selecting a starting point. Assume the starting number is 201. Although the population frame may be up to date, this design would systematically bias the sample toward the smallest firms. Number 1 on the list is the largest firm, but the sample would be drawn from numbers 201 through 441. This problem could be avoided by using a larger interval (such as 20) that would require returning to the beginning of the list after the number 500 was reached. This example illustrates that a researcher must be aware of the characteristics of the population frame before defining the n to use in systematic sampling.

Stratified Random Sampling

The *stratified random sampling* design requires stratification or segregation of the elements, followed by a random selection of subjects from the strata. To draw this type of sample, the Coastal City Club could stratify its members by age-groups corresponding approximately to education and career stages, such as 21 to 30, 31 to 40, 41 to 50, 51 to 60, and over 60. Then the club would determine what kind of sample it requires from each age-group to achieve the objectives of the study.

For proportionate sampling, the club would draw a number from each stratum that is proportionate to the percentage of the total population represented by elements in that stratum. The table in Illustration 11.2 shows the number of subjects to be drawn from each stratum if Coastal City Club wishes to draw a proportionate stratified random sample of 100 from its 1,000 members.

For disproportionate sampling, elements are drawn from each stratum based on the researcher's judgment. One factor that justifies disproportionate sampling is extreme imbalance in strata sizes warranting more or less than proportional representation of certain strata. That situation exists in the proportionate sample shown in Illustration 11.2. The disproportionate sample in that table shows how a researcher could adjust a sample to

ILLUSTRATION 11.2 PROPORTIONATE AND DISPROPORTIONATE STRATIFIED RANDOM SAMPLES

Population Strata	N	%	Proportionate ($N = 200$)	Disproportionate ($N = 200$)
21–30	200	20	40	40
31–40	250	25	50	47
41–50	300	30	60	50
51–60	190	19	38	38
Over 60	60	6	12	25
Total	1,000	100	200	200

compensate for small numbers in certain categories. Disproportionate sampling is also used at times because it is convenient, simple, and economical to administer.

Cluster Sampling

A *cluster sampling* technique may be appropriate when a targeted population is already divided into groups or can easily be clustered. After defining the clusters, the researcher randomly selects some of those clusters and studies all elements in each cluster. Ideally, the clusters demonstrate heterogeneity (diversity) within and homogeneity (similarity) across groups. In the Coastal City Club case, for example, ideal clusters would contain many different kinds of members (that is, varied by age, gender, profession, years of membership, etc.) but all clusters would represent the "typical" club member: an upper-middle-class business or professional person who enjoys fine food in an environment that permits him or her to expand relationships with similar business and professional people.

Naturally occurring clusters, such as clusters of students or residents, are often used in business research. But those clusters typically are relatively homogeneous *within* and heterogeneous *across* groups. For example, home owners clustered by neighborhoods tend to be similar within groups but different across groups. For that reason, naturally occurring clusters, although convenient for some kinds of research, tend to lack the precision and accuracy desired in samples.

Area Sampling

When research can be identified with some geographic region, area sampling is appropriate. Area sampling is a form of cluster sampling in which a sample is drawn from a defined geographic area.

This technique is efficient and relatively inexpensive. Suppose, for example, that Belle's Day Spa wants to survey the adult residents of the northeast section of the city to determine the feasibility of opening a branch in that area. Obtaining a complete list of all adults in that area would be virtually impossible. But it would be relatively easy to look at a map, define the area commonly considered the "northeast section," and draw a sample of homes by street addresses.

Nonprobability Sampling

Nonprobability sampling is appropriate when a researcher's objective is to gather preliminary information in a quick and inexpensive way rather than to make generalizations about a larger population. There are also times when nonprobability sampling is the only feasible technique. For example, probability sampling could not be used for an analysis of the content of internal reports because it would be impossible to construct the population frame of all internal reports. Some reports would be too confidential to release for research purposes, some would have been misplaced or destroyed, and some, such as oral reports, would not have been recorded in a permanent form. Nonprobability sampling takes two forms: convenience and purposive.

Convenience Sampling

A *convenience sample* is unrestricted; the researcher is free to choose elements according to their availability. This technique is easy and relatively inexpensive, and it satisfies the demands of some research designs.

Assume, for example, that Belle's Day Spa wants preliminary information about additional spa services in which customers might be interested. The spa might draw a convenience sample by placing a set of questionnaires at the door of the spa with a sign saying "Tell us how we can serve you." Although the sample could not possibly represent the total customer population, the results of the survey would provide worthwhile clues about customer interests. Similarly, interviewing a convenience sample of people as they leave the opening performance in a new concert hall could provide valuable information to the hall manager about the positive and negative aspects of the building (acoustics, seats, restrooms, etc.) and identify needed adjustments.

Purposive Sampling

A *purposive sample* is a nonprobability sample that conforms to certain criteria. There are two major types: judgment and quota sampling.

In a *judgment sample*, the researcher handpicks elements that conform to certain criteria. This technique is used when only limited numbers of people possess the information that is sought or when elements are chosen because of their predictive power in the past. For example, if you want to investigate what it takes for a woman to become a partner in a Wall Street law firm, you might appropriately seek information only from women who have achieved that status. Political analysts use judgment sampling when they predict the outcome of an election by projecting from results of a few precincts whose voting records in the past have predicted election results.

In a *quota sample*, the researcher tries to ensure that the sample is representative of the population from which it is drawn by specifying certain control dimensions. The dimensions selected must have a known distribution in the population, and they must be relevant to the topic studied.

Assume, for example, that you wish to conduct a study at your school to determine student opinion about required drug testing for student athletes. You may hypothesize that differences in attitudes may be related to gender, athletic team membership, and class level. You could assume two categories for each dimension and determine what percent of the student population fits into each category as follows:

Gender	*Female*	*57 percent*
	Male	*43 percent*
Athletic Team	*Member*	*29 percent*
	Nonmember	*71 percent*
Class Level	*Undergraduate*	*87 percent*
	Graduate	*13 percent*

You would then draw a convenience sample, choosing subjects until you have secured the same proportions of males and females, athletic team members and nonmembers, and undergraduate and graduate students that make up the student population.

An obvious weakness of quota sampling is that the sample may not be representative of the population; hence, the researcher's ability to generalize (draw conclusions) from the findings is limited. For example, you could conceivably draw your entire quota from students enrolled in the humanities, whose opinions might differ widely from those of students enrolled in business or engineering. Researchers can protect the sample from such bias, however, by careful selection of relevant dimensions that define the quota. In this example, including the course of study as a dimension would have forced you to avoid selecting all subjects from one academic area.

A special nonprobability method using a *referral*, or *snowball*, sample can be useful when the desired sample attribute is extremely hard to find. Snowball sampling relies on referrals from initial subjects to generate additional ones. For instance, a manufacturer of knitting kits is considering changing the product's image and redesigning its packaging to appeal to men and women ages 18 to 34. Not surprisingly, the manufacturer has difficulty finding people in that age-group who knit. Therefore, when the company's research associates identify a few subjects, they ask those respondents to refer to them other knitters they know. This useful sampling technique does introduce bias because it decreases the likelihood that the sample will truly represent the population. At the same time, referral sampling can lower research costs when subjects are scarce.

Evaluating a Secondary Data Source: Websites

As someone who has used the Internet from the earliest days of your academic career, you likely have confidence in your searching and surfing skills. And, by extension, you may have come to trust just about everything you read online—the kind of trust that previous generations had in the printed materials available to them. Several characteristics of the Internet, however, suggest that we learn to evaluate Web content before using it in a report. (Remember the GIGO reference at the beginning of this chapter?)

Reasons to Evaluate[3]

Many websites do not reveal who authored the content or what his or her qualifications are for writing on the topic. Rarely does a site include information for contacting the author. Besides, almost anyone can publish on the Internet, and, unlike printed publications, most Web content is not verified by editors/fact-checkers. Experience has shown that some websites include downright lies, and distortions, myths, and stereotypes are common. In addition, many websites do not link to credible outside sources. These qualities of the Internet make it necessary to evaluate a website's authority.

Generally, blogs show the date and even the time of posting, but many websites exclude both the origination date and when the site was updated. Another time-related problem: Even a relatively up-to-date site may include "dead" hyperlinks (links to sites that no longer exist or that are woefully outdated). These Internet qualities make it advisable to evaluate a website's currency.

Most websites give the impression of being objective, but some may pretend to be objective while giving only one viewpoint on a multifaceted issue. Most writers of printed materials are compelled by publishers to differentiate between advocacy and fact, but Web writers have no such requirement. While we expect commercial websites to present slanted information in order to promote a product or service, biased information is not limited to sales-oriented sites. As a result, it is wise to evaluate a website's objectivity.

Evaluation Criteria

Since 1936, the *Consumer Reports* testing laboratories have reviewed/compared consumer products and services and reported the results in the well-respected magazine. Once the

Internet became part of most Americans' everyday lives, Consumer Reports WebWatch launched research that determined Internet users' expectations. Besides navigability, Internet users in that early study were most concerned about (1) being able to trust website information, (2) being able to identify a site's information sources, (3) knowing that the site is updated often, and (4) being able to find important facts about the site.[4]

On the basis of these findings, Consumer Reports WebWatch generated Web evaluation guidelines in five broad areas: identity, advertising/sponsorship, customer service, corrections, and privacy.[5] (Customer service and privacy naturally relate to sites involving consumer transactions.)

The WebWatch guidelines are designed to promote website credibility. Guides call for showing where the site is produced (along with address, telephone number, or email address), naming the site's owner/parent company and stating its purpose. The consumer guidelines of WebWatch also ask website publishers to distinguish advertising from news and factual reporting, identify its sponsors, and disclose relevant business relationships, such as sponsored links to other sites. For example: A site that directs a reader to Amazon.com to buy a book should clearly state its financial relationship to Amazon. In addition, to promote credibility, the WebWatch guidelines say that people writing for the Web should show when content is posted and updated; strive to correct false, misleading, or incorrect information; and prominently display corrections at the website.[6]

Other organizations, especially university faculty and librarians, have set criteria for evaluating websites. For example, the University of Michigan Library established Web research guides consisting of three factors (intention, relevance, and reliability) with broad and narrow questions to be answered for each factor.[7] Twenty narrow questions aid Internet users to "get at" answers to these broad queries:

- Why was the site created, and what opinion does it represent?
- How old is the site?
- Who wrote the information, and what is the quality of the information and documentation?

Evaluation Tools

To help student researchers distinguish between valueless and valuable sites, academics have created website evaluation forms—both on paper and online. Most of these forms, designed for use in teaching Web evaluation skills, consist of evaluation guides written as questions and grouped in 3 to 10 categories. The forms include spaces for writing answers that let an instructor see students' ability to analyze Web content.

A tool called Evaluation Wizard created by the Illinois Mathematics and Science Academy at the 21st Century Information Fluency site (http://21cif.com/tools/evaluate) is an online example that uses an interactive evaluation form. First, Wizard users enter the URL of the site being evaluated, though the user, not the wizard, evaluates the site. Then users select one of eight question categories (*Author, Publisher, Objectivity, Links from this page, Date, Accuracy, Evidence,* and *Links to this page*), read the questions and criteria, and type their responses (few words, sentence, or paragraph) in a text box. They must toggle between Wizard and the site being evaluated (or review it carefully before opening Wizard), but this drawback is more than offset, especially for first-time users, by the tutorials provided for most categories.

Wizard's tutorials help users answer the evaluation questions for all but three categories (*Links from this page*, *Accuracy*, and *Evidence*). Each tutorial consists of a short reading for background information followed by three online applications with immediate feedback.

Although the wizard includes eight sets of evaluation questions, its creators noted that often a decision can be made about a website's authenticity with fewer queries. They recommended a minimum of three questions: *Author* (or *Publisher*), *Evidence*, and *Links to this page*.[8]

Users of Evaluation Wizard can print an evaluation report from the screen or transfer the text into a Microsoft Word document. Evaluation Wizard is recommended to clarify and reinforce your knowledge of Web evaluation guides and criteria. After using Wizard, you can be more confident about what to look for and where to find it on a Web page. Eventually, you may prefer to use an evaluation form designed as a yes-or-no checklist (see Illustration 11.3). Once the evaluation questions and criteria become automatic, you will be able to complete the checklist rather quickly. Then you can identify a reliable site by the ratio of Yes to No answers.

Ethical Considerations

As you choose data sources, you may again confront ethical dilemmas. For example, what are the ethical implications of using a convenience sample rather than a stratified random sample? There is no absolute answer to that question, but you should always attempt to use the most powerful sampling techniques available to you within your time and monetary budgets. Doing less than that could lead to faulty conclusions based on the data, with potential damaging outcomes—loss of customers, loss of goodwill, and so on—to your organization.

The relative importance of your research problem should also influence your choice of a sampling procedure. For example, a convenience sample of individuals entering a store may be adequate to test consumers' initial reactions to a new perfume. Although that sampling technique is easy to apply and relatively inexpensive, a perfumer would be unwise to base a major marketing campaign on the outcome of such a survey. A more difficult and costly technique, the stratified random sample, would be a better choice for identifying the socioeconomic group that should be targeted in a major marketing campaign.

Summary

A report can be no better than the data on which it is based, and data can be no more valid or reliable than the sources from which they are obtained. Therefore, your choice of data sources is a critical step in research planning. Both primary and secondary data sources are selected for their validity (ability to provide data related to the factors of analysis) and reliability (consistency). In addition, data sources are chosen for their practicality.

The impracticality of using an entire population of interest often requires the researcher to select a sample of that population and draw inferences based on data obtained from the sample. Accuracy and precision are desired in samples. When there is considerable variability in the population, sample accuracy and precision can be improved by increasing the sample size. When the population shows little variability, accuracy and precision may be possible with a small sample.

ILLUSTRATION 11.3 WEBSITE EVALUATION FORM

Website Evaluation Checklist		
If unsure of an answer while visiting the site, mark it No. Likelihood of a trustworthy site increases with each Yes answer.		
	Yes	No
Authority/Identity — Does anyone claim to be author (not same as webmaster) of the site? _____		
Are the author's credentials shown? _____		
Is the author's employment affiliation included? _____		
Do you recognize the author's name as someone qualified to write on this topic? _____		
Does the page include information for contacting the author? _____		
Objectivity — Is the author's aim clear? Is the aim to inform (rather than entertain, earn a profit, or persuade)? _____	/	/
Does the site present different viewpoints and/or discuss the options open to you? _____		
Is the emphasized viewpoint reasoned (rather than based on emotion)? _____		
If the site is sponsored by an organization, is that organization a known, reputable one? _____		
Does the text contain a minimum of words (adjectives and adverbs) suggesting how you should feel about the topic? _____		

continued

The research problem and purpose must be considered before deciding whether to use probability or nonprobability sampling. Probability samples include simple random, systematic, stratified random, cluster, and area samples. Nonprobability samples are either convenience or purposive samples. Two kinds of purposive samples are judgment and quota samples. To gather valid and reliable data, a researcher must choose the appropriate sampling technique.

Attributes of the World Wide Web make website evaluation necessary for sites to be used as secondary data sources. Many website evaluation forms have been

ILLUSTRATION 11.3 CONTINUED

Accuracy/Quality	Is the information detailed and thorough (rather than sketchy or shallow)? _____		
	Does the information square with your knowledge and experience? _____		
	Can you find the same information points in two other places? _____		
	But does the site offer "something different" or "something more" than other sources? _____		
	Does author support/explain statistics? For example, research results describe data sources and sample selection procedure and size. _____		
	Does the author avoid universal generalizations marked by words such as *all*, *always*, *completely*, *none*, *never*, and *only*. _____		
	Are the pages mostly free of grammatical and mechanical errors? _____		
	If visuals are present, do they support the text (rather than distract you from it)? _____		
	Do the sources and links seem scholarly (concerned with academic study)? _____		

continued

developed to aid researchers with this assessment. An interactive form, called Evaluation Wizard, exists online, while this chapter includes a yes-or-no checklist for assessing websites.

Topics for Discussion

1. Explain how a research question directs the choice of data sources.
2. Why should a researcher consult secondary data sources before primary sources?
3. Explain these terms: validity, content validity, and criterion-related validity.
4. Explain these terms: reliability, stability, and equivalence.
5. Explain the relationship of validity and reliability.
6. Why can validity and reliability not be the only criteria for selection of data sources?

ILLUSTRATION 11.3 CONTINUED

Currency	Does the page show the date it was posted or updated? _____		
	Was the page posted/updated recently enough for the purpose of your research? _____		
Coverage/Navigation	Is the site complete (no pages under construction)? _____		
	Can you find a list of references/sources? _____ _____		
	Do all the links to other websites work? _____ _____		
	Is the site easy to navigate (with minimal clicking and scrolling)? _____		
	Do you have any reservations about the site in question? _____		

© Cengage Learning 2013

7. Define these terms:
    a. Population
    b. Element
    c. Sample
    d. Subject
    e. Population frame
8. What are the characteristics of a valid sample?
9. Give four guides for determining sample size.
10. Compare and/or contrast the following sampling concepts:
    a. Probability and nonprobability
    b. Simple random, systematic, and stratified random
    c. Cluster and area
    d. Convenience and purposive
    e. Judgment and quota
11. Name three key factors to study when evaluating a website as a data source. (**Hint:** What factors recur throughout this chapter's website evaluation section?)

Applications

1. Plan the data collection for each of the following situations. Specifically, do the following:
    • Identify the kinds of information needed.
    • Identify the appropriate sources of data.

- Identify the likely sequence for collecting the data.
- Identity the best sampling technique and sample size for any necessary primary data.

   a. Carl Zumhoff, the manager of a large real estate firm, is concerned about the number of home owners in his community who are having difficulty meeting their mortgage payments. In an attempt to assist those home owners, Zumhoff wants to analyze the feasibility of adding rental services and property management to his company's offerings. His plan is to find appropriate tenants for home owners who may be facing foreclosure, enabling those home owners to keep their homes while shifting to less expensive housing. He would also be dealing in other rental properties so that he can help threatened home owners find appropriate housing while they rent out their homes. Elements of the research include determining potential benefits to home owners who face foreclosure on their homes, the demand for such services, how to determine whether the potential client is a good risk, costs to provide the services, fees to be charged, and legal considerations.

   b. Stella Linden, manager of human resources for an insurance company, is concerned about the number of productive hours lost by employees struggling to provide adequate child care, and she knows that some companies provide child care on their premises. Therefore, Ms. Linden wants to analyze the feasibility of providing child care for children of employees. Elements of the problem include methods of providing child care, success of other company-sponsored child care programs, costs, the company's responsibilities and potential liability when providing child care, government policies affecting child care centers, and the number of employees desiring child care on the company's premises.

   c. Letty Angler has learned that a newly organized national association of female college athletes is searching for an executive director. Ms. Angler has extensive experience in association management and has represented her current association effectively in promoting legislation that benefits its members. She is also an avid fan of female athletics, both amateur and professional. To prepare for an interview with the association, Ms. Angler has asked you to research this question: What opportunities exist for female athletes in college sports? Elements of the research include the history of college athletics for females, the current status of college athletics programs for females, changes in those programs during the past 10 years, the availability of scholarships for female athletes, changes in scholarship funding during the past 10 years, revenue generated by athletics programs for females, athletic opportunities for females after college, and public perceptions of female athletes.

2. For each of the following situations, identify the elements or scope of the research project and plan the data collection. With your instructor's approval, you may benefit by doing this application in groups of three or four people.

Specifically, do the following:

- Identify the elements of the research problem.
- Identify the kinds of information needed.
- Identify the appropriate sources of data.
- Identify the likely sequence for collecting the data.
- Identify the best sampling technique and sample size for any necessary primary data.

a. In an effort to revamp its image and attract new customers, McDonald's is going upscale. The upgrade involves installing flat-screen televisions, using wooden tables, and softening the color scheme (D. Gross, "Does Going Upscale Make Sense for McDonald's?," *The Daily Ticker*, last modified May 10, 2011, http://finance.yahoo.com/blogs/daily-ticker/does-going-upscale-sense-mcdonald-170612393.html). From its founding, McDonald's emphasized speedy service, but the chain will no longer rush customers in and out. Now it wants customers to linger and "tap into free Wi-Fi service … sip a cappuccino or smoothie while having a Snack Wrap" (B. Horovitz, "McDonald's Revamps Stores to Look More Upscale," *USA Today*, last modified May 9, 2011, http://www.usatoday.com/money/industries/food/2011-05-06-mcdonalds-revamp_n.htm). As the owner of Grove's, a long-standing local restaurant that features prime beef burgers and fried chicken, you are aware that other restaurants such as Starbucks and Panera Bread have drained away some of your business. Now, if McDonald's repackages its image in your community, you may lose even more business. You want to determine how Grove's can compete with this restaurant "hangout" concept.

b. SAS, a software development firm in Cary, North Carolina, provides an unusual range of employee benefits. Those benefits include high-quality child care at $410 a month, 90 percent coverage of the health insurance premium, unlimited sick days, a medical center staffed by four physicians and 10 nurse practitioners (at no cost to employees), a free 66,000-square-foot fitness center and natatorium, a lending library, and a summer camp for children. SAS's cofounder and chief executive officer initiated this corporate culture, which in his words is based on "trust between our employees and the company."[9] In 2011, SAS was named for the fourteenth consecutive year to *Fortune*'s list of 100 Best Companies to Work For.[10] As owner of a small but growing firm that offers computer-assisted design services to a variety of businesses, you are aware that employees often work late into the night on projects so that they can meet deadlines, or they become so captivated by their work that they forget to take time during the day for eating lunch and running errands. You want to retain such dedicated workers, but you also know they can find work with competing companies. You want to evaluate the positive and negative aspects of offering your employees some additional perks similar to some of those offered by SAS. (For a complete list of SAS employee benefits, see the company's website: http://www.sas.com/jobs/USjobs/benefits.html.)

c. Mitch Kallahan has been driving a diesel-powered automobile for about a year. With rapidly rising fuel costs, he is now considering adding a system that will permit him to burn alternate fuels, such as waste vegetable oil (WVO). He needs information about the costs of adding the system, how the system operates, where to obtain WVO, how to process WVO so that it can be used in his vehicle, the potential savings in fuel costs, any unique problems (or successes) that users have experienced with such systems, and so on.

d. Wendy Harvey recently completed a culinary arts program and also has three years' experience working as a chef with a well-known restaurant in your community. She wants to begin a personal chef business. Her idea is to offer in-home cooking services to clients (for example, retirees, busy professional people, etc.) who have little time or ability to prepare nutritious meals daily. Her plan is to go into a home once a week to prepare meals that can be frozen and cooked at a later time. She will plan the meals, shop for the ingredients, cook the meals, and package them for freezing and reheating. She wants to know the potential for success of such a business in your community.

e. Therapy animals have long been used effectively in lifting the spirits of patients recovering from long-term illnesses and injuries. Generally, therapy animals are taken to health care facilities by their owners and trainers. Consequently, their presence is dependent on the schedules of such volunteers. Andrew Ng, director of a First Choice Rehabilitation Center, recently heard about robotic pets that have been tested in therapeutic settings, with notable success. (One in particular, PARO, a pet seal designed by a Japanese company, seems most promising.) Ng wants information about the research that has been conducted so that he can decide whether robotic pets would be useful at First Choice. He thinks that pet therapy might be more reliable if he had the robots under his control rather than having to depend on volunteers to appear with their animals.

f. Because of the nursing shortage in your state, some hospitals are promoting accelerated nursing degree programs for nonnursing graduates in the state's colleges and universities. Offered at both baccalaureate and master's degree levels, these programs build on earlier learning experiences and move individuals with undergraduate degrees in other fields into nursing. As director of nursing at Health Help Hospital in your community, you want to determine the feasibility of starting accelerated nursing degree programs at institutions in your region.

g. Wilson Jones is planning to build a new home in western Iowa, where strong winds often sweep across the countryside. Jones wants information about the feasibility of installing wind turbines to supply electricity for his new home. Since several states are already offering incentives and tax rebates for the installation of wind turbines, solar panels, and/or geothermal heat pumps, be sure to include such options in the feasibility study.

h. Gina Richter, a recent college graduate, joined LinkedIn, a business network, during her senior year. Now that she works in a local accounting firm and is planning to sit for the CPA exam, Gina wants information to help her decide whether she should join another network, such as Ryze or Xing, for business professionals.

i. Replacements Ltd is known for its policy of letting employees take their companion animals (pets) to work. Before adopting such a policy, Don Nogami, owner of a start-up company that provides consulting services to construction companies about how to build "green" buildings, wants information about the successes or problems that Replacements Ltd and other firms have had when implementing such a policy.

j. Fireside Productions, a producer of videos for business clients, was launched as a part-time venture in February 2006 by a couple who formerly worked in television news. This video producer grew steadily over the next two years, and it became a full-time operation by late 2007. By 2010, Fireside Productions was "going strong," and the Metro Denver Chamber of Commerce named it the Denver Emerging Business of the Year. Aaron Pajevic wants information about the company, thinking he may want to launch a similar business.

3. After you have determined the appropriate data sources for items in Applications 1 and 2, as directed by your instructor, write a memo to report your recommendations regarding data collection for one or more of the studies.

4. This application relates to Chapter 10's Application 1d about the increase in strokes among young and middle-aged Americans. From the following list of nine websites, select three and evaluate them using Evaluation Wizard. Then choose three different websites and evaluate them using the checklist in Illustration 11.3. Finally, write a letter to your instructor reporting your evaluation procedures and outcomes. (**Note:** Use the block letter format with open punctuation shown in Illustration 6.5.)

a. *The New York Times* Health section (http://well.blogs.nytimes.com/2011/02/10/stroke-rising-among-young-people)

b. *CNI Review Medical Journal* (http://www.thecni.org/reviews/11-2-p03-marcoux.htm)

c. Physician Relations (http://physicianlink.uams.edu/casestudies/csstroke.asp)

d. Web MD (http://www.webmd.com/stroke/news/20110202/rare-form-of-stroke-affects-young-people)

e. Medscape Medical News (http://www.medscape.com/viewarticle/738013)

f. Exam Health (http://www.emaxhealth.com/1275/stroke-can-occur-teens-and-young-adults.html)

g. Vegsource (http://www.vegsource.com/news/2011/02/stroke-rising-among-young-people.html)

h. ABC News (http://www.abc12.com/story/15195436/statins-may-help-heart-in-some-young-stroke-patients)

i. Bloomberg Businessweek (http://www.businessweek.com/lifestyle/content/healthday/649766.html)

5. If you wrote a proposal for any of the Applications in Chapter 10, continue with that project, focusing at this time on appropriate data sources.

References

1.   This chapter deals with quantitative research methods that rely on numbers and statistics and deal with questions of *what*, *where*, and *when*. The qualitative method, used increasingly in business—especially for market research—studies the *why* and *how* of decision making through analysis of unstructured data (text, spoken words, and nonverbal responses) gathered from such sources as diaries and journals, emails, feedback forms, group discussions, interview transcripts, notes, open-ended survey questions, photos, and videos.

   Traditionally, qualitative methods were seen as generating information only for the specific cases studied. For that reason, qualitative researchers described a phenomenon in depth but did not try to generalize their results. Today, though, hypothesis testing and generalizing is done from qualitative research as well as quantitative. In addition, the long-standing quantitative-versus-qualitative debate is being settled by mixed-method studies. For more information about qualitative research methods, see books such as Merriam, Sharan B., *Qualitative research: A guide to design and implementation* (2nd ed.), Hoboken, NJ: Wiley, 2009, and Silverman, David, *Doing qualitative research: A practical handbook* (3rd ed.), Thousand Oaks, CA: Sage Publications, 2010.

2.   This discussion explains general concepts related to accuracy, precision, and sample size. For further study consult books such as Levy, Paul S., and Stanley Lemeshow, *Sampling of populations: Methods and applications* (4th ed., San Francisco: Jossey-Bass, 2008, and Fowler, Floyd J., *Survey research methods* (4th ed.), Thousand Oaks, CA: Sage Publications, 2009.

3.   Compiled from a slideshow, "website evaluation," Widener University, Wolfgram Memorial Library, last modified July 2011, http://www.widener.edu/libraries/wolfgram/evaluate.

4.   Princeton Survey Research Associates, A matter of trust: What users want from websites: Results of a national survey of Internet users for Consumer WebWatch, last modified January 2002, accessed August 8, 2011, http://www.consumerwebwatch.org/consumer-reports-webwatch-guidelines.cfm.

5.   "Consumer Reports WebWatch Guidelines," Consumer Reports WebWatch, accessed August 8, 2011, http://www.consumerwebwatch.org/consumer-reports-webwatch-guidelines.cfm.

6.   WebWatch.

7.   Research guides, University of Michigan Library, accessed August 4, 2011, http://guides.lib.umich.edu/content.php?pid=30524.

8.   Resources for teaching and learning: Evaluation Wizard, last modified July 5, 2011, 21st Century Information Fluency, http://21cif.com/rkitp/assessment/v1n4/evaluation_wizard.html.

9.   Working at SAS: An ideal environment for new ideas, accessed August 11, 2011, http://www.sas.com/jobs/corporate/index.html.sas.com/jobs/corporate/index.html.

10. 100 best companies to work for, *Fortune Magazine*, last modified February 7, 2011, http://money.cnn.com/magazines/fortune/bestcompanies/2011/full_list.

CHAPTER 12

Using Secondary Data Sources

LEARNING OBJECTIVES

After you have read this chapter, you should be able to:

1. Identify secondary sources for business research.

2. Evaluate secondary sources and data.

3. Demonstrate techniques for extracting and reporting secondary data.

4. Use standard procedures to acknowledge secondary data sources.

5. Observe ethical standards for using secondary data.

A LIBRARY IS AN EXCITING PLACE. In a library, including the global library known as the World Wide Web (Web), you can learn about the major current developments in business, science, education, politics, the arts, and other fields. Moreover, a library contains the accumulated wisdom and experience of many cultures, enabling you to link the past with the present.

Several types of libraries are prevalent today: academic, business or trade, online (Web), and public. Academic libraries, such as college or university libraries, contain strong research collections that support student and faculty research. Often these libraries maintain strong collections in certain areas but not in others. Business or trade libraries serve a specific clientele. Such libraries include those of companies, professional associations, trade associations, institutes, or research agencies. Narrow in focus, business or trade libraries offer depth in their specific areas. Many of these libraries, though not open to the public, offer advice and answer questions over the telephone. The Web, huge in scope and less organized than other library types, houses vast collections of accessible information on virtually every imaginable topic. Public libraries, general in nature, collect information for a broad user population.

The information accumulated in secondary sources can be valuable as you attempt to solve business problems. Secondary data constitute information already gathered and recorded or posted by someone else. When you review *Consumer Reports* (printed or online) before buying a car, plasma television, or DVD player, you use secondary data. The use of secondary data saves you time and money by avoiding unnecessary duplication. Efficient business researchers usually consult secondary sources before attempting to obtain data from primary sources (see Chapter 13). Secondary sources are important in business research for two reasons:

1. Secondary data can help you gain perspective on the problem and identify and define what must be investigated.

2. Secondary sources may contain adequate data to solve the problem (and for the report), eliminating the need to collect primary data. In fact, some secondary sources contain more extensive and more valid data than you would be able to collect from primary sources.

To gather secondary data, you must be able to identify appropriate sources, use secondary sources efficiently and ethically, and apply standard procedures for acknowledging your data sources. Generally, any data-gathering process should start with secondary research. Whatever your problem, similar ones likely have occurred in other organizations or have been researched by others. The solutions to these problems may be reported in business publications. Although these problems will differ slightly from your own, your knowledge of what other individuals and organizations concluded in similar situations can help to answer your questions.

Collecting secondary data includes four steps: (1) locating the data, (2) evaluating the data source, (3) extracting the data from its source, and (4) keeping records.

Locating Secondary Data

To locate secondary data for business research, you may consult the catalog of library holdings, reference books, specialized databases, the Web, and periodical indexes. Although online information services continually expand, you should expect to use a library's printed sources and CD and database subscriptions as well as generally accessible websites.

Catalogs

Today most libraries list books and periodicals and other items in an online catalog (electronic database) rather than in a card catalog. Thus users can search the catalog and produce a list of available items, along with full bibliographic information for each item, a brief description of its contents, and where and how to access it. Any of these terms can be used to search most online catalogs: author, title, library call number, subject, or keyword.

A *keyword search*, as you likely know, is a technique to narrow the scope of a data search. Assume, for example, that you are conducting research on labor force impacts of bank mergers in the southeastern United States. A manual search would necessitate looking under several subjects, such as labor force, bank mergers, displacement, retraining, and outplacement, and within those subject areas, you would have to select items that discuss impact in the Southeast. But by combining selected keywords in a database search—for example, labor force, bank mergers, and Southeast—you would likely locate pertinent material quickly and eliminate irrelevant items.

Typically an online catalog has a catchy name, like The Cat (Penn State University), UCB Pathfinder (University of California, Berkeley), CUNY UNION (City University of New York, all libraries), IUCAT (Indiana University catalog), InfoKat (University of

Kentucky catalog), or USCAN (University of South Carolina Access Network). Typically, too, first-time catalog users need help in addition to the online help provided. Libraries generally offer printed or online tutorials, and librarians give assistance readily when asked.

Using the website titled Gateway to the Library of Congress (http://www.loc.gov/z3950), one can search the immense Library of Congress collection and the library holdings of hundreds of other institutions.

A few libraries may continue to maintain a card catalog. A card catalog generally indexes all library holdings by subject, title, and author. Therefore, for each item in the library, three cards appear in the card catalog. Each card contains full bibliographic information for the item, a brief description of its contents, and a call number identifying its location in the library.

To find a book whose title or author you know, you may locate its card in either the title or the author section of the catalog, record the call number, and retrieve the book from its library location. In many situations, you will look for information on a particular subject. In such instances, you must search for the subject in the card catalog until you find items that appear to meet your needs.

Directories

Many directories can be accessed in a number of ways, such as by industry type or by geographic location. Some of the following business directories can be found on the Web. Type the full title of a directory in your browser's search box to determine if it's available on the Web.

Craighead's International Business, Travel, and Relocation Guide to 90 Countries (Detroit: Gale/Thomson). Two-volume publication provides destination-specific business and relocation information and business practices. Includes information about doing business and living and working conditions in 90 countries most important to international business. Acquaints readers with business and cultural environments.

Directory of American Firms Operating in Foreign Countries. Contains listings for American companies that have substantial investment in overseas operations—affiliate, branch, or partially or wholly owned subsidiary.

Directory of Corporate Affiliations (LexisNexis Group). Published annually with year in the title, shows the "family tree" of every major corporation in America. Indexed by name (parent and subsidiary), geographic location, Standard Industrial Classification (SIC) Code, and corporate responsibility.

D&B Million Dollar Directory: America's Leading Public and Private Companies (Dun & Bradstreet). Cross-indexed volume provides access by SIC (Standard Industrial Classification) number of geographic location. List of major U.S. companies ($9 million annual sales or 180 employees [900 if a branch]) with address, telephone number, officers, and business type. Separate publication titled *Million Dollar Directory Top 50,000.* Million Dollar Directory Series published in five volumes (three contain alphabetic listings; two are cross-referenced volumes grouped by state and SIC. Available as online database (http://www.dnbmdd.com/mddi) on a subscription basis.

Hoover's Handbook of World Business. Includes lists of top global companies from *Fortune* magazine and other publications. Indexes organized by headquarters location, industry, and company executives. Features 300 of world's most influential companies based outside the United States.

Political Risk Yearbook (New York: The PRS Group, Inc.). Eight-volume set reports extensively on political challenges (protests, general strikes, crime, civil violence, and outright war) that affect economic growth, inflation restraint, and maintenance of social order. Contains international trade reports for 150 countries. Available on CD-ROM, as a PDF file, and online as *International Country Risk Guide* (http://www.prsgroup.com).

Principal International Businesses. Lists top 100,000 companies worldwide (based on total employees). Provides key information on variety of businesses in 140 countries.

Ward's Business Directory of U.S. Private and Public Companies (Farmington Hills, MI: Gale Cengage Learning). A comprehensive guide to 112,000 companies (90 percent privately held) arranged alphabetically and geographically. Entries typically include company name, contact details (email and Web address), type and description of company, operating revenue, number of employees, and SIC and North American Industry Classification System codes.

Databases

Although directories may provide useful data for research, you may require more current information than that found in these books. Periodicals (bulletins, journals, magazines, and so on) also contain much current business information and can be located with the help of a periodical index or an online database.

A *journal* is a periodical on a single topic published by an academic or association press. A journal, which contains original research, is more scholarly than a magazine. Journal articles are signed by the authors and include a bibliography. A *magazine* is a periodical produced by a commercial publisher and covering multiple topics in one issue. Magazine articles, often reporting on events or a person's work, are usually unsigned and omit a bibliography.

Most libraries, especially academic and business or trade libraries, subscribe to commercial databases delivered on the Web and accessed by means of keyword search. Most databases offer full-text articles and/or entire journals. The following databases are widely used for collecting secondary business data. Some are *aggregated* databases: EBSCO, for example, includes several of the other databases on the list. (For you to access most databases on this list free of charge, your library must have subscribed to them.)

ABI/INFORM®. A database combining foremost business journals and leading sources of online business news with international and scholarly content. Includes full-text access to articles in *The Wall Street Journal* and *Financial Times*. Includes annual reports for over 1,000 North American companies; thousands of business cases; analysis of worldwide market conditions for 195 countries; 21,000 full-text doctoral dissertations and master's theses from over 1,000 colleges and universities; 11,300 SWOT analysis reports; and 125,000 author profiles, including email addresses. ABI product line includes AIB/INFORM Complete™ (almost 6,000 journals with information on a range of industries around the world); AIB/INFORM Global™ (business and financial information from 3,500 publications);

AIB/INFORM Research™ (1,865 journals on a variety of subjects); AIB/INFORM Trade and Industry,™ included in the ProQuest Direct database (companies, products, executives, and industrial trends from 2,300 publications); and AIB/INFORM Dateline™ (newspapers containing news about local and regional companies).

Business Source® Premier. An EBSCO database providing full-text access to more than 2,100 journals dating to 1965 in addition to company profiles; country, industry, and market research reports; and SWOT analyses. *Regional Business News,*™ a supplemental database, provides full-text coverage for nearly 100 U.S. and Canadian business publications. (Both Business Source and Regional Business News are trademarks of EBSCO Industries, Inc.)

Corporate Affiliations Online. Database provides a directory of American and international companies (private and public). Gives information about parent companies, global divisions, and subsidiaries.

Datamonitor 360. Provides coverage/analysis of more than 3,000 industries and 30,000 companies. Includes industrial profiles; news; opinion; reports and briefs; statistics on the political, economic, social, technological, legal, and environmental landscape of all major countries; and SWOT analyses.

Disclosure. A database containing 1.2 million company-related reports, back to 1997. Can be searched by date or company name. Subdivided into three sections: Image Repository (annual reports and interim reports that prospectus users can download as PDF files); SEC Edgar (current and historical securities filings that users can download as word-processing files); and Disclosure tearsheets (one-page summaries giving overview of companies' earnings estimates, financial standings, salaries, and the like).

EIU: Economist Intelligence Unit. Three-part database providing analysis and forecasts.

> *EIU Country Profiles* are annual reports on selected countries, supplying background and historical context of current economic and political events for each country. Analyzes infrastructure and major industrial factors of each economy and includes maps and tables of key economic data for the past five years.

> *EIU Country Reports* provides analysis of current economic and political trends. Each report examines and explains the issues shaping the country: domestic economy, economic policy, foreign trade and payments, and political scene. Includes 18- to 24-month forecasts in addition to two-year forecasts of economic and political changes and quarterly reports showing detailed analyses of the previous quarter. Updated monthly.

> *EIU ViewsWire* is a Web-based intelligence service offering analysis of key business, economic, and political developments around the world. Each day, it provides 100 to 150 analytical articles on 195 countries. Includes EIU's perspective on recent events and their impact on business, economic, and political conditions. Available at http://viewswire.eiu.com on a subscription basis.

Factiva (http://www.factiva.com) Business information and research tool providing access to 28,500 sources (such as newspapers, journals, magazines, television and radio transcripts, and photos) from 200 countries. Includes more than 600 continuously updated newswires.

Faulkner Advisory for Information Studies (FAITS). A database of 1,200 reports on developments in telecommunications, data networking, computer science, and related fields.

General BusinessFile ASAP. Database indexes and abstracts 900 periodicals and provides full-text articles for 460 titles. An important source of information about banking, business law, international trade, job-hunting strategies, management theories, mergers, and new technology. Indexes current year of *The Wall Street Journal* and financial section of *The New York Times* and current six months of the *Asian Wall Street Journal.*

HighBeam Research. A subscription database available on the Web (http://www.highbeam.com) delivers 80 million articles from the archives of 6,500 journals, newspapers, magazines, and other publications. Includes the *Boston Globe, Newsweek,* and *The Washington Post* and articles from several newswire services, including Business Wire. Also affords access to online almanacs, dictionaries, encyclopedias, and thesauruses, along with maps and photographs. Users can subscribe on the Web at http://www.highbeam.com. New articles are added to HighBeam daily. In addition, it provides an extensive article archive that includes newspapers, journals, and magazine back issues dating back more than 20 years.

Hoover's. A Web-based subscription service providing business information. Includes reports on companies, industries, and initial public offerings (IPOs). Includes reports on public and private companies, lists of top competitors, products and operations summaries, and lists of company officers. Users can access summary income statements and balance sheets and some marketing information. Additional links provide company-related news stories. "IPO Central" includes information about recent IPOs, lists of underwriters, lists of IPOs underwritten by a specific investment bank, pricing, and the like. Also offers information on business travel, career development, money management, and news. Available at http://www.hoovers.com.

IBISWorld. Covers every industry, the major enterprises in those industries, and the business conditions they face. In addition to the entire U.S. economy, also covers industries in the Asia/Pacific region with reports covering Australia and China. Recent addition of Global Industry Market Research Reports covers world industry analysis. Now publishes Industry Risk Rating Reports showing the level of risk an industry faces in the next 12 to 18 months. Available online (http://www.ibisworld.com), but membership is required to access data.

Investext® Archive. Database contains full-text of 2 million company, geographic, and industry research reports written by analysts in leading brokerage houses, consulting firms, and investment banks around the world. Reports most useful for competitive analysis, financial forecasting, market research, and strategic planning. Investext is a registered trademark of Thomson Research.

Kompass USA. Provides business and product information in directory files for thousands of U.S. companies with emphasis on manufacturing, industrial, and associated service sectors. Most records include complete company contact information, industrial information, products and activities, trade status, number of employees, and names of up to four senior executives. Updated annually. Besides the U.S. version, other Kompass versions include Canada, Central/Eastern Europe, Middle East/Africa/Mediterranean, New Zealand, and Western Europe.

LexisNexis® Academic. Database contains over 10,000 business, legal, and news sources (full text). News coverage includes extensive back files and current stories in broadcast transcripts, international news, national and regional newspapers, wire services, and non–English-language sources. *Company Dossier* module gives users access to company information and financial performance measures and allows them to identify and compare companies matching specific criteria. LexisNexis Academic also provides access to all federal and state court cases to 1789 (Shepard's Citations® service). LexisNexis and Shepard's Citations are registered trademarks of Reed Elsevier, Inc.

MRI+ Mediamark Internet Reporter. Database contains information on advertising media preferences, demographics, lifestyle, and product and brand usage reported by a sample of 250,000 U.S. consumers.

Mergent Online™. Database offers information on company descriptions, financials, history, property, subsidiaries, and officers and directors. Includes access to risk ratings and credit information; also, 200,000 executive profiles updated daily from all U.S. publicly traded companies. Profiles include biographies, compensation, and performance. Available at http://www.mergentonline.com on a subscription basis. Mergent Online is a trademark of Mergent, Inc.

Mintel. Covers global consumer market trends across all media, emphasizing U.S. and western European markets. Publishes 45 reports a month, divided among U.K.-specific, European, and U.S. reports.

NetAdvantage. Comprehensive source of business and investment information offering online access (http://www.netadvantage.standardandpoors.com) to Standard & Poor's independent research, data, and commentary on stocks, bonds, funds, and industries in academic, corporate, and public libraries. Includes hard-to-find data on 85,000 private companies. Allows users to download data into a spreadsheet for further analysis.

Proquest Direct. An online periodical database containing citations, abstracts, and many full-text articles from 10,000 journals, magazines, and newspapers, including *The Christian Science Monitor*, the *Los Angeles Times*, and *The Wall Street Journal*. Covers many fields and has many subordinate databases that can be searched separately or together.

PsychArticles. Full-text, peer-reviewed, scholarly articles in psychology and related disciplines (criminology, education, law, medicine, organizational behavior, psychiatry, social science, and social work). Features continuously growing number of behavioral science periodicals.

TDNet Journal Locator. Offers access to abstracts and full-text articles from 17,000 academic, medical, professional, and scientific journals.

Wilson Business Full Text. Database indexes and abstracts articles from English-language periodicals, including leading business magazines and trade and research journals, plus the full text of selected periodicals. Abstracts range from 50 to 150 words and describe content and scope of source articles. Full-text coverage began in January 1994.

Periodical Indexes

Mainly because of the high cost of database subscriptions, some small libraries maintain printed and bound copies of periodicals. In such situations, you can use printed periodical indexes and abstracting services to locate the most current information on your subject. Some indexes and abstracts (summaries) cover specific subject areas; others serve as general guides to current literature. The list that follows includes both types.

Accounting & Tax Index. An index of citations on accounting and taxation from 1992 to the present, including compensation, consulting, financial management, and the financial services industry.

Business Periodicals Index. Index of approximately 500 periodicals in business and management, including accounting, advertising and public relations, banking, communications, economics, finance and investments, industrial relations, insurance, international business, labor, marketing, and personnel as well as specific businesses, some industries, and some trades. Those broad areas are further divided into relevant subtopics. Also available on CD.

*The Gale Group F&S Index.*TM Database covers domestic and international company, product, and industry information. Contains information on corporate acquisitions and mergers, new products, technological developments, and socio-political factors. Also includes analysis of companies by securities firms, forecasts of company sales and profits by company officers, and reports on factors influencing future sales and earnings. Represents 2,500 trade journals, reports, prospectuses, newspapers, government documents, and bank letters from around the world. In addition, site contains news releases. F&S Index comes in three separate volumes: United States, Europe, and International.

New York Times Index. A detailed annual index of items in *The New York Times* the previous year, arranged alphabetically with many cross references.

PAIS International & Archives (Formerly, *Public Affairs Information Service Bulletin*). This Web-based index catalogs literature from 1972 to the present in the fields of business, economics, finance, government, international trade, law, political science, public administration, and public policy. Provides historical perspective on many of the twentieth century's public and social policies, including information on such topics as the civil rights movement, the Great Depression, space exploration, and the women's movement.

Each entry in a periodical index cites the author, article title, journal in which published, publication volume number and/or date, and page numbers. Most periodical indexes classify magazine, journal, or newspaper articles by author, subject, and title. Periodical indexes on CD or in a database may also allow for keyword searches.

Unless you are looking for an article by a specific author or title, begin your search by naming the subject(s) under which you are most likely to find relevant data. When doing a manual search, check all relevant subject headings for the time period to which you delimited your study. When doing a database search, try narrowing your search by combining keywords.

After locating specific journal or newspaper article citations, you must still locate the article itself. For citations located in a printed periodical index, obtain the call number of the journal or newspaper from the library catalog, locate that journal in the library, and then locate the specific pages cited in the index. For citations located by keyword search, you may need to obtain the call number from the online catalog, then locate the journal in the library. Often, though, you will be able to click a link in the citation to view a full-text rendering of the article.

Some libraries, especially those libraries that use a card catalog, list journals and newspapers in a separate serials index. And, often, a serials index is on microfiche—a sheet of film containing photographically reduced pages. The film is placed into a special fiche reader and moved manually until the desired pages or lines appear on the viewing screen. A typical microfiche in a serials index contains the names, call numbers, and holdings information for approximately 1,000 journals.

Special Issues of Business Periodicals

In addition to using periodicals for current information on a broad range of business and economic topics, you will find special issues of selected periodicals useful for specialized statistical data about the status of U.S. businesses.

Forbes. Published on the Internet (http://www.forbes.com/lists), the Annual Directory issue ranks the 500 largest U.S. corporations by sales, profits, assets, stock market value, and number of employees. Also ranks the Super 500—individual rankings of the firms that made one or more of the lists: sales, profits, assets, and market value. The Forbes 500 differs from the Fortune directories in that it includes industrial and nonindustrial corporations in one ranking. Each year's first January issue includes an Annual Report on American industry. It surveys major industries, ranking leading companies in each industry on profitability and growth.

Fortune. Annual rankings of companies by sales, assets, net income, stockholders' equity, employees, net income as percentage of stockholders' equity, earnings per share, and total return to investors. Lists include the "Fortune 500" list of U.S. industrial corporations, "Fortune 1000," "Fortune Global 500," "Fortune 40 (executives) Under 40," "Fortune 100 Best Companies to Work For," "Fortune America's Most Admired Companies," "Fortune 50 Most Powerful Women in Business," and "Fortune 100 Fastest-Growing Companies." Lists are available on the magazine's website (http://money.cnn.com/magazines/fortune) as well as the entire current print edition and an archive of editions for the past decade.

Sources of Statistical Data

The following statistical compilations will provide you with current social, political, and economic statistics.

Business Statistics of the United States (Year): Patterns of Economic Change (Lanham, MD: Bernan Press). Contains historical information about the U.S. economy since World War II and interpretation of new economic data. Presents annual data in regional, demographic, and industrial detail for key indicators, such as gross domestic product, personal income, spending, saving, employment, unemployment, and capital stock. Mostly graphics.

The Global Urban Competitiveness Report (Edward Elgar Publishing). Presents a study of competitiveness of 500 cities around the world. Ranks these cities and presents information about each city's strengths and weaknesses. Includes a full discussion of the factors that create urban competitiveness and the types of cities that are most competitive.

International Financial Statistics Yearbook (International Monetary Fund). Contains detailed statistics on all aspects of international and domestic finance. Covers 12 years for countries appearing in the monthly issues of *International Financial Statistics*.

Statistical Abstract of the United States 2010 (Washington, DC: U.S. Bureau of the Census and U.S. Government Printing Office). Presents data on social, political, and economic organization of the United States. Includes detailed tables on agriculture, business, communications, construction and housing, education, elections, federal government, finances and employment, energy, geography and environment, health, income, law, national defense and veterans affairs, population, science, transportation, and comparative international statistics. Available on CD and on the Web (http://www.census.gov/compendia/statab).

Reference Books

Reference books contain a wealth of current and historical business data. The reference section of a library contains, for example, several of the sources for company, industry, and statistical data as well as atlases, telephone directories, dictionaries, and encyclopedias. The reference section typically contains general business information sources, such as books about business careers and business and social customs around the world. Becoming familiar with the reference section of a library will acquaint you with valuable sources of secondary data.

Sources of Company and Industry Data

The following reference books will help you find data about companies and industries in and outside the United States.

Company Annual Reports. When researching a specific company, consult that company's latest annual report in addition to the sources cited in this section. Many university and public libraries maintain files of company annual reports.

Hoover's Handbook of World Business (Austin, TX: Hoover's, Inc.). Contains hard-to-find information on 300 influential private, public, and state-owned enterprises across the world (Canada to Europe and Asia to South America). Includes lists of top global companies from *Fortune* and other publications. Indexes are organized by company executives, headquarters location, and industry.

Standard & Poor's Register of Corporations, Directors and Executives (New York: Standard & Poor's Corp.). Alphabetically lists about 40,000 companies. For each company, information is provided about its officers, line of business, SIC codes, sales range, number of employees, accounting firm, primary bank and law firm, and stock exchange symbol. Contains brief biography of each company's executives and directors. Includes an index. Available online at Standard & Poor's NetAdvantage (http://www.netadvantage.standardandpoors.com).

Value Line Investment Survey (New York: A. Bernhard & Co.). Comprehensive research on 1,700 stocks. Three main sections include Ratings & Reports (full-page stock reports on 130 stocks in specific sectors, covering current and historical financial data), Summary & Index (a "wide-angle" view of the stock market), and Selection & Opinion (current economic, market statistics, and forecasts). Also available online at http://www.valueline.com (subscription basis).

Who Owns Whom (GAP Books in association with Dun & Bradstreet). Set of annual directories revealing the relationship between companies worldwide. Shows which company is the ultimate parent company and which companies are their subsidiaries. Details include parent name, address and telephone number, country of incorporation, and SIC code for each ultimate parent company along with the names of the subsidiaries. Divided into seven geographic regions: United Kingdom and Ireland; West Europe; North Europe; South, Central, and East Europe; North and South America; Australasia, Asia, Africa, and the Middle East.

This list should help you get started on any search for secondary data. If the data you require cannot be located in the sources listed, consult a reference librarian. A reference librarian, a highly trained individual, can guide you to appropriate sources if you clearly define your research problem and the kinds of data you need.

Information Sources on the Web

The World Wide Web offers a rich source of information for the business researcher. As discussed in Chapter 10, various search tools are available to the Web user, and you would do well to find the tools that best fit your purposes. Generally, use multiple search engines. For example, begin with one of the basic engines: Bing (http://www.bing.com), Google (http://www.google.com), or Yahoo! (http://www.yahoo.com); then use one or more meta-search engines, such as Dogpile (http://www.dogpile.com), Wolfram Alpha (http://www.wolframalpha.com), and Yippy (http://www.yippy.com). Sometimes you will need to search more intensely, and a deep-search engine, such as Biznar (http://biznar.com/biznar), DeepDyve (http://www.deepdyve.com), or Infoplease (http://www.infoplease.com), is recommended.

In addition to the subscription-only databases described earlier in this chapter, several business databases are now available on the Web.

Business.com (http://www.business.com). A search engine a search engine and directory to business products, jobs, and services, case studies, company profiles, magazine articles, and academic and business journal articles.

Economist (http://www.economist.com). A portal to *The Economist* and archive of that weekly journal's articles. Contains information useful to senior managers on the arts, business, finance, science, technology, and world politics. Website includes access to current and previous printed editions. Users must register to access some content, but registration does not involve a fee.

EDGAR: Electronic Data Gathering, Analysis, and Retrieval System of the SEC (http://www.sec.gov/edgar.shtml). Online database that provides free public access to corporate information, allowing users to research a company's financial information and operations by reviewing Securities and Exchange Commission (SEC) registration statements, prospectuses, and period reports filed on Forms 10-K and 10-Q. Includes Quick EDGAR Tutorial.

Market Research (http://www.marketresearch.com). Online database offers over 300,000 market research reports from more than 700 global publishers. Information categories include consumer goods, food and beverage, heavy industry, life sciences, marketing, public sector, service industries, and technology and media as well as company reports and reports by country.

World Exporters & Importers Trade Directory (http://www.eximdata.com). Guide to international companies and organizations. Helpful to companies interested in doing business outside the United States, especially in Japan. Gives details of specific products that countries look to import and export and services they want to provide. Includes extensive information about business conditions and locations. Users must register, but data access is free.

Pathfinder (http://www.pathfinder.com). A portal to the websites of Time, Inc., this site offers access to 21 of the company's publications, including *CNNMoney*, *Fortune*, and *Time*.

ThomasNet (http://www.thomasnet.com). An online database/directory of comprehensive information on industrial products and services and original equipment manufacturers. Includes white papers, product news, and CAD drawings. Users can find a supplier from the 67,000 categories listed and browse thousands of industrial product catalogs, searchable by specification, feature, or part number. Users must sign up to access the data, but registration does not involve a fee.

WWW Virtual Library (http://vlib.org). Database roughly maps the World Wide Web. Delivers a compilation of data sources (Web pages) in 16 broad categories (society, social and behavioral sciences, regional studies, recreation, natural sciences and mathematics, law, international affairs, information and libraries, humanities, engineering, education, computing and computer science, communications and media, business and economics, arts, and agriculture). Each broad category is subdivided into narrower categories that in turn are narrowed further, and a description accompanies each link. Navigation is simple both in the database and from it to the linked websites and back.

Following is a list of specific business information sources that may be useful as you conduct research related to your college major and specific report topics.

Sources of Accounting Information

A variety of accounting-related sites currently exists on the Web. These sites provide accounting students with a host of resources from which to examine career possibilities, research accounting technical issues, explore tax accounting issues, and examine financial statements, which are filed publicly with the SEC and posted by corporations for the benefit of prospective clients and customers.

American Accounting Association (http://aaahq.org). The American Accounting Association is an academic association of educators, practitioners, and business professionals. This site provides access to accounting research, teaching tools, practice references, association activities, and recent publications.

Department of Treasury, Internal Revenue Service (http://www.irs.gov). The two main uses for this site are to get IRS tax forms and publications and to seek answers to frequently asked tax questions.

Sources of Economic Information

The Web has many economics sites, most of them sponsored by the U.S. government. These sites contain not only important statistical data but also insightful data that may help you better understand economics.

BEA: Bureau of Economic Analysis (http://www.bea.gov). The BEA is responsible for integrating and interpreting economic data. The BEA's economic accounts—national, international, regional, and industrial—provide information on economic growth, regional development, and the world economy.

Commerce.gov (http://www.commerce.gov). The U.S. Department of Commerce maintains this website to carry out the department's mission to promote American business and trade. Available information includes statistics on U.S. population and housing and geographical breakdowns of the economy.

Federal Trade Commission (http://www.ftc.gov). Site covers a range of information related to FTC activities in competition, consumer information/protection, and policy planning arenas.

International Trade Administration (http://www.trade.gov/mac/index.asp). Site offers information on exporting, free-trade agreements, international finance and logistics, licenses and regulations, trade problems, and international trade barriers. Delivers a wealth of information designed to help American businesses plan their international sales strategies.

The Rand Journal of Economics (http://www.rje.org). Site supports and encourages research in the behavior of regulated industries, the economic analysis of organizations, and, more generally, applied microeconomics. It provides both theoretical and empirical manuscripts in economics and law. Includes the current issue and back issues to 1970; before 2006, the journal was known as *Bell Journal of Economics*.

The World Bank (http://www.worldbank.org). This site provides glimpses into activities of the World Bank, such as investments in education, health, public administration, infrastructure, financial and private sector development, agriculture, and environmental and natural resource management. Contains a wealth of information on the organization's fight against poverty by building capacity, forging partnerships in the public and private sectors, providing resources, and sharing knowledge.

Sources of Finance Information

Finance information on the Web is growing and covers topics from public finance policy to tax issues. Following are some helpful sites.

CME Group (http://www.cme.com). The Chicago Mercantile Exchange site is a rich resource for investors and students alike. It includes daily closing settlement prices on such items as agricultural commodities, foreign currencies, interest rates, and stock indexes.

The Institute of Internal Auditors (http://www.theiia.org). Established in 1941, the Institute of Internal Auditors is an international professional association of more than 100,000 members. This website offers varied information about the internal auditing profession and includes links to online resources.

The Wall Street Journal (http://online.wsj.com/public/us). This site has become a portal for news of all types, but it still specializes in U.S. and world financial news and analysis.

Sources of Global Business Information

Several websites, including two in the education domain, stand out as providers of information for students of international business.

JETRO: Japan External Trade Organization (http://www.jetro.go.jp). JETRO, a government-related organization, promotes foreign direct investment into Japan. This site provides a wide range of information through news and press releases, publications, electronic newsletters, current articles, and more.

Infogroup (aka *OneSource*) (http://www.infogroup.com/our-services/global-business-info.aspx). Site combines and organizes content from 2,500 information sources supplied by 50 content providers. Includes analyst reports, corporate families, executives, financials, industries, news, public and private company profiles, press articles, and trade and business categories (17 million companies and 21 million executives worldwide).

Sources of Marketing and Advertising Information

A wide assortment of websites awaits the student of marketing. Although each site has a slightly different take on marketing concepts, each provides valuable tools and ideas. A list of some marketing and advertising sites follows.

AdMarket International (http://www.admarketintl.com). This site provides information about marketing, media, advertising, and public relations. It also provides access to various advertising agencies, media producers, marketers, and marketing organization home pages. In addition, it identifies and references Web resources for advertisers.

Advertising Age (http://www.adage.com). Current week's issue of *Advertising Age*, a periodical devoted to marketing innovations, is accessible from this website. This site provides information on marketing, advertising, and media news along with coverage of marketing for consumers, businesses, and international clients. Includes white papers, webcasts, and a special Hispanic Marketing section.

American Marketing Association (http://www.marketingpower.com). The American Marketing Association, an international nonprofit society, serves the educational and professional needs of marketing executives. This website provides information about the study, practice, and teaching of marketing.

Sources of Real Estate Information

Real estate activities thrive on the Web. You can now view a potential purchase from the privacy of your home, whether the house is down the street or across the country. One-stop shopping centers that can provide everything from financing alternatives to information on home site selection are now available. Following are some useful real estate sites.

Fannie Mae (http://www.fanniemae.com). Site provides helpful information about refinancing mortgages, different mortgage programs, and two-step and asset integrated mortgages (AIMs) for home owners, home buyers, and investors.

homefair (http://www.homefair.com). This site provides relocation and mortgage services, homebuyer information, and classified services. Its sponsor, Move, Inc., intended the site "to provide resources and decision support tools for consumers and real estate professionals to help them navigate all stages of the home-buying cycle." The site includes links to real estate sites on the Web.

HSH.com (http://www.hsh.com). HSH is the world's leading publisher of mortgage and consumer loan information. At this site, HSH supplies current and accurate market information to consumers, real estate agents, lenders, the media, and other audiences.

HUD.gov, U.S. Department of Housing and Urban Development (http://www.hud.gov). At this site, HUD provides information about buying, owning, renting, and selling a HUD home, information about its fair housing and equal opportunity policies, a variety of reports, and news related to U.S. housing.

Sources of Small Business Information

The resources in the following list cater to the needs of entrepreneurs and small business owners.

BPlans (http://www.bplans.com/index.cfm). Sponsored by Palo Alto Software, this site covers business planning and strategy. Offers a collection of free business plans. Includes answers to frequently asked questions, interactive tools, such as Start-Up Cost Calculator, and practical planning advice.

Business Plans and Profiles Index (http://www.carnegielibrary.org/research/business/bplansindex.html). Site is a subject guide to sample business plans and profiles for specific business types. It also covers business resources and plans.

Center for Business Planning (http://www.businessplans.org/businessplans.html). Site gives strategy insights and provides business plan software and planning guidelines. Includes Web resources, a list of consultants, and sample business plans.

NOLO Law for All (http://www.nolo.com/index.cfm). This website is designed to help consumers and small business people handle their own everyday legal matters. Includes employment, human resources, intellectual property, real estate, taxes, and starting and running a small business.

SBA: U.S. Small Business Administration (http://www.sba.gov). The SBA provides information on many worthwhile topics, such as starting, financing, and managing your own business.

Sources of General Business Information

A number of general business topics—such as business ethics, technology in business education, and business law—are available on the Web. Following are some useful sites.

Business.gov (http://www.business.gov). The official business link to the U.S. government, this site provides regulatory, financial, labor, trade, and domestic commerce information to U.S. businesses.

D&B (http://www.dnb.com/us). Dun & Bradstreet helps customers locate, analyze, and interpret information in the areas of credit, marketing, purchasing, and risk and to use the information in making business decisions.

GPO Access (http://www.gpoaccess.gov/judicial.html). This site offers access to the catalog of U.S. government publications along with a huge database of government data, including the country's annual budget since fiscal year 1997. New information issued is generally posted promptly.

Although much valuable information can be derived from the preceding websites, you should adhere to the following guides to save time and money:

- Be aware that websites constantly change and move. Thus, a site you visited yesterday may be moved today.
- Use specific, concrete search terms. Avoid using articles and prepositions in your searches. Search engines usually ignore such words.
- Most sites with a large picture file offer a text-based alternative to shorten loading time.
- Bookmark (add to Favorites) any site to which you may return and take advantage of the History (Address) list to return to sites visited recently.

Evaluating Sources

A researcher must evaluate source reliability and continue to search for data until satisfied that, within the time and budget constraints of the research project, the most valid and reliable sources have been found. The following five criteria (which resemble the Web evaluation factors studied in Chapter 11) will help you evaluate the reliability of all secondary sources:

- Timeliness: Is the source current? If outdated, the source should not be used.
- Relevance: Does the source address the research problem? Even if extremely interesting and timely, sources should be used only if they address the problem specifically.
- Accuracy: Is the source reliable and unbiased? Is the author a recognized expert? Did the author use a reliable data collection method? Where and how were any statistics derived? Does the source include complete information? If any answer is "no" or "doubtful," the source should not be used. As advised in Chapter 11, evaluate sources on the Web extra carefully since that information constantly changes, website sponsors rarely employ fact-checkers like print publishers do, and many websites serve sponsors' commercial interests.
- Quality: Is the information verifiable, consistent, and properly referenced? What discrepancies do you expect? For example, while expert opinions may differ, data

discrepancies might result from differences in geography, population, or company size.

- Cost: Will the available data lead to an appropriate, cost-effective solution to the problem? If primary data would lead to a better solution, the data collection cost may be justifiable as opposed to using the lower-cost secondary data.

Extracting Data and Keeping Records

After you have found relevant information, you must extract it from its source for use in your data analysis and report. To use data effectively, you must know when and how to record data verbatim (word for word, exactly as written) from sources and when and how to paraphrase information. You must also develop a system for recording data sources.

Keeping records of data sources is an essential part of the research process. Efficient researchers keep those records carefully and constantly while collecting data, avoiding the need to return to the source later to verify documentation details.

Verbatim Data

Record information verbatim when you must preserve the exact nature of the data. For example, when you attribute a controversial statement to an individual, it is wise to quote the statement exactly as it was written or spoken. Similarly, when reporting certain statistics, the exact numbers, even to two or three places beyond the decimal, may be significant in your research.

Two commonly used techniques for recording secondary data verbatim are note taking and copying. Note taking involves writing the exact information onto a note card, into a loose-leaf notebook, or into a text file or Windows 7 Sticky Note on your computer. Alternatively, you might record notes (text or voice) on a PDA (personal digital assistant) or an iPod enabled as a hard drive. *Note:* Creating a Sticky Note involves three steps: (1) On the taskbar, click Start and click Sticky Notes; (2) right-click to change the note color from yellow to one of the other five colors; and (3) type the note. (Click + to add a new note. Right-click to pin notes to the taskbar or close the window [text automatically saved]). To use the note-taking technique, follow these suggestions:

- Prepare a reference card, sheet, or Sticky Note for each source used. (For Sticky Notes, use a unique note color, such as purple, for references.) Include complete *who*, *what*, *where*, and *when* information. Number each source record as you prepare it. (If listing sources in a word-processing file, include "Sources" in the file name, type only sources in the file, place each source on a separate page, and number each source.)
- Use a separate card, sheet, or Sticky Note for each quotation. (Again choose a note color, such as pink or white, to use only for quotations.) Write the number of the source (reference card) above the quotation. (Alternatively, open a separate word-processing file named "Quotations." Type the number of the source above each quotation; insert a page break below each quotation.)
- Copy material exactly as it appears in your source. Place quotation marks before and after the material to remind you that the material is directly quoted. Record the exact page reference beside the quotation. (In a word-processing file, check your typed text

word by word and correct even minor typing errors. When quoting from an online database or website, you may be able to copy and paste the text to your "Quotations" file. Then insert quotation marks before and after the material.)

Those suggestions, as well as suggestions for recording paraphrased information, are demonstrated in Illustration 12.1. Linking reference and note cards, sheets, or

ILLUSTRATION 12.1 REFERENCES AND NOTES

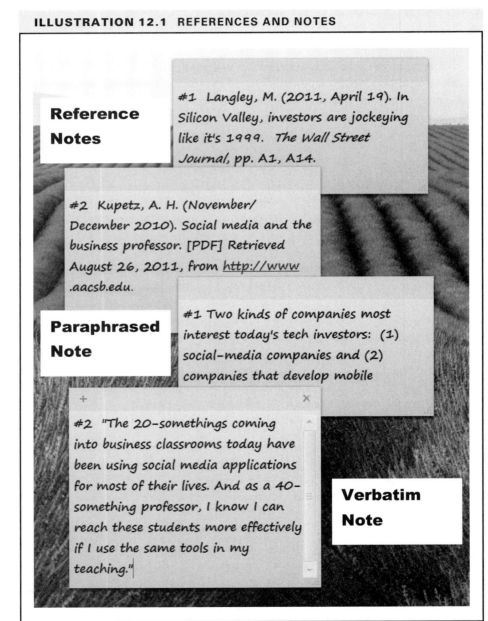

Reference Notes

#1 Langley, M. (2011, April 19). In Silicon Valley, investors are jockeying like it's 1999. *The Wall Street Journal*, pp. A1, A14.

#2 Kupetz, A. H. (November/ December 2010). Social media and the business professor. [PDF] Retrieved August 26, 2011, from http://www .aacsb.edu.

Paraphrased Note

#1 Two kinds of companies most interest today's tech investors: (1) social-media companies and (2) companies that develop mobile

#2 "The 20-somethings coming into business classrooms today have been using social media applications for most of their lives. And as a 40-something professor, I know I can reach these students more effectively if I use the same tools in my teaching."

Verbatim Note

Sticky Notes by numbers is a timesaving technique. It eliminates the need to write the full source on each note card yet ensures that sources can be relocated if needed when preparing the report.

Many people prefer the convenience of copying printed pages or printing Web pages containing desired data. However, copying can become costly and inefficient if a person copies or prints indiscriminately. (In academic libraries subscribing to full-text databases, students usually have a less costly alternative: emailing articles to their own email address.)

When you copy material from a printed publication or print material from a website, immediately prepare a reference card, sheet, or Sticky Note as you would when taking notes or *record the full source on the copy/printout itself*. The technique shown in Illustration 12.2 will help you correlate your data with other data by subject and will ensure that you have essential information for your report's references.

Although some verbatim data may be appropriate in a business report, excessive use of such data tends to suggest that the report writer lacks the ability to analyze and synthesize information. Therefore, you must become proficient at paraphrasing data.

Paraphrased Data

Paraphrased data are data that you have restated in your own words. When you write a paraphrase, you capture the essence of the information by summarizing key facts and stating them in a way that is relevant to your analysis. Paraphrased data are more desirable than exact quotations when the basic meaning is important but specific wording is not. For example, if you are reporting a company's growth for a three-year period, it may be more meaningful to compute and report a percentage of increase in gross revenues for each year than to report the exact gross revenues. Computing and recording percentages of increase based on exact revenues that you find in a secondary source is a form of paraphrasing.

Even when information is paraphrased, you must cite your data source. Therefore, you should record sources and extracted, paraphrased text similar to the records kept for verbatim data. The record for sources will be the same as those kept for verbatim data, but the notes will differ slightly: Since they will contain paraphrased data, you will use no quotation marks as you record information. The note should contain a subject heading, the number of the related source card, and, for printed sources, the page number of the original data from which you wrote your paraphrase (see Illustration 12.2).

An abstract is a form of a paraphrase. The term *abstract* usually refers to a summary of the contents of a blog post, a journal article, a special report, a book chapter, or an entire book. Whereas a paraphrased note summarizes one topic only, an abstract may include a summary of more than one topic covered in a particular publication. In some organizations, a report writer's duties may include abstracting

ILLUSTRATION 12.2 PRINTOUT WITH HANDWRITTEN REFERENCE

Top companies: Biggest employers

Rank	Company	Global 500 Rank	2010 Number of Employees
1	Wal-Mart Stores	1	2,100,000
2	China National Petroleum	6	1,674,541
3	State Grid	7	1,564,000
4	China Post Group	343	860,200
5	Hon Hai Precision Industry	60	836,000
6	Sinopec Group	5	640,535
7	U.S. Postal Service	109	627,798
8	China Telecommunications	222	493,919
9	Carrefour	32	471,755
10	Agricultural Bank of China	127	444,447
11	Compass Group	432	428,202
12	International Business Machines	52	426,751
13	Deutsche Post	93	418,946
14	Aviation Industry Corp. of China	311	404,042
15	Siemens	47	402,700
16	United Parcel Service	166	400,600

Subject: Personnel recruiting & hiring practices

(July 25, 2011) Top companies: Biggest employers. FORTUNE. Retrieved August 25, 2011, from http://money.cnn.com /magazines/fortune /global500/2011 /performers/companies/biggest.

current journal articles for managers or technical personnel. The duty of the person writing the abstract, also called an executive summary, is to capture the vital information in articles so that managers or technical personnel can be informed about current developments in their fields without having to read the contents of several journals. When writing an executive summary—or any report—follow the paraphrasing guidelines in Illustration 12.3. Additional guides for writing an effective abstract or executive summary are given in Chapter 8.

ILLUSTRATION 12.3 BASIC PARAPHRASING GUIDES[1]

Following these simple guides will help you avoid accidental plagiarism when explaining another writer's ideas in your own words.

1. First, read the material to understand it as a whole. Don't write anything until you get the information you need; then hide the source.
2. Write your note card without looking at the source. Cover up the printed page or minimize the computer screen.
3. Do *not* copy and paste text directly from a website into your report. Once in your document, it's too easy to think of the copied text as yours.
4. Notify readers at the beginning of a sentence that someone else originated the following text. Examples: In his 2010 article, Claffey reported that. ... Hall pointed out the. ... According to Okoro, ...
5. Write the idea in your own words—no peeking at the source. Imagine presenting the idea to a coworker or friend and use the words you would use in that situation.
6. Use only that part of the material that's needed to make the point you want to convey. And write a concise summary rather than including details from the source.
7. When finished recording your paraphrase, compare it to the source. Be sure you did not use the same words or phrases or simply rearrange /replace a word here and there.
8. If you have reason to use more than a six-word string from the source, put quotation marks around those words, turning them into a direct quotation within your paraphrase.
9. Compare your text and the original again to ensure that your facts are accurate and that you preserved the meaning of the source.
10. At the end of your paraphrased text, show where the idea came from, using the style of citation indicated by your employer or instructor.

© Cengage Learning 2013

Using Copyrighted Material Responsibly

Just about all manifestations of creativity can be covered by some form of "intellectual property" law. Intellectual property involves three areas (expression, ideas, and names), covered by three forms of misuse protection (copyright, patent, and trademark, respectively). Copyright law, which has important implications for all report writers, secures ownership of audio, print, and visual expressions as soon as they are made tangible. For example an article, a book or music on CD, a chart or table, a DVD, a photo, a report, a commercial software program, a textbook, or a Web page is *copyrighted the moment it exists*, with or without a copyright notice.[2] Copyright law is concerned with four criteria—purpose of use, nature of work used, proportion or extent of the work used, and the effect of use on marketability of the work.[3] Copyright law may be more complex than you think. You're likely aware that copyright law is concerned with giving credit to your data sources when you write a report, but did you know that overuse of a person's original work—even if the source is paraphrased and properly cited—may violate the copyright?[4]

True, both common knowledge and material in the public domain are exempt from copyright law. "Common knowledge," as Wikipedia defines it, "is knowledge that is known by everyone or nearly everyone, usually with reference to the community in which the term is used" (Wikipedia, The Free Encyclopedia, last modified August 28, 2011, http://en.wikipedia.org/wiki/Common_knowledge). *Public domain* refers to material that anyone can use and share without seeking permission, paying a fee, or even citing its source. Material enters the public domain if not copyrighted at its inception (exceedingly rare as already explained), if the copyright has expired (generally 70 years after the year of the author's death), or if the copyright is forfeited by the person or entity that owns it.

It's also true that a component of copyright law, called "fair use," allows for certain exceptions to the "purpose of use" criterion. In some instances, for example, an instructor may be permitted, under the fair use rule, to copy a chart from a business journal and distribute copies to your class. But fair use is also a complicated policy.[5]

Clearly, as you continue your academic career and begin your professional career, you would do well to learn all you can about intellectual property and copyright law and its implications for you as a report writer and presenter, including your and your company's rights as copyright owners. Good places to do so include the U.S. Copyright Office (http://www.copyright.gov) and the BitLaw Legal Resource (http://www.bitlaw.com/index.html). The government site includes an overview of copyright law for students and instructors, copyright cases, and a section on frequently asked questions. Two trends underscore the importance of knowing copyright law: that law is evolving to protect the rights of authors published on the Internet and that copyright cases traditionally held in civil courts have begun moving toward criminal courts.[6]

Defining Plagiarism

In all likelihood, your school's code of student conduct addresses the copyright violation known in academic circles as plagiarism, from a Latin word meaning "kidnapper."[7] The following definition of plagiarism is noteworthy for two reasons. "The intentional or unintentional failure to give credit to the originator of ideas, facts, words, and rhetorical structures that are not the writer's own."[8] This definition is notable because it brings up the possibility of unintentional plagiarism, and it indicates that text is not the only thing that copyright covers. (Rhetorical structure, as used here, refers to how an idea is expressed. John F. Kennedy's ask-not-what-your-country-can-do-for-you statement [1961 Inaugural Address] represents a unique rhetorical structure. To include the sentence in an oral or written report, replacing "country" with "fraternity" or "sorority," would be plagiarism. In addition, an updated definition of plagiarism would include visuals, such as charts, maps, and photographs, as intellectual property.)

Not all cultures view plagiarism as inappropriate behavior. In fact, in a collective culture, like China, the concept of intellectual property seems illogical, and students usually are taught, in the name of scholarship, to synthesize the ideas of many different authors and their own with no acknowledgment of sources. On the other hand, individualistic societies, like the United States, accept the notion of nonmaterial property or individual ownership of ideas and, in turn, equate plagiarism with theft. Therefore, as a student in an American institution, likely destined for employment in American business, learn all you can about copyright law and equip yourself to avoid plagiarism.

Avoiding Plagiarism

The leading way to avoid plagiarizing in a report is to be conscientious about acknowledging the secondary sources used in your document. Organizing your materials and managing your time goes a long way, too. In addition, continually improving your documentation skills will guard against accidental plagiarism. And knowing what plagiarism is and its consequences also helps you prevent it.

Acknowledge Secondary Sources

Whether paraphrasing or directly quoting an author, you must credit the sources in your report. Fully crediting sources, or documentation, consists of two parts:

- An alphabetical list of all references used, placed at the end of the report
- A citation in the report text wherever extracted data are used

Chapter 14 contains guides and examples for preparing a reference list and inserting citations.

Organize Materials and Manage Time

Plan your report-writing assignments carefully and start early. Generally, two things happen when one rushes to meet a due date: A person is more likely to make careless mistakes and to take foolish risks just to get done.[9]

To write reference information for a book, see the copyright page (near the front cover with "Copyright" and/or the © symbol displayed). For a periodical reference, look for a page showing the date, volume number, and issue number near the beginning of the periodical. To write a Web page reference, in addition to page title (top), last-modified date (bottom or top), and URL (Address box), record the article title and author's name (if any). Consider using two ink or font colors for writing notes, say, blue or black for paraphrased notes and red for verbatim notes (quotations).[10]

Don't overlook the obvious. *No matter where you find it*, give credit for words, information, and ideas that you learn during your research—even if it comes from your own daily newspaper, the encyclopedia you used in high school, or Wikipedia or another website.[11]

When forming a report-writing team, collaborate on writing procedures and policies for the team to follow. Include specific procedures for avoiding plagiarism and spell out how the team will deal with plagiarism and the plagiarizer if it occurs.

Enhance Your Citing Skills

Know the documentation style your instructor expects you to use, including where and how to place citations.[12]

Develop your ability to paraphrase properly, as described in Illustration 12.3. When citing multiple points from one source, cite them individually rather than giving one citation at the end of the paragraph.[13]

When unsure, ask. Besides your instructor, go to a reference librarian for answers to your research and documentation questions. For help in identifying common knowledge in a particular field, talk with your instructor. Doing so helps you build skill for future report-writing assignments. When in doubt about the need for a citation and there's no one you can ask, cite the source. It's better to err on the side of caution.[14]

Become Knowledgeable

Know the consequences at your school for a student caught plagiarizing and don't yield to the argument that "everybody does it."[15] Current technologies often allow instructors to uncover plagiarized text quickly and easily, so the chances of being caught are great, and usually the penalties are high (expelled from school, terminated from work).

Needless to say, students invite rather than avoid plagiarism when they buy reports from a website or elsewhere or pay someone to produce a report or part of one for them. Of course, the same might be said of copying all or part of another student's report.[16]

Plagiarism detection software may also help in avoiding the problem.

Use a Plagiarism Checker

Plagiarism checkers are search engines that scan documents, compare the text to that in the checker's database, and identify identical or similar text. In most checkers, the database contains many, varied articles, assignments, blogs, forums, and Web pages. Most checkers scan only selected phrases and rare words (chosen randomly by the software or entered by the user) rather than the entire document.

Most plagiarism checkers do not consider source citations or distinguish between paraphrased text and quotations. The general purpose of free online checkers is to help users *avoid suspicion of plagiarism* by their instructors, who themselves often use plagiarism detectors. (You may be familiar with Turnitin, an especially popular program among instructors, who often ask their students to use the checker in completing writing assignments.) If you inadvertently used the same sentence structure and similar vocabulary as a secondary source, running a plagiarism checker may alert you. Then you can revise your text before submitting the report to your instructor. Following is a list of free and low-cost checkers for your consideration.

- *Chimpsky* (http://chimpsky.uwaterloo.ca/index). Finds duplicated text within a set of documents the user specifies and searches Google for similar Web content. Includes a demonstration feature. Free but requires users to open an account.
- *CopyTracker* (http://copytracker.ec-lille.fr). Relatively complicated, requiring user to set up a text file (the document to test) and up to three reference files (potential sources of plagiarism). Checks for identical sentences and similar rare words. Highlights plagiarized sentences in red.
- *Paper Rater* (http://www.paperrater.com). Easy to use. Designed to identify entire or mostly plagiarized reports—or short, individual sections of a collaborative report. May not catch plagiarized paragraphs/sections in a long report. Shows links to the source(s) of matching text. Gives an originality score. Separated from the grammar-spelling checker described in Chapter 4.

- *Plagiarism Checker* (http://www.plagiarismchecker.com). User pastes snippets of text from different parts of the report into the checker, which then scans the Internet for matches. Has a slider bar for setting intensity of the search.
- *Plagiarism Detect* (http://www.plagiarismdetect.com). Includes a free option and a paid account costing 50 cents a page (275 words). Claims to help users be "99.9% sure that there is nothing uncited and/or unoriginal in your text." Reports the total plagiarism level and highlights suspected plagiarized text.
- *Plagiarisma* (http://www.plagiarisma.net). Cited as a free checker for students and an essay checker for teachers. Requires registration. User pastes plain text into the checker and types a URL or loads a file (most formats accepted) for comparison with that text. Checks each sentence for plagiarism. Originality score represents the percentage of original sentences. Shows yellow and gray highlights to distinguish unique and duplicate copy.
- *Plagium* (http://www.plagium.com). Accepts up to 25,000 text characters pasted to search box. Searches the Web and news feeds for identical text. Involves quick-search and deep-search modes. Results show actual plagiarized words and links to the sources.
- *Plagscan* (http://www.plagscan.com). Looks for relevant (thematically related) text. Can find three-word strings of duplicate text, so detects plagiarism even if the writer changed words. Reports results three ways: percentage of the test document found in other documents, list of links to the matching text, and comments. (Microsoft Word's Comment feature shows where duplicate text was found and a link to that source.)
- *WriteCheck for Students* (http://www.writecheck.com/static/home.htm). Uses the same database as Turnitin, including 14 billion Web pages, 150 million student papers, and 90,000 top publications, including textbooks. Unlike Turnitin, does not store your document. Besides plagiarism, checks for common grammar, spelling, and style errors. Involves a small fee.

Plagiarism checkers help report writers deal with a vital ethical/legal consideration. Related ethical matters call for report writers' attention.

Ethical Considerations

As you use secondary data sources, you may be confronted with ethical dilemmas, particularly with respect to selecting and acknowledging data sources.

Assessing Data

The quality of decisions based on a report can be no better than the quality of the data presented in the report. Therefore, as an ethical researcher, you must constantly assess the ABCD (accuracy, balance, credibility, and documentation) of the data you use. Evaluate sources when you find them as recommended earlier in this chapter. As you continue your search and report writing, continually ask yourself the following questions about your secondary sources; take the time to answer honestly; and replace any source for which the answer is "no." To do less jeopardizes the validity of your research.

- Accurate: Are statements factual—containing few superlatives and exclamation points—rather than opinionated or emotional? Did the author give the "whole story" or only part of it? Did the author include precise details or only sweeping generalities? Is the source correct right now?
- Balanced: Are the data sensible and practical? Do the data square with your existing knowledge and experience? Are data presented objectively, or can you detect a biased tone? Does the author seem concerned with truth and fairness? For example, if advantages are listed, disadvantages appear also.
- Credible: Do you intuitively trust or distrust the data? What are the author's credentials? Is the author and/or publication a known, respected authority on the subject? Did an organization sponsor publication of the data? If so, what kind?
- Documented: Do the data include a list of sources and information for contacting the author or publisher? Are all claims supported by evidence and/or references? Can you find at least two other sources that support the data?

Citing Sources

An ethical researcher acknowledges the sources that have contributed unique information to a research project. The ethical question usually concerns the uniqueness of the data and the degree to which one's credibility is affected by acknowledging sources.

Report writers generally do not cite the source of information that is common knowledge among the report readers; however, the more specific the data are, the greater is the need to cite sources. Data sources must be provided for three classes of secondary data:

- All direct quotations
- All paraphrased information that is not common knowledge among the report readers
- All visuals, such as charts, maps, and photographs, including visuals you create using data from a secondary source

Some writers erroneously think that their credibility is reduced when they recognize dependence on others for report data. In fact, the opposite is true. Student plagiarism represents a serious offense that may result in a failing grade on an assignment or for a course. Many academic institutions withhold or withdraw awards and diplomas from students who plagiarize. In business, plagiarists typically lose their jobs. In fact, a writer's credibility is enhanced by appropriate acknowledgment of sources. By citing sources that contributed unique information, a student demonstrates integrity. Moreover, by inference all information in your report that is not attributed to another source may be attributed to you. Those parts of the report demonstrate your ability to analyze and synthesize information.

Summary

Most researchers begin their research by consulting secondary data sources. Those sources help the researcher gain a perspective on the problem, and they often provide adequate data to solve the problem.

Appropriate use of secondary sources in research requires locating relevant, valid data; extracting that data from the source (either verbatim or paraphrased); and citing sources that contributed unique information to the report. The wide range of available secondary sources requires that you become proficient in the use of library catalogs, directories, online databases, periodical indexes, special issues of business periodicals, sources for statistical data, reference books, and sources for company and industry data as well as the Web. Responsible use of secondary sources also involves a basic understanding of copyright law, the consequences of violating it, and the steps you can take to comply with that law in school and the business world.

Topics for Discussion

1. Give at least five reasons why a businessperson would use secondary data sources in solving business problems.
2. Name four steps in collecting secondary data. Explain each step concisely (25 words or fewer).
3. Explain how directories, databases, and reference books help businesspeople search for secondary data.
4. Cite five criteria for evaluating secondary sources. Briefly explain each criterion.
5. With one or two classmates, recall your report-writing experiences. From experience, share tips for paraphrasing in a report. Generate at least three tips not found in Illustration 12.3.
6. Describe the record-keeping procedure for paraphrased data.
7. Identify your preferred record-keeping medium. Explain your preference to a member of your class.
8. Ask four members of your class about their experiences with plagiarism detectors. Which programs have they used (if any)? Do these students believe that detection software is helpful in avoiding plagiarism?
9. Name four characteristics of "good" secondary data. For each characteristic, give an example.
10. When must you acknowledge secondary sources in a written or oral report?

Applications

1. You have been asked to write a feasibility report for opening a cut-rate natural and organic food store in Milwaukee, Wisconsin. Answer the following questions using the latest information available. Provide a citation for each source.
   a. What is the population of Milwaukee? What percentage of this population is between the ages of 18 and 24, and what percentage is over 60?
   b. What is the per capita income of Milwaukee residents?
   c. What is the outlook for natural and organic food stores nationwide?
   d. Locate and skim a current (past three years) journal, magazine, newspaper, or Web article on the topic. (**Hint:** Look up 14 Carrot, Amaranth Whole Foods Market, Kimberton Whole Foods, and/or Whole Foods Market.)
2. Select three stocks traded on a major exchange that are of interest to you and relevant to your course of study. Use either the NASDAQ or S&P 500 website

to examine today's trading activity and activity for the past 12 months. Compare and contrast the three stocks in a three-page letter report to your instructor.

3. On the American Marketing Association's home page (http://www.marketingpower.com), click the Resource Library tab; then, under *Search by Topic*, select *Higher Ed. Marketing*. Choose and read two articles on the same topic, such as résumé writing or interviewing. Also, for each article, record data and source information. Following the guides presented and illustrated in Chapter 8, pages 218–221, write an abstract/executive summary of the articles for your instructor. *Notes:* Report information that will be most beneficial to your instructor in leading classes like yours. In the secondary heading, insert *by* and *your name* after *Executive Summary*. In the opening paragraph, include complete references for the two articles, as shown in Illustration 12.2 and Chapter 14.

4. At The Economist website (http://www.economist.com), identify five economies favorable to the United States on the basis of currency exchange rates. *Hints:* Use the table titled "Trade, Exchange Rates, Budget Balances and Interest Rates." Find the table by searching for the title or open the latest print version of the magazine and scroll to the list of economic and financial indicators. On the table, look for countries with current *and* year-ago exchange rates close to 1.00 unit per U.S. dollar (USD). In addition, find the name of the currency used in each of the five countries. (Wikipedia [http://en.wikipedia.org/wiki/List_of_circulating_currencies] may be used for collecting these basic facts.) In a memo report to your instructor, name each country and its currency; then describe its currency exchange rates now and a year ago (a rough indication of economic stability).

5. As directed by your instructor, collect secondary data for one of the following situations. Identify the kinds of data needed. (**Hint:** List several questions to be answered.) Then locate and evaluate at least three data sources. Finally, extract the necessary data and record reference information.
   a. You manage the delivery cars for LaRosa's Pizza. When replacing vehicles in the fleet, you look for economical, low-maintenance, and *green* (environmentally friendly) cars. In the next five years, these requirements may involve a gasoline alternative, such as biofuel, ethanol, hydroelectricity, solar, steam, wind, or some combination (hybrid). Examine any three of these power sources. Which power source(s) will new fleet cars likely use? Base your decision on advantages, disadvantages, and imminence of the power sources you studied.
   b. In your medium-sized organization, you are part of a team collecting data on electronic recycling. Your role: Identify U.S. businesses that methodically recycle electronics—keeping millions of discarded cell phones, personal computers, televisions, and the like out of the country's landfills. Describe each company's electronic recycling plan.
   c. Voice mail sometimes wastes time rather than saving it. For example, most of us know the frustration of unclear voice-mail messages or of voice-mail systems that make it impossible for callers to speak with a person. List

voice-mail advantages and disadvantages; draft a set of guidelines for voice-mail users (callers and person called).

    d. Your supervisor at a medium-sized publishing company has asked you to research the topic of speech recognition technology (SRT) and to answer three questions: How is SRT used by other businesses? For what types of messages is it useful? Does SRT have the potential to increase productivity for manuscript production?

    e. Your employer, Golden Goal Sports, relies heavily on outside research consultants to identify potential expansion sites outside the United States and serve as cultural informants for managers and their families preparing to live and work in an unfamiliar culture. Besides an oral report, each research team is asked to prepare a written report. Recently, your supervisor asked you to study commercial software for checking originality of these reports. *Hint:* Some brands to investigate include Attributor, Copyscape, Ithenticate, PlagScan, and Veriguide.

6. After you have collected the data requested in Application 5, write a memo report to your instructor. In the report, summarize the data and synthesize (blend) the ideas it contains. Also cite sources in your report. (*Hint:* Use Illustrations 12.1 and 12.2 as guides, or refer to Chapter 14.)

7. Visit three websites that list position openings in your major field and where you could post more than one résumé. Browse each site thoroughly, becoming familiar with its features. In a letter report to your instructor, identify and describe the potential usefulness of these sites in business education.

8. Prepare an annotated list of references on developments in communication as applied to one of the following fields. Include at least five journal articles published since 2009. (*Hint:* Articles may be located in print, in a database, or on the Web.) An illustration of an annotated list, or bibliography, appears in Chapter 14.

- Accounting
- Advertising
- Business law
- Economics
- Finance
- Global business
- Human resource management
- Marketing
- Real estate
- Robotics
- Small business management
- Telematics
- Text messaging for business
- Your major, if not listed above

9. In *Hoover's Handbook of World Business, Standard & Poor's Register of Corporations, Directors and Executives*, or another source of company data listed in this chapter, find information about a large international corporation. Write a short memo (one full page or less) to your instructor describing the kinds of information available in the source.

10. Use secondary sources to locate and record the information for any six of the following items. Record a full reference for each source.
    - Monetary unit in Dubai
    - Latest list of the Fortune 100 companies
    - Population of your hometown
    - Origin of the word "capitalism"
    - Definition of the term "agritourism"
    - Distance from Los Angeles to Beijing
    - Main cause of small business failures
    - Estimated trade-in value of the car you drive
    - Location of Cluj-Napoca, Romania, on world map
    - Locations of the three most recent winter Olympics
    - The *New York Times* headline on the day you were born
    - Web address (URL) for a site dedicated to your hobby or interest
    - Name of the first woman major party candidate for U.S. President
    - Size of continental United States compared to United Arab Emirates
    - Exact value of today's U.S. dollar in Argentine pesos and Japanese yen
    - Originator of this statement: "The only thing we have to fear is fear itself."
    - Names and locations of world's three richest countries and three poorest countries
    - *Fortune* magazine's top 10 employers and a distinctive characteristic of each organization

References

1. These guidelines compiled from three sources: Broyles, Robyn, "Tips for Avoiding Plagiarism," at Bright Hub, last modified June 20, 2009, accessed August 24, 2011, http://www.brighthub.com/education/homework-tips/articles/39394.aspx; "Plagiarism: What It Is and How to Recognize and Avoid It," Writing Tutorial Service, Indiana University—Bloomington, last modified April 27, 2004, accessed August 24, 2011, http://www.indiana.edu/~wts/pamphlets/plagiarism.shtml; "How to Paraphrase a Source," The Writer's Handbook, University of Wisconsin, Madison, last modified April 4, 2011, http://writing.wisc.edu/Handbook/QPA_paraphrase2.html.

2. "What Is Copyright?" Copyright website, accessed August 30, 2011, http://www.benedict.com.

3. Rockat, Alyssa, "Copyright Law for Dummies," Blogspot, last modified December 28, 2010, http://uvwriting.blogspot.com/2010/12/copyright-law-for-dummies.html.

4. Goad, Michael, "Copyright and Plagiarism: What's the Difference?" PDDOC.com, last modified 2005, accessed August 23, 2011, http://www.pddoc.com/index.html.

5. Templeton, Brad, "10 Big Myths about Copyright Explained," Brad Ideas, accessed April 23, 2011, http://www.templetons.com/brad/copymyths.html.

6. Templeton, Brad.

7. Goad, Michael.

8. Jameson, Daphne A. "The Ethics of Plagiarism: How Genre Affects Writers' Use of Source Materials." The Association for Business Communication Bulletin. June 1993: 18–28.

9. Hansen, Katharine, "10 Tips for Avoiding Plagiarism," My College Success Story, accessed August 28, 2011, http://www.mycollegesuccessstory.com/academic-success-tools/avoiding-plagiarism.html.

10. Hansen, Katharine.

11. "Avoiding Plagiarizing: Mastering the Art of Scholarship," University of California, Davis, last modified September 2006, accessed August 29, 2011, http://sja.ucdavis.edu/files/plagiarism.pdf.

12. Hansen, Katherine.

13. "Avoiding Plagiarism," The Writing Place, Northwestern University, last modified September 23, 2005, accessed August 30, 2011, http://www.writing.northwestern.edu/avoiding_plagiarism.html.

14. Hansen, Katherine.

15. Hansen, Katherine.

16. Stolley, Karl, and Allen Brizee, Contributors, Purdue Online Writing Lab (OWL), last modified August 24, 2011, http://owl.english.purdue.edu/owl/reHandbook/QPA_paraphrase2.html.

CHAPTER 13

Using Primary Data Sources

LEARNING OBJECTIVES

After you have read this chapter, you should be able to:

1. Identify ways to acquire primary data.

2. Construct effective data collection instruments.

3. Explain ethical issues related to using primary data.

4. Maintain accurate records that will contribute to ethical acknowledgment of data sources.

IF YOU DETERMINE THAT SECONDARY data are not adequate to answer your research questions, you must use primary data. To use primary data effectively, your first tasks are to select appropriate sources and to choose valid, reliable methods of collecting data from those sources.

Acquiring Primary Data

Primary data are data acquired at their source. Commonly used primary data sources for business research are company records; people, such as employees, customers, and suppliers; and phenomena, such as activities and processes. Methods to obtain information from those sources are either active or passive. *Passive data collection* involves observation of characteristics of the people or actions that are the elements of analysis; the person collecting the data does not actively interact or communicate with those subjects. *Active data collection* involves questioning the subjects; the person collecting the data interacts with the subjects who actively supply the data to the researcher.

Passive Methods

Passive data collection methods used by business researchers include search of company records, observation, and some forms of experimentation.

Search of Company Records

Company records contain much information generated during daily operations. Personnel, production, marketing, credit, accounting, and finance records are accumulated and modified daily. Those records are often used in day-to-day decisions and subsequently stored for possible future use. Although some of the information may be made available to the public in an annual report or a publicity release, much of the material is never published and distributed externally. But as new problems or challenges arise within the organization, the data that have been accumulated in the files often provide a perspective on the problems and information to solve them.

Company records are often the first primary data source consulted by a business researcher. Some researchers consider company records to be superior to other primary data sources for two reasons:

- The data are objective. The data were generated for purposes other than the immediate report that is being prepared.
- They are economical to use. Collecting data from company files is generally the least expensive method of gathering primary data.

Company files are especially useful when the research requires historical data about some aspect of the company's operations. For example, data from personnel files will show changes in the composition of the company's labor force, data from customer service files can identify a possible flaw in product design, and data from files in the information technology assistance center may be able to identify emerging user needs. When company records cannot provide adequate valid data, however, other strategies must be used.

Many companies store information about company activity in computerized databases and digitized files. A database is a collection of related records stored in a computer file. For example, a customer database might contain such information as name, street or post office address, city, state, ZIP code, telephone number, account number, and credit limit. A record is all of the information about one person or organization. Each category of information within the record is called a field. In this example, there would be eight fields: name, street or post office address, city, state, ZIP code, telephone number, account number, and credit limit. A digitized file, on the other hand, might consist of text and graphics. A proposal received via electronic mail, a sales report, a memo reporting the decisions at a meeting, and a status report of a project are examples of the types of documents stored as digitized files.

When information processing systems are integrated, personal computers are linked to other equipment so that information can be accessed by all authorized users. In an integrated system, you can relatively easily collect and process information that is stored in a database. You must first obtain authority to use the file, then gain access to the appropriate file, identify the correct record, identify the categories of data desired, and direct the computer to find the data. You can then organize the data in many ways: alphabetically or numerically, ascending or descending order, or by any category of information stored in the file.

Assume, for example, that as regional sales manager for Valdex Company you help sales representatives call on inactive customers, those who have not placed orders within the previous six months. While preparing to visit Ohio, you can access the database to identify customers in Ohio. Next, inactive accounts can be identified and arranged geographically by ZIP code so that your travel time is kept to a minimum. You can also sort the accounts alphabetically, by the date of the last order, or by the amount of the last order. If you desire, you can also insert this information in a letter or email report to Ohio sales representatives with a few simple keystrokes.

In contrast, if individual work stations are not linked, you must request the needed information from the division of the organization controlling that information. It is your responsibility to define the information needed and how it is to be organized. After receiving the information, you must integrate it into the report, often by reentering the data.

Report writers may also use digitized files to collect textual or statistical information. Documents stored digitally are coded with key words or phrases identifying the contents of the document. To locate information stored in files, you must first determine the appropriate criteria for the desired information and instruct the computer to locate files that match the criteria. You then select relevant documents from the list generated by the computer search. For instance, suppose you are the director of continuing education for a medical school. You know that many medical doctors practicing in rural communities find it difficult to leave their practices for a few days to travel to the medical school for the training needed to maintain their medical licenses. You want the medical school to develop online courses that will permit those rural doctors to participate in continuing education from their offices or homes. You think that several documents exist relating to this idea. To locate the documents, you would direct the computer to search for the key words *continuing education+medical+rural.* After the document list has been generated, you would select those that will support your proposal for online continuing education.

In fact, such a search in July 2011 located programs already in operation. After evaluating the programs located, you could conceivably conclude that your school should not develop such courses. At this point in your preliminary research, you might recommend a project to evaluate the existing courses to determine if they will meet the needs of the rural doctors in your region.

Observation

A second passive method is observation. In this technique the researcher (or a mechanical or electronic device) watches the data sources and records information about the elements that are being analyzed.

Assume, for example, that productivity is lower than average among the employees of one supervisor in a computer tech support call center. You may decide to collect data about working patterns of those employees. Company records are not likely to contain that information, except to the extent that it has been recorded in performance reviews. Asking employees about working patterns is unlikely to yield valid data because the technicians may be unwilling or unable to report how they work. Therefore, observation of the employees performing their tasks may be the best data collection method. In your observation, you could record several behaviors: how quickly they begin work after arrival, how they organize their work stations, how much call time is spent on "chit-chat" with the customer and how much is spent on solving the technical problem, the degree of direct supervision they receive, how they respond to the supervisor's comments, the percentage of time they are away from their work stations, and so on.

In some situations, observation can be accomplished mechanically. For example, highway departments regularly use traffic counting devices to help determine whether to install a traffic signal at a particular intersection. A time clock used to record when employees check in and check out of work is another type of mechanical or electronic observation.

Experimentation

Observation is often an integral part of another method, experimentation. Experimentation may employ both passive and active data collection methods. Assume that, as part of a wellness program, a company's dietician wants to encourage employees to eat fresh fruits and vegetables. You are assigned the task of determining how to increase employee consumption of those foods in the company cafeteria. In cooperation with the cafeteria staff, you decide to conduct an experiment in which you manipulate the location of the fruits and vegetables in the cafeteria layout. Then you observe employees' behaviors (looking at fruits and vegetables, not looking at them, selecting, not selecting, etc.) as they go through the line. That observation is a passive method. But you may supplement it with an active method, asking employees why they did or did not choose a fresh fruit or vegetable.

A major shortcoming of observation is that the observer must interpret what he or she sees, and different observers may assign different meanings to events. In the cafeteria experiment, for example, when an employee pauses in front of the fruits and vegetables, one observer may interpret that behavior as noticing the display. Another observer may interpret the behavior as a delay caused by other factors, such as a slow-down somewhere on the line. When an employee selects an item from the display, the observer might be tempted to assume that the decision was made at that time and was influenced by the attractiveness of the display. But the employee may have decided several hours earlier to eat an apple or a salad for lunch. Because of such potential shortcomings in observation, that method is often supplemented by an active method.

Active Methods

Active methods, also called communication methods, involve questioning subjects. Questioning is an appropriate data collection method when the information you need consists of knowledge, attitudes, opinions, or beliefs. In many situations, questioning is the only way to obtain necessary data. You can, for example, get data from personnel files about employee participation in a 401(k) plan; but you cannot determine employee attitudes toward the company's contribution to the plan from those files. Attitudes must be determined by questioning the employees. After the questioning, the results may be compiled and stored in company files; but those data then become historical data. Attitudes could change dramatically within a short time if company policy or economic conditions change.

Questioning can be accomplished by either personal or impersonal means. Interviewing is a personal means, whereas using questionnaires and electronic surveys tends to be impersonal.[1]

Interviews

In an interview, the researcher or an assistant orally presents instructions and questions to the subjects and records their answers. Interviews may be face-to-face or mediated.

The face-to-face interview is a rich communication medium that allows both the interviewer and the respondent to interpret nonverbal cues as well as verbal questions. For example, the respondent can ask for clarification of a question he or she does not understand. Likewise, the interviewer can use probes to encourage deeper thought if the responses seem superficial. Such richness may improve rapport between the researcher and the subject, thereby encouraging openness; but that same richness may stimulate the respondent to give socially acceptable answers, thereby biasing the data.

In a mediated interview, such as a telephone interview, the participants cannot see one another. Thus, trust and rapport must be established through oral means. Telephone interviews are considered by some researchers to be equal or perhaps superior to other active primary data collection methods in obtaining valid data, particularly when the subject matter is sensitive. For example, respondents may be more willing to answer questions about personal health matters in the relative anonymity of a telephone interview than in a face-to-face interview. Telephone interviews have been particularly successful in business-to-business situations because respondents may be willing to give a few minutes of telephone time when they are not willing to schedule an appointment for an interview.

The inability to show prompts, display materials, or present a long list of options is a severe limitation of telephone interviews. Another major disadvantage of telephone interviews is the increasing consumer resistance to that method of home intrusion for marketing purposes.

Interviews may be structured or unstructured. In a structured interview, the interviewer follows a formal guide that provides the exact wording of instructions and questions as well as the exact sequence in which questions are to be asked. If interviewers follow the guide as written, all subjects will be questioned in essentially the same manner. In an unstructured interview, the interviewee uses either no formalized questions or very loosely structured ones. The objective is to get the respondent to talk freely about the interview topic.

Today, researchers use computer assistance in both face-to-face and telephone interviews. For example, in telephone surveys, questions may be presented by a voice recording; the subject is asked to respond by pressing designated digits on the telephone keypad. Or a computer may be set up to provide an interviewer with a questionnaire and a means of recording responses. A particular advantage of this technique is the ability to branch easily to different paths in the interview, depending on a respondent's answer. Calculations can also be programmed into the questionnaire, enabling the interviewer to ask a simple question, such as how many glasses of milk each family member consumes daily, and immediately convert the answer into annual family consumption. Another advantage is the ability to randomize or rotate series of questions. In a face-to-face interview, the computer can also present visual stimuli.

Focus Group Interviews

Focus group interviews are often used to determine interest in a new product or service, the effectiveness of advertising and communications research, background studies on consumers' frames of reference, or consumer attitudes and behaviors toward an idea, organization, and so on.

The standard focus group interview involves 6 to 12 similar individuals, such as male college students, female lawyers, or Toyota Camry owners, who are brought together to discuss a particular topic. The respondents are selected according to the relevant sampling plan and meet at a central location that has equipment to make an audio or audiovisual record of the discussion. A moderator or facilitator is present to keep the discussion moving and focused on the topic, but otherwise the sessions are free flowing. The competent moderator attempts to develop three clear stages in a one- to three-hour interview:

1. Establish rapport with the group, structure the rules of the group interaction, and set objectives.
2. Pose questions to provoke intense discussion in relevant areas.
3. Summarize the group's responses to determine the extent of agreement.

Usually the moderator also analyzes the transcript or recording of the session and prepares a summary of the meeting. Focus groups can generate much data in a relatively short period. When little is known in advance of an investigation, the focus group may provide a basis for formulating research questions and problems.

Questionnaire Surveys

In a questionnaire survey (also called a self-completion survey), instructions and questions are presented to the subjects in a printed questionnaire, and the subjects record their answers on the questionnaire or another medium.

Questionnaire surveys are attractive to investigators for three reasons:

- The cost is low, relative to the amount of data that can be collected in one survey.
- The large geographic area from which the researcher can draw the sample may improve data validity.
- The assurance of anonymity and lack of pressure while the respondent completes the questionnaire contribute to data validity.

Response rates to questionnaire surveys are relatively low, however. Response rates can be influenced by questionnaire design, which is discussed later in this chapter. To increase response rates—and, thereby, data validity—researchers often offer inducements to the subjects. Market researchers have identified the relative effectiveness of various inducements, as follows:

Inducement	Influence
Prenotification	Increase in response
Personalization	Increase in response
Monetary incentives	Increase in response
Follow-up	Increase in response
Return postage	Increase in response
Sponsorship	Increase in response if subject identifies with sponsor
Appeal in cover letter	Ego, science, or social utility appeals tend to be most effective
Specification of deadline	No influence on number of returns; may accelerate speed of returns
Typewritten vs. printed; color; length; precoding	No influence on returns

Studies have shown that Web-based questionnaires, when skillfully designed, are completed more quickly than telephone, face-to-face, and paper questionnaire surveys. This medium also allows presentation of visual images, longer lists of options, and easy branching strategies. By involving the participant visually and manually, this medium tends to maintain the respondents' attention and promotes good-quality data to the end of the questionnaire.[2]

A later section of this chapter, "Online Surveys and Polls," discusses use of electronic surveys more extensively.

Comparison of Primary Data Collection Methods

Your choice of a data collection method must be based on its ability to obtain accurate data and satisfy other relevant research criteria. Factors that often influence the success of a project are the ability to identify subjects or to ensure subject anonymity, flexibility of the data-gathering technique, ability of the technique to tap sensitive data, protecting the data from researcher influence, scheduling requirements, time requirements, probable response rate, and cost.

As Illustration 13.1 shows, if your research design requires that subjects be identified, a search of company records, observation, or personal interview would be an excellent technique. On the other hand, if you wish to ensure subject anonymity, a search of company records or a personal interview would be a poor technique. Similarly, if you are concerned about the accuracy of sensitive data, you should choose the records search technique or a survey as opposed to observation or personal interviews. Some sensitive data, such as information about contributions to a political party or personal health practices, cannot be collected by observation and may be distorted in an interview. By weighing the relative importance of the nine dimensions, you can select a technique that best meets the requirements of your project.

After selecting your data collection method or methods, you must design a way to capture the data and make them available for analysis. The precision of your data collection instruments will influence the quality of your data.

Preparing Instruments to Collect Primary Data

Primary data collection tools consist of observation forms, questionnaires, and interview guides. To design those tools, you must understand some basic concepts about measurement and measurement scales.

Measurement and Measurement Scales

Measurement is the process of assigning numbers to an element or characteristic that is being observed or analyzed, and a measurement scale is any device used to assign numbers to the characteristic. Height—the distance from the bottom to the top of something standing upright—is a common measurement with which you are familiar. Height can be scaled in inches, feet, yards, centimeters, millimeters, or meters.

A primary purpose of measurement is to permit analysis and comparisons of relevant characteristics. For example, through measurement of an infant's height at birth and at age three months, you can learn something about the child's growth. By comparing those measurements with the average measurements for children in your culture, you obtain additional information about the child's growth rate.

In business research, you will frequently want to measure and compare behavior, attitudes, desires, or other characteristics of a target group of people. Four scales are

ILLUSTRATION 13.1 COMPARISON OF PRIMARY DATA COLLECTION METHODS

	Methods					
Dimensions	Search of Records	Observation	Personal Interview	Focus Group Interview	Questionnaire Survey	Electronic Survey
Subject identification	Excellent	Excellent*	Excellent	Excellent*	Fair	Excellent*
Flexibility	Excellent	Good to fair	Excellent	Excellent	Fair	Poor
Subject anonymity	Fair to poor	Excellent*	Poor	Excellent*	Excellent*	Excellent*
Accuracy of sensitive data	Excellent	Fair	Fair	Fair	Good	Excellent
Control of researcher effects	Good	Poor	Poor	Poor	Excellent	Excellent
Flexibility of scheduling	Excellent	Fair	Poor	Fair	Excellent	Good
Time required	Good	Fair	Fair	Fair	Fair	Excellent
Probable response rate	Good	Good	Good	Good	Fair to poor	Good
Cost	Excellent	Fair	Poor	Fair	Good	Good

*Dependent on design of study; subject identification or anonymity can be planned.

commonly used to measure or assign numbers to such data: nominal, ordinal, interval, and ratio.

Nominal

A *nominal* scale allows you to classify information and assign a number to each classification. The classifications used for nominal scales must be all-inclusive and mutually exclusive. For example, every survey respondent can be classified with respect to age if the group identifiers are defined correctly (for example, under 50 or 50 and older). In a customer survey, a private business/dining club may wish to categorize respondents by type of club services used:

1. Breakfast
2. Lunch
3. Dinner
4. Private banquet service
5. Private meeting rooms
6. Business networking events

A *nominal* scale merely permits assignment of numbers to the categories that are of interest to the researcher. Consequently, the statistics that can be computed from a nominal scale are limited to such descriptive items as the percentage of responses in each category and the mode—that is, which category has the greatest number of responses. A nominal scale provides no information about relative value of the items classified. A number does not indicate that items in any category are better or worse, weaker or stronger than items in another category.

Ordinal

An *ordinal* scale permits determination of a qualitative difference among categories. Assume the business-oriented club wants to know which proposed new services are most attractive to consumers. Respondents could be asked to indicate their preferences by ranking five services as shown in the following example. Assume the numbers in the "rank" column are one subject's responses, with 1 representing the most preferred and 5 the least preferred service.

Service	Rank
1. Half-price "Happy Hour" on Wednesday, 5–7 p.m.	4
2. "Quick Lunch" menu/service, Monday–Friday	3
3. Wireless Internet service	2
4. Reduced-priced dinner on member's birthday	5
5. Free use of private rooms for business meetings	1

An *ordinal* scale helps the researcher determine the percentage of respondents who consider half-price "Happy Hour" most important, the percentage who consider a "Quick Lunch" most important, and so on. Such a scale also shows that the individual who ranked the services as shown prefers free use of private rooms to all other services. The respondent also prefers a "Quick Lunch" menu and wireless Internet service to special prices for happy hour or birthday dinners. But the ranking does not indicate the relative strength of the preferences. The individual may consider the first-ranked item to be only slightly more important than the second-ranked item, but the respondent may think that the item given the second rank is considerably more important than the third-ranked service.

Interval

If the club wants to analyze the strength of differences in attitudes toward various services, the researcher must use an *interval* scale. Such a scale presents equally spaced (or equal-appearing) points on a continuum to represent order, differences, and magnitude of differences. Although five-point interval scales are common, any number of points may be used. On the basis of the research problem, the researcher must decide how refined the measure should be.

The following example illustrates how the club might use an interval scale to determine the strength of preferences for various services.

Indicate how important each of the following services is to you by circling the number on the scale that reflects your attitude:

1 = Very unimportant

2 = Unimportant

3 = Neutral

4 = Important

5 = Extremely important

Service	Rating
1. Half-price "Happy Hour" on Wednesday, 5–7 p.m.	1 2 3 4 5
2. "Quick Lunch" menu/service, Monday–Friday	1 2 3 4 5
3. Wireless Internet service	1 2 3 4 5
4. Reduced-priced dinner on member's birthday	1 2 3 4 5
5. Free use of private rooms for business meetings	1 2 3 4 5

An interval scale permits calculation of an arithmetic mean for each variable. Such a scale also permits calculation of the variance and standard deviation to analyze how responses are distributed around the mean.

An interval scale begins at an arbitrary point other than zero. The scale in the foregoing illustration begins at 1, but it could have started with any number. Since the scale does not begin at zero, it cannot measure the proportions of differences. Although the distances between points on the scale are assumed to be equal, a value of 5 cannot be interpreted as five times greater than a value of 1. Considering a Fahrenheit thermometer will help you understand that characteristic of an interval scale. A thermometer's scale range may be from a point below zero, −50 degrees for example, to a point above zero, such as +150 degrees. After using the thermometer to record outdoor temperature every day at noon for one month, you can compute the average noontime temperature for that month. But if the temperature is 80 degrees at noon one day and 60 the next day, you cannot say that the temperature has fallen 25 percent; you can say only that it has fallen 20 degrees.

Ratio

A *ratio* scale has an absolute zero point and equal intervals on the scale, making it the most powerful measurement scale. Some examples of ratio scales are income, age, height, and weight. This scale permits calculation of the magnitude of differences. For example, a $20,000 income is one-third of a $60,000 income; a 75-year-old person has lived three times longer than a 25-year-old person; a 90-foot structure is 50 percent taller than a 60-foot structure; and an object that weighs 260 pounds is twice as heavy as an object weighing 130 pounds.

Although the ratio scale is the most powerful scale, it cannot be used for some kinds of measurement. When measuring a behavioral characteristic, such as attitude, it is rarely logical to assume an individual completely lacks the characteristic that is being studied. For example, most club patrons have some attitude or opinion about the desirability of various services, even if the attitude is that a particular service is very unimportant. Logic requires, therefore, that scales used to measure most behavioral dimensions begin at a point above zero.

The type of measurement scale—nominal, ordinal, interval, or ratio—determines what kinds of statistics can be used for data analysis. Any statistic that can be computed from less powerfully scaled data (that is, nominal or ordinal) can be computed on more powerfully scaled data (that is, interval and ratio). But many statistics that can be computed for interval or ratio data cannot be applied to nominal or ordinal data. You will learn more about analysis of scaled data in Chapter 15.

To design an effective instrument for primary data collection, you must first decide which measurement scale or scales will help you collect and analyze the data needed to solve your research problem. After making that decision, you must design the instrument carefully and test it before beginning your actual collection. In addition, in some research, such as in questionnaire surveys, you must also prepare a transmittal message to stimulate potential respondents to participate in the study.

Criteria for Instrument Design

All primary data collection instruments must meet certain design standards. The overall objective is that the instrument must enable someone (the observer, interviewer, or subject) to record valid data in a manner that permits analysis. To achieve that objective, the tool must meet criteria related to content, language, format, and instructions. As you study the following criteria, notice their application in Illustration 13.2, Observation Form; Illustration 13.3, Interview Guide; Illustration 13.4, Checklist; Illustrations 13.5 and 13.6, Transmittal Message; and Illustration 13.7, Questionnaire.

Content

The content of the data collection instrument must be justified in terms of its relevance to the research problem. Research time and money are wasted if irrelevant items are included. To determine relevance, ask yourself what purpose each item serves:

- **Is the question required to establish rapport or to screen potential subjects?**
  Even though specific answers to such a question may not be part of the data analysis, the question may be relevant because it facilitates the data collection process. For example, the question "Approximately how long have you been a member of the club?" can establish rapport by providing an opening,

nonthreatening question that stimulates conversation. That question can also be a screening device. If you wish to interview members who have patronized the club for more than two years, the answer indicates whether to continue or discontinue the interview.

- **Is the information required for the data analysis plan?** Demographic data, such as gender or age of participant, may be relevant if data analysis calls for comparisons by gender or age. But if such comparisons are not planned, questions about gender or age should not be included.
- **Is this the best way to obtain the information?** If the information can be obtained in another way, the time of observers or respondents should not be wasted. For example, if club records show the date a customer joined the club, that information should not be sought unless it is used to establish rapport or to screen participants on the basis of length of membership.
- **Is this question (or observation) capable of generating valid data?** If a question is offensive or unduly taxes a respondent's memory, the person may refuse to answer or may fabricate an answer. If a question is biased or leading, the respondent may unknowingly provide invalid data. In some situations, subjects will provide answers they think are acceptable rather than admit lack of knowledge or understanding. An observer may also record inaccurate or fictitious data if the observation form demands more than the observer can handle capably.

Language

The overall effect of the language should be to encourage people to participate and provide accurate information. To achieve that effect, the language used in instructions and questions must be positive and confident (but not condescending), clear, unbiased, and neutral, or not leading. The following examples illustrate the effects of language.

> *Condescending: You may not know it, but the state legislature is debating whether to reduce the number of weeks that an unemployed person may be eligible for unemployment benefits.*
>
> *Positive, Confident: The state legislature is debating whether to reduce the number of weeks that an unemployed person may be eligible for unemployment benefits. The primary issue is that the recent high rate of unemployment has nearly depleted the unemployment insurance fund and is requiring the state to increase the unemployment taxes imposed on employers. What are your attitudes toward decreasing the number of weeks that an unemployed person may be eligible for unemployment benefits?*
>
> *Presumptuous: I'm sure you will agree that we all have an obligation to help unemployed individuals meet their basic needs. That's why I'm conducting this study.*
>
> *Encouraging, Confident: You can help improve the state's unemployment compensation program. Your answers, along with those of others, will help to identify critical unemployment issues for our legislators to consider during the coming legislative session.*

Unclear: Where were you married? (Respondent does not know whether to supply city, state, or exact site such as church, home, garden, county court. Recently a user of this book observed that the question is also inappropriate for a person who has been married more than once! The respondent could well ask, "Which time?")

Clear: Where was your wedding ceremony performed?

Church or synagogue _____
Judge's chambers _____
Home or private club _____
Other (specify) _____

Unclear, leading: What do you think the Chamber of Commerce should do to reduce the negative impact of cruise ships in Charleston Harbor? (Assumes respondent knows all options that the Chamber can pursue; assumes respondent opposes the presence of cruise ships in the local harbor.)

Clear: Which of the following actions would you support to improve relationships between local residents and cruise passengers? (Follow the question with a list of actions the Chamber is considering.)

Biased: Do you support public financing for all federal elections to take back control from the special interests? (Tends to lead toward "yes" because of negative connotation of "special interests.")

Unbiased: Do you support public financing for all federal elections?

Leading: Do you think there should be more public funding of the arts and arts education since private support of the arts has declined by more than 50 percent during the last 10 years? (A "no" to this question could suggest that the respondent lacks an appreciation for the arts.)

Neutral: Under what conditions should the state legislature continue to fund arts education in elementary and secondary schools?

Format

The format of observation forms, interview guides, and questionnaires must contribute to readability, ease of completion, and accuracy. In addition, questionnaire format should entice subjects to complete the questionnaire rather than discourage them from doing so. The following guides will help you achieve those objectives.

- **Provide enough space to record information neatly and clearly.** If insufficient space is provided, respondents may become discouraged and decide not to provide all data, or they may enter the information illegibly.
- **Use white space advantageously.** All margins should be at least one inch, and sufficient space should be placed between items to avoid a crowded, oppressive appearance.
- **Place spaces or boxes for responses near the items to be answered.** This practice contributes to accuracy. If the answer spaces are too far from the items, the respondent may accidentally use the wrong space or select an unintended answer.

- **Choose open and closed question formats wisely.** Open items state a question or make a statement to be completed by the respondent. No answer options are provided. Open items are appropriate when the researcher wants to probe for a range of responses or when the range is known to be so broad that it is impossible to list all options. Because the answers can vary considerably, responses to open items are difficult to process.

  Closed items provide a list of anticipated answers from which the respondent chooses. Closed items are appropriate when the range of responses can be anticipated or when the researcher wants to force responses into ranges that have been defined in the research problem. Options for closed items must be all-inclusive and mutually exclusive; that is, all possible answers must be included, and concepts or categories contained in the options must not overlap. The following example illustrates that criterion.

Incorrect:	*Under $10,000*
	$10,000–$20,000
	$20,000–$30,000
	$30,000–$40,000
	$40,000–$50,000
	Over $50,000
Correct:	*Under $10,000*
	$10,000–$19,999
	$20,000–$29,999
	$30,000–$39,999
	$40,000–$49,999
	$50,000 or more
Incorrect:	*Christian*
	Jew
	Protestant
Correct:	*Christian—Catholic*
	Christian—Eastern Orthodox
	Christian—Protestant
	Jew—Conservative
	Jew—Orthodox
	Jew—Reformed
	Muslim
	Other

- **Arrange questions logically and use branching techniques, if necessary, to help respondents avoid irrelevant questions.** Branching techniques are demonstrated in items B.1.a and B.1.g of the observation form shown in Illustration 13.2. Item C of the form also leaves additional space for the observer's comments.

ILLUSTRATION 13.2 OBSERVATION FORM

OBSERVATION—KIDS GYM

Address of Kids Gym Observed: _____

_____

Date of Observation: _____ Time in: _____ Time out: _____

Visit the assigned location on a weekday between 10:00 A.M. and 1:30 P.M. Your objective is to observe the cleanliness of the facility, adequacy of supplies, and interaction of instructors with children.

A. **Exterior Evaluation**

When you arrive at the site, evaluate the parking lot and exterior signage before entering the gym.

1. Was there adequate parking space?   Yes _____ No _____

2. Were the sidewalks and parking areas free of debris?   Yes _____ No _____

3. Was the gym easily identifiable from the parking lot?   Yes _____ No _____

4. Were windows and doors clean?   Yes _____ No _____

5. Were posters or announcements in the windows
   professional in appearance?   Yes _____ No _____ Not Applicable _____

B. **Interior Evaluation**

After observing the exterior features, enter the gym. Wait patiently for a Kids Gym team member to acknowledge your presence and ask to assist you. **Do not disturb any instructor who is working with children.** Introduce yourself to the team member and explain the purpose of your visit. Emphasize that you are an independent contractor working for a research company that has been hired by the Kids Gym franchisor to evaluate this gym. **Without disturbing any classes**, walk through the facility, checking all items noted on this observation form. If you are unable to complete any item, mark it with red ink.

1. **Signage, Promotional Materials, Supplies**

   (a) Were the Kool Kids posters visible?   Yes _____ No _____ (go to 1.c.)

   (b) Were the posters in good condition (clean, not torn)? Yes _____ No _____

   (c) Were Kool Kids coupons prominently displayed?   Yes _____ No _____

   (d) Were Kool Kids stickers on the lobby benches?   Yes _____ No _____

continued

ILLUSTRATION 13.2 CONTINUED

(e) Was Kool Kids soap available in the restrooms? Yes _____ No _____

(f) Were Kool Kids towels available in the restrooms? Yes _____ No _____

(g) Was a refreshing station available in the lobby? Yes _____ No _____ (go to 2.a.)

(h) Was the refreshing station fully stocked with cleansing cloths, lotion, and towels? Yes _____ No _____

2. **Training and Play Areas**

(a) Were all gym mats clean and in good repair? Yes _____ No _____

(b) Were all instructors wearing shirts bearing the Kids Gym logo? Yes _____ No _____

(c) Were all children wearing rubber-soled shoes? Yes _____ No _____

(d) Were observers seated off the gym floor? Yes _____ No _____

(e) What was the children: instructor ratio? _____

C. **Explanations.** Use this area to explain any item to which you answered "No." Identify the item and give a brief explanation.

D. **Conclusion**

After you have gone through the entire observation form, wait for a Kids Gym team member and ask for assistance on any items that you could not complete. **Do not interrupt anyone who is working with children**. If you have waited at least 15 minutes and no team member has come to assist you, you may leave the facility without answering the incomplete items. Report that fact on your observation guide.

Within 12 hours of completing this observation, log in to your account at www.westudy.com and complete the online version of the observation form. Keep this paper copy in your files for a minimum of six months.

Branching is further demonstrated in items 4 and 6 of the questionnaire shown in Illustration 13.7. The branches in item 4 direct the respondent to item 5 or item 7, depending on the person's answer. That branch also helps the researcher classify responses. Items 5 and 6 apply to individuals who favor the relocation and items 7 and 8 to those who oppose it. The branch after item 6 helps respondents avoid irrelevant questions.

Instructions

The instrument must contain clear, complete instructions to the user. Instructions must indicate how to complete the instrument and what to do with it after completion. Even a simple checklist, such as Illustration 13.4, must contain clear instructions.

ILLUSTRATION 13.3 INTERVIEW GUIDE

Perceptions of Hatfield-McCoy Mountains Region
Interview Guide

_____   _____   _____

Location of interview   Date of interview   Interviewer's initials

INSTRUCTIONS: Approach an adult (an individual who appears to be 18 or older) who is seated or standing at a rest area or waiting area in the tourist site in which you are conducting the survey. After greeting the individual, explain the study briefly. (For example, "I'm trying to find out what people know about one of West Virginia's tourist attractions.")

A. **Ask:** *Will you answer a few questions about tourism in West Virginia?*

   No _____ Offer one of our Hatfield-McCoy brochures and end the conversation cordially.

   Yes _____ Go to item B.

B. **Ask:** *Do you live at least 50 miles from this site?*

   No _____ Explain that we need participants who have traveled at least 50 miles to reach the site. Offer one of our Hatfield-McCoy brochures and end the conversation cordially.

   Yes _____ Go to item C.

C. **Say:** *We are trying to stratify our sample by age. Into what age range do you fit?*

   18–34 _____ *35–54* _____ *55+* _____

D. Indicate the participant's sex: Male ___ Female ___

E. **Say:** *I now have just 10 questions for you.* **Read each question clearly and slowly enough for the interviewee to understand the question and answer options.**

1. What is the primary reason for your trip to this location?

   Family/individual vacation   _____
   Weekend getaway   _____
   Business trip   _____
   Visiting friends   _____
   Other   _____

2. Have you visited this area before?

   Yes _____ How often within the past three years? _____

   No _____

continued

ILLUSTRATION 13.3 CONTINUED

3. Why did you choose to visit this area? (More than one answer may be given.)

   Recommended by family or friend   _____
   Recommended by travel agent   _____
   Required for business   _____
   Responded to advertising   _____
   Returning to a place I've enjoyed before   _____
   Interested in history and culture of area   _____
   Other   _____

4. What other areas of West Virginia have you visited on this trip?
   None _____
   Areas cited _____

5. How many nights have you spent/or plan to spend in West Virginia?

   None   _____
   1–3   _____
   4–6   _____
   7–9   _____
   10 or more   _____

6. Where will you spend/have you spent your nights? (More than one answer may be given.)

   Not staying overnight away from home   _____
   Home of family/friends   _____
   Camping site   _____
   Cabin in state park   _____
   Hotel/motel/bed-and-breakfast   _____
   Other   _____

7. What activities have you participated in while in this area? (More than one activity may be given.)

   Visiting friends/family   _____
   Camping/hiking   _____
   Visiting historical sites   _____
   General sightseeing   _____
   Shopping   _____
   Other   _____

8. Where have you eaten meals on this trip? (More than one location may be given.)

   Home of family/friends   _____
   Private restaurant   _____
   At campsite   _____
   At restaurant in park or other public facility   _____
   Other   _____

continued

ILLUSTRATION 13.3 CONTINUED

9. Are you familiar with the Hatfield-McCoy Mountains Region of West Virginia?

Yes _____   No _____

Give the interviewee the list of statements about the Hatfield-McCoy Mountains.

Say: *Here is a list of things that come to the minds of some people when they hear "Hatfield-McCoy Mountains of West Virginia." Please check any items that come to your mind when you think of this region.*

Collect Sheets. Say: *Thanks for your assistance. Here's a brochure that will tell you something about the Hatfield-McCoy region. I hope you will visit (it or again) sometime soon. Enjoy your visit to West Virginia.*

Return all interview guides and checklists to the Hatfield-McCoy Mountains Coalition office at the end of each working day.

In addition, the researcher should define any terms or scale values that may be interpreted in different ways, as is demonstrated in the opening instructions of Illustration 13.3, where *adult* is defined as a person who appears to be age 18 or older. Ambiguity must be avoided in instructions as well as in questions.

If the instrument is complicated or lengthy, the instructions should be broken into understandable units. For each new section of the instrument, meaningful headings or instructions related to that section should be provided. (Note the observer instructions in Illustration 13.2 and the interviewee instructions in Illustration 13.3.) When a rating scale is used, it should be repeated at the top of each page to which it applies so that users need not turn back to check the scale values. Many respondents will not expend that effort; they may, instead, supply inaccurate responses.

To ensure that the instructions for returning the instrument are not lost or misplaced, they should appear on the instrument itself, not in a separate letter or instruction sheet. Even when an addressed return envelope is provided, the instrument itself should show the address to which it must be returned. Envelopes can easily be lost, making response impossible if the questionnaire itself does not contain the address.

Although instructions tell respondents what to do with an instrument, the instrument itself must be presented to potential participants in such a way that they are motivated to respond. An effective transmittal message accomplishes that objective. No survey instrument should be distributed without a transmittal message, either contained in a separate message or placed on the instrument itself.

Guides for Transmittal Messages

An effective transmittal message builds researcher-subject rapport and motivates subjects to participate in the research. A transmittal message may be written, as in a cover letter that accompanies a questionnaire; or it may be spoken, as in an opening conversation with interviewees. In both situations, the message must be planned so that it will reveal enough information to stimulate interest and motivation without

ILLUSTRATION 13.4 CHECKLIST

Hatfield-McCoy Mountains of West Virginia
Visitor's Checklist

Your answers to this survey will help the Hatfield-McCoy Mountains
Coalition plan its programs and promotional campaigns.

A. Have you ever visited the Hatfield-McCoy Mountains region of West
Virginia? Yes _____ No _____

B. Whether you have or have not visited the Hatfield-McCoy Mountains
region, please check any items that you *currently* associate with the
Hatfield-McCoy Mountains.

1. A family feud long ago	1. _____
2. Coal mining region	2. _____
3. Chuck Yeager	3. _____
4. Cabins in state park	4. _____
5. Chief Logan	5. _____
6. Auto races	6. _____
7. Golf	7. _____
8. An interesting area of the state	8. _____
9. An economically depressed region	9. _____
10. Good hiking	10. _____
11. Mountaineer pride	11. _____
12. Historical monuments	12. _____
13. Outdoor drama about Shawnee princess	13. _____
14. Good restaurants	14. _____
15. Coal Mine Wars	15. _____
16. A building made entirely of coal	16. _____
17. Museums	17. _____

Please return this checklist to the person who interviewed you.

Thank you for participating in this survey. We wish you a pleasant and safe trip.

biasing responses. Since the questionnaire shown in Illustration 13.7 concerns a controversial issue, a transmittal letter would be useful to stimulate interest and encourage participation. The following guides, which have been applied in the transmittal
messages shown in Illustrations 13.5 and 13.6, will help you develop effective transmittal messages.

ILLUSTRATION 13.5 TRANSMITTAL MESSAGE TO ACCOMPANY ELECTRONIC SURVEY

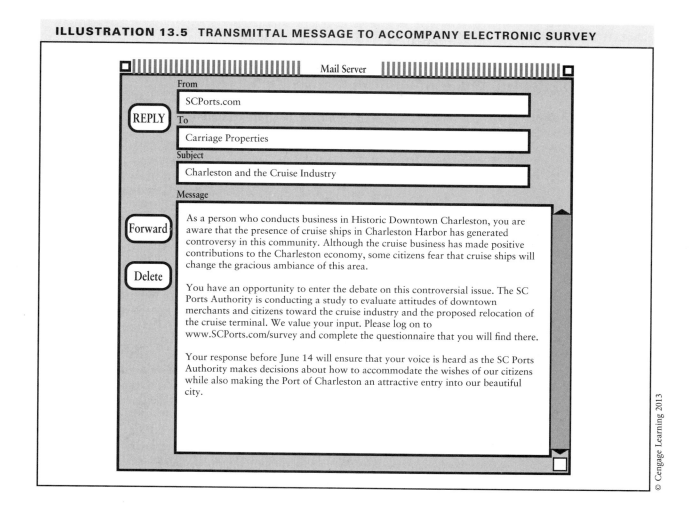

- **Use an interesting opening that focuses on the receiver, not the sender of the message.** When possible, identify a reader interest or need that may provide motivation to participate.
- **Provide enough identifying information to legitimize your request.** That information may include the purpose of the study, the company or agency for which it is being conducted, how the information will be used, and potential benefits of the study.
- **Indicate the role of the participants and the protections that are extended to them.** Role definition may include explanation of how participants were selected and what is requested of them (for example, five minutes of your time, answers to 10 questions, etc.). Protection usually includes assurance of confidentiality, particularly if sensitive information is sought.
- **Specify exactly what is required (for example, complete the questionnaire and mail it before August 15), and make that action as easy as possible.** Enclosing a stamped, addressed envelope with a mail survey or asking short, clearly worded questions in a telephone survey are ways to make response easy.

ILLUSTRATION 13.6 TRANSMITTAL LETTER

S. C. Ports Authority

P O Box 22288
Charleston, SC 29413
864.111.1111

May 15, 2011

Dear Ansonborough Resident:

As a resident of the Ansonborough District of Historic Charleston, you take pride in your home and the gracious ambiance of downtown Charleston.

In recent months the *Charleston News and Courier has* published comments about the presence of cruise ships in Charleston Harbor and cruise passengers in the historic district. Although many citizens realize that the cruise industry has a positive impact on the Charleston economy, some fear that its presence may distract from our traditional way of life.

The South Carolina Ports Authority wants to hear from you on this issue. On June 12 and 13 we will conduct town-hall meetings at St. Philip's Episcopal Church, 142 Church Street. At those meetings members of the Ports Authority will explain our tentative plans to relocate the cruise terminal and improve the Charleston Harbor waterfront. The entire project is intended to give Charlestonians and tourists better access to that wonderful resource.

Please plan to attend one of those meetings. You will be given an opportunity to discuss your views of the cruise industry and the proposed relocation of the terminal. The enclosed questionnaire should help you prepare for the meeting.

You may complete the questionnaire before the town-hall meeting, or you may wait to fill it in until after you have heard the discussion. We will collect completed questionnaires at the end of the meeting.

We look forward to seeing you at a meeting on June 12 or 13 at 7:30 p.m. to discuss what we can do to improve everyone's enjoyment of our downtown waterfront.

Sincerely,

Bryant T. Joseph

Bryant T. Joseph, VP, Terminal Development
Enc. Questionnaire

- **Offer an inducement to participate, if possible.** For example, enclosing a $1 bill and suggesting the recipient give it to her or his favorite charity has been known to induce response, even though the $1 does not adequately compensate the time spent on the questionnaire. If an inducement with material value cannot be offered, a realistic appeal to the individual's needs or interests may be sufficient

ILLUSTRATION 13.7 QUESTIONNAIRE

Questionnaire: Charleston and the Cruise Industry

Please share something about your knowledge, attitudes, and experiences related to the impact of the cruise industry in Charleston. There are no correct or incorrect answers. We are looking for your honest assessments.

1. Approximately how many jobs in the Charleston area are supported by the cruise industry?

   500___   400___   300___   200___   100___

2. Approximately how much economic output (in millions) is generated by the cruise industry in Charleston?

   $55___ $45___ $35___ $25___ $15___

3. Which of the following conditions do you associate with the presence of a cruise ship in port? (Check all that apply.)

   ___ Abrasive interactions with cruise passengers.
   ___ Decreased pedestrian traffic in neighborhood.
   ___ Decreased sales of food, lodging, and/or merchandise and services.
   ___ Environmental/noise pollution.
   ___ Increased pedestrian traffic in neighborhood.
   ___ Increased sales of food, lodging, and/or merchandise and services.
   ___ Pleasant interactions with cruise passengers.
   ___ Reluctance to leave home or place of business.
   ___ Smooth flow of vehicular traffic.
   ___ Traffic jams.
   ___ Other (please describe).

   One option the Ports Authority is considering is to relocate the cruise terminal to a point somewhat north of Union Pier.

4. At this time, do you favor or oppose relocation of the cruise terminal?

   Favor ___ **(Go to Item 5)**
   Oppose ___ **(Go to Item 7)**

5. Relocating the cruise terminal is projected to bring approximately 350 jobs to the Charleston region and contribute $45 million to the local economy during the 12 months of construction. Which of the following statements **best** reflects your attitude about those projections?

   ___ Projections are guesses, not facts.
   ___ The Charleston area needs that kind of economic boost; let's do it.
   ___ The Charleston historic district will receive little of that benefit.
   ___ The Charleston historic district will share in that benefit.

   continued

ILLUSTRATION 13.7 CONTINUED

6. If the cruise terminal is relocated:

___ My quality of life will very likely improve.
___ My quality of life may possibly improve.
___ I anticipate no change in my quality of life.
___ My quality of life may decline.
___ My quality of life will very likely decline.
Please go to item 9.

7. Relocating the cruise terminal is projected to bring approximately 350 jobs to the Charleston region and contribute $45 million to the local economy during the 12 months of construction. Which of the following statements **best** reflects your attitude about those projections?

___ Projections are guesses, not facts.
___ The Charleston area needs that kind of economic boost; let's do it.
___ The Charleston historic district will receive little of that benefit.
___ The Charleston historic district will share in that benefit.

8. If the cruise terminal is relocated:

___ My quality of life will very likely improve.
___ My quality of life may possibly improve.
___ I anticipate no change in my quality of life.
___ My quality of life may decline.
___ My quality of life will very likely decline.

9. **Please provide some information about yourself to help us process the answers to this survey.**

- Your age range is:
  Under 25___   26–35___   36–45___   46–55___   56–65___   Over 65___
- You are:
  Female ___   Male ___
- Your profession or occupation is best categorized as:

  _____ Artistic endeavors   _____ Education or religious services
  _____ Food services   _____ Full-time homemaker
  _____ Hospitality services   _____ Legal services
  _____ Medical/dental services   _____ Real estate services
  _____ Retail marketing   _____ Retired
  _____ Wholesale distribution   _____ Other (please describe)

Please return your completed questionnaire to:
South Carolina State Ports Authority
PO Box 22288
Charleston, SC 29413

inducement (for example, a desire for recognition, a sense of altruism, or the potential benefit to a group of which the person is a member).

After the instrument and transmittal message have been developed, one task remains before they are ready for use: testing and revision.

Testing and Revising Instruments

The objective of instrument testing is to detect errors or weaknesses in all aspects of the instrument before it is used. Instructions, questions, response modes, sequence of items, format, and level of language should be scrutinized. Ideally, two kinds of testing are used: in-house and field testing.

In-house testing involves presenting the instrument to colleagues or other impartial critics for their evaluation. To evaluate all aspects of the instrument, those critics should be knowledgeable about instrument design and about the kinds of data that are to be collected. Such evaluators can often detect shortcomings and provide suggestions for instrument revision.

Field testing involves presenting the instrument to a group of respondents typical of those with whom it will eventually be used. One way to do a field test is to ask potential participants to complete the instrument without informing them that they are a test group. After they have completed the instrument, the test group should then be asked to provide additional information about the effectiveness of the instrument—its clarity, format, time requirement, and so forth. Discussion of the respondents' reactions to the questionnaire will frequently yield valuable suggestions for instrument revision.

In the future, you will likely find yourself using online surveys and polls more frequently than traditional paper-and-pencil instruments.

Online Surveys and Polls

The large number of people who have access to the Internet has made it a popular tool for creating and distributing self-completion surveys. A more recent innovation in data collection is the one-question questionnaire, or poll.

Self-Completion Surveys on the Web

Websites such as Zoomerang (http://www.zoomerang.com) and SurveyMonkey (http://www.surveymonkey.com) automate many aspects of designing and transmitting a questionnaire, collecting results, and reporting and charting data. (Zoomerang is a copyright of Market Tools, Inc. SurveyMonkey is the registered trademark of a private American company of the same name.)

Uses of Web Surveys

Customer satisfaction surveys are commonly conducted by this medium, particularly after a major online purchase. At time of purchase, the customer is directed to a website to enter identifying information and answer questions about the purchase experience. Other common uses of online surveys include gathering responses to new or existing products and gaining insight into purchase behavior, including key influences. In addition, businesses use online questionnaires to analyze markets, determine product features and benefits, test hypotheses, evaluate product effectiveness, and measure brand perceptions. Increasingly, businesses use Zoomerang, SurveyMonkey, and less prominent sites in event planning (preferences and interests, scheduling and registration, and postevent feedback), employee training (course evaluation, quizzes and tests, and participant reactions), and employee feedback collection (performance reviews, satisfaction measures, workplace issues, and improvement suggestions).

Features of Internet Surveys

Most business questionnaire sites provide several closed-question types besides two-to-five-item multiple choice. SurveyMonkey, for example, specifies 15 question types. Having a range of question types allows you to pick the best type for collecting the data you need. However, no more than two or three types should be used in one questionnaire to avoid overwhelming the subjects. Top survey sites can handle open-ended questions in addition to closed questions. Zoomerang, for instance, creates a "tag cloud," or word list, of words in answers to an open-ended question. Then Zoomerang groups words on the list (qualitative data) to form numerical (quantifiable) categories that can be processed like closed-question data. This example from the Zoomerang Web site will suffice: "… if in 10 responses you find the phrases 'great,' 'best ever,' and 'excellent' it's easy to create a tag list titled 'good reviews' and know how many people answered your questions that way." At the same time, though, the respondents' original words will appear in any report of results.

Most business survey sites grant users ability to customize questionnaires using a variety of colors, fonts, and themes. For example, SurveyMonkey, producing questionnaires in any language, enables users to make survey appearance consistent with the company's Web site, including a company name and logo.

At first, businesspeople distributed questionnaires by posting them at the company's Web site; then they began contacting potential subjects by email, requesting their participation and including a link to the questionnaire. These days, Zoomerang users can post their surveys on Facebook and Twitter besides email and Web sites. In addition to these methods, SurveyMonkey users can post links to potential respondents in company blogs and in banner ads.

Naturally, as online competitors, each survey Web site continually adds appealing features to make itself stand out. In addition to features already mentioned, a few of the more salient features now offered by Zoomerang and/or SurveyMonkey include the following.

Address Book. At Zoomerang, you can store the contact information for survey respondents, adding the contacts one by one or importing them from your Gmail, Hotmail, Outlook, Yahoo!, or other email account. In addition, Zoomerang will send you a list of any invalid email addresses, called a "hard bounce report" because the emailed questionnaires "bounce back" to the sender unanswered. The address book also helps with survey management: Zoomerang will send survey reminders to the invited individuals who do not respond by a certain date.

Answer Validation Options. The survey software limits the kind of information a respondent can enter in a field. For example, if the question calls for a decimal number; the software would not allow a respondent to enter a whole number or alphabetic characters. For these cases, SurveyMonkey can send error messages in 21 languages. Related features are called "branch logic" and "skip logic." With the branch logic feature, respondents take different paths in the survey depending on their answers. With skip logic, the survey allows respondents to skip irrelevant questions and takes them to the next relevant item.

Automatic Survey Cutoff. Users can specify a cutoff date and time when creating a questionnaire, or the survey can be set to end based on the response count. Thus, a user can collect only as many responses as needed. This feature is especially valuable when each respondent receives an incentive for completing the questionnaire.

Restricted Usage. The survey can be set to require a password before entering responses. It can even be set to restrict responses to one per IP address to ensure that a participant completes the survey only once. For kiosks and computer labs, though, the same survey can be set to allow infinite responses.

Section 508 Certification. Under Section 508 of the U.S. Rehabilitation Act, federal agencies must make their Web sites accessible to people with disabilities. SurveyMonkey assures its users that the software is 508 compliant. For example, high-contrast themes are available for use by the visually impaired, while a screen reader is available for sightless individuals. Other adaptations are provided for entering responses.

Security Encryption. At top survey sites, responses can be encrypted with a secure sockets layer (SSL), much like the personal information you enter when ordering merchandise online. The shield protects the data entered from capture in transition from the respondent's browser to the data storage. (If this security is in place, the survey address will begin with "https.") This service is recommended any time you collect personal or private information, especially if you need to comply with the 1996 Health Insurance Portability and Accountability Act.

Sharing. Using Zoomerang, teams can collaborate on survey creation, management, and analysis from a common location. SurveyMonkey notes a variety of options for sharing survey results, from posting a summary only to allowing others to apply filters and export your data.

Survey Panel. Zoomerang has a profile database of 2.5 million people representing five demographic, lifestyle, occupational, and geographic attributes. Users can search the database for potential respondents in addition to or instead of naming their own subjects. This panel is particularly helpful for targeting ultraspecific respondents or a low-incidence group of subjects.

Telephone Surveys. SurveyMonkey's Precision Polling allows a user to design and record a survey in his or her own voice. Then the software calls the telephone numbers the user provides or creates a dedicated number for the respondents to dial.

Cost of These Online Services

While survey sites differ in the tools available for questionnaire creation, they differ even more in the collecting, analyzing, and reporting of survey results. For example, free survey sites, such as those on the following list, promote the ease and speed of creating a questionnaire but offer only minor service in dealing with survey results:

FreeOnlineSurveys (http://www.freeonlinesurveys.com)

KwikSurveys (http://www.kwiksurveys.com)

LimeSurvey (http://www.limesurvey.org)

Survey Pirate (http://www.surveypirate.com)

Toluna Quick (http://www.tolunaquick.com)

Business users generally are interested in customized questionnaires, targeted delivery to their audience, and sound analysis and reporting of results. Thus, most businesspeople will subscribe to a level of online service and pay a monthly or annual fee. In addition to SurveyMonkey and Zoomerang, the following sites offer subscription plans:

aytm (http://www.aytm.com)

Checkbox (http://www.checkbox.com)

eSurveyspro (http://www.esurveyspro.com)

Infosurv (http://www.infosurv.com)

Omniture (http://www.omniture.com)

StellarSurvey (http://www.stellarsurvey.com)

SurveyBuilder (http://www.surveybuilder.com)

SurveyGizmo (http://www.surveygizmo.com)

SurveyTool (http://www.surveytool.com)

The SurveyMonkey Web site describes four levels of service and pricing: Basic, $0; Select, $204; Gold, $300; and Platinum, $780. Zoomerang offers three levels of service: Basic, Pro, and Premium. The free Basic package permits 12 questions and 100 responses per survey, includes six basic questionnaire templates, and reports simple data (totals, percentages). The Pro package, costing $200 a year, allows unlimited questions and responses per survey, offers over a hundred questionnaire templates, involves filters for comparing data subsets, and charts data for each questionnaire item. At $600 a year, the Premium package offers the same templates, also allows unlimited questions and responses, and reports and charts seven statistical measures for each item. Survey templates, as you might guess, contain prewritten questions that the user can modify or simply replace.

Polls: Another Way to Collect Data on the Web

Many businesspeople advocate the use of one-question polls for determining customer needs, wants, and satisfaction. They note that all customer satisfaction surveys aim to answer just one question: Is Company X doing a good job? So, they ask, Why not design an instrument that focuses on that question?

Polls first appeared on social media sites. Perhaps that explains why many businesspersons still favor one-question polls as a simple way to engage people—to get them thinking and sharing about the business and its products or services. Virtually all polls are created to share results with respondents, enhancing the poll's value as an engagement tool. Polls continue to flourish on Facebook, LinkedIn, Twitter, and other social media. However, the ability now to put polls on an organization's Web site allows visitors to answer the poll while browsing or shopping on the site.

Besides audience engagement, increased product awareness, and customer satisfaction purposes, common uses of business polls include generating content for analyzing sales, blog, or newsletter articles; planning company events; gathering various feedback; assessing training/trainees; identifying employee/workplace issues; recruiting employees; and supporting strategy proposals. To say it more succinctly, businesspeople use polls to help them make better decisions.

Most Web sites that provide survey tools, including SurveyMonkey and Zoomerang, enable you to create polls. In addition, a large number of Web sites have sprung up just to fill the need for these miniature surveys. Some sites, such as MyPollCreator (http://www.mypollcreator.com) and 99 Polls (http://www.99polls.com), are popular for personal polls. For example, you might pose a question to friends about a just-released movie; or, as a planning committee member, you might use a poll to determine the preferred place to hold a graduation party. Sites for creating business polls include Micropoll (http://www.micropoll), the current leader Polldaddy (http://www.

polldaddy.com), and LinkedIn Polls (http://www.linkedin.com after joining LinkedIn and signing in).

The poll in Illustration 13.8 used a seven-item checklist to determine what content to include in a social media training program. The poll also encouraged use of a comment box below the single question: "If you have an opinion that is not represented in any of the above, or any other obstacles that are keeping you from using social media, please leave a comment below."

The poll in Illustration 13.9 highlights the absence of demographics in polls, using this statement: "Depending upon whether you're just starting out or you've been in online marketing for a while, your answers will likely differ." This poll asks respondents to check two items on a seven-item list. In addition, this illustration shows poll results from the 17 respondents.

Advantages of One-Question Polls

Businesspeople point out several advantages of single-question polls over longer surveys. First of all, the online survey tools for creating polls are plentiful and free.

Polls are extremely easy to set up and monitor. The question format can be flexible. Many polls involve a checklist and directions to select the best response or to select all that apply. The ideal format, some people say, is the yes-or-no question because the questions (Were you happy with your experience? Did we do a good job? Would you recommend us?) call for gut feelings rather than thoughtful answers.

People are more likely to answer a poll. Multiple-question surveys usually require respondents to think about their answers and often take 10 minutes, 20 minutes, or more to complete. A poll, especially in yes-or-no format, can be answered in 20 seconds or less.

ILLUSTRATION 13.8   A ONE-QUESTION POLL

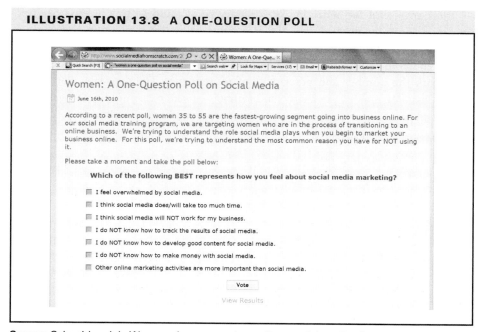

Source: Schneider, J. L. Women: A one-question poll on social media. *Social Media from Scratch*, September 21, 2011, http://www.socialmediafromscratch.com/2010/06/16/women-a-one-question-poll-on-social-media.

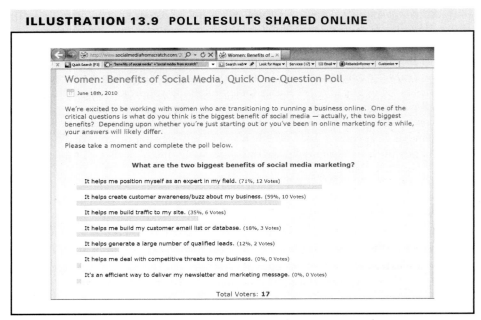

Source: Schneider, J. L. (2010, June 18). Women: Benefits of social media. *Social Media from Scratch*, September 21, 2011, http://www.socialmediafromscratch.com/2010/06/18/women-benefits-of-social-media-quick-one-question-poll.

In most instances, you have flexibility in how long you run each poll. At LinkedIn, for example, a poll, by default, stays open a month; but you can set it to close sooner or run for up to 90 days.

Polls are useful for collecting preliminary results and getting a sense of direction on a long, involved survey. Initial insights from polls can serve as a guide in writing the survey questions for the longer instrument.

In reporting results, some polls include a graphic representation of the voting along with the number and percentage of respondents. These visuals—bar/column graphs, line/area graphs, pie charts, and symbols—make outcomes easy to grasp at a glance and can be downloaded to a presentation, worksheet, or written report.

Disadvantages of Polls

The clearest limitation of one-question polls is the lack of detailed data. This lack can prevent you from addressing negative responses. Asking for a name/email address does not ensure that the respondent will supply it, leaving you no way to follow up on an acutely negative answer.

Votes in a customer satisfaction poll give you a general idea of how happy your customers are, but those answers do not provide specific information about what your organization does or does not do well. Thus, polls do not enable you to tap into specific areas of your business, such as customer service, pricing, or technical support. Some organizations partially offset this limitation by posting several polls at a time or by posting related polls over several weeks; conducting polls one or two days a week has become a standard practice for many businesses. Including an open-ended question or comment box is another way of partially offsetting this limitation.

Since most polls include no demographic data, the answers of one group cannot be compared with another. LinkedIn Polls is an exception, however. At LinkedIn, you can break down voting by age, gender, or seniority. Thus, you can compare the answers of people under 30/over 50, men/women, and office assistants/chief executive officers.

Generally, anyone who views a poll can also see the voting results. Seeing the results before voting could skew a poll's outcomes. Polls created and kept in a particular community like LinkedIn are inherently skewed because they are confined to a closed network of business professionals. However, the ability to migrate polls from LinkedIn to other networks and Web sites largely offsets this limitation. On the other hand, some dedicated sites list polls that pay people to take them, causing some Internet users to view poll taking as an income source—and possibly skewing the results of the polls they take.

One-question polls will likely never replace comprehensive, in-depth market research. Neither are such polls likely to go away. Instead, look for developments that will eliminate current drawbacks and expand and refine use of these miniature surveys.

Today, the Internet is home to practically all the research instruments described in this chapter, including focus group interviews. While technological advancement in this area is relatively unpredictable, two advancements seem likely. One likely development involves increased ability to analyze unstructured (text) data, to get a handle on the endless stream of words—from blog comments to Facebook "likes" and Twitter tweets. Another likely change is improved analytical tools until they are on a par with statistical measures used in offline research.

While planning and conducting primary research, you will confront ethical issues. The next section discusses some of those concerns.

Ethical Considerations

Much primary research requires gathering data from and about people. A major ethical issue concerns how people are used for the researcher's advantage. Three specific concerns must be considered: invasion of privacy, protection of subjects, and acknowledgment of primary data sources.

Invasion of Privacy

The right to privacy is a fundamental human right guaranteed by Supreme Court interpretations of the Fourth Amendment to the U.S. Constitution. Both passive and active data collection techniques have the potential to violate that right. An observation technique, for example, can be conducted in such a way that no rights are violated, as in observation of shoppers' responses to a store display. But observation may be a violation of the right to privacy when the observer secretly conducts an observation to which subjects would not likely consent. Is it ethical to place monitors in store dressing rooms to observe behaviors of shoppers without their knowledge or consent? Is it ethical to place secret recording devices on an employee's telephone to monitor communication practices or message content?

The invasion of privacy issue also relates to surveys conducted in homes. Is it ethical for a researcher to use the telephone to enter the privacy of homes primarily for the benefit of the researcher? The Federal Trade Commission's Telemarketing Sales Rule (TSR) requires that telemarketers disclose their identity and the purpose of the call promptly and restricts calls to the hours of 8 A.M. to 9 P.M. This rule also covers such things as a consumer satisfaction survey if a sales attempt is intended to accompany the survey. Most states have enacted similar protections.

Protection of Subjects

Humans also have the right to be free from injury to person or reputation—and to defend themselves against such harm. In experimental research, the researcher has an ethical obligation to protect subjects from harm. If the potential for injury exists, the researcher has an obligation to inform subjects and to give them the option not to participate. Is it ethical to test a new product on subjects when the full effect is not known? In the United States, the federal government attempts to protect subjects from potentially harmful food and drugs by requiring extensive records of research on nonhuman subjects before approving research on humans.

An interesting related issue concerns the ethics of prescribing a substance for an illness when the drug has not been approved for that particular use. Although this practice, known as off-label prescribing, is not illegal, the U.S. Food and Drug Administration (FDA) bars many forms of speech promoting off-label use. A physician who prescribes an off-label use makes the moral judgment that the potential for good results outweighs the risk to both patient and doctor of using an untested medication. In fact, many in the medical community view off-label prescribing as an essential component of good medical care for situations in which approved drugs have not been effective.

Acknowledgment of Primary Data Sources

After obtaining data from and about subjects, the researcher analyzes the data and reports the results of the analysis. In that report, the researcher has a continuing obligation to guarantee the right to privacy and to protect the subjects from injury to reputation, from reprisals by report readers, and so on. Those protections are usually accomplished by maintaining confidentiality—not identifying data sources unless authorized to do so.

When a researcher accepts the moral obligation to maintain the confidentiality of data sources, questions may arise about the appropriate ways to acknowledge primary data sources. The following guides will help you deal with that complex ethical issue.

- **Confidential sources.** When confidentiality has been promised to participants, primary data sources can be acknowledged only in a general way. However, confidential sources should still be recognized in the report body and in the source list. In the report body, provide a general description of the data collection method. In the source list, give a brief description of the data collection facts. The following examples illustrate accepted techniques:

    Report body: Data about EXACTO employees' attitudes toward the company's benefits plan were obtained by a mail survey. Questionnaires were mailed to employees' homes with the request that they send the completed questionnaire to the researcher. The researcher processed the data. No EXACTO managers had access to the data.

    Source list: EXACTO employees, mail survey conducted during April (year).

- **Identified sources.** When subjects grant permission to be identified, source acknowledgments are similar to those used for secondary data and should be recognized in both the report body and the source list. Essential facts include *who*, *what*, *where*, and *when*. In the report body, use the same techniques that you use to cite secondary data sources (footnote, endnote, or internal citation). The following examples show acceptable ways to list interviews, observations, and surveys.

    Interviews: (Name of interviewee) in an interview with (name of interviewer) at (place) on (date).

Observations: Observations of (describe people, activities) at (place) on (date).
Surveys: Survey of (describe subjects) conducted (state applicable details of method, place, date).

More extensive guides for documenting primary and secondary data sources are presented in Chapter 14.

Summary

You have several options for collecting data from primary sources: search of company records, observation, face-to-face and telephone interviews, and respondent-completed questionnaires. Tools for creating and distributing questionnaires abound on the Web along with one-question polling tools. To collect valid, reliable primary data, regardless of the medium used, you must carefully design and test content, language, format, and instructions of all data collection instruments and protect the privacy of subjects participating in the research. When reporting data obtained from primary sources, the researcher must reconcile the obligation to cite data sources with the obligation to respect the subjects' desires for confidentiality.

Topics for Discussion

1. Distinguish between active and passive data collection methods.
2. Describe two passive methods to collect primary data.
3. In what ways has electronic technology made the collection of primary data more efficient? If you have conducted or participated in an online survey, describe your experience. If you conducted the survey, also identify the online tools you used.
4. Identify three active methods to collect primary data.
5. In what ways do structured and unstructured interviews differ?
6. Identify the advantages and disadvantages of each primary data collection method discussed in this chapter.
7. Identify and describe four measurement scales.
8. What questions must be answered as you evaluate the content of a data collection instrument?
9. What aspects of language must be considered as you evaluate a data collection instrument?
10. What characteristics of format should you look for as you evaluate a data collection instrument? How would these considerations apply to single-question online polls?
11. What purposes are served by instrument instructions? by a transmittal message?
12. What guides should be followed in preparation of a transmittal message?
13. Why and how should instruments be tested?
14. Discuss three specific areas of ethics that must be considered when you use primary data sources.

Applications

1. Using the guidelines for effective primary data collection instruments and transmittal messages, critique one or more of the items shown on pages 403–407. Write a memo to your instructor detailing your evaluation.

2. As directed by your instructor, develop the data collection tools for one or more of the research problems in the Applications for Chapter 11. Follow these steps to complete your assignment:
   - Identify the appropriate method for collecting primary data.
   - Prepare a data collection instrument.
   - Write a transmittal message.
   - Identify potential ethical issues and ways to resolve them.

3. As directed by your instructor, develop primary data collection instruments for one or more of the following situations. Follow these steps to complete your assignment:
   - Identify the information needed.
   - Identify the best sources of information.
   - Identify appropriate methods for collecting primary data. If a questionnaire is an appropriate tool, specify the appropriate medium and distribution method—online (distributed by email, social media, or Web site), paper (distributed by handout or mailing), or other means.
   - Prepare data collection instruments.
   - Write a transmittal message.
   - Identify potential ethical issues and ways to resolve them.
     a. Snelling Wood Products has been making particle board for furniture manufacturers. Since the furniture industry has fallen on hard times, Snelling's market has declined, and the company has been forced to diversify. It recently spent about $40 million to modify its plant and install machinery to make quarter-inch tongue-and-groove laminate flooring. Home owners are buying more hardwood and laminate flooring, cutting into the market for carpet and sheet vinyl. The laminate floor market has been dominated by Pergo of Sweden and Wilsonart of the United States.

        Snelling is considering an additional investment of at least $100 million in machinery to make heavier-grade laminates in an attempt to capture a greater share of the U.S. market for laminate flooring. The company needs to know whether sellers of flooring materials would consider switching from Pergo or Wilsonart to a new U.S. supplier.
     b. The technology exists for universal electronic medical records. Such records could speed up medical service and reduce errors. However, some people have concerns about patient privacy and fears of what could happen if the information got into the wrong hands. Determine the attitudes of people in at least two different age groups (for example, 20–30 vs. 60–70) about the use of universal electronic medical records.
     c. You are wondering about job opportunities in the nonprofit sector. You want to get information from the chief executive officer of a nonprofit organization. You will seek information about the organization's history, its goals, its measures of success, its major sources of funding,

certification available or required for working in the organization, associations of which it is a member, and so on.

d. A group of investors is considering the restoration of a nineteenth-century opera house in Smalltown, a town with a population of approximately 11,000. The town is approximately 30 miles from a metropolitan area with a population of approximately 500,000. Although that larger city has a performing arts center, the investors believe that the residents of Smalltown, who are fiercely loyal to their town, would rather attend concerts in the restored opera house than drive 30 miles for performances in the larger city. Moreover, the investors, who are local residents, think that the restored opera house and its programs may attract tourists and residents of nearby towns and serve as a focal point for the revitalization of Smalltown's downtown area. Because the restoration is expected to cost about $5 million, the investors want to determine the potential success of the opera house.

e. You want to assess the nonmedical community's knowledge of and attitude toward the practice of off-label prescribing.

f. Many city residents want a space in which their dogs can get exercise and interact with other animals. Off-leash dog parks have met that need in some areas. A dog park may be a fenced-in area in a city or county park, or it may be a freestanding facility devoted solely to canine capers. A local service club, such as Kiwanis, wants to determine the level of interest in an off-leash dog park, desired amenities, acceptable fees, and so on. The club plans to use the instrument to get information from residents of a major apartment complex that allows tenants to have pets but has no exercise area for animals.

g. Technology has brought many supposed timesaving devices to the consumer market, such as automatic teller machines, self-serve gasoline pumps, and self-checkout stations in supermarkets and home improvement stores. Some consumers, however, are becoming increasingly frustrated with the loss of personal service in the self-service economy. A retail merchants' association in your area wants to evaluate consumer attitudes toward consumer service in a particular sector of the economy (for example, hospitality, industry, retail clothing sales, banking, etc.).

h. As the baby-boomer generation approaches retirement, many U.S. citizens and politicians are concerned about the continued viability of the Social Security system. Find at least three articles on the Internet that address this issue, particularly options for modifying retirement eligibility standards and the formula for retirement payments. Your representative to the U.S. Congress wants to determine attitudes about changes in Social Security retirement eligibility and benefits. Assume that the study will target a sample of men and women in two age-groups: 20 to 40 and 50 to 70.

i. A major manufacturer and distributor of energy-efficient replacement windows wants to survey its recent customers to determine their satisfaction with the entire process of buying and installing replacement windows. The company wants to be able to analyze the responses in terms of customer demographics, number of windows purchased, and payment option selected. You may add other items you think would be relevant in a decision to make this type of purchase.

j. The Young Lawyers Division of the South Carolina Bar offers a clinic to families who have purchased Habitat for Humanity homes to help those home owners draw up a will. A young lawyers group in your area wants to offer a similar service. They have asked you to develop a form that the potential clients could complete before they appear at the clinic site. The lawyers plan to deliver the form by mail, along with a letter inviting the target group to attend the clinic. The form is intended to help the client think of provisions he or she would like to include in a will.

k. Deconstruction is the careful removal of salvageable materials, such as flooring, light fixtures, cabinetry, doors, and so on, from homes that are being remodeled or destroyed. A primary objective of deconstruction is to reduce the amount of debris going into landfills. Much of the material can be reused in a remodeling job, or the materials can be donated to a nonprofit such as Habitat for Humanity ReStore. As a reporter for your local newspaper, you want to get information from a family that has employed deconstruction while remodeling *its* home.

l. In May 2011, the Texas legislature enacted a law that requires every college student to be vaccinated against bacterial meningitis. As a reporter for your college newspaper, determine students' knowledge of the threat of bacterial meningitis on college campuses and their attitudes toward required vaccinations to protect against the infection.

m. A growing trend in employee medical care is the establishment of on-site health centers in which a company's employees can see a nurse practitioner who is able to write prescriptions, a health coach, a medical assistant, or a collaborating physician for minor health issues. Some health centers also have pharmacies that can supply common prescription drugs. The employee often is assessed a lower co-pay than would be required if the employee went to a doctor's office. The on-site center is not meant to replace a relationship with a primary care physician. It is intended to provide easier access to basic, uncomplicated medical care. A major employer in your area wants to assess employees' uses of and reactions to services provided at its clinic.

4. In Application 4, identify any situations (a–m) for which necessary data could be collected using two or more single-question polls.

References

1. For further discussion of active methods of data collection, see Brace, I. (2004). *Questionnaire design.* London & Sterling, VA: Kogan Page; Bradburn, N., Sudman, S., & Wansink, B. (2004). *Asking questions.* San Francisco: Jossey-Bass; Stevens, R. E., Bruce, W., Sherwood, P. K., & Ruddick, M. E. (2006). *The marketing research guide* (2nd ed.). New York: Best Business Books.
2. Brace, I. (2004). pp. 37–42.

APPLICATION 13.1 ITEM 1

SPORT UTILITY VEHICLE SAFETY QUESTIONNAIRE

Name _____ Address _____

Occupation _____ Age _____ Sex _____

Vehicles Owned _____

INSTRUCTIONS: This questionnaire contains several statements about the growing practice of installing air horns on sport-utility vehicles (SUVs). Indicate the degree to which you agree or disagree with each statement by writing the number that best expresses your feelings: (1) strongly agree, (2) agree, (3) neither agree nor disagree, (4) disagree, or (5) strongly disagree.

___ 1.   I don't like to be startled while driving my car.

___ 2.   I drive safely and am intimidated by large SUVs.

___ 3.   I feel nervous when an SUV driver honks a loud horn at me.

___ 4.   SUV drivers should not crowd other drivers on the road.

___ 5.   The city should enforce the anti-noise laws more stringently.

___ 6.   Drivers should be able to report the license plate number of an SUV whose driver has blasted a loud air horn.

___ 7.   SUV drivers who use loud horns should be ticketed for a traffic violation.

___ 8.   I would consider installing an air horn on one of my vehicles.

___ 9.   A law should be enacted to prohibit the use of air horns on passenger vehicles, including SUVs.

___ 10.   I rarely sound the horn on my vehicle.

___ 11.   I always drive cautiously and considerately.

APPLICATION 13.2 ITEM 2

National Recreation and Parks Association

22377 Belmont Ridge Road, Ashburn, VA 20148
703-555-0784; www.nrpa.org

Instructions: Indicate your answers clearly with a check mark in the appropriate box. Then return the form in the enclosed envelope. Your name, address, and responses will remain confidential. Results will be published in an upcoming issue of P & R News.

1. Have you visited a national park within the past two years?

   Yes ____   No ____

2. What park activities do you enjoy?

3. Would you be willing to make a reservation to enter popular parks during the peak season if reservations would reduce crowding and help protect park resources?

   Yes ____   No ____

4. In general, how well do you think natural resources in the national parks are being protected?

5. For its size, Minnesota's Voyageurs National Park has more land for snowmobile use than any other national park. Congress is considering opening the remainder of the park wilderness areas to snowmobiles. Should these wilderness areas be opened to the noise and pollution of snowmobiles?

   Yes ____   No ____

6. At national parks like Grand Canyon and Great Smoky Mountains, companies offer low-flying airplane or helicopter sightseeing trips. Do you think these noisy flights should be limited or banned?

   Yes ____   No ____

7. Would you be willing to make a financial contribution if it could help prevent a full-scale crisis in our national park system?

   Yes ____   No ____

© Cengage Learning 2013

APPLICATION 13.3 ITEM 3

Good Life Recreation Research

P.O. Box 12345   Asheville, NC 28748   888.123.4567

February 1, 2013

Dear Winslow Hills Resident

When you chose a home in Winslow Hills, you demonstrated your appreciation for a gracious yet convenient lifestyle. We're sure you do not want that lifestyle threatened by businesses that would increase the traffic and noise in your neighborhood. On the other hand, you might welcome a facility that would give you easier access to a recreational activity that you enjoy.

A developer recently purchased property at 1924 Adger Road, approximately a half mile from the entrance to Winslow Hills. The developer wants to construct a recreational facility that will appeal to Winslow Hills residents. He is currently considering a skatepark, but he is open to other suggestions. By completing the enclosed questionnaire, you may influence the developer's decisions.

Please return the questionnaire before February 28. Send it to the address shown above.

Sincerely

Taylor Kelly

Enc. Questionnaire

APPLICATION 13.4 ITEM 4

Winslow Hills Recreation Survey

Instructions: Select one adult (age 18 or older) from your household to complete this questionnaire. That person should participate regularly in at least one recreational requiring physical exertion. That person should answer each question as it applies to him or her only.

1. Who is answering this questionnaire?

   Unmarried head of household   ( )

   Wife   ( )

   Husband   ( )

   Other (specify)   _____

2. What is your age?

   18–24   ( )

   25–34   ( )

   34–44   ( )

   45–54   ( )

   55–64   ( )

   65 or older   ( )

3. How long have you lived in Winslow Hills?

   1 year or less   ( )

   1–3 years   ( )

   3–5 years   ( )

   Over 5 years   ( )

4. Where did you live before moving to Winslow Hills? _____

5. How many adults (age 18 or older) live in this household? _____

6. How many full-time wage earners live in this household? _____

7. What leisure time activity do you enjoy most? (Please check only one.)

   Cycling ( )   Golfing ( )   Skateboarding ( )

   Swimming ( )   Playing tennis ( )   Walking or jogging ( )

   Other (specify) _____

continued

APPLICATION 13.4 CONTINUED

8. When do you primarily engage in that activity? (Please check no more than two items.)

Before going to work or school   (   ) After coming home from school or work   (   )

While at my place of work or school (   ) Primarily on weekends   (   )

Primarily on weekdays   (   ) Other (specify)   _____

9. What would be your reaction to the development of a membership-only, 24-hour, seven-day-a-week skate park at 1924 Adger Road (approximately a half mile from the entrance to Winslow Hills)?

Very pleased   (   )

Somewhat pleased   (   )

Indifferent   (   )

Somewhat displeased   (   ) (Go to item 12.)

Very displeased   (   ) (Go to item 12.)

10. How likely would you be to use a skate park at the proposed location?

Very likely   (   )

Somewhat likely   (   )

Unsure   (   )

Somewhat unlikely   (   )

Very unlikely   (   )

11. How much would you be willing to pay for a membership in the skate park? (Go to item 13.)

12. Please explain why you would be displeased.

13. Thank you for completing this questionnaire. Return it to the address given in the cover letter.

Documenting Data Sources

After you have read this chapter, you should be able to:

1. Prepare an annotated bibliography.

2. Construct a list of works cited in a report, using the style recommended by the American Psychological Association, the Modern Language Association, or the University of Chicago Press.

3. Construct references and in-text citations, using the style recommended by the American Psychological Association, the University of Chicago Press, or the Modern Language Association.

4. Use tools in Microsoft Word 2010 and on the Web to simplify the creation of citations and source lists.

5. Use standard explanatory abbreviations within the text and references of your reports.

THIS CHAPTER ILLUSTRATES THE MECHANICS of documenting the sources of data you use for your reports. Examples demonstrate the three styles most commonly used in business today: those recommended by the American Psychological Association (APA), the University of Chicago Press (CHIC), and the Modern Language Association (MLA). Each of those organizations publishes a style manual that is available in most bookstores.

Why You Should Acknowledge Data Sources

As you well know, ethical, experienced writers agree that every writer should acknowledge his or her unique sources of information for three reasons:

- The business and academic communities expect honesty in all transactions. When you indicate where or from whom you obtained unique information, you are following a standard academic and business practice.
- The business and academic communities appreciate the ability to build on previous knowledge. When you indicate where you obtained your information, you are enabling others to find the data and use it in their business or academic research.
- The business and academic communities respect individual contributions. When you document the sources of data that you acquired from others, including direct

quotations and paraphrased material, the readers may infer that any undocumented material is your contribution to the body of work.

In short, appropriate acknowledgment of data sources establishes your credibility as a writer and researcher.

Bibliography and Footnotes

Historically, source acknowledgments in a report consisted of footnotes placed at the bottom of the page and a bibliography. *Footnotes* cited the exact location of evidence or authority for specific statements. *Bibliographical entries* cited sources as whole entities.

A bibliography should list all references cited in the body of a report; it may also list other pertinent references of potential benefit to the reader. Technically, *bibliography* refers to writings on a particular subject; hence, interviews, speeches, and radio or television broadcasts would not logically be part of a bibliography.

A bibliography is sometimes prepared to direct the reader to useful sources of information about a subject. An *annotated bibliography,* a list of books or other publications with appropriate comments about each entry, is useful in such instances, as shown in Illustration 14.1. Note that the items in the annotated bibliography are printed in bold type merely to separate the citations from the descriptive information. This is not a standard requirement for an annotated bibliography, but it does contribute to readability. Note also that the entries are written in the bibliographic style recommended by *The Chicago Manual of Style.* Subsequent examples will be shown in the style recommended by that source for a reference list, which differs from its style for a bibliography.

APA, CHIC, and MLA reserve the term *bibliography* for a list that includes more than the works actually cited in the text. Current business practice permits—even encourages—variations that effectively combine footnote and bibliographic references. This chapter focuses on those techniques.

Reference List, Works Cited

For a list that includes only the works cited in the text, the APA, CHIC, and MLA manuals recommend the following practices. Illustrations 14.2 and 14.3 show a reference list and works cited page, respectively.

- APA: Use *References* to identify sources cited in the text.
- CHIC: Use *Reference List* to identify sources cited in the text; reserve *Bibliography* to identify works for background or further reading. In *The Chicago Manual of Style,* protocols for a reference list differ slightly from protocols for a bibliography.
- MLA: Use *Works Cited* to identify sources cited in the text. (*Literature Cited* may be used if the list contains only printed sources—a rare occurrence these days). Use *Works Consulted* if the list contains items used but not cited in the report.

Guides for Print Sources

Observe these general guides when preparing a bibliography, list of references, or list of works cited:

- Arrange entries in alphabetical order. In general, alphabetize entries by the author's last name, using the letter-by-letter system. That is, "remember that

ILLUSTRATION 14.1   ANNOTATED BIBLIOGRAPHY, CHICAGO MANUAL OF STYLE

Annotated Bibliography

Bradley, John. *Inside Egypt: The Land of Pharaohs on the Brink of Revolution.* New York: Palgrave Macmillan, 2008.

Book provided insight into politics and culture of Egypt. Author cautioned that history repeats itself and predicted 2011's political uprising. Author reported firsthand experience.

Bradley, Matt. "Egyptians Reach Out to Iran." *The Wall Street Journal,* April 19, 2011.

Newspaper article explained why warmer relationship between Egypt and Iran worried U.S., Israel, and Saudi Arabia. Author contrasted recent events with absence of Egypt-Iran diplomatic relations since 1980. Author predicted no radical change in Egypt and U.S. relationship as a result of this change.

Wilkins, Becca. "Boosting Brazil." *International Construction.* December 2009. Accessed October 10, 2011, in Business Source Premier.

Database article focused on construction plans in Brazil for 2014 FIFA World Cup and 2016 Olympic games. Author stated that huge capital investments are needed for development of airports, railways, roads, and sports arenas. *Note:* Important information for team members studying transportation issues and status of sporting events in relation to team's client.

"Brazil: Economic Policy and External Debt." World Bank. Accessed October 10, 2011. http://data.worldbank.org/country/brazil.

Website included database of Brazil's economic and social indicators. Showed line charts to convey data for the indicators and years you select. *Note:* A vital source of information information for comparing Cairo, Egypt, and São Paulo, Brazil.

© Cengage Learning 2013

'nothing comes before something': Brown, J. R. precedes Browning, A. R., even though *i* comes before *j* in the alphabet."[1]

- Use a solid seven-space line instead of repeating an author's name. To avoid possible errors when sorting the items, replace the name with the line in your final draft. See the entry for Martin and Chaney and the entry immediately below it in Illustration 14.2.
- Be consistent in preparing your list; select one style and follow it throughout your report. Follow the sequence, capitalization, and punctuation illustrated in this chapter or in the style manual cited.

ILLUSTRATION 14.2   REFERENCES LIST IN APA STYLE

References

Ball, D., & Bryan-Low, C. (2011, April 19). Arabic names spell trouble for banks. *The Wall Street Journal*, pp. A10.

Lauring, J. (2011, July). Intercultural organizational communication: The social organizing of interaction in international encounters. *Journal of Business Communication, 48*(3), 231-255.

Martin, J. S., & Chaney, L. H. (2009). *Global business etiquette: A guide to international communication and customs* (Reprint ed.). Westport, CT: Praeger.

_____ & _____. (2009). *Passport to success: The essential guide to business culture and customs in America's largest trading partners.* Westport, CT: Praeger.

Nikolaev, A. G. (Ed.). (2011). *Ethical issues in international communication.* New York: Palgrave Macmillan USA.

Ryall, C., & Luna, D. (2011, Fall). The other meaning of fluency: Content accessibility and language in advertising to bilinguals. *Journal of Advertising, 40*(3), 73-84. Retrieved October 10, 2011, from Business Source Premier.

Sall, A. M. (2010, April 13). Cross-cultural communication strategy—the 4 building blocks [Web log post]. Retrieved from http://thecrossculturalconnector.com

Siczek, M. M. (2011, March). Book Reviews Section [Review of the book *The global English style guide: Writing clear, translatable documentation for a global market*, by J. R. Kohl]. *Business communication quarterly, 74*(1):89-92.

Sokuvitz, S., & Reza, A. (2011). Crossing boundaries: A collaborative approach to teaching global communication. *Proceedings of ABC-SEUS conference.* http://businesscommunication .org/conventions/abc-conventions-proceedings/2011-abc-seus-conference-proceedings

Tips for traveling abroad. (n.d.). Retrieved from http://travel.state.gov

© Cengage Learning 2013

Examples in this chapter demonstrate the most common types of citations that appear in reference lists. The examples for APA, CHIC, and MLA styles come from the latest edition of each organization's style manual: *Publication Manual of the American Psychological Association*, 6th ed. (2010); *The Chicago Manual of Style*, 16th ed. (2010); and the *MLA Handbook for Writers of Research Papers*, 7th ed. (2009, respectively). The latter is available online (http://www.chicagomanualofstyle.org/tools_citationguide. html), and part of the APA guide is available, too (http://www.apastyle.org). The MLA style guide is accessible online by using an access code printed in your copy of the printed manual. In addition, many colleges and universities are licensed to incorporate all or part of these manuals—especially APA and MLA—on their library websites. If you must cite sources that are not illustrated here, refer to the appropriate manual.

Occasionally you may use a source that the style manual does not cover exactly. In those instances, combine the manual's basic guides and patterns in logical ways to help your readers find your sources if they choose. When in doubt, provide as much information as you can. More information is always better than less. Also, in the following reference examples, as well as in the manuals themselves, you may see abbreviations, such as *n.d.* or *n. pag.*, that are unfamiliar to you. In that case, see the Standard Abbreviations list on page 426.

For APA, MLA, and CHIC publication styles, follow the general rules for sequence, punctuation, and capitalization shown for periodicals (journals, magazines, and newspapers) and books. Remember, however, that you may have to provide additional information, such as the date on which you accessed an online source and its location (Web address). As described in Chapter 12, keeping detailed records while collecting your data will save time when you must cite your references.

Guides for Web-Based and Miscellaneous Sources

With Web-based sources now the rule rather than the exception, the latest editions of the APA, CHIC, and MLA style manuals differ from previous editions. In the following reference examples, you will notice the use of uniform resource locators (URLs) in APA and CHIC references for identifying and retrieving Web-based sources. The MLA manual recommends omitting URLs because (1) locations often change; (2) the URL may be specific to a member or subscriber or session (as when a deep-search engine pulls up a source "on the fly"); and (3) some URLs are extremely long and complicated, making them hard to type accurately. However, the MLA manual approves the use of a URL (at the end of the reference, enclosed in angle brackets) whenever your readers may be unable to find the source without a Web address.[2] In Illustration 14.3, notice the Sokuvitz entry.

Using Uniform Resource Locators (URLs)

Follow these guides for typing URLs in running text and especially in lists of sources:[3]

1. Always include the protocol (usually http://) in the URL.
2. To ensure an accurate URL, copy it from the address box in your browser and paste it into your report.
3. Omit a URL for sources in a full-text database.

ILLUSTRATION 14.3 WORKS CITED IN MLA STYLE

Works Cited

Ball, Deborah, and Cassell Bryan-Low. "Arabic Names Spell Trouble for Banks." *Wall Street Journal* 19 Apr. 2011. A10. Print.

Lauring, Jakob. "Intercultural Organizational Communication: The Social Organizing of Interaction in International Encounters." *Journal of Business Communication.* 48.3 (2011): 231-255. Print.

Martin, Jeanette S., and Lillian H. Chaney. *Global Business Etiquette: A Guide to International Communication and Customs.* Reprint ed. Westport, CT: Praeger, 2009. Print.

_____ & _____. *Passport to Success: The Essential Guide to Business Culture and Customs in America's Largest Trading Partners.* Westport, CT: Praeger, 2009. Print.

Nikolaev, Alexander G., ed. *Ethical Issues in International Communication.* New York: Palgrave Macmillan USA, 2011. Print.

Ryall, Carroll, and David Luna. "The Other Meaning of Fluency: Content Accessibility and Language in Advertising to Bilinguals." *Journal of Advertising.* 40.3 (2011): 73-84. *Business Source Premier.* Web. 10 Oct. 2011.

Sall, Amadou M. "Cross-cultural communication strategy—the 4 building blocks." *The Cross-Cultural Connector.* 13 Apr. 2010. Web. 10 Oct. 2011. <http:// thecrossculturalconnector.com>.

Siczek, Megan M. Rev. of *The Global English Style Guide: Writing Clear, Translatable Documentation for a Global Market*, by John R. Kohl. *Business Communication Quarterly*, Mar. 2011: 89-92. Print.

Sokuvitz, Sydel, and Amir Reza. "Crossing Boundaries: A Collaborative Approach to Teaching Global Communication." *Proceedings of ABC-SEUS Conference*, March 31-April 2, 2011: Communicating Across the Generations. Ed. Fiona Barnes. Web. 10 Oct. 2011. <http://businesscommunication.org/conventions/abc-conventions-proceedings/2011-abc-seus-conference-proceedings>.

"Tips for Traveling Abroad." *Travel.State.Gov.* Bureau of Consular Affairs, U.S. Department of State, n.d. Web. 10 Oct. 2011. <http://travel.state.gov>.

4. In running text, do not begin a sentence with a URL. Instead, within the sentence, give the title or sponsor of the website followed by the URL in parentheses.

5. To break a URL between lines, never insert a hyphen. (In Microsoft Word 2010, when Hyphenation is on, ensure that a hyphen is not inserted automatically in a long URL.)

6. Break URLs at punctuation points to prevent an excessively ragged right margin on the sources list. Divide *before* any of these marks: a comma, dot (.), hyphen, number sign (#), percent symbol (%), question mark, single slash (/), tilde (~), and underline (_). Break a URL *after* a colon or a double slash (//). If necessary, a URL may be divided before or after any other punctuation or symbol.

7. Test URLs in your references for each report draft. If the source you are citing has moved, change the URL to the new location. Of course, if a source is no longer available, you must substitute another source of the same quality or drop it from the report.

8. If you create your report in Microsoft Word 2010 and will post the report online, make sure each URL is an active hyperlink. Simply tap Enter after typing the URL or select the URL; then on the Insert tab, Links group, click Hyperlink. Then, on the Insert Hyperlink dialog, click OK.

9. If you will distribute a printout of your report created in Word 2010, remove each automatically inserted hyperlink from your final draft. Select the blue, underlined text. On the Insert tab, Links group, click Hyperlinks. On the Hyperlinks dialog, click Remove Link. Taking this step ensures that all text prints in the same color/shade.

Using Digital Object Identifiers (DOIs)

In the future, you may see the use of URLs in source lists give way to digital object identifiers (DOIs). (*Note:* The DOI system was developed by an international group of publishers. The DOIs serve as locators of textual content and links between bodies of text. The system greatly streamlines Internet use and aids publishers in content management—the easy, speedy handling of huge amounts of text.) In fact, current editions of the APA and CHIC style manuals refer to the DOI system.

A DOI is a string of alphanumeric characters assigned by the International DOI Foundation to identify a Web document, such as a journal, magazine, or newspaper article or report. A DOI contains information about the object it names, including where it can be found on the Internet. While data about the article—including its location on the Web—may change over time, its DOI name will not change. In an online article, a reader can click DOIs in the reference list to access each of those online references.

Since a DOI is assigned to an article, not to a specific version of it, a DOI is preferable to a URL, according to *The Chicago Manual of Style*. A single DOI applies to a Web article in multiple formats and in earlier and later print versions as well. Therefore, a DOI in your list of references would eliminate any need to specify the electronic format (for example, PDF or XML).[4]

Currently, only a relatively few organizations can assign DOIs—those willing to pay for membership in the DOI system that can also meet the contractual obligations of the system. A DOI name has two parts, separated by a slash (/). The first part (prefix) identifies who registered the name, and the suffix, chosen by the registrant, identifies the object associated with that DOI. Currently, all DOI names begin with "10." Thus, a DOI takes this form: 10.0000/00000. If an article has a DOI assigned, you will usually find it on the first page, near the copyright notice. Place it at the end of a reference in place of the more familiar Web address. (***Note:*** In some instances, your browser's address box may show a URL and DOI combined. Expect this combination to increase over time; eventually, though, you can expect to see only DOIs.)

The style manuals address diverse published media—from book reviews and concerts to television shows and videos—beyond the scope of this chapter. Additional examples include art works, DVDs, online maps, music recordings, photographs, plays, and podcasts.

Style Guides for APA, CHIC, and MLA

The following examples show the three most-used styles for listing sources.

Periodicals

Journal Article, One Author

APA: Lauring, J. (2011, July). Intercultural organizational communication: The social organizing of interaction in international encounters. *Journal of Business Communication, 48*(3), 231–255.

CHIC: Lauring, Jakob. "Intercultural Organizational Communication: The Social Organizing of Interaction in International Encounters." *Journal of Business Communication 48*, no. 3(2011): 231–255.

MLA: Lauring, Jakob. "Intercultural Organizational Communication: The Social Organizing of Interaction in International Encounters." *Journal of Business Communication. 48*.3(2011): 231. Print.

Journal Article, Multiple Authors

APA: Erickson, S. L., & Weber, M., & Segovia, J. (2011). Using communication theory to analyze corporate reporting. *Journal of Business Communication, 48*(2), 207–223.

CHIC: Erickson, Sheri L., Marsha Weber, and Joann Segovia. "Using Communication Theory to Analyze Corporate Reporting." *Journal of Business Communication 48*, no. 2(2011): 207–223.

MLA: Erickson, Sheri L., Marsha Weber, and Joann Segovia. "Using Communication Theory to Analyze Corporate Reporting." *Journal of Business Communication 48*.2 (2011): 207–223. Print.

Journal Article in Full-Text Database

APA: Ryall, C., & Luna, D. (2011, Fall). The other meaning of fluency: Content accessibility and language in advertising to bilinguals. *Journal of Advertising, 40*(3), 73–84. Retrieved October 10, 2011, from Business Source Premier.

CHIC: Ryall, Carrol, and David Luna. "The Other Meaning of Fluency: Content Accessibility and Language in Advertising to Bilinguals." *Journal of Advertising 4*, no. 3(2011): 73–84. Retrieved October 9, 2011. Business Source Premier.

MLA: Ryall, Carroll and David Luna. "The Other Meaning of Fluency: Content Accessibility and Language in Advertising to Bilinguals." *Journal of Advertising 40*.3(2011): 73–84. *Business Source Premier*. Web. 10 Oct. 2011.

Magazine Article

APA: Shinn, S. (2011, January/February). On the edge of innovation. *BizEd, 10*(1), 20–24.

CHIC: Shinn, Sharon. "On the Edge of Innovation." *BizEd*, January/February, 2011, 20–24.

MLA: Shinn, Sharon. "On the Edge of Innovation." *BizEd* Jan./Feb. 2011: 20–24. Print.

Magazine Article on Web

APA: Schulte, E. (2011, October 13). How Nobel peace prize winner Leymah Gbowee unified Liberian women. *Fast Company*, n.p. Advance online publication. Retrieved October 11, 2011, from http://www.fastcompany.com/1786780/nobel-peace-prize-winner-leymah-gbowee

CHIC: Schulte, Erin. "How Nobel Peace Prize Winner Leymah Gbowee Unified Liberian Women." *Fast Company*, October 13, 2011 (Advance online edition) Accessed October 11, 2011. http://www.fastcompany.com/1786780/nobel-peace-prize-winner-leymah-gbowee.

MLA: Schulte, Erin. "How Nobel Peace Prize Winner Leymah Gbowee Unified Liberian Women." *Fast Company*. 13 Oct. 2011: n.p. Web. Advance online issue 11 Oct. 2011. <http://www.fastcompany.com/1786780/nobel-peace-prize-winner-leymah-gbowee>. (Include the URL only if reader probably cannot locate the source without it or when your instructor requires it.)

Newspaper Article, Authors Cited

APA: Ball, D., & Bryan-Low, C. (2011, April 19). Arabic names spell trouble for banks. *The Wall Street Journal*, p. A10.

CHIC: Ball, Deborah, and Cassell Bryan-Low. "Arabic Names Spell Trouble for Banks." *The Wall Street Journal*, April 19, 2011, sec. A.

MLA: Ball, Deborah, and Cassell Bryan-Low. "Arabic Names Spell Trouble for Banks." *Wall Street Journal 19* Apr. 2011. A10. Print.

Newspaper Article, No Author Cited

APA: Photo ID bill a costly solution in search of a problem. (2011, March 15). *The State*, p. A11.

CHIC: "Photo ID Bill a Costly Solution in Search of a Problem." *The State*, March 15, 2011, sec. A11.

MLA: "Photo ID Bill a Costly Solution in Search of a Problem." *State* 15 Mar. 2011. A11. Print.

Newspaper Article on Web

APA: Holthaus, D. (2011, October 12). P & G releases sustainability report. *Cincinnati Enquirer*. Retrieved from http://news.cincinnati.com/article/20111012/BIZ01/310120020/P-G-releases-sustainability-report

CHIC: Holthaus, David. "P & G Releases Sustainability Report." *Cincinnati Enquirer*, October 12, 2011. http://news.cincinnati.com/article/20111012/BIZ01/310120020/P-G-releases-sustainability-report.

MLA: Holthaus, David. "P & G Releases Sustainability Report." *Cincinnati Enquirer* 12 Oct. 2011. n. pag. 14 Oct. 2011. Web. <http://news.cincinnati.com/article/20111012/BIZ01/310120020/P-G-releases-sustainability-report>. (Omit URL if instructor does not require it and reader likely can find the source without it.)

Newspaper Article, Full-Text Database

APA: Stuart, E. (2011, July 18). Mosaic marketing takes a fresh look at changing society [Electronic version]. *New York Times*, p. B3. Retrieved October 13, 2011, from EBSCO.

CHIC: Stuart, Elliott. "Mosaic Marketing Takes a Fresh Look at Changing Society." *New York Times*, July 18, 2011, sec. B, p. 3. Accessed October 13, 2011. EBSCO.

MLA: Stuart, Elliott. "Mosaic Marketing Takes a Fresh Look at Changing Society." *New York Times* 18 July 2011: B3. EBSCO. Web. 13 Oct. 2011.

Website Article

APA: Tips for traveling abroad. (n.d.). In Travel.State.Gov. Retrieved October 10, 2011, from http://travel.state.gov

CHIC: U.S. Department of State. "Tips for Traveling Abroad." Accessed October 10, 2011. <http://travel.state.gov>. (If a "last modified" date is available, use it in place of the "accessed" date.)

MLA: "Tips for Traveling Abroad." U.S. Department of State, n.d. Web. 10 Oct. 2011. <http://travel.state.gov>.

Books, Brochures, and Pamphlets

Entire Book, One Author

APA: Gbowee, L. (2011). *Mighty be our powers*. New York: Beast Books/Perseus.

CHIC: Gbowee, Leymah. 2011. *Mighty Be Our Powers*. New York: Beast Books/Perseus.

MLA: Gbowee, Leymah. *Mighty Be Our Powers*. New York: Beast Books/Perseus, 2011. Print.

Book, Multiple Authors

APA: Martin, J. S., & Chaney, L. H. (2009). *Passport to success: The essential guide to business culture and customs in America's largest trading partners*. Westport, CT: Praeger.

CHIC: Martin, Jeanette S., and Lillian H. Chaney. 2009. *Passport to Success: The Essential Guide to Business Culture and Customs in America's Largest Trading Partners*. Westport, CT: Praeger.

MLA: Martin, Jeanette S., and Lillian H. Chaney. *Passport to Success: The Essential Guide to Business Culture and Customs in America's Largest Trading Partners*. Westport, CT: Praeger, 2009. Print.

Book on Web

APA: Benedict, E. L., & Benedict, R. P. (2010). *How to analyze people on sight through the science of human analysis: The five human types* [Ebook version]. Retrieved October 13, 2011, from Project Gutenberg. http://www.gutenberg.org/files/30601/30601-h/30601-h.htm

CHIC: Benedict, Elsie Lincoln, and Ralph Paine Benedict. 2010. *How to Analyze People on Sight through the Science of Human Analysis: The Five Human Types. Ebook ed.* Project Gutenberg, http://www.gutenberg.org/files/30601/30601-h/30601-h.htm.

MLA: Benedict, Elsie Lincoln, and Ralph Paine Benedict. *How to Analyze People on Sight through the Science of Human Analysis: The Five Human Types.* 2010. *Project Gutenberg.* Web. 13 Oct. 2011. <http://www.gutenberg.org/files/30601/30601-h/30601-h.htm>.

Chapter in a Book

APA: Gallo, C. (2010). Master stage presence. In *The presentation secrets of Steve Jobs: How to be insanely great in front of any audience* (pp. 167–178). New York: McGraw-Hill.

CHIC: Gallo, Carmine. 2010. "Master Stage Presence." In *The Presentation Secrets of Steve Jobs: How to Be Insanely Great in Front of Any Audience,* 167–178. New York: McGraw-Hill.

MLA: Gallo, Carmine. "Master Stage Presence" in *The Presentation Secrets of Steve Jobs: How to Be Insanely Great in Front of Any Audience.* New York: McGraw-Hill, 2010. 167–78. Print.

Entry in a Reference Book

APA: Hoover's, Inc. Lego A/S. (2011). Lego A/S. In *Hoover's Handbook of World Business 2011: Profiles of Major Global Enterprises* (18th ed., pp. 207–208). Austin, TX: Author.

CHIC: Hoover's, Inc. 2011. *Hoover's Handbook of World Business 2011: Profiles of Major Global Enterprises,* 18th ed., s.v. "Lego A/S." Austin, TX: Hoover's, Inc.

MLA: Hoover's, Inc. *Hoover's Handbook of World Business 2011: Profiles of Major Global Enterprises.* 18th ed. Austin, TX: Hoover's, Inc., 2011. Print.

Work in a Compilation (Chapter in Edited Book)

APA: Hasnas, J. (2008). The normative theories of business ethics: A guide for the perplexed. In F. Allhoff & A. J. Vaidya (Eds.), *Business in ethical focus: An anthology* (pp. 79–99). Peterborough, ON: Broadview.

CHIC: Hasnas, John. 2008. "The Normative Theories of Business Ethics: A Guide for the Perplexed." In *Business in Ethical Focus: An Anthology,* ed. Fritz Allhoff and Anand J. Vaidya, 79–99. Peterborough, ON: Broadview.

MLA: Hasnas, John. "The Normative Theories of Business Ethics: A Guide for the Perplexed." *Business in Ethical Focus: An Anthology,* ed. Fritz Allhoff and Anand J. Vaidya. Peterborough, ON: Broadview, 2008. 79–99. Print.

Reports on the Web

Corporate Report

APA: *2011 annual report: Innovating for everyday life.* (2011, August 25). In Procter & Gamble. Retrieved October 16, 2011, from http://annualreport.pg.com/annualreport2011/_files/pdf/PG_2011_AnnualReport.pdf

CHIC: Procter and Gamble Company. 2011. *Annual Report: Innovating for Everyday Life.* http://annualreport.pg.com/annualreport2011/_files/pdf/PG_2011_AnnualReport.pdf.

MLA: "2011 Annual Report: Innovating for Everyday Life." Procter & Gamble, 25 Aug., 2011. Web. 16 Oct. 2011. <http://annualreport.pg.com/annualreport2011/_files/pdf/PG_2011_AnnualReport.pdf>.

Government Report, Corporate Author

APA: U.S. Department of Health and Human Services, National Institutes of Health, Office of Extramural Research. (2009). *Data book*. Retrieved from http://report.nih.gov/ndb/pdf/NDB_2009_Final.pdf

CHIC: National Institutes of Health, Office of Extramural Research. 2009. "Data Book" accessed October 14, 2011. http://report.nih.gov/ndb/pdf/NDB_2009_Final.pdf.

MLA: National Institutes of Health, Office of Extramural Research. "Data Book" *National Institute of Health*. U.S. Dept. Health & Human Services. n.d. Web. 14 Oct. 2011. <http://report.nih.gov/ndb/pdf/NDB_2009_Final.pdf>.

Task Force Report, Corporate Author, on the Web

APA: Executive Office of the President of the United States, White House Task Force on Childhood Obesity. (2010). *Report of the White House Task Force on Childhood Obesity to the President*. Retrieved from http://www.letsmove.gov/sites/letsmove.gov/files/TaskForce_on_Childhood_Obesity_May2010_FullReport.pdf

CHIC: Task Force on Childhood Obesity. 2010. *White House Task Force on Childhood Obesity Report to the President*, accessed October 15, 2011, http://www.letsmove.gov/sites/letsmove.gov/files/TaskForce_on_Childhood_Obesity_May2010_FullReport.pdf

MLA: Task Force on Childhood Obesity. *White House Task Force on Childhood Obesity Report to the President*. Washington: Executive Office of the President of the United States, 2010. Web. <http://www.letsmove.gov/sites/letsmove.gov/files/TaskForce_on_Childhood_Obesity_May2010_FullReport.pdf>.

Miscellaneous Sources

You may also obtain useful information from miscellaneous sources, such as blogs, conference proceedings, newsletters, and personal communication. Although such publications may seem relatively simple, they are often protected by copyright. Ethical standards also require acknowledgment of personal communications used in the preparation of your report.

Blog Post

APA: Sall, A. M. (2010, April 13). Cross-cultural communication strategy—the 4 building blocks [Web log post]. Retrieved from http://thecrossculturalconnector.com/?p=244

CHIC: Sall, Amadou M. *Cross-Cultural Communication Strategy*—The 4 Building Blocks," *The Cross-Cultural Connector* (blog), April 13, 2010, http://thecrossculturalconnector.com/?p=244.

MLA: Sall, Amadou M. "Cross-cultural communication strategy—the 4 building blocks." *The Cross-Cultural Connector*. n. pub. 13 Apr. 2010. Web. 10 Oct. 2011. http://thecrossculturalconnector.com/?p=244.

Conference Proceedings on Web

For conference proceedings in book form, replace locator information with publisher information and page numbers (see Chapter in a Book).

APA: Sokuvitz, S., & Reza, A. (2011). *Crossing boundaries: A collaborative approach to teaching global communication.* Paper presented at the ABC-SEUS Conference, Charleston, SC. Retrieved from http://businesscommunication.org/conventions/ abc-conventions-proceedings/2011-abc-seus-conference-proceedings

CHIC: Sokuvitz, Sydel and Amir Reza. Paper presented at the annual meeting of ABC-SEUS, Charleston, SC, March–April 2011, http://businesscommunication.org.

MLA: Sokuvitz, Sydel and Amir Reza. "Crossing Boundaries: A Collaborative Approach to Teaching Global Communication." *Proceedings of ABC-SEUS Conference*, March 31–April 2, 2011: Communicating Across the Generations. Ed. Fiona Barnes. Web. 10 October 2011. <http://businesscommunication.org/conventions/ abc-conventions-proceedings/2011-abc-seus-conference-proceedings>

Newsletter Article

Newsletter articles may be handled as magazine articles. An entire newsletter may be treated as a book. In any case, provide enough information to identify the document. For example, the company name [in brackets] did not appear in the newsletter title, but this detail would help someone locate the article. (If the newsletter involves a volume and issue number, show them between the newsletter title and page number.)

APA: Green with no compromise. (2011, Spring). *[Owens Corning] Retiree Update*, 3.

CHIC: "Green with No Compromise," 2011, *[Owens Corning] Retiree Update*, Spring, 3.

MLA: "Green with No Compromise." *[Owens Corning] Retiree Update*. Spring 2011: 1. Print.

Newsletter Article on Web

APA: EIP requires documentation for dependents. (2011, October). *EIP Direct*. Retrieved from http://www.eip.sc.gov/news/newsletter_detail.aspx?view=newsletters& id=371

CHIC: "EIP Requires Documentation for Dependents." *EIP Direct*, October 2011, http://www.eip.sc.gov/news/newsletter_detail.aspx?view=newsletters&id=371.

MLA: "EIP Requires Documentation for Dependents." *EIP Direct*. Employee Insurance Program, Oct. 2011. Web. 12 Oct. 2011. <http://www.eip.sc.gov/news /newsletter_ detail.aspx?view=newsletters&id=371>.

Personal Communications

The following pattern can be used for any type of personal communication: conversation, email, interview, letter, memo, and voice mail.

APA: *Because reader cannot verify the information, omit entry from reference list.*

CHIC: *Use only as an endnote or in-text note:* Jill Peek, email to author. February 8, 2011.

MLA: Peek, Jill. "Email & Survey." Message to the author. 8 Feb. 2011. Email.

In-Text Citations

With its strong emphasis on crediting, or documenting, sources, Chapter 12 explained that documentation consists of two parts: (1) an alphabetical list of all references used and (2) a citation in the report text. The American Psychological Association, the University of Chicago, and the Modern Language Association recommend source acknowledgments inserted in the main text in parentheses. (***Note:*** APA and CHIC refers to this citing method as author-date notes, and MLA refers to parenthetical citations.) This practice, as just discussed, requires an alphabetized list of all sources cited. Text in the following examples is paraphrased or quoted from previous reference examples.

Quotation from Book, One Author

APA: According to Carmine Gallo (2010), "When he's at his best, Jobs does three things anyone can, and should, do to enhance one's speaking and presenting skills: he makes eye contact, maintains an open posture, and uses frequent hand gestures" (Gallo, 2010).

CHIC: According to Carmine Gallo (2010, 170), "When he's at his best, Jobs does three things anyone can, and should, do to enhance one's speaking and presenting skills: he makes eye contact, maintains an open posture, and uses frequent hand gestures."

MLA: According to Carmine Gallo, "When he's at his best, Jobs does three things anyone can, and should, do to enhance one's speaking and presenting skills: he makes eye contact, maintains an open posture, and uses frequent hand gestures" (Gallo 170).

Paraphrase of Newspaper Article, Two Authors

APA: Ball and Bryan-Low (2011) noted that transliteration standards common to, say, Chinese and Japanese, are not present in Arabic. Thus, one name may be pronounced different ways in different places. Compounding the problem for banks, these variations in pronunciation carry over to the spelling of names. For example, language experts identify over a hundred alternative spellings for the family name "Gadhafi." (Ball & Bryan-Low)

CHIC: Ball and Bryan-Low (*Wall Street Journal*, April 19, 2011) noted that transliteration standards common to, say, Chinese and Japanese, are not present in Arabic. Thus, one name may be pronounced different ways in different places. Compounding the problem for banks, these variations in pronunciation carry over to the spelling of names. For example, language experts identify over a hundred alternative spellings for the family name "Gadhafi."

MLA: Ball and Bryan-Low noted that transliteration standards common to, say, Chinese and Japanese, are not present in Arabic. Thus, one name may be pronounced different ways in different places. Compounding the problem for banks, these variations in pronunciation carry over to the spelling of names. For example, language experts identify over a hundred alternative spellings for the family name "Gadhafi" (Ball & Bryan-Low A10).

Quotation from Web Article, No Author Cited

APA: The U.S. State Department advises travelers to "let us know your travel plans through the Smart Traveler Enrollment Program, a free online service at https://travelregistration.state.gov. This will help us contact you if there is a family emergency in the U.S., or if there is a crisis where you are traveling. In accordance with the Privacy Act, information on your welfare and whereabouts will not be released to others without your express authorization." ("Tips for Safe Travel")

CHIC: The U.S. State Department advises travelers to "let us know your travel plans through the Smart Traveler Enrollment Program, a free online service at https://travelregistration.state.gov. This will help us contact you if there is a family emergency in the U.S., or if there is a crisis where you are traveling. In accordance with the Privacy Act, information on your welfare and whereabouts will not be released to others without your express authorization." (U.S. Department of State 2011)

MLA: The U.S. State Department advises travelers to "let us know your travel plans through the Smart Traveler Enrollment Program, a free online service at https://travelregistration.state.gov. This will help us contact you if there is a family emergency in the U.S., or if there is a crisis where you are traveling. In accordance with the Privacy Act, information on your welfare and whereabouts will not be released to others without your express authorization." Text identifies corporate author, U.S. State Department. If omitting this ID from text, then quotation should end thus: ... authorization" (U.S. Dept. of State).

Paraphrase of Personal Communication

APA: In an email to the author on February 8, 2011, publisher Jill Peek admitted that the survey plan seemed too impersonal and too scripted. She suggested introducing the telephone survey in a more personal way and then using a checklist as subjects talk rather than asking them specific questions. *Omit personal communication from list of references.*

CHIC: The publisher admitted that the survey plan seemed too impersonal and too scripted. She suggested introducing the telephone survey in a more personal way and then using a checklist as subjects talk rather than asking them specific questions (Jill Peek, personal communication). *Omit personal communication from list of references.*

MLA: The publisher admitted that the survey plan seemed too impersonal and too scripted. She suggested introducing the telephone survey in a more personal way and then using a checklist as subjects talk rather than asking them specific questions (Peek).

Quick Citation Method

An even shorter version of in-text citations is used in some business reports. This system involves consecutively numbering alphabetized source list entries, prepared in APA, CHIC, or MLA, style. An in-text citation then identifies a source by its number in the source list, followed by a colon and page numbers if a page reference is required. In the following APA example, *9* refers to the ninth source listed; *211* refers to page 211 of that source.

Text Citation

Jameson (2011) explained a key difference between plagiarism and copyright infringement. An idea itself cannot be copyrighted (only the specific expression of it), but presenting another writer's idea as one's own is plagiarism (9:211).

Source List

9 Jameson, D. A. (2011, June). Who owns my words? Intellectual property rights as a business issue. *Business Communication Quarterly, 74*(2), 210–215.

Endnotes and Footnotes

In the previous section, you saw a demonstration of in-text citations—a simple, straightforward way to cite sources in a report. Traditionally, instead of in-text citations, writers used notes. In a report, a note is a line of text that contains the writer's comment about a point in the report body or that cites a source supporting the main text. Historically, writers placed notes at the bottom of a page (footnotes). Most contemporary writers who use notes group them immediately after the report body (endnotes). A superscript number in the report body signals a note. The superscript is placed just after the idea the note refers to. Then the same number identifies the footnote or endnote.

Notes used to cite a source appear similar to references; however, if you include a page titled Endnotes, include *an alphabetically arranged list of sources, too.* The APA, CHIC, and MLA style manuals explain how to use notes for citing sources. In addition, the following section explains how Microsoft Word 2010 can simplify the use of superscripts and endnotes. Academic reports often contain footnotes or endnotes, but instead of notes, business writers more often use in-text citations like the ones shown in this chapter.

Report Documentation Tools in Word 2010 and Online

Tools in Word 2010 and on the Web can aid you with in-text citations and lists of sources. Word's tools on the References tab offer advantages, but the online tools described here also deserve your consideration.

Microsoft Word 2010 Tools for Documenting Reports

Advantages of Word 2010 include (1) the ability to insert in-text citations or placeholders as you draft a report, (2) the ability to change a reference list from one style to another, and (3) the ability to reuse a reference as needed to document other reports.

As you type report text using Microsoft® Word 2010, you can place in-text citations and compile a references list automatically by responding to on-screen prompts, such as Author, Title, Publisher, and Year. Word's tools comply with earlier editions of the APA, CHIC, and MLA style manuals. Therefore, when you check each reference for accuracy, you may need to update some of them. Follow these steps whenever you begin drafting a report using Word 2010.

1. On the References tab, Citations & Bibliography group, click the Style down arrow. From the drop-down menu, choose the style of references (APA, Chicago, MLA, or one of seven other styles).

2. While typing your report text, instead of typing an in-text citation, click Insert Citation; then choose Add New Source or Add New Placeholder (to fill in later). Choosing Add New Source opens a dialog.

    a. At the top of the Create Source dialog, select the kind of source to be entered (see Illustration 14.4).

ILLUSTRATION 14.4   **CREATE SOURCE DIALOG IN WORD 2010'S CITATIONS & BIBLIOGRAPHY GROUP**

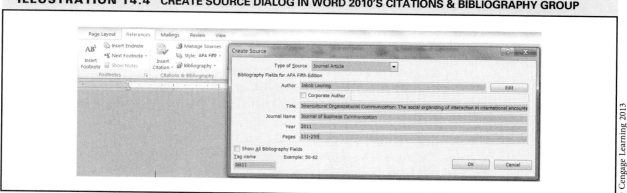

© Cengage Learning 2013

    b. Then type the appropriate information in each window. (To display more windows for additional details, select Show All Bibliography Fields.)

    c. Click OK and Word 2010 inserts an in-text citation in the proper place and style and saves a corresponding reference.

When ready to create your References or Works Cited page, place the insertion point at the top of a new page.

1. On the References tab, Citations & Bibliography group, click the Bibliography down-arrow.

2. At the bottom of the gallery, click Insert Bibliography.

As noted earlier, you will need to check this list and the in-text citations carefully for errors and omissions. An Edit feature enables you to alter the content of a reference: On the References tab, Citations & Bibliography group, click Manage Sources. Use the Source Manager dialog to edit references, consulting Word Help as needed. In addition, you can insert complete references between the existing ones—on those occasions when you need a type of reference unavailable in Word 2010.

Later, if necessary, you can change the documentation style of a report—from MLA to APA, for example. Word 2010 stores an added source in both a Master List and Current List (sources in the displayed report). Whenever you create a new report involving references on the Master List, you can select and copy any or all references into the new Current List, using Manage Sources. Thus, once a source is added to Word, it can be used again and again without retyping.

Incidentally, using Word 2010's Footnotes group (also on the References tab), you can insert a footnote or endnote and convert from one to the other.

Web Tools for Documenting Reports

The following four websites offer documentation tools and seem particularly worthy of your attention. Only one (EasyBib) involves a fee (after a three-day free trial); the others are free. Using Web tools to format sources, you will need to copy and paste each source into your list and then alphabetize the list.

- *KnightCite* (http://www.calvin.edu/library/knightcite). This website (maintained by Calvin College's Hekman Library staff) tops the list because it was among the first to support the latest editions of APA, CHIC, and MLA, and it's free. KnightCite provides a variety of source types, including multimedia sources.
- *Citation Machine* (http://www.citationmachine.net). This website is probably the best known of its kind and offers an impressive range of print and non-print types of references. At the time of this writing, Citation Machine supported the previous edition of CHIC and the latest editions of the APA and MLA style manuals.
- *BibMe* (http://www.bibme.org). This site allows you to search the Web for the book or article title you want to cite. In addition, you can search for website references by URL and films by title, director, or actor. BibMe supported previous editions of APA and CHIC and MLA's latest edition.
- *EasyBib* (http://www.easybib.com). This subscription-based documentation program supports the latest editions of APA, CHIC, and MLA. It offers 58 reference types, neatly categorized by tabs across the top, and includes a citation guide for MLA style. In addition to the subscription plans ($5 monthly, $15 biannually, or $20 annually), EasyBib provides free citation tools that support only the MLA style.

All four online tools are easy to use just by following the prompts. Each site also includes online Help. Do keep in mind, though, that none of the tools described can replace your keen eye and knowledge of the documentation guides.

Standard Abbreviations

To save writing and reading time, the following abbreviations may be used in reports. As you may have noted, some of the abbreviations, like *n.d.* and *n. pag.*, appear often in references. Other abbreviations, like *ibid.* and *op. cit.*, were once commonly used in academic reports by students at all levels but are less common today and are rather unusual in business reports. In any case, before using these abbreviations (except the ones that APA, CHIC, or MLA recommends in references), determine your readers' knowledge of them. When used, these abbreviations are the same in APA, MLA, and CHIC styles.

c. or ca.	about (from Latin *circa*; used in contexts of time; for example, c.1900)
cf.	compare (from Latin *confer*)
chap. or chaps.	chapter or chapters (followed by numbers)
ed. or eds.	editor or editors
ed. or edd.	edition or editions
eg.	for example (from Latin *exempli gratia*)
et al.	and other people (from Latin *et alii*)
etc.	and other things (from Latin *et cetera*)

f	and the following page (for instance, pp. 5f.)
ff.	and the following pages (for instance, pp. 5ff.)
ibid.	the same reference (from Latin *ibidem*; used, especially in footnotes, to repeat an immediately preceding source)
i.e.	that is (from Latin *id est*)
l. or ll.	line or lines continued
loc. cit	place cited (from Latin *loco citato*)
n.d.	no date (used especially concerning the details of publication)
n.n.	no name (used especially concerning the details of publication)
n.p.	no place (used especially concerning the details of publication)
n.pag	no page (used for online references lacking page number)
n. pub.	no publisher (used especially concerning details of publication)
no. or nos.	number or numbers
op. cit.	the work cited (from Latin *opere citato*)
p. or pp.	page or pages
par. or pars.	paragraph or paragraphs
passim	here and there (or throughout)
q.v.	which see (from Latin *quod vide*)
rev.	revised or revision
s.v. or s.vv.	"under the word" or "under the words" (from Latin *sub verbo*)
sec. or secs.	section or sections
sic	thus (usually placed within brackets, not parentheses, to indicate "thus it is in the original document or statement")
trans.	translator or translated
vol. or vols.	volume or volumes

Ethical Considerations

The ethical requirements for documentation were presented in Chapters 12 and 13. The opening section of this chapter also reminded you that the standard of giving credit where credit is due must be followed in all reporting. The *Publication Manual of the American Psychological Association* reminds writers that the purpose of careful documentation is to ensure the accuracy and integrity of information presented in reports and to protect the intellectual property rights of others whose knowledge you have tapped. Enough said: Ethical writers acknowledge their information sources accurately and as completely as possible.

Summary

To acknowledge all data sources that contributed to your report, you can use a brief in-text citation at the point at which you want to acknowledge a source, along with an alphabetized list of sources at the end of the report.

To ensure a degree of uniformity in such acknowledgments, three organizations have published style manuals: the American Psychological Association, the University of Chicago Press, and the Modern Language Association. Since the style manuals differ with respect to punctuation and sequence of information in a citation, you should follow just one style manual consistently throughout your report—after determining which one you are expected to use.

Each style manual publisher also maintains a website at which you can locate answers to frequently asked questions about documentation. In addition, Microsoft Word 2010 and the Internet contain tools that aid you in citing sources.

Topics for Discussion

1. Discuss three reasons why you should provide complete data sources as you write a business report just as you would in an academic one.
2. Compare the APA, MLA, and CHIC styles for citing a book with multiple authors. In what respects do the three styles differ from one another?
3. Compare the APA, MLA, and CHIC styles for citing a journal article with multiple authors and a journal article in a full-text database. In what respects do the three styles differ from one another for the two types of citations?
4. If you have had the experience of wanting to look up some information that is referred to in a newspaper, magazine, or journal article, were you able to find the source document relatively easily? Why or why not? What techniques did you use to find the source document?
5. In what ways does use of the Internet for research differ from use of print sources only? Consider both advantages and disadvantages of Internet research.
6. For the styles cited in this chapter, compare the online APA, CHIC, and MLA manuals. Which do you prefer? Why? (*Hint*: List specific questions about documentation, then search for answers in each manual.)
7. If you have had experience writing a report in a business or nonprofit organization, what documentation was expected? In what ways, if any, do business expectations differ from academic expectations?
8. Describe ethical challenges you have faced as you used data from print sources and/or the World Wide Web.

Applications

1. Find at least five sources (at least two print and two Web based) on one of the following topics or another topic approved by your instructor. Prepare an annotated bibliography of those sources.
   • Reflex sympathetic dystrophy/complex regional pain syndrome. What is it? How is it diagnosed and treated?
   • How business is reacting to terrorism
   • Investment opportunities in Romania
   • The future of private enterprise in the Czech Republic
   • The value of trip cancellation and/or medical evacuation insurance when traveling abroad
   • Why medical professionals encourage all adults to sign a health care power of attorney
   • What you should know about nonverbal communication when you travel for business purposes to (a country of your choice)

2. Form a group with two classmates and assign each person one of the manuals cited in this chapter. Each person is to write the following items in the appropriate reference list style as recommended by the manual he or she is responsible for. If you use BibMe, Citation Machine, EasyBib, or KnightCite, remember to check each reference against examples in the chapter. If illustrations are not given in the text, use the respective manual or online service.

- This fifth (2013) edition of *Contemporary Business Reports*. (See title and copyright pages.)
- A booklet titled "Discover Columbia South Carolina." Published Summer 2011 by Gardener Publications in West Columbia, SC.
- A chapter titled "Physical Grammar" on pages 167–182 of a book titled *Own the Room: Business Presentations That Persuade, Engage & Get Results*, authored by David Booth, Deborah Shames, and Peter Desberg and published by The McGraw-Hill Companies (New York) in 2010. *Hint*: As a general rule, abbreviate publisher names. In this example, using "McGraw-Hill" will clearly identify the publisher.
- An anthology edited by Robert W. Kates titled *Readings in Sustainability Science and Technology*. Publication information: CID Working Paper No. 213. Center for International Development, Harvard University. Cambridge, MA: Harvard University, PDF file, December 2010, on the Web http://www.hks.harvard.edu/var/ezp_site/storage/fckeditor/file/pdfs/centers-programs/centers/cid/publications/faculty/wp/213.pdf.
- An article, "Sustainable and Healthy Communities Research," on the Environmental Protection Agency (EPA) Website (http://www.epa.gov/sustainability). No author cited. Retrieved October 19, 2011. Site last updated September 21, 2011.
- An article in the Winter 2011 issue of *Management Accounting Quarterly* (Vol. 12 Issue 2, pp. 1–10) accessed in this database: Business Source Premier. Authors: Janet B. Butler, Sandra Cherie Henderson, and Cecily Raiborn. Title: "Sustainability and the Balanced Scorecard: Integrating Green Measures into Business Reporting."
- A flier titled "Inactivated Influenza Vaccine 2011–12: What You Need to Know" and published (interim version) on July 26, 2011, by Department of Health and Human Services, Centers for Disease Control and Prevention. (*Hint:* A current issue of the flier may be available online at the CDC's website at http://www.cdc.gov.flu.)
- A seven-page section (pages 65–71) labeled "Writing Style" in the reference book titled *Publication Manual of the American Psychological Association*, 6th edition. No author cited. A 2010 publication of the American Psychological Association of Washington, DC.
- In the 2011 summer issue of *World Ark* magazine, an article on pages 12–19 titled "Brain Drain" and authored by Lauren Wilcox. No volume number or issue number.
- Reporter Dan Vergano's article "Dangers of Space Junk Pile Up" in the September 1, 2011, issue of *USA Today* (on pages 1 and 2 of Section B), published by Gannett Co., Inc. No volume or issue numbers.

- A brochure containing a reprinted article, "It's a WaWa World," from the August 2011 issue of *Philadelphia Magazine*. Don Steinberg wrote the article, which was reprinted by The YGS Group with the permission of the magazine publisher, Metro Corp.
- A post by Jeff Hayden at the CBS Money Watch blog on September 28, 2011: "The Best Professional Advice I Ever Received." Accessed October 20, 2011, at http://www.cbsnews.com/8301-505143_162-47744612/the-best-professional-advice-i-ever-received/?tag=bnetdomain

3. The information in each of the following paragraphs was paraphrased from one of the items given in Application 2. Write each paraphrased item in APA, CHIC, or MLA:

   a. With an in-text citation, using the author's name in the paraphrase.

   b. With an in-text citation, not using the author's name in the paraphrase.

   - Is it okay to turn my back to the audience during a presentation? You bet it is. But only *once* in each talk. Save it for your most important point—the idea you want the audience to remember even if they forget everything else. Here's how to do it: (1) Finish the previous section and pause; (2) turn your back and—wordlessly—take a few steps away from the audience; (3) then stop, face the audience, and make your critical point. They'll get it! (Source: book titled *Own the Room*, page 178)

   - Green practices may increase or reduce a company's profitability. The balanced scorecard (BSC) is a way to relieve this tension. The BSC usually reflects four perspectives: customers, financial, growth, and internal processes. Options for involving sustainability include (1) adding a fifth perspective, (2) creating a separate BSC for sustainability, and (3) integrating sustainability throughout the four perspectives. (Source: article in *Management Accounting Quarterly*, page 4)

   - Since the mid-1980s, thousands of well-educated, highly skilled men and women have emigrated from their developing countries to America and other developed countries. From *the college-educated population*, a quarter of Sri Lankans, a third of El Salvadorans, up to half the people of African countries, and four out of five Jamaicans have emigrated to developed nations, seeking academic and employment opportunities unavailable at home. (Source: article titled "Brain Drain," page 14)

   - When you fire an employee, "We have to let you go" is all you should have to say. Even so, firing someone should feel awful. Firing, the last step in a series of manager-employee transactions, comes as no surprise to the employee. Still, firing someone affects her or his career, family, and life. If you are untouched by that, it's time for you to exit the management role. (Source: CBS Money Watch blog post).

4. Each of the following paragraphs is a quotation from an item given in Application 2 or an example in the chapter. For each quotation, write the item in APA, MLA, or CHIC style as:

   a. A direct quotation with in-text citation.

b. A paraphrase with in-text citation.

- "Toy blocks are the building blocks of success at LEGO. Keeping little hands busy worldwide for decades, LEGO Holding (dba LEGO Group) has made more than two billion of its interlocking toys. In a nod to kids' growing high-tech skills, the toymaker offers LEGO Mindstorms to build PC-programmable robots and BIONICLE sets that feature an evolving online storyline." (Source: Hoover's Handbook, page 207)

- "Another obvious compromise would be a grandfather—and grandmother—clause that would exempt, say, those born before 1945, from the picture ID requirement, since the bulk of the people for whom obtaining one would be a burden are elderly. This is in keeping with a state law that already exempts those 65 and older from providing a copy of a picture ID when they register to vote by mail." (Source: *The State* newspaper, p. A11)

- "How can we meet the needs of today without compromising those of future generations? More specifically, how can people protect our shared environment in a way that fosters human health and well-being, is socially just, and promotes economic prosperity?"

  "Providing the science to answer these questions is at the heart of EPA's sustainable and healthy communities research. EPA researchers and their partners and stakeholders are working together to form a deeper understanding of the balance between the three pillars of sustainability—environment, society, and economy." (Source: EPA website article)

5. Using one of the citation styles presented in this chapter, verify the form of all references you used recently in a report for this course, for another course, or at your place of business. Correct all inconsistencies you detect. (If you have not written a report recently, find one written by someone else and do the same. *Hint:* Ask your reference librarian or access a report online.)

6. On a blank page in Word 2010, create a Works Cited list in MLA style, including the following sources.

Create Source

Type of Source: Article in a Periodical
Author: Allen H. Kupetz
Title: Social Media and the Business Professor
Periodical Title: BizEd
Year: 2010
Month: November/December
Day:
Pages: 44–48

Create Source

Type of Source: Journal Article
Author: Carol M. Lehman, Debbie D. DuFrene, and Mark W. Lehman
Title: YouTube Video Project: A "Cool" Way to Learn Communication Ethics

Journal Name: Business Communication Quarterly
Year: 2010
Pages: 444–449

Create Source

Notes: Try using the "website" option if the Type of Source menu does not include "Blog." Click the checkbox at Show All Bibliography Fields.

Type of Source: Blog/Website
Year: 2011
Month: October
Day: 19
Year Accessed: 2012
Month Accessed: February
Day Accessed: 15
URL: http://soshable.com/law-enforcement-social-media

After adding all three sources, create the Works Cited list (click Bibliography and Insert Works Cited). Check each source against the MLA style guides in this chapter and edit as needed. Also ensure that items appear in alphabetical order.

Save your MLA Works Cited list. Then convert to APA style and change the heading to References. Again, compare the sources to style guides in this chapter and make changes as needed. For example, did Word 2010 give you the proper capitalization of all titles?

7. If you completed Application 4 by inserting in-text citations manually, type the Lego quotation in Word 2010. At the end of the quotation, instead of typing an in-text citation, click Insert Citation and Add New Source. Create the new source. Then insert a Reference page containing the single source and check/edit it. Finally, convert the source to Chicago style and compare with the CHIC guides in this chapter.

References

1. *Publication Manual of the American Psychological Association*, 6th ed. (2010). Washington, DC: American Psychological Association, p. 181.
2. *MLA Handbook for Writers of Research Papers*, 7th ed. (2009). New York: Modern Language Association of America, p. 182.
3. These items are a synthesis/adaptation of two sources: *Publication Manual of the APA, op cit.*, and the *Chicago Manual of Style*, 16th ed. (2010). Chicago: University of Chicago Press.
4. *Chicago Manual of Style, op. cit.*, p. 733.

CHAPTER **15**

Analyzing Data for Complex Reports

IN PREVIOUS CHAPTERS YOU LEARNED how to plan a research project and how to collect secondary and primary data. You learned that a thorough understanding of the managerial problem, a clear definition of the research question, and a comprehension of the purpose of the study must determine your data collection techniques.

As you collect relevant data from secondary and primary sources, you accumulate a mass of facts—your raw data. Perhaps the most crucial task of the entire research process remains. Since decision makers are rarely interested in the raw data, your duty as a researcher and report writer is to interpret those data, demonstrating their relationship to the project's problem and purpose and the context in which decisions must be made.

Data analysis is the entire process of converting raw data into meaningful information for decision makers. Analysis is a process of data reduction: the mass of raw data is reduced to classes or sets of information, those sets are reduced to major findings, and ultimately the findings are interpreted to yield conclusions and recommendations.

Assume, for example, that you are asked to conduct research to identify potential sites for a new FreshMart supermarket. Your data collection activities will yield many facts, which might include demographic data, responses to a consumer survey, and data about building sites currently on the market.

Your data analysis will require classification of the data into meaningful groups that will permit you to compare the desirability of different sites. One category could be the demographics of defined sections of the city. The many facts about each area—population growth, average household income, effective buying power, new home construction, and so on—can be reduced to major findings. Those findings would include the area that has shown the fastest growth in population, has the highest average household income, has the greatest effective buying power, and has had the most new home construction during a defined period of time. Those findings may be reduced further into a summary statement identifying one section of the city that demonstrates the greatest economic vitality. Similar data reduction would be required for the facts gathered in your consumer survey and the information about available building sites.

Conceivably, a data set containing hundreds of facts may finally be reduced to one recommendation. Assume that your findings indicate that a revitalized section of the central city shows the greatest economic vitality, consumers in that area expressed the greatest desire for a conveniently located supermarket, and a building site is available in an appropriate location and at an affordable price. Your single recommendation would likely be that the company purchase the site for a new supermarket.

Data that you collect are either qualitative or quantitative. To analyze data effectively, you must first understand the nature of those general data classes.

Qualitative and Quantitative Data

Qualitative data are nonnumeric data; *quantitative data* are numeric data. Both kinds of data are useful in business research.

Resume your role as a researcher who has been asked to identify potential sites for a new FreshMart supermarket. You might consult a source such as the *Sales and Marketing Management* "Survey of Buying Power" issue for demographic data about various sections of the county, talk to a real estate agent about available commercial sites in the county, and survey a sample of residents to determine their grocery-buying habits and preferences.

Your data set will contain both quantitative and qualitative data. The demographic data are quantitative and objective if the data were originally collected in a valid and reliable way. These data can be analyzed statistically. The information about site availability, however, may be both quantitative and qualitative. Dimensions of lots and quoted prices are quantitative; one site can be mathematically described as larger or smaller than another and more or less costly to acquire. Other aspects of site description, however, are qualitative and require subjective interpretation. For example, is a square plot of ground more or less desirable than a rectangular plot? Is a sloped site more or less desirable than a flat one? Is a parcel near other businesses more or less desirable than one near a residential area?

Data about consumer grocery-buying habits and preferences are largely qualitative; they are expressions of consumer qualities or characteristics, which generally are not numeric. An example of a specific qualitative fact is a consumer's expression that he or she would like to be able to shop for food on the way home from work or has recently moved to a central-city apartment and would like to be able to walk to the grocery. Interpretation of such data requires subjective judgment.

To improve objectivity when analyzing qualitative data, however, many researchers attempt to quantify the facts. Using a five-point ordinal scale, for example, to measure consumer preferences would permit you to compute the relative strength of various attitudes. You could also establish a set of criteria that a potential site must meet, assign weights to the relative importance of each criterion, and then evaluate each site by those criteria.

The following example illustrates such a weighting technique. In this example, three criteria are identified and their relative importance is determined. Location is the primary criterion and is given a weight of .60. Price and size are considered equally important but considerably less important than location. Each of those criteria is given a weight of .20. Weights for all factors must total 1 (100 percent). The maximum points to be allocated to each criterion must also be determined. In this example, a maximum of 50 was chosen. Then points for each criterion are assigned to each site. Criterion points are multiplied by criterion weight to get a weighted value. The total weighted values permit comparison of the two sites, with Site A scoring higher on the criteria than Site B.

Criterion	Weights	Site A		Site B	
		Points	Weighted Value	Points	Weighted Value
Location	.60	50	30	40	24
Price	.20	30	6	40	8
Size	.20	40	8	25	5
Total weighted value			44		37

Although such a procedure may improve objectivity, you must be aware that the choice of criteria, the weights given to each, and the values assigned to the criteria during site evaluation are all subjective judgments. Effective interpretation of qualitative data requires rational, logical, unbiased thinking throughout the entire process.

Interpretation of quantitative data also requires rational, logical, unbiased judgment. Although quantitative data are in themselves objective, their interpretation often involves subjective judgment. Your data may show that the average annual household income for a particular section of the city is $70,000. That figure is objective, but your interpretation that the neighborhood is a high-, middle-, or low-income community is subjective.

The author of this book was once asked to review a report about the selection of a site at which a professional football team would hold its summer training. The leader of the research team and the owner of the football team were alumni of a college that was approximately 80 miles from the home base of the team. Perhaps it comes as no surprise that the report recommended that college campus as the site for the team's summer training camp, although other sites also had desirable characteristics. Were the analysis, conclusions, and recommendations unbiased? Who knows? The owner did accept the recommendation, and the team still conducts its summer training on that campus.

As the foregoing examples suggest, data analysis is never a completely objective process. You can, however, actively monitor the accuracy and objectivity of your analysis by observing the four requirements discussed next.

Requirements for Accurate Data Analysis

To enhance the accuracy of your analysis, you must understand the research problem, maintain a critical mind-set, apply logical thinking, and understand basic statistical procedures.

Understand the Research Problem

Reviewing the research problem and purpose will remind you of what stimulated the research and of the objectives to be met by the study. Assume the following research problem and purpose.

> *Research Problem:* To evaluate potential sites for a new FreshMart supermarket.
>
> *Purpose:* To locate a site that will permit the company to operate profitably in a market that currently has inadequate supermarket service.

With that problem and purpose as guides, you will analyze all data (characteristics of available sites, demographic data, and survey results) in terms of what they contribute to identifying an area of the county that needs additional supermarket service and identifying a suitable site in that area. The analysis must move toward a conclusion and recommendation that will contribute to achieving the stated purpose—even if you conclude that no suitable site is currently available. You may recommend that the company conduct further site analyses and delay opening a new store until a satisfactory site is found.

Maintain a Critical Mind-Set

Maintaining a critical mind-set requires that you constantly evaluate your data and your interpretation of the data. Assume that you are a resident of the central city, which currently has no supermarket. As you conduct your research on potential market sites, you might feel the need for a central-city market keenly and find an excellent site in that area. Knowing your preferences, you should ask yourself several questions: Have I used valid sources? Have I gathered enough data? Have I gathered the right kinds of data? Have I permitted my biases to affect the interpretation of the data? Will others agree with my interpretation? If so, why? If not, why not?

One way to maintain a critical viewpoint is to discuss your research with others who are authorized to review the data, particularly during the data analysis. It is natural to develop some proprietary tendencies after working on a project for a while. You may become reluctant to discard data that are inadequate or irrelevant or to change tentative conclusions that are contradicted by the data. Individuals who have no vested interest in the project will be able to look at the data objectively and help you maintain your capacity to criticize your own work.

Apply Logical Thinking

Both qualitative and quantitative data must be interpreted logically. You can improve the quality of your analysis by understanding two basic styles of logic: induction and deduction.

Induction involves reasoning from specific facts, examples, or cases to generalizations based on those specifics. Assume that, in our FreshMart example, you look at specific data about population, family income, number of groceries, and locations of groceries in the central city. Based on those specific data, you generalize that the potential customers and the competitive environment are favorable for establishment of a FreshMart. That is inductive reasoning. When using induction, you must be especially careful to avoid such fallacies as the hasty generalization (reasoning that something true in one case is true in all cases) and the non sequitur (generalization based on inadequate data).

> **Example:** *The FreshMart in central-city Charlotte has exceeded sales projections for its first year; a FreshMart is bound to succeed in central-city Asheville. (Have you gathered enough data? Do the data show that the communities and conditions are similar?)*

In deduction, you reason from general concepts or principles to specific facts or cases. Deduction is based on the logical syllogism, which has three parts:

1. A major premise—a large assumption or primary fact
2. A minor premise—a small assumption or secondary fact
3. A conclusion—a logically inescapable inference based on the premises

In deductive reasoning, the major premise is broader than the minor premise, the minor premise is broader than the conclusion, and a specific fact is inferred from the more general premises. When using deduction, you must always test the accuracy of your premises, as demonstrated in the following examples.

If either the major or the minor premise is false, the conclusion is false.

> **False Major Premise; False Conclusion**
>
> *Major Premise:* Central-city residents are dissatisfied with current grocery services in their area. (False premise; possibly a hasty generalization.)
>
> *Minor Premise:* You are a central-city resident. (True premise.)
>
> *Conclusion:* You are dissatisfied with grocery services in your area. (Logically correct, but false conclusion.)
>
> **False Minor Premise; False Conclusion**
>
> *Major Premise:* The FreshMart in central-city Charlotte has exceeded sales projections for its first year. (True premise.)
>
> *Minor Premise:* Central-city Asheville is similar to central-city Charlotte. (False premise unless backed by sufficient data.)
>
> *Conclusion:* A FreshMart is bound to succeed in central-city Asheville. (Logically correct, but false conclusion.)

If both the major and minor premises are true, the conclusion is valid.

> **True Major and Minor Premises; Valid Conclusion**
>
> *Major Premise: The ratio of households to supermarkets in the central city is 2,000 to 0. (True premise.)*
>
> *Minor Premise: Industry statistics indicate that the ideal ratio is 1,500 to 1. (True premise.)*
>
> *Conclusion: There are enough households in the central city to support a Fresh-Mart supermarket. (Logically inescapable inference.)*

In addition to using accurate induction and deduction, you can sometimes improve the accuracy of your analysis by subjecting all or some of the data to statistical analysis.

Understand Basic Statistical Procedures

Statistics are the tools by which meaning is extracted from quantitative data. Through statistical computations, for example, you could determine average household income for an area, numbers of new homes constructed, rates of increase in both those variables, and relationships between the two. Those kinds of calculations will yield information that is more meaningful than the isolated facts represented by the raw data. Specific statistical concepts with which you should become familiar are presented later in this chapter.

Knowledge of the research problem, a critical viewpoint, knowledge of logic, and an understanding of statistics are essential throughout the data analysis process. The first step in that process is preparing the data for analysis.

Data Preparation

For most types of contemporary business research, data preparation includes editing, coding, and entering into a computer.

Editing

Data editing is inspection of the data to detect errors and omissions. Editing is done to ensure that data are accurate, consistent, complete, and arranged in a way that facilitates coding or classification.

Some editing can be done during or immediately after collection. For example, an interviewer should check the interview guide immediately after an interview to determine whether all items have been covered and whether any obvious inconsistencies exist. If an item has been omitted, the interviewer may be able to schedule a prompt follow-up interview and get the necessary information. If the interviewer notices inconsistencies in a respondent's answers, those items may also be reviewed in a follow-up interview.

When collecting data from a secondary source, you should verify the accuracy and legibility of direct quotations, paraphrases, and bibliographic references before you leave each source. Such editing ensures accuracy and saves valuable time by eliminating the need to return to a source for verification.

Data collected by questionnaire must be edited after questionnaires have been returned. Your objective is to detect missing answers and unusable (illegible or obviously inconsistent) responses. In some instances, you may be able to supply the correct information, as when a person provides annual instead of monthly income. In other situations, you may be able to determine the correct answer by a follow-up contact with the survey participant. Frequently, however, missing or unusable answers must be coded and handled as such.

How to deal with missing or incomplete data should not be an arbitrary decision. To protect the validity and reliability of data, the research design should include a decision about how to handle such data. For example, the research design might indicate that the number of missing or unusable answers will be reported for each item, but the findings will be based on usable answers.

Coding

Coding is the process of assigning numerals or other symbols to answers so that they can be categorized and interpreted, possibly statistically. Questionnaires and interview guides can be designed to eliminate the need for extensive manual coding. Closed questions, in particular, can be set up so that the responses are numbered with appropriate codes. Open-ended questions must be coded manually to fit into categories defined by the researchers. Any coding system used to establish categories of information must meet four criteria: appropriate, exhaustive, mutually exclusive, and one-dimensional.

Appropriate

As with all aspects of analysis, coding must be directed by the problem and purpose. Those factors, for example, must determine whether age or income ranges should be narrow or wide and how many scale points (values) should be used to measure attitudes. The following codes and ranges might be appropriate to measure annual earned income of students at a state university, but they would likely not be appropriate to measure income of faculty members at that institution because a disproportionate number would fall into category 5.

1. $0–$4,999.99
2. $5,000–$9,999.99
3. $10,000–$14,999.99
4. $15,000–$19,999.99
5. $20,000 or more

Exhaustive

The classification set must capture the full range of information. The set used in the previous example will provide little useful information about university professors' salaries. If the majority of responses fall into category 5, the only information acquired is that the majority of the faculty earns more than $20,000 annually.

Responses to open-ended questions must also be coded to identify the richness of the data. A question about plans for postsecondary education, for example, may originally have been grouped into three sets: college, technical school, no plans for postsecondary education. Closer examination of the data, however, may suggest the need for more classifications to identify the many dimensions of college and technical school education that the responses have indicated: Web-based college, community college, technical school, proprietary trade school, state college, private college, state university, private university, and so on.

Mutually Exclusive

The classifications must not overlap. This standard is met when an answer can be placed in only one category. In an occupational survey, the classifications may be professional, managerial, technical, sales, clerical, and operative. However, a nurse who supervises two assistants in a company health center may have difficulty choosing between the professional and managerial categories. In the previous example of student income ranges, each category is mutually exclusive. A respondent whose income falls near an extreme end of a category, such as $9,990, should have no difficulty selecting the appropriate category.

One-Dimensional

All items in a classification set must be related to the same concept. In a question asking what kind of automobile the respondent owns or leases, the responses may be subcompact, compact, intermediate, standard, full, premium, and none. The first six items refer to one dimension, size, but the last item deals with another dimension, current ownership status. That item is best handled in a separate category, perhaps as a screening question, such as "Do you currently own or lease an automobile?"

Preparing for Computer Analysis

Since virtually all business researchers use computers to analyze numerically coded data, an important step is to prepare the data for entry into the computer. In this step, the researcher defines and records the data structure. A data structure is the way the information is positioned on the storage medium, such as a magnetic tape, a magnetic disk, a CD, or a computer drive. A record of the data structure is called a codebook or code sheet.

Statistical programs generally permit you to enter data directly into a data editor, which resembles a spreadsheet, or to import the data from a database or spreadsheet. In any case, a codebook should be prepared before the data are entered so that each field of the data editor, spreadsheet, or database can be appropriately identified; data can be entered in the correct form; and data can be interpreted when they are processed.

A codebook for data to be entered directly into a spreadsheet or data editor might look similar to Illustration 15.1. The codebook identifies each variable (usually equivalent to a column or data field in a spreadsheet or database) by name, type, width, value, and value label.

After the codebook is prepared, the data are entered into the computer. For survey data, you will create a record for each participant or case. A record is all the information related to one case. For data translated into numerical codes, the record consists of a row of numbers entered onto the storage medium in the sequence defined by the data structure.

Some commonly used methods of data entry are optical scanning, manual entry, and direct entry by way of a computer-assisted survey. With optical scanning, survey participants or research assistants use pencils to mark data sheets with the appropriate

ILLUSTRATION 15.1 CODEBOOK

VARIABLE 1

Name: Case No.

Type: Numeric

Width: 4

Value: 0001–2000

Value label: None

VARIABLE 2

Name: State

Type: String

Width: 2

Value: AA–ZZ

Value label: Two-letter state abbreviations

VARIABLE 3

Name: Average monthly income

Type: Numeric

Width: 1

Value: 1–9

Value label: 1 = Under $3,000

                    2 = $3,000–$5,999

                    3 = $6,000–$8,999

                    4 = $9,000–$11,999

                    5 = $12,000–$14,999

                    6 = $15,000–$17,999

                    7 = $18,000–$20,999

                    8 = $21,000–$23,999

                    9 = $24,000 or more

response codes. The data sheets are then run through a scanner, which "reads" the pencil marks and records the codes onto a magnetic tape or computer drive. In manual entry, an individual keys the responses into the computer, using the numerical codes and sequence defined by the codebook. The data are then saved electronically for use with statistical software. In a computer-assisted survey, the program can be written to collect the data in a format and sequence that conforms to a predetermined codebook.

Since errors can occur during data entry, one preparation step remains before data can be processed: verification.

Verifying

Several techniques are used to ensure that edited, coded data are entered accurately into the computer. One procedure is to print a copy of the entire database and visually scan it for obvious omissions or errors, such as a 6 entered when the maximum code value is 5. Some researchers use two-person teams to orally and visually verify all data. One person reads the codes aloud from the questionnaires or scanning sheets while the second person verifies them on the database printout. For sizable databases, that manual technique may be used on a sample of the records. Verification is a tedious but necessary step to protect the validity of the data.

After much preparation, the data are finally ready for analysis. Most business research employs both nonstatistical and statistical analysis.

Nonstatistical Analysis

Nonstatistical analysis is the application of logical thought processes to extract meaning from the data. Traditionally, qualitative data were analyzed in that way only, but today qualitative and quantitative methods complement one another. For example, observations of communication behaviors in a group task can be observed, classified, coded, and converted to numeric values. Quantitative data also require a certain amount of nonstatistical analysis. Classification, analysis, and synthesis are three major forms of nonstatistical analysis.

Classification

As you have already seen in the discussion of data coding, *classification* is a form of data analysis whereby you assign data to categories on the basis of established criteria. Assume that you are conducting research to determine whether the general characteristics of the student body at your school have changed during the past 10 years. You could examine enrollments for year X and year Y and classify each student by gender, age, work experience, and marital status. You could then compare the student body in year X with the student body in year Y on those characteristics and ultimately draw conclusions about whether the general composition of the student body has changed.

When you group your secondary data notes by subject categories, you are also classifying data. In your study of the characteristics of your student population, you may also want to identify new student services that could benefit your students. As you read about student services in secondary sources, you could classify your data by subjects such as services for married students, for mature students, for part-time students, and so on.

For some data, classification may be the only form of analysis you perform. But frequently classification is a preliminary step that facilitates further analysis of the data. As you examine the characteristics of the student body, you may decide to survey students about attitudes toward various services. After classifying respondents by gender, you could then determine whether males and females differ in their attitudes toward specific student services.

Analysis and Synthesis

Analysis and synthesis require the application of deduction and induction. In *analysis* you break a large body of information into smaller elements for scrutiny and interpretation. Imagine a gourmet who orders an unfamiliar entrée from a restaurant menu and attempts to determine the ingredients while eating the food. That person is engaging in analysis—breaking the whole into parts to discover new information. Similarly, a business researcher who looks at response data from an employee opinion survey breaks the mass of data into parts to identify specific opinions or attitudes.

In *synthesis* you bring together individual facts and assimilate them into a broader finding or conclusion. The gourmet who attempts to duplicate at home the delicacy enjoyed in the restaurant brings together ingredients to synthesize a new recipe. Similarly, assume you have gathered secondary data—published reports—about the effectiveness of flexible benefits programs. You study the facts reported by individual managers who have used flexible benefits programs and summarize the overall success of such programs. The process of pulling together information reported by different individuals in various ways and summarizing that information is a synthesis process.

For most nonquantitative data, logical classification, analysis, and synthesis are the limits of data analysis. Nonetheless, those forms of analysis are critical to successful data interpretation. For quantitative data, statistical processing may also be used to enhance logical analysis and synthesis. Statistics do not replace logic; they complement it.

Statistical Analysis

Statistics is a branch of mathematics dealing with the analysis, interpretation, and presentation of numerical data. Statistical procedures range from relatively simple computations used to describe a data set to complex calculations used to analyze relationships between and among sets of data or to predict behaviors and events. The primary purpose of this discussion of statistics is to help you recognize possible statistical applications for your research. After choosing a potentially useful application, you should consult a business statistics text or a statistician for specific formulas and interpretations of results.

To comprehend any discussion of statistics, you must understand the relationship of measurement scales to statistical analysis. Such an understanding will help you select appropriate descriptive or inferential statistical applications for your data analysis.

Measurement Scales and Statistical Analysis

As you learned in Chapter 13, a measurement scale is a device used to assign numbers to an element or characteristic that is being analyzed. The type of measurement scale—nominal, ordinal, interval, or ratio—determines what kinds of statistics can be used for data analysis.

Any statistic that can be computed from less powerfully scaled data can also be computed on more powerfully scaled data. Conversely, many statistics that can be computed on more powerfully scaled data cannot be used for less powerfully scaled data. In terms of power, nominal scales are least powerful, and ratio scales are most powerful. Consequently, many of the more powerful statistics can be computed only for data measured by an interval or ratio scale.

The first step to effective statistical analysis occurs during the research design stage. While planning the study, you must determine the kinds of data you need, what you want to learn from the data, and what type of measurement is necessary. Those determinations will influence your choice of descriptive or inferential statistics when you reach the data analysis stage.

Descriptive and Inferential Statistics

Descriptive statistics describe and summarize data. The most frequently used descriptive statistics are measures of central tendency (arithmetic mean, median, mode) and measures of dispersion (range, variance, standard deviation).

Measures of central tendency examine how the data are clustered. Assume, for example, that you have collected data about income levels of survey participants. The *mean* is the arithmetic average, computed by adding the reported incomes of all respondents and dividing by the number of respondents. The *median* is the midpoint of the data; half of your respondents have incomes above that point, and half have incomes below that point. The *mode* is the most frequently occurring value; more respondents report that income figure than any other figure.

Measures of dispersion show how the data are scattered around a particular point. Although your data may show that the mean income of your respondents is $50,000 per year, you may need to know what differences exist among your subjects.

The *range* gives a concise statement of differences, showing the distance between the highest and the lowest values. Computing the range, as in the following example, may dramatize the fact that assumptions about an "average" customer may be quite inaccurate with respect to many of your respondents. In the example, no income falls near the mean.

Income	
$200,000	
$ 20,000	
$ 13,000	Mean income = $50,000
$ 10,000	Median income = $13,000
$ 7,000	Range = $193,000

The *variance* shows the average distance between the mean and the individual values. The variance is computed by determining the difference between the mean and each value and then squaring those differences. The squared differences are added and then divided by the number of observations. Because the deviations are squared, the variance is expressed in "square points," a relatively meaningless number to most people. To convert the variance into a meaningful number, you take the square root of the variance. That figure, the standard deviation, is a measure of dispersion expressed in the same units as the original data.

The *standard deviation* is a helpful statistic if the population has a normal distribution. The standardized normal curve is a theoretical distribution of sample means having these characteristics:

- The highest point of the curve represents the mean of the distribution.
- The curve is symmetrical about its mean.
- The curve has an infinite number of cases; thus, it is a continuous distribution.

If samples are drawn from a normally distributed population, it is expected that 99.7 percent of the observations will fall within plus or minus 3 standard deviations of the mean, 95.5 percent will fall within plus or minus 2 standard deviations, and 68 percent will fall within plus or minus 1 standard deviation (see Illustration 15.2).

The concepts of the normal curve and standard deviation are essential in selecting statistical analyses and interpreting their results. *Parametric statistics*, for example, assume that the population from which a sample is drawn is normally distributed, whereas that assumption is not required for *nonparametric statistics*. Therefore, before selecting a statistical procedure, you must know whether the procedure assumes a normal distribution. If you cannot make that assumption about your data, you must use nonparametric statistics.

When using inferential statistics, researchers make generalizations or forecasts about the population after analyzing data from a sample of that population. Inferential statistics permit you to estimate the degree of confidence that you can have in your inferences and forecasts. Results of analysis with inferential statistics are always interpreted in terms of level of significance, which is an estimate of the probability that the results observed in your sample are due to chance. A .05 significance level, for example, says that there is a 5 percent probability that your findings are chance findings and that what you observe in your sample is not typical of the population from which it was drawn.

Two primary concerns in business research are analysis of relationships (associations) and differences. Illustrations 15.3 and 15.4 are provided to help you select appropriate statistical measurements of association or tests for differences.

ILLUSTRATION 15.2 STANDARDIZED NORMAL CURVE

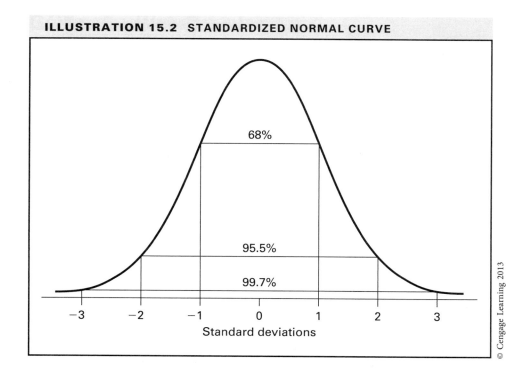

68%

95.5%

99.7%

−3   −2   −1   0   1   2   3

Standard deviations

© Cengage Learning 2013

ILLUSTRATION 15.3 MEASURES OF ASSOCIATION

Measurement Level, Independent Variable (X_1)	Nominal, dichotomous	Nominal, more than two categories	Ordinal	Interval or Ratio
			Measurement Level, Dependent Variable (X_2)	
Nominal, dichotomous	Phi coefficient	Pearson's contingency coefficient; Cramer's V coefficient	Rank-biserial correlation coefficient	Point-biserial correlation coefficient
Nominal, more than two categories	Pearson's contingency coefficient; Cramer's V coefficient	Pearson's contingency coefficient; Cramer's V coefficient		
Ordinal	Rank biserial correlation coefficient		Spearman rank order correlation; Kendall tau; tetrachoric correlation coefficient	1. Convert X_2 to ranks: Spearman rank order correlation; Kendall tau 2. Convert ordinal X_2 to dichotomous: Biserial correlation coefficient
Interval or ratio	Point-biserial correlation coefficient		1. Convert X_1 to ranks: Spearman rank order correlation; Kendall tau 2. Convert ordinal X_1 to dichotomous: Biserial correlation coefficient	Pearson product moment correlation (r)

© Cengage Learning 2013

ILLUSTRATION 15.4 TESTS FOR DIFFERENCES

Measurement Level	Univariate Tests		Group Differences—One Dependent Variable	
	Independent Samples	Related Samples	Independent Samples	Related Samples
Nominal	Contingency table analysis (χ^2)	McNemar test	(χ^2) for independent samples	Cochran-Q
Ordinal	Mann-Whitney test; Kruskal-Wallis	Wilcoxon matched-pairs signed-ranks test	One-way ANOVA—Kruskal-Wallis	Two-way ANOVA—Friedman
Interval or Ratio	t-test of differences (independent); F-test (independent)	t-test of differences (dependent; F-test (dependent)	Linear regression models	Linear regression models

© Cengage Learning 2013

To select a measurement of association from Illustration 15.3, you must do the following:

- Identify two variables (X_1 and X_2) to be analyzed (for example, income level and importance of supermarket within walking distance).
- Determine the level of measurement for each variable (nominal, ordinal, interval, or ratio).
- Identify the measurement in the intersecting column and row for the measurement levels.

To select a measurement of differences from Illustration 15.4, follow these steps:

- Identify the level of measurement for the variables of interest.
- Decide what you wish to test:
    - The significance of the distribution of a variable within a single sample or the significance of differences in distribution of a variable between groups. For that kind of analysis, select a test from the left side of Illustration 15.4 (univariate tests). An example of within-group differences would be to determine whether the average supermarket purchases in a single store location differ by age of shopper. An example of between-group variance would be to determine whether the average supermarket purchase at a central-city location differs significantly from the average purchase at a suburban location.
    - Whether groups that differ from one another on some defined characteristic also differ with respect to a specific dependent variable. For that kind of analysis, select a test from the right side of Illustration 15.4. An example of such analysis would be to determine whether managers of central-city and suburban supermarkets differ in their attitudes toward providing discount pricing on bulk purchases. The characteristic defining the group is store location. The dependent variable is the managers' attitudes.
- Identify whether comparisons are to be for independent or dependent samples. In independent samples, observations on a variable are completely independent of one another; no two observations for a particular variable can be based on the same individual. For example, in a customer preference survey, the responses of one customer are independent of responses made by another customer, if precautions are taken to prevent respondents from colluding on answers. With dependent samples (also called paired samples), the data are paired on a unit of analysis. Asking the same customers to respond to identical survey questions at two different times is an example of using paired samples.
- Select the statistical test from the intersection of the appropriate column and row in Illustration 15.4.

Illustrations 15.3 and 15.4 are initial aids for selecting statistics. The purpose of this text is not to present the calculations or the interpretation of the statistics. For those kinds of details, consult a statistics textbook, a statistical consultant, or the user guide accompanying the computer statistical software of your choice.

Using Statistical Software to Analyze Data

Spreadsheet and statistical software can help you prepare reports containing financial and statistical information. Conventional spreadsheets can be used to summarize data, make projections, or prepare data for complex calculations. Spreadsheets can also be used to create tables and, in some cases, figures or graphs representing the data. Those visual aids can then be imported into a report that is prepared in a word-processing program.

Most statistical programs today are integrated with spreadsheet or database software, permitting direct transfer of data from the spreadsheet or database into the statistical program. Commonly use programs include *Statistical Package for the Social Sciences* (SPSS), SAS, and SYSTAT. You are probably familiar with some of the relatively simple descriptive statistics that you can compute in Microsoft Excel; but to perform more sophisticated calculations, you would have to add a program such as XLSTAT or STATISIXL. To get an impression of how widely such programs are used for commercial or social research, check the companies' websites.

To illustrate the use of statistical software, assume that as the manager of training and development in your organization you must write a report summarizing supervisors' and subordinates' responses to a survey of training needs. You must organize the responses in a manner that will be meaningful to a reader. Responses could be grouped into categories, such as supervisors' perceptions of training needs and subordinates' perceptions of training needs. However, different readers may interpret the information in a different manner. You may choose to use a statistical technique that shows the relationship between the responses of supervisors and subordinates. If that is the case, you can decide to use statistical software to compute rank order correlations of employee and supervisor ranking of training needs. This analysis of the relationship of supervisors' and supervisees' perceptions of training needs would add a dimension to the analysis that could not be obtained by merely categorizing responses.

Statistical analysis software performs computations very quickly, but you must determine which statistical analysis is most appropriate. Statistical analysis software can free you of performing time-consuming, tedious calculations, but it cannot determine the appropriateness of the statistical analysis, nor can it interpret the calculations performed.

Data preparation, nonstatistical analysis, and statistical analysis are interrelated aspects of data analysis. To bring this subject into better focus, consider next the levels or stages of data interpretation through which you must progress.

Levels of Data Interpretation

Data analysis is a multistage process. In each stage you move further from the objectivity of the raw data and interject the subjectivity that inevitably accompanies data interpretation. When reporting the results of your analysis, you should carefully differentiate the levels of analysis: findings, conclusions, and recommendations.

Findings

Findings are what the data reveal. As you analyze your raw data by statistical or non-statistical methods, you find out certain things. Findings emerge as a result of data interpretation.

As you present your findings, follow these guides:

- Classify or summarize data; present such classifications or summaries in tables, charts, or graphs whenever appropriate.
- Interpret the data; don't merely repeat the raw data or the summary figures shown in visual aids.
- Show similarities and differences among groups of data. If differences exist, supply possible explanations for those differences.

Assume, for example, that you have asked a sample of FreshMart customers to rate the importance of five new services that you propose to offer. The rating scale used was the following:

1 = Very unimportant
2 = Unimportant
3 = Neutral
4 = Important
5 = Very important

The first step in data analysis would be to classify the data by tallying the survey participants' ratings for each service. That process would enable you to report a breakdown of the number or the percentage of participants rating a specific service in a particular way. You could report, for example, that 58 percent of the respondents considered Thursday afternoon wine-tasting parties to be unimportant. You could also report that respondents tended to value lower overall prices more highly than any other proposed service. That level of analysis, however, would not capture the subtleties of the evaluations. To get a better understanding of customers' attitudes, you would have to reduce the data further.

The next step would be to reduce the data to a summary figure by computing an average rating for each service. Assume that you computed the following averages:

Service	Average Rating
2 percent discount on purchases totalling $20 or more	4.50
5 percent senior discount on Wednesday	4.10
Free delivery of orders within a 10-mile radius of the store	1.75
Free Thursday afternoon wine tasting	1.3
Frequent-shopper discount card	3.97

The three highest-ranked items relate to ways in which customers can save money on grocery purchases; the two lowest-ranked items relate to special services for which most stores charge a nominal fee. An appropriate presentation of findings would be similar to the following example:

> *Average ratings indicate strong customer interest in new services that enable them to save money. Discounts on all purchases of $20 or more, a senior discount on Wednesday, and frequent-buyer discount cards all received average ratings above 3.95, indicating that FreshMart customers consider those services to be important or very important. In contrast, removing fees from seldom-used services appears to be of little importance to FreshMart customers. Free wine tastings and delivery service within a 10-mile radius of the store were rated very unimportant and unimportant, respectively.*

Those findings, along with others drawn from the study, should permit you to draw conclusions.

Conclusions

Conclusions are logical inferences based on the findings. As you draw conclusions, you are moving further from the objectivity of the data and relying on your perceptions of what the data mean. To avoid unwarranted subjectivity in conclusions and to state them effectively, follow these guides:

- Conclusions must not be a mere restatement of the findings.
- Conclusions must be objective and flow logically from the analysis. If the data contradict anticipated outcomes, you must put aside your expectations and base conclusions on the available data.
- Conclusions must be relevant to the stated problem and purpose of the report.
- Conclusions must not introduce new material. All relevant data and analysis must be presented before a conclusion can be drawn.
- Several findings may be used to support a single conclusion. You need not draw a conclusion from each major finding. On the other hand, one major finding may lead to more than one conclusion.

The following examples contrast inappropriate and appropriate conclusions related to the survey of FreshMart customer preferences.

> **Inappropriate Conclusions**
>
> **Restatement of Findings:** *FreshMart customers rated services providing discounts on purchases higher than eliminating fees for seldom-used services.*
>
> **Not Justified by Findings:** *FreshMart customers will not respond to reduced fees for seldom-used services. Customers want lower grocery prices, not parties or cheaper delivery service.*
>
> **Not Related to Problem of Report:** *FreshMart can gain a competitive edge by offering a variety of price-reduction strategies. (This conclusion is not justified if*

the stated problem is to determine customer preferences for new services and no data were gathered to determine their inclinations to choose a supermarket on the basis of the availability of those services.)

Appropriate Conclusion

Justified by Findings, Not Merely a Restatement of Findings, Related to Research Problem: *FreshMart customers are more interested in ways to save money on their grocery purchases than in saving money on peripheral services. FreshMart can satisfy some of the desires of current customers by offering discounts on purchases.*

Since research is problem oriented, you are usually expected to carry your analysis one step further—to make recommendations.

Recommendations

Recommendations are confident statements of proposed actions based on the conclusions. Recommendations must be context relevant; that is, they must respond to the purpose of the study and be appropriate for the specific audience. As you write recommendations, observe the following guides:

- Verify that specific conclusions and findings justify each recommendation. Some report writers number summary statements of findings and conclusions so that they can refer easily to such supporting information when they write recommendations.
- State recommendations in imperative sentence structure. Begin each with an action verb.
- State recommendations specifically, including a recommended plan for implementation, if appropriate.
- Suggest additional research to investigate unanswered questions that became evident during the study.

Assume that the purpose of FreshMart's survey was to increase customer satisfaction and loyalty by providing desired services. The following example shows an appropriate way to state your recommendations:

To increase customer satisfaction and loyalty, FreshMart should initiate two new services as soon as possible and determine the feasibility of a third. Specifically, FreshMart should:

1. *Give a 2 percent discount on orders totalling $20 or more. This recommendation can be implemented by:*
   - *Programming point-of-sale registers to compute a 2 percent discount on total orders of $20 or more.*
   - *Training checkout associates to highlight the savings on each receipt and point it out to the customer.*

> **2.** *Give an additional 3 percent discount to all seniors on Wednesday. This recommendation can be implemented by:*
>   - *Designing and publishing an attractive newspaper advertisement announcing the new policy.*
>   - *Training checkout associates on how to recognize customers who appear to be 60 years of age or older and how to enter the discount for such customers.*
> **3.** *Investigate the feasibility of issuing a frequent-shopper discount card. Specific facts needed include:*
>   - *How to identify frequent shoppers*
>   - *Type of discount that should be offered*
>   - *Cost of providing the card, maintaining records, and fulfilling the discount program*

By applying logic and statistics, you should be able to reach defensible conclusions and recommendations. But those conclusions and recommendations must also be ethically defensible.

Team Project Management Tools

Project managers use a variety of tools to keep projects on track, encourage the collaboration necessary to meet goals and deadlines, and manage content of documents (reports, user's guides, and so on) issuing from the project. This section focuses on three of those tools: project management applications, project blogs, and wikis.

Project Management Applications

Applications for managing projects are rich in features that help project managers with some or all of the many interrelated parts of a project: scheduling and tracking personnel, resources, and tasks; tracking time and progress; dealing with changes, issues, and risks; tracking and reporting expenses; reporting progress, resources, and status; storing, sharing, and backing up project files; and maintaining project security. In many instances, projects involve collaboration; and project applications help project managers encourage collaboration among team members.

Offline and Online Applications

Often, the project tracking applications found online make all features accessible from one location, called a dashboard (Illustration 15.5). In Microsoft's Project 2010® and ProjectWizard's Merlin 2.8, instead of a dashboard, the default view is the scheduling screen (Gantt chart), which resembles a spreadsheet. A Gantt chart displays tasks and time lines and is valued for its ability to differentiate project tasks that must be done together from those tasks that must be done consecutively.

Project management websites are many and varied. Many of them are best suited for traditional project management, called *waterfall*. A waterfall application is set up for completing one project phase before moving to the next phase and for not returning to a completed phase. Other sites are well suited for agile (also called *scrum*) project management, which breaks large projects into weeklong to monthlong sprints or cycles, allowing for changes in objectives and requirements between sprints. A scrum application provides additional tools for tracking unfinished tasks from one cycle to the next. Still other sites blend traditional and agile project management.

The following list of online project management tools gives a brief overview. Before choosing a project management package or website, a project manager should study and test it carefully over time to ensure compatibility with the types of projects involved. Many subscription-based Web applications (also available for installation on an organization's intranet) provide a 30-day free trial.

AceProject (http://www.aceproject.com) comes in both free and fee versions. Projects can be divided into phases or modules. The program is collaboration oriented, including a range of features for time tracking, timesheet management, and project cost tracking. It is also useful for bug tracking. The program is also available for mobile Web application devices.

AtTask (http://www.attask.com), an integrated help desk, enables organizations to track every issue submitted from initiation to resolution. Managers can set up queues where help desk users can submit issues and receive automatic status updates. AtTask organizes both structured, project-based work and unstructured, free-form work. A function

ILLUSTRATION 15.5 PROJECT MANAGEMENT DASHBOARD

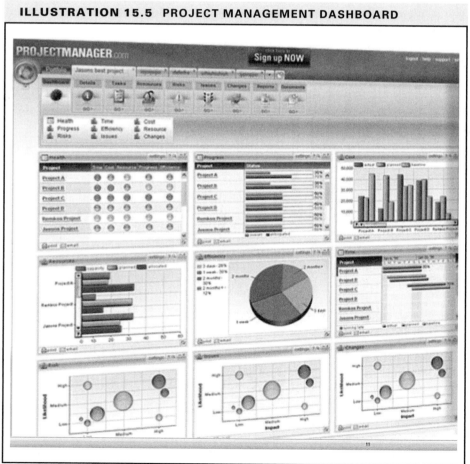

Source: ProjectManager. Accessed September 26, 2011, http://www.projectmanager.com/project-dashboard.php.

called Business Case Builder gives users tools for maximizing company resources by zeroing in on those projects that provide the most value. The program also includes tools aimed at improving how projects are conducted or managed. Because the program is browser independent, it works in Windows, Macintosh, or Linux and many mobile devices.

CentralDesktop (http://www.centraldesktop.com) is an enterprise-level application, that is, one intended to address a company-wide problem, not just an individual or departmental problem. CentralDesktop focuses on collaboration tools, including dashboards and reporting and a logging function. It delivers continuous feeds of client and industry news and includes a knowledge base that employees can search and contribute to.

Comindwork (http://www.comindwork.com) includes blogs for informing team and clients. It makes project status constantly available online.

GoPlan (http://goplanapp.com) enables issue tracking by capturing issues and allowing them to be prioritized and filtered. Thus, each defect in the project is attended to in a timely manner by the person best suited to address it.

HiTask (http://hitask.com) is a free application that is mostly useful for handling to-do lists and recording personal schedules and appointments. It also offers teamwork management features.

ProjectManager (http://www.projectmanager.com/index.php) incorporates exceptional project planning and reporting tools. It lets a user customize the dashboard, and all reports can be exported to Word, PDF, or Excel files.

Smartsheet (http://www.smartsheet.com) includes crowdsourcing in addition to the usual project management features. Crowdsourcing involves outsourcing tasks usually done by an employee or independent contractor to a large, open-ended group of people. The program enables project managers to use the research of anonymous workers. It comes in free trial and tiered subscription plans.

Task2Gather (http://task2gather.com) is a free online service containing simple applications for organizing business, family, personal, and social lives. With Task2-Gather, a user can upload all documents related to a project and manage them centrally. The program provides timesheets to track task time for client billing and supports multiple browsers. A subscription plan is available with additional features.

Wrike (http://www.wrike.com) pairs collaboration software with project management software. It includes an "intelligent email engine" that creates tasks and builds Gantt charts automatically from your emails. It is easy to change project plans and schedules as you go, and it even sends you reminders to help you meet project deadlines.

Guidelines for Using Project Management Applications

Follow these guidelines to avoid some common mistakes of managers and organizations when deciding on project management applications. (The guidelines given in this chapter for selection and use of project management software were adapted from "Criticisms of Project Management Software," Wikipedia, last modified September 18, 2011, http://en.wikipedia.org/wiki/Project_management_software.)

- **Don't try to adapt a project management application to management of an ongoing work flow.** For example, a publisher's marketing manager could benefit more from the use of so-called groupware than from project management tools (Chapter 2 contains a discussion of groupware). Groupware examples include IBM's LotusNotes and Microsoft's SharePoint and these websites: Atlassian (http://www.atlassian.com), Basecamp (http://basecamphq.com), Socialtext (http://www.socialtext.com), Teambox (http://teambox.com), TeamSpace (http://www.teamspace.com), WizeHive (http://www.wizehive.com), and Yammer (https://www.yammer.com).

- **Choose software consistent with the nature of your projects.** Analyze projects to determine the agility level and flexibility you need. Then seek an application with only the tools you will use. For example, be cautious about software that focuses too much on the planning phase while offering too few functions for project tracking, control, plan adjustment, and communication of plan changes.
- **Seek features that will enable you and your project team to work easier, faster, and better.** Study how the application works and also take a close look at the output. Avoid an application that involves a steep learning curve for you or that gives results that make no intuitive sense. Look out for features that replace tasks you can do manually just as easily, quickly, and well.
- **Test the application.** For example, while the project is being planned, does the software behave as expected whenever you shorten the duration of a task after assigning an additional person to it? Run tests using situations from your project management experience.

  If, after trying project management applications, you believe you can achieve better results using simpler techniques (pen-and-paper or Excel worksheets), avoid feeling pressured by colleagues or company policy into using project management software. If necessary, explain your reasons in a persuasive oral or written report, citing examples from your experience and reading.
- **Put first things first.** Focus on identifying purposes and objectives, audiences, context, deliverables, and requirements before engaging the software—regardless of the appealing look of the dashboard or Gantt charts.
- **Don't let project management shield you from interpersonal communication with the project team.** While application features can help you initiate and maintain communication—and reduce your need for team meetings—no software features can replace face-to-face communication altogether.

Project Blogs

A project blog is a frequently updated website, much like the blogs (Web logs) you visit. Think of a project blog as an online journal. The blogger—the project manager or a team member—details the project's goals, procedures, and status updates in narrative form. Members of the project team and others given access to the blog can, of course, comment on any journal entry (blog post).

Blog Features

To be sure, every blog contains a place for visitors to record comments, and the most recent post appears at the top by default. Some blogs include a header section showing the project start date, projected end date, current status, and an abstract of the project. The individual blog posts, with author identification, title, and date, represent milestones chronicling the project's background and ideas, research and development, and results.

The project blog for Microsoft's Word 2010 appears in Illustration 15.6. The last milestone, posted September 27, 2010, was written by a guest writer, a program manager on the Word team. With the project long since completed, this project blog is technically inactive and outdated, though, in fact, it still serves as a repository of useful information for the software developers and users alike.

A variety of Word team members posted updates, blogging about Word 2007 in July 2008 and then announcing the new version on the project blog a year later. The bloggers inserted photos, software screen captures, and videos to enliven their posts. Clicking the blogger's name reveals a list of that person's blog activity—the articles and follow-up remarks he or she posted and her or his responses to blog visitors' comments. When a visitor clicks "All Blogs," a pop-up menu gives access to eight other Microsoft Office 2010 projects. A sort feature enables visitors to sort posts three ways: most comments, most recent, and most views. A search box allows visitors to find specific information on this 19-page project blog.

Blog Advantages

The Microsoft Word blog (Illustration 15.6) helps us grasp the advantages and purposes of project blogs:

1. Team members visiting a project blog get a more holistic view of the project or product than their individual roles afford them.
2. Visiting a blog helps new team members get up to speed on a project.
3. If a blogger leaves the organization, other team members can still readily access his or her posts.
4. Linking other projects to the project blog helps accelerate knowledge creation.
5. Blog visitors' comments and questions give insights that can lead a project manager to change the project plan.

ILLUSTRATION 15.6   PROJECT BLOG FOR MICROSOFT'S WORD 2010 PROJECT

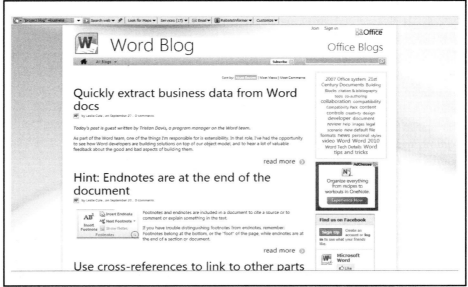

Source: Word Blog, Microsoft Corporation, last modified September 27, 2010, accessed September 28, 2011, http://blogs.office.com/b/microsoft-word.

6. Project blogs generally reduce time spent in meetings. Small concerns can be handled through posts and comments.

7. Posting a project blog on the Web instead of a company intranet helps blog visitors look forward to the project's outcome. For example, Word Blog built anticipation for the new version among Word 2007 users.

8. The project blog becomes a database that can be searched by author, key word, title, and the like. For instance, Word Blog's search function could be helpful to visitors during the project and later to technical support teams who must troubleshoot problems.

Specific Blog Sources

To create a project blog, you might use blog tools available in your project management application, if blog tools are available. Otherwise, you might use an offline program like BlogDesk (free) or Qumana to write and edit and then ping (submit) your blog to an online blogging site. Many bloggers forgo an offline program and start their project blogs with a blog service provider, such as Wordpress (http://wordpress.com), today's most-used provider. Other popular providers of blog service on the Web and company intranets include these organizations:

> Blogger by Google (http://www.blogger.com)
>
> Drupal (http://drupal.org)
>
> ExpressionEngine (http://expressionengine.com)
>
> LiveJournal (http://www.livejournal.com)
>
> Movable Type (http://movabletype.org)
>
> Serendipity (http://www.s9y.org)
>
> TypePad (http://www.typepad.com)

Posting a blog on the Web instead of a company intranet requires bloggers to be extra careful not to divulge confidential information. Having your blog on the Internet also increases your need for a comment editing feature (for example, to clean up the markup language, correct grammar and spelling errors, and delete profanity). To make a project blog an independent website (like the Word 2010 blog referred to earlier), you will need to choose a Web hosting service unless the blog provider, like Wordpress, can also be the Web host. A Web host is a company that provides clients space on its server and connection to its data center on the Internet. A few Web host examples include Bluehost (http://www.bluehost.com), DreamHost (http://dreamhost.com), JustHost (http://www.justhost.com), Laughing Squid (http://laughingsquid.us), and MediaTemple (http://mediatemple.net/wordpress-webhosting.php). Some Internet service providers offer free Web hosting to subscribers, and some Web hosts provide free (advertisement-sponsored) service for a basic Web page and small-scale files.

Wikis

A wiki, as you likely know, is a website that allows users to create and edit pages collaboratively by way of a Web browser. Whereas a blog promotes the publication of information from a single source (one to many), a wiki is meant for *shared content creation*, that is, collaborative writing (many to many).

Three Types of Wikis

Essentially, there are three types of wikis: general public type (can be read by anyone) with a large community of readers and editors, private enterprise type (meant to be used in an organizational setting for data management), and personal type (meant to be used by an individual to manage notes on a desktop computer).

You are surely familiar with the best-known public wiki, the website named Wikipedia. And you likely realize that you or anyone you know can edit Wikipedia articles. To prevent chaotic results, a great number of people watch over Wikipedia, checking facts and editing as needed to maintain information quality.

Likewise, in private enterprise wikis, users share responsibility for the accuracy, relevance, and suitability of information on the wiki. In some cases, private wiki servers require user verification to edit pages and in rare instances even to read them. Such access controls can be applied to individual wiki pages or to the entire wiki. Thus, a document created by one department or project team could be available for reading but not accessible for editing in another department or team. A wiki's built-in version control for those who have edit privileges also helps maintain the quality of information. Changes can be made only by creating a record of who made them, and a user can easily and quickly revert to an earlier version of the wiki text.

Another public wiki is Answers (http://wiki.answers.com), an ad-supported site that lets users submit and answer or edit questions. Wikia (http://www.wikia.com/Wikia) is a popular wiki farm, a single Web site that hosts multiple public wikis and allows users to start new wikis. Wikia hosts hundreds of wikis in entertainment, gaming, and lifestyle categories.

Incidentally, Microsoft makes extensive use of wikis, but employees do so under the organization's firewall security, not on the Web. Wikis for enthusiasts of games like Age of Empires and Champions Online abound on the Web, however, and these game wikis have notable differences as well as similarities with private enterprise wikis. The main page for Star Trek Online (STOWiki) devotees is shown in Illustration 15.7. Its colorful and richly illustrated appearance is unlike typical private enterprise wikis, which are plainer with minimum page and text formatting. STOWiki also includes a discussion forum, which is not recommended by business users, who note that a wiki's openness works against the structure (chronological order and separate threads) needed for coherent discussion. The contents list of STOWiki shows these features in common with enterprise wikis.

Announcements. This wiki page contains news about events in the wiki users' community.

Frequently Asked Questions. Any user can ask or answer a question about using the wiki or the project it supports.

Getting Started. Here, newcomers to the game or team project will learn the basics of using the wiki. Few project wikis may need this section, but some corporate wikis may rival the size of STOWiki (over 3,000 articles since May 2009 and almost 3,000 registered contributors).

Guidelines. Guidelines refer to the etiquette and common practice observed in creating, editing, and managing articles on the wiki to promote basic orderliness in the wiki's use and appearance. Guidelines include ways of organizing information and creating and using shared resources, such as templates.

Help. Although wikis are inherently simple to set up and use, pages devoted to how-to information have value, especially to newcomers.

ILLUSTRATION 15.7   MAIN PAGE OF AN INTERNET GAME WIKI

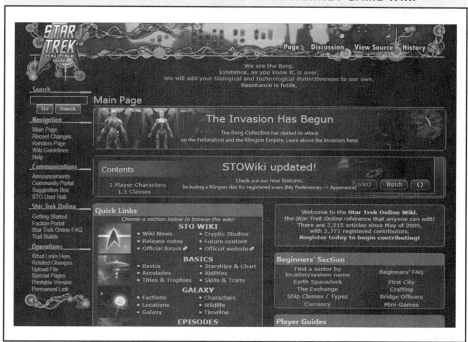

Source: Star Trek Online Wiki, Cryptic Studios, Inc. and CBS Studios Inc., accessed September 29, 2011, http://www.stowiki.org/Main_Page.

History. This wiki page shows the revision history. Through this page, each person's contributions can be identified, providing a sense of ownership for wiki users. The revision history page is central to undoing updates and enabling editorial oversight of the wiki.

Recent Changes. This page shows the wiki's revision history for the past couple of days. This information is a particular convenience to the person who oversees the wiki.

Search Function. With this feature, the wiki becomes a searchable knowledge base that everyone in the wiki community can share.

Suggestion Box. Users can write wiki-related feedback on this page. Another page is available for suggesting game features (STOWiki) or changes in the business team's project.

Wiki Uses

Collaborative writing is a wiki's strength; in addition, wikis are extremely flexible. Businesses use them in multiple ways:

- To create and track all the documentation (plans, schedules, team contract, specifications, status reports, and change proposals) needed to manage a team project
- To centralize all types of data files (word-processing files, spreadsheets, slide shows, PDF files—anything that a browser can display)
- To build a knowledge repository and keep it absolutely current since updates appear almost instantly online
- To brainstorm solutions to project-related problems
- To collect and share job know-how acquired "on the go" with teammates and other teams or communities

- To post meeting agendas and related handouts, allowing attendees to prepare for the meeting, suggest additional agenda items, and so on
- To store meeting minutes, enabling team members to record additional input about meeting topics on the wiki
- To provide information that can be used to solve common problems, like how to troubleshoot when the printer does not print
- To dispense up-to-date employment information—employee handbook, office procedures manual, and organization's mission statement and policies
- To let teams collaborate, using everyday skills and tools (an ordinary Web browser) to draft, organize, revise, and edit text, including product documentation (user's manuals), slides for oral reports, and all types of written reports (*Note:* Documents that require extensive formatting are exported to a word processor once the editing is done.)

Wiki Engines

Some wiki engines (software) are expressly made for public, private enterprise, or personal use. Other engines can be used for all three but contain functions (built-in or plug-in) explicitly for one or more of the usage types.

For public wikis, the dominant wiki engine is MediaWiki (http://www.mediawiki.org/wiki/MediaWiki), which powers both Wikia and Wikipedia. Other wiki engines used regularly for public wikis include MoinMoin (http://moinmo.in), PHPWiki (http://sourceforge.net/projects/phpwiki), and PmWiki (http://www.pmwiki.org).

Well-accepted wiki engines in the private enterprise category include Altassan's Confluence (http://www.atlassian.com/software/confluence), SamePage (http://www.etouch.net/home), Socialtext (http://www.socialtext.com), and TWiki (http://twiki.org).

Wiki engines designed for running personal wikis include an online notepad called NotePub (http://notepub.com), a personal information manager named Pimki (http://rubyforge.org/projects/pimki), and a desktop note-taking application called Tomboy (http://projects.gnome.org/tomboy). In addition, the public engine Moin-Moin offers a desktop edition for individual users.

Guides for Using Wikis

Your business career may involve setting up and/or overseeing an enterprise wiki. If so, keep the following guides in mind:

- At the outset, put just a few pages in the wiki with headings to suggest a structure for each wiki page. These starter pages will be especially helpful to anyone daunted by a fresh, blank screen. Don't overdo it, though; instead, let users create the structure for their wikis.
- Wikis need to be used by people with a shared cultural language so that the wiki structure and navigation make sense to all users. While people within one department at one location will share a corporate culture and speak the same jargon, people in other departments or locations may differ. Take steps to adopt a standard vocabulary and ensure that all users of your wiki know the terms.
- Use access controls sparingly to avoid stifling creativity and participation.
- Go with plain-vanilla formatting on the wiki pages. This practice will prompt users to use their time writing good content, not struggling with formatting issues. For

documents that need advanced formatting—such as a report for transmittal to a client—have text exported offline to a word-processing or other appropriate application.

- Always have a staff member who can take responsibility for the wiki. You will need somebody who can establish conventions for naming pages, maintaining links, and the like in addition to monitoring all revisions and taking needed corrective action.
- When writing in the wiki, avoid first-person style. Conform to the tone and flow of the existing articles. Omit your opinions. Include factual information and present it clearly and concisely in a neutral tone, neither negative nor overly positive.
- Promote the wiki by using it in all the ways that work for you and your team or organization. Gather innovative ideas from your associates and online information.
- Include a review page. Use it to capture feedback and ideas for fine-tuning the wiki to the project's and team's needs. In addition, this page may give you insight into the team's process.

View project management applications, project blogs, and enterprise wikis as natural extensions of your software skills. While in college, seek firsthand knowledge and hands-on experience with these tools in academic and business settings. Skill in using any project management tool is important to include on your employment résumé.

Ethical Considerations

You may be faced with ethical issues at all stages of data analysis. The presumed objectivity of numbers may lead some people to assume that statistical analysis is an objective, amoral process. You may, however, be confronted with ethical questions during statistical analysis. For example, your choice of a significance level may involve ethics. Your findings may be significant at the .10 level but not at the .05 or .01 level. Is it ethical to present findings as "significant" when there is a 10 percent probability that the observed relationships or differences are chance observations? To avoid this ethical dilemma, most researchers select a significance level before doing the analysis.

During the analysis of findings, you may also have to make choices about whether data should or should not be made public. When you have promised primary data sources that they will not be identified, you have a moral obligation to fulfill that promise. The assurance of confidentiality requires that you present the information in such a way that the data cannot be traced to specific participants. A similar obligation exists even when you have not promised confidentiality. In some situations, revelation of sources may cause financial, emotional, or other forms of injury to individuals. When that situation exists, you must decide which is the greater good: revealing or concealing source identity.

Similarly, you may have to decide whether certain data should be included in or excluded from the analysis. You may be tempted to exclude data that will not support your hypothesis or provide an outcome that you know your manager prefers. Ethical behavior, however, requires objective analysis of all relevant available data. Moreover, while drawing conclusions and making recommendations, ethical researchers test the logic of their conclusions and examine the likely impact of their recommendations.

Summary

Data analysis is the process of converting raw data into usable information for decision makers. The process involves reducing raw data into findings, interpreting those findings, drawing conclusions, and making recommendations.

Understanding the research problem, maintaining a critical mindset, and applying logic and appropriate statistical procedures are requirements for data analysis. Before data can be analyzed, they must be edited and coded. They may also be entered into a computer, after which their correct entry must be verified. Analysis may include statistical and nonstatistical procedures. Conclusions must be supported by findings, and recommendations must be related to the purpose of the study.

Topics for Discussion

1. Define the following terms:
    a. Raw data
    b. Data analysis
    c. Qualitative data
    d. Quantitative data
    e. Induction
    f. Deduction
    g. Mean
    h. Median
    i. Mode
    j. Findings
    k. Conclusions
    l. Recommendations
2. How does knowledge of the research problem assist in data analysis?
3. What is a critical viewpoint? How is it maintained?
4. Give examples of inductive reasoning and deductive reasoning other than those in the textbook.
5. Identify and explain the criteria for an effective data coding system.
6. What is the purpose of data verification?
7. For what purposes are descriptive statistics used?
8. For what purposes are inferential statistics used?
9. What are three guidelines for writing findings? Conclusions? Recommendations?
10. Identify ethical issues that may arise during and after data analysis.

Applications

1. As directed by your instructor, continue working on any study for which you prepared a proposal and data collection instruments in earlier assignments. Specifically, follow these steps to complete your assignment:
    *   Collect all necessary data for analysis.
    *   Select appropriate analysis techniques.
    *   Prepare the data.
    *   Analyze the data.
    *   Write a progress report to your instructor. In the report include a statement of preliminary findings and conclusions.
2. The World Factbook, published by the U.S. Central Intelligence Agency, contains a wealth of economic, political, and cultural information about nations worldwide (available at https://www.cia.gov/library/publications/the-world-factbook). Select

any consumer product that you are familiar with, then select three countries in which you would like to market the product. Go to that factbook and get information to compare the three countries on three economic indicators and one other factor, such as transportation or communication. Based on that information, conclude whether the product could be marketed successfully in any of the three countries. If so, which country appears to be the best target market? Present your findings and conclusions in a report to your instructor. Use memorandum format.

3. The recently organized Downtown Business Association hired you to conduct a survey to determine what citizens like and dislike about the downtown area. The purpose of the survey was to determine what kinds of people currently frequent the downtown area and what changes might encourage them to visit it more frequently. Your survey strategy was to conduct random interviews on the streets of the downtown area for a one-week period at six time intervals: 8:00 A.M. to 11 A.M., 11:01 A.M. to 2:00 P.M., 2:01 P.M. to 5:00 P.M., 5:01 P.M., to 8:00 P.M., and 8:01 P.M. to 11:00 P.M. You continued the data collection until you completed 500 interviews. The results of your interviews are summarized below. Analyze the data. Present your findings and conclusions in a report to the Downtown Merchants Association. Use memorandum format. Include at least one visual aid.

Age of Respondents

Age	No.
18–24	105
25–34	166
35–49	157
50–64	50
65 or over	22

Occupation of Respondent

Occupation	No.
Student	66
Professional	91
Administrative support	72
Service (including restaurant/bar employees)	77
Technical	52
Management	25
Blue collar (including construction)	25
Sales	38
Other	15
Retired	20
Unemployed	8
No response	11

Household Income

Income	No.
Less than $15,000	94
$15,000–$24,999	115
$25,000–$34,999	72
$35,000–$49,999	70
$50,000–$74,999	70
$75,000–$99,999	26
$100,000–$124,999	30
$125,000	16
No response	7

Type of Household

Household	No.
One adult, no children	216
Two adults, no children	109
Two-parent household	107
One-parent household	68

Place of Residence

Area	No.	Area	No.
Central city	111	Southeast suburbs	80
Northeast suburbs	121	Southwest suburbs	46
Northwest suburbs	115	Other	27

Reason for Being Downtown When Surveyed (only one response allowed)

Reason	No.
Working	236
Shopping	60
Dining/socializing	46
Going to school	29
Attending meeting	37
Running errands	22
Visiting art museum	25
Sightseeing	16
Going to library	21
Other	8

Reason for Ever Going Downtown Other Than Work (more than one response allowed)

Reason	No.
Shopping	127
None	119
Eating	91
Other	65
Going to school	40
Sightseeing	35
Going to city park	37
Going to library	24
Cultural events	29
Entertainment/clubs	34
Going to art museum	28

What People Like about Downtown (more than one response allowed)

Feature	No.
Atmosphere	105
Other	56
Convenience/proximity	72
City park	52
Cleanliness	40
Restaurants	45
Stores	39
Nothing	33
Buildings	23
Library	27
Safety	11
Art museum	30
Entertainment/clubs	30

What People Dislike about Downtown (more than one response allowed)

Feature	No.
Few stores	126
Parking	118
Other	87
Street people	65
Atmosphere	51
Lack of attractive, affordable housing	28
Boring	25
Nothing	25
Few restaurants	23
Unsafe	22

One Change That Would Bring People Downtown
(only one response allowed)

Feature	No.	Feature	No.
More specialty shops	141	More police/safety	35
More parking	72	Nothing	33
More housing options	49	Entertainment/clubs	31
No response	46	Department store	28
More dining options	39	Grocery store	26

4. Executives of companies considering expansion into the international market are often concerned about the level of corruption that exists among public officials in the countries in which they hope to establish a business presence. Transparency International publishes a Corruption Perceptions Index (CPI), which draws on polls and surveys from independent institutions to determine the perceptions of businesspeople, the general public, and country analysts regarding the level of corruption in 178 countries. Scores on the index range from 10 (highly clean) to 0 (highly corrupt). On the 2010 index, nearly three-quarters of the countries scored below 5.

The 2010 CPI can be found at http://www.transparency.org. Assume you are the marketing director for a U.S. company that wants to expand into the foreign market. Based on management's perception of the significance of corruption among public officials and the type of product or service you wish to introduce into other countries (you decide what your company wants to market abroad), select six countries that your company should investigate as possible target markets. Direct your report to the executive committee of your company. Use memorandum style and include sufficient information about your company and the countries' ratings on the CPI to support your recommendations.

5. African American, Asian American, and Hispanic consumers in the United States have made substantial gains in buying power over the last 10 years, and those gains are projected to continue. The growing populations and increased purchasing power in these groups have drawn the attention of all types of advertisers. Using the data given here and additional relevant data, prepare a report about the implications that such data have for marketers of discretionary goods and services, such as telephone service, electricity and natural gas, major appliances, vehicles, clothing, and footwear. Use memorandum style and direct the report to the chair of the marketing program in your school. Assume that the purpose of the report is to suggest changes in the advertising curriculum. (Source: http://www.tvb.org/planning_buying, retrieved August 23, 2011.)

Buying Power (billions of dollars)

	1990	2000	2009	2014 (projected)
African American	318.1	590.2	910.4	1,136.8
Asian American	116.5	268.8	978.4	696.5
Hispanic	211.9	489.5	951.0	1,330.4

Top States for Ethnic Buying Power

	African American			Asian American			Hispanic	
Rank	**State**	**$ (Billions)**		**State**	**$ (Billions)**		**State**	**$ (Billions)**
1	New York	86		California	163		California	253
2	Texas	72		New York	51		Texas	175
3	California	62		Texas	34		Florida	101
4	Georgia	61		New Jersey	32		New York	76
5	Florida	61		Illinois	23		Illinois	43
6	Maryland	52		Hawaii	22		New Jersey	37
7	Illinois	45		Washington	17		Arizona	31
8	North Carolina	41		Florida	15		Colorado	21
9	Virginia	38		Virginia	15		New Mexico	18
10	New Jersey	35		Massachusetts	13		Georgia	15

Percentage Change in Buying Power

	1990–2009	1990–2014	2000–2009	2009–2014
African American	186.2	257.3	54.3	24.9
Asian American	336.6	497.9	89.3	36.9
Hispanic	361.8	528.0	99.9	36.0

6. A growing trend in building construction is to convert shipping containers into vacation homes, suburban homes, apartments, and even office buildings. Gather information from the Web about this trend. Then construct a questionnaire to determine how likely a target group (such as young professionals, retirees, or second-home purchasers) would be to use that type of construction. Administer the questionnaires to a sample of your targeted population. Interpret the data and present your findings and conclusions in a memorandum report directed to your instructor.

7. Most of the Fortune 500 companies maintain a blog, according to the Fortune 500 Business Blogging Wiki. Recently, you learned that in the future the people at Fortune want to rate or rank the blogs. In fact, a Fortune staffer asked you to participate in this endeavor, starting with drafting an appropriate instrument. You choose to make it short and simple with six to ten items. You've already jotted several ideas for questionnaire items:

Audience engagement, such as freebies to download, contests to enter, polls to take

Appearance

Content (importance, interest, relevance)

Currency of the posts

Visitor traffic reflected by the number of comments

Before drafting the questions, though, you visit Fortune 500 Business Blogging Wiki (https://www.socialtext.net/bizblogs/index.cgi) and check out the following company's blogs: Boeing, Coca-Cola, Lowe's, United Parcel Service, and Wells Fargo.

   a. Write the six to ten questionnaire items, arrange them logically, and provide directions for completing the questionnaire. (Your instructor may have you collaborate with several other students or the class.)

   b. Return to the Fortune 500 wiki. Using your questionnaire, rate these five Fortune 500 blogs: Aflac, Colgate-Palmolive, Duke Energy, Nike, and Waste Management. Compute the mean rating for each blog as well as the mean for all five of them.

   c. Prepare a two- to three-minute oral report of your findings. In it, answer these questions: How well did your questionnaire distinguish among the five blogs? In other words, is the range in scores wide or narrow? If the range is narrow (all five blogs received basically the same score), how do you account for this fact? How might you "sharpen" the questionnaire so that it distinguishes among the business blogs more effectively? How did your ratings for each blog compare with those of classmates? Did this outcome surprise you? Why?

8. Assume that the following tables summarize the data collected by way of the interview guide shown in Illustration 13.3 and the checklist shown in Illustration 13.4. The interviews were conducted at two sites: Metro Valley State Park and New River-Greenbrier State Park. Analyze the data and write a report in manuscript format with a title page. The research problem was to determine tourists' current perceptions of the Hatfield-McCoy Mountains region and identify ways to increase tourist visits to the regions. Direct the report to Ms. Katherine Wilson, Hatfield-McCoy Mountains Coalition, 123 Main Street, Chapmanville, WV 25508.

TABLE 1 PROFILE OF INTERVIEWEES

Factor/Question	Metro Valley	New River-Greenbrier	Total N = 200	Percent of Total
Sex				
Male	48	49	97	48.5
Female	52	51	103	51.5
Age-group				
18–34	30	30	60	25
35–54	50	50	100	50
55+	30	30	60	25
Primary reason for trip				
Family vacation	42	54	96	48.0
Weekend getaway	16	34	50	25.0
Day trip	25	10	35	17.5
Business trip	8	2	10	5.0
Visiting family/friends	9	0	9	4.5
Visited area before				
Yes	26	19	45	22.5
No	74	81	155	77.5

continued

TABLE 1 CONTINUED

Factor/Question	Metro Valley	New River-Greenbrier	Total N = 200	Percent of Total
Why this area				
Family/friend recommendation	50	99	149	48.7
History/culture of region	13	40	53	17.3
Return trip	20	25	45	14.7
Advertising response	6	23	29	9.5
Travel agent recommendation	8	9	17	5.6
Business requirement	5	8	13	4.2
*Total			306*	
Other sites visited				
New River-Greenbrier	48	148	196	49.4
Metro Valley	111	64	140	35.2
Hatfield-McCoy	15	46	61	15.4
*Total			397*	
Activities engaged in				
General sightseeing	54	83	137	33.7
Visiting historical sites	50	56	106	26.0
Camping/hiking	35	29	64	15.7
Entertainment	23	0	23	5.7
Shopping	19	2	21	5.2
Gaming	17	0	17	4.1
Visiting family/friends	8	8	16	3.9
Hunting/fishing	10	13	23	5.7
*Total			407*	
Nights spent in West Virginia				
None	28	8	36	18.0
1–3	35	43	78	39.0
4–6	36	45	81	40.5
7–9	0	2	2	1.0
10+	1	2	3	1.5
Where lodged				
Hotel/motel/bed-and-breakfast	58	41	99	43.0
Campsite	25	38	63	27.4
Cabin in state park	13	16	29	12.6
Not staying overnight	20	8	28	12.2
Home of family or friends	6	5	11	4.8
*Total			230*	
Where ate meals				
Restaurant	83	95	178	69.9
At campsite	30	23	53	20.6
Home of family or friends	8	9	17	6.6
Food service at public facility	0	9		3.5
*Total			257*	
Familiar with Hatfield-McCoy Mountains				
Yes	13	40	53	26.5
No	87	60	147	73.5

*Total greater than 200 because more than one choice was permitted.

Source: © Cengage Learning 2013

TABLE 2 TOURISTS' PERCEPTIONS OF HATFIELD-MCCOY MOUNTAINS REGION

Prompt	Percent of Respondents Who Associated the Prompt with Hatfield-McCoy Mountains
A family feud long ago	96
An economically depressed region	68
Coal mining region	59
Mountaineer pride	55
An interesting area of the state	55
Coal Mine Wars	50
Beautiful scenery	45
Good hiking	41
Camping in state park	36
Good hunting and fishing	36
Trails for ATVs, motorcycles, bikes	35
Whitewater rafting	35
Cabins in state park	34
Museums	30
A building made entirely of coal	27
Chief Logan	25
Outdoor drama about a Shawnee princess	25
Historical monuments	23
Chuck Yeager	20
Golf	0
Auto races	0
Festivals	0
Good hotels	0
Good restaurants	0

Source: © Cengage Learning 2013

CHAPTER **16**

Writing Business Research Reports

LEARNING OBJECTIVES

After you have read this chapter, you should be able to:

1. Identify and prepare the preliminaries, body, and supplements for a formal business research report.

2. Use appropriate margins, spacing, headings, and page numbering for a formal report with the aid of Microsoft Word 2010 formatting features.

3. Describe the main collaboration features in Word 2010 and the security risks involved.

4. Be aware of ethical issues that may arise as you interpret and present the results of your research.

YOU HAVE STUDIED how to plan business research and how to collect and analyze data for a complex report. One aspect of the preparation of a formal business report remains: putting the information into an attractive, functional format that enables readers to absorb easily the information it contains and stimulates them to act on the contents of the report.

Business research reports are often classified as information or analytical reports. An *information* report provides comprehensive data related to a business problem along with interpretation of the data, but it offers no conclusions or recommendations. An *analytical* report includes conclusions and may also present recommendations.

Parts of the Formal Business Report

Many relatively lengthy reports are prepared in a formal style such as is presented in this chapter. A characteristic of a formal business report is the inclusion of several parts that are not included in less formal reports. Although you may adapt the parts of a formal report to suit the requirements of your reporting situation, the most comprehensive structure includes the factors listed in Illustration 16.1. Each part is explained in this chapter and demonstrated in a report illustrated at the end of this chapter[1] (see Illustrations 16.10, 16.11, 16.12, and 16.13, pp. 495–519). As you learned in Chapter 5, the preferred procedure is to display illustrations as soon as possible after they are introduced in the text. However, because of the length of the illustrated report and to be able to integrate other illustrations into the text of this chapter, the report illustrations are grouped at the end of the chapter and numbered in sequence from the last in-text illustration.

ILLUSTRATION 16.1 PARTS OF A FORMAL REPORT

1. Report Preliminaries (sometimes called front matter)
    1.1   Cover or binder
    1.2   Flyleaves
    1.3   Title page
    1.4   Transmittal message
    1.5   Authorization message
    1.6   Acceptance message
    1.7   Table of contents
    1.8   List of tables or figures
    1.9   Foreword or preface
    1.10 Acknowledgments
    1.11 Synopsis or executive summary

2. Report Body
    2.1   Introduction
    2.2   Presentation and discussion of findings
    2.3   Summary, conclusions, and recommendations (summary only for an information
          report; summary, conclusions, and recommendations for an analytical report)

3. Report Supplements (sometimes called end matter)
    3.1   Endnotes
    3.2   Bibliography, source list, or references
    3.3   Glossary
    3.4   Appendix
    3.5   Index

© Cengage Learning 2013

As you study the explanation of each part, examine its counterpart in the illustrations. Note also the writing style and the inductive structure of the report. Consider the report shown in this illustration to be the result of the research proposal presented in Illustration 10.2 (pp. 300–303). You should review that proposal at this time.

Report Preliminaries

The preliminary parts of a formal report help to make the report user friendly. Those parts provide a convenient way to physically transmit the report, establish a context for understanding it, and enable the reader to locate specific information easily. Some preliminary parts may be omitted when justified by the length of the report, the complexity of the topic, or the formality of the situation.

Although the report preliminaries are the first pages the report user sees, many of those parts can be compiled only after you have written the full report. The preliminary parts must accurately reflect the report's content and structure. If you revise your report in any way after you have written the preliminaries, be sure to check the accuracy of all preliminary parts and, if necessary, revise them before delivering the report. For example, be sure that your table of contents accurately shows the final content and page numbering of your report. Later sections of this chapter discuss ways to manage your draft of report preliminaries electronically.

Cover or Binder

A reader must be able to handle the report document conveniently. Although some readers may prefer that you present unbound pages, perhaps enclosed in an envelope or a file folder, many prefer that you bind the report securely, and some will request an electronic version. A cover or binder protects the pages of a printed report and prevents them from loosening while the reader uses the report. Your report cover should show at least the title of the report; if the title is long, a shortened form may appear on the cover. You may also include a design or illustration to suggest the content of the report and stimulate interest (see first page of Illustration 16.11, p. 496).

Flyleaves

A blank sheet may be placed at both the front and the back of the report to protect other pages and provide a space for readers' comments. Those sheets, called flyleaves, are optional. Since they tend to connote a higher level of formality, include flyleaves only when you think the situation justifies such formality. Note, for example, that most hardcover books contain flyleaves, but many softcover books do not.

Title Page

The title page usually contains four facts: the full title of the report; the identity of the person or agency for whom the report was prepared, including contact information; the author's identity, including contact information; and the submission date. Although inclusion of the author's identity is optional, it may be advantageous to include such information on all reports unless you are instructed not to do so. Such information will help readers provide feedback, such as questions, commendations, or requests for new projects.

The title of the report should provide a concise statement of the report's content. Include as much *who, what, why, when,* and *where* information as is possible without creating a cumbersome title. To achieve conciseness, avoid using unnecessary words and phrases such as "an analysis of" or "the determination of." A "talking" title may stimulate interest more readily than a purely descriptive title. The following examples contrast a cumbersome, verbose title with a descriptive title and a talking title.

> **Cumbersome, verbose:** *A Comprehensive Analysis of Charlestonians' Knowledge of and Attitudes toward the Cruise Industry in Charleston*
>
> **Descriptive:** *Assessing Charlestonians' Knowledge and Attitudes about the Cruise Industry*
>
> **Talking:** *What Should the Ports Authority Do to Improve Charlestonians' Attitudes about the Cruise Industry?*

For the title page you may use a traditional format or any creative format that effectively conveys the required information. A nontraditional format is demonstrated in Illustration 16.11 (p. 497). A traditional title page format is demonstrated in Illustration 16.12 (p. 517). Notice that no page number appears on the title page.

Transmittal Message

The transmittal message, in letter or memorandum format, presents the report to your primary reader(s). Generally, a letter is used for external reports and a memo for internal reports.

If you have written the report in an impersonal style, the transmittal message gives you an opportunity to speak more personally to your primary contact person and to reinforce goodwill. The message may include any comments that will stimulate interest in the report, confirm confidence in you as the researcher and writer, and perhaps lead to further interesting, responsible assignments. Appropriate content for the transmittal message includes some, but not necessarily all, of the following: a review of the research problem, purpose, and methodology; highlights of major findings; significant recommendations; comments about the research experience; an offer to discuss the report or assist with future projects.

The transmittal message is often bound within the report, either before or after the title page, but some writers prefer to present it as a separate message accompanying the report. See Illustration 16.10 (p. 495) for an example of a separate transmittal message accompanying the report. In this example, as the transmittal message indicates, the report will likely be circulated outside the organization for which it was prepared. Therefore, the separate transmittal memo is appropriate.

Authorization and Acceptance Messages

The authorization message provides evidence of permission to undertake the project, and the acceptance message gives evidence of agreement to do the task. Those messages are often exchanged before the project is undertaken, sometimes orally and sometimes in writing. If written, they may be included in the report as formal notice to secondary readers that the project was appropriately authorized and accepted. However, if the transmittal message includes reference to the authorization, as is done in Illustration 16.10, those messages may be omitted from the report.

If authorization and acceptance messages had been included in Illustration 16.11, they would be similar to the following examples:

Authorization Message

(Appropriate letter or memo format)

Please proceed with the study of citizens' attitudes toward the cruise industry and enhancements to the Port of Charleston.

As we discussed this morning, the State Ports Authority must be fully aware of current perceptions of the cruise industry and proposed port enhancements. The research proposal you presented convinced me that your department is the right one to undertake this study. You have my full support.

You agreed to submit a written report of your findings, conclusions, and recommendations no later than September 30. I would appreciate a progress report on July 30 about the first phase of the study.

Acceptance Message

(Appropriate letter or memorandum format)

Thank you for authorizing the Government Relations Division to analyze citizens' perceptions of the cruise industry and proposed port enhancements. My research team has already begun to prepare data collection instruments.

You will have a report of the research no later than September 25. As you requested, I will submit a progress report on July 30.

You may also occasionally submit unsolicited reports. In such an instance, authorization and acceptance messages do not exist, and the transmittal message must indicate clearly why you are submitting the report.

Contents

In a lengthy report, a table of contents (see Illustration 16.11, p. 498) and list of tables and figures (p. 499) help the reader get an overview of the report and easily refer to specific parts of the report.

The table of contents must list all items that appear after that page: any preliminary pages that follow and all chapter or section headings and subheadings used in the report. Do not list preliminary pages that appear before the table of contents. The number of the page on which each first-level division begins must be included. Many writers include page numbers to mark the beginning of each subdivision as well. Some writers use an outline numbering system, such as the decimal system demonstrated in Illustration 16.1 (p. 472), to identify the entries in the table of contents.

A list of tables or figures follows the table of contents when the report includes visual aids. When only one or two visual aids are used, some writers include them in the table of contents. However, the reader can locate the visual aids more easily if they appear in a separate list. If the list is short and space permits, the list may be included on the same page as the table of contents. The list of tables usually precedes the list of figures; but if few visuals are used, tables and figures may be grouped in a single list of illustrations.

Preface

A preface should present some special details about the report and create interest. The preface is not as comprehensive as the executive summary, which appears later. Comments about what stimulated the study and its significance are appropriate content for a preface. If that information already is conveyed in the authorization, acceptance, or transmittal messages, you may omit the preface. A preface is most appropriate in an unsolicited report.

The report shown in Illustration 16.11 contains no preface. The following example demonstrates an appropriate preface for that report.

Preface

Letters to the editor in the Charleston News and Courier *often indicate mixed attitudes about the docking of cruise ships at Union Pier in the Port of*

> *Charleston. Even after the implementation of a new cruise traffic plan for depart-ing ships, some residents and merchants continue to express negative opinions about pedestrian and motor traffic accompanying the presence of cruise ships in the port. It is essential that the Ports Authority use effective communication strategies to gain the support of Charlestonians as it proceeds with the proposed port enhancements. This report addresses the challenge of accurately identifying citizens' concerns and addressing those concerns openly and honestly.*

Acknowledgments

Include an acknowledgments page when you want to give credit to people who have as-sisted with the project. When such recognition is included in the transmittal message, the acknowledgments page is omitted. Acknowledgements are often written in the first person, even if the report itself is written in the third person. The following example de-monstrates appropriate acknowledgements for the report presented in Illustration 16.11.

> **Acknowledgments**
>
> *Many people contributed to the success of this study, and I am grateful to all of them. A special thank you goes to several who contributed in unique ways.*
>
> *Mary Ann Conrad of the Charleston Merchants Association generously shared the association's directory, from which a sample of merchants was drawn. Harry Hatfield of the Ports Authority's information technology division helped set up the electronic survey that was sent to the merchants. The vestry of St. Philip's Episcopal Church permitted use of its parish hall for the town-hall meetings held in the Ansonbourgh district. Individuals attending the town-hall meetings and merchants who completed the on-line survey willingly provided information about their perceptions of the impact of the cruise industry in Charleston. Their candid comments provided the data necessary to gain a needed perspective. Without their assistance, we would not have been able to produce this report.*
>
> *To all, a hearty "Thank you."*
>
> *Marvin L. Barbara*
>
> *VP, Government Relations*
>
> *S. C. Ports Authority*

Executive Summary

The executive summary, sometimes called a synopsis, immediately precedes the body of the report. In this summary, briefly state the research problem, purpose, research methods, major findings, conclusions, and recommendations. The summary must contain enough information to help a reader decide how much of the full report he or she should read (see Illustration 16.11, p. 500).

Although an analytical report may be written in inductive (indirect) structure, many readers prefer that the executive summary be written in deductive (direct) structure, be-ginning with the recommendations. One technique for drafting an executive summary is to reduce each major section of the report to one paragraph. After condensing the report in that way, you can revise the draft by arranging the paragraphs into the desired structure and adding transitions to link the paragraphs into a coherent summary.

Some executives prefer that the summary be no longer than one page. The length and complexity of the report, however, most often govern the length of the summary. Unless instructed to do so, do not feel that you must limit the summary to one page.

Report Body

Whereas the preliminaries provide a context for understanding the report and a summary of its contents, the body of your report must contain all details of the study. Since the report body should be a coherent unit, it begins with the report title, placed approximately 1½ inches from the top of the first page of the report body.

Write the report body so clearly and completely that a reader will understand its contents even if the person merely skims the preliminary parts. When the report is written in inductive structure, the title is followed by a coherent introduction; a complete presentation, discussion, and summary of findings; and—for an analytical report—conclusions and recommendations. For an information report, the summary marks the end of the report. The body of an analytical report written in inductive structure begins on the page immediately after the executive summary, as shown in Illustration 16.11.

Introduction

The introduction provides all information necessary to understand the remainder of the report. The introduction establishes the context for interpreting the findings and conclusions.

Typically, the introductory section for a report written in inductive structure includes the background to the problem, a statement of the research problem and purpose, the scope of analysis, and the research procedures. Delimitations, limitations, and definitions of terms may also be included. If you prepared a comprehensive research proposal, you can draw much of the information for the introduction from that document. Do not, however, merely copy the proposal. Use only those parts that are relevant and write in a style that is appropriate for a final report. Review the proposal shown in Illustration 10.2 (pp. 300–303) and note how its major points are included in the introduction to the report shown in Illustration 16.11. Note also that some parts of the proposal (such as the time schedule and budget) would be meaningless in the final report.

The report headings need not contain the words "introduction" or "problem." Indeed, descriptive headings, such as those used in Illustration 16.11, may increase reader interest.

Findings

The presentation and discussion of findings comprise the major portion of the report. In this section, you must present a complete and clear analysis of all data. For coherence, the final paragraph of the introduction or the first paragraph of the findings section should contain a preview of how this section will be organized.

The report need not contain an actual heading called "Findings." Instead, coherence should be achieved through descriptive headings and subheadings that provide clues about the information in each section and lead the reader through the analysis. Use your outline as a guide to ensure that your presentation is complete and organized logically.

The following headings were used in a report titled "Best ways to save gas."[2] Notice that the headings concisely summarize the content of each major division.

- Before you leave
  - Map it out
  - Check your tires
  - Get your car road-ready
  - Get the right rental
- On the road
  - Compare pump prices
  - Watch your speed
  - Drive smoothly
  - Don't be a drag
  - Avoid premium gas
  - Skip the gas-saving gadgets

Summary

Information and analytical reports should always contain an overall summary of the findings. When the analysis is lengthy and complex, you should also summarize your discussion of the findings at the end of each major section. For an information report written in inductive structure, the summary marks the conclusion of the report. In an analytical report, the summary may occupy a separate section, as is shown in Illustration 16.11 (p. 509), or may be included in a section with the conclusions and recommendations.

Conclusions and Recommendations

When analytical reports are written in inductive structure, the conclusions and recommendations constitute the final section or sections of the report (Illustration 16.11, p. 509). However, if the reader's preference or likely reaction justifies your using the deductive structure, recommendations and conclusions may be presented at the beginning of the report. The opening pages of a report presented in that manner are shown in Illustration 16.13 (p. 518).

Conclusions must be logical inferences supported by the data analysis. Recommendations propose actions that are justified by the analysis and conclusions; recommendations may also suggest other research that should be undertaken.

Recommendations are most meaningful when they are related to the stated purpose of the study. Notice, for example, the relationship of the purpose, conclusion, and recommendation in the following example:

> **Purpose:** *To assess the business and social climate in which the South Carolina Ports Authority will operate if it implements plans to relocate the cruise terminal. Knowledge of that climate will help the Authority develop operational and communication strategies relative to the relocation.*

> **Conclusion:** *Communication about the plans seems to have been understood and received favorably by downtown merchants. That communication, however, has done little to change the downtown residents' opinion about the value of the cruise industry.*

> **Recommendation:**
>
> 1. *Publicize the keys aspects of the Concept Plan. Specifically:*
>   - *Improved vehicular traffic flows and parking in the cruise terminal area and downtown Charleston*
>   - *Improved visual and human access to the waterfront*
>   - *Ecological reclamation and protection of the waterfront*
>   - *Reclamation and protection of historical structures in the Charleston Harbor*

Present all information to support the conclusions and recommendations in the data analysis sections. Some writers, perhaps in a mistaken attempt to compose a dramatic ending to the report, introduce new data with the conclusions or recommendations. That practice tends to confuse the reader and destroys report coherence. For example, in Illustration 16.11, a writer might be tempted to withhold the information about quality of life. Such a writer might think that the information would give final, solid justification for the recommendation to proceed with the proposed port enhancements in parallel projects. However, since the data about quality of life is closely related to respondents' perceptions of the cruise industry, it should be—and was—included as part of that analysis.

The conclusions and recommendations indicate completion of the analysis, but some situations warrant use of supplements, which provide supporting information.

Report Supplements

The supplements to a report include any information that may be useful—but not essential—for understanding the analysis, conclusions, and recommendations. Supplements may include endnotes, a bibliography or source list, a glossary, an appendix, and an index.

Source List

A reference list must be included when you decide to group specific source citations at the end of the report instead of using footnotes. Include in the list all sources that contributed data for the study. Illustration 16.11 demonstrates how to use in-text citations when you want to acknowledge specific sources within the text (see pp. 4 and 5 of that illustration). When in-text citations are used, all source information is given in a bibliography or a list of works cited (see Illustration 16.11, p. 511).

Glossary

A glossary—a list of selected words with their meanings—is required only when the report contains terms that may be unfamiliar to some readers. Including a glossary is advisable when the readership consists of some persons who know the technical terminology and others who do not. That practice provides definitions for readers who need them without cluttering the report with information that is unnecessary for many readers. If the report contains few technical or unfamiliar terms or words are given a specific meaning in the report, those terms may be included in the introductory section of the report, as is done on page 2 of Illustration 16.11.

Appendix

An appendix includes all items referred to but not displayed in the report body. Similarly, all items displayed in the appendix *must* be identified at some point in the report. Do not use the appendix to "share" interesting but nonessential information. Materials often displayed in an appendix include copies of transmittal letters and questionnaires or interview guides (Illustration 16.11, pp. 512–515), tabulations of data (Illustration 16.11, p. 516), statistical formulas, graphs, charts, and diagrams. Remember, however, that visual aids intended to clarify, emphasize, or summarize parts of the report should be incorporated into the report narrative unless you are specifically requested to group them in an appendix. Review Chapter 5 and see pages 5–8 of Illustration 16.11 for effective ways to incorporate figures and tables into the report narrative.

Index

An index is a list of key words or topics found in the report. Generally, an index is included only if the reader would not be able to locate specific information without that aid. In most situations, a comprehensive table of contents along with clear, concise division headings should be sufficient to direct the reader to specific topics.

The parts for a formal business report should be adapted to meet your specific reporting requirements. Be mindful of your audience and include all parts that will assist your readers. For example, when you must prepare an information report, you would include all parts except the conclusions and recommendations. In some contexts, the report summary may be included in the transmittal message, eliminating the need for a separate executive summary. As you select parts to include in your report, remember that your objectives are to establish rapport with report readers, stimulate interest in the report, and facilitate its use. Include all parts that will help you achieve those objectives.

Formatting Guides

Lengthy information and analytical reports are most frequently prepared in manuscript format. As you prepare your manuscript, attempt to determine your reader's preference for margins, spacing, headings, and page numbering. One way to determine a reader's preference is to ask; another way is to look in the company files to find examples of report styles in use. Some companies and government agencies publish office manuals (printed or online) for their employees. Those manuals often include document formats and the requirement that all reports follow the approved formats.

As noted in Chapter 6, some writers find that templates in word-processing software are useful; other writers think those templates give a "canned" look. If you use a template, select one that complements the overall tone and style of the report. Be sure also that the template applies protocols for margins, spacing, placement of headings, and pagination that are acceptable to your audience or modify the template to meet your reader's preferences and save it with a different file name. Microsoft Word 2010, for example, includes two report templates you might consider: one in the Academic Papers and Reports folder (XYZ Book template, about Row 7, labeled "Report Template with heading levels, table of contents, list of figures, list of tables and bibliography") and one in the Other Reports folder (Walnut & Birch template labeled Business Report). To access any of these templates, on the File tab, click New; then, under Available Templates, click the Reports icon. A template includes samples of default colors, fonts, graphics, headings, and visuals, as shown in Illustration 16.2.

Guides for Report Body

If you cannot determine the preferences of a specific reader, use the following formatting guides.

Margins and Spacing

Top, bottom, and side margins should contribute to the appearance and readability of the report. A guide for business report margins appears in Illustration 16.3, and Illustration 16.11 complies with it.

Although some readers may prefer double-spaced manuscripts, most contemporary business reports are printed in single-spaced, block format. Whenever you use single spacing, use double spacing (an additional stroke on the Enter key) between paragraphs.

Headings

Whether you use a single- or double-spaced format, you should use appropriate division headings to guide the reader through your report. The type style (capitalized, lowercase, bold, underlined, italicized) and placement of the headings must accurately reflect the organization of your report.

Style manuals differ slightly in their guides for style and placement of headings. Some manuals recommend typing the title in all capital letters; others (such as the *MLA Handbook for Writers of Research Papers*[3] and the *Publication Manual of the American Psychological Association*[4]) recommend capitalizing only the major words in the title. Although many reference manuals suggest that the title be centered on the first page, effective variations of title placement are shown in the Microsoft Word templates.

ILLUSTRATION 16.2 BUSINESS REPORT TEMPLATE IN WORD 2010

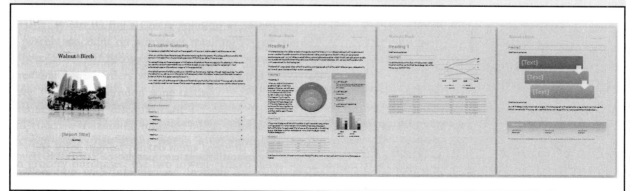

ILLUSTRATION 16.3 MARGINS FOR BUSINESS RESEARCH REPORT (IN INCHES)

Type of page	Top-Bound Manuscript				Left-Bound Manuscript			
	Top	Bottom	Left	Right	Top	Bottom	Left	Right
Title page	V*	V*	V*	V*	V*	V*	V*	V*
Transmittal message	V*	V* V*	V*	V*	V*	V*	V*	V*
Prefatory parts								
First page of each part	2	1	1	1	1.5	1	1.5	1
All other pages	1.5	1	1	1	1	1	1.5	1
Body of report								
First page	2	1	1	1	1.5	1	1	1
First page of each chapter	2	1	1	1	1.5	1	1	1
All other pages	1.5	1	1	1	1	1	1	1
Supplements								
First page of each part	2	1	1	1	1.5	1	1	1
All other pages	1.5	1	1	1	1	1	1	1

© Cengage Learning 2013

*Varies with design to achieve balanced appearance.

The American Psychological Association (APA) uses the following scheme to indicate division levels in a report.[5] When the entire report is prepared in block format (paragraphs not indented), all headings except Level 1 should begin at the left margin.

Level 1:
Centered Bold, Uppercase and Lowercase Heading

Level 2:
Flush Left, Bold, Uppercase and Lowercase Heading

Level 3:
> **Indented, bold, lowercase heading with a period.**

Level 4:
> ***Indented, bold, italicized lowercase heading with a period.***

Level 5:
> *Indented, italicized, lowercase paragraph heading ending with a period.*

Remember, most document designers recommend that you not underline headings because underlining can impair readability. Instead of underlining, headings may be distinguished from the report text and from other headings by variations in font style, color, and size. These headings (representing Microsoft Word's built-in Styles 1, 2, and 3) are used in Illustration 16.11.

> # REPORT TITLE: CENTERED UPPERCASE, BOLD, LARGE FONT
>
> ## Level 1. At Margin, Uppercase and Lowercase Headings, Bold, Dark Color, Large Font
>
> ### Level 2. At Margin, Uppercase and Lowercase Headings, Bold, Light Color, Medium Font
>
> **Level 3. At margin, sentence case headings, bold, light color, text-size font**

Chapter 6 referred to Word's nine built-in Heading Styles, called Heading 1, Heading 2, and so on. Each Style contains a particular font, font size, font color, and paragraph spacing; but Word allows you to change any or all of these features and save those Style changes whenever you save the file. These Styles have several advantages, including helping you with the consistency of your report headings. In addition, using the built-in Heading Styles enables you to construct a table of contents with only a few clicks. Follow these steps to apply and customize Heading Styles:

1. Select the text of a Level 1 heading.
2. On the Home tab, Styles group, point to Heading 1. Notice how the selected heading will look with this Style applied. If you do not like the appearance of your Level 1 heading, you have three options: (1) Choose a displayed Heading Style that you favor, (2) click the More down arrow to seek a more pleasing Style, or (3) click Heading 1 to apply it, knowing that you will modify it in one or more ways.
3. To modify a Heading Style you have applied, with the heading selected, you can click Change Styles (in the Styles group) and select the name of a Style Set (combination of font, size, color, and paragraph spacing) or select color, font, or paragraph spacing individually. Here is another way to modify the appearance of your Level 1 heading: With the heading selected, use tools in the Font and/or Paragraph groups, as shown in Illustration 16.4.
4. When the heading has the appearance you want, select it. Then right-click the style you applied. On the drop-down menu, select Update Heading _ to Match Selection. (Each time you apply this heading *in the current file*, it will contain your settings.)
5. Apply this same Heading Style to all Level 1 headings in your report.
6. Repeat steps 2 to 5 for Level 2 headings, applying a different style of your choice. Then repeat steps 2 to 5 for each additional heading level in the report.

Page Numbering

The report body and report supplements are numbered consecutively with Arabic numerals. The numeral "1" is usually omitted from the first page of the report body. If your report is printed on one side of each sheet, place numerals for subsequent pages in one of three locations: (1) about a half inch from the top, aligned with the right margin; (2) centered, about an inch from the bottom of each page; or (3) aligned with the right margin, about an inch from the bottom of the page. The first of these

ILLUSTRATION 16.4 HEADING STYLES CAN BE CHANGED

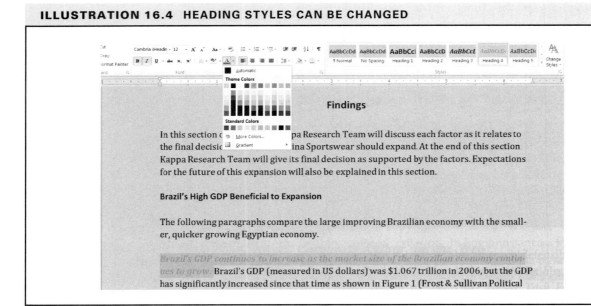

locations—which is shown in Illustration 16.11—is generally preferred. Leafing through a printed report or scrolling a report file to find a specific page is slightly easier when numbers are at the upper right. If you use two-sided printing, the first page of the report body (after preliminary parts) should be on a right-hand page, with no number printed. Unless centered page numbers are used, the numbers for subsequent odd-numbered pages are aligned at the right margin; even-numbered pages, at the left margin. The page number feature of your word-processing software will give you consistent placement of page numbers.

Follow these steps to insert page numbers using Microsoft Word 2010. (**Note:** If you want to include preliminary pages in the same file as the report body and supplements, see "Number Preliminary and Body Pages Differently" in this chapter.)

1. Click the Insert tab. In the Header & Footer group, click Page Number.
2. Click the page number location you want (Top or Bottom).
3. From the Simple gallery, choose left, centered, or right alignment—or scroll to one of the variations that fits the overall nature and appearance of your report.
4. To omit the number from page 1, click Header & Footer Tools. In the Options group, select Different First Page. If you will print on both sides of the sheet and are not centering page numbers, also click Different Odd & Even Pages.
5. Again, click the Insert tab and Page Number. Then click Format Page Numbers. In the Page Number Format dialog, at *Number format*, select the kind of page numbers you want. For the report body choose Arabic numerals, with or without hyphens before and after them. (**Note:** Word uses the Calibri, Size 11, font for all page numbers. If you prefer having page numbers match the serif font in

paragraphs, select the number on any page. Then click the Home tab and make choices from the Font group.)

6. To exit the Header/Footer view and return to the report body, on the Design tab, click Close Header and Footer or simply double-click outside the Header/Footer view.

Guides for Preliminary Pages

These additional guides will explore a few advanced features of Microsoft Word that can help you format the pages that precede the report body.

Insert Cover and Title Pages

Options for inserting a cover or title page include (1) using a cover page template or (2) preparing a title page to resemble Illustration 16.11 (p. 497) or Illustration 16.12 (p. 517). Word 2010 also lets you insert a cover and/or title page from the Insert tab.

1. On the Insert tab, Pages group, click Cover Page. Choose a suitable page and click to add it to the preliminaries. Click the selection a second time to add both a cover page and a title page to your report.
2. Replace original text with your report title and other title page information. Delete any original text that you do not replace.
3. If you want your title page to include information not represented, insert a text box: on the Insert tab, Text group, click Text Box; click the + insertion point where you want to add information; and then type in the box.
4. If desired, change the fonts, font sizes, and font colors using tools on the Home tab, Font group. To remove the fill or outline color of a text box, do the following:
   a. Click in the box.
   b. On the Drawing Tools tab, Shape Styles group, click Shape Fill (Shape Outline).
   c. Select No Fill (No Outline).

Insert Blank Page(s)

Sometimes you may want to insert a blank page between the text pages of your report. In the preliminaries, for example, you may want a blank page to serve as a placeholder for the transmittal letter instead of sending it as a separate document. You would print the letter on your company's letterhead as usual; then remove the blank page and insert the letter in its place before binding the report. Likewise, in the body of a report, you may need to insert a blank page in place of an oversized visual. In Word 2010, take two steps to insert a blank page:

1. Click the insertion point immediately before the text that is to follow the blank page.
2. On the Insert tab, Pages group, click Blank Page. Blank pages are numbered along with text pages because every page must be counted, though a number need not appear on every page.

Number Preliminary Pages

Traditionally, each of the preliminary parts begins on a new page. One exception to that practice concerns the list of tables or figures. If that list is short and space permits, you may place it on the last page of the table of contents. The preliminary pages are generally numbered with lowercase Roman numerals, centered about one inch from the bottom of the pages. (Using Word 2010, of course, you can follow the five guides for numbering pages in the report body. Just remember to choose "Bottom" in step 2; select a centered page number in step 3; and click on lowercase Roman numerals in step 5.) Use the following numbering scheme for preliminary pages:

Flyleaf, if used	No number
Title page	i, but no numeral is printed on that page
First page after title page	ii
Subsequent preliminary pages	iii, etc.

Number Preliminary and Body Pages Differently

Now, you are aware that preliminary pages are numbered with lowercase Roman numerals whereas the report body pages and supplements are numbered with Arabic numerals. The recommended placement of these page numbers also differs. You might handle these differences by creating the preliminaries in a separate file. However, Microsoft Word 2010 provides a way to include the two different numbering schemes in one file. The following steps involve creating separate sections in the report *and then* unlinking those sections.

1. Click at the beginning of the page where you want page numbering to change. (That is, click immediately before the text on the first report body page.)
2. On the Page Layout tab, Page Setup group, click Breaks. Under *Section Breaks*, click Next Page.
3. On the page that follows the Section Break, double-click in the header (top margin) or footer (bottom margin), wherever you will place page numbers in this section. (The Design tab opens, displaying Header & Footer Tools.)
4. On the Design tab, Navigation group, click Link to Previous to turn off the link. (This action unlinks the report body header from the preliminaries.)
5. Next, unlink the footer too: in the Navigation group, click Go to Footer (Illustration 16.5). Then click Link to Previous.
6. Now, follow page-numbering guides for each report section.

Insert a Table of Contents

Any report you create will likely have multiple readers now and in the future. Few of them, however, will read the entire report in sequence. Instead, they will read selectively, with some readers focusing on the executive summary, others on the conclusions and recommendations, and still others on the visuals included in the findings. A table of contents will enable each reader to find precisely the part that interests her or him.

ILLUSTRATION 16.5 UNLINK HEADER AND FOOTER TO NUMBER SECTIONS DIFFERENTLY

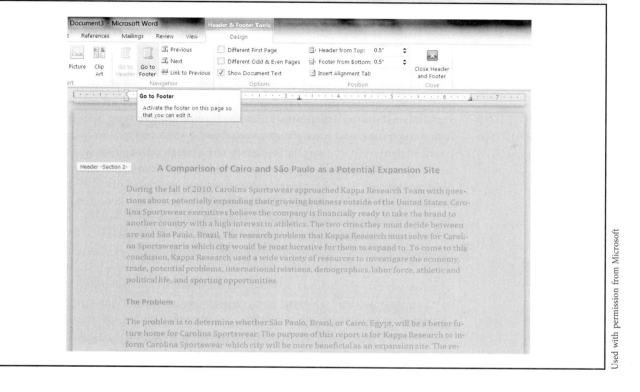

In Word 2010, the easiest way to create a table of contents is to use those built-in Heading Styles described in this chapter. Once you have applied Headings Styles as outlined on page 483, you are ready to build a table of contents (TOC):

1. Click where you want to insert the table of contents.
2. On the References tab, Table of Contents group, click Table of Contents.
3. Select a TOC option to fit the report medium. Naturally, if readers will see a printed report, then the table of contents should include each heading in the report and the page number where it appears. On the other hand, if readers will read your report online in Word, you might format the TOC headings as hyperlinks, as shown in Illustration 16.6. Then readers can click a link to go to a particular heading, which clearly makes navigating the report easier and faster.
4. If you add or remove headings in the report, you need to update the table of contents: On the References tab, Table of Contents group, click Update Table.

Word 2010 lets you customize this contents page. In Word Help, search for "custom table of contents." If you decide to delete the TOC, select Remove Table of Contents (after clicking References tab and Table of Contents).

ILLUSTRATION 16.6   INSERT LINKS IN TABLE OF CONTENTS OF ONLINE REPORTS

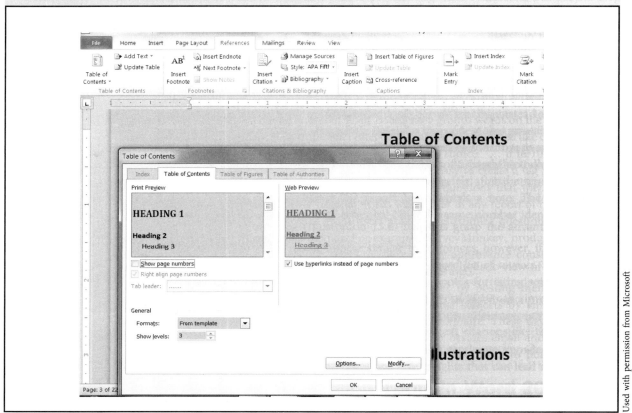

Used with permission from Microsoft

Microsoft Word 2010 Tools for Collaborative Writers

As you know from both experience and reading, many reports are produced through collaboration—two or more people working together to produce the final product. Today, the processes and technologies that support collecting, handling, and publishing information in any form or medium—including, of course, text and visuals in a word-processing file—is called *content management* (CM). The information or text itself is referred to as *content* or, more strictly, *digital content*. Whichever term you use—collaborative writing or content management—a vital part of it is handling communication among the collaborators and dealing with changes to a report in progress. Throughout this book, you came across tools that help people do these things. The following paragraphs focus on such tools in Microsoft Word 2010.

Insert Comments

Sometimes while drafting a report you may need to explain some aspect of your text to the other writers; or when reading what someone else has written, you may need to ask a question. Using Word 2010, you can include the remark or query in the report itself, using the Comments feature. Any comments inserted will appear in the margin, as shown in Illustration 16.7. Here, they are easy to spot and do not interrupt the flow of text. In Word 2010, insert a Comment in two steps:

1. Select the text (one word or entire paragraph) about which you want to ask or comment.
2. On the Review tab, Comments group, click New Comment. Type your remark or query in the balloon.

Each comment, by default, appears as a two-inch balloon in the right margin and automatically includes your identification (the user name entered in Microsoft Office). (To change these settings, on the Review tab, Tracking group, click bottom of Track Changes. To change the size and/or location of balloons, select Change Tracking Options. Make the desired changes under Balloons on the Track Changes Options dialog. To change your ID, select Change User Name.)

If you print a report draft, you can print the comments or omit them. (On the Print dialog under Settings, click Print Markup to omit comments from the printout.) Comments are easy to delete from a later draft. To delete a single comment, select it and click Delete (on the Review tab, Comments group). To delete all comments, click the Delete down arrow and choose Delete All Comments in Document.

ILLUSTRATION 16.7 WORD 2010 COMMENTS APPEAR IN A SIDE MARGIN

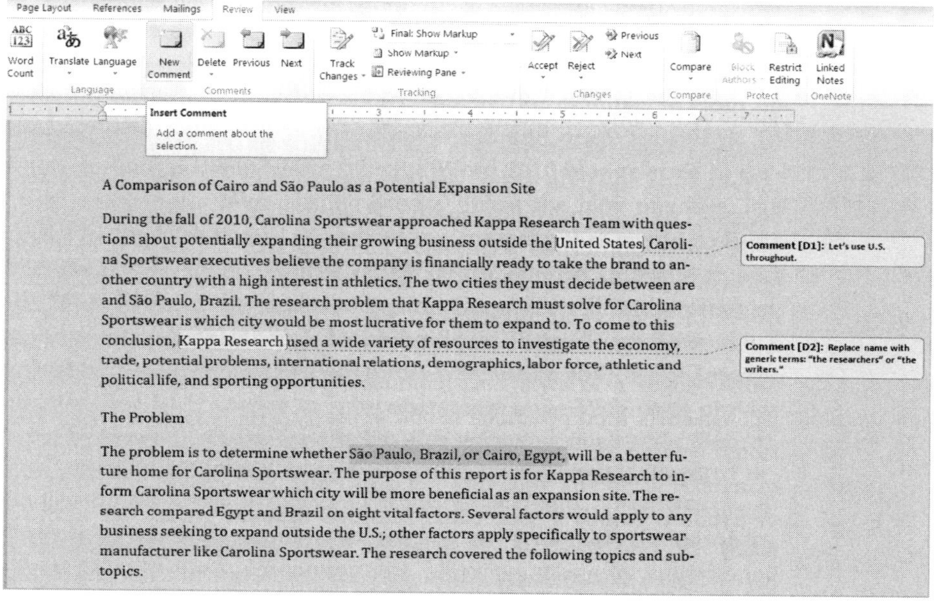

Used with permission from Microsoft

Track Changes

Collaborating writers may need to go back to a previous report draft because of inaccurate or inappropriate revisions. Word 2010 makes this possible by storing, as part of your report file, all the changes that you and your collaborators make to it. First, you need to tell Word to track changes and also how to display your changes. For such tracking to be useful, of course, Word must provide a way for you to accept or reject other writers' changes. Follow these guides to track and display changes in an existing Word file:

1. *If the words "Track Changes: On" appear on the status bar, go to step 2.* Right-click the status bar and select Track Changes from the pop-up menu. The words "Track Changes: On" now appear on the status bar. Alternatively, on the Review tab, Tracking group, click the top half of Track Changes. Word will now save changes to your text; performing step 2 will display those changes in the document.

2. On the Review tab, Tracking group, click Show Markup. This menu shows the kinds of changes Word can display. While drafting a report, do not display Formatting; do display Comments, Ink, and Insertions and Deletions. (Word will continue to save formatting changes although you chose not to display them. Later, when preparing the report for publication, you may return to Show Markup and select Formatting.) Thus, Word will display your comments in the right margin and a line on the left of each text line that contains a change. In addition, it will show your inserted text in a different color and will mark text that you delete rather than removing it. Some writers like to use Word's Reviewing Pane in addition to the text markups. Click Reviewing Pane (Review tab, Tracking group) and select a vertical (beside page on left) or horizontal (under the page) display. With step 3, you can control *how* these changes are displayed in your text.

3. Click the bottom half of Track Changes and select Change Tracking Options. On the Track Changes Options dialog, shown in Illustration 16.8, you can indicate how you want Word to mark your insertions, deletions, and changed text lines. Also, you can choose how to mark text that you move (cut and paste) and changes to any tables in the file. Here, too, you can turn the display of format changes on or off. In addition, you can indicate when to use balloons, their width and location, and whether balloons should be freestanding or connected by a line to the text. After changing the file, performing step 4 *hides* the changes, making the revised text easier to review. (If you like to review a printout, Word can print the tracked changes or hide them. Make this choice in the Print dialog at Print All Pages under Document Properties.)

4. On the Review tab, Tracking group, at Final: Show Markup, click the down arrow and select Final. Notice that all text markups disappear. Of course, clicking Original on this Display for Review menu shows the text before any changes were made. Most writers prefer to show changes while they work, using either Final: Show Markup or Original: Show Markup. After reviewing revised text, you will likely approve some changes and disapprove others. Performing step 5

ILLUSTRATION 16.8   CHOOSE DISPLAY SETTINGS IN THE TRACK CHANGES OPTIONS DIALOG

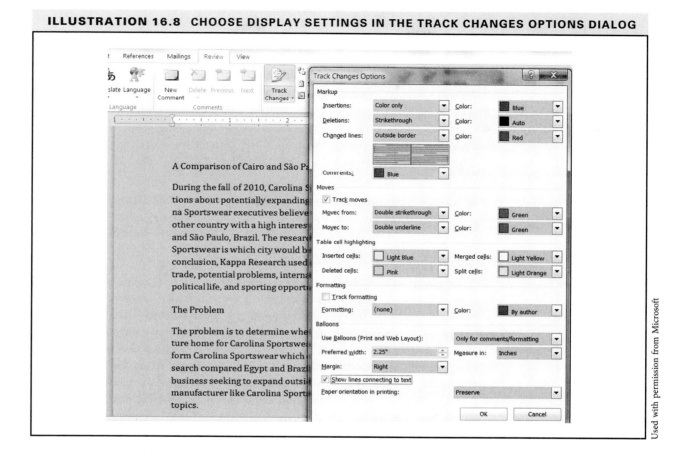

will make approved changes permanent and restore original text in place of dis-approved ones.

5. With changes displayed (Final: Show Markup), on the Review tab, Changes group, use Accept and Reject. Clicking either button will accept or reject one proposed change and move to the next change. (To accept or reject all proposed changes, click the Accept or Reject down arrow and select Accept/Reject All Changes in Document.)

Collaboration Security Issues

As you know, hiding your tracked changes does not delete them. Therefore, anyone to whom you send the Word file—including a client, for example—can view the tracked changes. In fact, any time you share a Microsoft Word file with colleagues or clients, review the file for hidden data or personal information that may be stored in the report document itself or in the so-called *document properties*. This information can disclose details about your organization or the file that you do not want to share. The following guides tell how to safeguard comments and tracked changes from the time you create a file containing them and how to remove hidden data and personal information.

Protect Tracked Changes in Word 2010

Take these five steps when you begin tracking changes in a Word file. This procedure will remind you of hidden tracking when you attempt to share that file:

1. On the File tab, click Options.
2. On the Word Options dialog, click Trust Center.
3. Click the Trust Center Settings button (right side of screen).
4. On the Trust Center dialog, click Privacy Options.
5. On the Privacy Options dialog, under Document-specific settings, select Warn before printing, saving or sending a file that contains tracked changes or comments. Click OK.

With this safeguard in place, you will be warned when attempting to print, save, or send the file. An example follows: "The document being saved contains comments and tracked changes. Continue with save?" You can select Cancel or OK.

Remove Hidden and Personal Data

Several types of hidden data and personal information can be saved in a Word file. Even though it may be imperceptible when you open the file in Word, other people may possibly view or retrieve that information. While comments and tracked changes can enable other people to see who worked on your documents and reviewers' comments, the document properties, or *metadata* (data about data), also include author, subject, and title of the file. In addition, "document properties" includes information automatically maintained by Microsoft Office programs, such as date a file was created and name of the person who saved it most recently. Your file might also contain document server properties, email headers, routing slips, and template names.

Of course, Word files can contain information in headers and footers, and using a watermark is another way that personal information gets into a file. But the most obvious risk involves objects that you format as invisible and text that you format (Font dialog) as hidden. Word's Document Inspector is designed to find and remove these types of hidden and personal information from a file. (**Note:** Document Inspector will not remove objects that are hidden behind other objects and text that is hidden by typing white text on a white background.)

Before sharing a Word file—as an email attachment, for example—you would be wise to inspect it. Since you may not be able to restore hidden content that Document Inspector removes, copy your file; then inspect and share that copy. Follow these steps:

1. In a copy of your Word file, click the File tab and select Info.
2. On the Info dialog, under Prepare for Sharing, click Check for Issues. Then click Inspect Document.
3. In the Document Inspector dialog, select the types of hidden content you want inspected. Generally, to minimize risk, choose to inspect all types, as shown in Illustration 16.9.
4. Click Inspect; in the Document Inspector dialog, review inspection results.
5. For each type of hidden content you want to remove from your file, next to the inspection results for it, click Remove All.

ILLUSTRATION 16.9 WORD'S DOCUMENT INSPECTOR REMOVES HIDDEN DATA FROM FILES

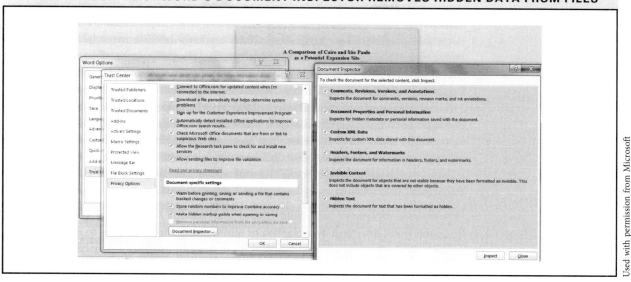

Word Help contains information about additional security measures for collaborators. Some terms to search for in Help include the following: Digital signature, Password, Protected documents, Protected view, Security warnings, and Suspicious websites.

Save Word Files in Other Formats

When saving files in Word 2010, you likely save most as Word Documents, the default file type. At various stages in collaborative report writing, though, other file formats, including Plain Text, Open XML, PDF, and XPS, offer advantages. (***Note:*** If you need to remove hidden data from a file, use Word's Document Inspector *before* converting to any other format.)

Plain Text Format

Plain text is the most portable format. That is, just about all word-processing software and every kind of computer can handle plain, or clear, text. But as its name implies, plain text cannot contain any formatting, objects, or pictures. (A file created and saved in Word as plain text appears to hold formatting and so on. However, when the file is reopened, only the plain text remains.) This combination of attributes makes plain text format suitable when sharing a first (or early) draft with people using diverse or unidentified equipment. To save a Word file in this format, on the Save As dialog, beside Save as type, select Plain Text from the drop-down menu. Supply a file name; a suffix (.txt) will be added.

Open XML

Word files saved in XML are automatically compressed up to 75 percent smaller. This compression (zip) technology decreases the disk space needed to store the files and the bandwidth needed to send them by email, networks, or the Internet. The file decompresses (unzips) when it is opened and then zips again when saved.

Another advantage of XML is the way it separates different data components from each other. This segregation allows files to open even if a segment in the file is corrupted or damaged. In addition, a file saved as an XML type can be opened and edited in most business applications by anyone equipped with a ZIP utility and XML editor, basic items in many offices. Thus, XML files may be considered the go-to file type for collaborators. To save a Word file in this format, on the Save As dialog, beside Save as type, select Word XML Document from the drop-down menu. Supply a file name; a suffix (.xml) will be added.

PDF and XPS Formats

The portable document format (PDF) and XML paper specification (XPS) have very similar advantages, and both are useful for sharing final drafts. Saving a file in PDF or XPS format makes it extremely difficult to change; it's intended only for printing and reading. Both PDF and XPS files retain the formatting that you put in and look the same on most computers. In addition, both formats reduce file size.

A PDF file is especially useful for commercial printing. To view a PDF file, you need a PDF reader, such as Acrobat Reader, on your computer. Acrobat Reader is available free from Adobe Systems (http://www.adobe.com). To save a Word file in this format, on the Save As dialog, beside Save as type, select PDF from the drop-down menu. Supply a file name; a suffix (.pdf) will be added. (Once you save a Word file in PDF format, you can convert it back to a Word document only with specialized software.)

An XPS file embeds all fonts in the file. Therefore, the fonts appear as intended even if the people who receive your XPS file do not have the font on their computers. In addition, XPS has higher image quality and coloring than a PDF when someone else opens your file. To save a Word file in this format, on the Save As dialog, beside Save as type, select XPS from the drop-down menu. Supply a file name; a suffix (.xps) will be added.

As a business report writer and Microsoft Office 2010 user, be aware of the file format options available to you and the advantages and disadvantages of each format for collaborators. Make a point of noting the file name suffix on any file you receive so you can be aware of its strengths and limitations.

Ethical Considerations

As you finalize a comprehensive report, review the comments about ethical considerations presented in previous chapters. For example, have you verified the need for the research? Have you reported all relevant data? Have you avoided manipulative language? Have you honored the privacy, accuracy, and ownership guides related to data sources? Have you honored your commitments to survey participants to maintain confidentiality? Have you avoided distortion of data in your visual aids? A final question might well be this: Does this report represent your best effort to convey information that will promote the good of others as you remain true to your own values and ideals?

Summary

Formal business reports often contain parts that do not appear in less formal reports. The preliminary parts of a formal report should set the stage for the report and enable the reader to access the information easily. The report body must be a complete document that presents all details of the study, from its introduction to its conclusions and recommendations, if those are included. Report supplements may be added to provide additional information that will be of interest to some readers.

Following format guides consistently will contribute to the readability and coherence of your report. Proper use of formatting features in Microsoft Word 2010 can help you achieve a consistent report format with minimal effort and time. This word-processing application also includes tools and file formats that can simplify collaboration.

ILLUSTRATION 16.10 TRANSMITTAL MESSAGE

S. C. Ports Authority

Memo

To: Bryant T. Joseph, VP, Terminal Development

From: Melvin L. Barbara, VP, Government Relations

Date: September 27, 2011

Subject: Citizens' Attitudes toward Cruise Industry and Port Enhancements

On January 15, 2011, you authorized me to proceed with a study of Charlestonians' attitudes toward the cruise industry and the proposed port enhancements. The accompanying report presents the results of that study. Although the study was initially intended for internal use only, subsequent events have suggested that the Ports Authority may want to share the report with other constituencies. Consequently, I have presented the report in a somewhat more formal style than we normally use for internal reports.

In addition to the survey proposed in January, my research team studied documents related to waterfront development and enhancement. We used that information to evaluate the 2010 Concept Plan for Union Pier Waterfront and to evaluate how the Ports Authority can best communicate with the public as it launches this major waterfront revitalization project.

My staff and I appreciate the opportunity to conduct this research. We are prepared to discuss the report at the September 30 management committee meeting.

ILLUSTRATION 16.11 FORMAL ANALYTICAL REPORT

Charleston and the Cruise Industry

September 2011

continued

ILLUSTRATION 16.11   CONTINUED

Charleston and the Cruise Industry

Charlestonians' Knowledge and Attitudes about the Cruise Industry

Prepared for—

Bryant T. Joseph, Vice President, Terminal Operations

SC State Ports Authority

P.O. Box 22287

Charleston, SC 29413

Prepared by—

Government Relations Division

South Carolina Ports Authority

September 2011

continued

ILLUSTRATION 16.11 CONTINUED

Table of Contents

continued

ILLUSTRATION 16.11 CONTINUED

iii

continued

ILLUSTRATION 16.11 CONTINUED

Executive Summary

The findings suggest that Charlestonians recognize the cruise business as an ongoing presence in the Port of Charleston and their lives. However, they want the negative aspects of that presence to be ameliorated.

To increase citizens' support for the proposed cruise terminal relocation and waterfront enhancements, the South Carolina Ports Authority must launch an extensive communication campaign. The campaign should publicize specific aspects of the concept plan, emphasizing the benefits to Charlestonians, such as improved vehicular traffic flows and parking, improved visual and human access to the waterfront, ecological reclamation and protection of the waterfront, and reclamation and protection of historical structures in the harbor. As the work progresses, the Authority should issue regular press releases to mark the progress of the project and to inform residents and merchants about construction activities that may temporarily inconvenience them. Constant communication should reassure the citizens of Charleston that the project is moving forward as planned and will soon show major benefits to residents and merchants as well as cruise passengers.

Further, as the Ports Authority proceeds with cruise terminal relocation, it would be wise to simultaneously begin the proposed waterfront improvements. Such a dual approach will most readily help downtown residents and merchants experience some of the benefits of the project. The following sequence is recommended:

- Complete street construction/traffic alteration projects first.
- Upon completion of the street improvements, begin making improvements to the waterfront at the same time that construction begins on the new terminal site.

The objective of this study was to assess the business and social climate in which the South Carolina Ports Authority will operate if it implements plans to relocate the cruise terminal. Knowledge of that climate will help the Authority develop operational and communication strategies relative to the relocation. Three factors were studied:

1. What business impacts do Charleston's downtown residents and merchants perceive to be related to the arrival and departure of cruise ships?
2. What personal and community impacts do Charleston's downtown residents and merchants perceive to be related to the arrival and departure of cruise ships?
3. What knowledge of and attitudes toward relocation of the cruise terminal are evidenced by Charleston's downtown residents and merchants?

The analysis revealed that the Port Authority's plan to relocate the cruise pier and enhance the Port of Charleston incorporates many principles generally considered essential in contemporary waterfront development. Yet there is no consensus among Charleston residents and merchants about the value of the cruise industry and the proposed waterfront development.

iv

continued

ILLUSTRATION 16.11 CONTINUED

CHARLESTON AND THE CRUISE INDUSTRY

For more than 25 years, Charleston's Union Pier has served as a home port and port of call for Carnival Cruises and a port of call for other cruise lines. The cruise industry currently contributes approximately $37 million to the region's economy, but the vehicular and pedestrian traffic associated with the departures and arrivals of cruise ships has been the subject of extensive debate among downtown residents, merchants, and professionals.

The South Carolina Ports Authority has begun plans to relocate the cruise terminal to a point north of its present location and relocate existing cargo operations. These changes will open 35 acres of harbor front that can be redeveloped to provide greater public access to the water's edge. Before implementing that plan, the Ports Authority officers wanted to know how much Charlestonians know about the economic impact of the cruise industry and what their attitudes are toward that industry and the proposed revitalization of the waterfront.

Determining Charlestonians' Perceptions of the Cruise Industry

A survey of downtown residents and merchants was conducted during the summer of 2011.

The Problem

The research problem was to assess Charlestonians' perceptions of the economic and social impact of cruise dockings in the Port of Charleston and the possible relocation of the cruise terminal.

The Purpose

The purpose of the study was to assess the business and social climate in which the South Carolina Ports Authority will operate if it implements plans to relocate the cruise terminal. Knowledge of that climate will help the Authority develop operational and communication strategies relative to the relocation.

Scope of Analysis

Three factors were studied:

1. What business impacts do Charleston's downtown residents and merchants perceive to be related to the arrival and departure of cruise ships?
2. What personal and community impacts do Charleston's downtown residents and merchants perceive to be related to the arrival and departure of cruise ships?
3. What knowledge of and attitudes toward relocation of the cruise terminal are evidenced by Charleston's downtown residents and merchants?

In addition, information related to waterfront development was studied to understand more fully the potential impact of community attitudes when a major urban revitalization project is undertaken. That

continued

ILLUSTRATION 16.11 CONTINUED

2

information was helpful while drawing conclusions about Charlestonians' attitudes and making recommendations to the South Carolina Ports Authority.

Delimitations

Because the area between the Charleston Harbor and King Street receives the greatest impact of the presence of cruise ships in the harbor, the analysis was limited to an area bounded by East Bay St. on the east, Broad St. on the south, King St. on the west, and Calhoun St. on the north. This area includes the downtown retail, hospitality, and professional facilities as well as the Ansonborough residential area.

Limitations

Confining the study to the historic Charleston area may have omitted some citizens and merchants who have strong positive or negative feelings about the cruise industry. However, since the downtown community absorbs the major direct impact of visiting cruise ships, the attitudes of that community can best direct decisions related to relocating the cruise terminal.

Since the data were collected during the summer cruise season, the participants' responses may differ slightly from responses they might have made during an earlier or later cruise season. Nonetheless, the responses obtained during a peak tourist season in Charleston were deemed to reflect the strongest feelings and most recent experiences of the participants.

Definitions

For purposes of this study, the term *residents* identifies respondents who live within the targeted Ansonborough section of downtown Charleston; the term *merchants* identifies respondents from the downtown business and professional community.

How the Study was Conducted

The Government Relations division of the Ports Authority used both secondary and primary data to meet the objective of this study.

Secondary Data

Secondary sources concerning waterfront development were studied. The information was useful in evaluating the South Carolina Ports Authority's Concept Plan for the Union Pier Waterfront and the citizens' views of that plan. A list of sources accessed appears in Works Cited given on page 11 of this report.

Primary Data

Primary data were obtained through a survey of downtown residents and merchants. All residents within the defined area were invited to participate in the study. A systematic random sample of 100 downtown businesses and professional offices was drawn from the Charleston Merchants Association Directory. A copy of the questionnaire and transmittal messages used for residents and merchants appears in Appendix A.

A summary profile of respondents appears in Appendix B. The median age range for both groups was 26-35. Thirty-eight percent of residents were engaged in professions or occupations that were most likely to

continued

ILLUSTRATION 16.11 CONTINUED

3

put them into direct contact with cruise passengers: food services, hospitality services, and retail marketing. Sixty percent of merchants were engaged in those occupations. When the two groups were combined, those occupations represented nearly 50 percent of respondents. Thus, the responses can be interpreted as heavily weighted by young adults who may have had direct contact with cruise passengers.

Downtown residents

On May 15 and August 1, 2011, letters were sent to all addresses in the Ansonborough district of Charleston. One half of the district was covered in each mailing. Recipients of the letters were invited to come to a town-hall type of meeting to discuss the impact of cruise dockings on the Charleston business and residential communities. The first meetings were held on June 15 and 16, the days following the departure of a home-port ship. The second series of meetings was held on August 14 and 15, the days after the arrival of a port-of-call ship. After an open discussion of the economic and social impacts of cruise dockings, the residents in attendance were asked to complete a questionnaire related to the presence of the cruise industry in Charleston and the plans to relocate the cruise terminal. Questionnaires were collected as soon as they were completed.

The meetings produced 127 usable questionnaires, 68 from females and 59 from males. The most frequent selections for profession/occupation were retired (25%), retail marketing (17%), food services (15%), and full-time homemaker (14%).

Downtown merchants

Email messages and an electronic questionnaire were sent to the sample of downtown businesses and professional offices on May 15 inviting them to complete the questionnaire on either June 1-2 or August 13-14. Cruise ships were docked at the Union Pier on June 1(a home-port ship) and on August 13 (a port-of-call ship). Merchants who completed the questionnaire in June were blocked from completing another in August. On August 1 a reminder message was emailed to any merchants who had not completed a questionnaire during the first round.

Ninety-two usable questionnaires were received, 26 from females and 66 from males. The most frequent selections for profession/occupation were food services (33 %), hospitality services (16%), and retail marketing (11%).

Data Analysis

Questionnaire responses were entered into a spreadsheet and summary statistics were computed. It was immediately noticed that residents and merchants were united in their desire to have the cruise terminal moved from its current location. Since over 90 percent of each group strongly favored the relocation, there appeared to be no value in cross-tabulating the data on that factor. Consequently, responses from the entire group of resident respondents were compared with responses from the entire group of merchants.

What the Study Revealed

The analysis produced guides for waterfront development and assessments of Charlestonians' knowledge and attitudes about the current economic impact of the cruise industry, projected economic benefits of

continued

ILLUSTRATION 16.11   CONTINUED

4

terminal relocation, personal and business experiences related to cruise dockings, and the potential impact of terminal relocation on quality of life.

Guides for Waterfront Development

One analyst of urban development has observed that few cities have viewed their waterfronts as distinctive elements that should be included in a systematic plan of urban development (Moss, 1999). Recently, however, some major cities have undertaken comprehensive programs of urban waterfront renewal or development. Notable examples of comprehensive planning exist in Baltimore, Maryland; Boston, Massachusetts; Louisville, Kentucky; and Salem, Oregon. Successful projects incorporate local residents' desires for recreational water space and tourist expectations of interesting target destinations (Craig-Smith, 1995).

The importance of planned, ethical waterfront development was acknowledged in 1999 in the Urban Waterfront Manifesto (The Waterfront Center, 1999). Several items included in the manifesto are especially relevant to the proposed relocation of the cruise terminal and related waterfront enhancements. They include the following:

- Meaningful community involvement is integral to valid waterfront planning and development. It should begin early and be continuous.
- Many conversions take 10, 15, or 25 years. The understandable desire to achieve instant results should be resisted in all except the smallest steps.
- Public access to and along the urban waterfront should be the hallmark of all projects, including residential developments. Visual access to the water likewise should be a pervading objective.
- Where possible, a diversity of uses should be included along waterfronts, from passive parks to vibrant commercial attractions. People of all income levels and cultures should feel welcome.

Another publication, Smart Growth for Coastal and Waterfront Communities (National Oceanic and Atmospheric Administration, 2009), presents ten elements that should be incorporated in waterfront development plans. Elements especially relevant to the current plans for Charleston Harbor include the following:

- Incorporate mix land uses, including water-dependent uses.
- Create walkable communities with physical and visual access to and along the waterfront for public use.
- Foster distinctive, attractive communities with a strong sense of place that capitalizes on the waterfront's heritage.
- Encourage community and stakeholder collaboration in development decisions, ensuring that public interests in and rights of access to the waterfront and coastal waters are upheld.

The Concept Plan for Union Pier Waterfront (Cooper, Robertson & Partners, 2010) prepared for the South Carolina State Ports Authority incorporates the concepts presented in the Urban Waterfront Manifesto and Smart Growth for Coastal and Waterfront Communities. The Concept Plan cites these goals:

- Create a financially viable plan including a new cruise terminal that is attractive and in keeping with the character of historic Charleston.
- Comply with today's enhanced cruise security requirements.

continued

ILLUSTRATION 16.11 CONTINUED

5

- Mitigate impacts on existing infrastructure and traffic.
- Identify additional uses for the Union Pier property that bring enjoyment to Charlestonians and enhance the local economy.
- Increase public access to Charleston's historic waterfront.

These principles of urban waterfront development and the goals cited in the Concept Plan are relevant in an assessment of Charlestonians' knowledge and attitudes about the proposed enhancements to the Port of Charleston.

Knowledge of Current Economic Impact

Whereas Charleston merchants appeared to have relatively accurate knowledge of both the current economic impact and the potential impact of the proposed relocation of the cruise terminal, Ansonborough residents tended to underestimate the economic impact of the cruise industry.

News reports about the relocation plans have consistently mentioned that the cruise industry is a vital player in the health of the state's economy and that of the Charleston area. In 2009 the cruise industry generated $64 million in direct spending in South Carolina and supported 1,177 jobs (2009 Economic Impact, 2009). A 2010 study by the College of Charleston found that the annual economic impact of the Charleston cruise industry exceeded $37 million and supported over 400 jobs (Smith, 2010).

However, 51 percent of Charleston residents attributed approximately 200 jobs to the industry, with only 17 percent reporting the accurate estimate of 400. Merchants, on the other hand, had an accurate perception of the number of jobs supported by the cruise industry; 74 percent of merchants indicated that the industry supported approximately 400 jobs and 21 percent placed their estimate at 300 jobs. (See Chart 1, page 6.) Similarly, Charleston residents underestimated the monetary impact of the industry; 54 percent of those respondents said that the impact was approximately $25 million. The majority of merchants (61 percent) accurately assessed that impact to be in the $35 million range. (See Chart 2, page 6.)

Overall, the Charleston citizens who participated in the study held incorrect perceptions of the number of jobs and the economic impact that could be attributed to the cruise industry, whereas Charleston merchants appeared to have accurate knowledge about those factors.

Attitudes about Projected Economic Benefits of Terminal Relocation

Ansonborough residents appear to be extremely skeptical about the potential economic benefits directly associated with relocation of the cruise terminal. The dominant attitude (over 60 percent) about projections of jobs and monetary contributions to the local economy was that these are guesses, not facts; and only 10-13 percent of respondents thought that the historic district will share in the economic benefits. Although only 13-18 percent of merchants anticipate that the historic district will share in the increased jobs and $45 million of expenditures, over 75 percent looked beyond the downtown area, saying that the Charleston area needs such a boost and the project should proceed. (See Charts 3 and 4, page 7.)

Personal and Business Experiences

In February 2010, the Ports Authority implemented a new cruise traffic plan (South Carolina State Ports Authority, 2010). Despite changes to traffic flows, a majority of both residents and merchants reported

continued

ILLUSTRATION 16.11 CONTINUED

6

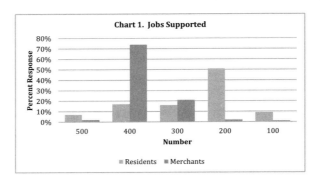

Chart 1. Jobs Supported

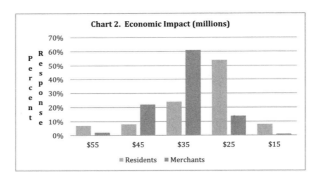

Chart 2. Economic Impact (millions)

negative experiences related to pedestrian and motor traffic; a complement to such reports is the fact that no one in either group reported having experienced decreased pedestrian traffic and a smooth flow of vehicular traffic. In addition, a majority of both groups reported having experienced noise and environmental pollution.

The major difference between the two groups of respondents related to how they interacted with cruise passengers. A larger percentage of residents (73%) than merchants (33%) reported reluctance to leave

continued

ILLUSTRATION 16.11 CONTINUED

7

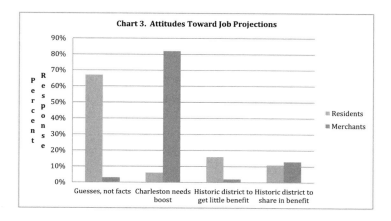

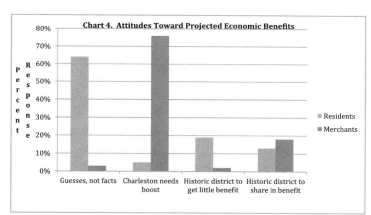

continued

ILLUSTRATION 16.11 CONTINUED

8

home or place of business, suggesting that the residents' contacts may have been more limited. In a related finding, a smaller percentage of residents (20%) than merchants (75%) reported pleasant interactions with the tourists. Fortunately, only five respondents in the residents group and none in the merchants group reported abrasive interactions. Understandably, no residents reported increased or decreased sales related to the presence of cruise ships. A considerably larger percentage of merchants reported increased sales (65%) as opposed to decreased sales (20%). (See Chart 5.)

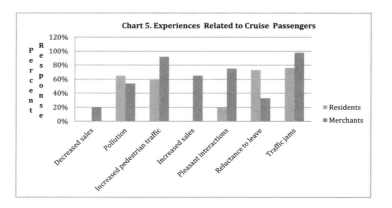

Chart 5. Experiences Related to Cruise Passengers

Impact of Terminal Relocation on Quality of Life

As was noted in the methodology section of this report, the strongest agreement between the two groups was their desire to relocate the cruise terminal. Over 90 percent of both groups favored the proposed relocation. A majority of both groups also thought that relocating the terminal would result in improved quality of life. Only five percent of each group projected that quality of life would decline if the terminal were relocated. The implications of these findings will be considered more extensively in the recommendations section of this report.

Table 1. Quality of Life

Quality	Residents	Merchants
Likely improve	30 %	15%
Possibly improve	43%	39%
No change	21%	41%
May decline	3%	3%
Very likely decline	2%	2%

continued

ILLUSTRATION 16.11 CONTINUED

9

Summary

The Ports Authority's plans for the cruise terminal and other waterfront enhancements generally adhere to contemporary guides for waterfront development. Ansonborough residents and members of the downtown business and professional community share some attitudes about the cruise industry, but the business community views it a bit more favorably than does the residential community. Overall, Ansonborough residents are less well informed about the economic benefits that the cruise industry has brought to Charleston and are less inclined to believe that the historic downtown community will benefit from a relocation of the cruise port. Both groups shared negative experiences related to pedestrian and vehicular traffic. Compared to the merchants, Ansonborough residents appeared to have had less direct contact and fewer positive interactions with cruise passengers.

Conclusions

The Ports Authority has attempted to apply sound waterfront development principles in its Concept Plan for Union Pier Waterfront, including public input. This study has been one attempt to obtain public input.

Communication about the plans seems to have been understood and received favorably by downtown merchants. That communication, however, has done little to change the downtown residents' opinion about the value of the cruise industry.

Downtown Charleston's residents and merchants both perceive that the presence of cruise ships in the Port of Charleston has negatively impacted pedestrian and vehicular traffic. Although residents and merchants have differing degrees of knowledge about the economic impact of the cruise industry, both groups strongly support relocation of the cruise terminal.

Recommendations

These findings suggest that Charlestonians recognize that the cruise business is going to continue to be a part of the Port of Charleston and their lives. However, they want the negative aspects of that impact to be ameliorated. To enhance citizens' support for the proposed cruise terminal relocation and waterfront enhancements the South Carolina Ports Authority should do the following:

- Publicize the keys aspects of the Concept Plan. Specifically:
    - Improved vehicular traffic flows and parking in the cruise terminal area and downtown Charleston
    - Improved visual and human access to the waterfront
    - Ecological reclamation and protection of the waterfront
    - Reclamation and protection of historical structures in the Charleston Harbor

- Proceed with port relocation and waterfront improvement plans presented in the Concept Plan in a sequence that will most readily show the greatest benefits to Charleston merchants and residents. Specifically:
    - Complete street construction/traffic alteration projects first. Improved traffic flow would immediately be felt by residents and businesses and may improve attitudes toward the presence of cruise ships in the Port of Charleston.

continued

ILLUSTRATION 16.11 CONTINUED

10

- Upon completion of the street improvements, begin making improvements to the waterfront at the same time that construction begins on the new terminal site. This simultaneous activity will demonstrate to residents and merchants that the Ports Authority is as serious about enabling greater recreational use of the waterfront as it is about improving cruise facilities.
- Issue regular press releases to mark the progress of the project and to inform residents and merchants about construction activities that may temporarily inconvenience them. Constant communication should reassure the citizens of Charleston that the project is moving forward as planned and will soon show major benefits to residents and merchants as well as cruise passengers.

continued

ILLUSTRATION 16.11 CONTINUED

11

Works Cited

2009 Economic Impact of the Cruise Industry in America by State. (2009). Retrieved July 4, 2011, from
    Cruiseline Industry Facts: http://www.cruiseindustryfacts.com/newsroom/data-and-reports/2009

Cooper, Robertson & Partners. (2010, July 18). *Concept Plan for Union Pier Waterfront.* Retrieved
    March 21, 2011, from Union Pier Cruise Terminal:
    http://www.scspa.com/UnionPierPlan/pdf/Union

Craig-Smith, S. J. (Ed.). (1995). *Recreation and Tourism as a Catalyst for Urban Waterfront
    Redevelopment.* Westport, CT: Praeger Publishers.

Johnson, Tashman & Elaine Howard. (2007, March). *South Waterfront Urban Renewal Feasibility Study.*
    Retrieved May 12, 2011, from City of Salem:
    http://www.cityofsalem/Departments/Urbandevelopment/UrbanRenewal/Documents/SWF

Moss, M. (1999). *The Urban Waterfront: Opportunities for Renewal.* Retrieved July 21, 2011, from
    Mitchall L. Moss: http://www.mitchellmoss.com/articles/urbanwaterfront.html

National Oceanic and Atmospheric Administration. (2009, Sept. 9). *Smart Growth for Coastal and
    Waterfront Communities.* Retrieved August 15, 2011, from Coastal Smart Growth:
    http://coastalsmartgrowth.noaa.gov

Ryckbost, P. (2005, April 14). *Redeveloping Urban Waterfront Property.* Retrieved Sept. 19, 2011, from
    http://www.umich.edu/~econdev/waterfronts/

Smith, B. (2010, Feb. 2). *Growing cruise industry means big money for Charleston, SC.* Retrieved April
    4, 2010, from USA Today: http://www.usatoday.com/travel/cruises/2010-02-02-south-carolina-
    cruise-industry_N.htm

South Carolina State Ports Authority. (2010, Feb. 11). *SCSPA Implements New Cruise Traffic Measures.*
    Retrieved Sept. 23, 2010, from SC State Ports Authority:
    http://www.scspa.com/about/news/pressroom/pressroom.asp?PressRelease=264

The Waterfront Center. (1999, July 10). *Urban Waterfront Manifesto.* Retrieved July 4, 2011, from The
    Waterfront Center: http://www.waterfrontcenter.org/about/manifesto.html

continued

ILLUSTRATION 16.11 CONTINUED

12

Appendix A. Data Collection Instruments

Text of Email Transmittal Message to Merchants

To: Carriage Properties

Subject: Charleston and the Cruise Industry

As a person who conducts business in Historic Downtown Charleston, you are aware that the presence of cruise ships in Charleston Harbor has generated controversy in this community. Although the cruise business has made positive contributions to the Charleston economy, some citizens fear that cruise ships will change the gracious ambiance of this area.

You have an opportunity to enter the debate on this controversial issue. The SC Ports Authority is conducting a study to evaluate attitudes of downtown merchants and citizens toward the cruise industry and the proposed relocation of the cruise terminal. We value your input. Please log onto www.SCPorts.com/survey and complete the questionnaire that you will find there.

Your response before June 14 will ensure that your voice is heard as the SC Ports Authority makes decisions about how to accommodate the wishes of our citizens while also making the Port of Charleston an attractive entry into our beautiful city.

continued

ILLUSTRATION 16.11 CONTINUED

13

Transmittal Letter to Residents

S. C. Ports Authority

P O Box 22288   Charleston, SC 29413   864.111.1111

May 15, 2010

Dear Ansonborough Resident:

As a resident of the Ansonborough District of Historic Charleston, you take pride in your home and the gracious ambiance of downtown Charleston.

In recent months the *Charleston News and Courier* has published comments about the presence of cruise ships in Charleston Harbor and cruise passengers in the historic district. Although many citizens realize that the cruise industry has a positive impact on the Charleston economy, some fear that its presence may distract from our traditional way of life.

The South Carolina Ports Authority wants to hear from you on this issue. On June 12 and 13 we will conduct town-hall meetings at St. Philips's Episcopal Church, 142 Church St. At those meetings members of the Ports Authority will explain our tentative plans to relocate the cruise terminal and improve the Charleston Harbor waterfront. The entire project is intended to give Charlestonians and tourists better access to that wonderful resource.

Please plan to attend one of those meetings. You will be given an opportunity to discuss your views of the cruise industry and the proposed relocation of the terminal. The enclosed questionnaire should help you prepare for the meeting.

You may complete the questionnaire before the town-hall meeting, or you may wait to fill it in until after you have heard the discussion. We will collect completed questionnaires at the end of the meeting.

We look forward to seeing you at a meeting on June 12 or 13 at 7:30 p.m. to discuss what we can do to improve everyone's enjoyment of our downtown waterfront.

Sincerely,

Bryant T. Joseph, VP, Terminal Development

Enc. Questionnaire

continued

ILLUSTRATION 16.11 CONTINUED

14

Questionnaire for Merchants and Residents

Questionnaire: Charleston and the Cruise Industry

Please share something about your knowledge, attitudes, and experiences related to the impact of the cruise industry in Charleston. There are no correct or incorrect answers. We are looking for your honest assessments.

1. Approximately how many jobs in the Charleston area are supported by the cruise industry?

     500____   400____   300____   200____   100____

2. Approximately how much economic output (in millions) is generated by the cruise industry in Charleston?

     $55____ $45____ $35____ $25____ $15____

3. Which of the following conditions do you associate with the presence of a cruise ship in port? (Check all that apply.)

    ____ Abrasive interactions with cruise passengers.
    ____ Decreased pedestrian traffic in neighborhood.
    ____ Decreased sales of food, lodging, and/or merchandise and services.
    ____ Environmental/noise pollution.
    ____ Increased pedestrian traffic in neighborhood.
    ____ Increased sales of food, lodging, and/or merchandise and services.
    ____ Pleasant interactions with cruise passengers.
    ____ Reluctance to leave home or place of business.
    ____ Smooth flow of vehicular traffic.
    ____ Traffic jams.
    ____ Other (Please describe.)

One option the Ports Authority is considering is to relocate the cruise terminal to a point somewhat north of Union Pier.

4. At this time, do you favor or oppose relocation of the cruise terminal?

     Favor _____   **(Go to Item 5)**

     Oppose _____   **(Go to Item 7)**

5. Relocating the cruise terminal is projected to bring approximately 350 jobs to the Charleston region and contribute $45 million to the local economy during the 12 months of construction. Which of the following statements **best** reflects your attitude about those projections?

    ____ Projections are guesses, not facts.
    ____ The Charleston area needs that kind of economic boost; let's do it.
    ____ The Charleston historic district will receive little of that benefit.
    ____ The Charleston historic district will share in that benefit.

continued

ILLUSTRATION 16.11 CONTINUED

15

6. If the cruise terminal is relocated:

_____ My quality of life will very likely improve.
_____ My quality of life may possibly improve.
_____ I anticipate no change in my quality of life.
_____ My quality of life may decline.
_____ My quality of life will very likely decline.

Please go to Item 9.

7. Relocating the cruise terminal is projected to bring approximately 350 jobs to the Charleston region and contribute $45 million to the local economy during the 12 months of construction. Which of the following statements **best** reflects your attitude about those projections?

_____ Projections are guesses, not facts.
_____ The Charleston area needs that kind of economic boost; let's do it.
_____ The Charleston historic district will receive little of that benefit.
_____ The Charleston historic district will share in that benefit.

8. If the cruise terminal is relocated:

_____ My quality of life will very likely improve.
_____ My quality of life may possibly improve.
_____ I anticipate no change in my quality of life.
_____ My quality of life may decline.
_____ My quality of life will very likely decline.

9. **Please provide some information about yourself to help us process the answers to this survey.**

- Your age range is:
  Under 25_____   26-35_____   36-45_____   46-55_____   56-65_____   Over 65_____

- You are:
  Female _____   Male_____

- Your profession or occupation is best categorized as:
  _____ Artistic endeavors   _____ Education or religious services
  _____ Food services   _____ Full-time homemaker
  _____ Hospitality services   _____ Legal services
  _____ Medical/dental services   _____ Real estate services
  _____ Retail marketing   _____ Retired
  _____ Wholesale distribution   _____ Other (Please describe.)

Please return your completed questionnaire to:

South Carolina State Ports Authority
P O Box 22288
Charleston, SC 29413

continued

ILLUSTRATION 16.11   CONTINUED

16

Appendix B. Profiles of Respondents

Gender	Residents	Merchants
Female	68	26
Male	59	66
Total	127	92

Ages of Respondents	Residents	Merchants
	No.	No.
46-55	3	8
56-65	21	10
36-45	24	22
26-35	31	27
Under 25	22	23
Over 65	26	2
Total	127	92

Profession/occupation	Residents	Merchants
Artistic endeavors	5%	8%
Education services	9%	4%
Food services	15%	33%
Full-time homemaker	14%	0%
Hospitality services	6%	16%
Legal services	2%	10%
Medical/dental services	5%	3%
Other	2%	4%
Real estate services	4%	7%
Retail marketing	17%	11%
Retired	25%	0%
Wholesale distribution	2%	3%

continued

ILLUSTRATION 16.12   TRADITIONAL TITLE PAGE

Charleston and the Cruise Industry

Prepared for

Bryant T. Joseph, Vice President Terminal Operations

South Carolina State Ports Authority

P.O. Box 22287

Charleston, SC 29413

Prepared by

Government Affairs Division

South Carolina State Ports Authority

Charleston, SC 22287

September 2011

© Cengage Learning 2013

ILLUSTRATION 16.13 OPENING PAGES OF REPORT IN DEDUCTIVE STRUCTURE

Charleston and the Cruise Industry

Recommendations

Charlestonians recognize that the cruise business is going to continue to be a part of the Port of Charleston and their lives. However, they want the negative aspects of that impact to be ameliorated. To enhance citizens' support for the proposed cruise terminal relocation and waterfront enhancements the South Carolina Ports Authority should do the following:

1. Publicize the keys aspects of the Concept Plan. Specifically:
    - Improved vehicular traffic flows and parking in the cruise terminal area and downtown Charleston
    - Improved visual and human access to the waterfront
    - Ecological reclamation and protection of the waterfront
    - Reclamation and protection of historical structures in the Charleston Harbor

2. Proceed with port relocation and waterfront improvement plans presented in the Concept Plan in a sequence that will most readily show the greatest benefits to Charleston merchants and residents. Specifically:
    - Complete street construction/traffic alteration projects first. Improved traffic flow would immediately be felt by residents and businesses and may improve attitudes toward the presence of cruise ships in the Port of Charleston.
    - Upon completion of the street improvements, begin making improvements to the waterfront at the same time that construction begins on the new terminal site. This simultaneous activity will demonstrate to residents and merchants that the Ports Authority is as serious about enabling greater recreational use of the waterfront is it is about improving cruise facilities.
    - Issue regular press releases to mark the progress of the project and to inform residents and merchants about construction activities that may temporarily inconvenience them. Constant communication should reassure the citizens of Charleston that the project is moving forward as planned and will soon show major benefits to residents and merchants as well as cruise passengers.

These recommendations are based on the conclusions that the South Carolina State Ports authority has attempted to apply sound waterfront development principles in its Concept Plan for Union Pier Waterfront, including public input. Communication about those plans seems to have been understood and received favorably by downtown merchants. That communication, however, has done little to change the downtown residents' opinion about the value of the cruise industry.

Downtown Charleston's residents and merchants both perceive that the presence of cruise ships in the Port of Charleston has negatively impacted pedestrian and vehicular traffic. Although residents and

continued

ILLUSTRATION 16.13 CONTINUED

merchants have differing degrees of knowledge about the economic impact of the cruise industry, both groups strongly support relocation of the cruise terminal.

Charlestonians' Perceptions of the Cruise Industry and Proposed Port Enhancements

For more than 25 years, Charleston's Union Pier has served as a home port and port of call for Carnival Cruises and a port of call for other cruise lines. The cruise industry currently contributes approximately $37 million to the region's economy, but the vehicular and pedestrian traffic associated with the departures and arrivals of cruise ships has been the subject of extensive debate among downtown residents, merchants, and professionals.

The South Carolina Ports Authority has begun plans to relocate the cruise terminal to a point north of its present location and relocate existing cargo operations. These changes will open 35 acres of harbor front that can be redeveloped to provide greater public access to the water's edge. Before implementing that plan, the Ports Authority officers wanted to know how much Charlestonians know about the economic impact of the cruise industry and what their attitudes are toward that industry and the proposed revitalization of the waterfront.

Research Plan

A survey of downtown residents and merchants was conducted during the summer of 2011.

The Problem

The research problem was to assess Charlestonians' perceptions of the economic and social impact of cruise dockings in the Port of Charleston and the possible relocation of the cruise terminal.

The Purpose

The purpose of the study was to assess the business and social climate in which the South Carolina Ports Authority will operate if it implements plans to relocate the cruise terminal. Knowledge of that climate will help the Authority develop operational and communication strategies relative to the relocation.

Scope of Analysis

Three factors were studied:

1. What business impacts do Charleston's downtown residents and merchants perceive to be related to the arrival and departure of cruise ships?
2. What personal and community impacts do Charleston's downtown residents and merchants perceive to be related to the arrival and departure of cruise ships?
3. What knowledge of and attitudes toward relocation of the cruise terminal are evidenced by Charleston's downtown residents and merchants?

Topics for Discussion

1. What are the purposes of report preliminaries?
2. Why should you bind a report? When should you not bind a report?
3. What information should be shown on a report cover?
4. What information should a title page contain?
5. What should a transmittal message accomplish?
6. What are the functions of authorization and acceptance messages?
7. What are the purposes of a table of contents and a list of tables?
8. When may the preface or acknowledgments be omitted?
9. What should be included in an executive summary? When may an executive summary be omitted?
10. What are the major sections of a report body? What information should be included in each section? Which sections are not included in an information report?
11. What are the purposes of report supplements? What items may be included in the supplements?
12. How do informative or "talking" headings differ from functional or structural headings? Which do you prefer? Why?
13. Describe an effective format for report headings.
14. Explain how to use these formatting features in Microsoft Word 2010: (1) custom margins, (2) heading styles, (3) multiple spacing, (4) page numbers (on preliminaries), and (5) table of contents with page numbers and leaders. Consult Word Help as needed.
15. Explain the page numbering systems for report preliminaries, report body, and report supplements. Why is it important to number preliminaries and report body separately?
16. With two or three other students, describe any experience you have had using Word's comments and/or tracking changes. Specify how these tools simplified the collaboration process.
17. Identify security risks involved in sharing Word files and two ways to reduce or eliminate those risks.

Applications

1. Access an XYZ book template in Microsoft Word 2010's template gallery. Discuss ways in which the template settings for margins, line spacing, placement and style of headings, and page numbering are similar to or differ from the guides given in this chapter. Compare the readability of a document prepared from that template and one prepared according to the guides given in this chapter.
2. As directed by your instructor, complete any research you began in conjunction with your study of previous chapters in this book. Write the body of a report that presents the results of your research.
3. After completing the body of your research report (Application 2), exchange reports with another student. (Suggestion: To ensure that your report cannot be

modified, save a copy in PDF or XPS Document format to send.) Each of you is to draft the executive summary for the other's report. Evaluate the executive summary that your classmate wrote for your report. Is it a highly effective, a marginal, or an ineffective summary? In a memo to your instructor explain your evaluation. Attach a copy of the summary to your memo. Insert an executive summary into your report and update the table of contents.

4. Complete the report you worked on for Applications 2 and 3.

    a. Include the following items and print the report:

- A title page
- A table of contents with page numbers and leaders
- An executive summary
- The report body
- A source list
- Appendixes, if appropriate

    b. Change the table of contents in 4a to one with hyperlinks instead of page numbers. Save this version of the file in PDF or XPS Document format.

5. As a collaborative research project, do the following:

    a. Interview managers in two to five companies in your area. Try to get the following kinds of information:

- What is the average length of reports produced by this company? If there is no average, what is the page-length range this manager has seen in the company's reports?
- What major types of internal reports does the manager use or prepare?
- What major types of external reports does the manager use or prepare?
- Does the company use a standard template or style guide for its reports? If the company has such a guide, ask for a copy. If the company does not have such a guide, determine the expectations for report structure and format that exist in the company and how those expectations are conveyed to employees.
- Does the manager prefer that illustrations be integrated into the report or grouped in an appendix at the end?

    b. Draft a report of your findings, showing whether expectations are consistent or inconsistent among those businesses. The working title for your report should be "Report Structures and Formats in Local Businesses." (You may, however, choose another title for your final report.) Be sure to include a full description of the objective of your report, your methodology, your findings, and your conclusions, particularly the implications of your findings for people entering the business world or transferring to a new company. Include any report preliminaries and supplements requested by your instructor. If all collaborators use Microsoft Word 2010, take advantage of comments and tracking changes. If some collaborators use other platforms, such as a Macintosh computer with Claris Works or a Mac-compatible version of Microsoft Word or Word Perfect, save the original file in Plain Text before sharing it.

    c. Present your findings in an oral presentation to your class, using a few illustrated PowerPoint slides to support your spoken words.

6. Select a research report that you have prepared for another class or at your job. In a memorandum to your instructor, describe how it is similar to or different from the model given in this chapter. If there are differences, explain how those differences improve or distract from the user-friendliness of the report.

7. Form a team with one or two of your classmates. Select one of the reports listed in the Works Cited of Illustration 16.11 and download it from the Web. In what ways do the structure, content, format, and writing style of the report resemble or differ from the items discussed in this chapter? What might account for those similarities and differences? If there are differences, explain how those differences improve or distract from the user-friendliness of the report. Communicate the results of your study in a written report to your instructor and an oral presentation to your class, using a few illustrated PowerPoint slides to support your spoken words.

References

1. The report shown in Illustration 16.11 is a combination of hypothetical and verifiable data, used for illustration purposes only. The names of South Carolina Ports Authority officers or employees are hypothetical, and the survey data are hypothetical. However, the author conducted a similar survey among a small sample of adults and projected the findings to the hypothetical sample. The guides for waterfront development and goals for the Port of Charleston were drawn from the sources cited in the report.

2. Best ways to save gas. (2011, July). *Consumer Reports*, pp. 52–54.

3. Modern Language Association of America. (2009). *MLA handbook for writers of research papers* (7th ed.). New York: Modern Language Association of America, 117.

4. American Psychological Association. (2010). *Publication manual of the American Psychological Association* (6th ed.). Washington, DC: American Psychological Association, p. 42.

5. American Psychological Association, *Publication manual of the American Psychological Association*, p. 62.

Index